Microeconomic Principles

Microeconomic Principles

FRANK A. COWELL
Reader in Economics
The London School of Economics and Political Science

Philip Allan

First published 1986 by

PHILIP ALLAN PUBLISHERS LIMITED
MARKET PLACE
DEDDINGTON
OXFORD OX5 4SE

and in the USA by

OXFORD UNIVERSITY PRESS, INC.

British Library Cataloguing in Publication Data
Cowell, F.A.
Microeconomic principles
1. Microeconomics
I. Title
338.5 HB172

ISBN 0-86003-067-9
ISBN 0-86003-172-1 Pbk

Typeset by MHL Typesetting Limited, Coventry
Printed and bound in Great Britain at The Camelot Press, Southampton

To Alexander and Frederick

Contents

Preface

For some years I have had the opportunity of teaching a course on Principles of Economics Treated Mathematically at the London School of Economics. This book is largely based on the material designed for the microeconomics component of that course.

The transition from lecture notes to book was a slow process, and along the way I have incurred many debts. Several LSE colleagues have helped in a variety of ways. S. Glaister, who leant on me to take on the course in the first place, bequeathed to me some questions which spurred me to provide the sets of exercises that follow the chapters. D. de Meza, J.H. Moore, V. Perotin and A. Zabalza all offered valuable comments on particular ideas in the course of the development of the main chapters. W. Leininger and A.F. Shorrocks warned me off some heinous errors. F. van der Ploeg patiently read a lot of the text and provided much encouragement. J.P.F. Gordon and A. Muthoo even more patiently ploughed their way through the galley proofs. Miss D. Montes laboured diligently on the Index. In addition I am much obliged to D.E.W. Laidler and M. Hoy for suggesting several improvements to a preliminary draft, and to the publisher, Philip Allan, who pleasantly bullied me along to completion. Naturally I exculpate them all for deficiencies that may remain.

My thanks also go to the several generations of students who have been taught using material in this book; in the process they have taught me quite a few things, and helped me to modify the presentation in many places. I am glad to acknowledge the University of London for permission to reproduce several examination questions as exercises: the University is in no way responsible for the correctness or otherwise of the suggested solutions in Appendix B. Finally, I am very grateful to, and impressed by, Miss S. Kirkbride who uncomplainingly typed the successive stages of the manuscript and artistically produced many of the diagrams.

Frank A. Cowell
London School of Economics
and Political Science

1

Introduction

1.1 The Scope of this Book

This book is a simplified story of the basic principles of microeconomics, expressed mainly in mathematical idiom. It is fairly basic in its economic content since, on the whole, it stays well within the shallow waters of equilibrium theory. The purpose is to show you the fundamental techniques of modern economic analysis, to introduce you, as far as possible, to the wide range of application of these techniques, and to demonstrate some of the more important general propositions on which a lot of applied economic reasoning is based.

The story begins with production, partly because it seems to make sense to look first at some of the basic components of a general microeconomic model (in this case firms), and partly because certain results that are obtained most readily in the theory of the firm can then be simply applied to the theory of the household which follows. We then look at the problem of 'assembling' all the components of the economy and examine how the combined system behaves; and we consider the difficulties raised by some important departures from the main story line. The story ends with the beginning of another story: how we can use the principles discussed in this book as a basis for judging the performance of the economic system and for deciding what ought to be done.

We are going to use mathematical language as an expository device and as a powerful method of proof. There are a number of reasons for this: it is often easier to state one's economic assumptions more precisely if one has to put the analysis in mathematical terms; many economic results simply drop out from well-known mathematical results; it is easy to construct illustrative examples and problems. For those readers who may be nervous about the extent of mathematics required, Section 1.3 reviews this, and Section 1.4 sets out the mathematical conventions I shall use (incidentally, the concepts used in Chapter 2 are about the most abstract of the whole book – so do not despair!). However, despite the use of formulae in the text and the presence of exercises at the end of each chapter, it cannot be overemphasised that the book is not about 'mathematical puzzles and problems in economics', but about economic principles.

Let us briefly review some of the methodology we shall be using.

1.2 Methods

There are not many basic tricks that the student of standard microeconomics has to perform. In fact one simplified example will serve to illustrate most of what the book is about. The example concerns the equilibrium method.

The Equilibrium Method

Suppose that in a particular economy there are n distinct goods, labelled 1, 2, . . ., n, and that we wish to investigate the supply of and demand for good 1. We shall suppose that there is a free market in good 1; in particular each supplier of the good is prepared to announce a particular quantity of the good he is willing to supply at any given price p_1, and each user of the good will announce the amount that he would want to buy at any given price p_1 (why each party should appear to behave in this obliging fashion is a topic to which we shall return with some curiosity). For convenience let us suppose that all this information has been collated and that the suppliers' offers can be summarised by the formula

$$y_1 = -A + ap_1 \tag{1.1}$$

for $p_1 \geqq A/a$ (and $y_1 = 0$ otherwise), where y_1 is the aggregate amount of

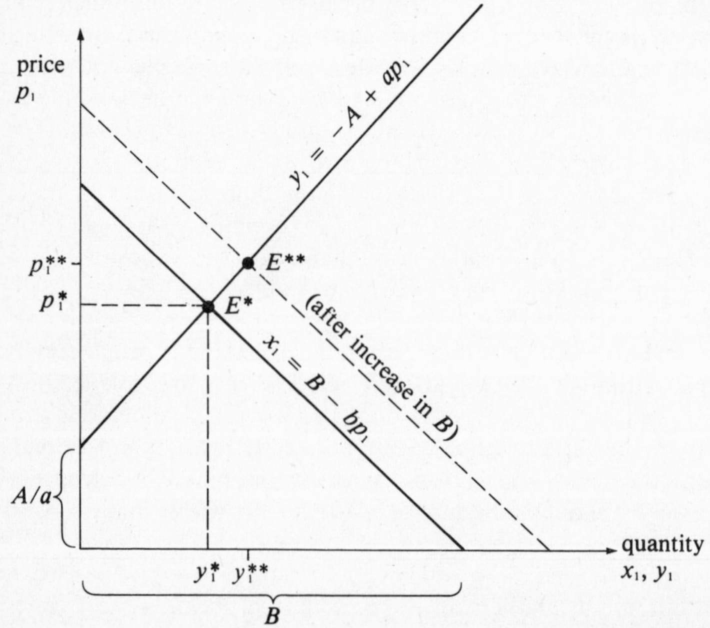

Figure 1.1

good 1 produced. Likewise suppose that the consumers' total demand can be summarised by the formula

$$x_1 = B - bp_1 \tag{1.2}$$

for $p_1 \leqslant B/b$ (and $x_1 = 0$ otherwise), where x_1 is the quantity demanded. A, a, B, b are all non-negative numbers. Equations (1.1) and (1.2) represent two sets of behavioural relations, and may be simply represented as the two straight lines in Figure 1.1. To make use of these we impose the simple condition that must obtain at an equilibrium, 'supply equals demand':[1]

$$y_1 = x_1 \tag{1.3}$$

Applying the condition (1.3) to the two behavioural relations (1.1), (1.2) immediately to derive p_1^*, the particular value of the price that is consistent with this equilibrium, namely

$$p_1^* = \frac{A + B}{a + b} \tag{1.4}$$

This yields the equilibrium amount supplied (and demanded):

$$y_1^* = \frac{aB - bA}{a + b} \tag{1.5}$$

– see point E^* in Figure 1.1. Deriving p_1^* and y_1^* as functions of the given data of the problem A, a, B, b is all there is to the equilibrium method. Obviously the linearity of the example is not particularly important. In general (1.1) and (1.2) could be replaced by more general formulations

$$y_1 = S(p_1; \alpha) \tag{1.6}$$

$$x_1 = D(p_1; \beta) \tag{1.7}$$

where α and β are each sets of parameters which determine the shape and position of the supply function and the demand function respectively. Applying the equilibrium condition one would then find a solution of the form

$$p_1^* = F(\alpha, \beta) \tag{1.8}$$

and, if $p_1^* > 0$, the equilibrium quantity would be found by substituting from (1.8) back into (1.6) or (1.7). This procedure is an essential step in much of the economic modelling which follows. By itself the equilibrium method is not enormously interesting. Where can we take it?

1 Strictly speaking it should be 'supply is at least as great as demand'. We pursue this technicality in Chapter 7.

Behavioural Modelling

One of the most obvious steps to take is to provide an explanation of the shape and position of the demand and supply functions. This normally involves two steps: (a) the behaviour of each particular agent – the individual, household, firm – must be modelled. Usually this involves specifying a particular form of optimisation behaviour on the part of each agent. This is discussed in detail in Chapters 3 and 4. (b) the behaviour of individual agents may need to be aggregated – if there are many suppliers and many demanders for example. This can raise a number of problems – see Chapter 6.

General Systems

Manifestly the system described by (1.1)–(1.3) is of only limited usefulness. The supply of good 1 will depend on the prices of labour and other inputs; the demand for good 1 will be affected by the prices of other goods and by individuals' incomes – which in turn will be affected by the wages paid by firms. In short we need to model the dependence of parameters such as A, a, B, b on prices of other goods $p_2, p_3, \ldots$ in the economy. Instead of considering the *partial* equilibrium analysis of a single good, one attempts a *general* equilibrium approach that simultaneously solves for the equilibrium values of all prices, quantities and incomes allowing for all the interactions between markets. We attempt this in Chapters 7 and 8.

Comparative Statics

Whatever the underlying structure of the equilibrium model, it is interesting to enquire how different the equilibrium would have looked had the original data been slightly different. Note this does not say 'how the system will look if the data are altered'. Therein lies the deceptive beauty of the comparative static method. There is no analysis of disequilibrium, of the adjustment mechanism to the new equilibrium, or whether the model will even tend to a new equilibrium at all. What one does is notionally to alter the parameters of the system (A, a, B, b, in (1.1) to (1.5) or more generally α and β in (1.6) to (1.8) and note how equilibrium price(s) and quantity(ies) change). For example, if good 1 is a so-called 'normal good' and if everyone gets richer so that the parameter B increases, shifting the demand curve to the right in Figure 1.1, then the equilibrium prices rises to p_1^{**} and equilibrium quantity rises to y_1^{**} – see point E^{**}. The partial equilibrium models of Chapters 3 and 4 are subjected to this treatment and the comparative statics of the general equilibrium model are examined in detail in Chapter 9.

Disequilibrium Adjustment

So far in Figure 1.1 considerable attention has been devoted to the equilibrium points E^* and E^{**} corresponding to the situations before and after the notional increase in B. But what of the rest of the diagram? How does the system behave if it is not already at rest? There is no easy answer to this question that is also uniformly satisfying. We shall examine one of the possibilities in Chapter 7.

The simplistic equilibrium model will take us on to more interesting issues. Chapters 10 to 12 introduce the complications of uncertainty in various forms and of strategic behaviour, in contrast to the models of Chapters 2–9 wherein, in the main, agents act meekly as price takers under conditions of certainty. Finally Chapter 13 shows how the mechanisms discussed in earlier chapters can be used to analyse questions of policy.

1.3 Mathematics

Economic principles can often be expressed very succinctly in mathematical terms and, fortunately, one does not need particularly heavyweight machinery to deal with the most important ideas.

Of course techniques that are second nature to one person may seem forbidding and fearsome to another. So I shall state now the range of mathematical concepts and methods which will be employed: you should ensure that you are familiar with them. The ones marked with a * are only infrequently employed, but you should be thoroughly conversant with the rest.

Algebra

Basic manipulation of expressions involving real variables; solution of simple simultaneous equations; the concept of a function of one or more variables; addition of vectors; multiplication of a vector by a scalar; elementary matrix operations*; the concept of a limit.

Calculus

Differentiation of functions of one variable; definite and indefinite integrals of functions of one variable; first- and second-order partial derivatives of a function of several variables; total differentiation of functions of several variables; ordinary differential equations of the first order*.

Set Theory and Analysis

The meaning of the symbols $\in$, $\subset$, $\cap$, $\cup$; convexity, boundedness*; closedness*.

Optimisation

Classical unconstrained and constrained optimisation; the interpretation of Lagrange multipliers; the concept of a linear or non-linear programme and its dual*.

Probability and Statistics

The concept of a random variable; expectation; variance; moments*.

There are a few specific concepts which are so useful in economics that special attention should be drawn to them. Since they crop up time and again in diverse applications, it is worthwhile briefly checking through (a)–(h) below now with the aid of pen and paper.

(a) Homogeneity of a function. If r is an integer, then a function f of n variables is homogeneous of degree r if, for any positive number λ and any $(x_1, \ldots, x_n)$ one finds

$$f(\lambda x_1, \ldots, \lambda x_n) = \lambda^r f(x_1, \ldots, x_n)$$

Euler's theorem states that a differentiable function f is homogeneous of degree r if and only if

$$\sum_{i=1}^{n} x_i \frac{\partial f(x_1, \ldots, x_n)}{\partial x_i} = r f(x_1, \ldots, x_n)$$

(b) Homotheticity of a function. Briefly, what is meant is as follows. Let $g(x_1, \ldots, x_n) = \phi(f(x_1, \ldots, x_n))$ where f is a homogeneous function; then g is homothetic. Clearly homogeneity is a special case of homotheticity.

(c) Convex combination of vectors. Suppose $\mathbf{x}^1, \mathbf{x}^2, \ldots, \mathbf{x}^k$ is a collection of k vectors, each of which is of dimension n. Then for *any* collection of k non-negative scalars $\alpha_1, \alpha_2, \ldots, \alpha_k$ which has the property that $\alpha_1 + \alpha_2 + \ldots + \alpha_k = 1$ the vector $\mathbf{y}$ formed thus:

$$\mathbf{y} = \sum_{i=1}^{k} \alpha_i \mathbf{x}^i$$

is known as a *convex combination* of the **x**s.

(d) Convexity of a set. Suppose X is a set of vectors. Pick *any* two points $\mathbf{x}^1$ and $\mathbf{x}^2$ belonging to the set. Then X is convex if and only if all convex combinations of the form

$$\mathbf{y} = \alpha \mathbf{x}^1 + [1 - \alpha] \mathbf{x}^2 \quad \text{where} \quad 0 \leqslant \alpha \leqslant 1$$

also belong to X.

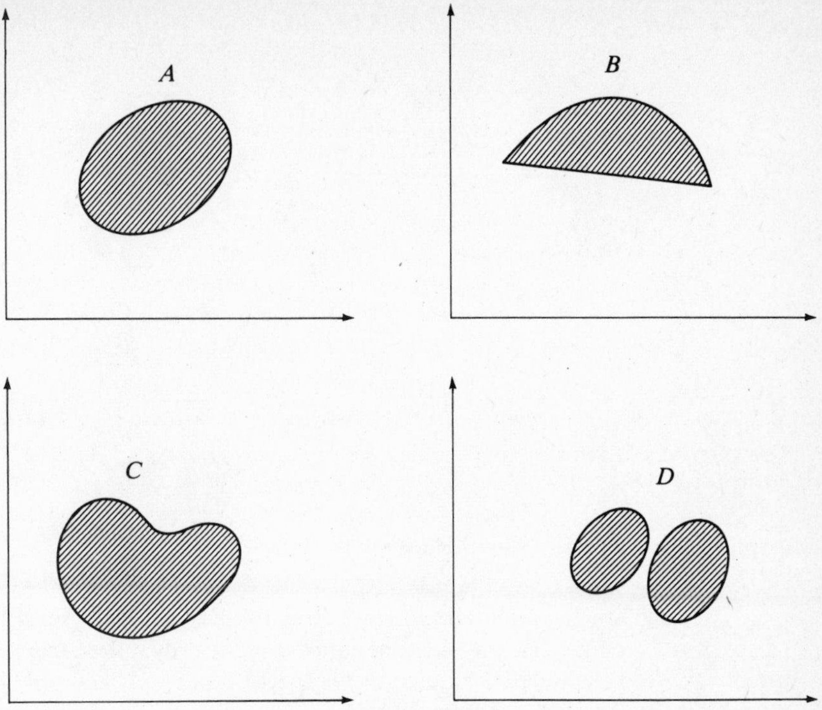

Figure 1.2

(e) Strict convexity[2] *of a set.* This is a useful special case of convexity. Suppose X is a convex set and that $\mathbf{x}^1$ and $\mathbf{x}^2$ are any two *boundary* points of X. Consider all convex combinations of the form

$$\mathbf{y} = \alpha\mathbf{x}^1 + [1 - \alpha]\mathbf{x}^2 \quad \text{where} \quad 0 < \alpha < 1$$

note that here α and $1 - \alpha$ are strictly positive. If all such $\mathbf{y}$ lie in the *interior* of X (i.e. they belong to X but not to the boundary of X) then the set X is strictly convex. In Figure 1.2 the set A is strictly convex, the set B is convex but not strictly convex and the sets C and D are not even convex. You should check this from the definitions.

(f) Convex and concave functions. Consider a function f of n variables and consider the set A of all points (vectors) given by $(x_1, x_2, \ldots, x_n, y)$ where $y \geqq f(x_1, \ldots, x_n)$. The function f is said to be convex if and only if A is

2 Also known as strong convexity.

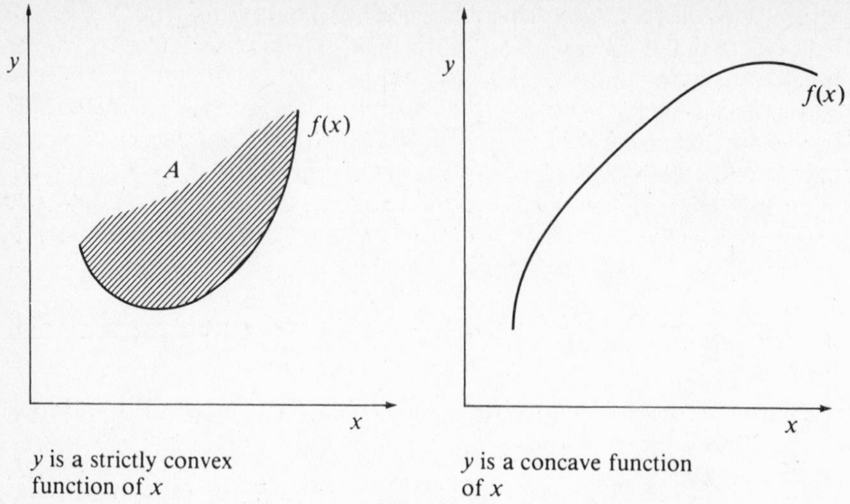

Figure 1.3

convex. The function f is said to be *strictly* convex if and only if the set A is strictly convex. The function f is said to be concave if and only if the function $-f$ is convex. And of course the function f is strictly concave if and only if $-f$ is strictly convex. These properties can be easily illustrated in the case where f is a function of one variable – see Figure 1.3.

(g) Convex/concave-contoured functions.[3] Consider a function f of two or more variables and pick some *particular* value y which that function f may yield. Now consider the set B of all points $(x_1, \ldots, x_n)$ such that $y \geqq f(x_1, \ldots, x_n)$. The set B is known as a level set of f (in this case defined at the particular chosen level y) and the boundary of B is a contour of f. The function f is convex-contoured if the set B is convex; likewise the function f is concave-contoured if $-f$ is convex-contoured. The definitions of strictly convex-contoured functions and strictly concave-contoured functions follow in a similar fashion.

It is fairly easy to illustrate this idea in the case of a function f of two variables x_1 and x_2. Lay a piece of graph paper on a table and draw two axes on it along which you will measure x_1 and x_2. Now take an empty grapefruit skin (from half a grapefruit) and put it, hollow side down, on the graph paper. Let y be the height of any part of the grapefruit skin above the table: you will see that y is a (strictly) concave function of x_1 and x_2. Moreover if you, in the manner of a cartographer, drew a contour map[4] of the grapefruit

---

[3] Also known as quasi-convex/quasi-concave functions.
[4] Each contour, of course, corresponds to a particular height above the table.

skin you would find that each contour viewed from the inside of the grapefruit was (strictly) concave. This confirms the obvious point that a concave function must be concave-contoured. Now replace the grapefruit skin by a bowler hat,[5] and let y be the height of any part of the hat above the table. It is easy to see that now y is *not* a concave function of x_1 and x_2 (if you don't see this, examine the bit of the hat near the brim!). But if you draw the contours of the bowler hat you will find that their shape is quite similar to the contours of the grapefruit skin. So the bowler hat example is one of a function that is strictly concave-contoured without being concave.

(h) The Hessian property. Consider a twice-differentiable function f of n variables $(x_1, \ldots, x_n)$, and consider an arbitrary vector $(w_1, \ldots, w_n)$. Write the partial derivative $\frac{\partial^2}{\partial x_i \, \partial x_j} f(x_1, \ldots, x_n)$ as $f_{ij}(x_1, \ldots, x_n)$; the n-by-n symmetric matrix with elements $f_{ij}(x_1, \ldots, x_n)$, $i = 1, \ldots, n, j = 1, \ldots, n$ is known as the Hessian matrix of f. If it is true that for the above arbitrary weights one has $\sum_{i=1}^{n} \sum_{j=1}^{n} w_i \, w_j \, f_{ij}(x_1, \ldots, x_n) \leqslant 0$ then the Hessian at $(x_1, \ldots, x_n)$ is said to be *negative semi-definite*. A twice differentiable function f is concave *if and only if* its Hessian matrix is negative semi-definite at every point $(x_1, \ldots, x_n)$ where the differential is defined.

Again consider a twice differentiable function f of n variables and let $(w_1, \ldots, w_n)$ be an arbitrary set of weights that *are not all zero*. Its Hessian matrix at $(x_1, \ldots, x_n)$ is said to be *negative definite*, if for any such set of weights it is true that $\sum_{i=1}^{n} \sum_{j=1}^{n} w_i \, w_j \, f_{ij}(x_1, \ldots, x_n) < 0$. If a twice differentiable function f has a negative definite Hessian matrix everywhere then, as shorthand, we shall say 'f has the Hessian property': a function f that exhibits the Hessian property must be strictly concave.[6] Examining a function's second partial derivative to see whether or not it exhibits the Hessian property is a useful way of checking whether the function is strictly concave.

All of these topics are discussed in more detail in the references given at the end of this chapter: check them out at an early date if you feel uneasy about any of them.

1.4 Economics

When I was an undergraduate the lecture list contained two thoughtful provisions for aspiring economists who needed to brush up – or work up

---

5 Bare-headed non-British readers may substitute 'bell' for 'bowler hat'.

6 But the reverse is not true: you can have a strictly concave function f for which the Hessian is only negative *semi*-definite and not negative definite. Note also that there is a corresponding relationship between (strictly) convex functions and positive (semi-)definiteness, although we shall not have occasion to use it.

from scratch – their ability to work with mathematics. One lecture course was entitled 'elementary mathematics for economists'; the other bore the humiliating title of '*very* elementary mathematics for economists'.

This book is about elementary economics. As such it will assume that most readers have already encountered some very elementary economics, although none of the essential economic concepts are taken completely for granted, so that relative newcomers to the subject who have a reasonable mathematical background will also be able to find their way around. This having been said, it will be helpful if you have already encountered the economic analysis of the firm, the household and the market in some form before. Isoquants, average and marginal cost curves, indifference curves, demand and supply schedules and the idea of equilibrium will all be properly introduced, but it would be useful if they were recognised as nodding acquaintances, if not old friends.

1.5 Conventions

Unfortunately notation and terminology often vary confusingly from one text and author to another. Throughout Chapters 2–13 a uniform, fairly standard, and – I hope – readily understandable notational system is used. For ease of reference the most important notation in each chapter is summarised in a table within the chapter. Ordinary scalar variables are usually denoted by lower-case letters, although a few upper case letters also appear in this role. Vectors are denoted by bold type thus, $\mathbf{w}$; components of those vectors are written in normal type with an appropriate subscript; n-dimensional Euclidean space is denoted by $\mathbb{R}^n$. So the statement 'the vector $(x_1, x_2, \ldots, x_n)$ lies in n-dimensional Euclidean space' could be written more compactly, and equivalently: '$\mathbf{x} \in \mathbb{R}^n$'. Superscripts, asterisks and other symbols written *over* the letter are used to distinguish different vectors. Thus $\mathbf{x}^1$ and $\mathbf{x}^2$ might denote two different vectors in $\mathbb{R}^n$, and if written out in full would be

$$\mathbf{x}^1 = (x_1^1, x_2^1, x_3^1, \ldots, x_n^1)$$
$$\mathbf{x}^2 = (x_1^2, x_2^2, x_3^2, \ldots, x_n^2)$$

Sets other than $\mathbb{R}^n$ are denoted by ordinary upper case letters and, where necessary, are defined in the following way. The statement

$$\text{'}X = \{\mathbf{x} : \mathbf{x} \in \mathbb{R}^n, x_i \geqslant 1, i = 1, \ldots, n\}\text{'}$$

should be read 'X is the set of n-dimensional vectors which have the property that every component is greater than or equal to unity'. Very often the particular set to which a vector belongs ('all n-vectors', 'all strictly positive n-vectors', 'the subset X of $\mathbb{R}^n$', etc.) will not need to be written down explicitly each time: where it is obvious from the context, qualifying statements such as '$\mathbf{x} \in X$' will be left understood.

The following convention on vector inequalities will be employed, for any two n-vectors:

(1) '$\mathbf{x} > \mathbf{y}$' means '$x_i > y_i$ for every $i = 1, \ldots, n$'
(2) '$\mathbf{x} \geqq \mathbf{y}$' means '$x_i \geqq y_i$ for every $i = 1, \ldots, n$'
(3) '$\mathbf{x} \geqslant \mathbf{y}$' means '$x_i \geqq y_i$ for *every* $i = 1, \ldots, n$ and for *at least one* component i it is true that $x_i > y_i$'.

Hence, let $\mathbf{x}$ be the vector (1, 1), let $\mathbf{y}$ be the vector (1, 0), denote the zero vector (0, 0) by $\mathbf{0}$, and let $\mathbf{z} = \mathbf{0}$. Then the following are all true (check them):

$$\mathbf{x} \geqslant \mathbf{y}$$
$$\mathbf{x} \geqq \mathbf{y}$$
$$\mathbf{x} > \mathbf{z}$$
$$\mathbf{x} \geqslant \mathbf{z}$$
$$\mathbf{x} \geqq \mathbf{z}$$
$$\mathbf{y} \geqslant \mathbf{z}$$
$$\mathbf{y} \geqq \mathbf{z}$$
$$\mathbf{z} \geqq \mathbf{0}$$

But in this case it would *not* be correct to write $\mathbf{y} > \mathbf{z}$ or $\mathbf{z} \geqslant \mathbf{0}$, for example.

It is only very seldom that reference will be made to set operators other than the usual ones of union $\cup$, intersection $\cap$ and inclusion $\subset$. (Indeed it is not *very* often that we have to use set notation at all.) Occasionally we shall also require the operation of *addition* of sets (as distinct from union) that are subsets of $\mathbb{R}^n$. The following convention is used:

$$X + Y \equiv \{\mathbf{z} : \mathbf{z} = \mathbf{x} + \mathbf{y} \text{ for all } \mathbf{x} \in X \text{ and all } \mathbf{y} \in Y\}$$

This is illustrated in Figure 1.4. To familiarise yourself with this concept it is well worth taking a piece of graph paper and trying the exercise for yourself: do it with both convex and non-convex sets.

A final point on notational conventions concerns derivatives of functions. Because we shall be using the differential calculus time and again in our analysis of optimisation problems and in examining the comparative statics of economic models, we have to write down many expressions involving partial derivatives. To make these expressions a little easier on the eye it is convenient to use a subscript shorthand for such derivatives. Accordingly if, for example, U is a function of $\mathbf{x} \equiv (x_1, x_2, \ldots, x_n)$ we write

$$\frac{\partial U(\mathbf{x})}{\partial x_i} \quad \text{as} \quad U_i(\mathbf{x})$$

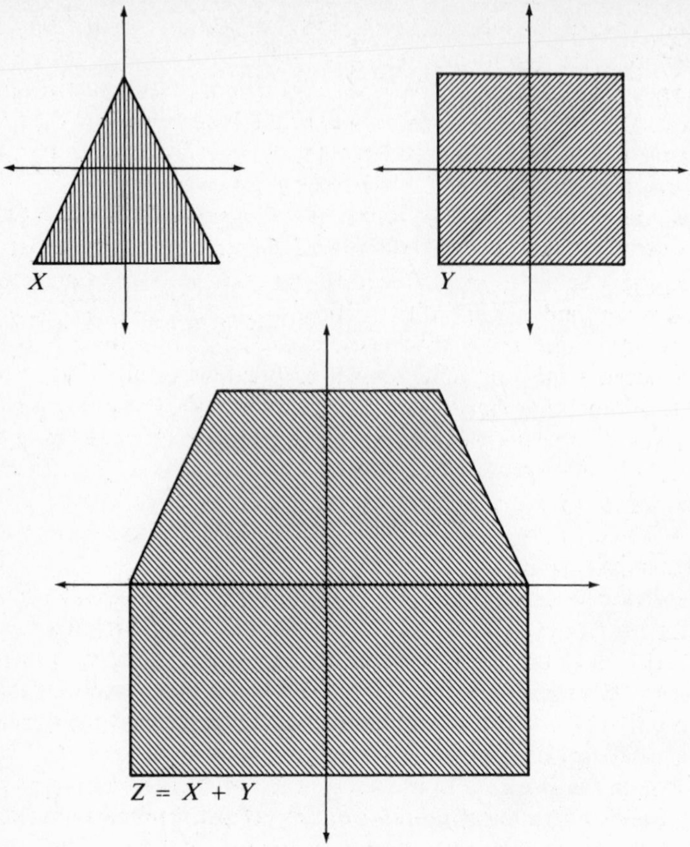

Figure 1.4

1.6 How to Use the Book

The main part of this book – Chapters 2 to 13 – takes you on a fairly brief and compressed tour of mainstream microeconomics, from the 'fact of life' about the technology with which one works, through to the objectives and tools of policy making. It is not essential to read each chapter in strict order of appearance, although there are some logical dependencies which ought to be noted. Chapters 2 to 4 form a natural sequence and also provide the foundation blocks for the rest of the book. Chapters 5 and 6 each provide essential preliminaries to the general system models of Chapters 7 to 9. If you do prefer to 'dip' you will find that there is fairly free usage of backward reference on definitions, assumptions, proofs and results (this is in an attempt to save space and patience). To make this referencing easier equations are numbered, key results are dated formally as numbered theorems, and a consistent notation system has been adopted.

The main arguments are developed using formal theorems and informal discussion. The formal statements are important both because of the necessity of referring back to precise, specific results and because of the desirability of putting down in black and white the assumptions required.

Your understanding and appreciation of the economic significance of several results will be enhanced by working through the proof. Where these appear in the main text, you are encouraged to do so. However, not all the results that we shall use and discuss have the proofs provided with them. Several follow immediately from earlier results. A few are left to you as exercises because they are quite similar to previous results. But some are, frankly, too much like hard work for the main text. In these cases I have usually given a simplified discussion in the main text and the formal proof in Appendix A. Finally some proofs are just not very interesting to the economist, since they do not provide any great insight on the economic processes involved. Where this is so I have omitted them altogether and given a suitable bibliographical reference.

Every chapter except this one has a set of exercises at the end. They are important for two reasons. Solving them can help you develop a facility in working with some of the formal analyses of the text. Also they provide the opportunity of introducing you to a number of important applications and more specialised developments of the argument in the main text. A full set of answers is provided in Appendix B to encourage you to persist in your attempts on the problems.

It is a good policy to make sure you understand – intuitively as well as formally – why certain results come out the way they do. So use the exercises and answers along with the theorems to improve your insight on microeconomic principles.

Further Reading

General Mathematics for Economists:

Birchenhall, C.R. and Grout, P. (1984) *Mathematics for Modern Economics*, Philip Allan.

Chiang, A.C. (1984) *Fundamental Methods of Mathematical Economics* (3rd edn), McGraw-Hill.

Glaister, S. (1984) *Mathematical Methods for Economists* (3rd edn), Basil Blackwell.

Lambert, P.J. (1985) *Advanced Mathematics for Economists*, Basil Blackwell.

Sydsaeter, K. (1981) *Topics in Mathematical Analysis of Economics*, Academic Press.

Weintraub, E.R. (1982) *Mathematics for Economists*, Cambridge University Press.

Convexity, concavity of functions:

Birchenhall and Grout (1984), Ch. 7.
Chiang (1984), pp. 348–52.
Intriligator, M.D. (1971) *Mathematical Optimization and Economic Theory*, Appendix A5, Prentice-Hall.

Optimisation:

Chiang (1984), Ch. 12.
Dixit, A.K. (1976) *Optimization in Economic Theory*, Oxford University Press.
Glaister (1984), Chs 15, 17.
Intriligator (1971), Chs 2–5.

2

Production

2.1 Preliminaries

Before we discuss the economic analysis of the way firms behave and how production is organised, we need to think carefully about the facts of life. How are we to model production possibilities?

One way to proceed might be to write down – for each firm or plant in the economy – a production function of the following sort

$$Q = G(z_1, z_2, \ldots, z_m) \tag{2.1}$$

which gives the maximum amount of output Q obtainable from the quantities of $z_1, z_2, \ldots, z_m$ of the inputs labelled 1, 2, ..., m. Indeed in subsequent chapters we shall adopt this conventional approach. But this begs a number of questions. What properties should one impose on the function G? On what economic principles should such properties be based? And may not such a functional representation as (2.1) *in itself* be unduly restrictive? After all to write it thus assumes that one can identify single-output production units within the economy. It is interesting to look at the production process in a more general way in order to discover the intellectual underpinnings of a form such as (2.1).

Let us begin, then, by introducing a convenient and concise way of describing the production possibilities in the entire economy. Suppose that there is an exhaustive list of *all n* commodities in the economy, whether they be consumer goods, primary resources or intermediate goods. To handle this general approach conveniently we need a new nomenclature and notation that treats outputs and inputs symmetrically. Accordingly, we shall refer to y_i as the *net output* of any one such commodity i; a number of physical units. The convention is that if more of commodity i is being produced than is being used as input, then y_i is positive, whereas if more is used up than is produced, then y_i is negative. So to illustrate this usage, consider Figure 2.1 where labour, land, pigs and potatoes are used as inputs, and pigs, potatoes and sausages are obtained as output. Netting out intermediate goods and combining the three separate production stages illustrated, we find the

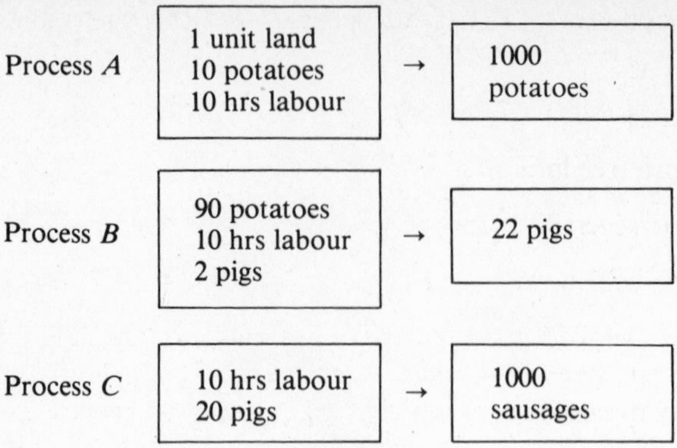

Figure 2.1

overall result described by the net output vector

$$\mathbf{y} = \begin{bmatrix} -30 \\ -1 \\ 0 \\ +900 \\ +1000 \end{bmatrix} \begin{matrix} \text{labour} \\ \text{land} \\ \text{pigs} \\ \text{potatoes} \\ \text{sausages} \end{matrix}$$

This simply describes *one* possible set of production activities. It is useful to be able to describe the 'state of the art', the set of all available processes for transforming inputs into outputs – i.e. the technology. We shall accordingly refer to Y, a subset of Euclidean n-space, $\mathbb{R}^n$, as the *technology set*. If we write $\mathbf{y} \in Y$ we mean simply that the list of inputs and outputs given by the vector is technically feasible. We assume the set Y is exogenously given – a pre-ordained collection of blueprints of the production process. Our immediate task is to consider the possible structure of the set Y: the characteristics of the set which incorporate the properties of the technology.

2.2 The Technology

We approach this task by imposing on Y a set of axioms which seem to provide a plausible description of the technology available to the community. These axioms will then form a basis of almost all our subsequent discussion of production, although sometimes one or other of them may be relaxed. We shall proceed by first providing a formal statement of the axioms, and then considering what each means in practical, intuitive terms.

The first four axioms incorporate, in a formal fashion, some very basic ideas about what we *mean* by the concept of production: zero inputs mean zero outputs; production cannot be 'turned around' so that outputs become inputs and vice versa; it is technologically feasible to 'waste' outputs or inputs.

AXIOM A1 (possibility of inaction): $\mathbf{0} \in Y$

AXIOM A2 (no free lunch): $Y \cap \mathbb{R}^n_+ = \{\mathbf{0}\}$[1]

AXIOM A3 (irreversible sausage machine) : $Y \cap (-Y) = \{\mathbf{0}\}$

AXIOM A4 (free disposal): $(\mathbf{y}^1 \in Y \text{ and } \mathbf{y}^2 \leqslant \mathbf{y}^1) \Rightarrow \mathbf{y}^2 \in Y$

The next two axioms introduce rather more sophisticated ideas and, as we shall see, are much more open to question. They relate, respectively, to the possibility of combining and dividing production processes.

AXIOM A5 (additivity): $(\mathbf{y}^1, \mathbf{y}^2 \in Y) \Rightarrow \mathbf{y}^1 + \mathbf{y}^2 \in Y$

AXIOM A6 (divisibility): $(0 < \alpha < 1 \text{ and } \mathbf{y}^1, \mathbf{y}^2 \in Y) \Rightarrow \alpha\mathbf{y}^1 + [1 - \alpha]\mathbf{y}^2 \in Y$

Let us see the implications of all six axioms by using a diagram. Accordingly take Process *C* in Figure 2.1 and consider the technology of turning labour and pigs into sausages. In Figure 2.2 $\mathbf{y}^1$, $\mathbf{y}^2$, $\mathbf{y}^3$, $\mathbf{y}^4$, $\mathbf{y}^5$ represent five different techniques for combining the two inputs to produce the output: note that $\mathbf{y}^1, \ldots, \mathbf{y}^5$ all lie in the $(-, -, +)$ orthant indicating that labour and pigs are inputs, sausages the output. Axiom A1 simply states that the origin $\mathbf{0}$ must belong to the technology set – no pigs, no labour: no sausages. Axiom A2 rules out there being any points in the $(+, +, +)$ orthant – you cannot have a technique that *produces* sausages *and* pigs *and* labour time to be enjoyed as leisure. Axiom A3 fixes the 'direction' of production – if $\mathbf{y}^3$ is technically possible, then there is no feasible vector $-\mathbf{y}^3$ lying in the $(+, +, -)$ orthant whereby labour time and pigs are produced from sausages. Axiom A4 just says that outputs may be thrown away and inputs wasted, so that the entire negative orthant belongs to *Y*. The implications of Axiom A5 are easily seen if we introduce $\mathbf{y}^6 = (0, -12, 0)$ which is another feasible (but not very exciting) technique, whereby if one has pigs but not labour one gets zero sausages. Now consider $\mathbf{y}^5 = (-5, -10, 500)$; then Axiom A5 simply says that $\mathbf{y}^7 = \mathbf{y}^5 + \mathbf{y}^6 = (-5, -22, 500)$ must also be a technically feasible net output vector. Clearly a further implication of Axiom A5 is, for example, that $2\mathbf{y}^5 = \mathbf{y}^5 + \mathbf{y}^5 = (-10, -20, 1000)$ is a technically feasible vector. Axiom A6 says that if we have two points representing input/output combinations then any point on the line segment joining them must represent a feasible technique too. Hence because $\mathbf{y}^3 \in Y$ and $\mathbf{0} \in Y$ we have $\frac{1}{2}\mathbf{y}^3 \in Y$; hence also the entire cone shape in Figure 2.2 must belong to *Y*.[2]

---

1 $\mathbf{0}$ denotes the zero vector $(0, 0, \ldots, 0)$; $\mathbb{R}^n_+$ is the non-negative orthant $\{\mathbf{x} : \mathbf{x} \in \mathbb{R}^n, \mathbf{x} \geqslant \mathbf{0}\}$; $-Y$ means the set $\{-\mathbf{y} : \mathbf{y} \in Y\}$.

2 Obviously in view of Axiom A5, this cone should be projected towards infinity; for clarity we have shown just a segment of it here.

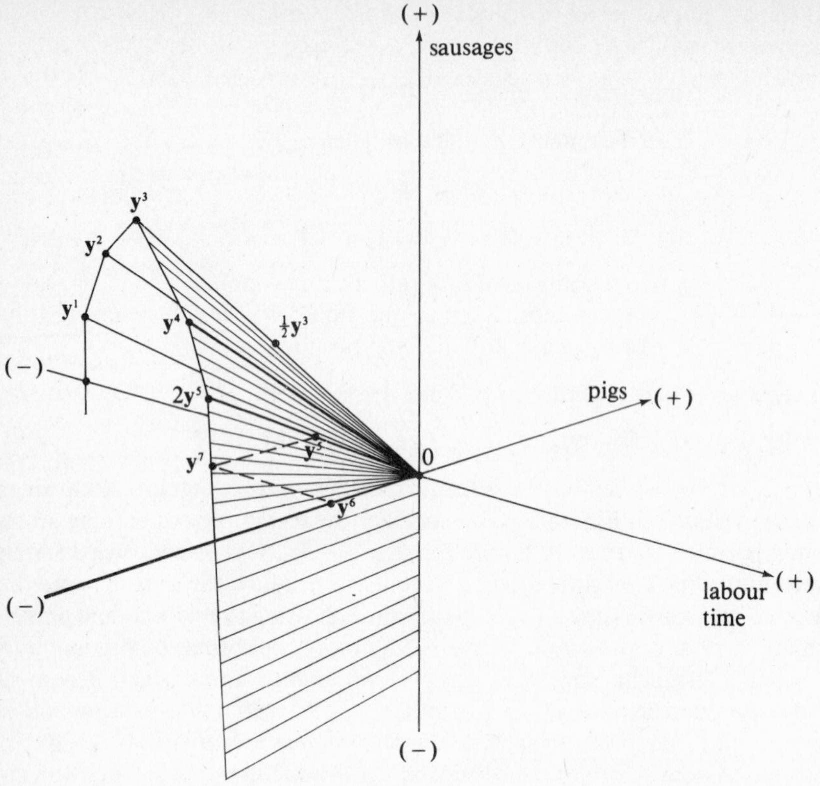

Figure 2.2 The technology set Y for process C

Axioms A1, A2, A3 are fairly unexceptionable, and it is not easy to imagine circumstances under which one would want to relax them.[3] Axiom A4 is almost innocuous: perhaps only the case of noxious wastes and the like need to be excluded. Axiom A5 rules out the possibility of 'diminishing returns to scale' – i.e. doubling the inputs producing *less* than double the

[3] One possible case where A1 would be violated is if one were to assume that at the level of the *individual firm* there is a precommitment to certain inputs before even zero output is produced (it is assumed that the firm cannot costlessly pack up production altogether). Then, in this special interpretation of the production model, one has to 'run in order to stand still' after the fashion of the Red Queen.

outputs. As long as every single output is correctly identified this axiom seems reasonable: if, say, land were also required for sausage making then it might well be the case that multiplying $\mathbf{y}^5$ by 2000 would produce less than a million sausages, because the sausage makers might get in each other's way – but this is clearly a problem of incomplete specification of the model, *not* the inappropriateness of the axiom. However, at the level of the individual firm (rather than across the whole economy) apparent violations of Axiom A5 may be relevant. If certain essential features of the firm are non-expandable, then diminishing returns may apply within the firm; in the overall economy A5 would still apply if 'clones' of individual firms could be set up. Axiom A6 rules out increasing returns (since this implies that any net output vector can be 'scaled down' to any arbitrary extent) and is perhaps the most suspect. Clearly some processes *do* involve indivisibilities, and whilst it is reasonable to speak of single pigs or quarter pigs in process C, there is an obvious irreducible minimum of two pigs required for process B! However, in view of the fact that if Axiom A6 holds, Y must be a convex set, and because of the tremendous importance of convexity (as in much of economic theory as we shall see), for most of the time we shall assume that Axiom A6 does hold. Evidently if both Axiom A5 and Axiom A6 are valid then decreasing and increasing returns to scale are ruled out. We then have *constant returns to scale*, whereby if $\mathbf{y}$ is feasible then so is $\lambda\mathbf{y}$ where λ is any non-negative scalar.

Even a casual glance at Figure 2.2 reveals that some parts of Y are a lot more interesting than others. In particular the 'top surface' is appealing since everywhere else involves some sort of waste of inputs or of output. Hence we introduce the following:

DEFINITION 2.1: the *technically efficient* set Y_e is given by

$$Y_e = \{\mathbf{y} : \mathbf{y} \in Y, \mathbf{y}^1 \geqslant \mathbf{y} \Rightarrow \mathbf{y}^1 \notin Y\}$$

If $\mathbf{y} \in Y_e$ then $\mathbf{y}$ is *technically efficient.*

This is to be distinguished from the idea of economic efficiency (discussed in subsequent chapters). Briefly the economically efficient points form a subset of Y_e which is further delimited by the market or other constraints which confront the production unit. The idea of technical efficiency leads on immediately to a very useful device.

2.3 The Production Function

The production function is simply a convenient way of describing points in the technology set and in the technically efficient set. It is a function Φ from $\mathbb{R}^n$ to the real line that is increasing in each of the y_i and where

$$\Phi(\mathbf{y}) = 0 \quad \text{if} \quad \mathbf{y} \in Y_e \tag{2.2}$$

Equation (2.2) may not *look* much like a production function, but it is actually a very useful format when dealing with multi-product entities such as a model of an entire economy. It is, in effect, a simple description of the *condition* for technological efficiency. Amongst other things what it says is that if you increase y_i (i.e. raise some output or lower some input level) then, if you are producing efficiently, you *must* reduce some other variable y_j in order to maintain the equality (2.2). This 'tradeoff' is the very essence of meaning of 'efficient production'. Again if you unilaterally decrease some y_i (cut some output, or raise some input level without altering anything else) then the above implies that $\Phi(\mathbf{y})$ becomes negative: you are then producing inefficiently. So $\Phi(\mathbf{y}) \leqslant 0$ for all $\mathbf{y} \in Y$.

An extremely simplified example of Φ may be useful at this point. Take the case in which two inputs ($y_3 \leqslant 0, y_4 \leqslant 0$) are used to produce two outputs ($y_1 \geqslant 0, y_2 \geqslant 0$) in the very special circumstances where three units of input 4 can always be 'traded off' – that is substituted – for exactly one unit of input 3, and where one unit of input 3 can produce either one unit of output 1 or ten units of output 2. The production function for this technology, using the sign convention noted above, is:

$$\Phi(\mathbf{y}) = 30y_1 + 3y_2 + 30y_3 + 10y_4 \leqslant 0 \tag{2.3}$$

which can be written more illuminatingly as

$$y_1 + \frac{1}{10}y_2 \leqslant [-y_3] + \frac{1}{3}[-y_4] \tag{2.4}$$

The left-hand side of (2.4) gives the possible output combinations for any arbitrarily specified combination of inputs on the right-hand side. (Recall that the expressions in the [ ] will be positive or zero.) For example, in this *special* case, we could just use good 3 to produce good 2 in which case, setting $y_1 = y_4 = 0$, (2.4) becomes:

$$y_2 \leqslant -10\,y_3 \tag{2.5}$$

which says that one unit of good 3 can produce up to 10 units of good 2.

The contours of Φ are of particular interest. Take first of all contours in pig–labour space by 'slicing horizontally' through Figure 2.2 at the 500-sausage mark and at the 1000-sausage mark – see Figure 2.3, where the interior of the set Y at each level has been shaded. Note that each contour, known as an *isoquant*, is a set of line segments, the kinks corresponding to the different basic techniques[4] $\mathbf{y}^1, \ldots, \mathbf{y}^5$. The reason for its being made up of line segments, rather than a set of isolated points, is simply the divisibility assumption A6. Note too that because of assumptions A5 and A6 any contour

[4] For the purists: a technique $\mathbf{y}^* \in Y$ is a *basic* technique if there exists no set of other techniques $\{\mathbf{y}^1, \ldots, \mathbf{y}^S\} \subset Y$ such that $\mathbf{y}^*$ can be written as a convex combination of $\mathbf{y}^1, \ldots, \mathbf{y}^S$.

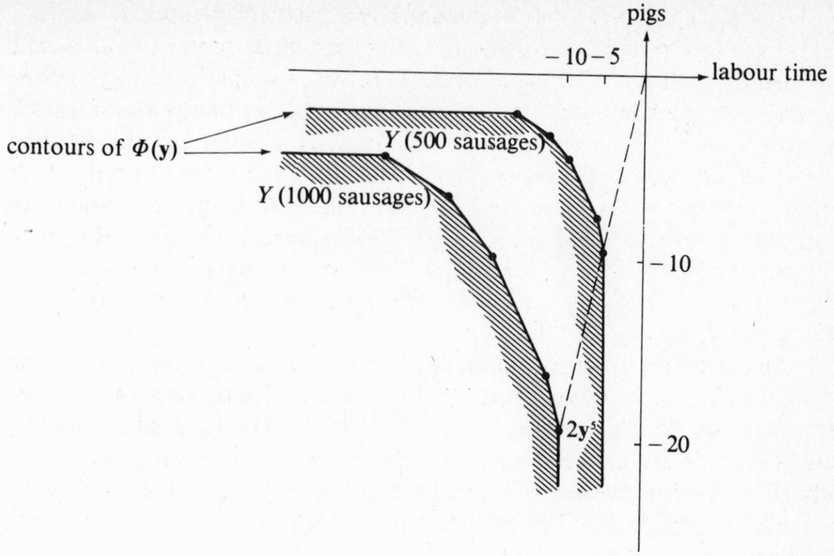

Figure 2.3 Isoquants

can be constructed from any other contour by 'radial projection' through the origin (draw dotted lines like the one shown, and measure the distance from the origin to each contour: observe that the distance to the 1000-sausage isoquant is always twice that to the 500-sausage isoquant).

Now look at the effect on output of increasing just one input whilst the other is held constant. This can be seen in pig–sausage space in Figure 2.4. Clearly whether the level of labour input is fixed at 5 units, 10 units or any other level, output per unit of input (the sausage/pig ratio) at first remains constant and then falls as successive techniques are brought into use. This illustrates the so-called principle of diminishing returns to one factor: it is a consequence of there being more than one essential input and the convexity of Y.

Let us return to the economy-wide production process – the amalgam of A, B and C which turns land and labour into potatoes and sausages via the intermediate good of pigs. Clearly we may *in principle* draw diagrams like those of Figures 2.2 to 2.4 for this general case, but it would be a messy task because of the number of dimensions involved. However, one interesting aspect of the composite production process is the shape of contours of the production function drawn in the space of two *outputs*. That is, *given* a fixed number of units of land and hours of labour time, what is the set of points giving the maximal outputs of potatoes and sausages? This must look something like Figure 2.5 where Y is, of course, the technology set for the amalgamated processes A-B-C. The reason for this is that in view of Axiom

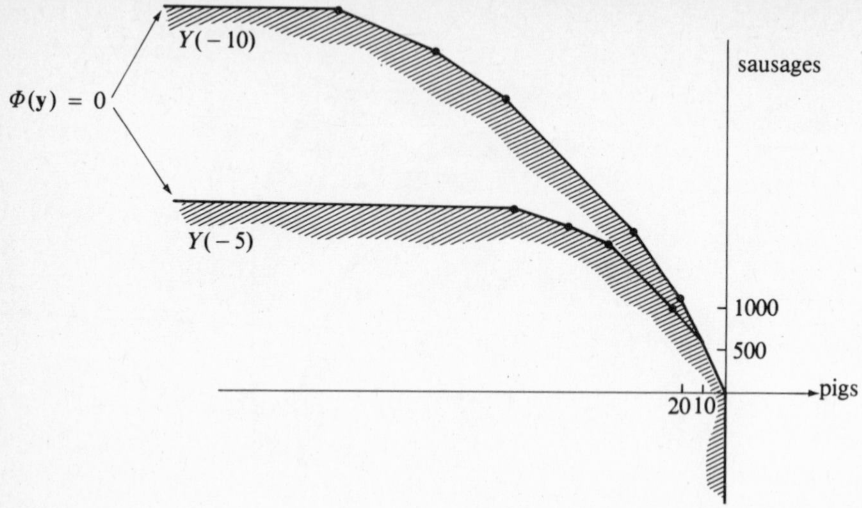

Figure 2.4

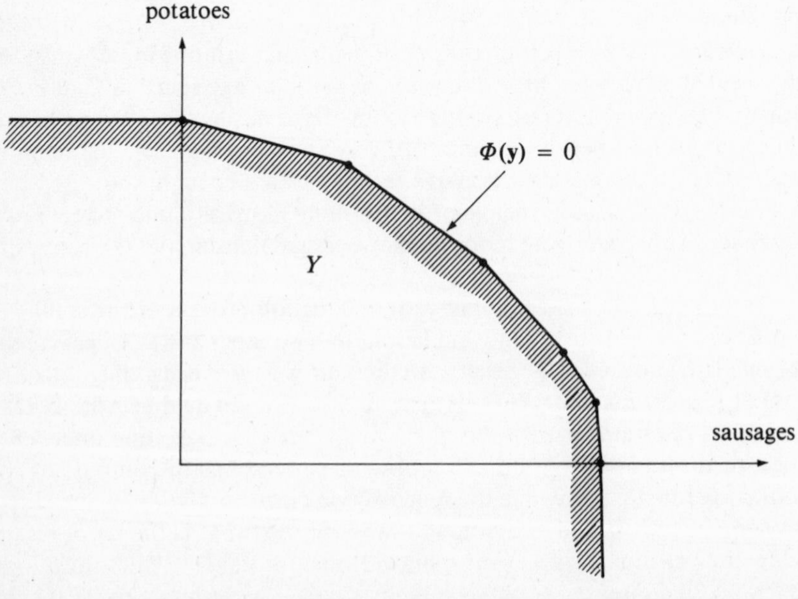

Figure 2.5 The production possibility frontier

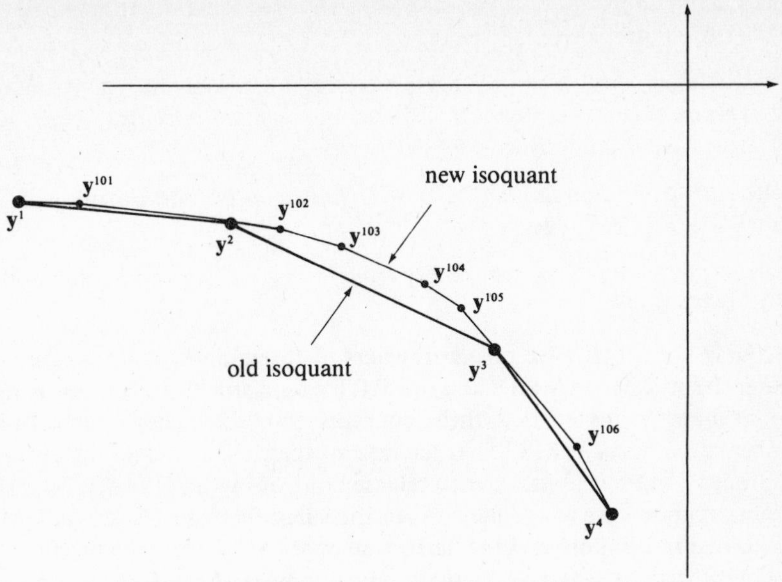

Figure 2.6 More of the basic techniques

A6 Y must be a convex set, so the two dimensional 'slice' of it illustrated here must also be convex.[5] The number of kinks in its 'upper boundary' (along which $\Phi(\mathbf{y}) = 0$) will depend on the technology of processes A and B as well as on that of process C which we have already examined. The sausage–potato frontier is usually known as the *production possibility frontier* or as the *transformation curve*. It represents the set of technically efficient combinations of outputs that are obtainable from given quantities of non-produced inputs (in this case land and labour).

Whilst virtually all the essential results of production theory can be obtained with as simplistic a framework as this, it must be admitted that the 'kinkiness' of Y_e – arising out of there being a finite number of basic techniques – makes manipulation rather unwieldy. Intuition suggests that if there were more and more of the basic techniques eventually Y_e would become a smooth surface in $\mathbb{R}^n$. For example, note in Figure 2.6 how the isoquants corresponding to the techniques ($\mathbf{y}^1$, $\mathbf{y}^2$, $\mathbf{y}^3$, $\mathbf{y}^4$) alter when new techniques ($\mathbf{y}^{101}, \ldots, \mathbf{y}^{106}$) are introduced. Indeed it is convenient to assume that there are infinitely many such techniques.

---

5 For the purists: Y is a convex set; sausage–potato plane P is a sub-space of $\mathbb{R}^n$, also a convex set; so $Y \cap P$ must be a convex set. We are ignoring for the moment the problem of pig-indivisibility in process B.

AXIOM A7 (smoothness): $\Phi(\mathbf{y})$ is everywhere twice differentiable and its second partial derivative commute.

This enables us to make extensive use of calculus methods. Let i and j denote any two *inputs* ($y_i, y_j < 0$); let h and l denote any two *outputs* ($y_h, y_l > 0$); and write the partial derivative $\partial\Phi(\mathbf{y})/\partial y_i$ as Φ_i.

DEFINITION 2.2: *the marginal rate of technical substitution* of input i for input j, MRTS_{ij}, is Φ_j/Φ_i.

DEFINITION 2.3: *the marginal rate of transformation* of good h into good l, MRT_{hl} is Φ_l/Φ_h.[6]

Of course even if Φ were not *everywhere* differentiable (as in the case of Figures 2.2 to 2.5) the MRTS and the MRT would still be useful – it is just that we have to accept that these concepts will be undefined at a finite number of points. The MRTS_{ij} is the rate at which we introduce input i into the production process in order to release units of input j; the MRT_{hl} is the amount of good h we would have to sacrifice in order to get one extra unit of good l. Figure 2.7 illustrates the derivation of the MRT from the production possibility frontier where y_1, y_2 are assumed to be outputs. If $y_3, \ldots, y_n$ are taken to be constant then differentiate equation (2.2) to obtain

$$\Phi_1\,\mathrm{d}y_1 + \Phi_2\,\mathrm{d}y_2 = 0$$

which implies

$$\mathrm{MRT}_{21} \equiv \Phi_1/\Phi_2 = -\frac{\mathrm{d}y_2}{\mathrm{d}y_1}\text{[7]} \tag{2.6}$$

Clearly the MRT is the (absolute) slope of the production possibility curve. Likewise the MRTS is the (absolute) slope of the isoquant. In the simplified example of equation (2.3) we see that $\mathrm{MRT}_{21} = 10$ and $\mathrm{MRTS}_{43} = 3$.

2.4 Single-Output Production

The form of the production function Φ can be rather unwieldy for some purposes such as the analysis of a single firm or plant in the economy. So it is often convenient to assume that the processes in the economy be suitably defined such that for each process there is *no joint production* – i.e. to assume that there are possibly many inputs producing but a single output. This is certainly true of the processes A, B and C illustrated in Figure 2.1, but would not be true if pigs were used to produce a second good (pigskin for

[6] In principle the MRT could be applied to *any* pair of goods – inputs or outputs (so that the MRTS is just a special case of MRT), but it is common to restrict its use to a pair of outputs.
[7] Note that this differential is taken along $\Phi(\mathbf{y}) = 0$, with $y_3, \ldots, y_n$ constant.

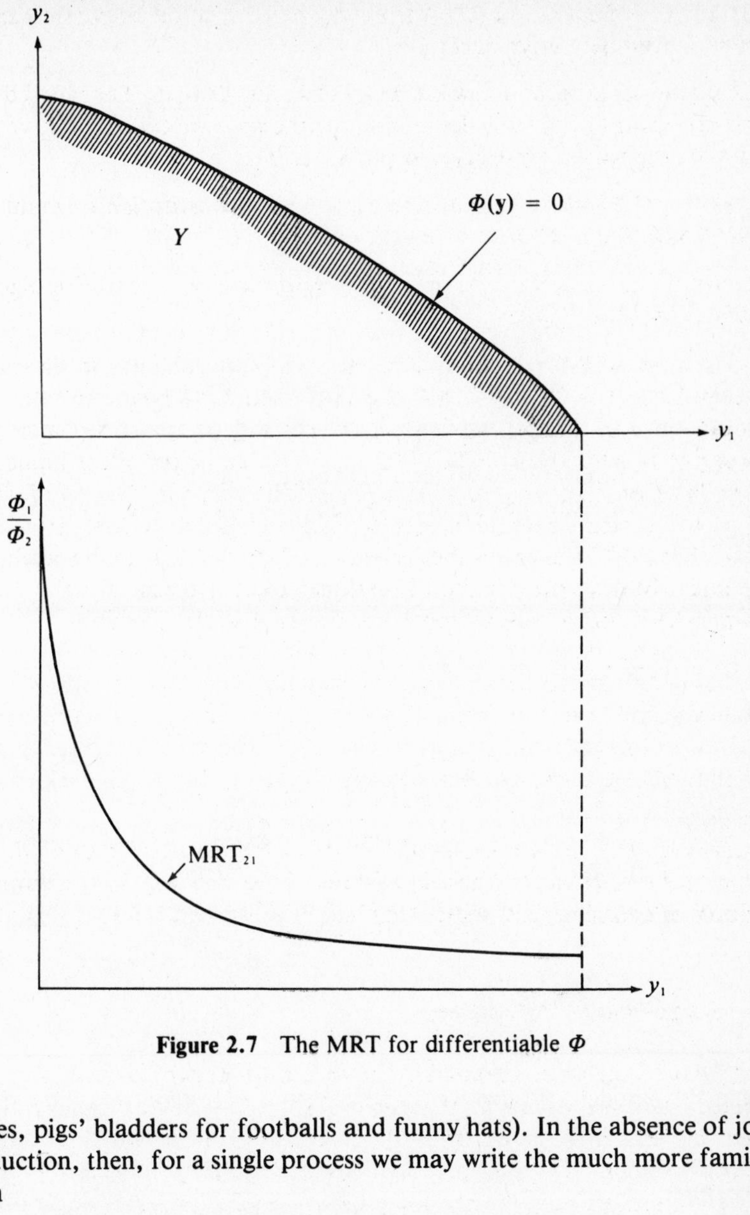

Figure 2.7 The MRT for differentiable Φ

purses, pigs' bladders for footballs and funny hats). In the absence of joint production, then, for a single process we may write the much more familiar form

$$Q \leqslant G(z_1, \ldots, z_m) \tag{2.7}$$

a slight generalisation of (2.1) where again Q is the output of that process, and $z_1, \ldots, z_m$ the (non-negative) quantities of m inputs. We now are distinguishing notationally between inputs and outputs, and it is helpful to measure Q and each of the z_is along the positive axis. Obviously (2.7) could be simply rewritten

$$-G(-y_1, \ldots, -y_m) + y_{m+1} \leqslant 0 \tag{2.8}$$

where $-y_i \equiv z_i$, $i = 1, \ldots, m$, $y_{m+1} \equiv Q$: the expression on the left of (2.8) is none other than $\Phi(\mathbf{y})$ for this case. Compare the two ways of writing down the production relationship set out in Table 2.1. Written as (2.7) the production function is said to be in *explicit* form; written as (2.8) the production function is in *implicit* form. From the definition (f) on page 8 of Chapter 1 we see that G must be *concave* function. Obviously too we must have equality in (2.7) and (2.8) for technically efficient production. The explicit form enables one to describe overall changes in scale of production more conveniently. If, for some $\lambda > 1$ we have $G(\lambda\mathbf{z}) > \lambda G(\mathbf{z})$ we say there are increasing returns to scale; if $G(\lambda\mathbf{z}) < \lambda G(\mathbf{z})$ we say there are decreasing returns to scale. Using (2.7) we may now introduce a further concept unambiguously.

DEFINITION 2.4: given the differentiable explicit production function (2.7), the *marginal product* of any input i is $\partial G(\mathbf{z})/\partial z_i$, $i = 1, \ldots, m$, a non-negative number.[8]

Once again we shall write G_i as shorthand for the marginal product. Evidently in Figure 2.4 the (absolute) slope of the boundary of the set $Y(-5)$ gives the marginal product of pigs in producing sausages when there are 5 hours of labour in use; the slope of the boundary of the set $Y(-10)$ gives the marginal product when there are 10 hours of labour used as input. In view of the convexity of the set Y (the *concavity* of the function G) we see that the marginal product of i must be non-increasing in z_i. Clearly the MRTS_{ij} can also be written G_j/G_i.

Now let us investigate the significance of Axioms A5 and A6 (constant returns to scale) for the shape of G. Since a proportionate expansion of all inputs by a scalar λ results in expansion in output by λ we may write

$$\lambda Q = G(\lambda\mathbf{z}) \tag{2.9}$$

that is:

$$G(\lambda\mathbf{z}) = \lambda G(\mathbf{z}) \tag{2.10}$$

so that the (explicit) production function must be *homogeneous of degree one*. Differentiating (2.10) with respect to λ and then putting $\lambda = 1$ we immediately get *Euler's Theorem* for the case of a function homogeneous of degree one:

---

[8] We can all think of practical examples where more input leads to *fewer* outputs so that marginal products are negative. However in the technically efficient set Y_e the marginal products *must* be non-negative.

Table 2.1 Essential notation for Chapter 2: Production

Single output		*Multiple outputs*	
$(z_1, \ldots, z_m)$	: vector of inputs	$(y_1, \ldots, y_n)$	: vector of 'net outputs'
$z_j \geqq 0$	: level of input j	$y_j < 0$	: input
$Q \geqq 0$	: level of output	$y_i > 0$	: output
G	: production function	Φ	: production function
$Q = G(\mathbf{z})$	: technical efficiency	$\Phi(\mathbf{y}) = 0$	: technical efficiency
		Y	: the technology set

$$\sum_{i=1}^{m} z_i G_i(\mathbf{z}) = G(\mathbf{z}) \tag{2.11}$$

– the so-called 'adding up' property of constant returns to scale. So the sum of each input multiplied by its own marginal product must equal the total output. And this leads us immediately to write

$$z_i G_i(\mathbf{z}) = G(\mathbf{z}) - \sum_{j \neq i} z_j G_j(\mathbf{z}) \tag{2.12}$$

Since every term in (2.12) is non-negative we must have

$$G_i(\mathbf{z}) \leqq G(\mathbf{z})/z_i \tag{2.13}$$

– i.e. the marginal product is less than or equal to the average product.[9] Finally note a very important feature of the MRTS. Consider two input vectors $\mathbf{z}$ and $\lambda\mathbf{z}$ where λ is any positive scalar. The marginal product of input i at $\lambda\mathbf{z}$ is $\partial G(\lambda\mathbf{z})/\partial(\lambda z_i) = \frac{1}{\lambda}\partial G(\lambda\mathbf{z})/\partial z_i = \partial G(\mathbf{z})/\partial z_i$ in view of (2.10). Hence, for any $\lambda > 0$:

$$\text{MRTS}_{ij}(\lambda\mathbf{z}) = \text{MRTS}_{ij}(\mathbf{z}) \tag{2.14}$$

So, if we draw a ray through the origin every isoquant will have the same slope as it intersects that ray – a point which we note from Figure 2.3. This illustrates the result that a homogeneous function (of any degree) must be *homothetic* – i.e. its contours have the 'radial blow up' property illustrated in Figure 2.3 (see also page 6 of Chapter 1).

So a constant-returns-to-scale production function has all its contours of the 'same shape'. But how can this shape be described?

DEFINITION 2.5: *the elasticity of substitution* of input i for input j in

---

9 This is also true of *any* concave G, not just those exhibiting constant returns to scale: see Exercise 2.10.

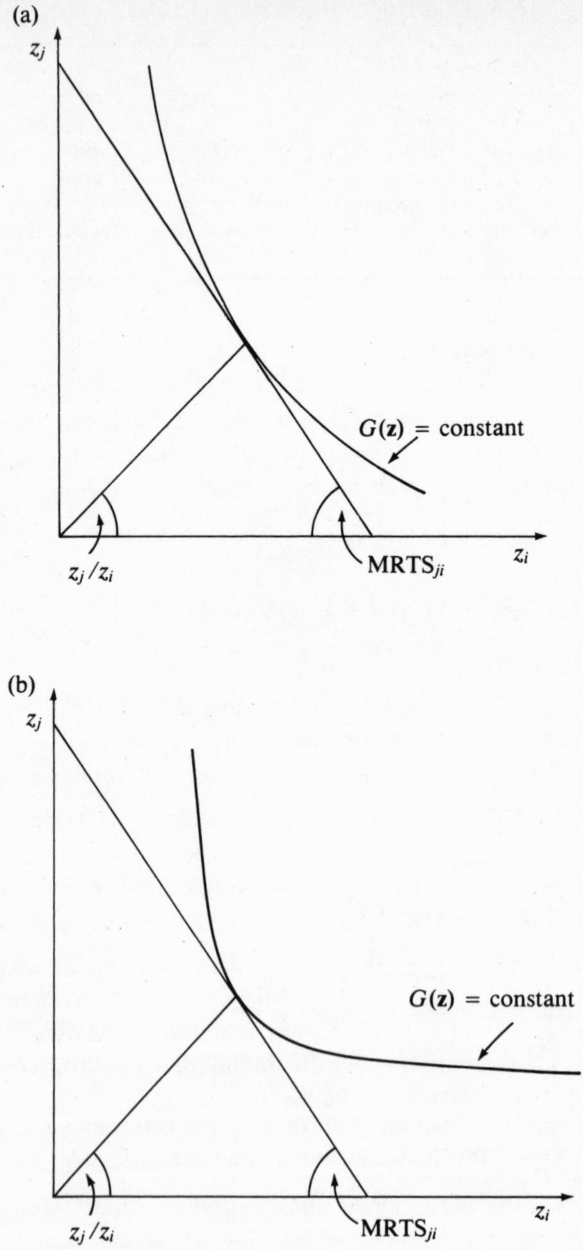

Figure 2.8 (a) High elasticity of substitution; (b) Low elasticity of substitution

production, σ_{ij}, is given by

$$\sigma_{ij} = \frac{\partial \log(z_j/z_i)}{\partial \log(G_i/G_j)} \tag{2.15}$$

The interpretation of this is most easily seen by taking the reciprocal of σ_{ij} – this is then the percentage increase in the MRTS_{ji} resulting from a 1 per cent increase in the input ratio z_j/z_i. Hence, conversely, if a 1 per cent increase in MRTS_{ji} is associated with a *large* percentage increase in z_j/z_i we say that σ_{ji} is *high* – see Figure 2.8a; and if a 1 per cent increase in MRTS_{ji} is associated with a *small* percentage increase in z_j/z_i we say that σ_{ji} is *low* – see Figure 2.8b. The operational importance of the elasticity of substitution will become evident in subsequent chapters.

2.5 Summary

Much of the essential framework for a suitable general economic model of production is contained in a handful of axioms: A1–A3 which in effect make precise what we mean by production; A4 which says that waste is possible; and the more controversial A5 and A6 which rule out decreasing and increasing returns to scale. Simple models using this basic framework will recur time and again in our examination of microeconomic principles. Usually we shall work with the convenient device of the production function in explicit form rather than with production sets. Sometimes, however, the implicit form of the production function is particularly useful (see Chapters 6–8) and the possibility of technical inefficiency in production should not be overlooked.

Marginal products, the marginal rate of transformation and the elasticity of substitution in production will make constant appearances in the following chapters, and you should make sure that you understand these concepts thoroughly before proceeding to Chapter 3.

Further Reading

Chiang, A.C. (1984) *Fundamental Methods of Mathematical Economics* (3rd edn), McGraw-Hill, sections 20.3 and 20.4.

Koopmans, T.C. (1957) *Three Essays on the State of Economic Science*, Essay 1, McGraw-Hill.

Exercises

(Those marked * are especially important).

2.1 Suppose that a unit of output Q can be produced by any of the following combinations of inputs

$$\mathbf{z}^1 = \begin{bmatrix}0.2\\0.5\end{bmatrix} \quad \mathbf{z}^2 = \begin{bmatrix}0.3\\0.2\end{bmatrix} \quad \mathbf{z}^3 = \begin{bmatrix}0.5\\0.1\end{bmatrix}$$

(a) Construct the isoquant for $Q = 1$.
(b) Assuming constant returns to scale, construct the isoquant for $Q = 2$.
(c) If the technique $\mathbf{z}^4 = [0.25, 0.5]$ were also available would it be included in the isoquant for $Q = 1$?

2.2 Illustrate Axioms A1–A6 in a 1-input 1-output model.
2.3 Show that Axioms A3 and A4 together imply Axiom A2.
2.4 A firm uses two inputs in the production of a single good. The input requirements per unit of output for a number of alternative techniques are given by the following table:

Process	1	2	3	4	5	6
Input 1	9	15	7	1	3	4
Input 2	4	2	6	10	9	7

The firm has exactly 140 units of input 1 and 410 units of input 2 at its disposal.

(a) Discuss the concepts of technological and economic efficiency with reference to this example.
(b) Describe the optimal production strategy for the firm.
(c) Would the firm prefer 10 extra units of input 1 or 20 extra units of input 2?

2.5 Sketch the MRTS and the MRT corresponding to Figures 2.3 and 2.5.
2.6 Write down the production functions for each of the following production sets and sketch their isoquants:

(a) $Y = \{\mathbf{y} : y_1^2 + y_2^2 \leqslant -y_3 - y_4, y_1 \geqslant 0, y_2 \geqslant 0, y_3 \leqslant 0, y_4 \leqslant 0\}$
(b) $Y = \{\mathbf{y} : y_1^\alpha - [-y_2]^\beta - [-y_3]^\gamma \leqslant 0, y_1 \geqslant 0, y_2 \leqslant 0, y_3 \leqslant 0\}$
(c) $Y = \{\mathbf{y} : \log y_1 \leqslant \frac{1}{2}\log(y_2 y_3), y_1 \geqslant 0, y_2 \leqslant 0, y_3 \leqslant 0\}$
(d) $Y = \{\mathbf{y} : y_1 + y_2 \leqslant \min(-y_3, -y_4/\alpha), y_1 \geqslant 0, y_2 \geqslant 0, y_3 \leqslant 0, y_4 \leqslant 0\}$

Check whether the basic axioms are satisfied in each case, and, where relevant, sketch the production possibility frontiers.

2.7 Sketch a production set Y that violates Axiom A6 – i.e. that has indivisibilities.

*2.8 (a) Give an example of a production function $G(z_1, z_2)$ that is

(i) homogeneous of degree 1,
(ii) homogeneous of degree 2,
(iii) homogeneous of degree $\frac{1}{2}$,
(iv) homothetic but *not* homogeneous

in each case illustrating the function diagrammatically.

(b) Let $G(\mathbf{z})$ be homogeneous of degree γ in $\mathbf{z}$, where $\mathbf{z} \equiv (z_1, \ldots, z_m)$. Show that $G_i(\mathbf{z})$ is a function that is homogeneous of degree $\gamma - 1$.

2.9 A certain firm can employ two types of labour – Greeks and Italians. Workers of each type are identical except for the language they speak. Hence the marginal product of a Greek is much higher if he works with Greeks than if he works with Italians (and correspondingly for the Italian workers). What are the problems involved in sketching the production function of such a firm? Which of the axioms A1–A6 may be violated?

2.10 Show that if $G(\mathbf{z})$ exhibits decreasing returns to scale in the neighbourhood of $\mathbf{z}$ then $\partial G(\alpha\mathbf{z})/\partial\alpha < G(\mathbf{z})$ in the neighbourhood of $\alpha = 1$. Write down the equivalent result for a locally increasing returns to scale function.

*2.11 In an economy with two inputs z_1, z_2 and one output, and where production is given by the constant returns-to-scale differentiable production function

$$Q \leqslant G(z_1, z_2)$$

show: (i) that for all non-zero values of z_2 the technology can also be represented by the function

$$q \leqslant g(k)$$

where $k \equiv z_1/z_2$ and $q \equiv Q/z_2$, and $g(\xi)$ is the function $G(\xi, 1)$; (ii) that the marginal product of input 1 may be written $g'(k)$, where g' is the first derivative of g; and (iii) that the marginal product of input 2 may be written $g(k) - kg'(k)$.

If the function G is twice differentiable everywhere and satisfies the conditions

$$G(0, z_2) = G(z_1, 0) = 0$$

$$\left.\begin{array}{l} G_1(z_1, z_2) > 0 \\ G_2(z_1, z_2) > 0 \end{array}\right\} \quad 0 < z_1, z_2 < \infty$$

G strictly concave-contoured

$$\lim_{z_i \to 0} G_i(z_1, z_2) = \infty, \qquad i = 1, 2$$

$$\lim_{z_i \to \infty} G_i(z_1, z_2) = 0, \qquad i = 1, 2$$

find the corresponding restriction on g. Sketch the isoquants of G and the function g. Discuss the interpretation of the function g.

*2.12 Given the production function

$$Q = \left[\sum_{i=1}^{n} \alpha_i z_i^{\beta}\right]^{\gamma/\beta}$$

where $0 < \alpha_i < 1$, $\sum_{i=1}^{n} \alpha_i = 1$, $\gamma > 0$, $\beta < 1$, explain the significance of the parameters β and γ and show that the elasticity of substitution for any pair of inputs is

$$\sigma = \frac{1}{1 - \beta}$$

Draw isoquants for the cases $\sigma = 0$, $\sigma = 1$, $\sigma = \infty$. [Hint: in the case $\sigma = 1$, use the result $\lim_{r \to 0} [x^r - 1]/r = \log x$.] Assuming that inputs receive as payments exactly their marginal products, show that if $\gamma = 1$ payments for inputs exactly exhaust the product.

2.13 Investigate the production function

$$Q = [z_1^{\alpha} + [z_2 - b]^{\alpha}]^{1/\alpha}$$

with respect to (i) returns to scale, and (ii) the elasticity of substitution at different levels of production given

(a) $z_1 > 0$, $z_2 > b > 0$
(b) $z_1 > 0$, $z_2 > 0 > b$

*2.14 Consider a production process with two inputs and one output given by

$$Q = G(z_1, z_2)$$

where G is concave and exhibits constant returns to scale. Show that the elasticity of substitution can be written as

$$\sigma = \frac{G_1 G_2}{G\, G_{12}}$$

Show that in the notation of Exercise 2.11 we may also write

$$\sigma = \frac{g'}{g''}\left[\frac{g'}{g} - \frac{1}{k}\right]$$

3

The Firm

3.1 The Nature and Objectives of the Firm

We now introduce an anonymous, and in some ways rather curious, actor to our scene. The neo-classical firm is simply an agency that is assumed to exist to organise the production process to achieve certain objectives. *Why* it exists, what motives there are for individuals to set up such an institution, we do not question. Assuming that it does exist, however, we can make some reasonable suggestions about its objectives.

First of all we must establish the stage-setting in which this actor appears, and some more notation. In the main it is useful to consider the firm within a market environment freely choosing its output and input levels in the light of known prices, although some exceptions to this will appear below. So, corresponding to the net outputs $y_1, \ldots, y_n$ discussed in Chapter 2 we suppose that there are prices $p_1, \ldots, p_n$; in the case where we distinguish a particular *output* (Q) from m inputs ($z_1, \ldots, z_m$) we shall write the output price as P and the input prices as $w_1, \ldots, w_m$. Note that in either notation prices may be assumed to be *parametrically given* to the firm (the case of perfect competition), or they may actually depend on the quantities $\mathbf{y}$, Q, $\mathbf{z}$ – the case of (quasi-) monopoly or monopsony.[1] We may now define the following.

DEFINITION 3.1: the *profits*[2] of the firm are

(i) $\tilde{\Pi}(\mathbf{y}) = \sum_{i=1}^{n} p_i y_i$

or, equivalently,

(ii) $\Pi(Q, \mathbf{z}) = PQ - \sum_{j=1}^{m} w_j z_j$

---

1 The various situations covered by these terms are analysed on pp. 55–57.

2 We avoid the use of the term 'profit function' which has a special meaning discussed in Exercise 3.7.

It should be emphasised that these are merely two ways of writing the same thing. The first form is slightly more convenient when (as in Chapters 6–8) we consider many firms with different types of output and input. The second form is more convenient for the purposes of this chapter and in Chapters 9 and 11, in that the expression 'revenue (PQ) minus costs ($\Sigma w_j z_j$)' is made explicit.

It seems fairly safe to say that all firms will, at the very least, be interested in their profits. If we assume that (a) the economic environment is free from uncertainty, and (b) those who own the firm have effective control over its management, then intuition suggests – and Chapter 5 formally shows – that an optimal strategy is to maximise $\Pi(Q, \mathbf{z})$ by an appropriate choice of Q and $\mathbf{z}$. In an uncertain world this objective becomes somewhat blurred. Moreover, it may be that those who run the firm do so to suit their own ends rather than those who legally own it – a state of affairs that is made all the more possible in a world of uncertainty. However, for the moment, because of its theoretical importance we confine our attention to profit-maximising behaviour.

3.2 The Profit-Maximising Firm's Problem

For convenience we shall continue to assume that the firm produces a single output Q from m inputs $z_1, \ldots, z_m$. We shall also assume that the price P at which it can sell Q units of output is known – though clearly P may vary with Q. Likewise we shall also assume that the price w_i at which it can purchase z_i units of input is known – though once again w_i may depend on z_i. Then at any set of input levels $\mathbf{z}$ and output level Q profits are

$$\Pi(Q, \mathbf{z}) = P(Q)Q - \sum_{i=1}^{m} w_i(z_i) z_i \tag{3.1}$$

Obviously in view of the discussion of Section 3.1 the firm wishes to maximise (3.1) subject to the 'relevant' constraints. Apart from the obvious non-negativity restrictions on Q and $\mathbf{z}$ and the technology constraint, these may include short-run constraints on the availability of certain inputs ($z_i \leqslant \bar{z}_i$, $i = 1, \ldots, m_1$) and short-run fixed values of some inputs ($z_j = \bar{z}_j, j = m_1 + 1, \ldots, m_2$).[3] Formally the problem is

$$\max_{(Q,\, \mathbf{z})} \Pi(Q, \mathbf{z}) \quad \text{subject to}$$

$$Q \geqslant 0 \tag{3.2}$$

[3] Of course m_1 could be zero and/or $m_2 = m_1$ when either or both of these sets of short-run constraints are absent.

$$\mathbf{z} \geqslant \mathbf{0} \tag{3.3}$$
$$Q \leqslant G(\mathbf{z}) \tag{3.4}$$
$$z_i \leqslant \bar{z}_i,\ i = 1, \ldots, m_1 \tag{3.5}$$
$$z_i = \bar{z}_o,\ i = m_1 + 1, \ldots, m_2 \tag{3.6}$$

The solution to this problem characterises *economic efficiency* for the firm: there are three types of solution that may be relevant. (i) The analytically trivial (but often economically important) solution $Q = 0$, $\mathbf{z} = \mathbf{0}$: at no positive output level can the firm make a profit; (ii) an input-constrained maximum where at least one of the constraints (3.5) is binding: here the scale of operation of the firm is limited by something like a short run-capacity constraint; (iii) an interior maximum: short-run constraints (3.5) are not binding and the solution may be characterised by conventional calculus. Of course it may be that no solution to the problem exists because profits are unbounded above on the set of technically feasible points. The scale of operation of the firm is then indefinitely large. If such a state of affairs arises it usually means that the model has been mis-specified and some essential constraint such as (3.5) or (3.6) has been omitted.

A general solution to (3.1)–(3.6) is rather unwieldy, so we shall examine a number of illuminating special cases.

3.3 The Competitive Firm

If we assume that the firm can buy *as much as it wants to*[4] of each input i at a fixed price w_i and can sell its output at a uniform price P, then the optimisation problem may be solved by maximising the Lagrangean function.

$$\mathscr{L}(Q, \mathbf{z}, \lambda) = PQ - \sum_{i=1}^{m} w_i z_i + \lambda\,[G(\mathbf{z}) - Q] \tag{3.7}$$

subject to (3.2) and (3.3). The first-order conditions[5] for maximising this function are:

$$\frac{\partial \mathscr{L}}{\partial Q} \leqslant 0 \tag{3.8}$$

$$Q\frac{\partial \mathscr{L}}{\partial Q} = 0 \tag{3.9}$$

$$\frac{\partial \mathscr{L}}{\partial z_i} \leqslant 0, \qquad i = 1, \ldots, m \tag{3.10}$$

---

[4] That is, constraints (3.5) and (3.6) are irrelevant.

[5] The second-order conditions are automatically satisfied because $G(\mathbf{z})$ is concave. This means that we are maximising a concave function $\mathscr{L}$ over a convex subset of $\mathbb{R}_{+}^{m+2}$.

$$z_i \frac{\partial \mathscr{L}}{\partial z_i} = 0, \qquad i = 1, \ldots, m \tag{3.11}$$

$$\frac{\partial \mathscr{L}}{\partial \lambda} \leqslant 0 \tag{3.12}$$

$$\lambda \frac{\partial \mathscr{L}}{\partial \lambda} = 0 \tag{3.13}$$

If we assume an interior solution $Q>0$, then clearly from (3.8) and (3.9) we must have (3.8) satisfied with *equality*. Moreover, in view of the No Free Lunch axiom (A2) at least *some* inputs must be used in positive amounts and so, from (3.10) and (3.11), for each such input we have that (3.10) must be satisfied with equality. Evaluating (3.8) for $Q > 0$ therefore, we find

$$P - \lambda = 0 \tag{3.14}$$

Obviously P cannot be zero for an interesting solution, so (3.14) reveals that λ must be positive. In which case (3.13) reveals that $\frac{\partial \mathscr{L}}{\partial \lambda} = 0$ and so we find

$$G(\mathbf{z}) - Q = 0 \tag{3.15}$$

– i.e. the firm is on the boundary of its technology set. Now evaluate (3.10) and (3.11). Using (3.14) we obviously have

$$-w_i + PG_i = 0 \qquad \text{if } z_i > 0 \tag{3.16}$$

and

$$-w_j + PG_j \leqslant 0 \qquad \text{if } z_j = 0 \tag{3.17}$$

where PG_i is the value of the marginal product of input i – that is output price times marginal (physical) product. From (3.16) and (3.17) we also get

$$G_{i'}/G_i = w_{i'}/w_i, \quad \text{if } z_i > 0 \text{ and } z_{i'} > 0 \tag{3.18}$$

and

$$G_j/G_i \leqslant w_j/w_i, \quad \text{if } z_i > 0 \text{ but } z_j = 0 \tag{3.19}$$

This is illustrated in Figures 3.1 and 3.2 and is summarised in the following theorem.

THEOREM 3.1: (a) profit-maximising output under perfect competition is technically efficient.

(b) At the profit-maximising technique, for any input the value of the marginal product of the input must be no greater than the price of that input. If the input is purchased in positive amounts, the value of its marginal product must equal its price.

(c) For any two inputs, i, i' purchased in positive amounts $\text{MRTS}_{ii'}$ must equal the input price ratio $w_{i'}/w_i$.

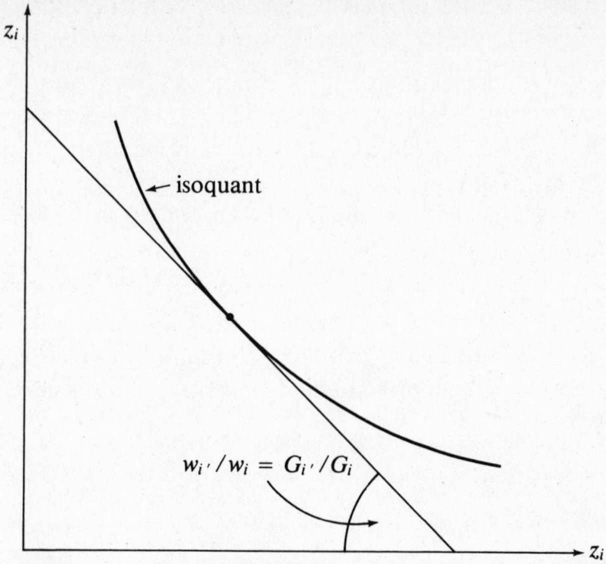

Figure 3.1

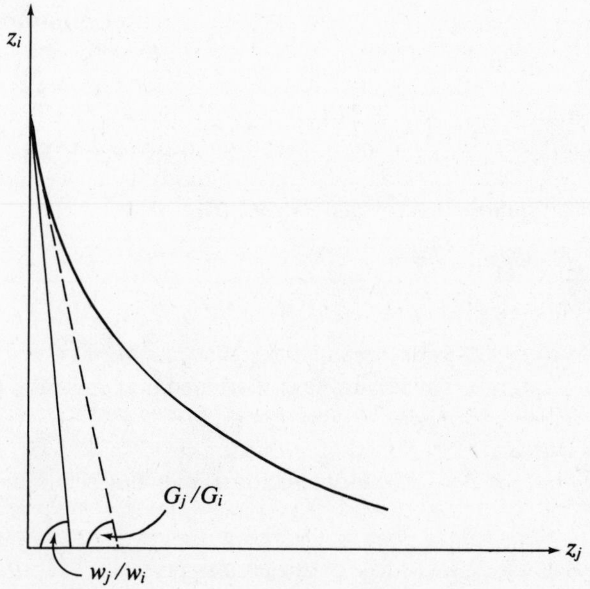

Figure 3.2

(d) If i is an input that is purchased, and j is an input that is not purchased then MRTS_{ij} will be less than or equal to the input price ratio w_j/w_i.

This characterises the optimum, but it tells us little about the nature of the firm's demand for inputs and its supply of output in response to different market conditions. Nor indeed does it reveal what happens when there are exogenous changes such as shifts in the technology set. Hence we shall examine the explicit solution to the first-order conditions (3.14) to (3.19), and the comparative statics of this system.

The key to this is the convenient device of splitting the optimisation problem into two stages:

(1) For any given output level Q_0, find the optimum combination of inputs.
(2) Given the optimised input combinations for any output level, find the optimum output level.

3.4 The Cost Function

Suppose the firm's output is arbitrarily fixed at $Q = Q_0$. Then the maximand (3.7) becomes

$$\hat{\mathscr{L}}(\mathbf{z}, \lambda_0) = \text{constant} - \sum_{i=1}^{m} w_i z_i + \lambda_0 [\, G(\mathbf{z}) - Q_0] \tag{3.20}$$

where the new Lagrange multiplier λ_0 must depend on the arbitrary Q_0 that has been chosen. This can obviously be rewritten as the problem 'minimise the cost of inputs $\Sigma_i w_i z_i$ subject to $G(\mathbf{z}) \geqslant Q_0$'. Obviously, we can follow through the argument in Section 3.3 to obtain solutions very similar to (3.16) and (3.17). Let us assume that all inputs are demanded in positive amounts – this can easily be arranged by a renumbering of goods. Then we end up with $m + 1$ equations from the first-order conditions:

$$w_i = \lambda_0 G_i(\mathbf{z}), \quad i = 1, \ldots, m \tag{3.21}$$

$$Q_0 = G(\mathbf{z}) \tag{3.22}$$

If $(\mathbf{z}^*, \lambda_0^*)$ is a set of $m + 1$ variables satisfying these equations then clearly $\mathbf{z}^*$ is a set of input demands that solves the constrained maximisation problem (the cost-*minimisation* problem) of equation (3.20).

Whilst we can always be sure that a solution $(\mathbf{z}^*, \lambda_0^*)$ will exist even if G does *not* satisfy Axiom A6[6,7], the input vector $\mathbf{z}^*$ may not be unique. Figure

---

6 Because $\sum_{i=1}^{m} w_i z_i$ is a continuous function of $\mathbf{z}$ and the set $\{\mathbf{z}{:}\mathbf{z} \geqslant \mathbf{0}, Q_0 = G(\mathbf{z})\}$ is closed and bounded below.

7 See Chiang, W. (1984) *Fundamental Methods of Mathematical Economics*, 3rd edn, p. 376 or Sydsaeter, K. (1981) *Topics in Mathematical Analysis of Economics*, Academic Press, New York, p. 290 for an interpretation of the Lagrange multiplier λ_0.

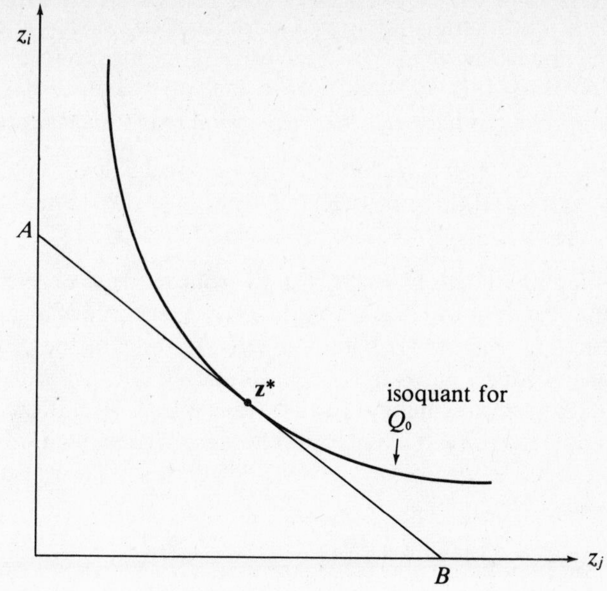

Figure 3.3

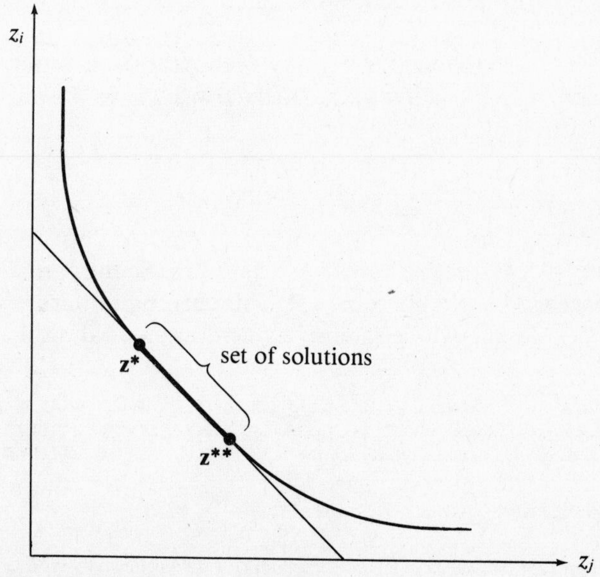

Figure 3.4

3.3 illustrates a case where $\mathbf{z}^*$ is unique for the given Q_0. Figure 3.4 illustrates a case where $\mathbf{z}^*$ is not unique, though Axiom A6 is satisfied – anywhere on the line segment between $\mathbf{z}^*$ and $\mathbf{z}^{**}$ is a cost-minimising input combination; Figure 3.5 illustrates the case where points $\mathbf{z}^*$ and $\mathbf{z}^{**}$ are two possible cost-minimising input combinations.[8] We may now introduce a central concept.

DEFINITION 3.2: the *cost function* $C(\mathbf{w}, Q)$ is a real valued function of the input price vector and the output level which gives the minimum value of $\sum_{i=1}^{m} w_i z_i$ subject to $z_i \geqslant 0$, $i = 1, \ldots, m$ and $Q \leqslant G(\mathbf{z})$.

Obviously the cost function will be found from the first-order conditions (3.21) and (3.22) and so will depend on the known technology as summarised in the production function G. Let us investigate some of the properties of this function. In what follows let $\mathbf{z}^*$ be a solution input vector derived from (3.21) and (3.22) and assume that the arbitrary output level is Q_0.

Firstly, note that $C(\mathbf{w}, Q_0)$ is nondecreasing and concave in $\mathbf{w}$.[9] Secondly, C is homogeneous of degree one in $\mathbf{w}$. Thirdly, a standard result of constrained maximisation is that

$$\lambda_0^* = C(\mathbf{w}, Q_0)/\partial Q_0 \equiv C_Q(\mathbf{w}, Q_0) \tag{3.23}$$

the *marginal cost* at output Q_0, a positive number for a non-trivial solution. Fourthly $C_j(\mathbf{w}, Q_0)$, the derivative of the cost function with respect to w_j is simply z_j^*, the jth component of the optimal input demand vector. To see this, note first of all that (3.22) and the fact that Q_0 is fixed implies that

$$0 = \sum_{i=1}^{n} G_i(\mathbf{z}^*)\mathrm{d}z_i = \sum_{i=1}^{n} w_i \mathrm{d}z_i/\lambda_0 \tag{3.24}$$

where the second step follows from (3.21). Hence the fixed output condition means that any input variation must satisfy $\Sigma\, w_i \mathrm{d}z_i = 0$. Now differentiate the cost function with respect to w_j:

$$\frac{\partial C(\mathbf{w}, Q_0)}{\partial w_j} = \frac{\partial}{\partial w_j}\sum_{i=1}^{n} w_i z_i^* = z_j^* + \sum_{i=1}^{n} w_i \partial z_i^*/\partial w_j \tag{3.25}$$

But, in view of (3.24), the last term in (3.25) is zero. So the partial derivative of C with respect to w_j simply equals z_j^*. This very important result, known as *Shephard's Lemma*, will be extensively used in the analysis that follows.

---

8 Obviously the first-order conditions are no longer *sufficient* to locate the interior solution since $G(\mathbf{z})$ is no longer a concave function. It is easy to check that whenever there is more than one solution, each solution vector must be linearly dependent on the others since

$$\text{minimum cost} = \sum_{i=1}^{m} w_i z_i^* = \sum_{i=1}^{m} w_i z_i^{**} \text{ implies } \sum_{i=1}^{m} w_i[z_i^* - z_i^{**}] = 0$$

9 Obviously it must be increasing in any w_i for which $z_i > 0$. On concavity see Exercise 3.1: this also implies that it is continuous in $\mathbf{w}$. See page 35 in the Fuss and McFadden reference at the end of this chapter for a more detailed discussion of the cost function.

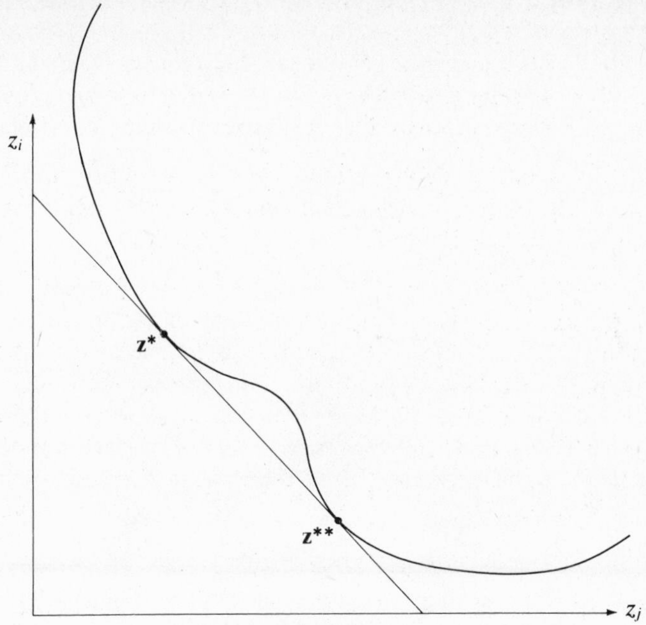

Figure 3.5

It should be stressed that these properties are *always* true whatever the shape of the underlying production function – even if it should be non-concave as in Figure 3.5.

THEOREM 3.2: the competitive firm's cost function $C(\mathbf{w}, Q)$ is nondecreasing and continuous in **w**, homogeneous of degree one in **w** and concave in **w**. It is strictly increasing in Q and in at least one w_i. At every point where the differential is defined

$$\partial C(\mathbf{w}, Q)/\partial w_i = z_i^* \tag{3.26}$$

the optimal demand for input i.

There is an attractive duality introduced by the use of the cost function. We can represent the firm's optimisation problem with fixed output as *either* minimising costs subject to an output constraint as in (3.20), *or* as maximising output subject to a cost constraint $C(\mathbf{w}, Q) \leqslant C_0$ where $C_0 = C(\mathbf{w}, Q_0)$.

Finally we note an interesting property of the relationship between the cost function and the underlying technology. Consider Z_0, the set of all possible input combinations that would *always* cost as least as much as the minimum-cost combination required to produce Q_0, whatever the input price vector **w** happened to be: $Z_0 \equiv \{\mathbf{z} : \sum_{i=1}^{n} w_i z_i \geqslant C(\mathbf{w}, Q_0) \text{ for all } \mathbf{w} \geqslant \mathbf{0}\}$. In Figure 3.3 it is clear that at prices **w**, where the optimal input combination is

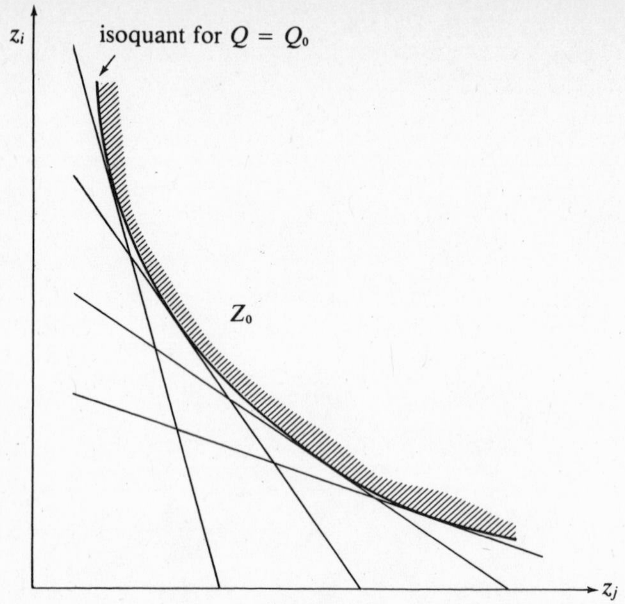

Figure 3.6

z*, any point on, or above and to the right of, the line AB must cost as least as much as $C(\mathbf{w}, Q_0)$: call this set of points $Z(\mathbf{w})$. Now change the input prices arbitrarily and again compute minimum cost of producing Q_0: the line AB shifts and a new set of 'at-least-costly-inputs' is defined. We can go on repeating this exercise for different input prices and clearly Z_0 is none other than the intersection of all the sets $Z(\mathbf{w})$ where **w** ranges over all possible input prices. This is illustrated in Figure 3.6 where the boundary of Z_0 is apparently the original Q_0-isoquant. Is this always so? Certainly it is always true that any point lying 'above' the isoquant must be a member of Z_0: this is obvious from the definition of the cost function $C(\mathbf{w}, Q_0)$. But there may be points in Z_0 other than those lying in the set $\{\mathbf{z} : G(\mathbf{z}) \geqslant Q_0\}$. To see this note that Z_0 must be a convex set, since it is the intersection of a collection of convex sets, and examine an isoquant such as that in Figure 3.5. If we trace out the boundary of the set Z_0 we shall end up with a diagram like that in Figure 3.7. The interesting thing to note about this is that non-convexity A_2A_3 in the isoquant, and the portions where it 'curls back' at each end, above A_1 and to the right of A_4, have been 'ironed out' in the construction of Z_0. In fact if you constructed the set Z_0 for the isoquant in Figure 3.4 you would end up with *the same* figure as Figure 3.7.

What has happened then is that in the process of cost-minimisation we have simply ignored those bits of the isoquant that violate Axioms A4 and A6 – they are treated as economically irrelevant, so that for practical

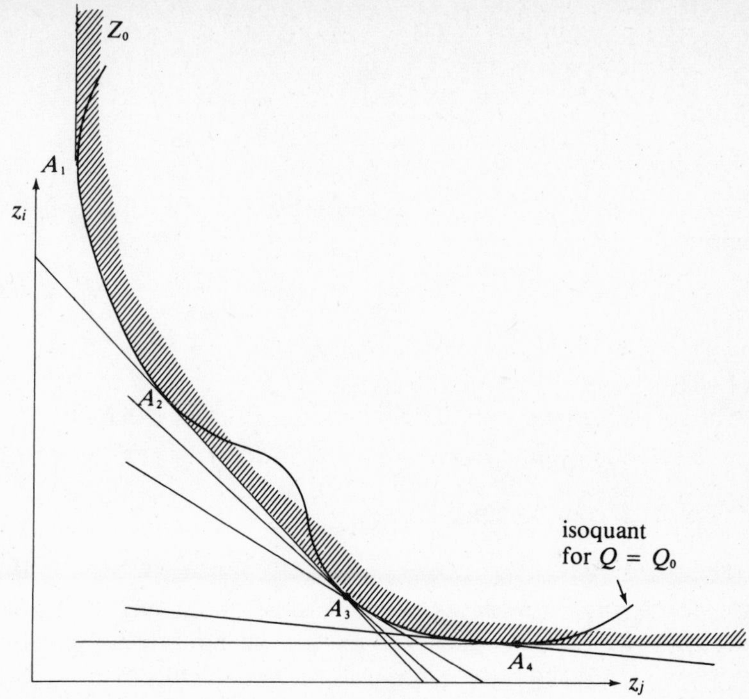

Figure 3.7

purposes we might just as well have started with a more conventional isoquant such as that in Figure 3.4. And of course if we attempt to 'work back' from a given cost function to find the underlying technology we will find that the unconventional bits in Figure 3.5 will have simply disappeared. So for cost-minimising firms that can buy inputs freely at a given price we do not have to worry about 'perverse' production functions. We shall find a similar useful result holds when we examine the theory of the household in Chapter 4.

Now let us turn to the 'second half' of the original problem – the determination of an optimum output level.

3.5 Output of the Competitive Firm

Once the cost function $C(\mathbf{w}, Q)$ has been found as a solution to the first part of the optimisation problem, we may now respecify the problem (3.1)–(3.6) as

$$\max \hat{\Pi}(Q)$$

where

$$\hat{\Pi}(Q) \equiv PQ - C(\mathbf{w}, Q)$$

subject to

$$Q \geqslant 0, \hat{\Pi}(Q) \geqslant 0 \tag{3.27}$$

The first-order condition for this maximisation problem yields an optimum quantity Q^* where

$$P = C_Q(\mathbf{w}, Q^*) \qquad \text{if } Q^* > 0 \tag{3.28}$$

$$P \leqslant C_Q(\mathbf{w}, Q^*) \qquad \text{if } Q^* = 0 \tag{3.29}$$

i.e. price is less than or equal to marginal cost.

The second-order conditions for a maximum require that

$$\partial^2\hat{\Pi}(Q)/(\partial Q^2) \leqslant 0$$

at Q^* which, of course, implies that

$$C_{QQ}(\mathbf{w}, Q) \geqslant 0 \tag{3.30}$$

at $Q = Q^*$: so the optimum must be on a constant or rising portion of the marginal cost curve. However we must also take into account the obvious restriction (3.27), that no firm will stay in business if it makes a loss. Clearly this requires

$$C(\mathbf{w}, Q)/Q \leqslant P \tag{3.31}$$

'average cost less than or equal to price' at the optimum.

If for all Q greater than or equal to some output Q_1 we find $C_{QQ} > 0$, then a maximum must exist: *either* maximum profit is at the trivial point $Q = 0$, $\hat{\Pi}(Q) = 0$, *or* profit $\hat{\Pi}(Q)$ is at first positive, and then eventually negative as Q is increased. But will Q^* be unique? Figure 3.8 illustrates a case where it is unique, and Figure 3.9 a case where it is not (any output in the range Q^* to Q^{**} is a solution). Certainly non-uniqueness is a problem that may well arise in practice for a firm whose technology includes a marginal cost curve containing 'horizontal segments'. However, abstracting from such cases[10] it is useful to introduce the following concept.

DEFINITION 3.3: the *supply function* $S(P)$ of the competitive firm is a non-negative, real-valued function of one variable such that $Q^* = S(P)$ is a solution to (3.28)–(3.31).

---

[10] For example by assuming C_Q is everywhere a strictly increasing function of Q. This is in fact inconsistent with Axiom A5 of Chapter 2 since A5 explicitly rules out 'diminishing returns to scale'. However for a particular firm it may make sense to drop A5. See the discussion on page 19 of Chapter 2 and Exercise 3.2 of this chapter.

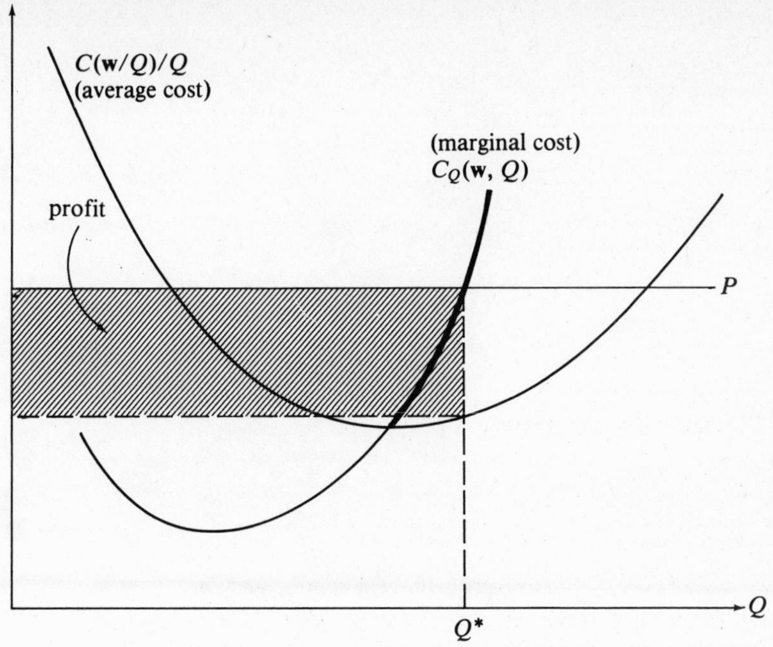

Figure 3.8

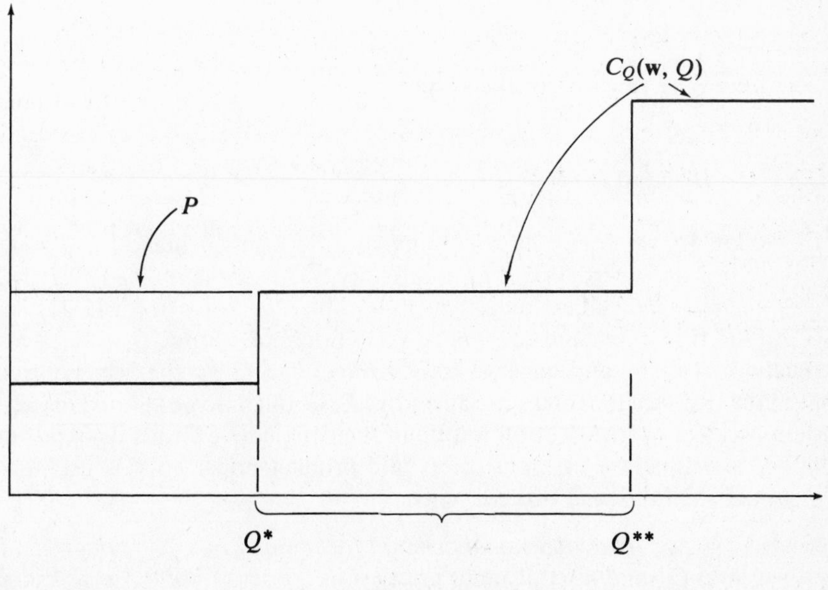

Figure 3.9

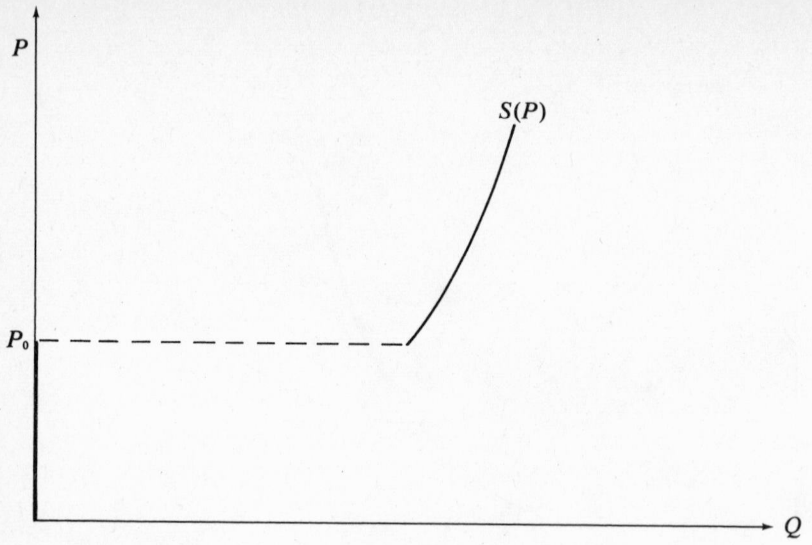

Figure 3.10 The supply function

It is easily seen that S must be an increasing or constant function with a discontinuity at P_0 where $P_0 = C(\mathbf{w}, Q)/Q$ – see Figure 3.10 where $S(P)$ is drawn using the Marshallian convention of output quantity on the horizontal axis.

THEOREM 3.3: the output of the competitive profit-maximising firm is a non-decreasing function of the output price.

3.6 The Demand for Inputs

In Section 3.4 we were only able to look at the firm's demand for inputs $\mathbf{z}$ *conditional* on a particular output quantity Q_0 being maintained. We shall now examine the subject more generally. Since we know from (3.21) and (3.22) the firm's demand for inputs, conditional on output Q, and its cost function $C(\mathbf{w}, Q)$, and since we know from (3.28)–(3.31) the firm's output given the cost function and a product price P, we ought to be able to combine these two bits of information to obtain the competitive firm's demand for inputs as a function of input prices and product price. So it is useful to introduce the following two concepts.

DEFINITION 3.4: the *conditional demand for inputs* $i = 1, \ldots, m$ given an output level Q_0, and a set of input prices $\mathbf{w}$, is the set of vectors $\mathbf{z}$ satisfying (3.21) and (3.22). Where the set has only one member for any Q_0 and $\mathbf{w}$ the

Table 3.1 Essential notation for Chapter 3: The Firm

variables		*functions*	
$z_1, \ldots, z_m$	: levels of inputs	$G(\mathbf{z})$	: production function
$w_1, \ldots, w_m$	: prices of inputs	$C(\mathbf{w}, Q)$	: cost function
Q	: level of output	$\hat{D}^j(\mathbf{w}, Q)$	: conditional input demand
P	: price of output	$D^j(\mathbf{w}, P)$	: unconditional input demand
Π	: profits	$S(P)$	: supply function

conditional input demand function for input i is written

$$z_i^* = \hat{D}^i(\mathbf{w}, Q_0), \qquad i = 1, \ldots, m \tag{3.32}$$

DEFINITION 3.5: the *demand for inputs* $i = 1, \ldots, m$ given output price P and input price $\mathbf{w}$ is the set of vectors $\mathbf{z}$ satisfying (3.21) and (3.22) and (3.27)–(3.31). Where the set has only one member for any P and $\mathbf{w}$, the (unconditional) *input demand function* for input i is written

$$z_i^* = D^i(\mathbf{w}, P), \qquad i = 1, \ldots, m \tag{3.33}$$

Notice that (3.33) has to be homogeneous of degree zero in all its arguments. This is because originally it was derived from (3.16), and multiplying $\mathbf{w}$ and P by some positive constant clearly leaves (3.16) – and hence (3.33) — unchanged. So a uniform proportionate increase in the prices of all inputs and the price of output of a firm leaves its equilibrium unaltered.

These two functions and other essential notation are displayed for easy reference in Table 3.1. The wording of the two definitions alerts us to the fact that an input vector providing a solution to the optimisation problem may well not be unique, though it is not hard to find restrictions that will ensure uniqueness so that $\hat{D}^i$ and D^i are well defined.

THEOREM 3.4: (a) if the production function is strictly concave-contoured, conditional input demand functions are always well defined and continuous for all positive input prices.

(b) if the production function is strictly concave, input demand functions are always well defined and continuous for all positive input prices.

The proof of these two theorems is given in Appendix A. Let us note a couple of restrictive features of the conditions in Theorem 3.4.

The technical qualification 'for all positive input prices' is inserted to ensure that attention is restricted to the particular region in which the 'strict concavity' implies the 'Hessian property' cited on page 9 of Chapter 1. If we want to guarantee that the demand functions are defined *everywhere* (i.e. including situations where one or more $w_j = 0$) then we would have to impose the Hessian property directly on the production function.

Note that *strict* concavity of G in Theorem 3.4(b) is inconsistent with Axiom A5 for the reasons given in the footnote on page 44 of this chapter. We have already seen (in Figure 3.9) that optimal output (and hence the demand for inputs) may be indeterminate if the production function were not strictly concave, but what would happen to the conditional demand for inputs? We can get the right answer by non-rigorous manipulation of Figures 3.4 and 3.5. Imagine a change in input prices that shifts the line AB around to different positions on the diagram. Obviously in Figure 3.4 the top left-hand corner and the bottom right-hand corner of the isoquant look like the strictly concave case so that conditional input demands (for given Q_0) change smoothly in response to prices. But as the line AB becomes coincident with the flat section as shown, multiple solutions to the optimisation problem suddenly emerge and at that set of prices, input demands are no longer well defined. Likewise in Figure 3.5: start with input j relatively expensive, so that AB is very steep. Now make the line AB progressively flatter. Optimal input demands (for given Q_0) change smoothly as we move along the isoquant until we reach $\mathbf{z}^*$: then we 'jump' to $\mathbf{z}^{**}$. A similar argument applies to ordinary (unconditional) demands. So *non-convexities in the production set (non-concavities in the production function) give rise to discontinuities in input demands.*

For the sake of convenience let us suppose that $\hat{D}^i$ and D^i are well defined so that we may easily examine the response of the firm to changes in its market environment. Our basic relationships are (3.26), (3.28) and (3.33). Let us examine first a change in the price of one input, w_j. Differentiate equations (3.26) and (3.28) in the neighbourhood of $\mathbf{z}^*$ and Q^* with respect to w_j, allowing Q^* and z_i^* to vary. We obtain

$$C_{ij}(\mathbf{w}, Q^*) + C_{iQ}(\mathbf{w}, Q^*)\frac{\partial Q^*}{\partial w_j} = \frac{\partial z_i^*}{\partial w_j} \tag{3.34}$$

$$0 = C_{Qj}(\mathbf{w}, Q^*) + C_{QQ}(\mathbf{w}, Q^*)\frac{\partial Q^*}{\partial w_j} \tag{3.35}$$

Substituting from (3.35) into (3.34) so as to eliminate $\partial Q^*/(\partial w_j)$ and rearranging, we obtain

$$\frac{\partial z_i^*}{\partial w_j} = C_{ij}(\mathbf{w}, Q^*) - \frac{C_{iQ}(\mathbf{w}, Q^*)C_{jQ}(\mathbf{w}, Q^*)}{C_{QQ}(\mathbf{w}, Q^*)} \tag{3.36}$$

This can be simplified a little further. Clearly using (3.26) and (3.32) we have

$$C_i(\mathbf{w}, Q) = \hat{D}^i(\mathbf{w}, Q) \tag{3.37}$$

so

$$C_{ij}(\mathbf{w}, Q) = \hat{D}^i_j(\mathbf{w}, Q)^{11} \tag{3.38}$$

Hence (3.36) becomes

$$D^i_j = \underset{\text{[substitution effect]}}{\hat{D}^i_j} - \underset{\text{[output effect]}}{C_{iQ}C_{jQ}/C_{QQ}} \tag{3.39}$$

The first term on the right-hand side of (3.38) is known as the 'substitution effect' because it represents that component of the change in demand that would arise if w_j were to increase and the firm were *constrained to keep on the same isoquant*, output stays constant and all that happens is that inputs are substituted for one another because of the relative price changes. The second term is the 'output effect' because it reflects the change in input demand resulting from the change in optimal output induced by the shift in the marginal cost curve. Figure 3.11 shows a possible outcome of an increase in w_j. In part (a) we see that the increase in w_j has shifted the marginal cost curve upward,[12] reducing optimal output from Q^* to Q^{**}; in part (b) we see that were output to be maintained at Q^*, the increase in w_j shifts optimal input demand from $\mathbf{z}^*$ to $\hat{\mathbf{z}}$ (substitution effect); but of course optimal output has changed, so there is a further shift $\hat{\mathbf{z}} \to \mathbf{z}^{**}$ (output effect). The new equilibrium is at $(\mathbf{z}^{**}, Q^{**})$.

Let us have a closer look at the substitution term $\hat{D}^i_j$. Since we may assume that C is twice differentiable, clearly $\partial^2 C(\mathbf{w}, Q)/\partial w_i \partial w_j = \partial^2 C(\mathbf{w}, Q)/\partial w_j \partial w_i$; so we see immediately that $\hat{D}^i_j = \hat{D}^j_i$ wherever the derivatives are defined – i.e. the matrix $\hat{\mathbf{D}} \equiv \|\hat{D}^i_j\|$ must be symmetric. Moreover because C is concave in $\mathbf{w}$, its matrix of second partial derivatives $\|C_{ij}\|$ must be negative semi-definite. Hence $\hat{\mathbf{D}}$ must be negative semi-definite; i.e. for an arbitrary m-vector $\mathbf{x}$:

$$\sum_{i=1}^{m}\sum_{j=1}^{m} x_i \hat{D}^i_j x_j \leqslant 0 \tag{3.40}$$

In particular we must have $\hat{D}^i_i \leqslant 0$. In fact we can show that if G were everywhere smooth and concave contoured, then for all $\mathbf{w} > 0$ we have $\hat{D}^i_i < 0$. Hence the *conditional demand for input i must be a decreasing function of its own price.*

Now it is also obvious that the output effect term, $-C_{iQ}C_{jQ}/C_{QQ}$ is also symmetric in i and j and that for the *own price* case ($i = j$) it must be strictly negative ($-C_{iQ}^2/C_{QQ}$) as long as input price w_i has *some* effect on marginal cost C_Q. Hence we immediately see also that $D^i_i < 0$: *(unconditional) demand for input i is a decreasing function of its own price.*

---

11 Following our previous convention $\hat{D}^i_j(\mathbf{w}, Q) = \partial \hat{D}^i(\mathbf{w}, Q)/\partial w_j$ etc.

12 The marginal cost curve *need not* be shifted upwards, since C_{iQ} can be of any sign – see Exercise 3.4.

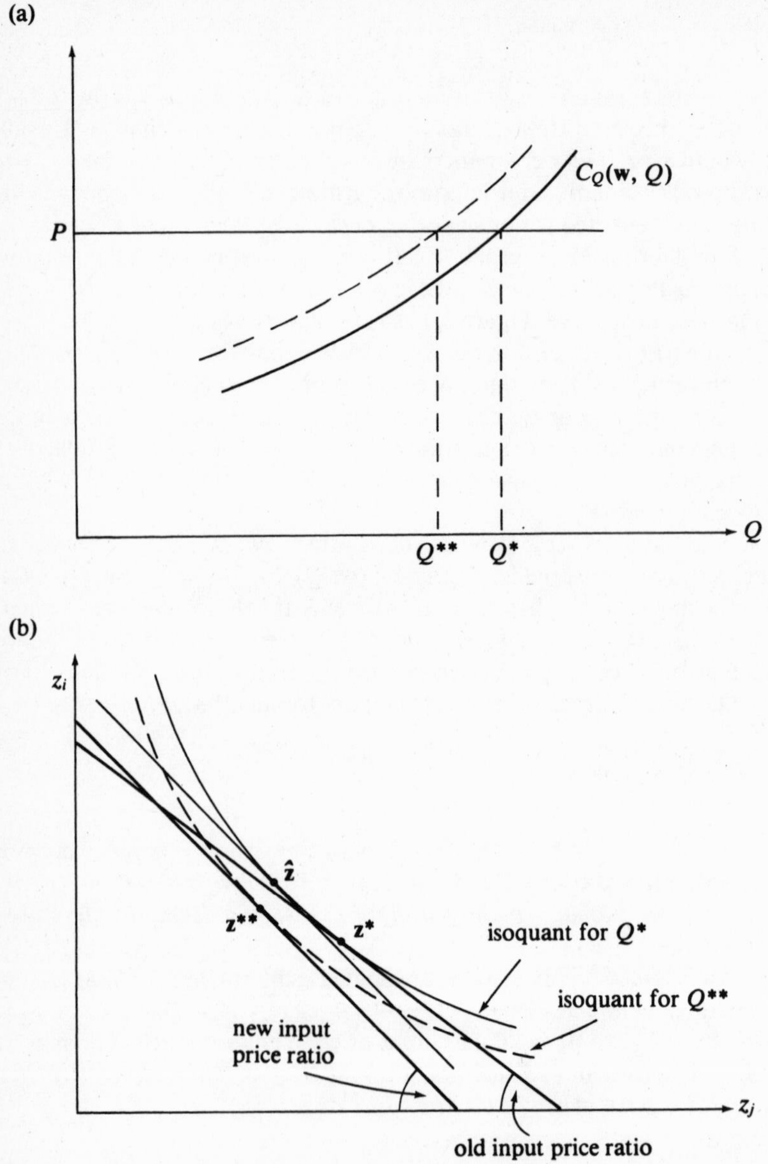

Figure 3.11 Increase in price of input j

Next consider the effect of a change in the output price P keeping $\mathbf{w}$ constant. Differentiating (3.26) and (3.28) in the neighbourhood of $(\mathbf{z}^*, Q^*)$ with respect to P one obtains

$$C_{iQ}(\mathbf{w}, Q^*)\,\mathrm{d}Q^* = \mathrm{d}z_i^* \tag{3.41}$$

$$\mathrm{d}P = C_{QQ}(\mathbf{w}, Q^*)\,\mathrm{d}Q^* \tag{3.42}$$

from which we obtain immediately

$$\frac{\partial z_i^*}{\partial P} = \frac{C_{iQ}}{C_{QQ}} \tag{3.43}$$

This is positive or negative as an increase in w_i raises ('normal' case) or lowers ('regressive' case) marginal cost C_Q. We can summarise all these results as follows.

THEOREM 3.5: (a) the effect of an increase in w_j on the conditional demand for input i equals the effect of an increase in w_i on the conditional demand for input j.

(b) the same result holds for the unconditional input demands.

(c) The *own price* effect of an increase in the price of input i on both the conditional demand for input i ($\hat{D}_i^i$) and on the unconditional demand for input i (D_i^i) must each be non-positive.

(d) the absolute size of D_i^i must be at least as great as $\hat{D}_i^i$.

Finally, a simple geometrical experiment with Figure 3.11 suggests that the higher the elasticity of substitution, the more elastic will input demand be in response to changes in input price (see Definition 2.5 and Figure 2.8). In the case of two inputs and constant returns to scale this is easily confirmed since the own-price elasticity of input demand is given by[13]

$$\frac{w_j}{z_j} D_j^j = -\sigma\,[1 - v_j] \tag{3.44}$$

where σ is the elasticity of substitution and v_j is the share of payments to input j as a proportion of the value of total output, $j = 1, 2$; $v_1 + v_2 = 1$.

We shall now extend this basic analysis in the next two sections by considering what happens if there are some constraints on the choice of inputs, and what happens if the firm has some control over prices.

3.7 The Short and Long Run

The 'short run' is not next Tuesday. However it is convenient to distinguish in principle between a period so short that a certain set of inputs is fixed and

---

13 See Exercise 3.8.

a period that is sufficiently long for the input to be varied. For notational simplicity assume that input m is fixed in the short run, so that $z_m = z_m^0$, but is variable in the long run.

DEFINITION 3.6: if $z_m = z_m^0$, then *short-run variable costs* $V(\mathbf{w}, Q, z_m^0)$[14] are the solution to

$$\left.\begin{array}{l} \min\limits_{\{z_1, \ldots, z_{m-1}\}} \sum\limits_{i=1}^{m-1} w_i z_i \text{ subject to} \\ \left\{\begin{array}{l} Q \leqslant G(z_1, \ldots, z_m) \\ z_m = z_m^0 \\ z_i \geqslant 0, i = 1, \ldots, m-1 \end{array}\right. \end{array}\right\} \tag{3.45}$$

Fixed costs are $w_m z_m^0$. The sum of variable costs and fixed costs is *short-run total costs*. The idea of these short run costs is that they are the best you can do *given* that you are committed to $z_m = z_m^0$.

Clearly, by definition of the cost function (Definition 3.2) we must have

$$C(\mathbf{w}, Q) \leqslant V(\mathbf{w}, Q, z_m^0) + w_m z_m^0 \tag{3.46}$$

with equality in (3.46) at Q_0 where $Q_0 = G(z_1^0, \ldots, z_m^0)$ and $(z_1^0, \ldots, z_m^0)$ is the (long-run) cost-minimising input combination. Dividing both sides of (3.46) by Q, we must have long-run average cost less than or equal to short-run average cost. Writing in the conditional demand function $z_m^0 = \hat{D}^m(\mathbf{w}, Q_0)$ we see that exactly at the point $Q = Q_0$, it is true that:

$$C(\mathbf{w}, Q) = V(\mathbf{w}, Q, \hat{D}^m(\mathbf{w}, Q)) + w_m \hat{D}^m(\mathbf{w}, Q) \tag{3.47}$$

which in turns equals $\sum_{i=1}^{m} w_i z_i^0$.

Let us look at the first-order behaviour of long- and short-run costs. First of all, let us see what happens when the arbitrary output level Q_0 is changed. Differentiating (3.47) with respect to Q we obtain, on simplification:

$$C_Q(\mathbf{w}, Q) = V_Q(\mathbf{w}, Q, z_m^0) + \frac{\partial C(\mathbf{w}, Q)}{\partial z_m} \hat{D}_Q^m(\mathbf{w}, Q) \tag{3.48}$$

again, *evaluated at* $Q = Q_0$. The last term in (3.48) is the effect on (long-run) costs that is transmitted via a change in optimal z_m. But by definition $C(\mathbf{w}, Q_0)$ is the *minimum* of $\sum_{i=1}^{m} w_i z_i$ at Q, and so $\partial C(\mathbf{w}, Q)/\partial z_m = 0$.[15] Hence the second term in (3.48) vanishes and so, at $Q = Q_0$, we have

$$C_Q(\mathbf{w}, Q_0) = V_Q(\mathbf{w}, Q_0, z_m^0) \tag{3.49}$$

---

14 Although it is convenient to write V this way, it is clear that whilst $\partial V/\partial w_i \geqslant 0$ for $i = 1, \ldots, m-1$, $\partial V/\partial w_m = 0$ – i.e. V does not depend on w_m *directly*, but only indirectly through z_m.

15 This is an application of a standard result known as an *envelope theorem* – see Dixit, A.K. *Optimization in Economic Theory*, pp. 27–30.

Thus when output is at the optimum level for the fixed input z_m^0, long-run marginal costs (C_Q) equal short-run marginal costs (V_Q). Hence it is obvious that at Q_0 the slope of the long-run average cost curve must equal the slope of the short-run average cost curve. We may also define the short-run input demands as the input combinations which satisfy the short-run cost minimisation problem (3.45). Since these depend on **w**, Q and z_m^0 we may write these demand functions as $\tilde{D}^i(\mathbf{w}, Q, z_m^0)$ for $i = 1, 2, \ldots, m - 1$.[16] Putting $Q = Q_0$ in (3.47) and differentiating for any i from 1 to $m - 1$ we have

$$C_i(\mathbf{w}, Q_0) = V_i(\mathbf{w}, Q_0, z_m^0) + \frac{\partial C(\mathbf{w}, Q_0)}{\partial z_m} \hat{D}_i^m(\mathbf{w}, Q_0) \tag{3.50}$$

Using the same reasoning as before, the second term in (3.50) must vanish, and applying Theorem 3.2 to the short-run cost function, we see that we have

$$C_i(\mathbf{w}, Q_0) = V_i(\mathbf{w}, Q_0, z_m^0)$$

which implies

$$\hat{D}^i(\mathbf{w}, Q_0) = \tilde{D}^i(\mathbf{w}, Q_0, z_m^0) \tag{3.51}$$

So *in the neighbourhood of* Q_0, short-run and long-run conditional input demands are identical.

Now let us look at the second-order conditions. Using the conditional input demand function $z_m = \hat{D}^m(\mathbf{w}, Q)$, differentiate (3.49) with respect to Q in the neighbourhood of $Q = Q_0$. We obtain:

$$C_{QQ} = V_{QQ} + \frac{\partial V_Q}{\partial z_m} \hat{D}_Q^m \tag{3.52}$$

Now differentiate (3.49) with respect to w_m:

$$C_{Qm} = \frac{\partial V_Q}{\partial z_m} \hat{D}_m^m \tag{3.53}$$

But from Theorem 3.2 we know that wherever the derivatives are defined $C_{Qm} = C_{mQ} = \hat{D}_Q^m$. So, making this substitution and simplifying (3.52) and (3.53) we get

$$C_{QQ} = V_{QQ} + [\hat{D}_Q^m]^2/\hat{D}_m^m \tag{3.54}$$

But we know from Theorem 3.5 that the *own price substitution effect* $\hat{D}_m^m$ must be non-positive (and if the production function is smooth $\hat{D}_m^m < 0$). Hence for a (locally) smooth production function we have

---

16 Once again note that $\partial \tilde{D}^i / \partial w_m = 0$ – the short-run conditional input does not depend *directly* on w_m.

$$C_{QQ} < V_{QQ} \tag{3.55}$$

– short-run marginal cost is steeper than long-run marginal cost.

In like manner differentiate (3.51) with respect to w_i ($i = 1,2, \ldots, m - 1$):

$$\hat{D}^i_i = \tilde{D}^i_i + \frac{\partial \tilde{D}^i}{\partial z^0_m} \hat{D}^m_i \tag{3.56}$$

and differentiate (3.51) with respect to w_m:

$$\hat{D}^i_m = \frac{\partial \tilde{D}^i}{\partial z^0_m} \hat{D}^m_m \tag{3.57}$$

Simplifying (3.56) and (3.57), and using the symmetry of $\hat{D}^i_m$ we get:

$$\hat{D}^i_i = \tilde{D}^i_i + [\hat{D}^m_i]^2 / \hat{D}^m_m \tag{3.58}$$

Immediately we see that $\hat{D}^i_i < \tilde{D}^i_i$ so that short-run input demand is less elastic (to its own price) than is long-run input demand.[17]

We can summarise our results thus:

THEOREM 3.6: (a) Where output is at the optimal level for the fixed input, short-run and long-run total costs are equal.

(b) At this output level, short- and long-run marginal costs are equal.

(c) At this output level, short- and long-run input demands are equal.

(d) The short-run marginal cost curve is at least as steep as the long-run marginal cost curve.

(e) Long-run input demands are at least as elastic as short-run demands.

Figure 3.12 illustrates these results in the case where long-run marginal costs are rising.[18] For example input *m* might represent the computer the firm has just installed: technological change may have shifted the production function so that it now wishes it had a larger computer, but in the mean time it is committed to the installation. The broken average cost curve through *A* represents the situation with the existing computer (allowing programmers' hours and materials to be varied in the short run); the broken average cost curve through *B* represents the short-run situation given that a computer of ideal size had been installed; the solid curve through *A* and *B* represents average costs given that size of computer installation can itself be taken as a variable input. In fact, as the opening remarks to this section suggest, the results may be easily generalised. Instead of just one constraint, $z_m = z^0_m$, let a further input be constrained, and then another and then another.

---

17 These results are examples of the *Le Chatelier Principle* – see the Samuelson (1983) reference at the end of this chapter.

18 For an example where long-run marginal costs are constant (where the production function satisfies both Axioms A5 and A6 of Chapter 2) see Exercise 3.6.

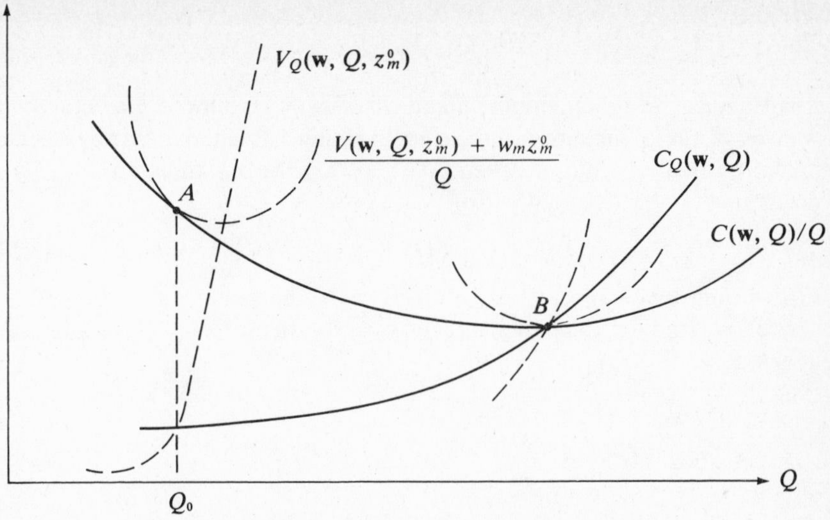

Figure 3.12 Short- and long-run cost curves

Then we have:

$$\left.\frac{\partial z_i}{\partial w_i}\right|_{\substack{\text{no}\\\text{constraints}}} \leqslant \left.\frac{\partial z_i}{\partial w_i}\right|_{\substack{\text{one}\\\text{constraint}}} \leqslant \left.\frac{\partial z_i}{\partial w_i}\right|_{\substack{\text{two}\\\text{constraints}}} \leqslant \ldots \leqslant 0 \quad (3.59)$$

– a result which makes the 'short run' as 'short' as you like.

3.8 The Price-Setting Firm

Let us briefly examine the behaviour of the profit-maximising firm which is *not* a price taker in all markets. There is an enormous range of possible alternative assumptions; many of which depend on special assumptions about the characteristics of the market in which the firm operates. We shall examine some of these special cases more closely in Chapters 6 and 10. For the present we shall merely assume that the firm faces either an output price that depends (in a determinate fashion) on the quantity of output sold, or input prices that depend on the quantities of inputs bought in.

Take first the case of the *monopolist*[19] who can buy as much of each

---

[19] He may not strictly be a monopolist. For example he may just have a localised monopoly; but the important thing is that he has a determinate downward-sloping demand curve. This is in sharp contrast to the situation discussed in Chapter 11. See also pp. 119–122 of Chapter 6.

input as he likes at prices $w_1, \ldots, w_m$, but whose output price is given by

$$P = P(Q) \tag{3.60}$$

Clearly the conditional input demand curves will be found in much the same way as in the competitive case, since nothing has altered with respect to assumptions about input markets. We may take the cost function $C(\mathbf{w}, Q)$ as determined in Section (3.4). Profits are now

$$\hat{\Pi}(Q) = P(Q)Q - C(\mathbf{w}, Q) \tag{3.61}$$

Maximising this subject $Q \geqslant 0$, $\hat{\Pi}(Q) \geqslant 0$ (the same condition as (3.27) above), we find the following necessary conditions for an interior maximum at $Q^* > 0$:

$$P_Q Q^* + P - C_Q = 0 \tag{3.62}$$

$$P(Q^*)Q^* - C(\mathbf{w}, Q^*) \geqslant 0 \tag{3.63}$$

$$\hat{\Pi}_{QQ} \leqslant 0 \tag{3.64}$$

where all the partial derivatives are evaluated at $Q = Q^*$. Note that (3.62) has the interpretation 'marginal revenue equals marginal cost' – cf. the rule (3.28) for the competitive firm. Let us investigate this a little further. Let the elasticity of product demand be $\eta \equiv \mathrm{dlog}Q/\mathrm{dlog}P = P(Q)/QP_Q(Q)$, a negative number. Then a slight rearrangement of (3.62) yields

$$P = \frac{C_Q}{1 + 1/\eta} \tag{3.65}$$

Since the maintainable sale price is likely to *fall* (or remain constant) as output increases, $\eta < 0$. It is also easily checked that condition (3.63) requires $1 + 1/\eta \geqslant 0$, so that $\eta \leqslant -1$. Hence we see that

$$P \geqslant C_Q \tag{3.66}$$

price is *greater* than marginal cost; moreover the discrepancy between price and marginal cost is greater the less is the absolute size of the elasticity $|\eta|$. If a monopoly faces inelastic demand then it will charge a higher price than it would were it to face conditions approximating horizontal demand curves (similar to the competitive case). Hence $\eta/[1 + \eta]$ might be interpreted as the differential the monopolist is able to command on account of his market power, and so this expression is sometimes known as the *degree of monopoly*.

Furthermore, note an interesting implication of condition (3.64). It imposes a requirement on a combination of the second derivatives of C and P, and not just on C alone (contrast this with (3.30) above in the competitive case). Specifically it requires that $P_{QQ} + 2P_Q - C_{QQ} \leqslant 0$. It is easy to see that this condition could be satisfied *(for some demand curves)* even if C_{QQ} were in fact *negative*. So a monopolist might well produce profitably under conditions of decreasing marginal costs – that is, in a situation where no set of competitive price-taking firms would produce.

Having seen the solution for the monopolist we find our second case may be easily resolved: take now the *monopsonist* who sells his product in a perfect market, but whose input prices are each functions of the amount of the input purchased $w_i(z_i)$. The expression for profits (3.1) may now be rewritten as

$$\Pi(Q, \mathbf{z}) = PQ - \sum_{i=1}^{m} w_i(z_i)z_i \tag{3.67}$$

Defining the elasticity of the supply of input i as $e_i = \text{dlog}z_i/\text{dlog}w_i$, and reasoning as before it is easy to see that we must now have

$$PG_i = w_i(z_i^*) + z_i^* \frac{\partial w_i(z_i^*)}{\partial z_i} \tag{3.68}$$

for an interior solution; this implies

$$w_i = \frac{PG_i}{1 + 1/e_i} \tag{3.69}$$

Equation (3.68) clearly reveals that the value of the marginal product is no longer equal to the input price, but to the 'marginal factor outlay', $\partial(w_i z_i)/\partial z_i$. In fact, if the input price increases with the amount of input bought – so that $e_i > 0$ – we see that the input clearly receives at the margin *less* than the value of its marginal product.

The case of the competitive firm assumes that the firm has absolutely no market power – that is, it is incapable of setting its price. What we have seen is that even if we allow the firm to have market power (over output or inputs) – as *long as its maximum profit is still well defined* – the previous results carry over with minor modifications. What exactly is meant by market power is discussed more fully in Chapter 11.

3.9 Summary

The principal lessons to be derived from the analysis of optimising behaviour by the firm can be simply restated:

- Economic efficiency for a price-taking firm can be characterised by a few elementary marginal conditions – Theorem 3.1.
- The optimisation procedure in a sense 'convexifies' the opportunity set.
- Competitive price-taking firms with strictly concave production functions have well-defined input–demand functions and out-

put–supply functions which have (positive) market prices as arguments.

- Short-run marginal cost curves and short-run input demand schedules are less elastic than their longer-run counterparts.
- Firms with a measure of market power use it to 'distort' prices by, for example, forcing the price of output above its marginal cost. Their perception of market responses (elasticities of demand for their output, elasticities of supply of their inputs, and not just the level of market prices), is essential to determining their optimal strategy.

We shall find that all of these principles are useful in subsequent chapters. In particular there are some important parallels between optimisation by firms and optimisation by households, to which subject we now turn.

Further Reading

Fuss, M. and McFadden, D. (1980) *Production Economics: A Dual Approach to Theory and Applications*, North Holland, Chs I.1, I.3.

Intriligator, M.D. (1971) *Mathematical Optimization and Economic Theory*, Prentice-Hall, Ch. 8.

Samuelson, P.A. (1983) *Foundations of Economic Analysis* (enlarged edn), Harvard University Press, Chs III and IV.

Exercises

3.1 Show that the cost function is homogeneous of degree one in $\mathbf{w}$. Show that the cost function is concave in $\mathbf{w}$. [Hint: show that $C(\alpha\mathbf{w}^1 + [1-\alpha]\mathbf{w}^2, Q) \geqslant \alpha C(\mathbf{w}^1, Q) + [1-\alpha]C(\mathbf{w}^2, Q)$ for any $0 \leqslant \alpha \leqslant 1$.] If the production function is homogeneous of degree γ show that the cost function is convex in Q if $\gamma \leqslant 1$ and concave in Q if $\gamma \geqslant 1$. [Hint: show that for any α: $C(\mathbf{w}, \alpha^\gamma Q) = \alpha C(\mathbf{w}, Q)$.] Comment on the result.

*3.2 Show that if the production function exhibits strictly decreasing returns everywhere, then average cost must be less than marginal cost. What must happen to average costs as output increases? What is the relationship between average and marginal costs if there are increasing returns everywhere?

*3.3 (a) Suppose a firm has the production function

$$Q = z_1^\alpha z_2^\beta, \qquad \alpha + \beta < 1$$

(b) Find the cost function corresponding to the production function in Exercise 2.12. Find the cost function and sketch it.

3.4 An input i is sometimes known as *inferior* if $\partial Q^*/\partial w_i > 0$. Show what conditions on the second partial derivative of $C(\mathbf{w}, Q)$ must hold if this is to be the case. Illustrate inferiority of a factor by drawing diagrams of $C(\mathbf{w}, Q)$ and $C_Q(\mathbf{w}, Q)$ when w_i increases. Show that for a competitive firm an input is inferior if and only if it is regressive – see equation (3.43). Give a verbal example of such a phenomenon.

3.5 Consider the following structure of the cost function: $C(\mathbf{w}, 0) = 0$, $C_Q(\mathbf{w}, Q) = \text{int}(Q)$ where $\text{int}(x)$ is the smallest integer greater than or equal to x. Sketch total, average and marginal cost curves.

*3.6 Let the production function be

$$Q = [\alpha_1 z_1^{-1} + \alpha_2 z_2^{-1} + \alpha_3 z_3^{-1}]^{-1}$$

where z_3 is a factor that is fixed in the short run. Find the short-run and long-run cost functions and comment on their form. Sketch short-run and long-run marginal cost and average cost curves.

3.7 It is sometimes convenient to work with the *profit function* of the firm – the *maximised* profits of the firm expressed as a function of P and $\mathbf{w}$ alone. This is found by substituting the supply function $S(P)$ and the cost function $C(\mathbf{w}, Q)$ into the Definition 3.1 (ii) of profits to give

$$\pi(\mathbf{w}, P) \equiv PS(P) - C(\mathbf{w}, S(P)) \equiv PQ - \Sigma w_i z_i$$

The mathematical properties of this are very similar to the cost function.

(a) Find simple expressions for

(i) $\partial \pi/\partial P$
(ii) $\partial \pi/\partial w_j$

(b) Show that π is a convex function.

3.8 For a firm that has a constant returns to scale technology and purchases two inputs in competitive markets, show that the elasticity of the demand for input 1 with respect to its own price is

$$-\sigma[1 - v_1]$$

where σ is the elasticity of substitution and v_1 is the share of input 1 in the final product. [Hint: differentiate the relationship $G_1(z_1, z_2)/G_2(z_1, z_2) = w_1/w_2$ with respect to w_1, use the formula for σ given in Exercise 2.14, and apply Euler's theorem to $G(z_1, z_2)$ and to $G_i(z_1, z_2)$.]

*3.9 (a) Draw a diagram of the equilibrium of the monopolist, showing clearly the profit made by the monopolist.

(b) Show that for a monopoly to produce at a determinate $Q^* > 0$, the elasticity of demand must satisfy $|\eta| \geqslant 1$.

3.10 Will a profit-maximising monopoly be technically efficient?

3.11 Show that, similarly to the competitive firm, an input purchased by a monopolist (*not* a monopsonist) is inferior if and only if it is regressive for a firm selling its output monopolistically. [Hint: show that $\partial Q/\partial w_i > 0$ if and only if $\partial z_i/\partial Q < 0$.]

*3.12 A monopolist produces a single output with the production function

$$Q = [\alpha_1 z_1{}^{\beta} + \alpha_2 z_2{}^{\beta}]^{1/\beta}$$

where $\alpha_1 + \alpha_2 = 1$ and $\beta < 1$. Inputs 1 and 2 are purchased in competitive markets and aggregate demand for the output is a linear function of the price charged. Determine the output and price set by monopolist. Describe the reaction of the monopolist to taxes levied as a fixed proportion of:

(a) total profits
(b) the price charged
(c) total outlay on input 2.

3.13 A monopolist has a cost function

$$C(Q) = 100 + 6Q + \tfrac{1}{2}Q^2$$

If the demand function is given by

$$Q = 24 - P/4$$

calculate the output-price combination which maximises profits. Now assume that it becomes possible to sell in a *separate* second market with demand determined by

$$Q = 84 - 3P/4$$

Calculate the prices which will be set in the two markets and the change in total output and profits. What would be the result of abandoning discrimination?

3.14 Derive equations (3.56) to (3.58).

*3.15 Draw a diagram showing the equilibrium of the monopsonist. Suppose a minimum price $\bar{w}_i$ is fixed exogenously for input i. Show that this may increase, decrease or leave constant the amount of input demanded depending on the level of $\bar{w}_i$. Contrast this with the purely competitive case.

3.16 Vastco Inc. is run by a set of managers whose aim is to maximise the *sales revenue* of the firm $P(Q)Q$, subject to a profit constraint $\Pi(Q, \mathbf{z}) \geqq \Pi_0$. Analyse the equilibrium of such a firm with reference to

(a) its technical efficiency;

(b) its input demand function, in comparison to that of a profit-maximising firm;

(c) its price/output decision.

3.17 Assume that a price-setting firm faces a downward sloping demand function with constant elasticity η and has a production function

$$Q = AK^{\alpha}L^{1-\alpha}$$

where K and L represent, respectively, capital and labour inputs. Assume that capital goods can be rented at a price r and labour hired at a wage w. Write down expressions for optimal K and L in terms of output price P, r and w. Show how the *investment* demand of the firm is linked (a) to output price changes; and (b) to changes in the rental price of capital.

Discuss the factors which will determine the rental price of capital in practice.

4

The Consumer

4.1 The Consumer and his Environment

'Who or what is a consumer?' may seem like a silly question. But once one recalls that the decisions about spending on consumption goods are sometimes made by persons in isolation, sometimes by families, and sometimes by larger groups, it is clear that specifying who or what forms the 'basic unit' of consumption analysis is by no means a trivial task. It is further complicated by the observation that persons, families or other groups may themselves be the objects of concern in forming government policy. The two concepts may not be identical: we may, for example, spend as families, but the government may view us as individuals.

Accordingly, we shall suppose that the basic social unit is the 'household'. This may contain one person or many, but two things will *always* be assumed: (a) the composition of the household is *fixed* exogenously; (b) each household acts as an individual agent with coherent objectives.[1] We do not question how consumption is allocated *within* the household.

We assume that there is a given list of all the goods in the economy, labelled $1, 2, \ldots, n$. These goods are clearly defined – the consumer cannot, for example, invent new goods of his own – and are perceived as objects of *direct* satisfaction by the consumer. We defer until the next chapter consideration of consumers who desire certain goods that contribute *indirectly* to consumption – lawnmowers, foodmixers, gasoline. The consumption by the household is denoted by an n-vector $\mathbf{x} \equiv (x_1, \ldots, x_n)$. The set of all physically conceivable vectors with which the consumer might be confronted is denoted X. If all goods are perfectly divisible and no one good is essential to survival then clearly X is the entire non-negative orthant $\mathbb{R}^n_+$. It is fairly easy to imagine the restrictions on X that would be required if there were certain minimum physical consumption requirements (one redefines X with

[1] Coherence should not be taken for granted. It does not usually apply in larger social groups, as anyone who has attempted to organise a group vacation trip will know. See Section 13.2 of Chapter 13.

a non-zero lower bound), or indivisibilities (X may be represented by an integer set), for example. Although much of the analysis which follows also goes through with these refinements, we shall usually neglect them in the main text, for the sake of clarity.

We further assume households are rational, in that they pursue the best objectives for themselves subject to the constraints of their environment. If we assume that all relevant information about the environment is known with certainty, and all time is collapsed into the present, this becomes very simple. The household then attains the best possible bundle of consumption goods subject to whatever constraints are imposed by the world around it. These constraints are *additional* to the physical requirement $\mathbf{x} \in X$ and may be illustrated by the following examples. (i) The perfect market: in Figure 4.1 the household has an exogenously fixed amount of money M to spend. It faces prices p_1, p_2 and may buy as much as is desired of each (divisible) commodity subject to this amount M. *Hence the entire shaded area is available.* (ii) Alternatively as in Figure 4.2, the consumer might have an exogenously fixed initial endowment $(\bar{x}_1, \bar{x}_2)$ of the two goods and is allowed to buy and sell freely. The set of attainable points is just the same in this case. (iii) Figure 4.3 illustrates the case when the selling price and the buying price differ – you get less per unit when you sell loaves of bread than you would have to pay to buy them. (iv) Figure 4.4 illustrates the case where a quantity *ration* is imposed. The consumer may buy as much as is desired of good 1 as long as this quantity does not exceed x_1^R and total expenditure does not exceed income.

It is obvious that how the household chooses its consumption, and how that choice responds to price changes, will depend on the type of constraint it faces. Constraints such as Figure 4.1 are convenient for analysis but may not be appropriate. We turn now to the preferences on which households base their choices.

4.2 Revealed Preference

When dealing with goods and services that are desired in their own right as consumption objects, we do not generally have the luxury of an independently observable objective function and set of constraints. Contrast this with the firm whose objectives may (in principle) be unambiguously clear – to make as much profit as possible[2] – and whose production constraints may be examined by any engineer, economist or industrial spy. Whilst we might be able to determine with some degree of objectivity the constraints within

---

[2] Though there may also be problems here too as noted in Section 3.1.

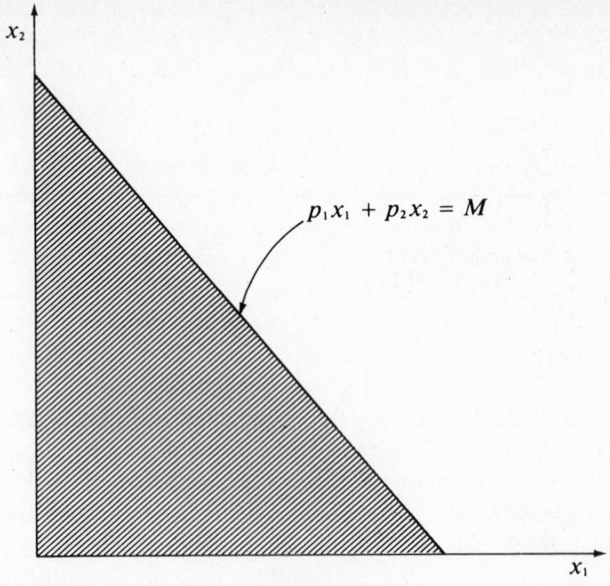

Figure 4.1

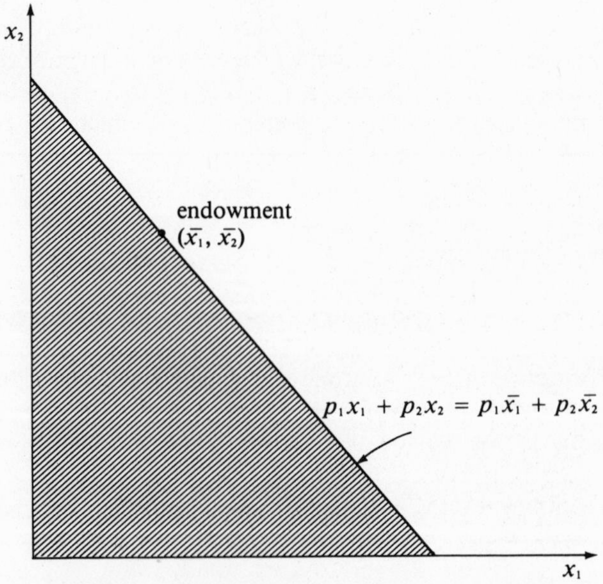

Figure 4.2

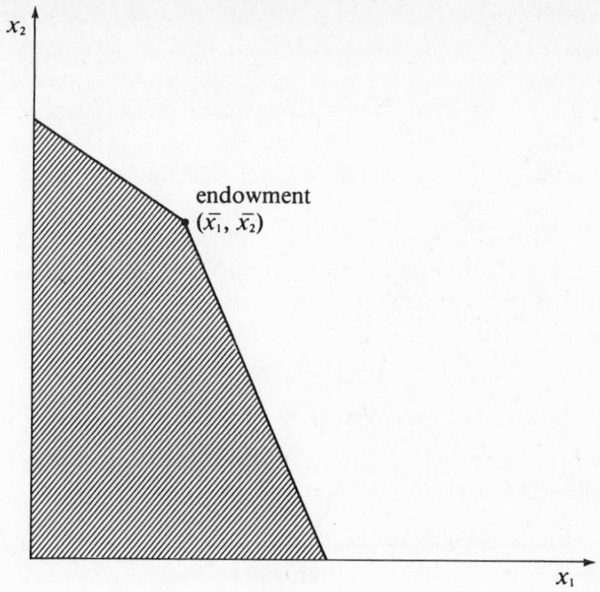

Figure 4.3

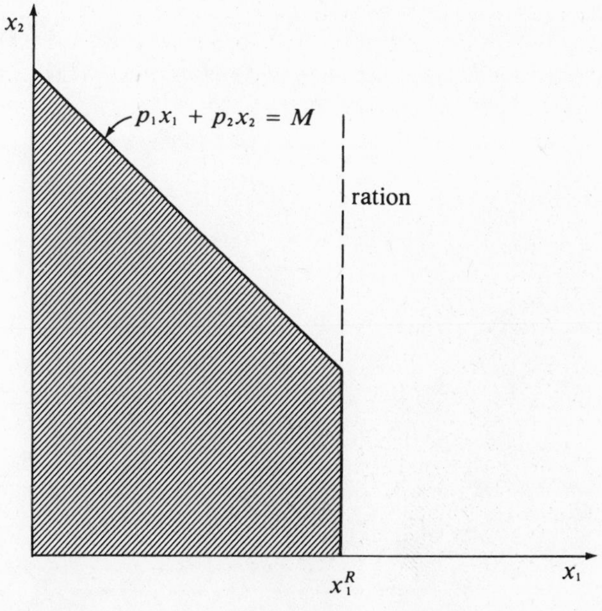

Figure 4.4

which the consumption plan must be made, how can we determine the objectives the consumer is presumed to pursue in carrying out the plan? We could ask people of course, but at worst this is likely to invite lying and dissimulation; at best it runs the risk of people being unable to express their preferences clearly.

Hence it has been suggested that the best one may do is to observe people's actual behaviour, and given one or two elementary assumptions about their (presumed) economic rationality infer what their underlying preferences must be. In this section we shall see how far it is possible to get using only the most rudimentary assumptions. To do this we introduce the following concept.

DEFINITION 4.1: a bundle $\mathbf{x}^1$ is *revealed preferred* to a bundle $\mathbf{x}^0$ (in symbols: $\mathbf{x}^1 \circledS \mathbf{x}^0$) if $\mathbf{x}^1$ is actually selected when $\mathbf{x}^0$ was also available to the consumer.

The idea is almost self-explanatory and is given operational content by the following axiom.

AXIOM OF RATIONAL CHOICE: the consumer always makes a choice, and selects the most preferred bundle that is available.

This enables one to draw the amazingly simple Figure 4.5. If $\mathbf{x}^1$ is the chosen point when the consumer can spend its income freely on the two goods at given prices $\mathbf{p}^1$ then $N^*(\mathbf{x}^1)$ is the set of points to which $\mathbf{x}^1$ is revealed to be preferred (note that $N^*(\mathbf{x}^1)$ includes all points on the line segment A_1B_1 except for the point $\mathbf{x}^1$). This may seem to be obvious. Nevertheless it is a step of fundamental importance to assume that consumers do not act capriciously, or completely irrationally – after all why shouldn't they? The next axiom is also more powerful than it might at first appear.

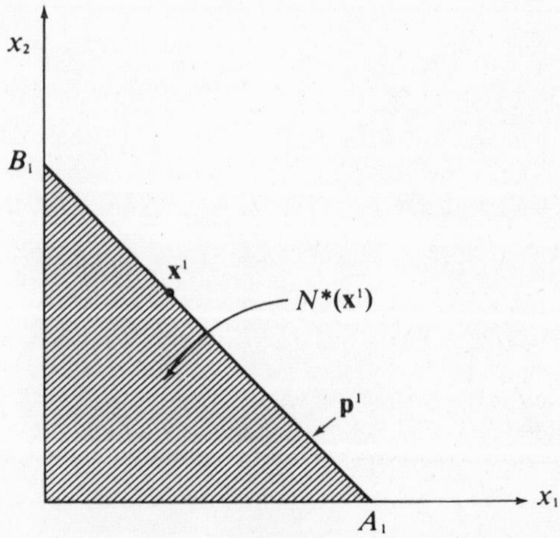

Figure 4.5

WEAK AXIOM OF REVEALED PREFERENCE (WARP): if $\mathbf{x}^2 \circledcirc \mathbf{x}^1$ then $\mathbf{x}^1$ not $\circledcirc$ $\mathbf{x}^2$.

In other words if we find that $\mathbf{x}^1 \in N^*(\mathbf{x}^2)$ then we immediately know that $\mathbf{x}^2 \notin N^*(\mathbf{x}^1)$. In the case where purchases are made in a free market this has a very simple interpretation. Suppose the household's income remains the same but prices change from $\mathbf{p}^1$ to $\mathbf{p}^2$. If the household now selects a new bundle $\mathbf{x}^2$ even though $\mathbf{x}^1$ is still purchasable, then WARP states that $\mathbf{x}^2$ cannot have been purchasable originally when the prices were $\mathbf{p}^1$. Thus WARP means that if

$$\sum_{i=1}^{n} p_i^2 x_i^2 \geqslant \sum_{i=1}^{n} p_i^2 x_i^1 \tag{4.1}$$

then

$$\sum_{i=1}^{n} p_i^1 x_i^2 > \sum_{i=1}^{n} p_i^1 x_i^1 \tag{4.2}$$

This is illustrated in Figure 4.6. Note an interesting result to which we shall return in Section 4.5. Obviously if the budget constraint shifts from that labelled $\mathbf{p}^1$ to that labelled $\mathbf{p}^2$ as shown, we may regard this as an increase in the relative price of good 1 with a further compensating adjustment in the budget such that the consumer is still just able to buy the previously optimal bundle $\mathbf{x}^1$. Instead a bundle is chosen that has *less* of the good whose price has increased. This suggests that WARP may yield a result very similar to the result on the own-price effect on a firm's conditional input demand in

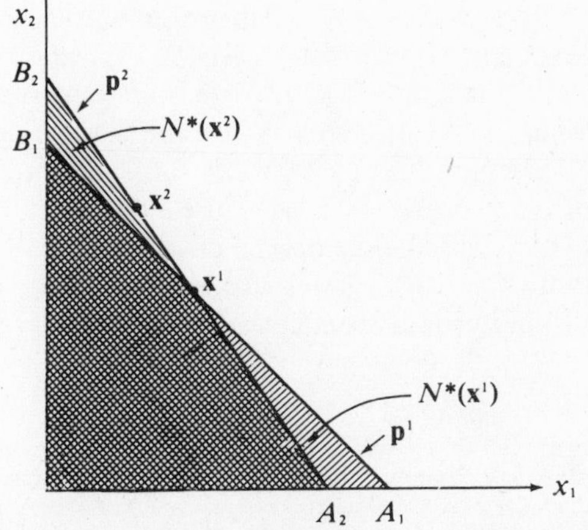

Figure 4.6

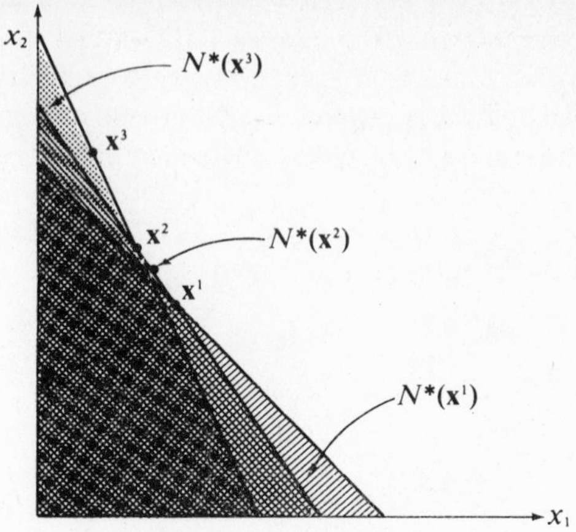

Figure 4.7

Theorem 3.5, namely that the own-price substitution effect for any good is non-positive.[3] This suggestion is in fact quite correct.

In fact if we pursue this idea we see that WARP may lead on to some very useful analogies with the analysis of input demands in the theory of the firm. Suppose the budget is altered yet again – to $\mathbf{p}^3$ such that at $\mathbf{p}^3$ bundle $\mathbf{x}^2$ could still just be afforded – see Figure 4.7. If $\mathbf{x}^3$ is chosen then $\mathbf{x}^3 \circledS \mathbf{x}^2$ and we might suggest that $\mathbf{x}^3$ is also *indirectly* revealed preferred to $\mathbf{x}^1$ (because we already know $\mathbf{x}^2 \circledS \mathbf{x}^1$). We could then be interested not only in $N^*(\mathbf{x}^3)$, the set of points to which $\mathbf{x}^3$ is directly revealed preferred, but in $N^*(\mathbf{x}^1) \cup N^*(\mathbf{x}^2) \cup N^*(\mathbf{x}^3)$ the set of points to which $\mathbf{x}^3$ has been directly or indirectly revealed preferred in our market experiment; in fact of course one could go on to indefinitely many experiments in this fashion tracing out a series of points such that $\mathbf{x}^t \circledS \mathbf{x}^{t-1} \circledS \ldots \circledS \mathbf{x}^2 \circledS \mathbf{x}^1 \circledS, \ldots$ then examine $\bar{N}(\mathbf{x}^t) \equiv \cup_{j=1}^{t} N^*(\mathbf{x}^j)$. The whole shaded area in Figure 4.7 suggests clearly what this grand set of 'worse than $\mathbf{x}^t$' points must look like. Indeed it invites comparison with the construction of Figure 3.6. Consider $B(\mathbf{x}^t)$ = the set of points that lie in X but *not* in $\bar{N}(\mathbf{x}^t)$. This must be convex for reasons similar to those by which we showed the convexity of the set Z_0 in Figure 3.6.

This suggests that we *might* be able to proceed from observed choices, via the weak axiom of revealed preference, to tracing out a contour map rather like the pattern of isoquants in Chapters 2 and 3. In fact this is antici-

[3] The substitution effect here, of course, is defined as the effect on the demand for good i when the price of i increases but the person is compensated so *as to be just able to buy the same bundle as before*. This is slightly different from the substitution effect we shall examine in detail in Section 4.6. See Exercise 4.2.

pating a little too much: other technical restrictions need to be imposed.[4] Moreover the device of revealed preference, though appealingly primitive in its nature, becomes rather cumbersome for some of the manipulations that one wishes to perform in consumer theory. Accordingly we proceed to a *direct* axiomatic consideration of a consumer's preferences.

4.3 The Preference Map

What we shall do in this section is examine a set of proposed axioms about people's preferences that might conceivably command wide acceptance. Though it might appear as though we are abandoning the approach of Section 4.2 and starting afresh, in fact we shall find that much of what follows is in fact complementary to the revealed preference analysis. Since we are now being so bold as to suggest the unobservable structure of people's actual likes and dislikes (rather than merely posit rationality about their behaviour) we need a new, stronger basic concept of preference.

DEFINITION 4.2: the *weak preference relation* $\succcurlyeq$ is a binary relation defined on the set of all consumption vectors. If $\mathbf{x}^0, \mathbf{x}^1 \in X$ then the statement '$\mathbf{x}^0 \succcurlyeq \mathbf{x}^1$' is to be read '$\mathbf{x}^0$ is no worse than $\mathbf{x}^1$'.

To make this concept useful we shall now consider three basic axioms on preference.

AXIOM C1 (completeness): for every $\mathbf{x}^0, \mathbf{x}^1 \in X$, *either* $\mathbf{x}^0 \succcurlyeq \mathbf{x}^1$ is true, *or* $\mathbf{x}^1 \succcurlyeq \mathbf{x}^0$ is true, *or* both statements are true.

AXIOM C2 (transitivity): for any $\mathbf{x}^0, \mathbf{x}^1, \mathbf{x}^2 \in X$, if $\mathbf{x}^0 \succcurlyeq \mathbf{x}^1$ *and* $\mathbf{x}^1 \succcurlyeq \mathbf{x}^2$ then $\mathbf{x}^0 \succcurlyeq \mathbf{x}^2$.

AXIOM C3 (continuity): for any $\mathbf{x}^0 \in X$ the sets $B(\mathbf{x}^0) \equiv \{\mathbf{x}:\mathbf{x} \succcurlyeq \mathbf{x}^0\}$, $N(\mathbf{x}^0) \equiv \{\mathbf{x}:\mathbf{x}^0 \succcurlyeq \mathbf{x}\}$ are each closed in X.

The meaning of the first two axioms should be pretty obvious and, perhaps, unexceptionable: though maybe there are people who cannot say whether they think A is as good as, better than or worse than B (violating Axiom C1) or indeed people who say that though they think A is better than B and B is better than C nevertheless they prefer C to A (violating Axiom C2). The

---

4 Most notably we need the strong axiom of revealed preference: given any sequence $\mathbf{x}^1, \ldots, \mathbf{x}^t$ such that $\mathbf{x}^t \circledS \mathbf{x}^{t-1} \circledS \ldots \circledS \mathbf{x}^1$, then it must not be the case that $\mathbf{x}^1 \circledS \mathbf{x}^t$. See also Exercise 4.3. Observe also that in attempting to employ the concept of 'indirect revealed preference' we are introducing the idea of 'transitivity' by the back door – see Axiom C2 below. On the relationship between various concepts of transitivity and acyclicity of choice see Suzumura, K. (1983) *Rational Choice, Collective Decisions and Social Welfare*, Cambridge University Press, pp. 7–11 and 23, 24.

continuity axiom is, perhaps, less obvious. Since it is introduced for the sake of technical convenience rather than deep economic significance we shall not discuss it at length, but a brief example may suffice. Write '$\mathbf{x}^0 \succ \mathbf{x}^1$' when '$\mathbf{x}^0 \succcurlyeq \mathbf{x}^1$' is true but '$\mathbf{x}^1 \succcurlyeq \mathbf{x}^0$' is *not* true – the symbol '$\succ$' is one of *strict* preference. Now suppose that $\mathbf{x}^2 = 2\mathbf{x}^1$ – that is $\mathbf{x}^2$ is a bundle very much like $\mathbf{x}^1$ but with twice as much of everything in it. Suppose also there is some other bundle $\mathbf{x}^0$ that has the property that $\mathbf{x}^2 \succ \mathbf{x}^0 \succ \mathbf{x}^1$ (note the strict preference relation here). Clearly we can *construct* a bundle $\mathbf{x}^\alpha$ that is intermediate between $\mathbf{x}^1$ and $\mathbf{x}^2$ simply by letting $\mathbf{x}^\alpha = \alpha\mathbf{x}^1$ where α can have any value between 1 and 2. For values of α close to 1 we expect $\mathbf{x}^0 \succ \mathbf{x}^\alpha$, and for α close to 2 we expect $\mathbf{x}^\alpha \succ \mathbf{x}^0$; but is there a value of α in between such that $\mathbf{x}^\alpha \succcurlyeq \mathbf{x}^0$ *and* $\mathbf{x}^0 \succcurlyeq \mathbf{x}^\alpha$ – that is a bundle that is regarded as *just* as good as $\mathbf{x}^0$? Axiom C3 ensures that there is, and it is a vital step enabling one to partition X into 'indifference classes' i.e. subsets of bundles that are regarded as just as good as each other. It further enables us to simplify the business of the technical representation of preferences.

THEOREM 4.1:[5] given Axioms C1 to C3 there exists a continuous function U from X to the real line such that for all $\mathbf{x}^1, \mathbf{x}^2 \in X$:

$$U(\mathbf{x}^1) \geqq U(\mathbf{x}^2) \quad \text{if and only if} \quad \mathbf{x}^1 \succcurlyeq \mathbf{x}^2 \tag{4.3}$$

U is usually known as the *utility function*. It should be obvious that only the *ordinal* characteristics of U are important so that, for example, if $\hat{U}(\mathbf{x}) \equiv \psi(U(\mathbf{x}))$ and ψ is a continuous monotonically increasing function, then $\hat{U}$ is just as good a representation of the same set of consumer preferences. The contours of the utility function, given by $\{\mathbf{x} : U(\mathbf{x}) = \text{constant}\}$ are known as *indifference curves* or indifference surfaces. The remaining axioms can be stated either in terms of the preference relation $\succcurlyeq$, or in terms of the equivalent continuous utility function U. For convenience we shall use the latter in the main text: the exercises at the end of the chapter give examples of some idiosyncratic cases that violate Axioms C1 to C3.

AXIOM C4 (greed): if $\mathbf{x}^1 \geqslant \mathbf{x}^2$, then $U(\mathbf{x}^1) > U(\mathbf{x}^2)$.[6]

AXIOM C5 (strictly concave contours): let $\mathbf{x}^1$ and $\mathbf{x}^2$ be two vectors such that $U(\mathbf{x}^1) = U(\mathbf{x}^2)$ and let α be a number such that $0 < \alpha < 1$. Then

$$U(\alpha\mathbf{x}^1 + [1 - \alpha]\mathbf{x}^2) > \alpha U(\mathbf{x}^1) + [1 - \alpha]\, U(\mathbf{x}^2) \text{ for all } \alpha.$$

AXIOM C6 (smoothness): $U(\mathbf{x})$ is everywhere twice differentiable and its second partial derivatives commute.

---

5 For proof of this see Debreu, G. (1983) 'Representation of a Preference Ordering by a Numerical Function', in Debreu's *Mathematical Economics: Twenty Papers*, Cambridge University Press, reprinted from R. Thrall et al. (eds): *Decision Processes*, Wiley, 1960.

6 Recall that when ordering vectors '$\mathbf{x} \geqslant \mathbf{y}$' means '$\mathbf{x} \geqq \mathbf{y}$ and $\mathbf{x} \neq \mathbf{y}$'.

It should be noted that the particular forms in which Axioms C4 to C6 are expressed are rather stronger than is necessary to obtain many of the results which follow. In particular Axiom C4 states that more of *any* commodity always makes the person 'better off' in the sense of reaching a preferred point. Often this may be relaxed to simply ruling out the existence of *bliss points* (a bliss point $\hat{\mathbf{x}}$ is one at the peak of a utility 'hill' such that, for all $\mathbf{x} \in X$, $U(\hat{\mathbf{x}}) \geqslant U(\mathbf{x})$: if a person were able to reach $\hat{\mathbf{x}}$ he would feel on top of the world, and would not want any more of anything, even if you gave it to him.) Also we may occasionally weaken C5 to

AXIOM C5′ (concave contours): $U(\alpha\mathbf{x}^1 + [1 - \alpha]\mathbf{x}^2) \geqslant \alpha U(\mathbf{x}^1) + [1 - \alpha]\, U(\mathbf{x}^2)$, where $0 < \alpha < 1$ and $U(\mathbf{x}^1) = U(\mathbf{x}^2)$

which merely requires that the contours of U be concave rather than strictly concave. If we insist on strict concavity we are assuming that, for example, if $U(1, 2) = U(2, 1)$ then $U(1\frac{1}{2}, 1\frac{1}{2}) > U(1, 2)$ – i.e. the averaged bundle is strictly preferred – see Figures 4.8 and 4.9.[7] Likewise Axiom C6 may sometimes be relaxed to allow a finite number of non-differentiable points – as in the case of the production function in Chapter 2. We may use the differentiability assumption once again to introduce an important concept.

DEFINITION 4.3: the *marginal rate of substitution* of good i for good j MRS_{ij} is U_j/U_i.[8]

This is none other than the slope of the indifference curve, of course. It is the amount of good i that the person is just willing to give up to get another unit of good j. Axiom C5 requires that MRS_{ij} be a monotonically decreasing function of x_i whilst Axiom C6 requires that MRS_{ij} be a continuous function of x_i.

The marginal rate of substitution plays a key role in optimisation, to which we now turn our attention.

4.4 Optimisation in a Perfect Market

Now that we have the individual household's objective function $U(\mathbf{x})$ (from Section 4.3) and budget constraint (from Section 4.1) we may set up a constrained optimisation problem in order to characterise economically efficient behaviour.

---

7 It is difficult to think of really convincing examples that violate C5′. Beer and cider constitute my favourite case: an evening spent drinking either one is strictly preferable to an evening spent mixing one's drinks. But this, like most such examples, merely illustrates that C5′ is probably quite reasonable if commodities are defined broadly (food, drink, clothing) rather than restrictively (specific drinks on a particular evening). Notice that Axiom C5 implies that the set $B(\mathbf{x}^0)$ (defined in C3) is strictly convex; Axiom C5′ requires only that it be convex – see the discussion on p. 7 of Chapter 1.

8 In line with the convention used previously $U_i \equiv \partial U(\mathbf{x})/\partial x_i$.

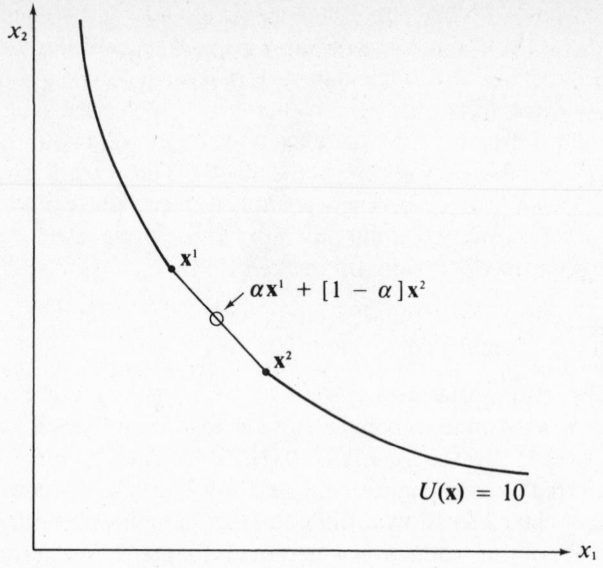

Figure 4.8 Concave contours

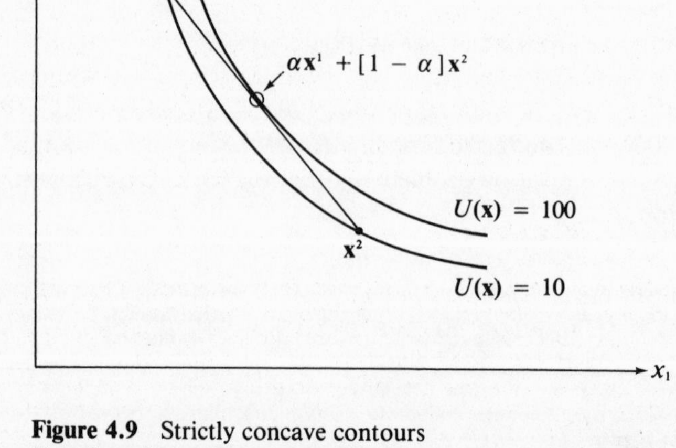

Figure 4.9 Strictly concave contours
Note: in each case the contours of U have been labelled arbitrarily.

Intuitively this involves finding a point on the highest utility contour (for example Figure 4.8 or 4.9) within the appropriate constraint set (for example Figures 4.1 to 4.4). In the case of a perfect market with exogenously fixed income M we have:

$$\left.\begin{aligned}&\max_{\{\mathbf{x}\}} U(\mathbf{x})\\ &\text{subject to}\begin{cases} x_i \geqslant 0 \qquad i = 1, \ldots, n\\ \sum_{i=1}^{n} p_i x_i \leqslant M\end{cases}\end{aligned}\right\} \tag{4.4}$$

However we can if we wish rewrite (4.4) as an equivalent problem which may be regarded as its economic 'dual':

$$\left.\begin{aligned}&\min_{\{\mathbf{x}\}} \sum_{i=1}^{n} p_i x_i\\ &\text{subject to}\begin{cases} x_i \geqslant 0\\ U(\mathbf{x}) \geqslant u_0\end{cases}\end{aligned}\right\} \tag{4.5}$$

where u_0 is an exogenously specified utility level; obviously we would take u_0 as being the maximum utility obtainable under (4.4). So (4.4) says 'maximise the utility obtainable under a given budget'; (4.5) says 'minimise the cost of getting to any given utility level'. We shall return to the 'primal' problem (4.4) but for the moment let us look at the solution to (4.5).

We form the Lagrangean

$$\mathscr{L}(\mathbf{x}, \mu) = \sum_{i=1}^{n} p_i x_i + \mu\,[\,u_0 - U(\mathbf{x})] \tag{4.6}$$

Now inspection of (4.6) and comparison with equation 3.7 of Section 3.3 reveals that the problem of cost minimisation subject to a utility constraint is formally equivalent[9] to the firm's cost minimisation problem for *given* output $Q = Q_0$, where all input prices are given. So we may exploit all the results in Chapter 3 that dealt with this problem.

4.5 Cost Minimisation

Since the problem (4.5) is really the same as that in Sections 3.3 and 3.4, with a change of notation, we may move rapidly on to the next concept and then state a number of results without proof.

---

[9] The only minor difference is that as we have seen there is no cardinal significance to the function $U(\mathbf{x})$, in contrast to the interpretation of $G(\mathbf{z})$ in physical units of output.

DEFINITION 4.4: the consumer's *cost function* or *expenditure function* $C(\mathbf{p}, u)$ is a real valued function of the price vector and the utility index which gives the minimum value of $\sum_{i=1}^{n} p_i x_i$ subject to $x_i \geqslant 0, i = 1, \ldots, n$ and $u \leqslant U(\mathbf{x})$.

THEOREM 4.2: the consumer's cost function $C(\mathbf{p}, u)$ is non decreasing and continuous in $\mathbf{p}$, homogeneous of degree one in $\mathbf{p}$ and concave in $\mathbf{p}$. It is strictly increasing in u and in at least one p_i. At every point where the differential is defined

$$\partial C(\mathbf{p}, u_0)/\partial p_i = x_i^* \tag{4.7}$$

where x_i^* is the demand for good i found as a solution to (4.5).

We may use the consumer's cost function to provide an interesting tie up with the revealed preference theory of Section 4.2. Given any point $\mathbf{x}^0$ on the indifference curve $U(\mathbf{x}) = u_0$ we may define the 'better set' (strictly speaking, the 'at least as good set') $B(\mathbf{x}^0)$ and the 'not better set' $N(\mathbf{x}^0)$ as in the statement of Axiom C3. These are sketched in Figure 4.10 for a utility function that satisfies Axioms C1–C4, C5′ and C6.

Now consider the set $\hat{B}_0$, the set of all possible combinations of goods that would always cost as least as much as $C(\mathbf{p}, u)$ for any vector of prices $\mathbf{p}$. In Figure 4.10 where the utility function is concave-contoured and everywhere increasing in its arguments it is easily seen (by analogy with Figure 3.6) that $\hat{B}_0 = B(\mathbf{x}^0)$. However, in a case such as Figure 4.11, where both Axioms C4 and C5′ are violated $\hat{B}_0$ is a convex set that strictly contains $B(\mathbf{x}^0)$. Note that the boundary of $\hat{B}_0$ is the same in both Figure 4.10 and in Figure 4.11 – as with the firm's input demand in Section 3.4 we find that the cost-minimisation procedure simply ignores the bits of the indifference curve that are 'dents' violating Axiom C5′ or where utility *falls* with an increase in the consumption of some good. Let us define $\hat{N}_0$ as the set of points that lie in X but that do not lie in $\hat{B}_0$. It turns out that $\hat{N}_0$ is contained by or is equal to $\bar{N}(\mathbf{x}^0)$, the set of all points to which $\mathbf{x}^0$ is revealed preferred (directly or indirectly).

Now consider the interpretation of (4.7). Reading from right to left it appears to yield optimal consumption of good i as a function of prices $\mathbf{p}$ and the *given* utility level u_0. In fact, analogous to Definition 3.4 we introduce:

DEFINITION 4.5: the *compensated demand* (or Hicksian demand) for goods $i = 1, \ldots, n$ given a utility level u_0 and a set of prices $\mathbf{p}$ is the set of vectors $\mathbf{x}$ providing a solution to (4.5). Where the set has only one member for any u_0 and $\mathbf{p}$, the *compensated demand function* for good i is written

$$x_i^* = \hat{D}^i(\mathbf{p}, u_0) \tag{4.8}$$

The compensated demand function may be seen as a rule which yields the consumer's demand for a particular good, at any vector of prices where money income M is always adjusted as necessary to keep the consumer on the indifference curve $U(\mathbf{x}) = u_0$. Writing the partial derivative $\partial\hat{D}^i(\mathbf{p}, u_0)/\partial p_j$

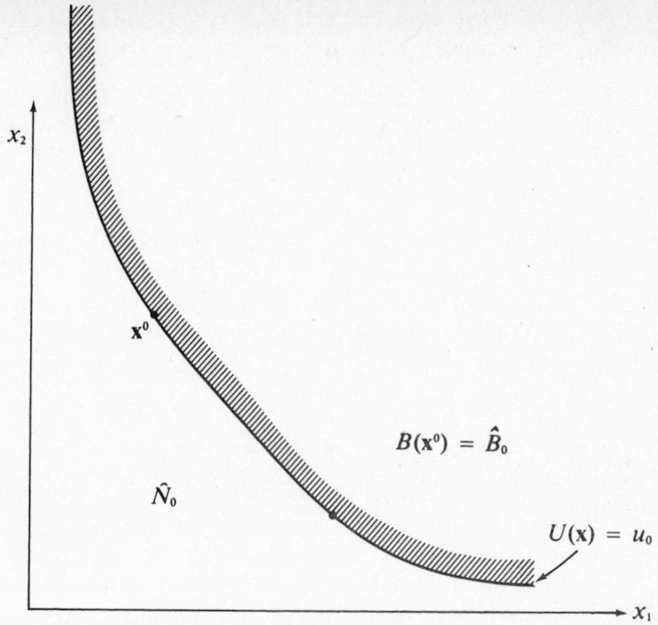

Figure 4.10

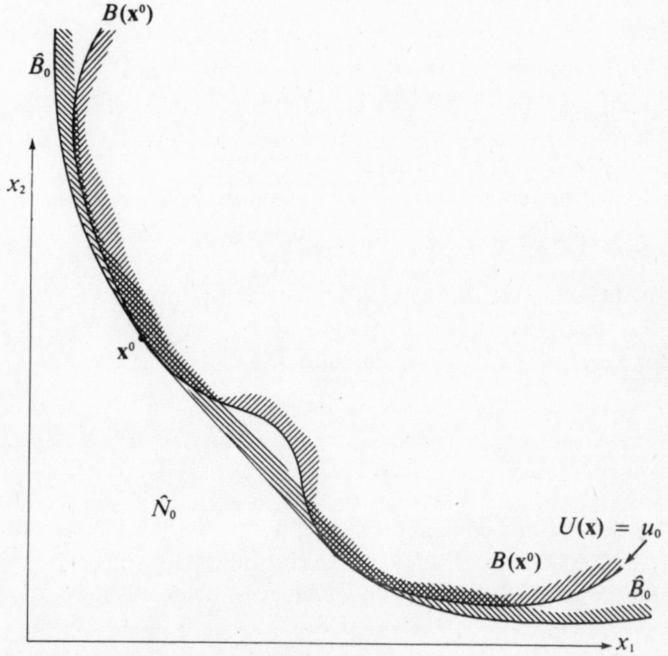

Figure 4.11

as $\hat{D}^i_j$, the following two theorems carry over directly from Theorem 3.4(a) and Theorem 3.5(a) and (c).

THEOREM 4.3: if the utility function is strictly concave-contoured then compensated demand functions are always well defined and continuous for all positive prices.[10]

THEOREM 4.4: (a) $\hat{D}^i_j$, the effect of an increase in the price of good j on the compensated demand for good i, is equal to $\hat{D}^j_i$, the effect of an increase in the price of good i on the compensated demand for good j.

(b) $\hat{D}^i_i$, the effect of an increase in the price of good i on the compensated demand for good i must be non-positive. If Axiom C6 holds, then $\hat{D}^i_i$ is strictly negative.

Once again, in fact, the *substitution matrix* $\hat{\mathbf{D}} \equiv \|\hat{D}^i_j\|$ is symmetric and negative semi-definite – a property which we showed in Section 3.6 follows directly from the properties of the cost function: so once again we have the useful results $\hat{D}^i_i < 0$ and $\hat{D}^i_j = \hat{D}^j_i$.

4.6 Utility Maximisation

Now let us return to the consumer's optimisation problem in its more straightforward form (4.4). We may evidently solve this by maximising the Lagrangean

$$\hat{\mathscr{L}}(\mathbf{x}, \nu) = U(\mathbf{x}) + \nu\,[M - \sum_{i=1}^{n} p_i x_i] \tag{4.9}$$

where ν is the Lagrange multiplier.

The first-order conditions for the maximum yield

$$U_i(\mathbf{x}^*) \leqslant \nu^* p_i \quad \text{if} \quad x_i^* = 0 \tag{4.10}$$

$$U_i(\mathbf{x}^*) = \nu^* p_i \quad \text{if} \quad x_i^* > 0 \tag{4.11}$$

$$\sum_{i=1}^{n} p_i x_i^* \leqslant M \quad \text{if} \quad \nu^* = 0 \tag{4.12}$$

$$\sum_{i=1}^{n} p_i x_i^* = M \quad \text{if} \quad \nu^* > 0 \tag{4.13}$$

where $\mathbf{x}^*$ is the optimal consumption vector.

Note that Axiom C4 is sufficient to rule out (4.12), since $\nu^* = \partial U(\mathbf{x}^*)/\partial M$, the *marginal utility of income*, which must be positive.[11]

---

10 On the restriction to 'positive prices' see the discussion on page 47 of Chapter 3.
11 See footnote 7 on page 38 of Chapter 3.

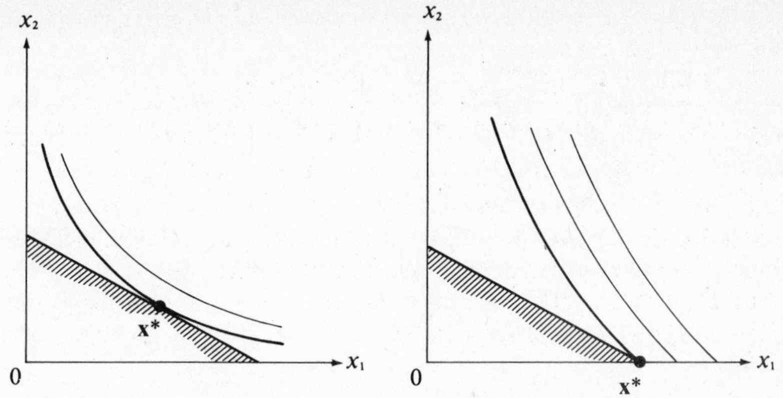

(i) $MRS_{12} = p_2/p_1$ (ii) $MRS_{12} < p_2/p_1$

Figure 4.12

Also note that $MRS_{ij} = p_j/p_i$ if x_j^* and x_i^* are positive, but we may have $MRS_{ij} < p_j/p_i$ if $x_j^* = 0$, $x_i^* > 0$. This is illustrated in Figure 4.12. We summarise these results thus:

THEOREM 4.5: (a) if the consumer is not satiated all income M is spent at the optimum; (b) at the optimum, for any pair of goods i, j that are consumed in positive amounts the marginal rate of substitution MRS_{ij} must equal the price ratio p_j/p_i; (c) if i is a good that is purchased and j a good that is not purchased at the optimum then MRS_{ij} will be less than or equal to p_j/p_i.

If we restrict attention to commodities that are consumed in positive amounts at the optimum, then clearly the $n + 1$ unknowns $\mathbf{x}^*$, ν^* are to be found as solutions to the following $n + 1$ equations:

$$\left.\begin{aligned} \nu^* p_i &= U_i(\mathbf{x}^*),\ i = 1, \ldots, n \\ M &= \sum_{i=1}^{n} p_i x_i^* \end{aligned}\right\} \tag{4.14}$$

DEFINITION 4.6: the *(ordinary) demand* for good $i = 1, \ldots, n$ given prices $\mathbf{p}$ and income M is the set of vectors $\mathbf{x}$ satisfying (4.14). Where the set has only one member for any $\mathbf{p}$ and M, the *(ordinary) demand function* for good i is written

$$x_i^* = D^i(\mathbf{p}, M), \quad i = 1, \ldots, n \tag{4.15}$$

THEOREM 4.6: if the utility function is strictly concave-contoured then ordinary demand functions are well defined and continuous for all positive prices.

PROOF: as for the proof of Theorem 3.4(a).

The demand curve – a representation of the demand function that plots values of x_i^* against values of p_i for given values of other prices and income – can easily be derived graphically from Figure 4.12 by rotating the budget constraint and observing how optimal quantities change. You are strongly invited to do this – see Exercise 4.5. Also note the discontinuities in demand that arise when Axiom C5′ is violated: the significance of such discontinuities will be discussed further in Chapter 7.

Let us now investigate further the properties of the functions D^i. Note that $D^i(\mathbf{p}, M)$ must satisfy the second restriction in (4.14) and so we have

$$\sum_{i=1}^{n} p_i D^i(\mathbf{p}, M) = M \tag{4.16}$$

– the *adding up* property. If we define the *income elasticity* of commodity i as $\varepsilon_{iM} \equiv \dfrac{M}{x_i^*}\dfrac{\partial D^i(\mathbf{p}, M)}{\partial M}$ and the *expenditure share* of commodity i as $v_i \equiv p_i x_i^*/M$, then differentiation of (4.16) with respect to M immediately yields

$$\sum_{i=1}^{n} v_i \varepsilon_{iM} = 1 \tag{4.17}$$

Note also that in view of equation (4.16) the D^i are homogeneous of degree zero in $\mathbf{p}$, M – the *absence of money illusion*. Define the elasticity of consumption good i with respect to price j as $\varepsilon_{ij} = \dfrac{p_j}{x_i^*}\dfrac{\partial D^i(\mathbf{p}, M)}{\partial p_j}$. Then Euler's theorem applied to equations (4.15) immediately yields

$$\sum_{j=1}^{n} p_j \frac{\partial D^i(\mathbf{p}, M)}{\partial p_j} + M\frac{\partial D^i(\mathbf{p}, M)}{\partial M} = 0, \quad i = 1, \ldots, n \tag{4.18}$$

which implies

$$\sum_{j=1}^{n} \varepsilon_{ij} + \varepsilon_{iM} = 0 \tag{4.19}$$

The elasticity conditions (4.17) and (4.19) are just another way of stating our next theorem.

THEOREM 4.7: (a) the ordinary demand functions are subject to a linear restriction in that the sum of the demand for each good multiplied by its price must equal total income;

(b) the ordinary demand functions are homogeneous of degree zero in all prices and income.

Finally we examine an important decomposition for the effects of a price change on the quantities of goods demanded. Suppose the utility level

u_0 in Section 4.5 is in fact equal to $U(\mathbf{x}^*)$ then clearly the demands $\mathbf{x}^*$ are the solution to both cost-minimisation and utility-maximisation problems, and we may write

$$\hat{D}^i(\mathbf{p}, u_0) = x_i^* = D^i(\mathbf{p}, M) \tag{4.20}$$

which implies

$$\hat{D}^i(\mathbf{p}, u_0) = D^i(\mathbf{p}, C(\mathbf{p}, u_0)) \tag{4.21}$$

because of course $M = \sum_{i=1}^{n} p_i x_i^* = C(\mathbf{p}, u_0)$. Differentiate (4.21) with respect to p_j:

$$\hat{D}_j^i = D_j^i + D_M^i C_j \tag{4.22}$$

Now use (4.7) to give

$$D_j^i = \underset{\text{[substitution effect]}}{\hat{D}_j^i} - \underset{\text{[income effect]}}{x_j^* D_M^i} \tag{4.23}$$

the so-called *Slutsky equation*.[12] Defining the compensated price elasticity as $\hat{\varepsilon}_{ij} \equiv \dfrac{p_j}{x_i^*}\dfrac{\partial \hat{D}^i(\mathbf{p}, u)}{\partial p_j}$, we see that (4.23) yields

$$\varepsilon_{ij} = \hat{\varepsilon}_{ij} - v_j \varepsilon_{iM} \tag{4.24}$$

In view of the fact that $\hat{D}_j^i = \hat{D}_i^j$ we must also have $v_i \hat{\varepsilon}_{ij} = v_j \hat{\varepsilon}_{ji}$ and so we may write either of the equivalent expressions

$$D_j^i + x_j^* D_M^i = D_i^j + x_i^* D_M^j \tag{4.25}$$

$$v_i \varepsilon_{ij} + v_i v_j \varepsilon_{iM} = v_j \varepsilon_{ji} + v_i v_j \varepsilon_{jM} \tag{4.26}$$

the *Slutsky symmetry condition*. Also from (4.24) and (4.19) we immediately find

$$\sum_{j=1}^{n} \hat{\varepsilon}_{ij} = 0 \tag{4.27}$$

Finally, summing (4.26) over i, we find

$$\sum_{i=1}^{n} v_i \varepsilon_{ij} + v_j = 0 \tag{4.28}$$

The signs of the elasticities (or, equivalently, the signs of the derivatives of $\hat{D}^i$ and D^i) yield a useful classification of goods. If for two distinct goods

---

[12] Compare this with equation (3.39) on p. 49, where the appropriate decomposition is into substitution and *output* effects.

$\hat{\varepsilon}_{ij} > 0$ we say that goods i and j are *net* (or *Hicksian*) *substitutes*; whereas if $\hat{\varepsilon}_{ij} < 0$ we say that the goods are *net complements*. So, for a tea and coffee drinker with a sweet tooth it might be that tea and coffee were net substitutes, tea and sugar net complements, coffee and sugar net complements. Correspondingly if $\varepsilon_{ij} > 0$ we say that i is a gross substitute for j whereas if $\varepsilon_{ij} < 0$ we say that i is a gross complement for j.[13]

The elasticity ε_{iM} can be of either sign. If it is negative then good i is known as *inferior* because the richer you get, the less you buy of it – an example of this is brown rice in India.[14] Otherwise we shall refer to goods as 'normal'. Moreover, *in sharp contrast to the case of a firm's demand for an input*, ε_{ii} can take either sign: if it is positive (most unusual!)[15] then it is known as a *Giffen good*. However, as we have seen, if the utility function is everywhere differentiable, then the *compensated elasticity* $\hat{\varepsilon}_{ii}$ must be negative – a result that we intuited from the revealed preference analysis, and which we formally showed in Theorem 4.4. So there follows what has been described by Samuelson as 'the fundamental Theorem of consumer theory':

THEOREM 4.8: if a consumer's demand for a particular good never decreases when his income (alone) increases, then his demand for that good must definitely decrease when its price (alone) increases.

PROOF: take the own-price Slutsky equation as a special case of (4.23) where $i = j$:

$$D^i_i = \hat{D}^i_i - x^*_i D^i_M \qquad (4.29)$$

We know that $\hat{D}^i_i < 0$. So if $D^i_M \geqslant 0$, then $D^i_i < 0$.

The Slutsky equation thus yields a simple and interpretable restriction on the derivatives of any demand function D^i. More than that: because (4.23) enables one to compute the substitution effect directly from these derivatives, we can thus deduce the 'unobservable' indifference curves from market data. However one should exercise care in using market data to infer the shape of individual demand curves – see Chapter 6.

---

13 Note the difference in wording here: we may have $\varepsilon_{ij} > 0$ but at the same time $\varepsilon_{ji} < 0$ – see Exercise 4.7.

14 This example illustrates a simple point about the way in which the list of goods {1, 2, . . ., n} is specified. If goods are to be distinguished in very fine detail – {patna rice, basmati rice, brown rice, . . ., white flour, high gluten flour, granary flour, . . .} – then, as we have seen, some of the items in this long list may be inferior goods for some consumers over some range of income. However, if goods are classified more broadly {rice, flour, meat, . . .} then it will be less likely that we shall find inferior goods among this shorter list of generically-defined items. See also the footnote about Axiom C5′ on p. 71 of this chapter.

15 A practical example of such a good is given in: Bopp, A.E. (1983) 'The demand for kerosene: a modern Giffen good', *Applied Economics*, **15**, pp. 459–67.

Table 4.1 Essential notation for Chapter 4: The household

$x_1, \ldots, x_n$	: quantities consumed	$x_i = \hat{D}^i(\mathbf{p}, u)$	: compensated demand
$p_1, \ldots, p_n$	: goods prices	$x_i = D^i(\mathbf{p}, M)$	: ordinary demand
$M = \Sigma p_i x_i$	: budget constraint	$M = C(\mathbf{p}, u)$	: cost function
$u = U(x_1, \ldots, x_n)$	: utility function	$u = V(\mathbf{p}, M)$	: indirect utility function

4.7 Consumer Welfare

We have now examined how a consumer determines his optimum consumption bundle $\mathbf{x}^*$, and how this optimum choice responds to changes in prices and income. Clearly increases in income make him better off, and increases in prices makes him worse off (or leave him where he is). But can we quantify the severity of these effects? Is the consumer worse off if the price of butter doubles than if the price of wine trebles? And how do these compare with a cut in his income of 10 per cent? Obviously we would look at how far on the indifference map each change would take us from a *given* utility level u_0. But since the function $U(\mathbf{x})$ has purely ordinal significance, it is generally meaningless to compare *differences* in U, and thus to attempt to measure changes in how well off the consumer is at different utility levels. There is a simple way round this: measure the changes in welfare by corresponding changes in the budget by use of the cost function. To do this we introduce the final piece of essential notation listed in Table 4.1 – the *indirect utility function*. This is the value of the maximised utility, expressed as a function of prices and income. In practice it is derived from the regular utility function using the demand functions (4.15), thus:

$$V(\mathbf{p}, M) \equiv U(D^1(\mathbf{p}, M), D^2(\mathbf{p}, M), \ldots, D^n(\mathbf{p}, M)) \tag{4.30}$$

It is easy to see that this function has the property $\partial V/\partial p_i \leqslant 0$, $\partial V/\partial M = v^* > 0$. Substituting in the cost function we have

$$V(\mathbf{p}, C(\mathbf{p}, u_0)) = u_0 \tag{4.31}$$

Differentiating (4.31) with respect to p_i we get, on rearrangement:

$$x_i^* = -\frac{\partial V}{\partial p_i} \bigg/ \frac{\partial V}{\partial M} \tag{4.32}$$

a result known as *Roy's Identity*.

Now we may measure the welfare change induced by, say, an exogenous change in prices from $\mathbf{p}^0$ to $\mathbf{p}^1$ in a straightforward fashion. One approach is to compute that change in M which would bring the consumer back from $u_1 = V(\mathbf{p}^1, M)$ to $u_0 = V(\mathbf{p}^0, M)$, with prices remaining at their new values $\mathbf{p}^1$: this is the *compensating variation* (CV). We may implicitly define CV as an amount of income such that

$$u_0 = V(\mathbf{p}^0, M) = V(\mathbf{p}^1, M - \mathrm{CV}) \tag{4.33}$$

Alternatively we may compute that change in M which brings the consumer from $u_0 = V(\mathbf{p}^0, M)$ to $u_1 = V(\mathbf{p}^1, M)$ whilst prices remain at their original values $\mathbf{p}^0$: this is the *equivalent variation* (EV). We define this as

$$u_1 = V(\mathbf{p}^1, M) = V(\mathbf{p}^0, M + \mathrm{EV}) \tag{4.34}$$

We can clearly see that CV and EV will be positive if and only if the change $\mathbf{p}^0 \rightarrow \mathbf{p}^1$ increases welfare – the two numbers always have the same sign as the welfare change. We can also see that, by definition:

$$\mathrm{CV}(\mathbf{p}^0 \rightarrow \mathbf{p}^1) = -\mathrm{EV}(\mathbf{p}^1 \rightarrow \mathbf{p}^0) \tag{4.35}$$

Clearly also:

$$\mathrm{CV}(\mathbf{p}^0 \rightarrow \mathbf{p}^1) = C(\mathbf{p}^0, u_0) - C(\mathbf{p}^1, u_0) = \sum_{i=1}^{n} \int_{p_i^1}^{p_i^0} \hat{D}^i(\mathbf{p}, u_0)\, dp_i \tag{4.36}$$

$$\mathrm{EV}(\mathbf{p}^0 \rightarrow \mathbf{p}^1) = C(\mathbf{p}^0, u_1) - C(\mathbf{p}^1, u_1) = \sum_{i=1}^{n} \int_{p_i^1}^{p_i^0} \hat{D}^i(\mathbf{p}, u_1)\, dp_i \tag{4.37}$$

CV can thus be interpreted as 'the change in cost of getting to the original utility level'; analogously EV is 'the change in cost of getting to the new utility level'. Neither CV nor EV can be claimed as the unique, 'correct' measure of welfare change. Each has a claim to usefulness, and the choice must depend on whether one views the change *'ex-ante'* (with reference to u_0) or *'ex-post'* (with reference to u_1).

In the case of a *normal* good i, we may represent the situation as in Figure 4.13. If, *ceteris paribus*, the price of i *falls* from p_i^0 to p_i^1 there has been a welfare *increase*. The CV measure is (+) the area under the curve $\hat{D}^i(\mathbf{p}, u_0)$, namely $ABEF$. Note that this is less than the change in the so-called Marshallian *consumer's surplus*, the area under $D^i(\mathbf{p}, M)$, namely $ABGF$. The EV measure is (+) the area under $\hat{D}^i(\mathbf{p}, u_1)$, namely $ACGF$; this of course is greater than the change in consumer's surplus (CS). For *inferior* goods the relative magnitudes of the slopes of D^i and $\hat{D}^i$ are reversed; so

$$\text{normal goods:} \quad \mathrm{CV} \leqslant \mathrm{CS} \leqslant \mathrm{EV} \tag{4.38}$$

$$\text{inferior goods:} \quad \mathrm{CV} > \mathrm{CS} > \mathrm{EV} \tag{4.39}$$

Only if the income effect is zero, so that $D^i = \hat{D}^i$ will we have CV = CS = EV.

Clearly it makes sense to use CV or EV to derive, respectively, a base-weighted or current-weighted, cost-of-living index (price index):

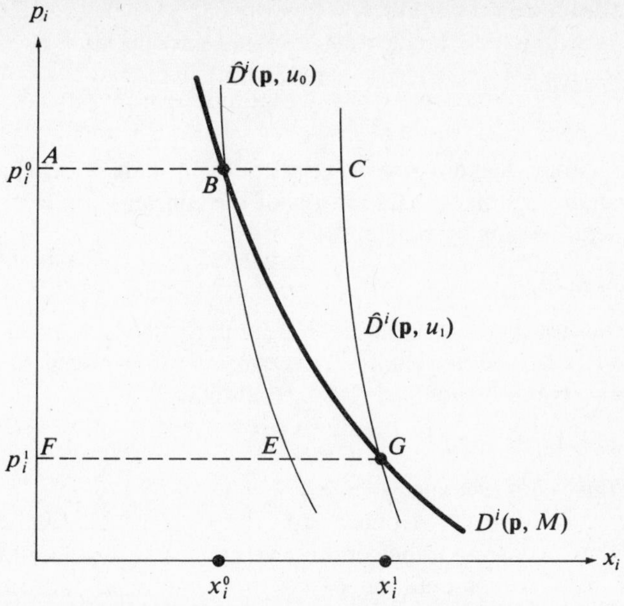

Figure 4.13

$$I_{CV} \equiv \frac{C(\mathbf{p}^1, u_0)}{C(\mathbf{p}^0, u_0)} \tag{4.40}$$

$$I_{EV} \equiv \frac{C(\mathbf{p}^1, u_1)}{C(\mathbf{p}^0, u_1)} \tag{4.41}$$

However, (4.40) and (4.41) in general require a complete evaluation of the cost function, and may well depend on the particular reference level of utility. It may be expedient, then, to use two corresponding approximations, the *Laspeyres* and the *Paasche* indices which are, respectively:

$$I_L = \frac{\sum_{i=1}^{n} p_i^1 x_i^0}{\sum_{i=1}^{n} p_i^0 x_i^0} \tag{4.42}$$

$$I_P = \frac{\sum_{i=1}^{n} p_i^1 x_i^1}{\sum_{i=1}^{n} p_i^0 x_i^1} \tag{4.43}$$

Note that the bottom line of (4.42) is simply $C(\mathbf{p}^0, u_0)$. The top line of (4.42) cannot, by definition, be smaller than $C(\mathbf{p}^1, u_0)$ since the latter is the minimum cost of reaching U-level u_0 at prices $\mathbf{p}^1$. Hence

$$I_L \geqslant I_{CV} \tag{4.44}$$

with equality only if the change in prices does not induce any change in the relative magnitudes of the components of the consumption vector.

By similar reasoning we can see

$$I_P \leqslant I_{EV} \tag{4.45}$$

However, notice that in general there is no particular relationship between I_{EV} and I_{CV}, so there is *no particular relationship* between I_P and I_L. If preferences were to be homothetic we would have

$$I_P \leqslant I_{EV} = I_{CV} \leqslant I_L \tag{4.46}$$

although this is a rather special case.

Finally, two words of qualification concerning CV and EV. First, although they may seem to be concepts yet more ethereal than Marshallian consumer surplus, computation of CV or EV requires no more special information than does computation of CS.[16] In either case one needs a reliable estimate of the ordinary consumer demand curve: this point is not really surprising in view of our observation concerning the Slutsky equation at the end of Section 4.6.

Secondly, although CV or EV gives one a money metric for welfare changes, this does *not* by itself imply that one may automatically compare one household's welfare change with another. To make the assertion 'my \$5 welfare gain outweighs the \$2 welfare loss to each of households two and three' involves a number of further important assumptions which we shall address in Section 8.5 of Chapter 8 and in Chapter 13.

4.8 Summary

Perhaps the single most interesting thing about the discussion of optimisation by consumers is how much of an overlap there is with the theory of the firm. By way of a reminder, Table 4.2 summarises some of these points of similarity.

Nevertheless, it is perhaps worth recalling the salient differences between the analysis of the firm and of the consumer. These relate to both the nature of the objective function and the form of constraint that is being faced. So:

---

16 See Vartia, Y.O. (1983) 'Efficient methods of measuring welfare change and compensated income in terms of ordinary demand curves', *Econometrica*, **51**, pp. 79–98.

Table 4.2

	Firm	*Household*
'Dual' problem	$\min_{\mathbf{z}} \Sigma w_i z_i$ subject to $G(\mathbf{z}) \geqslant Q_0$	$\min_{\mathbf{x}} \Sigma p_i x_i$ subject to $U(\mathbf{x}) \geqslant u_0$
First-order conditions (for interior optimum)	$\frac{w_j}{w_i} = \frac{G_j}{G_i} = \text{MRTS}_{ij}$	$\frac{p_j}{p_i} = \frac{U_j}{U_i} = \text{MRS}_{ij}$
Cost function	$C(\mathbf{w}, Q_0)$ increasing in Q_0, concave in $\mathbf{w}$	$C(\mathbf{p}, u_0)$ increasing in u_0, concave in $\mathbf{p}$
Conditional (compensated) demand	$z_i^* = \hat{D}^i(\mathbf{w}, Q_0) = C_i(\mathbf{w}, Q_0) \geqslant 0$	$x_i^* = \hat{D}^i(\mathbf{p}, u_0) = C_i(\mathbf{p}, u_0) \geqslant 0$
Substitution effects	$\hat{D}^i_i < 0;\ \hat{D}^j_i = \hat{D}^i_j$	$\hat{D}^i_i < 0;\ \hat{D}^j_i = \hat{D}^i_j$

- Unlike the production function G, the utility function U is defined only up to an increasing transformation.
- The consumer faces a fixed budget; the firm does not.

The former point implies, for example, that whilst we have a perfectly natural way of measuring and comparing firms' performances (in terms of profits), there is no obvious way of measuring and comparing households' 'well-offness'. We have examined two different possible types of money-metric for consumers' welfare in Section 4.7; but even then there are several pitfalls involved in comparing welfare levels of different households.

The second point implies that the (ordinary) demand functions for firms and for households will be specified rather differently, and hence will have different properties. In particular it makes sense to decompose the effects of price changes into *output and substitution* effects for firms, but *income and substitution* effects for households. Whilst each type of demand function can display 'inferiority' there is no counterpart to Giffen goods in the theory of the firm.

But one might question whether this subdivision of economic agents into 'producers' and 'consumers' is not a little arbitrary. We shall pursue this point in the next chapter.

Further Reading

The first two references are highly recommended and give a thorough grounding in the basic theory:

Deaton, A.S. and Muellbauer, J. (1980) *Economics and Consumer Behavior*, Cambridge University Press, Chs 2 and 7.

Green, H.A.J. (1976) *Consumer Theory* (2nd edn), Macmillan, Chs 2–5.

The classic reference on the use of indifference curve analysis is:

Hicks, J.R. (1946) *Value and Capital* (2nd edn), Oxford University Press.

The mathematics of demand functions is examined further in:

Arrow, K.J. and Intriligator, M.D. (eds) (1982) *Handbook of Mathematical Economics*, North-Holland, Vol. II, Ch. 9.

Intriligator, M.D. (1971) *Mathematical Optimization and Economic Theory*, Prentice-Hall, Ch. 7.

Two useful references on the empirical applications are:

Brown, J.A.C. and Deaton, A.S. (1972) 'Models of consumer behaviour: a survey', *Economic Journal*, Vol. 82, pp. 1145–236.

Phlips, L. (1974) *Applied Consumption Analysis*, North-Holland.

Some difficult, but interesting topics in the area of revealed preference and utility theory are covered in:

Chipman, J.S. *et al.* (1971) *Preferences, Utility and Demand*, Harcourt Brace.

Exercises

4.1 You observe a consumer in two situations: with an income of \$100 he buys 5 units of good 1 at a price of \$10 per unit and 10 units of good 2 at a price of \$5 per unit. With an income of \$175 he buys 3 units of good 1 at a price of \$15 per unit and 13 units of good 2 at a price of \$10 per unit. Do the actions of this consumer conform to the basic axioms of consumer behaviour? (Assume he may purchase fractions of a unit of either good.)

4.2 Using the weak axiom of revealed preference show that the own-price substitution effect must be negative. What problem is there in defining the substitution effect using revealed preference theory?

4.3 Consider the following price vectors $\mathbf{p}^1$, $\mathbf{p}^2$, $\mathbf{p}^3$ and corresponding observed consumption choices $\mathbf{x}^1$, $\mathbf{x}^2$ and $\mathbf{x}^3$

$$\begin{matrix} \mathbf{p}^1 & \mathbf{p}^2 & \mathbf{p}^3 & ; & \mathbf{x}^1 & \mathbf{x}^2 & \mathbf{x}^3 \\ \begin{bmatrix} 2 \\ 1 \\ 1 \end{bmatrix} & \begin{bmatrix} 1 \\ 2 \\ 1 \end{bmatrix} & \begin{bmatrix} 1 \\ 1 \\ 2 \end{bmatrix} & & \begin{bmatrix} 2 \\ 3 \\ 1 \end{bmatrix} & \begin{bmatrix} 1 \\ 2 \\ 3 \end{bmatrix} & \begin{bmatrix} 3 \\ 1 \\ 2 \end{bmatrix} \end{matrix}$$

Verify that these choices are consistent with WARP. Are they also consistent with a conventional utility function?

4.4 Old George is a dipsomaniac. Friends speak in hushed tones about his *lexicographic* preference map (this comment has nothing to do with his research appointment in the English Faculty): he always strictly prefers the consumption bundle that has the greatest amount of booze in it (regardless of the amount of other goods in the bundle); if two bundles contain the same amount of booze then he strictly prefers the bundle containing the larger amount of other goods.

Sketch old George's preferences in a diagram. Extend the idea of a lexicographic ordering to an n-good model. Which of the axioms in Section 4.3 are violated by such an ordering?

*4.5 Sketch (i) the marginal rate of substitution and (ii) the compensated and ordinary demand curves that would arise from each of these four types of indifference maps:

(a) All of Axioms C1 to C6 are satisfied.
(b) C1 to C4, C5′, C6 are satisfied, but *not* C5.
(c) C1 to C4 and C6 are satisfied, but *not* C5′.
(d) C1 to C5 are satisfied, but the indifference curves have 'kinks'.

4.6 Show that the following three utility functions are equivalent:

$$U^1(\mathbf{x}) = x_1^{\alpha 1} x_2^{\alpha 2} \ldots x_n^{\alpha n}$$
$$U^2(\mathbf{x}) = \textstyle\sum_{i=1}^{n} \alpha_i \log x_i$$
$$U^3(\mathbf{x}) = x_1^{2\alpha 1} x_2^{2\alpha 2} \ldots x_n^{2\alpha n}$$

where $\alpha_i > 0$, $i = 1, \ldots, n$. Derive the cost function and demand functions and comment on their form.

4.7 (a) Explain why for uncompensated cross price elasticities we may have $\varepsilon_{ij} > 0$ but $\varepsilon_{ji} < 0$ for given i and j.
(b) Show that at least one pair of goods *must* be net substitutes.

*4.8 An individual maximises the utility function

$$U(x_1, \ldots, x_n) = \sum_{i=1}^{n} b_i \log(x_i - a_i)$$

where $a_i, b_i \geqslant 0$ for all i and $\sum_{i=1}^{n} b_i = 1$.

Prices are given by $p_i (i = 1, \ldots, n)$ and income by

$$M > \sum_{i=1}^{n} p_i a_i$$

(a) Obtain the ordinary demand functions and explain how the parameters may be interpreted.
(b) Examine whether the goods are normal or inferior and whether pairs of goods are complements or substitutes.
(c) Describe the conditions under which the goods are 'luxuries' (such that their income elasticities exceed unity).
(d) Show that all goods are price inelastic.

4.9 In a two-good economy a person's utility function is given by $U(\mathbf{x}) = x_1x_2/[x_1 + 2x_2]$, $\mathbf{x} \geqslant \mathbf{0}$. Verify that marginal utilities are positive, and that U is concave-contoured. Write down the first-order conditions for a maximum of U subject to the constraint $p_1x_1 + p_2x_2 = M$ where $M > 0$ and $\mathbf{p} > \mathbf{0}$, and find the demand functions for x_1 and x_2.

Verify that the demand functions are homogeneous of degree zero in prices and income and establish whether the goods are normal/inferior/Giffen commodities. Write down the indirect utility function $V(\mathbf{p}, M)$, and verify the result

$$x_i = -\frac{\partial V}{\partial p_i} \Big/ \frac{\partial V}{\partial M}, \quad i = 1, 2$$

4.10 Sketch the income and substitution effects for a Giffen good.

*4.11 Illustrate the consumer's budget constraint when he faces a *quantity discount* on good 1. What special problems may this raise for demand analysis?

*4.12 Consider a consumer with a utility function defined over three goods (which he always consumes in positive amounts). Suppose the *relative price* of good 3 in terms of good 2 *always* remains the same. Show that maximising $U(x_1, x_2, x_3)$ subject to $p_1x_1 + p_2x_2 + p_3x_3 \leqslant M$ is equivalent to maximising a function $\bar{U}(x_1, \bar{x})$ subject to $p_1x_1 + \bar{p}\bar{x} \leqslant M$

where $\bar{p} \equiv p_2 + p_3, \bar{x} \equiv \alpha x_2 + [1 - \alpha] x_3, \alpha \equiv p_2/\bar{p}$. Comment on this result and its obvious generalisation (known as the *composite commodity* theorem).

*4.13 Suppose a consumer is rationed in his consumption of commodity 1, so that his consumption is constrained $x_1 \leqslant a$. Analyse the demand functions for commodities 2, ..., n of a consumer for whom the rationing constraint is binding. (Hint: use the analysis that leads up to Theorem 3.6 of Chapter 3.)

4.14 A consumer has the utility function

$$U(x_1, x_2, x_3) = x_1 + x_2 x_3$$

which he maximises subject to the budget constraint

$$p_1 x_1 + p_2 x_2 + p_3 x_3 = M$$

where

$$M > \frac{2 p_2 p_3}{p_1}$$

(a) Find the demand functions for the three goods and comment on their form.

(b) Use Slutsky's equation to find the pure substitution effect of a change in the price of good 2 on the demand for good 1 and demonstrate its symmetry.

(c) Derive the indirect utility function. Illustrate its properties and show how the demand function for good 3 can be used to estimate the benefit of a fall in its price. Can the same thing be done for goods 1 and 2? If not, why not?

*4.15 A consumer has the two-period utility function

$$U(x_1, x_2) = \log x_1 + \alpha \log x_2, 0 < \alpha < 1$$

and initial wealth A, which is partly spent on consumption in the first period x_1 and the remainder invested in an asset paying a rate of interest r. Obtain the optimal allocation of $\mathbf{x}$, the consumption over the two periods, and explain how consumption varies with A, r and α (the index of impatience). Comment on your results and examine the 'income' and 'substitution' effects of the interest rate on consumption.

4.16 Suppose gasoline is rationed by the government: each household is issued a fixed number of ration coupons and may buy gasoline at a low, regulated price by surrendering one coupon per litre along with the purchase price. However consumers can drive across the border to buy gasoline at a higher, unregulated price.

(a) If the government prevents the resale or transfer of coupons, but keeps the border open, use diagrams similar to Figure 4.12 to illustrate the equilibrium of two consumers: Alf who drives little and Bill who wants to drive more than his coupon allocation would permit.
(b) If the government closes the border, again illustrate the equilibrium for the two consumers.
(c) If the government were to allow people to trade the coupons freely, what would be the market price of the coupons?

4.17 The elasticity of demand for domestic heating oil is -0.5, and for gasoline is -1.5. The price of both sorts of fuel is 60¢ per litre: included in this price is an excise tax of 48¢ per litre. The government wants to reduce energy consumption in the economy and to increase its tax revenue. Can it do this (a) by taxing domestic heating oil? (b) by taxing gasoline?

4.18 Show that if preferences are homothetic then $I_{CV} = I_{EV}$.

4.19 In a two-commodity model suppose that good 1 has a strictly positive income effect. Illustrate the effect of a fall in the price of good 1 using indifference curve analysis.

(a) Using good two as *numéraire*, show how compensating variation and equivalent variation may be represented on this diagram.
(b) Use the diagram to prove that the equivalent variation is larger than the compensating variation.

5

Households, Workers and Producers

5.1 Introduction

So far we have considered one production unit on its own and one consumer on its own, and in either case took the rest of the universe for granted. This approach begs a number of questions which we deal with in the next few chapters. The most immediate issues seem to be these: why the profit-maximising firm? Why suppose that production is organised this way? Why assume an exogenously fixed income for the consumer? If a household is faced with the entire range of decision making – from basic production to final consumption – how will it organise this? Under what circumstances will it specialise so as to separate out the production and consumption activities?

To do this we shall begin with an extremely primitive hypothetical single-agent economy, without trade. We then introduce an additional agent, and then access to free markets in some of the goods. At each stage we shall consider how the range of opportunities for the original economic agent is enlarged. Once again we assume there is a given state of the art represented either by the constraint on net production vectors $\mathbf{y} \in Y$, or by the production function $\Phi(\mathbf{y}) \leqslant 0$ where Y or Φ are exogenously given. In order to 'close' the system we also have to assume the existence of a finite, exogenously given list of resources which are present before our story begins.

5.2 Robinson Crusoe

Robinson Crusoe is the ideal prototype for our present purposes: a single-person economy with a stock of natural resources (including his own labour), an endowment of other consumption goods and intermediate goods, well-defined technology, and no contact with other producers or consumers (before the arrival of Man Friday and the cannibals).

Formally, Crusoe is endowed with resources $(R_1, \ldots, R_n)$ – many components of the vector $\mathbf{R}$ may be zero of course (items lost overboard in the shipwreck that he would subsequently have to manufacture); he has a concave production function $\Phi(\mathbf{y}) \leqslant 0$ where $\mathbf{y}$ is the n-vector of net outputs (see Chapter 2). And he has a utility function $U(\mathbf{x})$ where $\mathbf{x}$ is the n-vector of consumption. Hence the Crusoe problem is

$$\max_{(\mathbf{x},\, \mathbf{y})} U(\mathbf{x})$$

subject to

$$\mathbf{x} \geqslant \mathbf{0} \tag{5.1}$$

$$\Phi(\mathbf{y}) \leqslant 0 \tag{5.2}$$

$$\mathbf{x} \leqslant \mathbf{y} + \mathbf{R} \tag{5.3}$$

Constraint (5.3), known formally as the 'materials balance condition', is simply a statement of the facts of life: for any commodity i, consumption (x_i) cannot exceed the net output of that commodity (y_i) plus the initial stock of that commodity (R_i). For obvious reasons we call the set $\{\mathbf{x}$: (5.1)–(5.3) are satisfied$\}$ the *feasible* set. Employing Axioms A1–A7 and C1–C6 of Chapters 2 and 4, respectively, we find a solution at a differentiable point $\mathbf{x}^0$, $\mathbf{y}^0$ where, for every good i consumed in positive amounts:

$$U_i(\mathbf{x}^0) = \lambda \Phi_i(\mathbf{y}^0) \qquad i = 1, \ldots, n \tag{5.4}$$

$$x_i^0 = y_i^0 + R_i \tag{5.5}$$

where λ is the Lagrange multiplier in the maximisation problem and where 5.2 holds with equality. Obviously (5.4) implies $\text{MRS}_{ij} = \text{MRT}_{ij}$ for any pair of goods i and j. This rather obvious solution is illustrated in Figure 5.1.

Certain features of this solution are most easily demonstrated in the case of a fixed proportions technology – although the results are quite general. Suppose goods 1 and 2 are consumption goods, of which Crusoe has no stocks ($R_1 = R_2 = 0$). He does have positive amounts of three resources R_3, R_4, R_5, and the production of a unit of consumption good i requires at least a_{ij} units of resource j, ($i = 1, 2; j = 3, 4, 5$). Assuming constant returns to scale y_i units of good i therefore require at least $y_i a_{ij}$ units of input j. Hence the feasible set is simply the non-negative values of $\mathbf{x}$ satisfying:

$$\left.\begin{aligned} x_1 a_{13} + x_2 a_{23} &\leqslant R_3 \\ x_1 a_{14} + x_2 a_{24} &\leqslant R_4 \\ x_1 a_{15} + x_2 a_{25} &\leqslant R_5 \end{aligned}\right\} \tag{5.6}$$

This is illustrated in Figure 5.2 bounded by the heavy kinked line through A. Given the preference map illustrated by the particular indifference curve drawn as $U(\mathbf{x}) = u_0$ Crusoe's optimum is clearly at A.

Now suppose Crusoe found some more of resource 3 (gunpowder) aboard the shipwreck. It is easy to see that such a discovery may in fact be worthless. To see this shift the R_3-constraint outwards a small distance parallel to itself, and note that the optimum remains unchanged at point A.

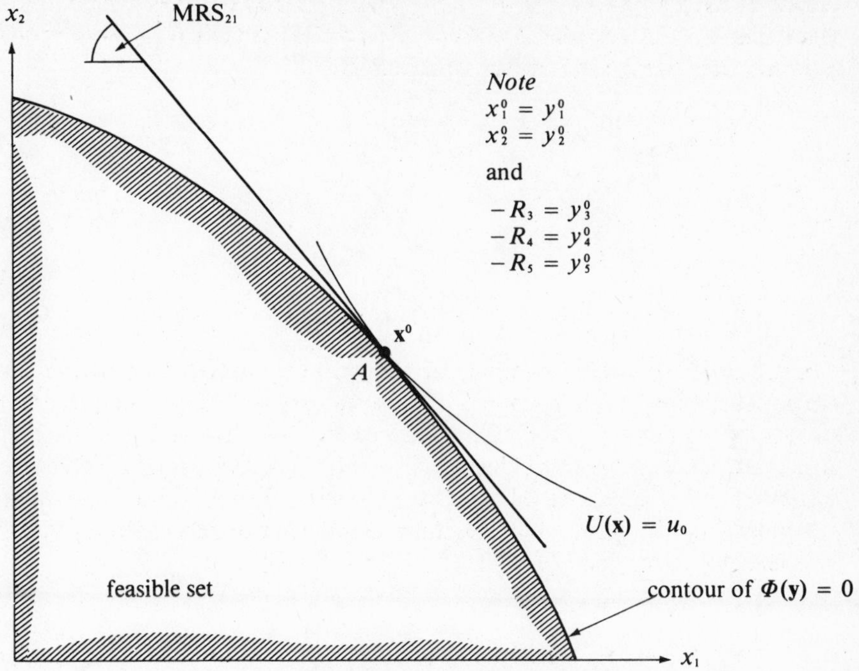

Figure 5.1

Of course exactly the same point could be noted if, say, Crusoe discovered some gunpowder-saving invention (which effectively reduced a_{13} and a_{23} slightly). Although the feasible set is enlarged, Crusoe is no better off in any relevant sense. Clearly Crusoe would be unwilling to pay anything at all to secure extra units of resource 3. Indeed, at point A he is underutilising the R_3 he already has. This illustrates the point that although certain inputs may be used in positive amounts at the optimum, their valuation at the margin may in fact be zero. Their 'shadow price' is zero if they do not locally present an effective constraint on production.

Clearly the MRS_{21} represents Crusoe's relative valuation of good 1 in terms of good 2. Suppose now there is a change in the feasible set which *apparently* yields the same 'income' at this valuation – namely let R_5 decrease and R_4 increase so that the boundary now runs through point B, where B lies on the tangent through A. Clearly Crusoe would be *worse* off – point A is no longer feasible, and he would end up consuming at a point B which is on a lower indifference curve.[1] By extension we can see that any change in resource

---

[1] At the new equilibrium MRS_{21} may have changed, thus changing the shadow prices.

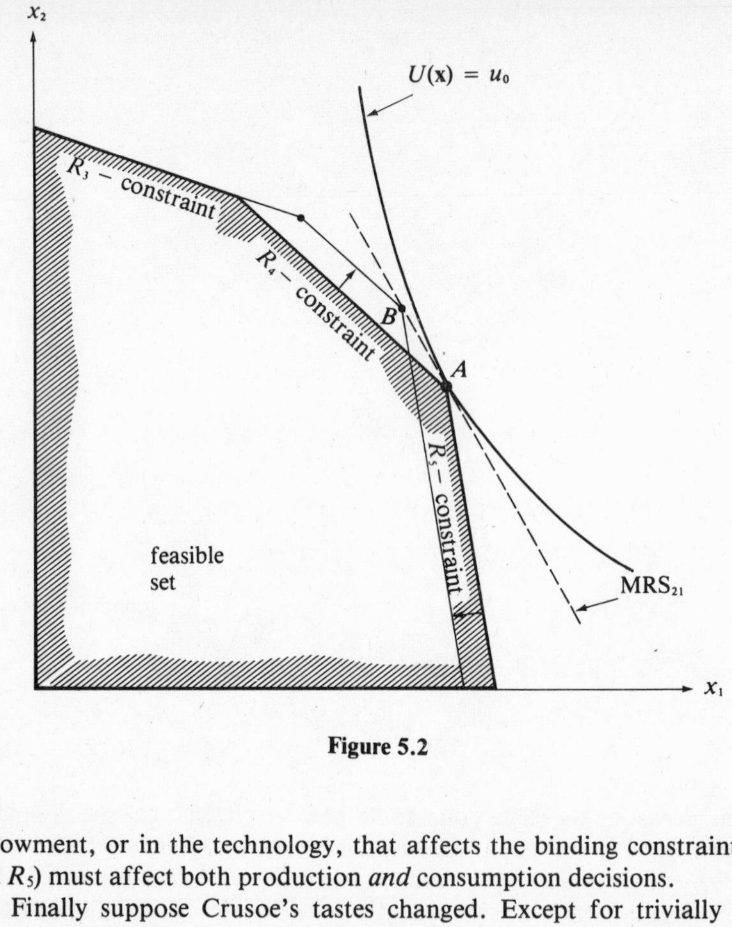

Figure 5.2

endowment, or in the technology, that affects the binding constraints (R_4 and R_5) must affect both production *and* consumption decisions.

Finally suppose Crusoe's tastes changed. Except for trivially small changes whereby he does not move from the corner A, we can see that both consumption *and* production decisions must alter when tastes alter.

5.3 Crusoe and Man Friday

Man Friday enters our make-believe world for an entirely immoral purpose – to act as a slave to Robinson Crusoe. He has no property rights and his tastes are not respected when Crusoe makes consumption decisions. He is in fact just part of the technology, and his food, shelter and so on can just be subsumed as inputs to the production process.

The big advantage of Man Friday is that Crusoe might be able to delegate some of the economic activities. Indeed, if we regard Man Friday's labour time and Crusoe's labour time as distinct resources, substituting the former for the latter might result in a clear welfare improvement for the despotic

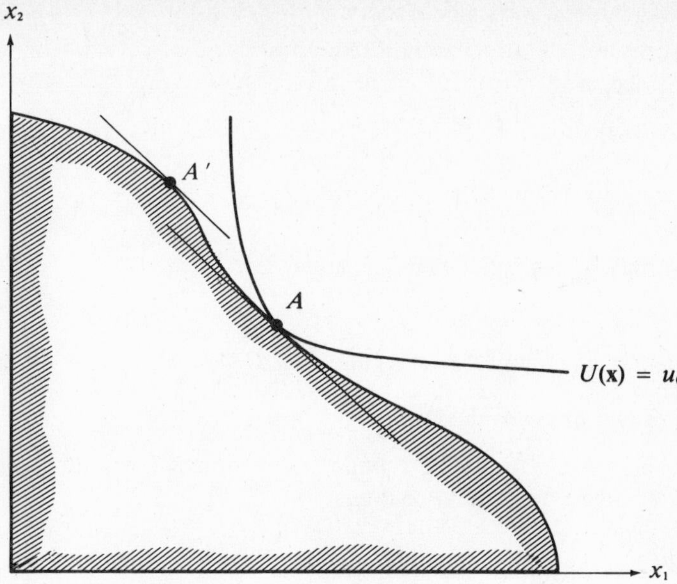

Figure 5.3

Crusoe. Re-examination of Figure 5.1 reveals a simple way of doing this. The slope of the tangent through point $\mathbf{x}^0$ is of course MRS_{21}, Crusoe's relative valuation of good 1 in terms of good 2, U_1/U_2. So Crusoe could write down the list of all these relative values as a set of shadow prices $(\pi_1, \ldots, \pi_n)$, give them to Man Friday, tell him to treat the economic organisation of the desert island as a firm and instruct him to maximise profits $\Sigma\pi_i y_i$. Friday would automatically produce at point A.[2] This might seem rather a roundabout way of going about matters, though one's intuition suggests that with more complex 'households' consisting of master and slaves, of family members or of other agents this might be quite a useful idea – see Section 5.4 and Chapter 8.

What is perhaps even more interesting is the case where this *cannot* be successfully done. Examine Figure 5.3. Here the technology set is *not* convex (Φ is not a concave function) – locally there are increasing returns in production. Suppose Crusoe announces the shadow prices as those pertaining to the tangent through A, where he actually maximises utility. Friday will actually go and produce at point A' if he acts as a profit-maximising firm. Delegating production by using shadow prices does not work. The convexity or non-convexity of the technology is in fact crucial.

2 To see this note that $x_1 = y_1$, $x_2 = y_2$, and sketch on Figure 5.1 the family of lines $\pi_1 x_1 + \pi_2 x_2 = \Pi$ for different values of Π given π_1, π_2; Π is then maximised on the feasible set at A.

THEOREM 5.1 (separating hyperplane):[3] if the feasible set is convex and the utility function is concave-contoured, then there exists a set of imputed shadow prices π such that the problem

$$\max_{\mathbf{x}} U(\mathbf{x}) \text{ subject to (5.1)–(5.3)}$$

is equivalent to the two-stage problem

$$\begin{cases} (1): \max_{\mathbf{y}} \sum_{i=1}^{n} \pi_i y_i \text{ subject to (5.2) and (5.3)} \\ (2): \max_{\mathbf{x}} U(\mathbf{x}) \text{ subject to (5.1) and } \sum_{i=1}^{n} \pi_i x_i \leqslant M \text{ where } M \text{ is the maximal value of problem (1).} \end{cases}$$

This is the first example of *economic decentralisation* which plays an important role in subsequent chapters.

5.4 Trade

Crusoe now makes contact with the rest of civilisation. A free market opens up in gunpowder, goats, Gorgonzola cheese and everything else: he may buy or sell as much as he likes of good i at price p_i. Consider the new feasible set. Clearly it is no smaller than before, because all the production possibilities that were available before are still available now. But now if $\mathbf{x}^0$ is attainable so also is any $\mathbf{x}^1$ where $\sum_{i=1}^{n} p_i x_i^1 \leqslant \sum_{i=1}^{n} p_i x_i^0$ – simply because of the possibility of unlimited buying and selling at the price vector $\mathbf{p}$. So in Figure 5.4 all points 'south west' of the line through $\mathbf{x}^0$ must be feasible. But of course the feasible set includes other points as well – for example $\mathbf{x}^2$ is clearly feasible (since it lies in the original frontier) and all points below the line running through $\mathbf{x}^2$ must also be feasible. Obviously the full feasible set can be found by maximising $\Sigma p_i x_i$ subject to the relevant constraints (5.1)–(5.3). In view of (5.5), maximising $\sum_{i=1}^{n} p_i x_i$ is equivalent to maximising $\sum_{i=1}^{n} p_i [R_i + y_i]$. So the new feasible set is $\{\mathbf{x} : \mathbf{x} \geqslant \mathbf{0}, \sum_{i=1}^{n} p_i x_i \leqslant M\}$ where

$$M = \max_{\{\mathbf{y}\}} \sum_{i=1}^{n} p_i [R_i + y_i] \tag{5.7}$$

subject to

$$\Phi(\mathbf{y}) \leqslant 0$$

[3] See Dixit, A.K. (1976) *Optimization in Economic Theory*, Ch. 4. Also see Theorem 8.3 of Chapter 8 and its proof in Appendix A for a slightly stronger application of the 'separating hyperplane' result.

Table 5.1 Essential notation for Chapter 5: Households, Workers and Producers

x_i	: consumption of good i
y_i	: net output of good i
R_i	: resource endowment of good i
p_i	: price of good i
$D^i(\mathbf{p}, \Sigma_j p_j R_j)$	: demand for good i given resources $\mathbf{R}$

Since the vector $\mathbf{R}$ is exogenously fixed, the problem implicit in (5.7) is equivalent to maximising $\Sigma p_i y_i$ subject to the technology. In other words the feasible set is a simple budget set with 'income' M found by valuing the resources at their market prices and adding the (maximised) profits from the production process. Note that these profits will never be negative because Crusoe has the option of not producing at all, but just selling his gunpowder, his goats and possibly his labour on the free market.

The rest of the optimisation problem is easy since it amounts to 'maximise $U(\mathbf{x})$ subject to $\Sigma p_i x_i \leqslant M$' – a conventional consumer optimisation problem, as examined in Chapter 4. Since the new feasible set is obviously con-

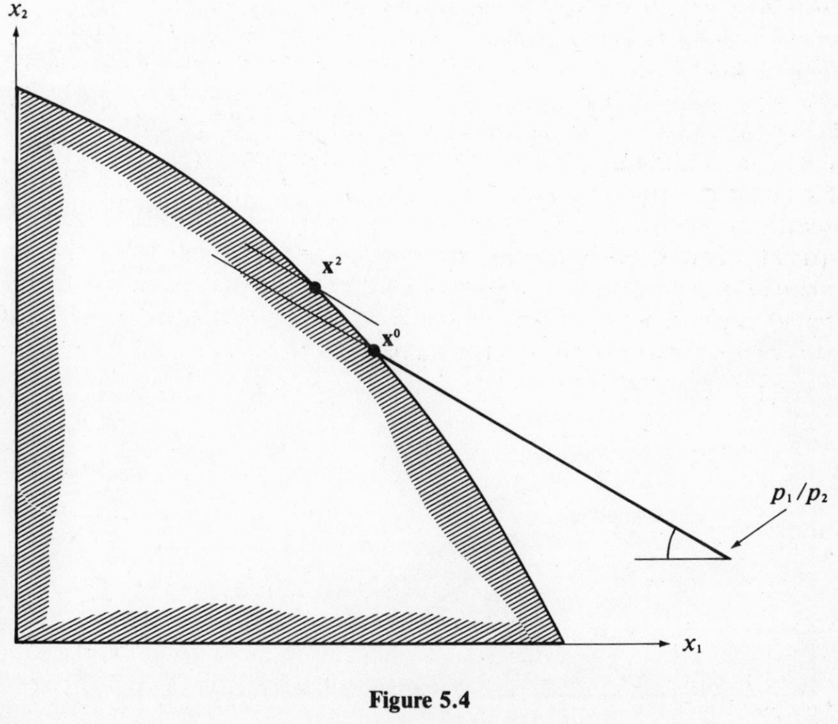

Figure 5.4

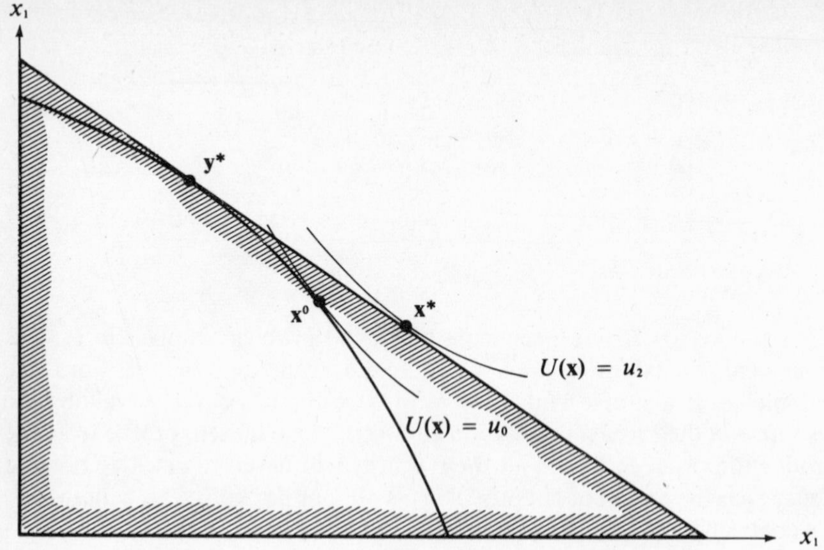

Figure 5.5

vex, we can immediately apply the separating hyperplane theorem with the *actual* prices **p** playing the role of the shadow prices **p**, of course. So we immediately see that *irrespective of whether the Crusoe/Friday technology is convex*, decentralisation is always possible given a free world market in all commodities.

To understand this further, examine Figures 5.5 and 5.6 corresponding to Figures 5.1 and 5.3. We assume that the 'firm' owned by Crusoe and run by Friday does in fact produce at the optimum (it is not optimal for Crusoe just to sell his goats to the Europeans and his gunpowder and Man Friday to

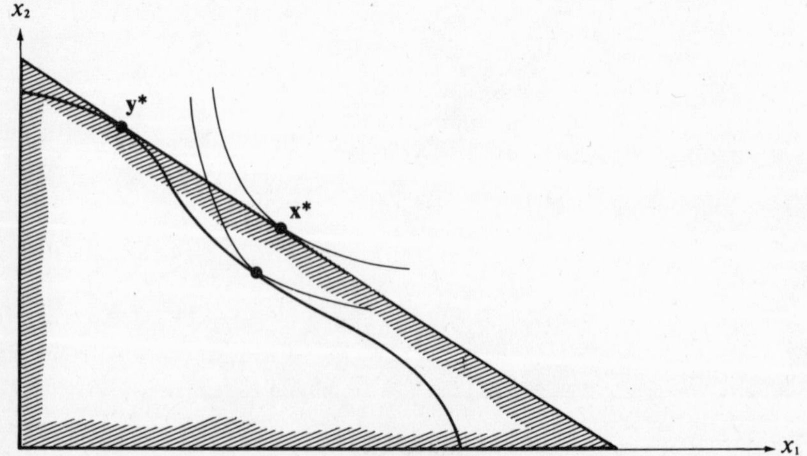

Figure 5.6

the cannibals). Then the feasible set is as shown, shaded in. Net outputs of the firm are at the point $\mathbf{y}^*$; Crusoe consumes at point $\mathbf{x}^*$; he buys in some extra good 1 from the market in exchange for selling some good 2 and it is clear that regardless of whether the underlying technology is convex or not Crusoe can safely delegate production to Friday, instructing him to maximise profits at prices $\mathbf{p}$. It must be emphasised that this result depends crucially on the access to competitive markets which 'convexify' the feasible set. Clearly trade can never make Crusoe worse off and it can (as in the figures) make him better off. Also if we were to reconstruct the example with the linear technology (Figure 5.2) it is clear that some of the interactions that were inevitable in the no-trade model are now no longer present. For example, if Crusoe has a taste change, this affects $\mathbf{x}^*$, but not $\mathbf{y}^*$, the optimum production point (try redrawing the indifference map) – the altered consumption pattern is accommodated purely by a change in the amounts of goods traded. Likewise a change in resource endowment or in the technology that leaves M unaltered would alter $\mathbf{y}^*$, but *not* $\mathbf{x}^*$. In passing it is interesting to note that resources that do not present a binding constraint on Crusoe's production (such as R_3 in the example of Section 5.2) will not now be worthless if they command a positive price in the open market.

5.5 Factor Supply

Now let us suppose that we ignore the production that Crusoe might undertake (it may be that it is inefficient, compared to the technological possibilities elsewhere). Crusoe then trades some of his resource endowments $R_1, \ldots, R_n$ to obtain additional quantities of other goods.

The problem can be expressed: 'maximise $U(\mathbf{x})$ subject to $\sum_{i=1}^{n} p_i [x_i - R_i] \leqslant 0$'. Form the Lagrangean:

$$\mathscr{L}(\mathbf{x}, \nu) = U(\mathbf{x}) + \nu \sum_{i=1}^{n} p_i [R_i - x_i] \tag{5.8}$$

Clearly the first-order conditions for a maximum are the same as in equation (4.14) except that now the 'income' is endogenously defined as

$$M \equiv \sum_{i=1}^{n} p_i R_i \tag{5.9}$$

the market value of the resource endowments. Accordingly the demand for good i, $D^i(\mathbf{p}, M)$ can be written $D^i(\mathbf{p}, \sum_{j=1}^{n} p_j R_j)$. Obviously if, for some i, the optimum x_i^* is greater than R_i we have a fairly conventional case of consumption demand for this good; but if $x_i^* < R_i$ (and $p_i > 0$) then an amount $R_i - x_i^*$ is being *supplied to* the market. Factor supply by households can thus be treated symmetrically with consumption demand by households within this simple model.

Now let us examine the comparative statics of these demand functions (since R_i is fixed, to get the effect on the *supply* in each case below, simply put a minus sign in front). Firstly consider the effect of an increase in the endowment R_j:

$$\frac{\partial x_i^*}{\partial R_j} = D_M^i p_j \tag{5.10}$$

– a simple modification of the effect of a change in income in the theory of the consumer modelled in Chapter 4. Next consider a change in p_j the price of good j: note that this now has both a *direct* effect through the first argument of D^i *and* an indirect effect through the size of M, because increasing p_j increases the value of resource R_j (contrast this with the model of Chapter 4 where M was exogenously fixed). So clearly

$$\frac{\partial x_i^*}{\partial p_j} = \left.\frac{\partial x_i^*}{\partial p_j}\right|_M + \frac{\partial x_i^*}{\partial M} R_j \tag{5.11}$$

Obviously the last term in (5.11) is just $D_M^i R_j$; and the first term on the right-hand side of (5.11) is the expression that we wrote as D_j^i in Chapter 4 – the effect of an increase in p_j on x_i^* when M is held constant. But of course we know a simple result on D_j^i – the Slutsky equation (4.23), namely

$$D_j^i = \hat{D}_j^i - x_j^* D_M^i \tag{5.12}$$

where $\hat{D}^i(\mathbf{p}, u)$ is the compensated demand for good i, so that $\hat{D}_j^i$ is the substitution effect of an increase in p_j. Substituting (5.12) into (5.11) we get

$$\frac{\partial x_i^*}{\partial p_j} = \hat{D}_j^i - [x_j^* - R_j]\, D_M^i \tag{5.13}$$

Equation (5.13) can be treated as a *modified* Slutsky equation, with the modification arising in the interpretation of the 'income effect' of course.

Take the case where $j = i$ in equation (5.13). If the household is a net *demander* of good i, then the analysis goes through much as in Chapter 4, but with an income effect smaller in absolute size. However, suppose that the household *supplies* good i to the market. Let us make the conventional assumption that $D_M^i > 0$, so that i is not an inferior good. Then, recalling that $\hat{D}_i^i < 0$, we can see that the 'substitution' and 'income' effects are of opposite signs. Clearly it is quite possible that x_i^* initially decreases with p_i and then, when p_i is large and x_i^* is small, the income effect dominates so that x_i^* actually *increases* with p_i – see Figure 5.7.

If we plot the resulting *supply* of good i by the household as a function of p_i we would then get a shape such as Figure 5.8. Of course, depending on household preferences, the supply could be everywhere forward rising, or everywhere backward bending.

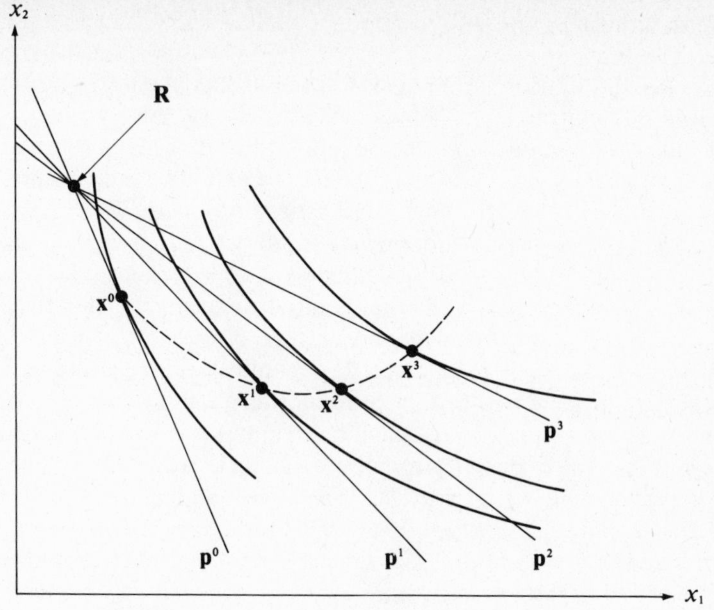

Figure 5.7 Demand for x_1 and x_2 as p_2 increases

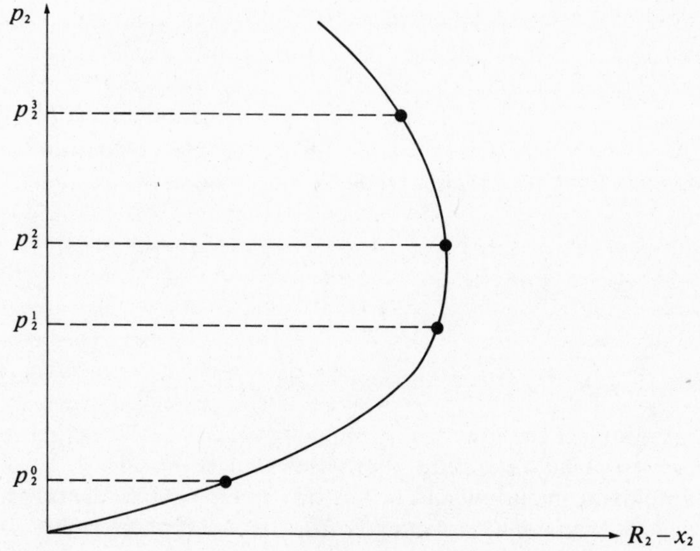

Figure 5.8

5.6 Household Production

We can use the Crusoe model to examine further important features of household decision making. It may well be the case that certain items of household consumption *cannot* be bought and sold on the market – or at least there are no obvious close substitutes. Instead they must be produced within the household using other purchased goods as inputs. Some would argue that the child care performed by a mother falls into this category. Family home movies are an obvious example. Likewise there are many other leisure activities where time and other goods are expended within the household to produce 'commodities' that are enjoyed directly but which cannot be bought or sold. Suppose the Crusoe 'household' faces a perfect market in some commodities but that certain consumption goods are not purchasable: fresh milk, let us say, is unobtainable on the market because it perishes on the sea journey. To fix ideas, let us suppose that there are $n + m$ commodities[4] in the economy, n of which have (direct) positive marginal utility, but cannot be bought or sold, and m which do not yield utility directly, but which may be purchased (or sold) at prices $\mathbf{w}$ (an m-vector) and transformed by the household into 'outputs' $x_1, \ldots, x_n$.

Take first the fixed proportions technology outlined in Section 5.2. The production function here for outputs $x_1, \ldots, x_n$ from inputs $z_1, \ldots, z_m$ is given by

$$x_i = \min\{z_1/a_{i1}, \ldots, z_m/a_{im}\} \qquad i = 1, \ldots, n \tag{5.14}$$

Clearly as long as at least one good x_i has positive marginal utility, Crusoe would wish to transform inputs into outputs efficiently. Hence the minimum cost of producing say a bundle $\mathbf{x}^0$ would be $\sum_{i=1}^{n} \sum_{j=1}^{n} x_i^0 a_{ij} w_j$, where a_{ij} is the minimum amount of input j needed to produce one unit of output i. His income, we know, is given by $M = \sum_{j=1}^{m} R_j w_j$. Hence the feasible set of vectors $\mathbf{x}$ that can be reached by Crusoe with resources $\mathbf{R}$ and facing input prices $\mathbf{w}$ is

$$\{\mathbf{x} : \mathbf{x} \geqslant \mathbf{0} \sum_{i=1}^{n} \pi_i x_i \leqslant M\} \tag{5.15}$$

where $\pi_i \equiv \sum_{j=1}^{m} a_{ij} w_j$ (the shadow price of output i). This is the equivalent to a simple linear budget constraint – see Figure 5.9.

The problem becomes more interesting if it is possible to substitute amongst inputs in the household production process. Once again we may assume that the 'firm' will be operated as an efficient economic unit, so that

---

4 There is in principle no difficulty in having goods that are used both as inputs and which yield utility directly; however this device simplifies the presentation a little.

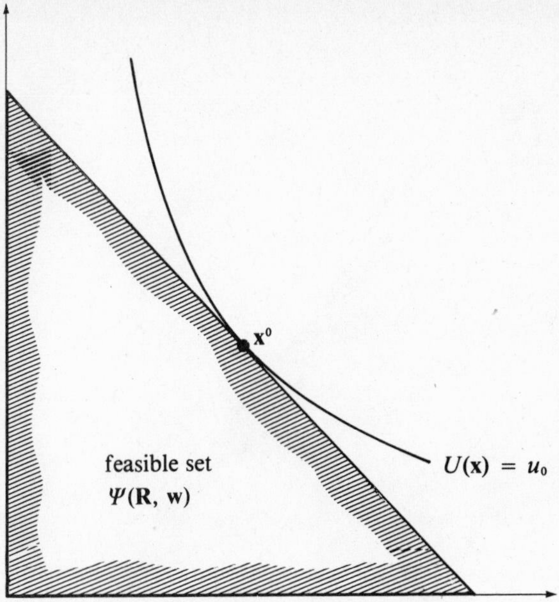

Figure 5.9

inputs $z_1, \ldots, z_m$ are adjusted to minimise cost. This yields a cost function $C(\mathbf{w}, \mathbf{x})$ – which is simply the minimum value of $\sum_{j=1}^{m} w_j z_j$ required to obtain the specified n-vector of output $\mathbf{x}$. Obviously this cost must not exceed M, the value of Crusoe's resources, so the feasible set of outputs is given by

$$\Psi(\mathbf{R}, \mathbf{w}) \equiv \{\mathbf{x} : C(\mathbf{w}, \mathbf{x}) \leqslant \sum_{j=1}^{m} R_j w_j\}$$

We may conveniently write the boundary of this set as

$$\psi(\mathbf{x}; \mathbf{R}, \mathbf{w}) \equiv C(\mathbf{w}, \mathbf{x}) - \sum_{j=1}^{m} R_j w_j = 0 \tag{5.16}$$

It is easy to see that ψ must be concave[5] in $\mathbf{x}$. For, suppose that $\mathbf{x}^0$ and $\mathbf{x}^1$ are two points on the boundary of $\Psi(\mathbf{R}, \mathbf{w})$, that $\mathbf{z}^0$ is the minimum cost combination of inputs to produce $\mathbf{x}^0$, and that $\mathbf{z}^1$ is the minimum cost combination

---

[5] In fact it can be shown that if the household production function is *strictly* concave contoured, then ψ must be *strictly* concave in $\mathbf{x}$.

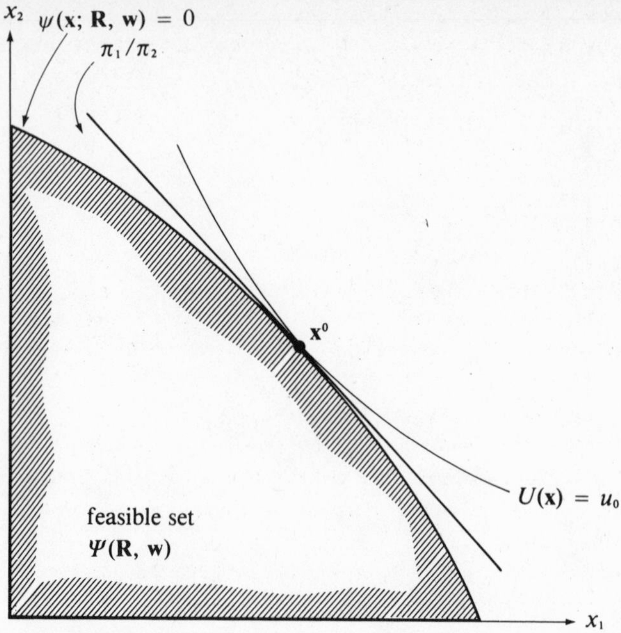

Figure 5.10

required to produce $\mathbf{x}^1$. If the technology is convex, then the vector $\mathbf{x}^\alpha \equiv \alpha\mathbf{x}^0 + [1 - \alpha]\mathbf{x}^1$ (where $0 < \alpha < 1$) can be produced from the input combination $\mathbf{z}^\alpha \equiv \alpha\mathbf{z}^0 + [1 - \alpha]\mathbf{z}^1$. But $\Sigma_j w_j z_j^\alpha = \alpha\Sigma w_j z_j^0 + [1 - \alpha]\,\Sigma w_j z_j^1 = \alpha M + [1 - \alpha]M = M$; so $\mathbf{z}^\alpha$ can certainly be purchased, and $\mathbf{x}^\alpha$ must lie in $\Psi(\mathbf{R}, \mathbf{w})$ – see Figure 5.10. Clearly the effective budget constraint need no longer be a straight line.

The remainder of Crusoe's optimisation problem can easily be illustrated in Figures 5.9 or 5.10. Given the budget constraint, he merely selects the optimum combination of non-market goods in the usual fashion by a constrained maximisation of $U(\mathbf{x})$.[6] This determines a point such as $\mathbf{x}^*$, which in turn determines the optimal combination of purchased inputs through the appropriate technique in the household production set.

Once again let us see what effects certain exogenous changes have upon Crusoe's consumption plan. In the fixed proportions case it is clear that a change in *any* of the input prices $w_1, \ldots, w_m$, or indeed a change in any of the production coefficients a_{ij} will shift the budget constraint – see (5.14). This is hardly surprising, because *every* input is always essential. However if some

---

6 If we like we can introduce a set of shadow prices such as π in Figure 5.10; then (applying Theorem 5.1) household production is carried out to maximise 'profit' at input prices $\mathbf{w}$, output prices π; household consumption maximises $U(\mathbf{x})$ subject to $\Sigma\pi_j x_j \leqslant M$.

substitution is possible, a rather more interesting picture emerges. To see this, consider another special case – the general linear technology. Let input j have a constant marginal productivity b_{ij} in the production of output i. Then, if the input vector $z_1, \ldots, z_m$ is selected, the amount of consumption good i that is produced is given by

$$x_i = \sum_{j=1}^{m} b_{ij} z_j \tag{5.17}$$

Contrast this with the fixed proportions technology (5.4). If $m > n$, not all the inputs will in fact be purchased – in fact at least $m - n$ will be redundant, i.e. optimal purchases of them will be zero. *Which* of these are redundant depends on the input prices $\mathbf{w}$ and on the particular objective function U. The situation is illustrated in Figure 5.11 for the case $n = 2$, $m = 5$. The feasible set is a polyhedron, so that $\psi(\mathbf{x}; \mathbf{R}, \mathbf{w})$ is piecewise linear. Any point A_j shows the amount of x_1 and x_2 that could be purchased if the entire budget was spent on input z_j, namely $b_{1j}M/w_j$, $b_{2j}M/w_j$. The slope of the frontier between adjacent vertices A_j, A_{j+1} is $[w_j b_{2j+1} - w_{j+1} b_{2j}]/[w_j b_{1j+1} - w_{j+1} b_{1j}]$, i.e. the shadow price ratio π_1/π_2. So it is clear that a simple increase in the budget

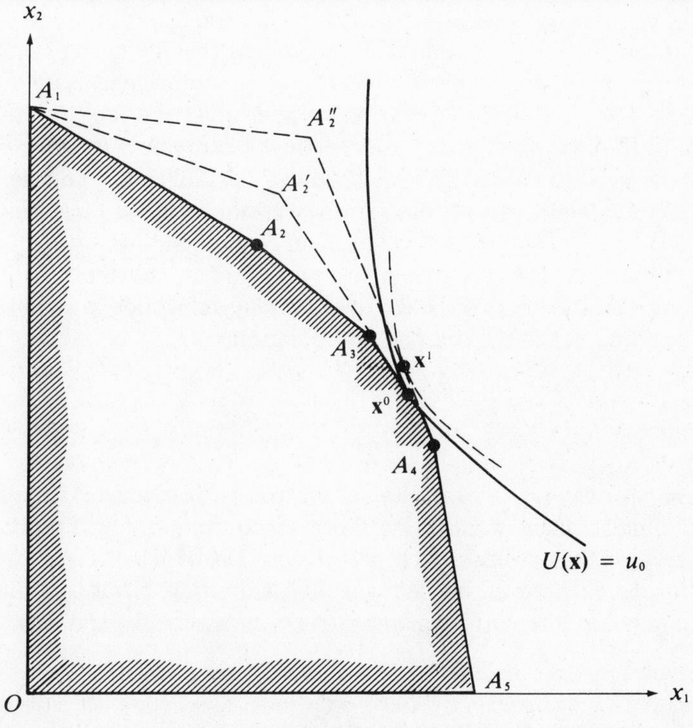

Figure 5.11

(from a larger resource endowment) just 'inflates' the feasible set without altering the relative slopes of different parts of the frontier, whilst changes in input prices or productivities will change the shape of the frontier.

As illustrated Crusoe would consume at $\mathbf{x}^0$ using a combination of cutlasses (input z_3) and rope (input z_4) to provide himself with food (output x_1), and shelter (output x_2). He does not bother buying gunpowder (input z_2) because its market price is too high. Now suppose gunpowder becomes cheaper – w_2 falls. Clearly the frontier is deformed by this – vertex A_2 is shifted out along a ray through O. If the price of gunpowder falls only a little absolutely nothing happens to Crusoe's equilibrium, *unless* of course he has a stock of gunpowder ($R_2 > 0$) which he can sell, in which case his budget M increases and the frontier moves outwards at *all* points. Let us assume $R_2 = 0$. Then the new frontier is $A_1A_2'A_3A_4A_5$ and Crusoe carries on consuming at $\mathbf{x}^0$. But suppose the price w_2 falls a lot, so that the vertex moves out to A_2''. Note that the technique of using cutlasses to provide food and shelter is now inefficient, and it lies *inside* the new frontier $A_1A_2''A_4A_5$. Gunpowder is now so cheap he uses it to hunt for food and to light fires to keep him warm and cancels his arrangement with the South Seas Cutlass Rental Store. His new consumption point is at $\mathbf{x}^1$.

The fact that some commodities are purchased by households not for direct consumption but as inputs to produce other goods within the household enables us to understand a number of phenomena that are hard to reconcile in the simpler model of Chapter 4. Firstly, if $m > n$, some market goods may not be purchased.[7] Secondly, if the market price of a good falls, or indeed if there is a technical improvement in some input (more powerful gunpowder) this may lead to no change in the consumer's equilibrium. Thirdly, even though all the x_i's may be 'normal' goods, certain purchased market goods may appear 'inferior' if preferences are non-homothetic.[8] Fourthly, the demand for inputs purchased in the market may be quite unstable; for as the price of an input drops to a critical level we may get a sudden switch from one facet to another in the optimal consumption plan.

5.7 Summary

The principal message of this chapter is that perfect markets make life extremely simple. They enable us to 'separate' consumption and production decisions within the optimisation process – see Theorem 5.1. Hence we find one rationale for separating out profit-maximising firms and utility-maximising households in the manner of the previous two chapters. They

---

7 By contrast if all indifference curves are strictly convex to the origin, *all* goods must be consumed in positive amounts in the model of Chapter 4.

8 See Exercise 5.8.

also make it easy to discuss factor supply as a 'mirror image' of commodity demand by the household, a feature that we shall exploit further in Chapters 7 and 8.

Where such markets cannot be assumed – for example in cases where the technology for producing consumer goods is inextricably bound up with each household – then a kind of 'hybrid' of the analysis of Chapters 3 and 4 emerges. The household demands marketable commodities in a manner similar to firms' demands for inputs. Results then emerge that may appear unusual in the light of the 'pure consumption with fixed budget' model of Chapter 4.

Further Reading

A good reference for insight in the workings of the Robinson Crusoe economy is:

Koopmans, T.C. (1957) *Three Essays on the State of Economic Science*, Essay 1, McGraw-Hill.

Two useful references on the extension of consumer theory to include household production are:

Deaton, A.S. and Muellbauer, J. (1980) *Economics and Consumer Behavior*, Cambridge University Press, Ch. 10.

Green, H.A.J. (1976) *Consumer Theory*, Macmillan, Ch. 10.

And the classic articles on this topic are also worth consulting:

Becker, G.S. (1965) 'The economics of the allocation of time', *Economic Journal*, Vol. 75, pp. 493–517.

Lancaster, K.J. (1966) 'A new approach to consumer theory', *Journal of Political Economy*, Vol. 74, pp. 132–7.

Exercises

*5.1 A consumer has a utility function

$$U(x_1, x_2) = x_1 x_2^2$$

and an original endowment vector (R_1, R_2).

(a) Obtain the demand function for each of the goods and verify that these are homogeneous of degree zero in prices. Under what circumstances will the individual wish to obtain additional quantities of good 1?

(b) Derive expressions for the effects of changes in prices and endowments on the demand for good 1. Is this good normal or inferior?

(c) Separate the own-price and cross-price effects for demand for good 1 into substitution and income terms, explaining how the income term is to be interpreted.

5.2 A firm produces two goods using a single input. The input requirement z corresponding to outputs y_1, y_2 is determined by the production relation

$$\phi(y_1, y_2, z) = y_1^2 + y_2^2 - z^2 \leqslant 0$$

What is (a) the marginal physical product of the input in the manufacture of good i? (b) the marginal rate of transformation between the produced goods?

If the outputs are sold at prices p_1, p_2 per unit, write down the first-order condition for maximising revenue μ from some fixed quantity of the input, $\bar{z}$. Examine the effect of changes in the prices on the outputs produced, and show that

$$\lambda = \left.\frac{\partial \mu}{\partial \bar{z}}\right|_{\substack{\text{prices}\\ \text{constant}}} \div \left.\frac{\partial \phi}{\partial \bar{z}}\right|_{\substack{y_1,\, y_2\\ \text{constant}}}$$

where λ is the Lagrange multiplier in the maximisation problem. Give an economic interpretation of your result.

*5.3 A consumer has the following utility function

$$U(x_1, x_2, L) = x_1^{1/6} x_2^{1/6} [24 - L]^{2/3}$$

where x_i is the quantity of good i, L is the quantity of labour he supplies in one day measured in hours. His only income is derived from working for a wage of w per hour. p_1, p_2 are the prices of the two goods. Prove that he will work for a fixed number of hours per day independent of his wage. What is this number? Show that the demands for the two goods are homogeneous of degree zero in p_1, p_2, w.

5.4 A firm at present operates an overtime system paying £2 per hour for the first 40 hours and then £3 per hour for overtime. An employee, who is at present working 50 hours per week, is given the option of being paid a straight £2.20 for each hour, which would maintain earnings at £110 for the 50 hours. The employee claims that under the new system his income would fall; the firm claims that he would be better off. With whom do you agree?

5.5 A particular household consists of two individuals who are both potential workers and who pool their budgets and whose preferences are represented by a single utility function $U(x_0, x_1, x_2)$ where x_1 is the amount of leisure enjoyed by person 1, x_2 is the amount of leisure enjoyed by person 2 and x_0 is the amount of the single, composite consumption good enjoyed by the household. Each member of the household has T hours which he/she can either enjoy as leisure or can spend at work. The hourly wage rates for the two individuals are w_1 and w_2 respectively, they jointly have non-wage income of $\overline{M}$, and the price of the composite consumption good is unity. Write down the budget constraint for the household.

If the function U takes the form

$$U(x_0, x_1, x_2) = \sum_{i=0}^{2} \alpha_i \log(x_i - \gamma_i)$$

where the α_i and γ_i are parameters such that $\alpha_i > 0$, $\gamma_i \geqslant 0$ and $\alpha_0 + \alpha_1 + \alpha_2 = 1$, interpret these parameters. Solve the household's optimisation problem and show that the demand for the consumption good is

$$x_0 = \gamma_0 + \alpha_0[\overline{M} + Tw_1 + Tw_2 - \gamma_0 - w_1\gamma_1 - w_2\gamma_2]$$

Write down the labour supply function for each of the two individuals. What is the response of an individual's labour supply to an increase in (a) his/her own wage, (b) the other person's wage, and (c) the non-wage income?

5.6 (a) Consider a household with a two-period utility function of the form specified in Exercise 4.15. Suppose that the individual receives an exogenously given income stream (M_1, M_2) over the two periods in question, assuming the individual faces a perfect market for borrowing and lending at a uniform rate r. Examine the effects of varying M_1, M_2 and r on the optimal consumption pattern. Will first period savings rise or fall with the rate of interest?

(b) How would your analysis be affected if the household faced a total ban on borrowing?

5.7 Consider the model of Exercise 5.6 but suppose that income is exogenously given at M_1 for the first period only. Income in the second period can be obtained by investing an amount z in the first period. Suppose $M_2 = \phi(z)$ where ϕ is a twice differentiable function with positive first derivative and negative second derivative, and $\phi(0) = 0$. Assuming a perfect market for lending/borrowing:

(a) write down the budget constraint;

(b) find the household's optimum and compare it with that of Exercises 4.15 and 5.5;

(c) suppose $\phi(z)$ were replaced by $\alpha\phi(z)$ where $\alpha > 1$; how would this affect the solution?

(d) discuss possible interpretations of this model.

5.8 In the context of the household production model, show how the phenomenon of an inferior market good may arise even though all home-produced consumption goods are normal goods.

6

Aggregation

6.1 Introduction

So far we have dealt in the main with one firm in isolation, or one consuming unit making decisions in isolation. This chapter and the following two chapters build up a framework which enables us to proceed beyond this to an analysis of several decision makers together. In this chapter we consider some taxonomical problems which must be settled before proceeding to general equilibrium analysis and also some problems involved in grouping different consumers together or grouping different firms together and examining their composite behaviour.

The sort of questions we shall deal with are:

What does the nature of each firm's technology imply about the technology of the entire economy?

Can households' consumption plans be analysed independently of each other?

How are individual firms' and consumers' supply curves and demand curves related to market supply and demand curves?

Is there such an animal as 'the representative consumer'?

Since we now consider many consumers and many firms we need a slightly more elaborate notation. Suppose there are altogether F firms indexed $f = 1, \ldots, F$; we let $\mathbf{y}^f \equiv (y_1^f, y_2^f, \ldots, y_n^f)$ be the n-vector of net production by firm f: of course if production is specialised into particular firms many of the components y_i^f will be zero. Call $[\mathbf{y}^1, \ldots, \mathbf{y}^F]$, or more compactly $[\mathbf{y}^f]$, the *allocation* of net output vectors amongst the F firms. Let $\mathbf{y} = (y_1, \ldots, y_n)$ be the n-vector of net output for the economy as a whole: we shall see below how $\mathbf{y}$ is related to the allocation $[\mathbf{y}^f]$. Likewise let Y^f be the technology set for firm f, and Y the technology set for the whole economy – see pp. 15, 16 of Chapter 2.

On the consumption side, suppose that there are H households indexed $h = 1, \ldots, H$; we let $\mathbf{x}^h = (x_1^h, x_2^h, \ldots, x_n^h)$ be the n-vector of consumption

Table 6.1 Essential notation for Chapter 6: Aggregation

Households			*Firms*		
Individual level					
x_i^h	:	consumption by h of good i	y_i^f	:	net output by f of good i
$\mathbf{x}^h$	$\equiv$	$(x_1^h, x_2^h, \ldots, x_n^h)$	$\mathbf{y}^f$	$\equiv$	$(y_1^f, y_2^f, \ldots, y_n^f)$
U^h	:	utility function of h	Y^f	:	technology set for firm f
$[\mathbf{x}^h]$	$\equiv$	$[\mathbf{x}^1, \mathbf{x}^2, \ldots, \mathbf{x}^H]$ allocation of consumption vectors	$[\mathbf{y}^f]$	$\equiv$	$[\mathbf{y}^1, \mathbf{y}^2, \ldots, \mathbf{y}^F]$ allocation of net output vectors
Aggregate level					
x_i	:	aggregate consumption of good i	y_i	:	aggregate net output of good i
$\mathbf{x}$	$\equiv$	$(x_1, x_2, \ldots, x_n)$	$\mathbf{y}$	$\equiv$	$(y_1, y_2, \ldots, y_n)$
			Y	:	technology set for the whole economy

by household h, and call $[\mathbf{x}^1, \ldots, \mathbf{x}^H]$ (written more compactly $[\mathbf{x}^h]$) the *allocation* of consumption bundles amongst the H households. The consumption of goods in the economy as a whole is denoted by the n-vector $\mathbf{x} = (x_1, \ldots, x_n)$: once again the relationship between $\mathbf{x}$ and $[\mathbf{x}^h]$ will be discussed later. Each household has its own consumption set X^h, its own utility index U^h, and its own income M^h; alternatively we may assume (as we do in Chapters 5 and 8) that incomes M^h are endogenously determined, and that each household has a given endowment of resources. The most important features of this notation system are noted in Table 6.1. One dangerous step which must be warned against straightaway is to suppose that there is an aggregate counterpart to U^h defined instead on either the set of allocations $[\mathbf{x}^h]$ or on the set of aggregate consumptions $\mathbf{x}$. This presupposes a degree of unanimity and coherence in personal preferences which, frankly, may not exist; further discussion of this issue is deferred until Chapter 13.

However, we can turn straightaway to two rather similar problems – the relationship between Y and $\{Y^1, \ldots, Y^F\}$ and the relationship between $\mathbf{x}$ and $[\mathbf{x}^h]$. These are discussed in the next two sections.

6.2 Aggregation of Production Sets

What is the relationship between the set of technically feasible vectors in the economy as a whole, and the technology set of each firm? This is straightforward in the absence of the following two problems:

(1) non-convexities
(2) technological externalities

The idea of convexity of production sets and its implications should be familiar from Chapter 2, but obviously problem (2) needs elucidation. A *technological externality* arises when Y^f, the set of feasible vectors for firm f, itself depends on the production decision of some other firm f' (the vector $\mathbf{y}^{f'}$). Note that in general such an effect is quite distinct from firm f having its *choice of production vector* $\mathbf{y}^f$ within a *given* set Y^f influenced by the vector $\mathbf{y}^{f'}$. The latter case could arise simply because a change of policy by f' might alter market prices of outputs and inputs which in turn affects the optimum policy of firm f: no change in the technology possibilities facing firm f need have occurred.[1]

If Y^f is independent of $\mathbf{y}^{f'}$ for any two arbitrary distinct firms f and f', then it is clear that if $\mathbf{y}^1, \ldots, \mathbf{y}^F$ are each technologically feasible for firms $1, \ldots, F$ then $\mathbf{y} = \Sigma_{f=1}^F \mathbf{y}^f$ is the corresponding feasible vector for the economy as a whole. More formally

$$Y = \{\mathbf{y} : \mathbf{y} = \sum_{f=1}^{F} \mathbf{y}^f, \mathbf{y}^f \in Y^f\}$$

So, in the absence of technological externalities the procedure for deriving the production set for the whole economy is simple: it is the *summation* (as distinct from the union) of the production sets of the individual firms. In the absence of non-convexities for each firm's technology a simple result is then available:

THEOREM 6.1: in the absence of technological externalities, if each firm's production set is convex, the economy's production set is convex.

PROOF: suppose $\hat{\mathbf{y}}^1, \tilde{\mathbf{y}}^1 \in Y^1$
$\hat{\mathbf{y}}^2, \tilde{\mathbf{y}}^2 \in Y^2$
$\ldots \ldots \ldots$
$\hat{\mathbf{y}}^F, \tilde{\mathbf{y}}^F \in Y^F$

then by the assumption of convexity of each Y^f, it is known that for an arbitrary scalar α lying between zero and unity we have

$$\alpha\hat{\mathbf{y}}^f + [1 - \alpha]\tilde{\mathbf{y}}^f \in Y^f, \qquad f = 1, 2, \ldots, F$$

However from the assumption that there are no technological externalities:

$$\sum_{f=1}^{F} \hat{\mathbf{y}}^f \in Y \quad \text{and} \quad \sum_{f=1}^{F} \tilde{\mathbf{y}}^f \in Y \tag{6.1}$$

[1] Somewhat confusingly this pure price-linkage effect is sometimes known as a 'pecuniary' externality. I shall not use this term.

but also from this assumption

$$\sum_{f=1}^{F} [\alpha \hat{\mathbf{y}}^f + [1 - \alpha]\tilde{\mathbf{y}}^f] \in Y$$

$$\Rightarrow \alpha \sum_{f=1}^{F} \hat{\mathbf{y}}^f + [1 - \alpha] \sum_{f=1}^{F} \tilde{\mathbf{y}}^f \in Y \tag{6.2}$$

Clearly (6.1) and (6.2) imply that Y is convex.

The obvious question that this raises is, if there are technological externalities can Y be non-convex even though each individual Y^f is convex? This is in fact so, and may be illustrated by an example.

Consider pest control. Imagine an island divided into F identical farms. To increase the output in any one farm by 10 per cent, *given that the other farms do not change their outputs or inputs* may involve a more than 10 per cent increase in inputs, including pesticides. (The greenfly keep coming back.) But if all farms wish to increase their output by 10 per cent *together* this may involve *less* than 10 per cent increase in pesticides. The reason is that each farm's pest control helps other farms and all farms increase pest control together. (The greenfly do not come back.)

Now let us turn to the problem of non-convexities in individual Y^f. Of course, as long as there are no externalities we may use the simple aggregation rule of summing production sets $Y = Y^1 + Y^2 + \ldots + Y^F$. But will Y be non-convex also? It is in fact possible to have one or more of the production sets of individual firms exhibiting non-convexities, and yet the aggregate production set itself having the property of convexity. This phenomenon is illustrated in Figure 6.1. Although the set Y^1 is clearly non-convex the effect of the set Y^2 'counteracts' this, so to speak, so that the aggregate technology is convex.

Moreover even if *all* firms exhibit non-convexities an interesting result on the aggregate is available. Imagine an economy in which there is just one firm with production set Y^1 as depicted in Figure 6.2(a). Now duplicate the economy, so that there are two firms with $Y^2 = Y^1$ (also exactly double the consumers resources, etc.). The new production set, drawn to half-scale is illustrated in Figure 6.2(b). Duplicate the economy again: the result (again rescaled in the drawing) is in Figure 6.2(c); Figure 6.2(d) shows the result of a further duplication. It is intuitively obvious that if we can appeal to the existence of a large number of firms in the economy, each of which is in a reasonable sense 'small', the resulting aggregate production set may be taken to be 'arbitrarily close' to convex, *even though* each individual firm exhibits non-convexities.

The great advantage of these results is that many of the results in subsequent chapters require only that the *aggregate* technology be convex which, as we can see, may be consistent with indivisibilities – increasing returns to scale – for specific firms.

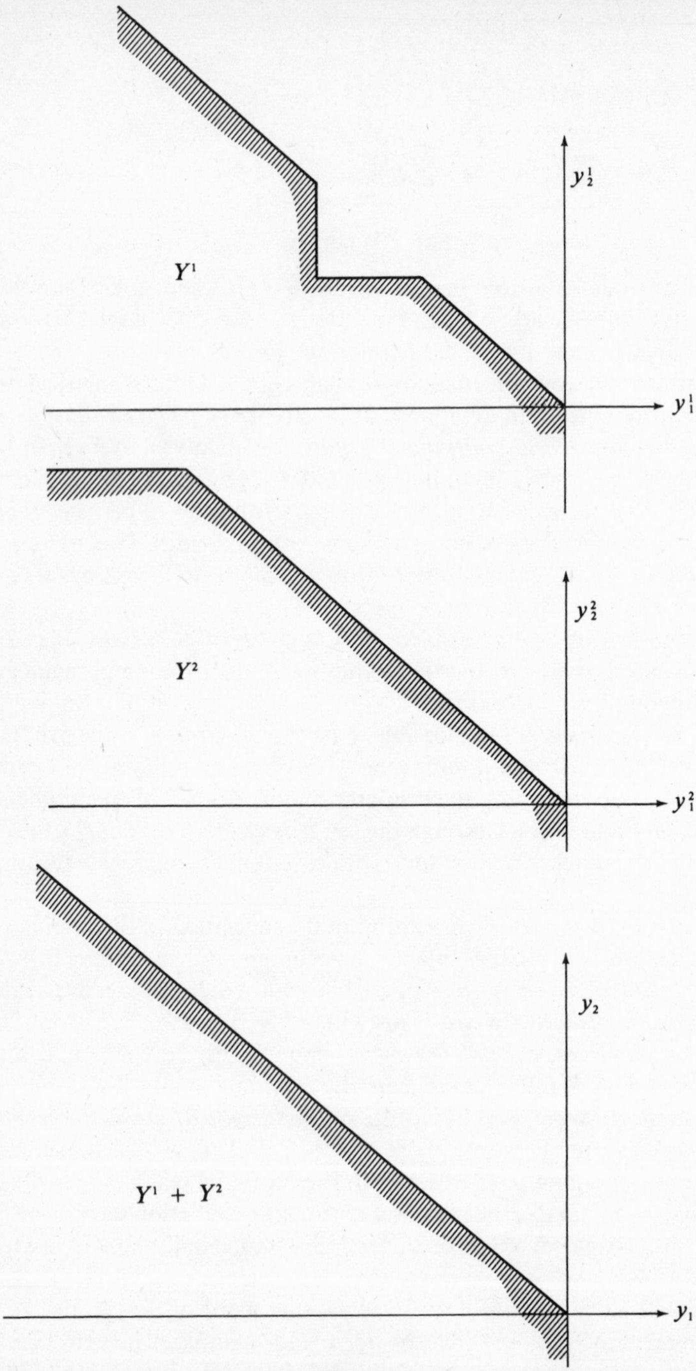

Figure 6.1

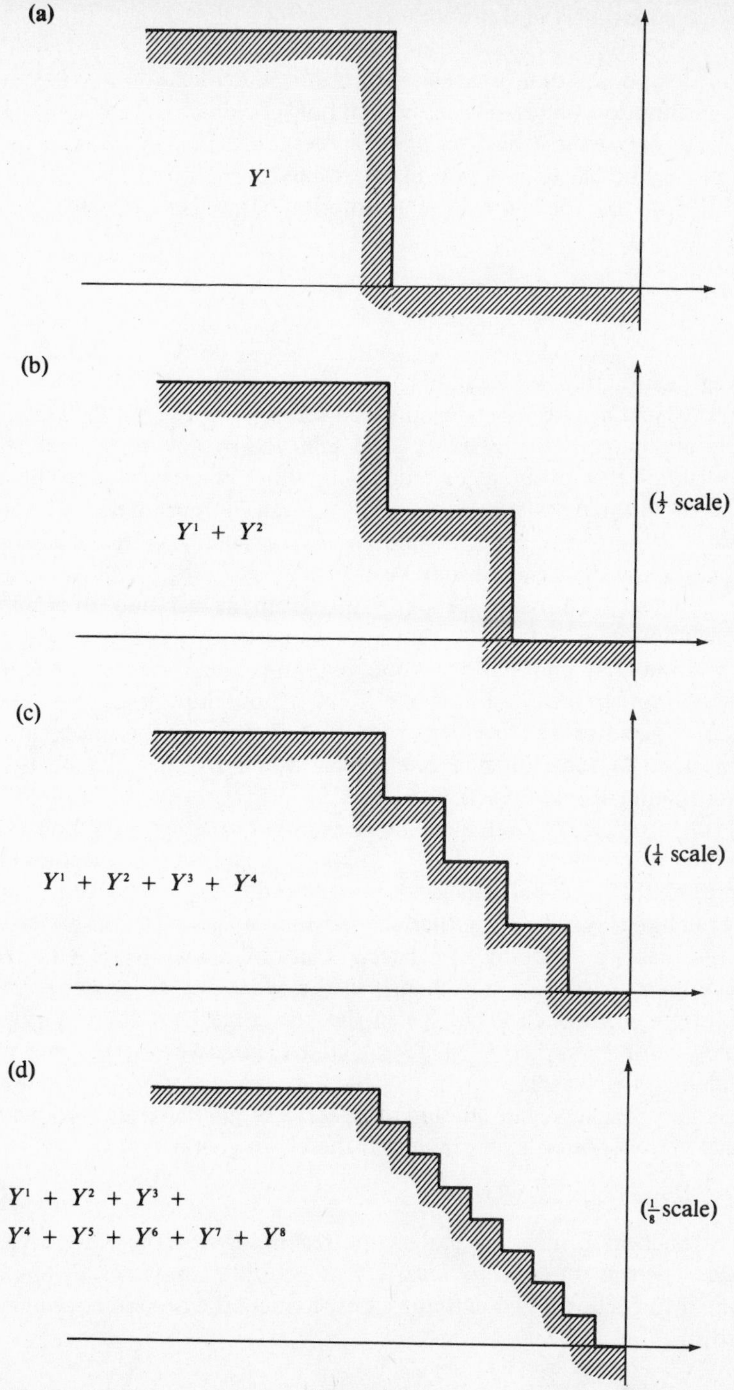
(a)
Y¹
(b)
Y¹ + Y²
(½ scale)
(c)
Y¹ + Y² + Y³ + Y⁴
(¼ scale)
(d)
Y¹ + Y² + Y³ +
Y⁴ + Y⁵ + Y⁶ + Y⁷ + Y⁸
(⅛ scale)

Figure 6.2

6.3 Aggregation of Consumption

It might be supposed that, given a set of utility functions $U^1, \ldots, U^H$ and a set of consumption vectors for individual households $\mathbf{x}^1, \ldots, \mathbf{x}^H$, all that is required to analyse the behaviour of consumers collectively is to assume that each household h has its utility level determined solely by its own particular $\mathbf{x}^h$, and to note that the aggregate consumption of goods is given by a vector $\mathbf{x}$ where

$$x_i = \sum_{h=1}^{H} x_i^h$$

This is misleading on two accounts.

Firstly, just as one firm's production set may depend on the decisions made by other firms, so the utility level achieved by household h given $\mathbf{x}^h$ may depend on the consumption enjoyed by other households; the value of $U^h(\mathbf{x}^h)$ is conditional on $[\mathbf{x}^1, \ldots, \mathbf{x}^{h-1}, \mathbf{x}^{h+1}, \ldots, \mathbf{x}^H]$. As with the production set analogy, the effect of the other households' consumptions may be favourable or unfavourable. Also it may be a purely psychological phenomenon, arising from envy or altruism, or it may arise from the technique of exchange and consumption of goods. A simple example of this is the smoking of tobacco (good i) by household h': one might have $\partial U^h/\partial x_i^{h'} < 0$ if household h is a non-smoker, but $\partial U^h/\partial x_i^{h'} > 0$ if household h appreciates the aroma of a good cigar. Another example is that it may be impossible to provide street-lighting outside one's own home without the next-door neighbour being able to benefit too.

If the technique of exchange and consumption permits any household h' to enjoy its consumption of good i without benefiting (or harming) any other household h, we shall call good i an *excludable good*: food and clothing usually fall into this category. Otherwise we shall call good i a *non-excludable good*: the 'passive' smoking of tobacco is an obvious example. Obviously there are many cases where a change in the technique of exchange or of consumption – through a change in the law, or a change in marketing technology, for example – where excludable goods could become non-excludable and vice versa.

Secondly, the aggregate amount of a good x_i required to satisfy individual demands x_i^h may not be a simple sum of the x_i^h. In general

$$x_i = \Xi(x_i^1, \ldots, x_i^H) \tag{6.3}$$

and the function Ξ may depend on the technology of the economy, for example. There is an enormous variety of possible forms for Ξ, but it is convenient to focus on two extreme cases, namely the one we have already referred to

$$x_i = \sum_{h=1}^{H} x_i^h \tag{6.4}$$

and alternatively

$$x_i = \max_h(x_i^1, \ldots, x_i^H) \tag{6.5}$$

The former case (6.4) we shall call a pure *rival* good; the latter a pure *non-rival* good. The logic of this terminology is simple. Consider a 1-household economy with a consumption x_i^1 of good i. Now introduce a second household with a consumption demand x_i^2. If i is a rival commodity x_i^2 can only be satisfied by increasing production of good i, running down stocks of good i, or diminishing x_i^1; but if i is non-rival and $x_i^2 \leqslant x_i^1$, no further production and no further sacrifice will be required elsewhere in the economy to meet the new household's demand. A non-rival good (for example a very wide bridge) often exhibits a substantial component of indivisibility in its production, but this is not essential to its consumption characteristics.

A clear distinction between the properties of excludability and of rivalness should be made. It is possible to have excludable, non-rival goods, or rival, non-excludable goods. In the special case where i is *both* excludable *and* a pure rival good, we shall call i a *pure private good*; in the special case where i is non-excludable and a pure non-rival good, we shall call i a *pure public good* – see Figure 6.3. In the case of a pure public good i such that $\partial U^h / \partial x_i^h \gtreqless 0$ for all households and all x_i^h, it is notationally convenient to write (6.5) in the stronger form

$$\begin{aligned} x_i^1 &= x_i^2 = \ldots = x_i^H \\ &= x_i \end{aligned} \tag{6.6}$$

This feature is sometimes known as 'non-optionality' since the same amount

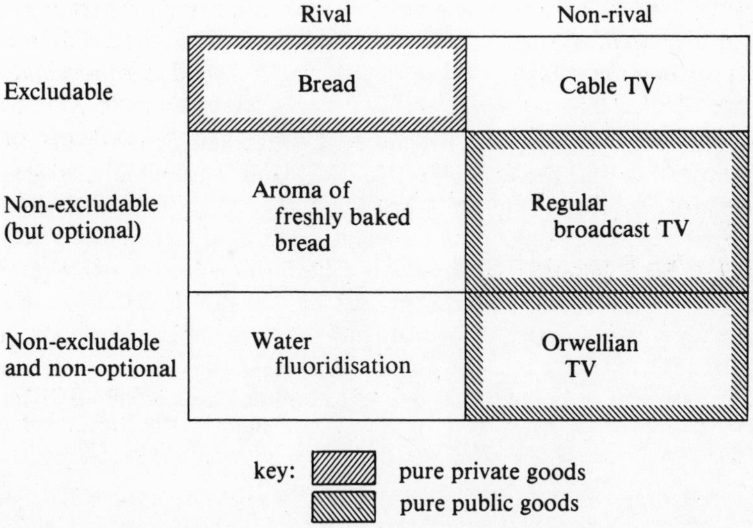
Rival
Non-rival
Excludable
Bread
Cable TV
Non-excludable
(but optional)
Aroma of
freshly baked
bread
Regular
broadcast TV
Non-excludable
and non-optional
Water
fluoridisation
Orwellian
TV
key:
pure private goods
pure public goods

Figure 6.3 A 'bread and circuses' example of different categories of goods

of the good *has* to be consumed by everyone. TV is sometimes cited as a (not quite perfect) example of a public good; cable TV is an example of that intermediate case, a non-rival good with exclusion; and though TV viewing might nowadays be regarded as theoretically optional George Orwell's 1984 version is an example of TV as a non-optional, public good. The interesting thing about this classificatory exercise is that it illustrates the way in which the major economic characteristics of certain goods may alter radically with a technological advance, or with the social and legal background institutions.

6.4 Market Supply and Demand Curves

We now extend the analysis of Chapters 3 and 4 (Sections 3.5, 3.6 and 4.6) concerning supply and demand functions for *individual* agents.

Consider first competitive firms in a free market. 'Competitive' means that they act as price takers both with respect to their output and with respect to their inputs; the free market means that each faces the same set of prices. So every firm has a supply function for outputs and demand function for inputs as in Definitions 3.3 and 3.5, where the arguments of these functions are the prices of the relevant outputs and inputs. We can summarise these functions in a compact fashion by writing for each firm a vector-valued *net output* function $\mathbf{y}^f = \mathbf{y}^f(\mathbf{p})$. Picking out the appropriate component from this n-vector yields the firm's supply of output or its demand for a particular input (recall the convention of y_i^f positive for outputs and negative for inputs).

Now let us suppose that in the production of any good there are no externalities whatever. From the work of Section 6.2 we may then write the net output function as

$$\mathbf{y}(\mathbf{p}) = \sum_{f=1}^{F} \mathbf{y}^f(\mathbf{p}) \tag{6.7}$$

If we consider any one input, then clearly the aggregate demand curve must be downward sloping (because each firm's demand for input i is a decreasing function of the price of input i + see Theorem 3.5). Likewise for any one output the aggregated supply function must be upward sloping (see Theorem 3.3). This latter point is illustrated in Figure 6.4 for the production of commodity 1 – an *output* – in the case of two firms.[2] (Recall that each firm's supply curve $y_1^f(\mathbf{p})$ will be formed from the segment of the marginal cost curve for output 1 that lies above the average cost curve – see Figure 3.10). However if there are production externalities, changes in the output of

[2] Of course the number of firms is, in principle, endogenous to the system if there are no restrictions on the setting up of new firms. New firms will wish to enter as long as there is the prospect of a positive profit to be made. See Exercise 6.2 and the discussion below.

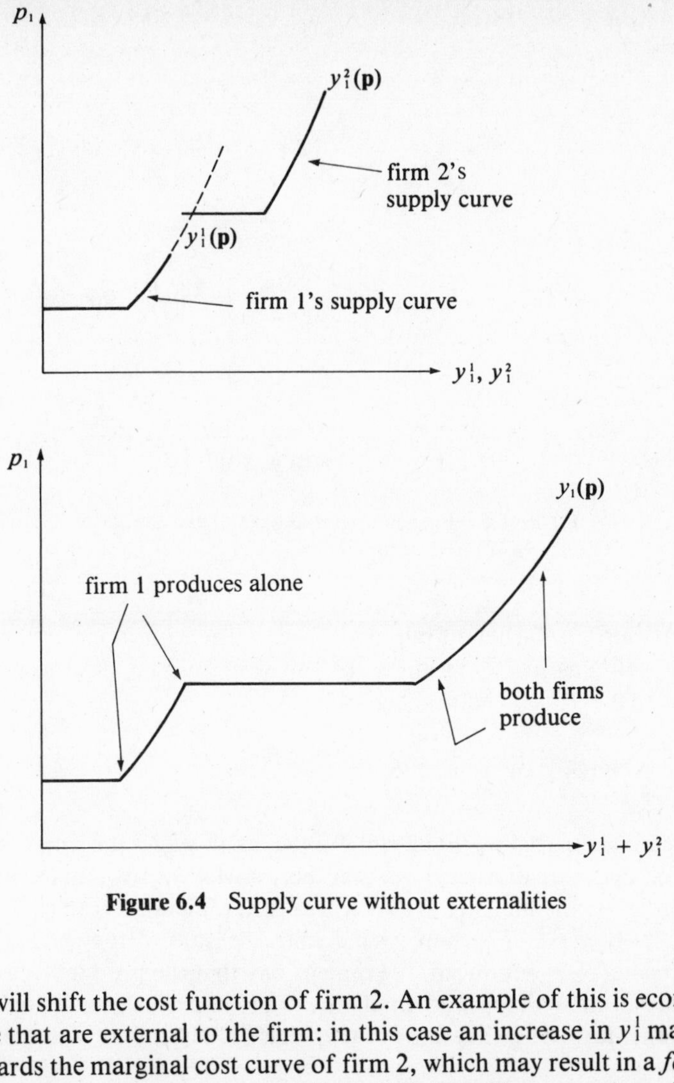

Figure 6.4 Supply curve without externalities

firm 1 will shift the cost function of firm 2. An example of this is economies of scale that are external to the firm: in this case an increase in y_1^1 may shift downwards the marginal cost curve of firm 2, which may result in a *forward falling* aggregate supply curve (see Figure 6.5). This illustrates the point that positive production externalities may introduce non-convexities into the aggregate production set, even if individual firm production sets are convex.

As a final point on market supply let us turn to a different case of interdependence amongst firms. Recall that externalities, as discussed above, involved an apparently exogenous shift in the cost curve of a particular firm, brought about as a side effect of other firms' input or output decisions. It is reasonable to consider the possibility that there might be similar 'spillover effects' in respect of the demand curve which confronts an individual firm. Suppose the price vector that any particular firm faces were to depend

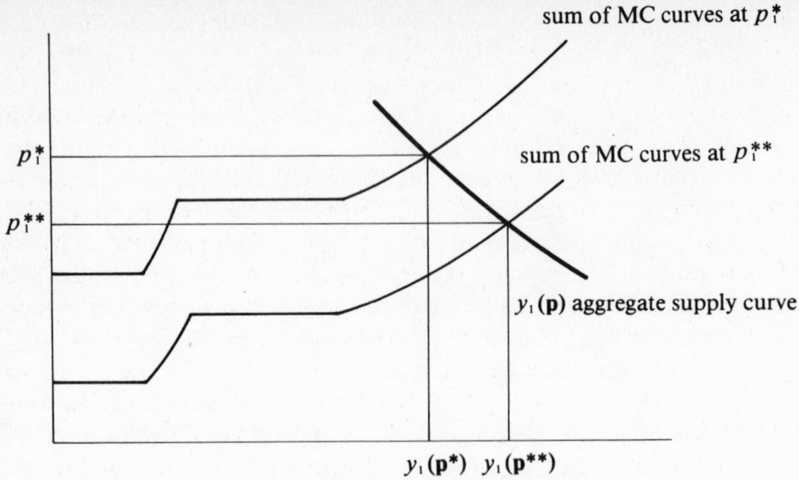

Figure 6.5 Positive externalities: an extreme case

parametrically on the net output of all firms in the economy, then instead of writing profits as in Definition 3.1(i), we would now write the profits of firm 1 as:

$$\sum_{i=1}^{n} p_i([\mathbf{y}^f])y_i^1 \tag{6.8}$$

One phenomenon that might be represented in this way is the situation where there is competition of a sort – in that there are lots of firms in the industry, or able to enter the industry – but where each individual firm has a 'quasi-monopoly' because of certain special characteristics of the product – the location where it is produced, the time of day that the product is delivered, the colour of the wrapper, or simply the brand name is not matched exactly by any other firm. This situation in a market is usually known as 'monopolistic competition'.

Consider firm 1 that finds itself in such a quasi-monopolistic position with respect to its output. By this we mean that firm 1 faces a *known* negatively-sloped demand curve for its output; for simplicity we shall assume that it is a single-output firm (producing good 1) and that all input prices are parametrically fixed. So, we may interpret (6.8) as follows. Firm 1 recognises (a) that $\partial p_1([\mathbf{y}^f])/\partial y_1^1 < 0$, and (b) that the exact shape of $p_1(\cdot)$ depends on the particular net output choices by other firms. But it takes these net outputs by other firms as *exogenously given*.

Maximising (6.8) subject to the technology constraint $\Phi^1(\mathbf{y}^1) \leqslant 0$ yields the first-order condition

$$y_1^1 \frac{\partial p_1}{\partial y_1^1} + p_1 - \lambda \Phi_1^1(\mathbf{y}^1) = 0 \tag{6.9}$$

assuming positive output of good 1 with, of course, a conventional condition $p_i - \lambda \Phi_i^1(\mathbf{y}^1) \leqslant 0$ for all other goods $i = 2, \ldots, n$. The first two terms in (6.9) represent 'marginal revenue' whilst, at the optimum, the last term in (6.9) represents 'marginal cost' (compare this with equation (3.62) of Chapter 3). Assuming the second-order conditions to be satisfied (6.9) yields the standard 'marginal revenue equals marginal cost' rule for the firm in this situation: this is illustrated in Figure 6.6 where the firm produces output y_1^1 and charges a price p_1. Note that, given the position of the demand curve in Figure 6.6, the firm makes a positive profit, represented by the shaded area; and it is the presence of these profits which may mean that the situation is *not* an equilibrium for the economy as a whole. If other firms can set up to supply goods that are perceived by consumers to be 'reasonably' close substitutes to good 1 as supplied by firm 1, then they could capture some of this profit opportunity. In view of the price of good 1 depending on the whole allocation $[\mathbf{y}^f]$, this entry will shift the demand curve in Figure 6.6. (If there was an indefinite number of firms waiting in the wings whose products were *exact* substitutes for good 1, then the demand curve for the particular firm in Figure 6.6 would collapse into a horizontal straight line: the 'perfectly

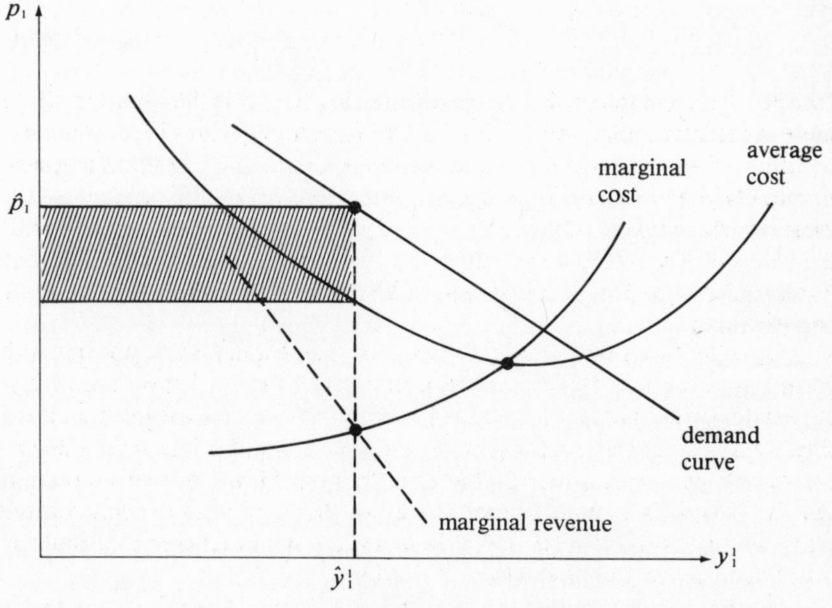

Figure 6.6

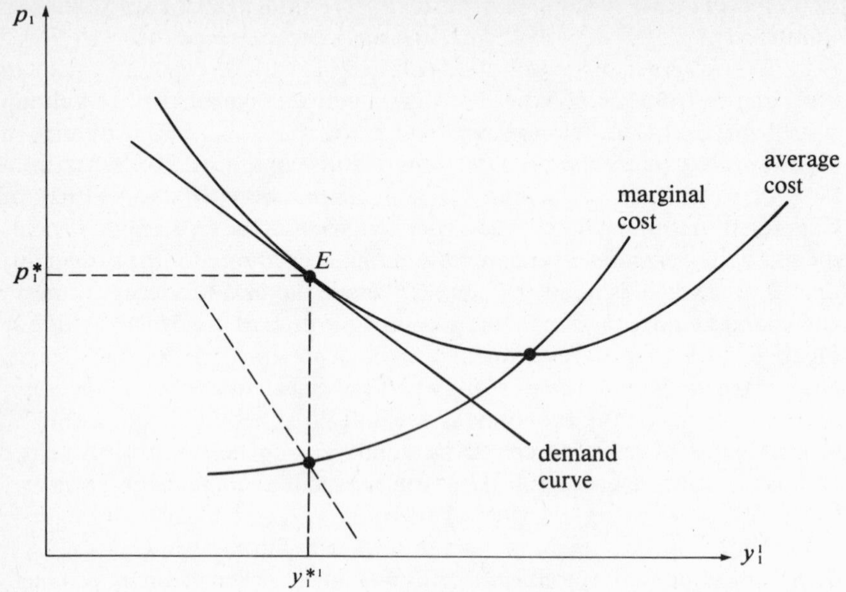

Figure 6.7

competitive' case where the firm faces a parametrically given price.) If no firm produces a good that is regarded exactly as a perfect substitute, then the long-run equilibrium will find each firm in a position such as that in Figure 6.7. Note that the monopolistic profit has been eliminated by the entry of other firms (as would also have happened in the perfectly competitive case), but that because each firm's output is differentiated from that of any other firm, the individual firm's perceived demand curve is downward sloping and so long-run equilibrium does *not* occur at the minimum point of the average cost curve but at point E (quite unlike the perfectly competitive case) – see Exercises 6.1 and 6.2.

Because each firm is a quasi-monopolist there is no simple relationship between price and output for any one firm. So what happens as the industry expands will depend not only on the cost structure of newly entering firms (as in the discussion on pages 118–120 above) but also on the 'position' of new and slightly different goods that are introduced by these firms. The 'position' of these new goods – the way in which consumers perceive them as substitutes for other products – will affect the shape of other firms' demand curves, and therefore their equilibrium point E as the industry is expanded. However, for a large number of small firms and an appropriate redefinition of a 'commodity' (so that different brands of toothpaste are lumped together as quantities of a single good) it may be satisfactory to treat this situation as though it were one of perfect competition.

Of course the assumption of exogeneity is crucial to all the above analysis of interrelationships between firms. This apparent exogeneity of other firms' actions – whether of pollution activity (in the case of externalities) or of setting up new products (in the case of monopolistic competition) – is clearly a strong assumption. We shall return to an examination of this in Chapters 11 and 12. Let us now turn to issues on the demand side of the market.

A particularly interesting problem arises with the aggregation of consumers' demands: if we take consumers' money incomes as exogenously given, will *aggregate* demands **x** be determined by the vector of prices and aggregate income according to some 'overall' demand function? To make this question more precise we proceed as follows. In view of (4.15) for any household h with income M^h we may write

$$x_i^h = D^{hi}(\mathbf{p}, M^h) \tag{6.10}$$

as the household demand function for good i when prices are p. Now, can x_i, the demand for private good i, likewise be written as some function $\bar{D}^i$ where

$$x_i = \bar{D}^i(\mathbf{p}, \bar{M}) \tag{6.11}$$

$\bar{D}^i$ has the same general properties as described in Section 4.6, and $\bar{M}$ is some function of $M^1, M^2, \ldots, M^H$? Will such a function, if it exists, have the properties of a conventional neoclassical demand function for a 'representative' consumer? The answers to these questions are far from self-evident; and in fact only if the demand functions D^{hi} have certain special characteristics may this functional aggregation be carried out in general.

As a special case of some interest, take equation (6.11) where $\bar{M} = \Sigma_{h=1}^{H} M^h/H$: aggregate consumer demand is a function of prices and *average* income. Now consider an arbitrary variation in the *distribution* of the incomes $M^1, M^2, \ldots, M^H$ such that the average $\Sigma_h M^h/H$ remains unchanged. In particular let there be an infinitesimal transfer from household 2 to household 1, with no other income being changed (any pair of households would do, in fact). Differentiating (6.11), we find that the resulting effect on x_i is

$$\frac{\partial D^{1i}}{\partial M^1} - \frac{\partial D^{2i}}{\partial M^2}.$$

Obviously x_i can only remain constant if this expression – and similar expressions for every pair of households – is zero. This implies that

$$\frac{\partial D^{hi}}{\partial M^h} = b_i(\mathbf{p}) \tag{6.12}$$

where $b_i(\mathbf{p})$ is an expression independent of M^h and h. Integrating (6.12) we have

$$D^{hi}(\mathbf{p}, M^h) = a_i^h(\mathbf{p}) + b_i(\mathbf{p})M^h \tag{6.13}$$

where $a_i^h(\mathbf{p})$ is a number which may differ between households, but is independent of M^h. Equation (6.13) simply says that, for each commodity, household *Engel curves* – the relationship between demand and income – must be linear and have the same slope for each household.

Suppose (6.10) is derived from utility maximisation. Then, using (4.7) and substituting in the consumer's cost function $C^h(\mathbf{p}, u^h)$ where $u^h = U^h(\mathbf{x}^h)$ we find that (6.13) yields

$$\partial C^h(\mathbf{p}, u^h)/\partial p_i = a_i^h(\mathbf{p}) + b_i(\mathbf{p})C^h(\mathbf{p}, u^h) \tag{6.14}$$

We may treat this as a first-order differential equation in p_i: indeed there will be H such equations. Solving this we find

$$C^h(\mathbf{p}, u^h) = A^h(\mathbf{p}) + B(\mathbf{p})K^h(u^h) \tag{6.15}$$

where $K^h(u^h)$ is the constant of integration; $B^{-1}\partial B/\partial p_i = b_i$, $\partial A^h/\partial p_i - b_i A^h = a_i$. Averaging (6.15) over the H households:

$$\bar{M} = \bar{A}(\mathbf{p}) + B(\mathbf{p})\bar{u} \tag{6.16}$$

where $\bar{A}(\mathbf{p}) \equiv \sum_{h=1}^{H} A^h(\mathbf{p})/H$ and $\bar{u} = \sum_{h=1}^{H} K^h(u^h)/H$. Since (6.15) is consistent with utility maximisation for any h, (6.16) must be consistent with maximisation of some utility index $\bar{u}$. Hence the aggregated demand curve 'looks' as if it were that belonging to some representative consumer.

THEOREM 6.2: if each consumer's demand functions take the form (6.13) then aggregate demand functions (6.11) exist and will be consistent with utility maximisation.

It should perhaps be stressed that whilst (6.13) is the only form consistent with aggregation as long as $\bar{M}$ is interpreted as average household income, other more general aggregation results are available where $\bar{M}$ is some other function of $[M^1, \ldots, M^H]$.

Theorem 6.2 and its generalisations are obviously of central interest in any empirical study that involves estimating demand functions from *market* data involving groups of households. But suppose that one is not immediately concerned with investigation of functions of the form (6.11) – does the aggregation over households consuming private goods still raise problems? It can do. To see this, suppose that all the M^h are endogenously determined by the $\mathbf{p}$ through the endowments of the individual households, so that households demand functions may be written $\mathbf{x}^h = \mathbf{x}^h(\mathbf{p})$ – clearly if all n goods are private, aggregate consumer demand functions $\mathbf{x}(\mathbf{p})$ always exist because

$$\mathbf{x}(\mathbf{p}) = \sum_{h=1}^{H} \mathbf{x}^h(\mathbf{p}) \tag{6.17}$$

However the mere existence of such functions is not the only interesting issue. There still remains the question: will the functions **x(p)** exhibit characteristics that would be consistent with utility maximisation by some mythical representative consumer?

It may well be the case that in the *aggregate* rather weird things occur. In Figure 6.8 each consumer's behaviour satisfies WARP, but the market demands *do not* satisfy WARP! There is no sense in which the consumption behaviour of the economy as a whole could be represented as though it were the outcome of the maximisation process by a 'typical' consumer. If we want that (as we shall do for some results in subsequent chapters) some kind of aggregation result like Theorem 6.2 is needed.

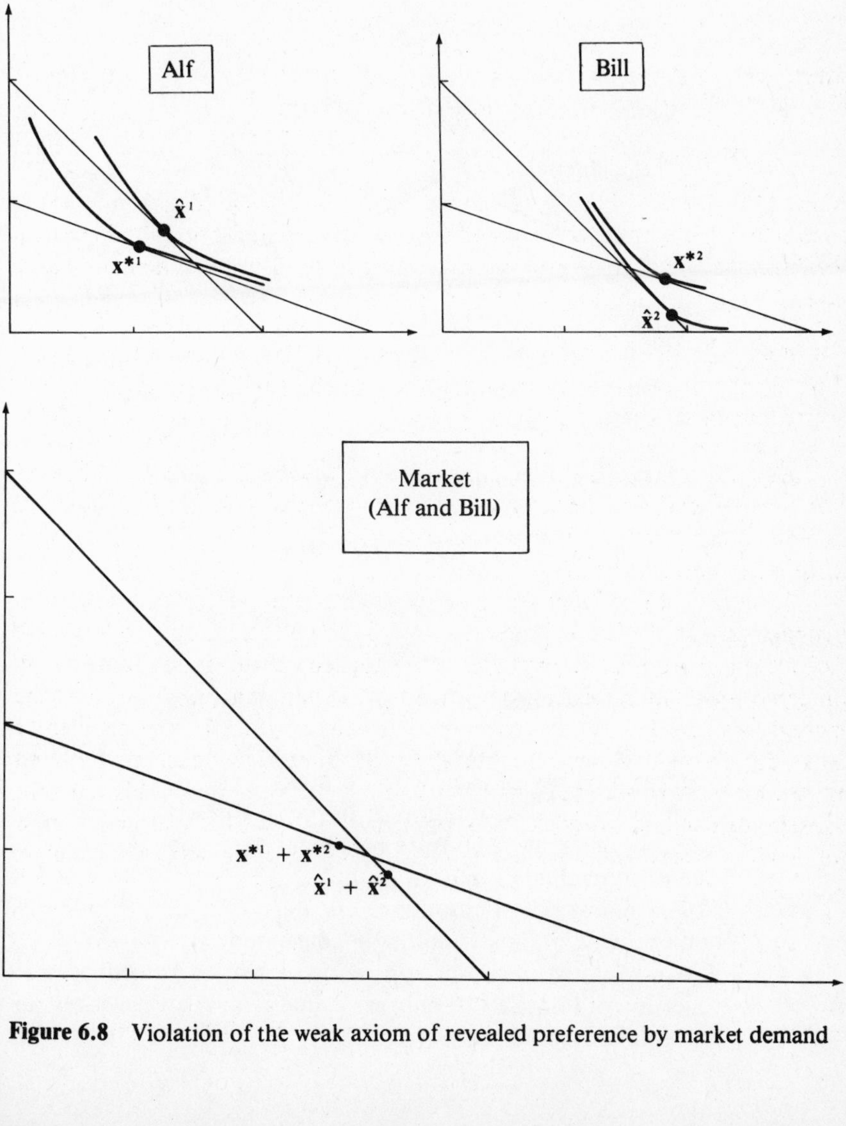

Figure 6.8 Violation of the weak axiom of revealed preference by market demand

Armed with demand functions **x(p)** and supply functions **y(p)** we can, presumably, proceed to analyse market equilibrium, industry by industry in the classic fashion illustrated in the classic diagram depicted in Figure 6.9. But, whilst this partial approach may be suitable for the product of one particular industry, the *general* approach to equilibrium raises further problems in its own right which we discuss in Chapter 7.

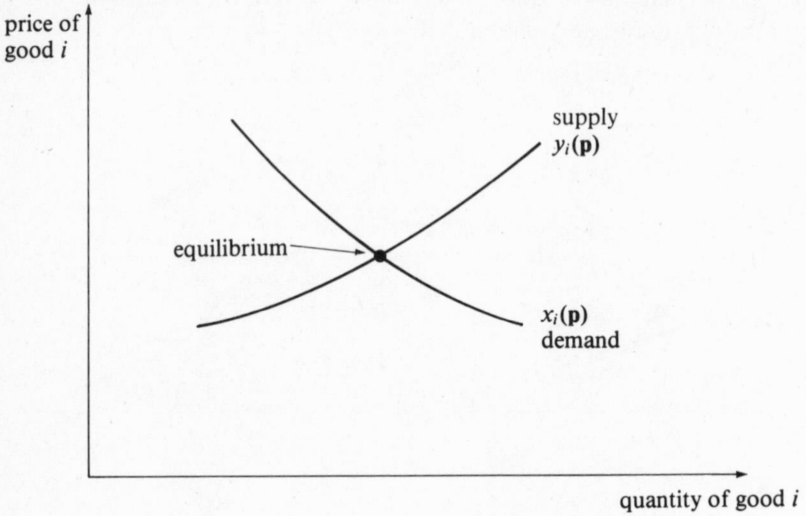

Figure 6.9 Equilibrium in the market for good i

6.5 Summary

In subsequent chapters we need to remember the following points:

- Convexity of the aggregate production set does not generally require convexity of each firm's production set.
- Externalities in consumption or in production create problems. Roughly speaking, aggregate behaviour cannot be taken as the sum of individual agents' behaviour.
- Non-rivalness in consumption is a property that is independent of non-excludability (externalities in consumption).
- A representative consumer (in terms of market behaviour of a collection of households) only exists under fairly stringent restrictions on household preferences.

Further Reading

On aggregation over consumers see:

Deaton, A.S. and Muellbauer, J. (1980) *Economics and Consumer Behavior*, Cambridge University Press, Ch. 6.
Green, H.A.J. (1976) *Consumer Theory*, Macmillan, Ch. 10.

On monopolistic competition see:

Chamberlin, E.H. (1964) *The Theory of Monopolistic Competition* (8th edn), Harvard University Press, Chs 4 and 5.
Dixit, A.K. and Stiglitz, J. (1977) 'Monopolistic competition and optimum product diversity', *American Economic Review*, Vol. 67, pp. 297–308.

Exercises

*6.1 Suppose that in a competitive industry with no technological externalities the elasticity of *supply* of inputs to firms is positive but finite. What will happen to each firm's costs as output of the industry is expanded? Sketch the relationship between supply curves of output of individual firms and the supply curve of the industry.

*6.2 Consider the model of Exercise 6.1, but where all inputs are available at fixed prices. What will the industry supply curve look like if identical firms can be easily set up? What will the long-run equilibrium look like for each firm?

6.3 In a particular industry there are n profit-maximising firms each producing a single good. The costs for firm i are $C(Q_i) = C_0 + mQ_i$ where C_0 and m are parameters common to all firms and Q_i is the output of firm i. The goods are not regarded as being exactly identical by the consumers and the inverse demand function for firm i is given by

$$p_i = AQ_i^{\alpha-1}/\sum_{j=1}^{n} Q_j^{\alpha}$$

where A is a positive constant characterising the scale of the industry and α is a measure of the degree of substitutability between the firms' products; $0 < \alpha \leqslant 1$.

Assuming that each firm takes the output of all other firms as given, write down the first-order condition yielding firm 1's optimal output conditional on the outputs $Q_2, \ldots, Q_n$ of all the other firms. Hence, using the symmetry of the equilibrium, show that in equilibrium optimal output for any firm is

$$Q_i = A\alpha[n-1]/n^2m$$

and that the elasticity of demand for firm i is

$$\frac{n}{n - n\alpha + \alpha}$$

Consider the case where $\alpha = 1$. What phenomenon does this represent? Show that the number of firms in the industry must be less than or equal to

$$\sqrt{(A/C_0)}.$$

6.4 Consider an economy containing three different types of goods, with good i priced at p_i per unit. An individual with money income M spends a proportion $v_i(M, \mathbf{p})$ of his income on good i where

$$v_i(M, \mathbf{p}) = \frac{1}{M} a_i(\mathbf{p}) + b_i(\mathbf{p})$$

The terms $a_i(\mathbf{p})$, $b_i(\mathbf{p})$ may vary with prices but do not depend on income. Show that the Engel curves for the three goods are straight lines and explain why one finds

$$\sum_{i=1}^{3} a_i(\mathbf{p}) = 0 \quad \text{and} \quad \sum_{i=1}^{3} b_i(\mathbf{p}) = 1$$

for all sets of prices.

Now assume that the economy contains three individuals with incomes M^1, M^2 and M^3 where $M^3 = \frac{1}{2}[M^1 + M^2]$. If α_i denotes the aggregate budget share of good i, show that for all sets of prices and any income values M^1, M^2

$$\alpha_i = \frac{\text{aggregate expenditure on good } i}{\text{aggregate income}} = v_i(M^3, \mathbf{p})$$

*6.5 Let the demand by household 1 for good 1 be given by

$$\begin{aligned} x_1^1 &= \tfrac{1}{4}M/p_1 \quad \text{if} \quad p_1 > a \\ &= \tfrac{1}{2}M/p_1 \quad \text{if} \quad p_1 < a \\ &= \frac{M}{4a} \quad \text{or} \quad \frac{M}{2a}, \text{ at } p_1 = a, \text{ where } a > 0 \end{aligned}$$

Draw this demand curve and sketch an indifference map that would yield it. Let household 2 have identical income M. Write down the average demand of households 1 and 2 for good 1 and show that at $p_1 = a$ there are now *three* possible values of $\frac{1}{2}[x_1^1 + x_1^2]$. Extend the argument to H identical consumers. Show that as $H \to \infty$ the possible values of the consumption of good 1 per household becomes the entire segment $\left[\frac{M}{4a}, \frac{M}{2a}\right]$.

7

General Equilibrium

7.1 Introduction

In Chapters 3 to 6 we have built up the rudiments of an equilibrium system in a piecemeal fashion. Chapter 3 yields sufficient information to describe the behaviour of the firm with respect to its supply of outputs and its demand for inputs – more compactly its n-vector of net outputs $\mathbf{y}^f$ – *given* that it acts as a price taker and *given* a price vector $\mathbf{p}$. Chapter 4 establishes each household's vector of demands $\mathbf{x}^h$ again *given* that it acts as a price taker and *given* $\mathbf{p}$. Chapters 5 and 6 show respectively the issues involved in dealing separately with consumption and production decisions of a single agent and of aggregating the behavioural responses of price-taking consumers and firms. This clearly leaves a number of big issues to be resolved.

The most obvious of these, which we deal with in Section 7.2, is how to extend the ideas of Chapters 3 and 4 concerning equilibrium of each agent given the state of the rest of the world to a *general* simultaneous equilibrium, whilst taking into account the constraints on the whole system which were discussed in the single-agent Robinson Crusoe example of Chapter 5. Secondly, and much more difficult, we need to consider why firms and households meekly accept prices in a full-scale model of the economic system. We examine this, at least in outline, in Section 7.3. Thirdly, assuming that everyone does act as a price taker, can one be sure that a general equilibrium exists? If it does exist, is it unique? Where does the equilibrium price vector come from? Will the economy actually have a tendency to approach the equilibrium?

Throughout all the discussion of this chapter we retain a number of assumptions that were basic to our previous discussion. We assume that the number of households is fixed, and that their composition and preferences are fixed. We assume also a given number of firms each with a given technology. Finally, everyone has perfect information so that there is no risk or uncertainty and everyone acts as rational utility maximisers or profit maximisers.

7.2 The Definition of Competitive Equilibrium

The first, straightforward, step is to draw together the concepts of an allocation of consumption bundles, and of an allocation of net production vectors (introduced in Chapter 6) into a single definition. We retain all the notation of Chapter 6: see Table 7.1.

DEFINITION 7.1: an *allocation* in an economy consists of an allocation of consumption vectors to each household, and an allocation of production vectors to each firm thus:

$$\mathscr{a} \equiv ([\mathbf{x}^h], [\mathbf{y}^f]) \tag{7.1}$$

where

$$[\mathbf{x}^h] \equiv [\mathbf{x}^1, \ldots, \mathbf{x}^h, \ldots, \mathbf{x}^H] \tag{7.2}$$

$$[\mathbf{y}^f] \equiv [\mathbf{y}^1, \ldots, \mathbf{y}^f, \ldots, \mathbf{y}^F] \tag{7.3}$$

and

$$\mathbf{x}^h \equiv (x_1^h, x_2^h, \ldots, x_n^h)$$

$$\mathbf{y}^f \equiv (y_1^f, y_2^f, \ldots, y_n^f)$$

The allocation $\mathscr{a}$ could be imposed exogenously, as in the extreme version of a command economy. More interestingly, $\mathscr{a}$ may be determined endogenously (at least in part) by the actions of the individual agents – the households $1, \ldots, H$ and the firms $f = 1, \ldots, F$. For both theoretical and practical reasons we are interested in *market allocations* i.e. allocations where for each $\mathscr{a}$ there is also specified a price vector $\mathbf{p}$. The idea of a market allocation *by itself* does not take one very far since the way in which agents respond to the prices $\mathbf{p}$ has not been specified. To make the idea more useful let us introduce a scalar M^h for each household $h = 1, \ldots, H$ to be known as the household's *money income* as in Chapter 6. Exactly *how* the M^h are fixed is a topic we discuss below. Also, as in Chapter 6, let household h have a utility function $U^h(\mathbf{x}^h)$, let the profits of firm f be $\Pi^f, f = 1, \ldots, F$, and the production function of firm f be $\Phi^f(\mathbf{y}^f)$.

DEFINITION 7.2: a *competitive allocation* is a market allocation $(\mathscr{a}, \mathbf{p})$ where $\mathscr{a}$ is given by (7.1) and

(1) $\mathbf{x}^h$ is chosen by household h to maximise $U^h(\mathbf{x}^h)$ subject to

$$\sum_{i=1}^{n} p_i x_i^h \leqslant M^h$$

(2) $\mathbf{y}^f$ is chosen by firm f to maximise profits $\Pi^f \equiv \sum_{i=1}^{n} p_i y_i^f$ subject to

$$\Phi^f(\mathbf{y}^f) \leqslant 0.$$

Notice that implicit in Definition 7.2 is a specific assumption about maximising behaviour by each household and each firm *and* an assumption that each agent acts as a price taker. Clearly either of these assumptions may be relaxed to some extent in order to examine other potentially interesting

Table 7.1 Essential notation for Chapter 7: General Equilibrium

R_i^h	endowment of household h with resource i
s_f^h	share of household h in the profits of firm f
$\mathscr{d} \equiv ([\mathbf{R}^h], [\mathbf{s}^h])$	property distribution
x_i^h	consumption by h of good i
y_i^f	net-output by f of good i
$\mathscr{a} \equiv ([\mathbf{x}^h], [\mathbf{y}^f])$	allocation
p_i	price of good i
R_i	aggregate stocks of good i
$x_i(\mathbf{p})$	aggregate consumption of good i
$y_i(\mathbf{p})$	aggregate net-output of good i
$E_i(\mathbf{p})$	excess demand for good i

systems of allocation that are not competitive in this strict sense. This leads us swiftly towards the idea of a (general) competitive equilibrium. One further restriction is required, as in the equilibrium of the Crusoe economy of Chapter 5. Let $\mathbf{R} \equiv (R_1, \ldots, R_n)$ be the stock of resources already in existence in the economy where, of course $R_i \geqslant 0$. Let $\mathbf{y}$ be the net output vector for the whole economy and let $\mathbf{x} \equiv (x_1, \ldots, x_n)$ be the vector of aggregate consumption by all households together: in general this is determined by (6.3). The *materials balance* condition, first introduced as inequality (5.3), may thus be restated here:

$$\mathbf{x} \leqslant \mathbf{y} + \mathbf{R} \tag{7.4}$$

If there are only pure private goods in the economy, and if there are no externalities in production, then the aggregate consumption vector $\mathbf{x}$ and the aggregate net output vector $\mathbf{y}$ can each be expressed very simply as in Sections 6.2 and 6.3 of Chapter 6; condition (7.4) may then be rewritten:

$$\sum_{h=1}^{H} x_i^h \leqslant \sum_{f=1}^{F} y_i^f + R_i \quad \text{for all} \quad i = 1, \ldots, n \tag{7.5}$$

The materials balance condition now allows us to introduce the following important definition.

DEFINITION 7.3: a *competitive equilibrium* is a competitive allocation ($\mathscr{a}^*$, $\mathbf{p}^*$) where $\mathscr{a}^* = ([\mathbf{x}^{*h}], [\mathbf{y}^{*f}])$ such that

(i) $U^h(\mathbf{x}^{*h}) \geqslant U^h(\mathbf{x}^h)$ for every $\mathbf{x}^h$ such that $\sum_{i=1}^{n} p_i^* x_i^h \leqslant M^h$; and

(ii) $\sum_{i=1}^{n} p_i^* y_i^{*f} \geqslant \sum_{i=1}^{n} p_i^* y_i^f$ for every $\mathbf{y}^f$ such that $\Phi^f(\mathbf{y}^f) \leqslant 0$; and

(iii) the materials balance condition (7.4) holds.

This, of course, is simply a combination of the definition of a competitive allocation with the materials balance condition (7.4). Hence the three parts of Definition 7.3 have a simple interpretation, namely: (i) the consumption vectors in the allocation must maximise utility for every price-taking household at prices **p***; (ii) the net output vectors in the allocation must maximise profits for every price-taking firm at prices **p***; (iii) the aggregate consumption of any good cannot exceed the net production plus the pre-existing stocks of that good.

However the equilibrium in Definition 7.3 obviously depends crucially on the specification of the household incomes $M^1, \ldots, M^H$. What determines these? Again these could be exogenously fixed, by a paternalistic government, for example; or they could be endogenously determined. Notice that this issue is *logically separate* from the above discussion of the competitive equilibrium. That discussion refers to a system of behaviour given assumptions about the agents' rationality, their information and their assumed response to prices. What now needs to be done is to discuss the ground rules which fix the 'starting point' incomes $M^1, \ldots, M^H$ which act as constraints upon the consumers' behaviour. To start with we consider the case of private ownership: other political and social ground rules can easily be obtained as a variant on this. Accordingly let R_i^h be the amount of resource i that is owned by household h. The firms are also owned by the households who are entitled to the firm's profits; let s_f^h be the share of household h in the profits of firm f. By definition we have:

$$\sum_{h=1}^{H} R_i^h = R_i \quad \text{for every} \quad i = 1, \ldots, h \tag{7.6}$$

$$\sum_{h=1}^{H} s_f^h = 1 \quad \text{for every} \quad f = 1, \ldots, F \tag{7.7}$$

Then, if a household's money income is determined solely by its ownership of property, we have, given the price vector **p** and profits $\Pi^1, \ldots, \Pi^F$:

$$M^h = \sum_{i=1}^{n} p_i R_i^h + \sum_{f=1}^{F} \Pi^f s_f^h \tag{7.8}$$

However, we also have for each firm f, by definition:

$$\Pi^f = \sum_{i=1}^{n} p_i y_i^f \tag{7.9}$$

where y_i^f is the net production by firm f of commodity i. And so we obtain

$$M^h = \sum_{i=1}^{n} p_i \left[R_i^h + \sum_{f=1}^{F} s_f^h y_i^f \right] \tag{7.10}$$

so that M^h is obviously homogeneous of degree 1 in prices. Using the notational conventions introduced earlier we may write $[\mathbf{R}^h]$ as shorthand for the list of resource endowment vectors for each household $[\mathbf{R}^1, \mathbf{R}^2, \ldots, \mathbf{R}^H]$ and $[\mathbf{s}^h]$ as shorthand for the list of share-ownership vectors for each household $[\mathbf{s}^1, \mathbf{s}^2, \ldots, \mathbf{s}^H]$. Then we may call $\mathscr{d} \equiv ([\mathbf{R}^h], [\mathbf{s}^h])$ the *property distribution* and write $\mathscr{D} = \{\mathscr{d} : \Sigma_h \mathbf{R}^h = \mathbf{R}, \Sigma_h \mathbf{s}^h = \mathbf{1}, \mathbf{R}^h \geqslant \mathbf{0}, \mathbf{s}^h \geqslant \mathbf{0}\}$ for the set of all such distributions. We shall not discuss further the social and political issues which determine $\mathscr{d}$ but take it as being given outside the economic system.

DEFINITION 7.4: a *private ownership competitive equilibrium relative to a property distribution* $\mathscr{d}$ is a competitive equilibrium where households' money incomes are determined by (7.8).

This definition highlights a central feature of general equilibrium analysis: for each $\mathscr{d} \in \mathscr{D}$ there may be a different competitive equilibrium $(\mathscr{a}^*, \mathbf{p}^*)$. So a change in the property rights of just one group of households, leaving other households' property rights unchanged may nevertheless affect the incomes and hence the utilities of *all* households. The reason is that the change in $\mathscr{d}$ may require a new equilibrium price vector $\mathbf{p}^*$; this will of course potentially alter every household's income M^h defined in (7.10); and of course the resulting change in the equilibrium allocation $\mathscr{a}^*$ may affect everyone's utility. It also highlights a fundamental distinction between two types of economic policy within the equilibrium framework. Suppose that, for whatever reason, it is desired to shift the economy away from a particular equilibrium allocation $\mathscr{a}^*$. One way of doing this is to leave $\mathscr{d}$ as it is and to intervene in the market mechanism so that allocations are no longer competitive. An alternative approach is to allow the competitive mechanism to remain in force, but to manoeuvre $\mathscr{d}$ by redistributing property rights until the desired competitive allocation emerges.[1]

However the 'rules of the game' that underlie a competitive equilibrium evidently consist of two parts. First there is the acceptance of and respect for the pre-existing distribution of property rights, second there is the acceptance of price-taking behaviour. Whilst the first part of these rules is outside the scope of our discussion, the second clearly ought not to be. Why *should* people behave as price takers? Or, perhaps more to the point, why should we assume that they do?

---

1 Of course, practical policies for social control will not be as simple as this. We return to this issue in Chapter 13, Section 13.6.

7.3 The Logic of Price-Taking Behaviour

In order to examine the merits of the price-taking assumption we need to set up some alternative system of behaviour. To do so we shall look at a rather general way of modelling the resolution of the conflict of interests by the participants in the economic 'game'. To keep this discussion manageable we shall simplify the model of the economy in two ways: all goods are taken to be pure private goods, and there is no production. It is important to realise that the concepts that will be discussed in this section are *not* restricted to such economies; it is just that the analysis gets very complicated without these simplifications. In such a model, known as an 'exchange economy', an allocation $\mathscr{a}$ is simply $[\mathbf{x}^h]$ and the property distribution $\mathscr{d}$ is just $[\mathbf{R}^h]$. Clearly in such a simple world $\mathscr{d}$ is just a special allocation which happens to have been fixed by history. The set-up is analogous to life in a prisoner of war camp where $\mathbf{R}^h$ would be the contents list of prisoner h's food parcel.

Clearly there must be some tacitly accepted rules governing the economy – at the very least we should rule out theft – though such rules are best kept to a minimum, for the purposes of our analysis. We shall assume that:

(1) all initial property rights in $\mathscr{d}$ are respected;
(2) any bilateral or multilateral trade agreement may be freely made;
(3) there is perfect, instantaneous information so that no trade takes place until all persons agree, and all persons tell the truth.[2]

This obviously allows people to form any private trading groups they like. Such trading groups will be known as *coalitions*. These coalitions can prevent certain allocations from coming into force. For, suppose that allocation $\hat{\mathscr{a}}$ is proposed to the households; if a coalition Θ of some households can be formed such that by trading their parcels amongst themselves the members of Θ could be better off than under $\hat{\mathscr{a}}$, then obviously the Θ-people will never agree to $\hat{\mathscr{a}}$ but will *block* its implementation.

DEFINITION 7.5: a coalition Θ *blocks* an allocation $\hat{\mathscr{a}}$ if there exists a set of consumption vectors $\{\mathbf{x}^h : h \in \Theta\}$ such that

$$\text{for } \textit{every } h \text{ in } \Theta: \quad U^h(\mathbf{x}^h) \geqslant U^h(\hat{\mathbf{x}}^h) \tag{7.11}$$

$$\text{for } \textit{at least one } j \text{ in } \Theta: \quad U^j(\mathbf{x}^j) > U^j(\hat{\mathbf{x}}^j) \tag{7.12}$$

$$\text{and} \quad \sum_{h\in\Theta} \mathbf{x}^h \leqslant \sum_{h\in\Theta} \mathbf{R}^h \tag{7.13}$$

The idea of blocking yields the solution concept to the problem of exchange in an economy of truthful agents. It is simply:

---

2 This assumption can be problematic for economies with small numbers of traders. See Sections 11.6 and 12.3 of Chapters 11 and 12.

DEFINITION 7.6: the *core* is the set of unblocked feasible allocations given the preferences $(U^1, \ldots, U^H)$ and the property distribution $\mathscr{d}$.

So the core as an equilibrium concept is defined *relative to* a particular distribution $\mathscr{d}$. It is of fundamental importance in the analysis of economic conflicts of interest, and is thus worth examining in more detail. The core may of course contain a great many allocations, or perhaps even none at all, but there is one very important set of allocations which, if they exist, *always* lie in the core.

THEOREM 7.1: if no consumer has a bliss point, any competitive equilibrium allocation must always be in the core.

PROOF: let $\mathscr{a}^*$ be a competitive equilibrium allocation with associated price $\mathbf{p}^*$. Now suppose, contrary to the proposition, that this does *not* lie in the core. Then there is a set of households Θ with a set of consumption bundles $\{\mathbf{x}^h : h \in \Theta\}$ such that (7.11) and (7.12) hold. However since all the members of Θ are price-taking optimisers we must assume that the only reason that they are not already consuming $\{\mathbf{x}^h\}$ rather than $\{\mathbf{x}^{*h}\}$ is that they cannot afford it. Otherwise condition (i) of Definition 7.3 would not be fulfilled. So:

$$\sum_{i=1}^{n} p_i^* x_i^h \geqslant \sum_{i=1}^{n} p_i^* x_i^{*h} \tag{7.14}$$

with strict inequality holding for at least one h. Also, given non-satiation, the RHS of each of (7.14) must equal $\sum_{i=1}^{n} p_i^* R_i^h$, the budget. So:

$$\sum_{h \in \Theta} \sum_{i=1}^{n} p_i^* x_i^h > \sum_{h \in \Theta} \sum_{i=1}^{n} p_i^* R_i^h \tag{7.15}$$

Now if coalition Θ is to block the equilibrium allocation in this fashion (7.13) must hold. But this implies

$$\sum_{h \in \Theta} \sum_{i=1}^{n} p_i^* x_i^h \leqslant \sum_{h \in \Theta} \sum_{i=1}^{n} p_i^* R_i^h \tag{7.16}$$

a direct contradiction of (7.15). Therefore no such blocking coalition exists, and $\mathscr{a}^*$ must lie in the core.

This result is easily illustrated in the case of a two-good exchange economy with two persons Alf and Bill. Draw a box of dimensions R_1, R_2, the total amounts available of two goods, as in Figure 7.1. Alf's allocations and his indifference curves are drawn with respect to origin O^a, Bill's allocations and his indifference curves are drawn with respect to origin O^b. The indifference curves are labelled u_1^a, u_2^a, u_3^a, etc. The property distribution $\mathscr{d}$ is represented by point D with co-ordinates (R_1^a, R_2^a) with reference to origin O^a (and of course co-ordinates (R_1^b, R_2^b) with reference to origin O^b). Consider the

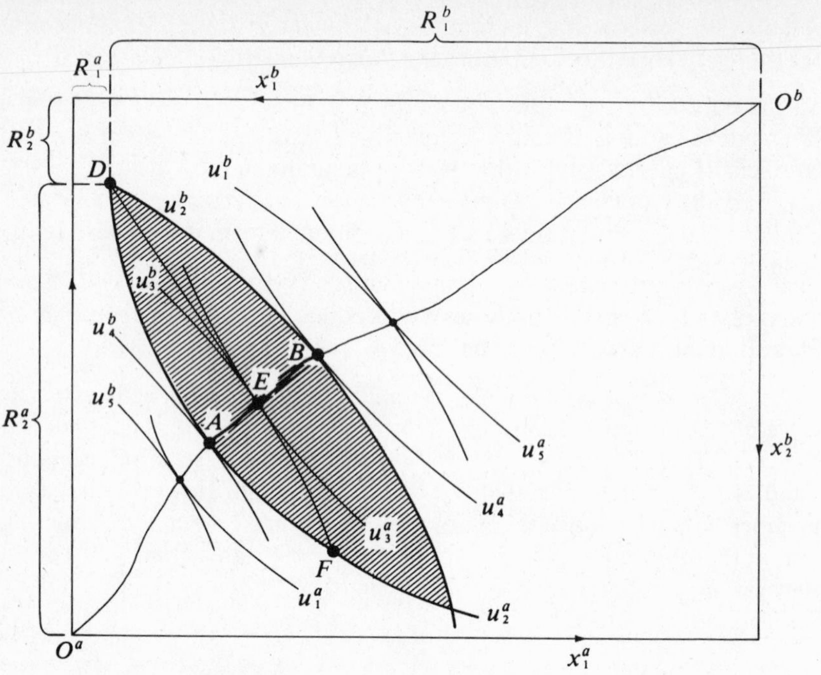

$$x_1^b = R_1 - x_1^a$$
$$x_2^b = R_2 - x_2^a$$

Figure 7.1 The Edgeworth trading box

locus of the points of common tangency of a-indifference curves and b-indifference curves, the so-called 'contract curve' O^aAEBO^b. Clearly Alf and Bill will not agree to an allocation that lies off this curve (assuming that they tell the truth); the reason is that if an allocation is proposed corresponding to, say, point G then there is some other allocation on the contract curve such that utility is higher for one trader and certainly no lower for the other. In Figure 7.1 this is clearly so for point A compared with point F: A and F lie on the *same* a-indifference curve, but A is on a higher b-indifference curve than F. All allocations off the contract curve are blocked. Now we can also be sure that Alf will not agree to any allocation that leaves him on a lower a-indifference curve than that which passes through D (u_2^a); Bill will not agree to anything that leaves him on a lower b-indifference curve than that which passes through D (u_2^b). Hence any allocation outside the shaded area shown will be blocked. The core thus consists of the segment AEB of the contract curve.

Now let us find the point that corresponds to the competitive equilibrium allocation $\mathscr{a}^*$. Since any point in the box in Figure 7.1 represents a feasible allocation, all we need to do is to find that point at which each household is maximising its utility subject to the budget constraint determined by its initial endowment. Clearly this is given by selecting a line through the point D that is tangential to *both* an a-indifference curve *and* a b-indifference curve at the same point. In Figure 7.1 this is shown as E; obviously E must lie on the contract curve (since it is a point of double tangency) and in particular within the core segment AB.

So if a competitive equilibrium exists in an exchange economy the core will not be empty since it will contain that equilibrium allocation. But allocations other than the competitive equilibria may lie in the core and may thus be a solution to the trading game. This is evident in Figure 7.1, since at points on AB other than E the common tangent does *not* pass through D. So why are competitive equilibria of such special interest amongst the numerous core allocations?

An answer to this may be found by examining a similar economy with a larger number of traders. Consider a 'clone' economy: two a-type persons Alf and Arthur (each with allocations $\mathbf{R}^a$ and identical preferences), and two b-type persons, Bill and Ben. Again allow free formation of trading groups. Note first of all that in an economy of any size a core allocation must entail identical consumption vectors for any pair of identical households[3] (that is, any pair of households with the same preferences and the same endowment of resources). Next note that if Figure 7.1 is now interpreted as depicting the consumption of a typical a-person (either Alf or Arthur) and a typical b-person (Bill or Ben), a point such as A can no longer lie in the core.

To see this consider a coalition formed of Alf, Arthur and Bill. Alf and Bill would be prepared to switch from point D, the original allocation, to A; but then Alf and his brother Arthur (who is still at D) realise that if they pooled their resources they could *both* enjoy the consumption bundle represented by point G, the midpoint of AD in Figure 7.2. (Bill is left at point A and Ben, cut out of the coalition, is still at D.) Clearly G is strictly preferred by Alf and Arthur to A, and so the three-person coalition has, from its members' own resources in the initial distribution, secured an outcome which satisfies (7.11) to (7.13). Thus the Alf–Arthur–Bill coalition *blocks* the allocation where everyone is at point A. Of course a point such as G will not be in the core since it is not on the contract curve. In fact Alf and Arthur will not settle for any point on the contract curve to the left of A' in Figure 7.2. A similar argument applies to the point B. Hence the core has shrunk. In fact with every replication of the economy the core may shrink further as new coalitions become possible, and in the limit it reduces to the set of competitive equilibria.

---

[3] See Exercise 7.1.

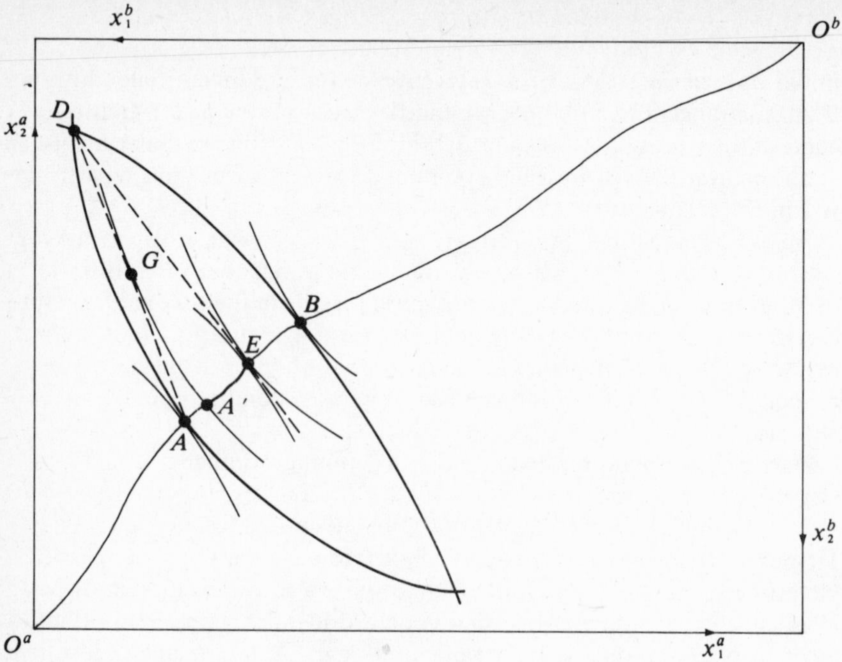

Figure 7.2

Because the core shrinks asymptotically to the set of competitive equilibria there appears to be an argument that if there are enough agents in the economy the rules of the trading game would *compel* everyone to act as a price taker. This is not quite true because the 'large' economy discussed above has been constructed in rather a special way by doubling and redoubling a group of identical persons. Nevertheless the 'limit theorem' on the core can be generalised to other large economies. However if, say, there are only a few of certain types of trader who possess large stocks of a certain resource, or if perfect information is not available, the argument of the limit theorem may no longer be applicable.

Notice also that this section has left the existence of a non-empty core in a particular economy as an open question. We shall return to the issue of the existence of a competitive equilibrium allocation in Section 7.5 and to the uniqueness of that allocation for a given $\mathscr{d}$ in Section 7.6. We now introduce a device that facilitates the analysis of more complex economies in which all agents act as price takers.

7.4 The Excess Demand Function

Much of the discussion of general equilibrium problems can be greatly simplified by a device that is a simple extension of the demand and supply functions discussed in Chapters 3–6. To make the analysis simple we shall assume a private ownership economy, so that (7.10) holds. If each firm is a profit maximiser we may write its net output supply function thus:

$$y_i^f = y_i^f(\mathbf{p}), \quad \text{for all} \quad i = 1, \ldots, n \tag{7.17}$$

as in Section 6.4 of Chapter 6. Now, substituting (7.10) into the consumer's demand function

$$x_i^h = D^{hi}(\mathbf{p}, M^h) \tag{7.18}$$

we find

$$x_i^h = D^{hi}(\mathbf{p}, \sum_{j=1}^{n} p_j [R_j^h + \sum_{f=1}^{F} s_f^h y_j^f]) \tag{7.19}$$

On substituting from (7.17) into (7.19) we find

$$x_i^h = D^{hi}(\mathbf{p}, \sum_{j=1}^{n} p_j [R_j^h + \sum_{f=1}^{F} s_f^h y_j^f(\mathbf{p})]) \tag{7.20}$$

So it is clear that, given the property distribution $\mathscr{d}$ and the firm's supply functions, each household's demand function (7.20) could be written more compactly as a function of **p** the price vector:

$$x_i^h = x_i^h(\mathbf{p}) \tag{7.21}$$

Accordingly, from (7.17) and (7.21) we may derive the *aggregate* demand function, and aggregate net supply function each in terms only of the vector **p**:

$$x_i = x_i(\mathbf{p}) \tag{7.22}$$

$$y_i = y_i(\mathbf{p}) \tag{7.23}$$

It should be carefully remembered, though, that each demand function will depend on the property distribution $\mathscr{d}$.

Since each $y_i^f(\mathbf{p})$ is homogeneous of degree zero in $p_1, \ldots, p_n$ and since each D^{hi} is homogeneous of degree zero in its arguments, it is clear that $x_i(\mathbf{p})$ and $y_i(\mathbf{p})$ must each be homogeneous of degree zero in $p_1, \ldots, p_n$.[4] If there are no consumption externalities then, of course, $x_i(\mathbf{p}) = \Sigma_{h=1}^{H} x_i^h(\mathbf{p})$; and if there are no production externalities we also have $y_i(\mathbf{p}) = \Sigma_{f=1}^{F} y_i^f(\mathbf{p})$ – see

[4] See pp. 47, 78 above.

equation 6.7. Irrespective of whether there are externalities or not we may now introduce:

DEFINITION 7.7: the *excess demand function* $E_i(\mathbf{p})$ for commodity i is given by

$$E_i(\mathbf{p}) \equiv x_i(\mathbf{p}) - y_i(\mathbf{p}) - R_i \tag{7.24}$$

where $x_i(\mathbf{p})$ and $y_i(\mathbf{p})$ are, respectively, the aggregate demand and aggregate net supply functions, and R_i is the aggregate resource endowment of good i.

The idea is simplicity itself: if at prices $\mathbf{p}$ more of good i would be demanded than would be available from firms' outputs plus pre-existing stocks then there is (positive) excess demand for good i: $E_i(\mathbf{p}) > 0$. If at $\mathbf{p}$ more of good i would be made available ($y_i(\mathbf{p}) + R_i$) than is being demanded ($x_i(\mathbf{p})$) then there is negative excess demand, or *excess supply*: $E_i(\mathbf{p}) < 0$.

Let us now assume that all consumers are greedy, non-satiated and have perfect information. Then each will be on his budget constraint, so that at any *given* price vector $\mathbf{p}$, for every household h:

$$\sum_{i=1}^{n} p_i x_i^h = M^h \tag{7.25}$$

If we assume that the economy contains only pure private goods then combining (7.10) and (7.20)–(7.25) we immediately obtain *Walras' Law*:

THEOREM 7.2: for *any* price vector $\mathbf{p}$ and fully-informed, rational, non-satiated agents in a private-ownership economy

$$\sum_{i=1}^{n} p_i E_i(\mathbf{p}) = 0 \tag{7.26}$$

PROOF: See Exercise 7.12.

In other words, the sum of *all* the excess demands, correctly weighted by their corresponding prices, must be exactly zero. Notice that this holds for any competitive allocation regardless of whether $\mathbf{p}$ is a price vector corresponding to an equilibrium allocation. Just as we defined the competitive equilibrium in Section 7.2 by simply incorporating the materials balance condition, so we may correspondingly introduce

DEFINITION 7.8: let $\{E_i(\mathbf{p})\}$ be a set of excess demand functions, as defined in Definition 7.7, for $i = 1, \ldots, n$. Then $\mathbf{p}^*$ is a *competitive equilibrium price vector* if:

$$\text{for all } i: \quad \begin{cases} E_i(\mathbf{p}^*) \leqslant 0 & (7.27) \\ p_i^* E_i(\mathbf{p}^*) = 0 & (7.28) \\ p_i^* \geqslant 0 & (7.29) \end{cases}$$

In other words $\mathbf{p}^*$ cannot be a set of competitive equilibrium prices if there is positive excess demand anywhere; and if in equilibrium $E_i(\mathbf{p}^*)$ is strictly negative then p_i^* must be zero, if $\mathbf{p}^*$ is to be a set of equilibrium prices. Hence, at the equilibrium, for any good with a positive price the excess demand must be exactly zero; for any good with zero price – a free good – the excess demand may be exactly zero, or there may be excess supply.

It should be emphasised that this only covers the ground of Section 7.2 again by a convenient alternative route. For any given property distribution $\mathscr{d}$ the $\mathbf{p}^*$ in Definition 7.8 is the same as the $\mathbf{p}^*$ in Definition 7.3.

So if a $\mathbf{p}^*$, satisfying (7.27) to (7.29) is used in the demand and supply functions of households and firms (equations 7.17, 7.21) we will find the equilibrium allocation $\mathscr{a}^*$ at which $x_i^{*h} = x_i^h(\mathbf{p}^*)$ and $y_i^{*f} = y_i^f(\mathbf{p}^*)$ for every f, h and i. Thus we may conveniently summarise the two logical steps in the determination of a general competitive equilibrium:

(1) find the price vector that is consistent with equilibrium, given the *aggregate* excess demand functions;
(2) 'plug in' the equilibrium price vector to the *individual* demand and supply functions to get the detail of the allocation that is consistent with that equilibrium.

The complete system in a private ownership economy is illustrated in schematic form in Figure 7.3: the numbers in brackets represent the equation numbers of the relationships we have discussed. Notice the central role of prices in the process of transforming the property distribution $\mathscr{d}$ into the allocation $\mathscr{a}$. Plugging in *any* particular price vector $\mathbf{p}$ – in the manner just described – affects firms' net outputs, firms' profits, households' incomes and households' demands. Figure 7.3 takes the story from the starting point of a given property distribution and an arbitrary price vector $\mathbf{p}$ through to the excess demands $\mathbf{E}(\mathbf{p})$. If these $\mathbf{E}(\mathbf{p})$ satisfy (7.27)–(7.29) – step 1 – then the equilibrium system is solved: much of Sections 7.5 to 7.7 is concerned with questions involved in this step. In Section 7.7 we return to step 2.

7.5 The Existence of an Equilibrium

If we can prove that there is at least *one* vector $\mathbf{p}^*$ that satisfies (7.27)–(7.29) for a given set of excess demand functions, we have proved the existence of a competitive equilibrium, because then the equilibrium allocation is found merely by mechanically substituting $\mathbf{p}^*$ in (7.17) and (7.21). We wish to see whether such a vector actually exists. Note that this appears to reduce to finding a solution to n equations

$$p_i^* E_i(\mathbf{p}^*) = 0, \qquad i = 1, \ldots, n \tag{7.30}$$

in n unknowns $p_1^*, \ldots, p_n^*$ subject to the conditions (7.27) and (7.29). Actually

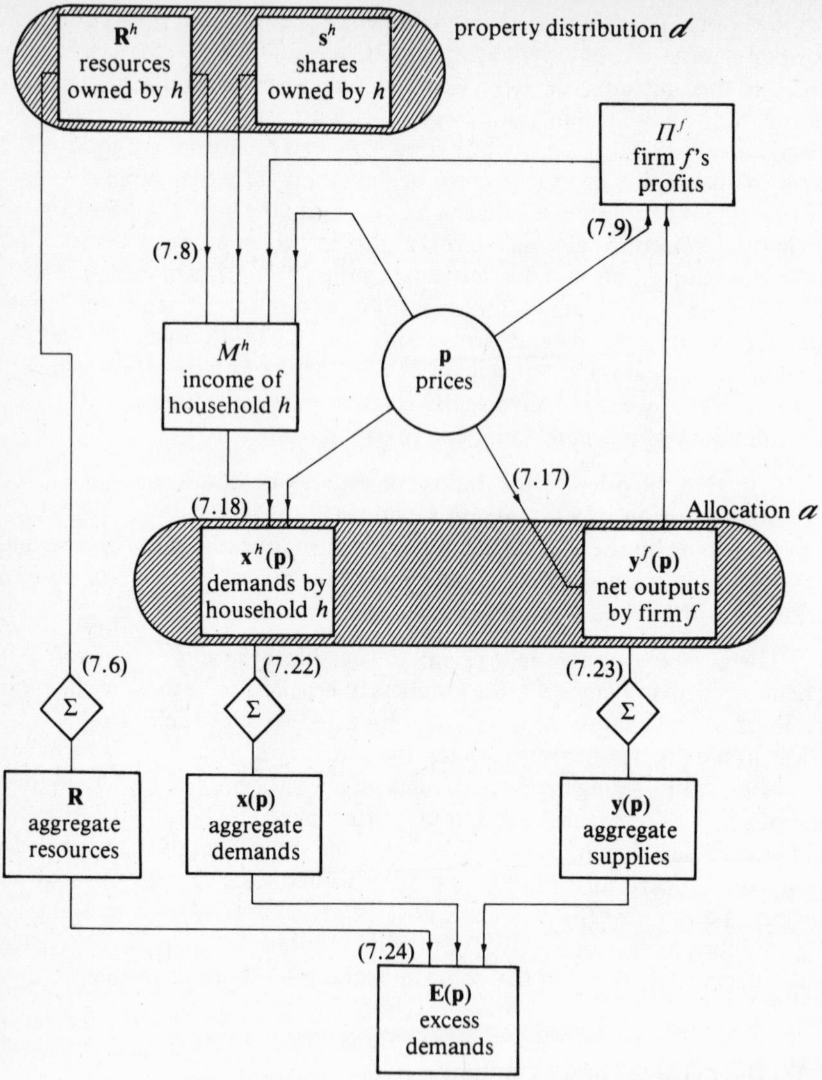

Figure 7.3

there are only $n - 1$ independent unknowns, because each equation is clearly homogeneous of degree zero in $p_1^*, \ldots, p_n^*$; halving, doubling or trebling all prices would leave excess demands unchanged so that, for example, we may arbitrarily divide one price, p_j into all the others to yield prices $\left[\frac{p_1}{p_j}, \ldots, \frac{p_{j-1}}{p_j}, 1, \frac{p_{j+1}}{p_j}, \ldots, \frac{p_n}{p_j}\right]$ without affecting the excess demand.

One price is therefore redundant and may be arbitrarily scaled. Also one equation in the system is redundant. Walras' Law implies that the excess demand for good j, $E_j(\mathbf{p})$, may always be found by the simple formula

$$E_j(\mathbf{p}) = -\frac{1}{p_j}\sum_{i \neq j}^{n} p_i E_i(\mathbf{p})$$

Hence in fact we have a system of $n - 1$ equations in $n - 1$ unknowns.

We now need to discover the conditions under which we may be sure that such a non-negative solution exists. The general procedure involves two stages. Firstly one examines what mathematical restrictions on the *form* of the excess demand functions $E_i(\mathbf{p})$ will guarantee a solution. Secondly one has to interpret those mathematical conditions in terms of their economic content.

Note that the fact that we may scale the prices arbitrarily leads to a convenient simplification. Choose $p_1, \ldots, p_n$ such that $\Sigma_{i=1}^{n} p_i = 1$; obviously we may always ensure this by dividing each p_i by $\Sigma_{j=1}^{n} p_j$. Since no price can be negative all such price vectors must lie in the set $J = \{\mathbf{p} : \mathbf{p} \geqslant \mathbf{0}, \Sigma_{i=1}^{n} p_i = 1\}$. Clearly J, the set of *normalised prices*, is convex and compact (i.e. it is bounded and contains all its boundary points).

Considerable insight into the formal conditions that ensure a solution can be found by examining a two-good example. In this case, using the normalisation just described, $p_1 + p_2 = 1$ and the set J is simply the interval $[0, 1]$. Figure 7.4 illustrates three possible excess demand functions. Obviously in cases (a) and (b) there is no equilibrium. In case (a) the excess demand function is *discontinuous* between points A and B so that there is no value of p_1 at which $E_1 = 0$ (and, of course, E_1 is positive as $p_1 \to 0$). In case (b) E_1 stays positive for all possible prices. Observe that, since Walras' Law implies $E_2 = -p_1E_1/p_2 = -p_1E_1/[1 - p_1]$, as p_1 tends to 1 (and consequently p_2 tends to 0) we find $E_2 \to -\infty$. Case (c) suffers from neither of these difficulties: there is an equilibrium price p_1^* (for the moment ignore the two sets of arrows on the curve). This suggests two conditions which might ensure the existence of an equilibrium: excess demands should be continuous and they should never reach minus infinity. Indeed this condition translates to the general case, summarised in our next theorem, which is proved in Appendix A.

THEOREM 7.3: if each $E_i(\mathbf{p})$ is a *continuous* function from J to the real line and is bounded below, then there exists $\mathbf{p}^* \in J$ which is an equilibrium price vector.

Let us examine and interpret the conditions required for Theorem 7.3. The requirement that each $E_i(\mathbf{p})$ is bounded below is not very restrictive. Obviously $x_i(\mathbf{p}) \geqslant 0$ and so the only way that $E_i(\mathbf{p})$ *could* equal minus infinity is for either $y_i(\mathbf{p})$ or R_i to equal plus infinity. So as long as there is neither an infinite stock of good i, nor at any price vector would there be infinite supply by firms, the condition is assured. However it is evident that a lot turns on

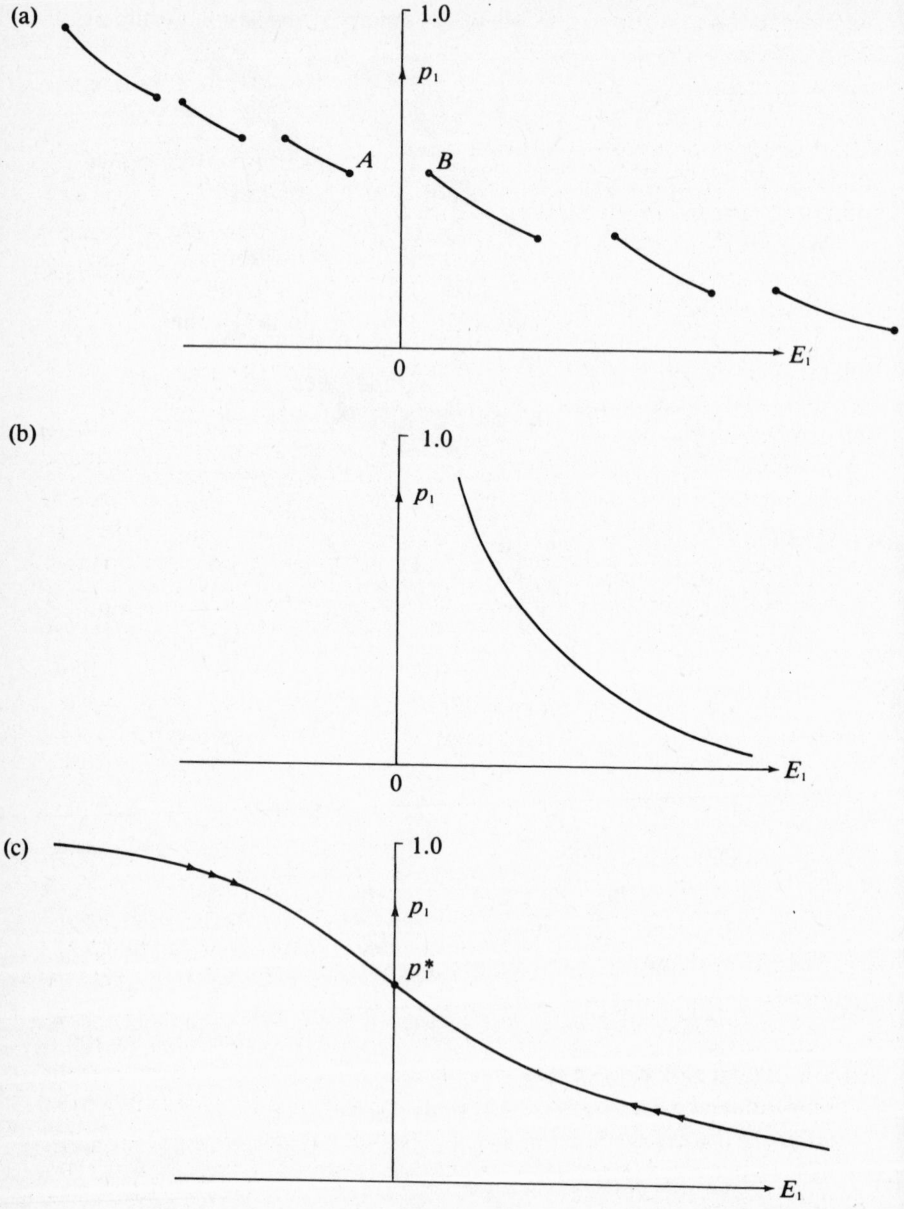

Figure 7.4 Excess demand in a two-good model

the economic assumptions required to ensure the other principal condition: that excess demands are single-valued, continuous functions of price. A *sufficient* condition for this to be so (at strictly positive prices) would be strictly concave-contoured utility functions for each household, no external effects in consumption or production, and a strictly convex aggregate production set. This is too strong for comfort really, since this requirement would imply decreasing returns everywhere in the aggregate. Fortunately similar results to Theorem 7.3 exist when utility functions are merely concave contoured, and the production set is convex.

Why are these 'convexity' assumptions so important? Recall the discussion on this topic in Chapters 3 and 4 concerning the behaviour of *individual* firms and households. If technology sets are strictly convex and if indifference curves are strictly convex to the origin, then we know that each firm's input demand functions are well defined and continuous, its supply function is well defined and continuous and each household's demand functions are well defined and continuous (Theorems 3.4 and 4.6). If we have only convexity rather than strict convexity then similar but more complicated results are obtainable. But if we have *non-convexities* – indivisibilities in production, a preference for 'extremes' rather than 'mixtures' by households – then, as we have seen, we get 'jumps' in demand or supply at certain critical prices. Because of these jumps it *may* happen that no equilibrium exists. We return to this point when we discuss *aggregate* production and consumption in Section 7.7.

7.6 Uniqueness of Equilibrium Prices

Will the equilibrium $\mathbf{p}^*$ be unique for a given $\mathscr{d}$? Of course this question only has a meaning if we talk about *normalised* price vectors because, as we noted in the general equilibrium system of Section 7.5, the price vector $\mathbf{p}^*$ is equivalent to $\alpha\mathbf{p}^*$ where α is any positive scalar multiple. But there might well be circumstances where there is more than one normalised price vector that yields a competitive equilibrium relative to $\mathscr{d}$. To see this, examine Figure 7.5 – which is designed to be very similar to Figure 7.1, except that the indifference curves have been deliberately altered. As you can see there are now at least *two* distinct lines through the point D which each produce a common tangent to an a-indifference curve and a b-indifference curve. According to the argument in Section 7.3 each will correspond to a different equilibrium price vector $\mathbf{p}^*$, $\mathbf{p}^{**}$ in the exchange economy and, if one carries out the clone-like replication of the economy described in that section, the limit of the core will contain *all* the allocations $\mathscr{a}^*$, $\mathscr{a}^{**}$, ... which correspond to each price vector $\mathbf{p}^*$, $\mathbf{p}^{**}$, ... that yields a common tangent in the manner of Figure 7.5. And of course if multiple equilibria can crop up in a

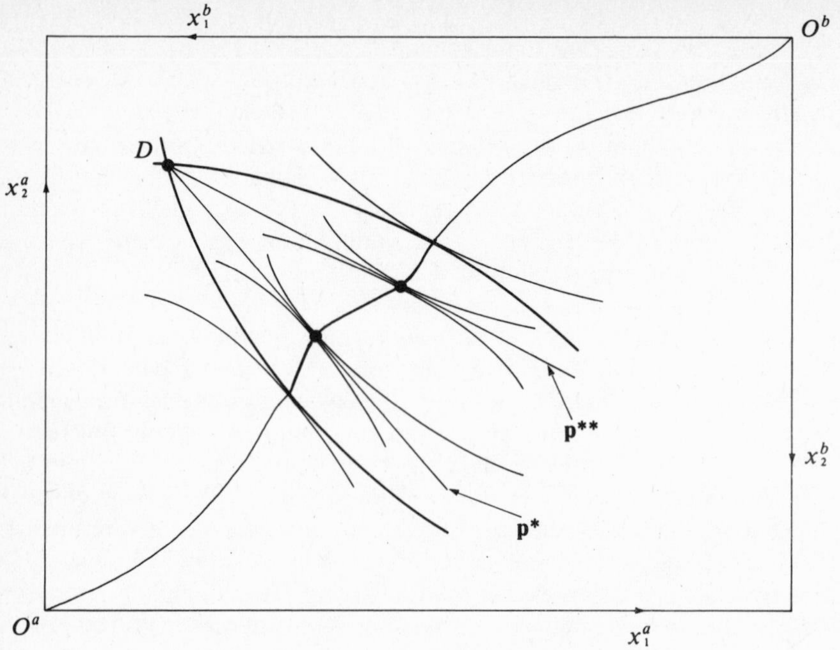

Figure 7.5

simple exchange economy, it is certain that they can arise in more complex economies that include production.

How can this situation arise? After all, if we take the excess demand function in the two-commodity model depicted in Figure 7.4(c), we can see at a glance that there is one and only one $\mathbf{p}^*$ at which $\mathbf{E}(\mathbf{p}^*) = \mathbf{0}$. In *that* economy the equilibrium is unique; so what must the excess demand functions look like in order to yield multiple solutions? It is not hard to see that they must appear something like Figure 7.6. Here each crossing point of $E_1(\mathbf{p})$ on the vertical axis yields an equilibrium price vector (since Walras' Law implies $p_1E_1(\mathbf{p}) + p_2E_2(\mathbf{p}) = 0$, whenever E_1 is zero p_2E_2 must be zero). So multiple equilibria can occur if the excess demand functions 'wiggle about'. It is quite easy to see why this happens. Consider a two-commodity, two-person exchange economy and let us suppose that person *a* owns all the stock of commodity two, R_2. Now refer back to Figure 5.8. We noted there that the person's net supply of good two to the market might 'bend back' on itself. The reason was that as p_2 rose there was a substitution effect leading him to consume *less* of good two; but at the same time there was a powerful effect from the concomitant increase in the component of his income p_2R_2, which of course led him to consume more of both goods one and two. So because of this 'income effect' $x_2^a(\mathbf{p})$, consumer *a*'s net demand for good 2, sometimes

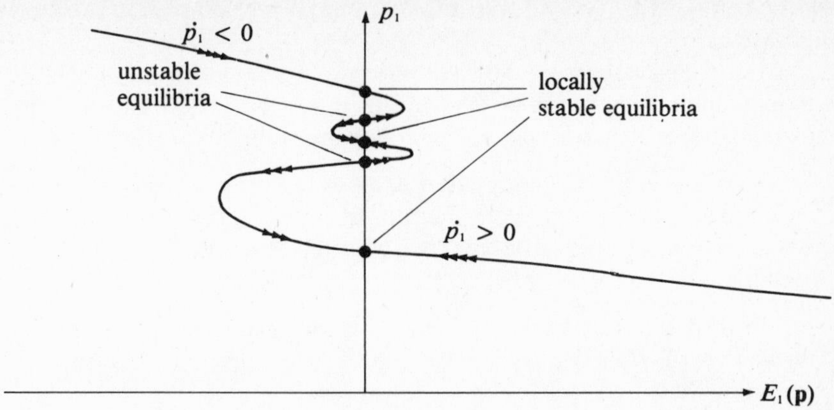

Figure 7.6 Multiple equilibria in a two-commodity model

increases and sometimes decreases in p_2. Well of course consumer b may have a completely different preference map and it may well be that *his* demand function $x_2^b(\mathbf{p})$ is monotonic in p_2. So, loosely speaking, if consumer a's income effect is 'strong enough' the market excess demand function $x_2^a(\mathbf{p}) + x_2^b(\mathbf{p}) - R_2$ 'bends back' on itself at some point. Naturally what actually happens depends on the shape of each agent's indifference curves and the particular property distribution $\mathscr{d}$. It is the powerful impact that prices have on the incomes M^h in (7.10) – and in particular on the distribution of those incomes amongst different households – that makes the excess demand function behave in this strange fashion.

Multiple equilibria are of more interest than mere curiosities. Suppose the economy is in equilibrium. For some reason it is decided by the government (or whoever else it is that decides the rules about property rights) that the equilibrium allocation should be changed. So, let us say, a redistribution from $\mathscr{d}$ to $\mathscr{d}'$ takes place as a parcel of land is reassigned from household h to household h'. What then happens? Obviously we may expect prices to adjust in response to the consequent shift in demands; but *where* will they settle, if indeed they settle at all? If the world looks like Figure 7.6 it is no good computing just *any* set of new equilibrium prices $\mathbf{p}^*$ with its accompanying allocation $\mathscr{a}^*$: as we can see there are four other candidate equilibria and it may be that quite the 'wrong' equilibrium in fact emerges.

Obviously to deal with these issues fully one needs a full model not only of the competitive equilibrium system but also of the *dis*equilibrium system – the system that deals with the movements of prices and/or quantities of goods in real time when the economy is not at rest. An adequate discussion of such issues is beyond the scope of this chapter, though we shall discuss one process below. However, *if* one could be sure that the equilibrium relative to any given $\mathscr{d}$ would be unique, then it is obviously quite likely that the analysis of the disequilibrium process will be relatively less complicated than in a case such as Figure 7.6.

Clearly if all excess demand functions $E_i(\mathbf{p})$ were monotonic in $p_1, \ldots, p_n$ multiple equilibria could not arise – cf. Figure 7.4(c). But such a requirement may be unnecessarily restrictive. The following is slightly weaker:

THEOREM 7.4: if $\mathbf{p}^*$ is a normalised equilibrium price vector in a private ownership economy and if *aggregate* consumer demands $\mathbf{x}(\mathbf{p})$ always satisfy the weak axiom of revealed preference with reference to $\mathbf{p}^*$, then $\mathbf{p}^*$ must be unique.

PROOF: if $\mathbf{p}^*$ is an equilibrium price vector, then by definition $E_i(\mathbf{p}^*) \leqslant 0$. Also in view of Walras' Law, for *any* vector $\mathbf{p}$ we have $\sum_{i=1}^{n} p_i E_i(\mathbf{p}) = 0$. Combining these two facts we have, for any $\mathbf{p}$:

$$\sum_{i=1}^{n} p_i E_i(\mathbf{p}^*) \leqslant \sum_{i=1}^{n} p_i E_i(\mathbf{p}) \tag{7.31}$$

where the right-hand side of (7.31) is zero. Now if producers always maximise profits at any vector $\mathbf{p}$ we also have $\sum_{i=1}^{n} p_i y_i(\mathbf{p}) \geqslant \sum_{i=1}^{n} p_i y_i(\mathbf{p}^*)$ where $y_i(\mathbf{p}^*)$ is the net output of i that would be supplied at price vector $\mathbf{p}^*$. Now using this result and the materials balance condition (7.4) we find that (7.31) implies

$$\sum_{i=1}^{n} p_i x_i(\mathbf{p}) \geqslant \sum_{i=1}^{n} p_i x_i(\mathbf{p}^*) \tag{7.32}$$

for *any* conceivable price vector $\mathbf{p}$.

Now suppose that WARP holds with respect to aggregate demands at $\mathbf{p}^*$. Then (cf. equations 4.1 and 4.2) (7.32) implies

$$\sum_{i=1}^{n} p_i^* x_i(\mathbf{p}) > \sum_{i=1}^{n} p_i^* x_i(\mathbf{p}^*) \tag{7.33}$$

Define a function $\phi(\mathbf{p}^1, \mathbf{p}^2) \equiv \sum_{i=1}^{n} [p_i^1 + p_i^2]\, x_i(\mathbf{p}^2)$. Then, we find that (7.32) and (7.33) imply

$$\phi(\mathbf{p}^*, \mathbf{p}) > \phi(\mathbf{p}, \mathbf{p}^*) \tag{7.34}$$

However, if there were a separate distinct normalised price vector $\mathbf{p}^{**}$ that was *also* an equilibrium vector (7.34) would imply that for equilibrium $\mathbf{p}^*$:

$$\phi(\mathbf{p}^*, \mathbf{p}^{**}) > \phi(\mathbf{p}^{**}, \mathbf{p}^*)$$

but for equilibrium $\mathbf{p}^{**}$ (7.34) implies:

$$\phi(\mathbf{p}^{**}, \mathbf{p}^*) > \phi(\mathbf{p}^*, \mathbf{p}^{**})$$

an obvious contradiction. So a distinct $\mathbf{p}^{**}$ cannot exist.

This condition amounts to requiring that perverse income effects be not so strong that the situation illustrated in Figure 6.8 arise around an equilibrium point. As we noted in the discussion of Chapter 6 this can be guaranteed if household preference maps have certain regularity properties. One should not, perhaps, be too sanguine about these properties always being present. However we can now say something about the *stability* of the system of markets we have described, though as we have noted above, this amounts to the merest sketch. To do this let $\mathbf{p}(t)$ denote the price vector at time t and let $\dot{\mathbf{p}}(t)$ denote the time derivative vector $(\mathrm{d}p_1(t)/\mathrm{d}t, \mathrm{d}p_2(t)/\mathrm{d}t, \ldots, \mathrm{d}p_n(t)/\mathrm{d}t)$.

DEFINITION 7.9: the economy follows a *linear tâtonnement* process if

$$\dot{p}_i(t) = \alpha_i E_i(\mathbf{p}(t)) \qquad i = 1, \ldots, n \tag{7.35}$$

where α_i is some positive scalar.

Tâtonnement processes, linear or non-linear, are very convenient analytical simplifications, but are rather strange in terms of their economic interpretation.[5] Condition (7.35) implies that if there is positive excess demand for a good then that good's price rises, and vice versa. But the $E_i(\mathbf{p})$ functions are defined *relative* to a given distribution $\mathscr{d}$, so that (7.35) implicitly assumes that $\mathscr{d}$ does not change during the process. Obviously once people *do* trade, these resource endowments for the 'next period' will change; so the *tâtonnement* process effectively assumes that no trading occurs before equilibrium is reached. In many cases this is a manifestly absurd assumption. However, let us see how the system adjusts under this simple-minded process where, for convenience we shall take $\alpha_i = \alpha$ for all i.[6]

Consider the distance of prices at time t from equilibrium prices given by

$$\delta(t) \equiv [\sum_{i=1}^{n} [p_i(t) - p_i^*]^2]^{\frac{1}{2}} \geqslant 0 \tag{7.36}$$

Differentiating this with respect to time we have

$$\delta(t)\dot{\delta}(t) = \sum_{i=1}^{n} [p_i(t) - p_i^*]\,\dot{p}_i(t) \tag{7.37}$$

---

5 They are sometimes rationalised in terms of a simple parable: at the centre of Figure 7.3 one imagines that there sits an auctioneer who scrutinises the excess demands that emerge and adjusts the prices accordingly.

6 This is not a serious restriction. Some readers will recognise (7.36) as a simple Lyapunov function. For the more general case simply define a different Lyapunov function

$$\delta(t) = [\sum_{i=1}^{n} \alpha_i^{-2}[p_i(t) - p_i^*]^2]^{\frac{1}{2}}$$

The analysis goes through as before.

which in the case of the linear *tâtonnement* system reduces to

$$\dot{\delta}(t) = \alpha \sum_{i=1}^{n} [p_i(t) - p_i^*] E_i(\mathbf{p}(t))/\delta(t)$$

$$= -\alpha \sum_{i=1}^{n} p_i^* E_i(p(t))/\delta(t) \tag{7.38}$$

where the last line follows because Walras' Law implies that $\sum_{i=1}^{n} p_i(t) E_i(\mathbf{p}(t))$ vanishes.

However, if aggregate consumption demands $\mathbf{x}(\mathbf{p})$ obey WARP with reference to $\mathbf{p}^*$, so also do the excess demand functions $\mathbf{E}(\mathbf{p})$ (cf. the argument concerning equations (7.31) and (7.32)). So, since we know that (7.31) is true for any $\mathbf{p}$ and the equilibrium vector $\mathbf{p}^*$, WARP implies

$$\sum_{i=1}^{n} p_i^* E_i(\mathbf{p}^*) < \sum_{i=1}^{n} p_i^* E_i(\mathbf{p}(t)) \tag{7.39}$$

But the left-hand side of (7.39) is zero, again because of Walras' Law. So, combining (7.38) and (7.39) we find that under these circumstances

$$\dot{\delta}(t) < 0 \tag{7.40}$$

So the distance to equilibrium monotonically decreases over time. The system is stable.

This is illustrated in Figure 7.4(c) where the arrows show the direction of motion under the *tâtonnement* process. By contrast look at Figure 7.6 where the WARP condition does not hold with reference to the equilibrium price vector: again the arrows depict the *tâtonnement* process. We see that there are in fact three locally stable equilibria and two unstable equilibria. The precise choice of the starting point $\mathbf{p}(0)$ will determine which locally stable equilibrium is eventually reached.

7.7 Convexity and the Equilibrium Allocation

Suppose there is a unique equilibrium price vector $\mathbf{p}^*$. Then the equilibrium allocation is found by evaluating the individual household demand functions and firm net supply functions to obtain $x_i^{*h} = x_i^h(\mathbf{p}^*)$ and $y_i^{*f} = y_i^f(\mathbf{p}^*)$ for every $i = 1, \ldots, n$, $h = 1, \ldots, H$ and $f = 1, \ldots, F$. As in Figure 5.1 of Chapter 5 we can represent this equilibrium as a price hyperplane separating two sets. Let us examine Figure 7.7 which represents the case where there are two consumer goods (and the resources do not enter anyone's utility function directly). One convex set is clearly bounded by a contour of $\Phi(\mathbf{y})$ and is the set of all consumption vectors that can be produced in the economy. The other convex set is

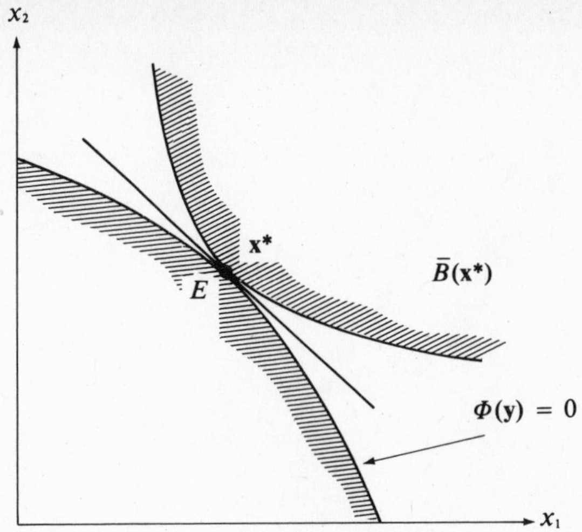

Figure 7.7

$$\bar{B}(\mathbf{x}^*) = \{\mathbf{x} : \mathbf{x} = \sum_{h=1}^{H} \mathbf{x}^h \text{ and } U^h(\mathbf{x}^h) \geqslant U^h(\mathbf{x}^{*h})\} \tag{7.41}$$

$\bar{B}(\mathbf{x}^*)$ is the set of all aggregate consumption vectors that correspond to situations where nobody is worse off than at the original equilibrium allocation $\mathscr{a}^*$. If everyone's indifference curve is convex to the origin then clearly the set $\bar{B}(\mathbf{x}^*)$ must be convex.

Consider first the interpretation of $\mathbf{p}^*$. Clearly the point marked E *maximises* $\Sigma_i p_i^* x_i$ over the set of production possibilities, and it *minimises* $\Sigma_i p_i^* x_i$ over the set $\bar{B}(\mathbf{x}^*)$. No firm could attain higher profits than at the allocation corresponding to E, and likewise, given its budget, no household could attain higher utility than at $\mathbf{x}^{*h}$.

As we argued in the case of the single-agent Robinson Crusoe economy (Theorem 5.1) the convexity of the two sets in Figure 7.7 is extremely important. If either set is non-convex it may be that no 'separating hyperplane' exists. Figure 7.8 reproduces the familiar case of the non-convex production possibility set: the allocation at E is no longer a competitive equilibrium because higher profits could be made at A – but at A we would find that for at least some households utility was not being maximised. Figure 7.9 illustrates a similar case where the set $\bar{B}(\mathbf{x}^*)$ is non-convex. Once again it is clear that the sets cannot be separated by a straight line (the price hyperplane), and so neither in Figure 7.8 nor in Figure 7.9 does a competitive equilibrium exist. In fact it can be shown that these provide two examples where the excess demand functions $\mathbf{E}(\mathbf{p}^*)$ are discontinuous, so that in Figure 7.4 there is no value of p_1 at which E_1 cuts the vertical axis.

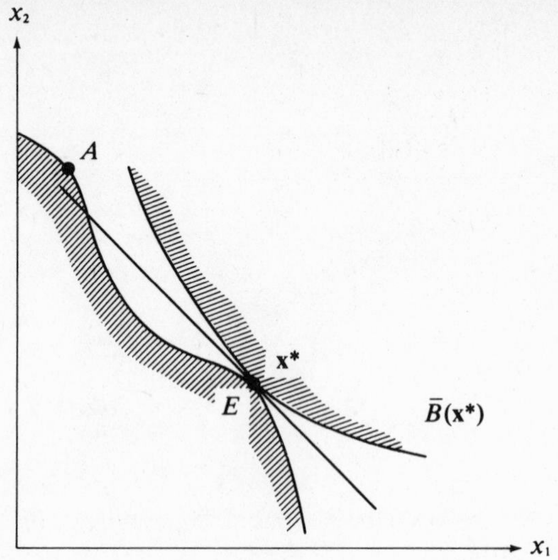

Figure 7.8

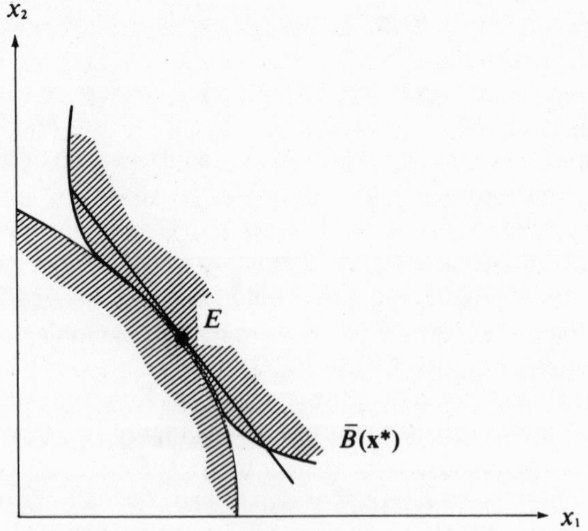

Figure 7.9

How serious is this sort of problem? Recall that, as we saw in Chapter 6, for a number of reasons the production set for the whole economy may be convex even if the production sets of individual firms are non-convex. One such reason is that each firm that exhibits locally increasing returns to scale may actually be very small in comparison to the whole economy, in which

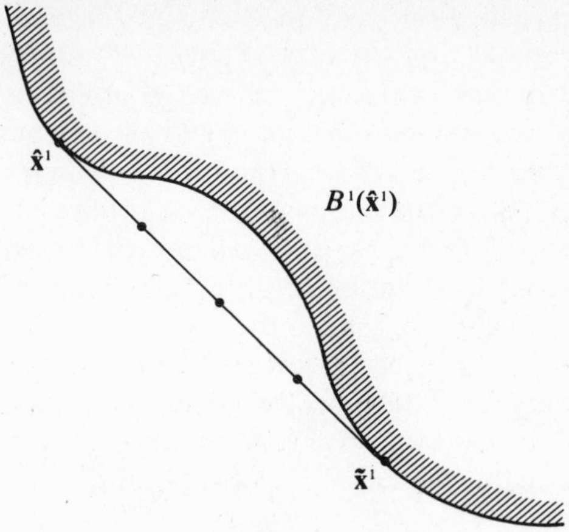

Figure 7.10 An indifference curve that is not convex to the origin

case the sum of the production sets is 'approximately' convex; sheer weight of numbers ensures this. A similar result is available for consumers where individual household utilities violate Axiom C5′ of Chapter 4 so that isoquants are *not* convex to the origin. To see this consider Figure 7.10. This represents the indifference curve for a particular household through a point $\hat{\mathbf{x}}^1$. The set $B^1(\hat{\mathbf{x}}^1) \equiv \{\mathbf{x}^1 : U(\mathbf{x}^1) \geqslant U(\hat{\mathbf{x}}^1)\}$ clearly is that which has been shaded in, and $\tilde{\mathbf{x}}^1$ obviously belongs to this set. Let household 2 be *identical* to household 1, so that $B^2(\hat{\mathbf{x}}^2)$ is an identical set. Now consider $\bar{B}(\hat{\mathbf{x}})$ as defined in (7.41); where $\hat{\mathbf{x}} \equiv \hat{\mathbf{x}}^1 + \hat{\mathbf{x}}^2 = 2\hat{\mathbf{x}}^1$. Obviously $2\hat{\mathbf{x}}^1$ and $2\tilde{\mathbf{x}}^1$ belong to $\bar{B}(\hat{\mathbf{x}})$ but *so does* the point $\hat{\mathbf{x}}^1 + \tilde{\mathbf{x}}^1$ which is of course the *average* of $2\hat{\mathbf{x}}^1$ and $2\tilde{\mathbf{x}}^1$. From this it can be seen that $\bar{B}(\hat{\mathbf{x}})$ is *not* just a 'photographic enlargement' of the set $B^1(\hat{\mathbf{x}}^1)$ but will also include points such as that corresponding to the mid-point of the straight line in Figure 7.10 (amongst others). If there were four people then $\bar{B}(\hat{\mathbf{x}})$ would contain vectors such as $3\hat{\mathbf{x}}^1 + \tilde{\mathbf{x}}^1$ or $2\hat{\mathbf{x}}^1 + 2\tilde{\mathbf{x}}^1$ or $\hat{\mathbf{x}}^1 + 3\tilde{\mathbf{x}}^1$ which, *when scaled down*, correspond to points $\frac{1}{4}$, $\frac{1}{2}$ and $\frac{3}{4}$ of the way along the straight line. In the limit, if there were infinitely many such consumers each of infinitesimal size, $\bar{B}(\hat{\mathbf{x}})$ would be found simply by 'convexifying' the diagram in Figure 7.10 – i.e. by 'filling in' the non-convexity, shading in the area above the straight line.

7.8 Summary

The *theoretical existence* of a competitive equilibrium can be proved under conditions that do not appear to be unduly demanding: convexity of the aggregate technology set, and a similar condition imposed on preferences. We have argued that the effect of large numbers in itself might be sufficient to ensure that such conditions hold 'near enough'. Somewhat more stringent conditions are required if one is to be sure that, for a given distribution of property, the equilibrium allocation is unique. Non-uniqueness may give rise to problems when the system is disturbed away from equilibrium.

However, the story in this chapter pays little attention to (i) why everyone should act as price-taking, maximising agents; (ii) what adjustment process is used if the economy does not happen to be in equilibrium and whether this affects the underlying distribution of property. And it pays no attention at all to (iii) the importance of goods other than purely private goods in the equilibrium; and (iv) the effect of uncertainty on the equilibrium. Further treatment of points (i) and (ii), beyond the discussion of Sections 7.3 and 7.6, would be outside the scope of this book. Point (iii), which incorporates the treatment of externalities and public goods, is discussed in the next chapter.

Further Reading

Most of the issues in this chapter are discussed in great depth in:

Arrow, K.J. and Hahn, F.H. (1971) *General Competitive Analysis*, Oliver and Boyd, Edinburgh.

The game theoretic analysis of the core and equilibrium is presented in:

Bacharach, M.O.L. (1976) *Economics and the Theory of Games*, Macmillan.

The classic article on the shrinking core and equal treatment in coalitions is:

Debreu, G. and Scarf, H. (1963) 'A limit theorem on the core of an economy', *International Economic Review*, Vol. 4, pp. 235–46.

An easier treatment of their main result is given in:

Schweizer, U. (1982) 'A Lagrangian approach to the limit theorem on the core of an economy', *Zeitschrift für Nazionalökonomie*, pp. 23–30.

More general, but more difficult, analysis is available in:

Hildenbrand, W. and Kirman, A.P. (1976) *Introduction to Equilibrium Analysis*.

Quirk, J. and Saposnik, R. (1968) *Introduction to General Equilibrium Theory and Welfare Economics*, McGraw-Hill. Ch. 3, provides a very valuable summary of the standard models used to analyse the existence of competitive equilibrium and stability. This latter issue is comprehensively treated in:

Hahn, F.H. (1982) 'Stability', in K.J. Arrow and M.D. Intriligator (eds), *Handbook of Mathematical Economics*, North-Holland, Vol. II, Ch. 16.

Farrell, M.J. (1959) 'The convexity assumption in the theory of competitive markets', *Journal of Political Economy*, Vol. 67, pp. 377–91, gives a useful and largely non-technical discussion of the issue of convexity in competitive equilibrium.

Exercises

7.1 (a) Prove that in a core allocation all persons of the same type must have the same consumption.

(b) Suppose the economy in Figure 7.2 has been cloned many times so that there is the same large number of both a-people and b-people, and consider any point K in the segment AE such that DK is *not* tangential to the indifference curves through K. Construct an argument similar to that on page 137 to show that the allocation which places all consumers at point K could be blocked.

7.2 Which of the following sets of functions are legitimate excess demand functions?

(a)
$$E_1(\mathbf{p}) = -p_2 + A/p_1$$
$$E_2(\mathbf{p}) = p_1$$
$$E_3(\mathbf{p}) = -A/p_3$$

(b)
$$E_1(\mathbf{p}) = [p_2 + p_3]/p_1$$
$$E_2(\mathbf{p}) = [p_1 + p_3]/p_2$$
$$E_3(\mathbf{p}) = [p_1 + p_2]/p_3$$

(c)
$$E_1(\mathbf{p}) = p_3/p_1$$
$$E_2(\mathbf{p}) = p_3/p_2$$
$$E_3(\mathbf{p}) = -2$$

*7.3 Let $E_1(\mathbf{p}), \ldots, E_n(\mathbf{p})$ be a set of excess demand functions in an economy incorporating all the assumptions of Section 7.5. Suppose $E_1(\mathbf{p}) = A$ for all *strictly positive* price vectors, where A is a positive constant. Show that this implies either (i) at least one of the $E_i(\mathbf{p})$ must be discontinuous at some point, or (ii) at least one of the $E_i(\mathbf{p})$ must have the value $-\infty$ at some point. (Hint: use Walras' Law and examine behaviour as various prices go to zero.)

7.4 Consider the following excess demand function in a two-commodity economy:

$$E_1(\mathbf{p}) = 3\rho^2 - 2\rho - \rho^3 \quad \text{where} \quad \rho \equiv p_1/p_2$$

Find the other excess demand function $E_2(\mathbf{p})$. Sketch the excess demand function E_1. How many equilibria are there? Which of these are locally stable?

*7.5 The two individuals in a two-commodity exchange economy have utility functions

$$U^a(\mathbf{x}^a) = \log x_1^a + 2 \log x_2^a$$
$$U^b(\mathbf{x}^b) = 2 \log x_1^b + \log x_2^b$$

The property distribution is given by the endowments

$$\mathbf{R}^a = (9, 3)$$
$$\mathbf{R}^b = (12, 6)$$

Obtain the excess demand function for each good and verify that Walras' Law is true. Find the equilibrium price ratio. Given that the total resources available remain fixed at $\mathbf{R} = \mathbf{R}^a + \mathbf{R}^b = (21, 9)$, derive the contract curve.

7.6 Suppose there are 200 traders in a market all of whom behave as price takers. Suppose there are three goods and the traders own initially the following quantities.

100 of the traders own 10 units of good 1 each
50 of the traders own 5 units of good 2 each
50 of the traders own 20 units of good 3 each

All the traders have the utility function

$$U = x^{\frac{1}{3}}{}_1 x^{\frac{1}{3}}{}_2 x^{\frac{1}{3}}{}_3$$

What are the equilibrium relative prices of the three goods? Which group of traders has members who are the best off?

*7.7 Consider an exchange economy with two goods and three persons. Alf always demands equal quantities of the two goods. Bill's expenditure on good 1 is always twice his expenditure on good 2. Charlie never uses good 2.

Describe the indifference maps of the three individuals and suggest utility functions consistent with their behaviour.

If the original endowments are respectively (5, 0), (3, 6) and (0, 4), compute the equilibrium price ratio. What would be the effect on equilibrium prices and utility levels if (i) 4 extra units of good 1 were given to Alf; (ii) 4 units of good 1 were given to Charlie?

*7.8 In a two-person, two-commodity exchange economy the households have the following utility functions:

$$U^a(\mathbf{x}^a) = -\tfrac{1}{2}[x_1^a]^{-2} - \tfrac{1}{2}[x_2^a]^{-2}$$
$$U^b(\mathbf{x}^b) = x_1^b x_2^b$$

The property distribution is as follows: person a has $(R_1, 0)$; person b has $(0, R_2)$.

Assuming both persons act as price takers find their demand functions. How many equilibria does this system have? Find the equilibrium price ratio if $R_1 = 5$, $R_2 = 16$.

7.9 The economy consists of two types of people: capitalists and workers. All capitalists are identical and have the utility function:

$$U^a(x_1^a, x_2^a) = x_1^a x_2^a$$

All workers are identical and have the utility function:

$$U^b(x_1^b, L) = x_1^b - [L]^2$$

where L is the amount of labour that the worker supplies. The production constraint is

$$[y_1]^2 + [y_2]^2 = AL$$

where A is a constant. Find the equilibrium allocation of goods and the share of profits in total income. What would happen to this share if A increased?

7.10 In a two-person private ownership economy persons a and b have the indirect utility functions

$$V^h(p_1, p_2, M^h) = \log(M^h - p_1\beta_1^h - p_2\beta_2^h) - \tfrac{1}{2}\log p_1 p_2$$

where $h = a, b$ and the β_i^h are parameters. Find the equilibrium price ratio as a function of the property distribution ($\mathbf{R}^h$).

7.11 Construct a diagrammatic example of an exchange economy where the *same* equilibrium allocation $\boldsymbol{a}^*$ is generated for several different property distributions each yielding different equilibrium prices.

7.12 Prove Theorem 7.2.

8

Efficiency

8.1 The Pareto Criterion

We have already looked briefly at the issue of efficiency in several of the preceding chapters. Chapter 2 discussed the ideas of *technical* efficiency (being on the upper boundary of the technology set) and of economic efficiency in production (being at the right part of the boundary of the technology set). Implicit in Chapter 4's discussion of the rational consumer is the idea of an efficient allocation of the budget. And in the discussion of the core in Chapter 7 we had the idea of each participant avoiding wasteful allocations. We now want to generalise the ideas and put them in a formal and precise fashion. We also see how these separate ideas of efficiency fit in the more general context.

An efficient state of the economy can be described in an abstract way, without a detailed description of the economy's internal mechanisms. Let states of the economy be indexed by $\mathscr{s}$ – associated with $\mathscr{s}$ is a complete description of every single piece of relevant information about the economy. The only essential piece of equipment from previous chapters is the utility function U^h, $h = 1, 2, \ldots, H$. We assume that each household knows how well off it is given a state $\mathscr{s}$ (including an allowance for any possible externalities); so let the value of U^h given $\mathscr{s}$ be $u^h_{\mathscr{s}}$. Also let $\mathscr{S}$ be the set of all feasible states.

DEFINITION 8.1: for any two states $\mathscr{s}$, $\mathscr{s}'$, the state $\mathscr{s}$ is *Pareto superior* to the state $\mathscr{s}'$ if and only if

(1) for all households h: $u^h_{\mathscr{s}} \geqq u^h_{\mathscr{s}'}$
(2) for at least one household l: $u^l_{\mathscr{s}} > u^l_{\mathscr{s}'}$

If states are adequately described there is a clear presumption to reject as 'inefficient' any state $\mathscr{s}'$ when a Pareto superior alternative exists. This leads to a definition of efficiency.

DEFINITION 8.2: a state $\mathscr{s}$ is *Pareto efficient* if (i) $\mathscr{s} \in \mathscr{S}$, (ii) there is no other $\mathscr{s}' \in \mathscr{S}$ that is Pareto superior to $\mathscr{s}$.

Table 8.1 Essential notation for Chapter 8: Efficiency

$s \in \mathcal{S}$	:	social states
u^h_s	:	utility of household h in state s
x^h_i	:	consumption of good i by household h
y^f_i	:	net output of good i by firm f
$[\mathbf{x}^h]$	$\equiv$	$[\mathbf{x}^1, \mathbf{x}^2, \ldots, \mathbf{x}^H]$
$[\mathbf{y}^f]$	$\equiv$	$[\mathbf{y}^1, \mathbf{y}^2, \ldots, \mathbf{y}^F]$
a	$\equiv$	$([\mathbf{x}^h], [\mathbf{y}^f])$: an allocation
x_i	:	aggregate consumption of good i
y_i	:	aggregate net output of good i
R_i	:	total resource stock of good i

Call the vector $(u^1_s, \ldots, u^H_s)$ corresponding to such a s a Pareto efficient point. Clearly the set of Pareto efficient points form part of the boundary of the *utility possibility* set $\Upsilon = \{(u^1_s, \ldots, u^H_s) : s \in \mathcal{S}\}$, which is illustrated in Figure 8.1 where $H = 2$. Of course a Pareto efficient state need not be Pareto superior to an arbitrary Pareto inefficient state. Note that Υ, and hence the set of Pareto efficient points, can only be defined *with reference* to a particular $\mathcal{S}$. Alter $\mathcal{S}$ by changing the technology or the legal system, for example, and the set of Pareto efficient points will alter. The set of feasible social states thus depends on the resources available $\mathbf{R}$, on the technology Y and on any legal or other social constraints on the class of permissible pro-

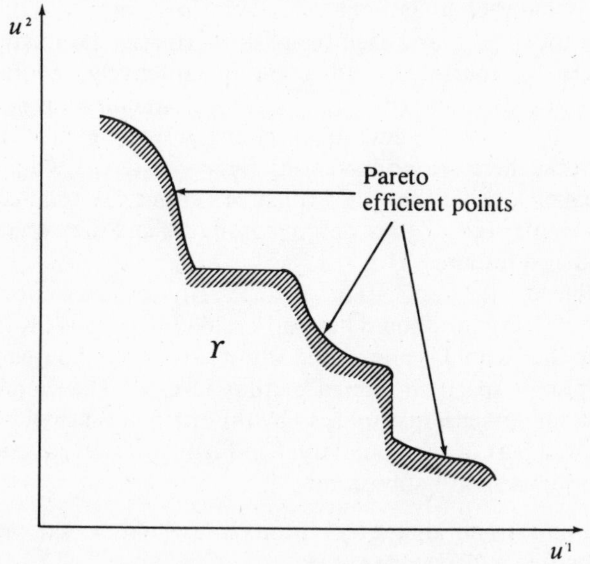

Figure 8.1

perty distributions $\mathscr{d}$. However other issues may be relevant too. For example the number of different social states that can be distinguished is clearly greater if one takes into account the consumption of each *individual person* rather than merely the consumption of household units, which has been our practice so far. Again, if households' utility functions have as arguments prices, along with quantities of consumption goods, then if the same competitive allocation $\mathscr{a}$ was consistent with, say, three distinct price vectors, we would have to count *three* distinct social states and not one.

Thus the set $\mathscr{S}$ is in principle much richer than the set $\mathscr{A}$ of all allocations $\mathscr{a}$ defined in Definition 7.1 of Chapter 7. Nevertheless, in order to keep the discussion to manageable proportions, we shall assume that $\mathscr{S}$ and $\mathscr{A}$ are identical. Thus we take it that any allocation $\mathscr{a} = ([\mathbf{x}^h], [\mathbf{y}^f])$ provides all the information that is needed about the corresponding social state and take as given the composition of the population, the list of firms, the technology Y and the vector of non-produced resources $\mathbf{R}$. We shall also suppose that, subject to these provisos, we may legitimately consider *any* property distribution $\mathscr{d}$.

8.2 Efficiency with Pure Private Goods

There are some very useful results obtainable just by considering private goods in isolation. Accordingly we shall defer discussion of public goods and of externalities in consumption and production until Sections 8.3 to 8.5. We shall assume that each household h has a concave-contoured differentiable utility function $U^h(\mathbf{x}^h)$, and each firm f has a concave production function $\Phi^f(\mathbf{y}^f)$ where of course $\mathbf{x}^h$ and $\mathbf{y}^f$ are, respectively, consumption by household h of the n goods $(h = 1, \ldots, H)$ and net output by firm f of the n goods $(f = 1, \ldots, F)$. These assumptions ensure 'regular' indifference curves and that there are *no* increasing returns to scale. We also need the materials balance condition (7.4) which constrains the total consumption possible given the vector of net outputs produced and the exogenous vector of non-produced resources $\mathbf{R}$.

Now consider the application of the Pareto efficiency criterion in such an economy. Clearly we should have a Pareto efficient state if the utility of one arbitrary household is maximised whilst every other household h is kept on or above some specified reference utility level $\bar{u}^h$. The exercise could be repeated for any other household, so by this method we shall indeed arrive on the required part of the boundary Υ in Figure 8.1. Let us then maximise the utility of household 1 subject to:

(a) the constraint that every other household be on or above the specified indifference curve:

$$U^h(\mathbf{x}^h) \geqslant \bar{u}^h, \quad h = 2, \ldots, H \tag{8.1}$$

(b) the condition that the output of every firm f is technically feasible:

$$\Phi^f(\mathbf{y}^f) \leqslant 0, \quad f = 1, \ldots, F \tag{8.2}$$

(c) the materials balance condition holds for every good i

$$\sum_{h=1}^{H} x_i^h \leqslant \sum_{f=1}^{F} y_i^f + R_i, \quad i = 1, \ldots, n \tag{8.3}$$

where of course the vector $\mathbf{R}$ is exogenously fixed. For expositional convenience we shall for the moment assume that all the U^h and Φ^f are differentiable; though the argument can be generalised, it becomes a little cumbersome.

$$\begin{aligned}\mathscr{L}([\mathbf{x}^h], [\mathbf{y}^f], \lambda, \mu, \nu) = U^1(\mathbf{x}^1) &+ \sum_{h=2}^{H} \lambda_h [U^h(\mathbf{x}^h) - \bar{u}^h] \\ &- \sum_{f=1}^{F} \mu_f \Phi^f(\mathbf{y}^f) \\ &+ \sum_{i=1}^{n} \nu_i [R_i + y_i - x_i]\end{aligned} \tag{8.4}$$

where $y_i \equiv \sum_{f=1}^{F} y_i^f$, $x_i \equiv \sum_{h=1}^{H} x_i^h$ and $\lambda_2, \ldots, \lambda_H, \mu_1, \ldots, \mu_F, \nu_1, \ldots, \nu_n$ are Lagrange multipliers associated with constraints (8.1), (8.2), (8.3).

Maximising $\mathscr{L}$ with respect to $[\mathbf{x}^h]$, $[\mathbf{y}^f]$, λ, μ and ν we find the first-order conditions:

$$x_i^h \frac{\partial \mathscr{L}}{\partial x_i^h} = x_i^h [\lambda_h U_i^h - \nu_i] = 0, i = 1, \ldots, n; h = 1, \ldots, H \tag{8.5}$$

$$y_i^f \frac{\partial \mathscr{L}}{\partial y_i^f} = y_i^f [-\mu_f \Phi_i^f + \nu_i] = 0, \; i = 1, \ldots, n; f = 1, \ldots, F \tag{8.6}$$

$$\lambda_h \frac{\partial \mathscr{L}}{\partial \lambda_h} = \lambda_h [U^h(\mathbf{x}^h) - \bar{u}^h] = 0, \; h = 2, \ldots, H \tag{8.7}$$

$$\mu_f \frac{\partial \mathscr{L}}{\partial u_f} = \mu_f \Phi^f(\mathbf{y}^f) = 0, f = 1, \ldots, F \tag{8.8}$$

$$\nu_i \frac{\partial \mathscr{L}}{\partial \nu_i} = \nu_i [R_i + y_i - x_i] = 0, \; i = 1, \ldots, n \tag{8.9}$$

where subscripts on U^h and Φ^f denote the relevant partial derivatives, and for presentational convenience we have introduced a dummy variable $\lambda_1 = 1$ in equation (8.5). Let us now interpret these conditions.

Firstly consider a commodity that is consumed in positive amounts by some household that is not satiated at the efficient allocation. From (8.5) we see that, in view of the fact that $\lambda_h > 0$, if x_i^h and U_i^h are positive then ν_i must be positive. Hence, if $\nu_i > 0$, (8.9) reveals that $x_i = y_i + R_i$; so we have the common-sense rule that if good i is scarce ($U_i^h > 0$ for some h) stocks of good i should not stand idle. Moreover if we take a *pair* of goods i, j that are consumed in positive amounts[1] (8.5) yields

$$\lambda_h U_i^h = \nu_i \tag{8.10}$$

$$\lambda_h U_j^h = \nu_j \tag{8.11}$$

independently of h. Recalling the definition of the marginal rate of substitution of good j for good i (Definition 4.3) on dividing (8.11) by (8.10), we find for any household h:

$$\text{MRS}_{ij}^h = \frac{U_j^h}{U_i^h} = \frac{\nu_j}{\nu_i} \tag{8.12}$$

Next consider a firm that is producing or using at least one scarce good i. If $x_i > 0$, $\Phi_i^f > 0$ for at least one i in firm f, then obviously $\mu_f > 0$. So, from (8.8) we see that we ought to have $\Phi^f(\mathbf{y}^f) = 0$. Hence Pareto efficiency requires technical efficiency in production on the part of every 'active' firm – again a common-sense rule. Again consider any *pair* of goods i and j for which the net output of firm f is non-zero. From (8.6) we find

$$\mu_f \Phi_i^f = \nu_i \tag{8.13}$$

$$\mu_f \Phi_j^f = \nu_j \tag{8.14}$$

Using Definition 2.3, on dividing (8.13) by (8.14) we find for any firm f:

$$\text{MRT}_{ij}^f = \frac{\Phi_j^f}{\Phi_i^f} = \frac{\nu_j}{\nu_i} \tag{8.15}$$

Now, notice that the right-hand side of (8.12) and (8.15) is an identical constant *independent* of the household index h or the firm index f. Hence we immediately find the result:

THEOREM 8.1: in a Pareto efficient state without externalities for any pair of pure private goods i and j that are consumed by each household and produced by each firm:

$$\text{MRS}_{ij}^1 = \text{MRS}_{ij}^2 = \ldots = \text{MRS}_{ij}^H = \frac{\nu_j}{\nu_i}$$

$$= \text{MRT}_{ij}^1 = \text{MRT}_{ij}^2 = \ldots = \text{MRT}_{ij}^F \tag{8.16}$$

---

[1] Of course if $x_i^h = 0$ we may have $\lambda_h U_i^h < \nu_i$, and a simple modification may be made to the results summarised in Theorem 8.1 – see Exercise 8.5.

Everywhere households' marginal rates of substitution and firms' marginal rates of transformation are the same. This, of course, is exactly the same property that characterises the competitive equilibrium allocation – see Section 7.7 – and the ratio v_j/v_i is in effect a ratio of shadow efficiency prices. The 'consumer price ratios' (MRS) should everywhere be equal to 'producer price ratios' (MRT). In fact we can state a somewhat stronger result which imposes no requirement of differentiability on utility or production functions. The proof is left as Exercise 8.8.

THEOREM 8.2: if consumers are non-satiated, in a private ownership economy, without externalities and consisting entirely of pure private goods, then for any property distribution $\mathscr{d}$, any competitive equilibrium allocation is Pareto efficient.

So, in the very special circumstances of a pure private economy, competitive equilibrium must be Pareto efficient. This is illustrated in the case of the exchange economy in Figure 7.7 of Chapter 7. For, consider what the set of Pareto efficient allocations must be in this model: fix household a's utility at an arbitrary level $\overline{u}^a$; now keeping a on the given indifference curve $\overline{u}^a$, maximise b's utility; one obviously ends up on the contract curve. Hence in the exchange economy it is the contract curve itself which forms the set of Pareto efficient allocations. We know that the core is a subset of the contract curve and that the competitive equilibrium allocation, if it exists, must lie in the core.

However Theorem 8.2 says only that *if* for a *given* property distribution $\mathscr{d}$ there happens to exist a competitive equilibrium $\mathscr{a}^*$, then $\mathscr{a}^*$ must be Pareto efficient. A second, and perhaps more interesting, question is as follows. In any economy pick an arbitrary Pareto efficient allocation $\hat{\mathscr{a}}$: then, given the total stock of resources $\mathbf{R}$, can one find *some* property distribution $\hat{\mathscr{d}}$ such that $\hat{\mathscr{a}}$ could be attained as a competitive equilibrium? In the jargon, can *any* Pareto efficient allocation be 'supported' by a competitive equilibrium? If two additional assumptions are introduced then indeed this is possible.

THEOREM 8.3: if the conditions of Theorem 8.2 hold; and if (i) the technology set of each firm is convex, (ii) if consumers are greedy and have concave-contoured utility functions, then any Pareto efficient allocation $\hat{\mathscr{a}}$ in which $\hat{x}_i^h > 0$ for all h and i can be supported by a competitive equilibrium.

The detail of the proof is relegated to Appendix A, but the outline of the method of proof is as follows. What is needed is to prove the existence of a price vector $\hat{\mathbf{p}}$ such that for some property distribution $\hat{\mathscr{d}}$ each household maximises its utility exactly at the point $\hat{\mathbf{x}}^h$ (using of course the prices $\hat{\mathbf{p}}$ in its budget contraint); also that if each firm uses these prices it maximises profits exactly at $\hat{\mathbf{y}}^f$. To do this one again needs a version of the 'separating hyperplane' theorem that we applied in Theorem 5.1 of Chapter 5. Of course

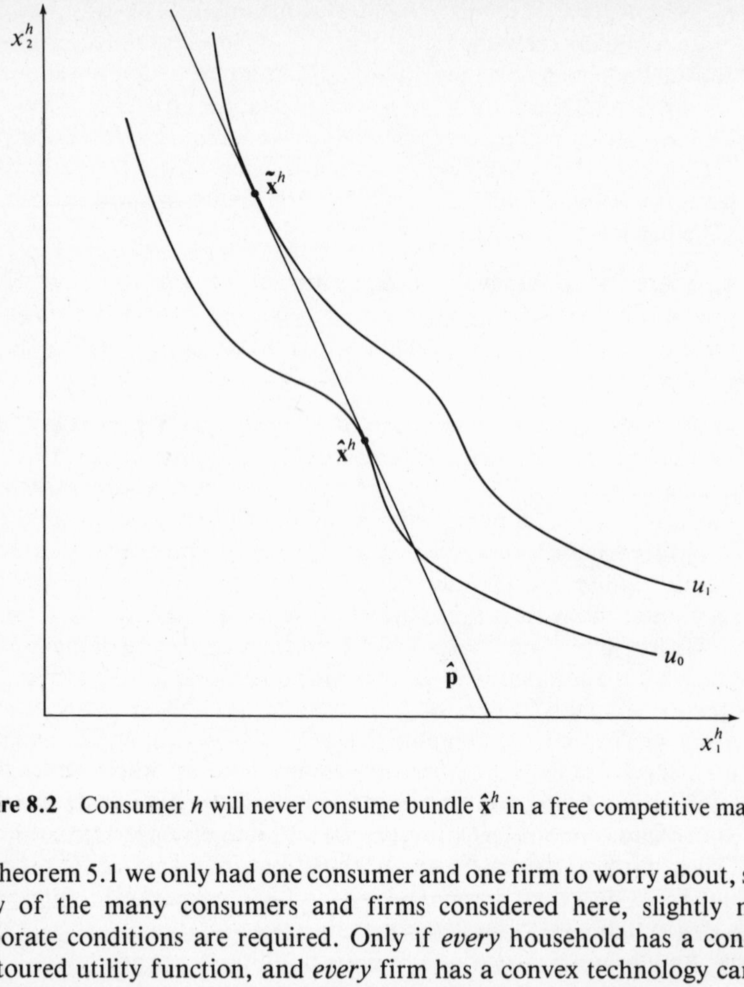

Figure 8.2 Consumer h will never consume bundle $\hat{\mathbf{x}}^h$ in a free competitive market

in Theorem 5.1 we only had one consumer and one firm to worry about, so in view of the many consumers and firms considered here, slightly more elaborate conditions are required. Only if *every* household has a concave contoured utility function, and *every* firm has a convex technology can we *always* be sure that such a separating hyperplane exists. For, otherwise, consider Figures 8.2 and 8.3: if the selected Pareto efficient allocation happens to require household h and firm f to be at the points $\hat{\mathbf{x}}^h$, $\hat{\mathbf{y}}^f$ shown, it is just not possible to 'persuade' them to go there using prices $\hat{\mathbf{p}}$; if faced with the prices $\hat{\mathbf{p}}$ they choose $\tilde{\mathbf{x}}^h$ and $\tilde{\mathbf{y}}^f$ instead.

Consider the implications of Theorem 8.3. If, for whatever reason, a particular Pareto efficient allocation with positive consumption is considered 'desirable', then this can apparently be achieved in a 'convex economy' in two steps: (a) rearrange the property distribution by legal decree, 'lump-sum' taxation or revolution; (b) allow competition to take place amongst all agents. Other than the property redistribution no government intervention is needed. The implications of this for government policy are considered further in Chapter 13; but notice straightaway that attainment of

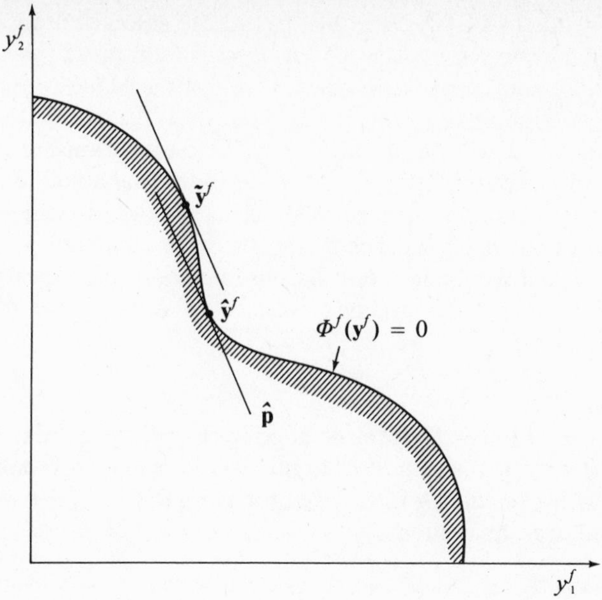

Figure 8.3 Firm f will never produce at $\hat{\mathbf{y}}^f$ in a free competitive market

$\hat{a}$ through this mechanism may be impeded if there are informational, ethical, administrative or political reasons inhibiting the redistribution of property needed to reach $\hat{a}$. Next notice that even if $\hat{a}$ cannot be supported by a competitive equilibrium in a particular economy, it might be possible to support it in an economy that is very similar. For example suppose firms 1 and 2 had production sets Y^1 and Y^2 illustrated in Figure 6.1; firm 1's production set is clearly non-convex and so certain Pareto efficient allocations may appear to be unattainable through the competitive mechanism. Now let firms 1 and 2 merge: as one can see in Figure 6.1 the *combined* production set is convex, so decentralisation of any particular allocation now becomes possible in the modified economy with some of the firms merged.

8.3 Non-rivalness and Efficiency

To restrict one's attention solely to economies in which there are pure private goods is, of course, terribly restrictive. As we noted in Chapter 6, Section 6.3, there are two principal features of economic goods which need to be examined in more depth: the extent of their 'rivalness', and the extent of their 'excludability'. Pure private goods – absolutely rival and absolutely excludable – appear only at one end of a very complex spectrum. In this section we shall see what modifications to our earlier work need to be made when non-rivalness is considered. We continue to assume the absence of production and consumption externalities (hence we continue to assume excludability) and we continue to assume concave-contoured utility functions and convex production sets.

'Rivalness', it will be recalled, refers to the relationship between the *aggregate* consumption of a good x_i and the individual household consumptions $x_i^1, x_i^2, \ldots, x_i^H$. For convenience, let us take the first $n-1$ goods to be pure private (hence rival) goods: this does not entail any serious loss of generality since it will be seen that the ensuing argument is easily applied to as many non-rival goods as one wishes. Now consider the nth good. In general we have

$$x_n = \Xi^n (x_n^1, x_n^2, \ldots, x_n^H) \tag{8.17}$$

– compare equation (6.3). If the nth good were a private good then of course Ξ^n would simply be the sum of its arguments. The materials balance condition (8.3) whilst remaining unchanged for every $i = 1, \ldots, n-1$ must, for the nth good, now be written

$$\Xi^n (x_n^1, \ldots, x_n^H) \leqslant \sum_{f=1}^{F} y_n^f + R_n \tag{8.18}$$

Now let us look again at the conditions for efficiency in (8.5) to (8.9). Clearly very little has altered: all we need to do is to re-evaluate the marginal conditions where the nth good is involved. As before equation (8.6) holds for good n:

$$y_n^f \frac{\partial \mathscr{L}}{\partial y_n^f} = y_n^f [-\mu_f \Phi_n^f + \nu_n] = 0, f = 1, \ldots, F \tag{8.19}$$

However equation (8.5) no longer holds. Take the case of a *pure non-rival good* where we have:

$$x_n = \Xi^n (x_n^1, \ldots, x_n^H) = \max_h \{x_n^1, \ldots, x_n^H\} \tag{8.20}$$

– cf. equation 6.5. Obviously in this case if, for some household h we have $x_n^h < x_n$ and yet $U_n^h > 0$, then a Pareto superior allocation can be attained by allowing household h's consumption of good n to increase (as long as x_n^h is strictly less than x_n no additional resources have to be used up to increase h's consumption of this non-rival good, so we might as well let household h increase its own utility since it will not thereby reduce any one else's utility). Therefore at the Pareto efficient allocation for each household h *either* (i) $x_n^h = x_n$, so that the household is consuming the non-rival good to its maximum capacity, *or* (ii) $x_n^h < x_n$ and $U_n^h = 0$ so that the household is consuming less than it could, but is satiated with good n. So everyone who is non-satiated (households $1, \ldots, h^*$, let us say) must consume exactly the same amount at a Pareto efficient allocation. Thus we put $x_n^h = x_n$, $h = 1, \ldots, h^*$ in equation (8.4). Differentiate (8.4) with respect to x_n and set it equal to zero:

$$\sum_{h=1}^{h^*} \lambda_h U_n^h - v_n = 0 \tag{8.21}$$

But, by definition, households $h^* + 1, h^* + 2, \ldots, H$ are satiated, so for each of them $U_n^h = 0$. Hence we may rewrite (8.21) as

$$\sum_{h=1}^{H} \lambda_h U_n^h = v_n \tag{8.22}$$

Now pick any other pure private good i that is being consumed in positive amounts by everyone: we know that (8.10) must hold. So, divide (8.22) by (8.10) and we get

$$\sum_{h=1}^{H} U_n^h / U_i^h = v_n / v_i \tag{8.23}$$

But of course from (8.15) we have

$$\Phi_n^f / \Phi_i^f = v_n / v_i, f = 1, \ldots, F \tag{8.24}$$

So we find:

THEOREM 8.4: in a Pareto efficient state without externalities for any pure private good i consumed by everyone and a non-rival good n we have:

$$\text{MRS}_{in}^1 + \text{MRS}_{in}^2 + \ldots + \text{MRS}_{in}^H = \frac{v_n}{v_i} \tag{8.25}$$
$$= \text{MRT}_{in}^f, \quad f = 1, \ldots, F$$

Contrast this with the result for two pure private goods (8.16). There we equate the MRS for *each* household to the MRT; here we *sum* the MRS for all households and equate *that* to the MRT.

Other intermediate cases could of course be constructed. If Ξ^n was differentiable, instead of (8.5) or (8.21) we would have the result

$$x_n^h \frac{\partial \mathscr{L}}{\partial x_n^h} = x_n^h \left[\lambda_h U_n^h - v_n \frac{\partial \Xi^n}{\partial x_n^h} \right] = 0 \tag{8.26}$$

but the resulting rule on the MRSs and MRTs will of course be more complicated.

8.4 Externalities and Efficiency

We shall deal with production externalities first and then consider cases where there are non-excludable goods – externalities in consumption.

In the case of production externalities condition (8.6) obviously no longer holds. To see what modification needs to be made, let us suppose that the output of good 1 from firm 1 affects the technology set of every other firm *directly*. It might be, for example, that firm 1 is a glue factory. The noxious fumes from this factory would have to be filtered by other firms round about so that their workers are not nauseated by the smell. The more glue firm 1 produces, the more inputs the other firms have to use up in cleaning and filtering. However, whether the externality is positive or negative we shall continue to assume, throughout this section, that the *aggregate* technology set is convex. Accordingly, let the net output from firm 1 of good 1 enter the production function of every other firm, and let each Φ^f be concave in $\mathbf{y}^f$. We have

$$\Phi^f(\mathbf{y}^f; y_1^1) \equiv \Phi^f(y_1^f, y_2^f, \ldots, y_n^f; y_1^1) \leqslant 0 \quad f = 2, \ldots, F \tag{8.27}$$

as the production constraint. Introducing (8.27) into (8.4) and examining once again the conditions for an interior maximum, we find that (8.5), (8.7), (8.8) and (8.9) still hold, and that (8.6) holds for all f and $i = 2, 3, \ldots, n$, and for $i = 1$ and $f = 2, 3, \ldots, F$. For $i = f = 1$, instead of (8.6) we have:

$$y_1^1 \left[- \sum_{f=1}^{F} \mu_f \frac{\partial \Phi^f(\mathbf{y}^f; y_1^1)}{\partial y_1^1} + \nu_1 \right] = 0 \tag{8.28}$$

For convenience let us assume that $y_1^1 > 0$, and write $e_1^f \equiv -\partial \Phi^f(\mathbf{y}^f; y_1^1)/\partial y_1^1$ for $f = 2, 3, \ldots, F$, the *external effect* of a change in output y_1^1 on the production constraint of firm f. We then find, instead of (8.15):

$$\frac{\Phi_1^1}{\Phi_i^f} - \sum_{f=2}^{F} \frac{e_1^f}{\Phi_i^f} = \frac{\nu_1}{\nu_i} \tag{8.29}$$

for any other commodity i. So, suppose commodities 1 and i are each outputs, and that $e_1^f < 0$ for each f: the production of an additional unit of good 1 impedes the production of other goods. Then clearly the optimal solution for firm 1, producing the externality is to have $\mathrm{MRT}_{i1}^1 < \dfrac{\nu_1}{\nu_i} = \mathrm{MRS}_{i1}$; hence less of good 1 will be produced at the efficient point than if the externality e_1^f did not exist – see Figure 8.4.

Now let us consider consumption externalities. As noted in Section 6.3 of Chapter 6 this can be done by a simple modification which allows the consumption of one household directly to affect the utility of others. Clearly there are several ways of doing this; consider the following alternatives to writing $U^h = U^h(\mathbf{x}^h)$.

(i) Suppose the consumption of good j by any household l directly affects the utility of household h: household l might be a smoker

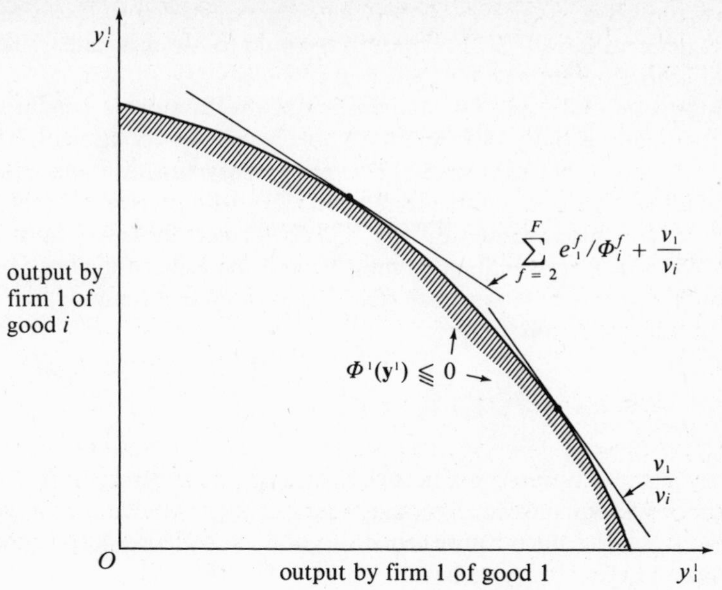

Figure 8.4

and household h an asthmatic non-smoker. We would then write:

$$U^h = U^h(\mathbf{x}^h; x_j^1, x_j^2, \ldots, x_j^H) \tag{8.30}$$

where presumably $\partial U^h/\partial x_j^l < 0$ for any $l \neq h$.

(ii) The *living standard* of every other household l might affect the utility of household h: for example the person may be upset or delighted by the amount of income inequality he perceives. We could let the utility level of each other household enter as an argument to household h's utility function. Alternatively, in a market economy we might adopt an equivalent approach by introducing the money measure of any household's utility $M^l = C^l(\mathbf{p}, u^l)$ where $C^l(.,.)$ is the cost function of household l, and M^l is its money income. We then may write

$$U^h = U^h(\mathbf{x}^h; M^1, M^2, \ldots, M^H) \tag{8.31}$$

(iii) More generally the entire allocation $\mathscr{a}$ may shift household h's utility function. This could occur if there were 'bandwagon effects' whereby the shape of one's indifference curves is modified by other people's consumption choices. We would then write simply:

$$U^h = U^h(\mathbf{x}^h; \mathscr{a}) \tag{8.32}$$

Several other specific examples could be expounded. Let us just consider in detail example (i), since the others would follow in a similar manner, but with more notational complexity.

Substitute (8.30) in (8.4) and work out the first-order conditions as before. Equations (8.6), (8.8) and (8.9) hold as before, equation (8.7) holds with the minor modification (8.30) to each utility function and equation (8.5) holds for every good other than good j. So, let us look at the remaining first-order condition, namely $\partial \mathscr{L}/\partial x_j^h$. Since x_j^h enters the utility function of household h as a conventional argument, and the utility function of *every* household $l = 1, \ldots, H$ as an external effect we find that for good j we have, instead of (8.5) the condition:

$$x_j^h \frac{\partial \mathscr{L}}{\partial x_j^h} = x_j^h \left[\sum_{l=1}^{H} \lambda_l \frac{\partial U^l}{\partial x_j^h} - v_j \right] = 0$$

Obviously if there were no externality $\partial U^l/\partial x_j^h$ would be zero for every $l \neq h$ and would equal U_j^h for $l = h$ and so this equation would then simplify to (8.5). Now, taking any other pure private good i that is consumed in positive amounts and using (8.5), we have:

$$\sum_{l=1}^{H} \frac{\partial U^l}{\partial x_j^h} \bigg/ U_i^l = \frac{v_j}{v_i} \tag{8.33}$$

or equivalently

$$\frac{U_j^h}{U_i^h} + \sum_{l \neq h} \frac{\partial U^l}{\partial x_j^h} \bigg/ U_i^l = \frac{v_j}{v_i} \tag{8.34}$$

Compare (8.33) and (8.34) with equations (8.12) and (8.29). Note that the first term on the left-hand side of (8.34) is MRS_{ij}^h. So the rule now is that the MRS of each household *adjusted for the marginal externalities imposed on each of the other households* (the second term in (8.34)) should equal v_j/v_i which in turn equals the MRT. This is obviously very similar to the case of the production externality in equation (8.29).

Alternatively, we could interpret the rule using the equivalent expression (8.33). Take an interesting special case here. Suppose the external effect was everywhere *positive* (so I get direct benefit from your consuming more of good j) and in particular that $\partial U^l/\partial x_j^h$ equals U_j^l for *all* l and h (so I get as much benefit from a marginal increase in *your* consumption of good j as I do from a marginal increment in my own consumption). Then in this special case (8.33) immediately yields:

$$\sum_{l=1}^{H} \text{MRS}_{ij}^l = v_j/v_i \tag{8.35}$$

But this is the same rule as (8.25). In fact we have now analysed the case of a *pure public* good (see Section 6.3 of Chapter 6). A public good of course is (i) absolutely non-rival – as in the last section; and (ii) absolutely non-excludable – as in the special case just described.

So, to summarise, we find that for pure private goods the efficiency rule implies the equation of *each* household's MRS to the MRT, but for a pure public good it is the *sum* of each household's MRS that is equalled to the MRT. Of course other less extreme cases can be discussed in exactly the same way using conditions such as (8.33) or (8.34).

8.5 Non-convexities and Efficiency

Non-convexities *need* not raise problems for the efficiency rules, but they might. For, if a competitive equilibrium exists, as long as there are no externalities we know from Theorem 8.2 that it must be efficient.

However, we may not in general be able to take comfort in Theorem 8.2, if the aggregate technology set is non-convex – i.e. if there are somewhere increasing returns in the economy as a whole. This is apparent from the more restrictive requirements of Theorem 8.3. One of the principal difficulties is that the first-order conditions of (8.5) to (8.9) are no longer sufficient to ensure a maximum of $\mathscr{L}$: so there may be lots of local maxima, because of the non-convexity of the problem and of course many of these will not be global maxima, so they will not correspond to efficient allocations.

To see the problem consider a simple two-good example in Figure 8.5. Here good 1 exhibits substantial fixed costs – i.e. a large lump of good 2 has to be given up to get the first unit of good 1 and thereafter only small sacrifices of good 2 need to be made for additional units of good 1. Clearly the corresponding production possibility frontier drawn in Figure 8.5 implies that the technology set is non-convex (in other words the production function $\Phi(\mathbf{y})$ is non-concave). Furthermore, let us suppose that all consumers are identical clones so that we need only draw one representative set of indifference curves.

Three of the possible outcomes are illustrated in Figure 8.5. The efficient state in case (i) – point A – is much the same as if the non-convexity in the production set were not present. With a slight shift in preferences, however, the efficient state becomes point B, even though A is still a point of tangency – see case (ii). Finally, for a further shift in preferences, states A and B are regarded as indifferent – case (iii). Notice, however, that whenever it is efficient to produce the good in positive amounts (at point A) then the marginal rule MRS = MRT will hold.

Hence in the case of fixed cost there is a two-part rule as follows: (1) experiment to see whether individual utilities would be higher at a positive production point such as A or at a zero production point, such as B. (2) if it is

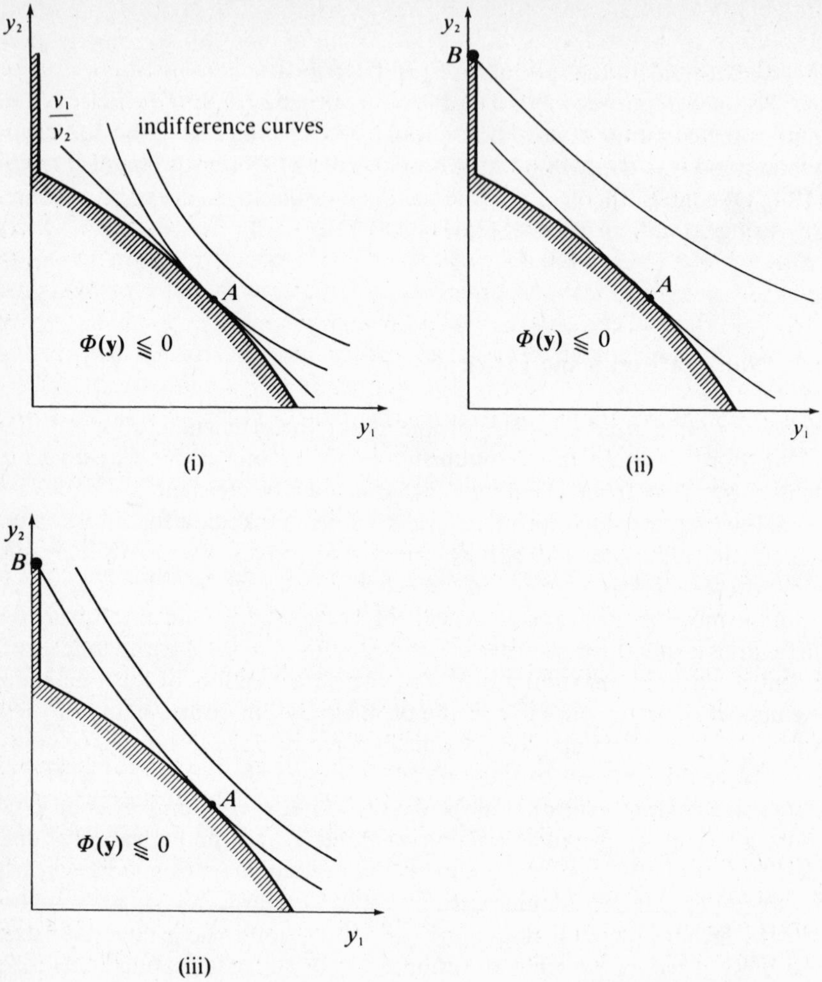

Figure 8.5

decided to produce, then select A such that the marginal rules (8.16) are satisfied.

There remain two final problems. The first is that one has yet to specify *how* A is to be implemented: competitive firms would make a loss at that point, and a monopolist (as we know from Section 3.8) will set a price *above* marginal cost, which will violate (8.16); we return to this point in Section 12.5 of Chapter 12. The second problem is that, in practice, when one compares A and B in a heterogeneous population some people will have higher utility at A, and some will have higher utility at B, so that step (1) may become a rather complex one: see Sections 12.6 and 13.3 in Chapters 12 and 13 for further discussion.

8.6 Waste

The observation (on p. 163 above) that the efficiency conditions for an economy can be simply stated in terms of 'prices' for households and for firms prompts a further question. Granted that the real world is very probably inefficient, can one quantify how far away from efficiency the actual state of the economy is?

To begin with an answer to this let us return to the analysis of measuring welfare changes in Section 4.7 of Chapter 4. The concepts of compensating variation and equivalent variation provide a natural way of measuring the effects of price changes on a particular household's welfare. It may be that we can use this analysis to provide an *aggregate* measure of waste in the economy if (i) one can specify the appropriate 'reference' state of the economy with which one wishes to compare the actual distorted economy; (ii) the analysis is modified to take into account the feedbacks through the price system of any hypothetical adjustment of one price, and (iii) one has an agreed system of aggregating the effects on individual households.

For the sake of simplicity of exposition, let us take as one point of reference a private ownership economy without externalities that, for a given property distribution $\mathscr{d}$, has a unique competitive equilibrium with prices $(p_1^*, \ldots, p_n^*)$. In fact we do not observe this equilibrium, because the economy has been distorted. Suppose, for example, that the consumer price of good 1 has been deliberately forced above marginal cost of good 1 (so that $\text{MRS}_{i1} > \text{MRT}_{i1}$) by a factor $1+\tau$ – this might be due to an *ad valorem* tax on good 1 or a mark up on costs by firms producing good 1, for example. This will have repercussions in at least two ways. First, the excess of consumer price over marginal costs means that there is a surplus to be distributed: for convenience we shall assume that this surplus is distributed to shareholders in the firms along with other profit income. Second, in a market clearing system, prices of *other* goods will also be shifted away from their competitive equilibrium levels. Let us suppose that we actually observe the consumer prices $(p_1, p_2, \ldots, p_n)$ and producer prices $(\tilde{p}_1, \tilde{p}_2, \ldots, \tilde{p}_n)$ where $\tilde{p}_1 = p_1/[1+\tau]$ and $\tilde{p}_i = p_i$, $i = 2, 3, \ldots, n$; we suppose that all prices are positive and that all markets clear. Write the deviations from the reference prices as $\Delta p_i = p_i - p_i^*$, $i = 1, \ldots, n$. Note that we have

$$\text{MRS}_{ij} = \frac{p_j}{p_i} \text{ for all } i \text{ and } j$$

$$\begin{cases} \text{MRT}_{i1} = \dfrac{p_1/[1+\tau]}{p_i} \\[2ex] \text{MRT}_{ij} = \dfrac{p_j}{p_i}, \; j \neq 1 \end{cases}$$

Write the factor income accruing to household h from its ownership of resources $\mathbf{R}^h$ and its shares in firms $\mathbf{s}^h$ as M^h in the observed state and as M^{*h} in the reference competitive equilibrium: remember that the property distribution $\mathcal{d}$ is the same in each state.

Consider the transformation of the economy from the (unobserved) undistorted reference state to the observed, distorted state. For each household we may write down the *equivalent variation* for this transformation. This may be expressed

$$\mathrm{EV}^h = [C^h(\mathbf{p}^*, u^h) - M^{*h}] - [C^h(\mathbf{p}, u^h) - M^h] \tag{8.36}$$

The expression in the first set of brackets is the net income adjustment that household h would require to achieve its observed utility level u^h if the prices and factor incomes were at their undistorted values $\mathbf{p}^*$, M^{*h}. The expression in the second set of brackets is the net income adjustment that h would require to achieve the observed utility level u^h given that prices and factor income are their observed values $\mathbf{p}$, M^h: this term must be zero since by definition $M^h = C^h(\mathbf{p}, u^h)$.

Now let us evaluate the loss for the economy as a whole. There are many ways of doing this, but a simple way of illustrating the principles involved is simply to use $(-)\ \Sigma_h \mathrm{EV}^h$, the (negative of the) sum of the individual equivalent variations i.e. the sum of the *compensating* variations from the status quo to the reference state. This gives us a measure of loss:

$$\Lambda = \Sigma_h [C^h(\mathbf{p}, u^h) - C^h(\mathbf{p}^*, u^h) - M^h + M^{*h}] \tag{8.37}$$

To help evaluate Λ let us recall three points from previous chapters. First recall[2] Shephard's Lemma: that if we differentiate the consumer's cost function $C^h(\mathbf{p}, u^h)$ with respect to p_i, we find $C_i^h(\mathbf{p}, u^h) = \hat{D}^{hi}(\mathbf{p}, u^h) = x_i^h$, the consumer's compensated demand for good i; likewise if we differentiate $\Sigma_{i=1}^n \tilde{p}_i y_i^f(\tilde{\mathbf{p}})$, the profits for firm f, with respect to $\tilde{p}_i$, we obtain simply y_i^f, the net output of good i by firm f. Second,[3] recall that the household's compensated demands have the property that $\Sigma_{i=1}^n \Sigma_{j=1}^n w_i w_j \hat{D}_j^{hi} \leqslant 0$ for arbitrary weights $(w_1, w_2, \ldots, w_n)$; likewise for the firm we find $\Sigma_{i=1}^n \Sigma_{j=1}^n w_i w_j S_{ij} \geqslant 0$ where $S_{ij} \equiv \partial y_i(\tilde{\mathbf{p}})/\partial \tilde{p}_j$. Third, note that in a private ownership economy the income of household h may be written down as[4]

$$M^h = \Sigma_i p_i \left[R_i^h + \sum_{f=1}^{F} s_f^h y_i^f \right] \tag{8.38}$$

where the terms on the right-hand side represent the valuation of the household's resource endowment and its share in profit income of each firm.

---

[2] See Theorem 4.2 and Exercise 3.7.
[3] See p. 76 of Chapter 4 and p. 49 of Chapter 3.
[4] See equations (7.8)–(7.10) of Chapter 7.

Writing $p_i^* = p_i - \Delta p_i = \tilde{p}_i - \Delta\tilde{p}_i$ we may then express (8.37) as

$$\Lambda(\Delta\mathbf{p}) = \Sigma_h [C^h(\mathbf{p}, u^h) - C^h(\mathbf{p} - \Delta\mathbf{p}, u^h)] - \Sigma_i [R_i\Delta p_i + y_i(\tilde{\mathbf{p}})p_i - y_i(\tilde{\mathbf{p}} - \Delta\tilde{\mathbf{p}})[\tilde{p}_i - \Delta\tilde{p}_i]] \quad (8.39)$$

where the last term represents $-M^h + M^{*h}$ and follows from (8.38) and the observation that $\Sigma_h s_f^h = 1$. We may now evaluate Λ by using a Taylor expansion:

$$\Lambda(\Delta\mathbf{p}) = \Lambda(\mathbf{0}) + \Sigma_i\Lambda_i(\mathbf{0})\Delta p_i + \tfrac{1}{2}\Sigma_i\Sigma_j\Lambda_{ij}(\mathbf{0})\Delta p_i\Delta p_j + \ldots \quad (8.40)$$

where $\Lambda_i(\mathbf{0})$ denotes $\partial\Lambda/\partial\Delta p_i$ evaluated at $\Delta p_i = 0, i = 1, \ldots, n$. Ignoring the small higher terms, and noting that $\Lambda(\mathbf{0}) = 0$, we find that the Taylor expansion on (8.39) yields

$$\Lambda(\Delta\mathbf{p}) \simeq \Sigma_i [x_i - R_i - y_i]\Delta p_i - \tfrac{1}{2}\Sigma_i\Sigma_j [\Sigma_h C_{ij}^h(\mathbf{p}, u^h)\Delta p_i\Delta p_j + \tfrac{1}{2}S_{ij}(\tilde{\mathbf{p}})\Delta\tilde{p}_i\Delta\tilde{p}_j] \quad (8.41)$$

where the first term follows from the application of Shephard's Lemma noted above and the observation that $x_i = \Sigma_h x_i^h$; in view of the market clearing conditions this term must be zero. So (8.41) simplifies to

$$\Lambda(\Delta\mathbf{p}) = -\tfrac{1}{2}\Sigma_i\Sigma_j\Sigma_h\hat{D}_j^{hi}(\mathbf{p}, u^h)\Delta p_i\Delta p_j + \tfrac{1}{2}\Sigma_i\Sigma_j S_{ij}\Delta\tilde{p}_i\Delta\tilde{p}_j \quad (8.42)$$

This is non-negative in view of the properties of $\hat{D}_j^{hi}$ and S_{ij} discussed above.

The loss in (8.42) is composed of two parts, the first being attributable to substitution effects of each household for each good in response to the price changes, $\hat{D}_j^{hi}$, the second being due to the supply responses $\partial y_i/\partial p_j$. Clearly the more elastic compensated demand is (and the more elastic supply is) the greater will be the loss. This has a simple interpretation in the case where the effects on markets other than good 1 are so small as to be negligible. Suppose that the economy is very, very nearly competitive: there is just one good (good 1) that is being taxed at an *ad valorem* rate τ, and this good is only consumed by an eccentric in Oshkosh, Wisconsin (household 1). All the producer prices change so slightly that they may effectively be assumed to be fixed and the revenue from the tax is returned to our Oshkosh resident. The situation is illustrated in Figure 8.6. The distorted equilibrium is at point A. Were the tax to be eliminated, so that the effective price of good 1 is lowered to p_1^* the competitive equilibrium price, there would be a substitution effect resulting in an increase in consumption of $\Delta x_1 = -\hat{D}_1^{11}\Delta p_1$ where $\hat{D}_1^{11}$ is the compensated own-price effect of a change in p_1 (we have not modelled the income effect here). The tax by itself reduces welfare by an amount proportional to the whole shaded area in the figure; but the lightly shaded area – equal to $T = \tau x_1^1 p_1$ the revenue raised by the tax – is returned to the consumer; this leaves the little heavily-shaded triangle, whose area is $-\hat{D}_1^{11}\Delta p_1^2 = -T\tau\hat{\varepsilon}_{11}^1 > 0$ where $\hat{\varepsilon}_{11}^1$ is household 1's own-price elasticity. In simplified

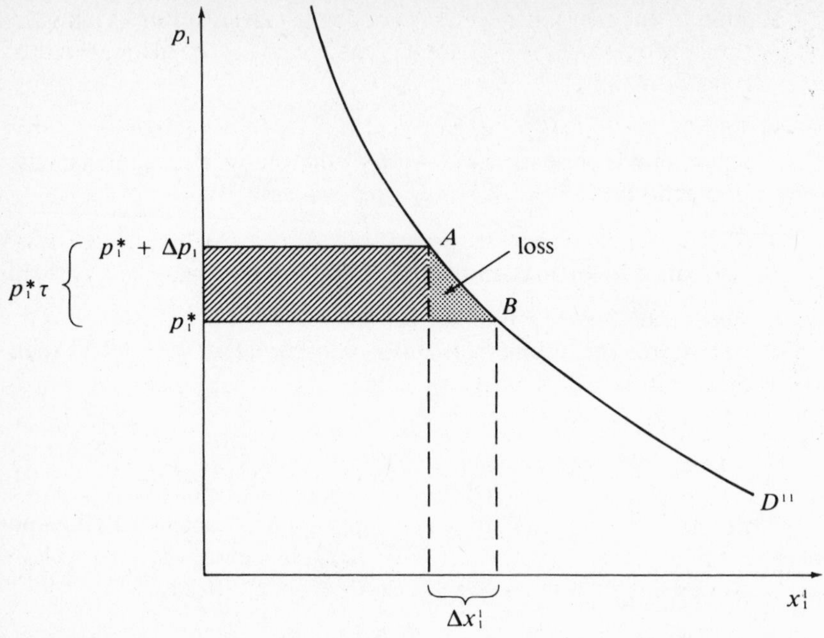

Figure 8.6

terms, then, the loss through price distortions depends on (i) the absolute size of the net expenditure involved in the distortion (the tax revenue T in the above example); (ii) the proportionate deviation in price (τ in the above example); (iii) the compensated price elasticities.

Finally, two words of qualification.

Although our discussion of the measurement of waste has concentrated on deviations from a private ownership, no-externality, competitive equilibrium, the same principles can be applied in other situations where some imperfection forces prices away from the 'ideal'. And, although the above criterion for measuring loss is useful, it is not the only way of defining the loss, nor should such a measure of loss be taken as definitive in terms of ranking the performance of an economy. We return to this issue in Chapter 13.

8.7 Summary

The main results of this chapter can be condensed into six simple rules. Of course, in each case one should be careful to refer back to the main text to recall their precise statement and applicability. Nevertheless, this abbreviated form should be useful for future reference.

- Rule 1: for any pair of *private* goods the marginal rate of substitution is equated across households, and is equal to the marginal rate of transformation.
- Rule 2: the marginal rate of transformation for a private good into a pure public good equals the sum of the households' marginal rates of substitution.
- Rule 3: for a firm generating a production externality, the marginal rate of transformation plus the marginal damage equals the marginal rate of substitution for any household.
- Rule 4: for a household generating an externality the marginal rate of substitution plus the marginal impact on other households equals the marginal rate of transformation.
- Rule 5: if the aggregate production set exhibits non-convexities the marginal rules 1 and 2 will no longer be sufficient to characterise efficiency.
- Rule 6: a measure of the departure from efficiency is provided by the 'triangle rule' using the *compensated* demand curve.

Further Reading

The relationship between competitive equilibrium and Pareto efficiency is discussed further in:

Quirk, J. and Saposnik, R. (1968) *Introduction to General Equilibrium Theory and Welfare Economics*, McGraw-Hill, pp. 116–46.

Much of the received wisdom on the subject is to be found in the following two references:

Graaf, J. de V. (1957) *Theoretical Welfare Economics*, Cambridge University Press, esp. Ch. IV.

Little, I.M.D. (1956) *A Critique of Welfare Economics*, Oxford University Press, esp. Ch. VIII.

Two classic articles on the characterisation of efficiency in the economic system and the possible failure of the market to achieve efficiency are:

Bator, F.M. (1957) 'The simple analytics of welfare maximization', *American Economic Review*, Vol. 47, pp. 22–59.

Bator, F.M. (1958) 'The anatomy of market failure', *Quarterly Journal of Economics*, Vol. 72, pp. 351–79.

The incorporation of public goods into the efficiency conditions is elegantly presented in:

Samuelson, P.A. (1954) 'The pure theory of public expenditure', *Review of Economics and Statistics*, Vol. 36, pp. 387–9.

Exercises

8.1 Draw a utility possibility set for two persons that has, respectively (i) no Pareto efficient states, (ii) exactly three Pareto efficient states, (iii) infinitely many Pareto efficient states.

8.2 Show that if the greed axiom is not satisfied, even if no consumer has a bliss point, a Pareto efficient point may not be sustainable by a competitive equilibrium.

8.3 In Exercise 7.5 show that the equilibrium allocation is Pareto superior to the allocation given by the original property distribution.

8.4 Show diagrammatically that if consumers' indifference curves and firms' production functions are not smooth then there may be many price vectors attaining a Pareto efficient allocation via competition.

8.5 Restate Theorem 8.1 for the case where, for some i, $x_i^h = 0$ or $y_i^f = 0$. [Hint: check Theorem 3.1 and Theorem 4.5.]

*8.6 In a certain 1-good economy the hth consumers utility is given by

$$U^h(x_1^h, x_2^h, x_2)$$

where x_i^h is consumer h's consumption of good i ($h = 1, \ldots, H$; $i = 1, 2$) and $x_2 \equiv \Sigma_{j=1}^{H} x_2^j$. Production in the economy is carried out by a single firm with production function

$$\Phi(y_1, y_2) \leqslant 0$$

where y_i is the net output of good i. Discuss the phenomenon that this model might represent (i) if $\partial U^h/\partial x_2 > 0$, (ii) if $\partial U^h/\partial x_2 < 0$. Analyse the economic efficiency of the economy with special reference to the pricing policy of the firm.

*8.7 The inhabitants of Etruria are identical clones with utility function

$$U = 2^{\alpha x_1} x_2$$

where α is a positive parameter. Good 1 represents consumption of radio and TV programmes. Good 2 represents all other goods. The quantity of these two goods currently available is given by $\mathbf{x}^0 \equiv (0,1)$. To build a broadcasting system of capacity 1 requires $\frac{1}{2}$ unit of all other goods; because of the production technology no smaller and no larger broadcasting system can be constructed. Consider whether or not building the broadcasting system is an efficient outcome when

(i) $\alpha = 1$
(ii) $\alpha = 1.1$
(iii) $\alpha = 0.9$

What is the MRS_{21} in each case?

8.8 (a) Consider the exchange economy of Section 7.3. Prove that any allocation that lies in the core must be Pareto efficient.
(b) Prove Theorem 8.2.

8.9 Consider an economy where each household's utility U^h depends on the utility level achieved by every other household, thus:

$$U^h = U^h(\mathbf{x}^h; u^1, u^2, u^3, \ldots, u^H)$$

What are the first-order conditions for a Pareto efficient allocation?

*8.10 In a 2-good exchange economy there are two equal-sized groups of traders. Each trader of the first group has an endowment of 10 units of good 1 and the utility function $\log x_1^1 + 2\log x_2^1$. Each trader of the second group has an endowment of 10 units of good 2 and a utility function $2\log x_1^2 + 4\log x_2^2 - \log x_1^1$, where x_i^h is the consumption of good i by a trader in group h. Find the competitive equilibrium and show that it is not Pareto efficient. Why not?

8.11 (a) Consider a 2-good economy in which there is an *ad valorem* tax on good 1. Illustrate the equilibrium using the production possibility frontier (i.e. in a diagram similar to Figures 8.3 to 8.5).
(b) Apply the analysis to the case where one good is supplied monopolistically.

8.12 The following is an example of the 'isolation paradox' of saving.[5] Take the model of Exercise 5.7 and modify it in the following ways. (i) Let there be H identical households who enjoy their own consumption now, x_1^h, the prospect of their own children's consumption, x_2^h, and the prospect of the standard of living of posterity $\bar{x} = \frac{1}{H}\Sigma_l x_2^l$: thus preferences are given by $U(x_1^h, x_2^h, \bar{x})$ where U is increasing in each of its arguments. (a) Discuss the reasons why preferences might have this form. (b) Show that a market equilibrium will lead to too little saving being carried out. (c) How might an efficient solution be achieved?

[5] Sen, A.K. (1961) 'On optimising the rate of saving', *Economic Journal*, Vol. 71, p. 479.

9

The Equilibrium System

9.1 The Model

In Chapter 7 we examined the specific characteristics of any one equilibrium state taking as given such parameters as the technology Y, preferences U^1, ..., U^H and the property distribution $\mathscr{d}$. This enables one to deal with a number of interesting questions but leaves open other issues with obvious practical relevance. For example: what would happen to the equilibrium allocation $\mathscr{a}^*$ if there were an unanticipated technological improvement? A change in tastes? A different endowment of resources $\mathbf{R}$? A different system of ownership? To deal with such matters properly requires a model of *disequilibrium* behaviour of the economy which raises a whole host of problems that we have not yet discussed. A possible way of side-stepping this – and not all economists are persuaded of its usefulness in general – is to use the method of *comparative statics*.

Comparative statics involves an 'as if' exercise. The sort of question one asks is, 'what would the global equilibrium look like if, instead of the underlying parameters we now have, one or more of these parameters were to have a different value?' What is glossed over to some extent is the *actual process* by which the economy would move from one equilibrium to another. Instead the economy is fictionalised as a smoothly operating machine so that one may arbitrarily move around various 'levers' (the economy's parameters) and observe how its visible components (the equilibrium allocations) then move. We can do this either directly by examination of consumption and production decisions, or indirectly by looking at the behaviour of equilibrium prices as parameters change.

However the general n-commodity model gets rather complicated even under the restrictive assumptions of the comparative static method. To simplify matters yet further we shall assume a four commodity system – two consumer goods and two natural resources. This permits a certain simplification of notation for the purposes of this chapter. In particular we make the following assumptions:

ASSUMPTION S1: there are two consumer goods, labelled 1 and 2 of which there are no stocks *ex-ante*: $R_1 = R_2 = 0$.

Table 9.1 Essential Notation for Chapter 9: The Equilibrium System

K_i	:	amount of K-resource (good 3) used in sector i (i = 1,2)
L_i	:	amount of L-resource (good 4) used in sector i (i = 1,2)
k_i	:	(K/L)–ratio for sector i (i = 1,2)
q_i	:	output per unit of L in sector i (i = 1,2)
g_i	:	production function (intensive form) in sector i (i = 1,2)
θ	:	(price of L-resource)/(price of K-resource)
ρ	:	(price of sector 1 output)/(price of sector 2 output)

ASSUMPTION S2: there are two resources used only as production inputs. Stocks of these resources are given by $R_3 = \bar{K} > 0$ and $R_4 = \bar{L} > 0$. For obvious reasons these will be known as the K-resource and the L-resource.
ASSUMPTION S3: there is no joint production and there are no externalities.
ASSUMPTION S4: there are constant returns to scale.
ASSUMPTION S5: each resource is essential in the production of each good.
ASSUMPTION S6: isoquants are strictly convex to the origin.
ASSUMPTION S7: production functions are everywhere twice differentiable.

Assumptions S1 to S3 mean that we may write the production of the two goods as

$$Q_1 \lesseqgtr G^1(K_1, L_1) \tag{9.1}$$
$$Q_2 \lesseqgtr G^2(K_2, L_2) \tag{9.2}$$

where K_i is the amount of the K-resource, and L_i the amount of the L-resource that is devoted to the production of good i, i = 1,2. For efficiency, as long as both goods 1 and 2 are scarce, we know from Chapter 8 that (9.1) and (9.2) must be satisfied with equality, and also:

$$K_1 + K_2 = \bar{K} \tag{9.3}$$
$$L_1 + L_2 = \bar{L} \tag{9.4}$$

Assumption S4 means that for *any* positive scalar α: $G^i(\alpha K_i, \alpha L_i) = \alpha Q_i$. Setting $\alpha = 1/L_i$ we obtain from (9.1) and (9.2):

$$\frac{Q_i}{L_i} = G^i\left(\frac{K_i}{L_i}, 1\right)$$

or more simply

$$q_i = g_i(k_i) \tag{9.5}$$

where

$$q_i \equiv Q_i/L_i \tag{9.6}$$
$$k_i \equiv K_i/L_i \tag{9.7}$$

and where $g_i(\cdot)$ is a function of one variable defined so that $g_i(\zeta) = G^i(\zeta, 1)$. The function g_i is known as the production function for good i written in *intensive form*. It gives output per unit of L as a function of the input ratio k_i, and in fact much of the subsequent analysis is facilitated by being able to use the single variable k_i rather than having to write two variables K_i, L_i explicitly. High values of k_i are said to indicate a *K-intensive technique* in the production of good i and, correspondingly, low values of k_i indicate an *L-intensive technique* in the production of good i. In view of assumption S7 first- and second-order derivatives of g_i exist and we shall denote these by g_i' and g_i'' respectively. Assumptions S4 to S6 imply that:[1]

$$\frac{\partial G^i}{\partial K_i} = g_i'(k_i) > 0 \tag{9.8}$$

$$\frac{\partial G^i}{\partial L_i} = g_i(k_i) - k_i g_i'(k_i) > 0 \tag{9.9}$$

$$g_i''(k_i) < 0 \tag{9.10}$$

$$g_i(0) = 0 \tag{9.11}$$

$$g_i(\infty) = \infty \tag{9.12}$$

The shape of the function $q_1 = g_1(k_1)$ is shown in Figure 9.1.[2]

Just as it is possible to economise on notation by using k_i rather than K_i and L_i, so one may simplify the representation of efficiency prices. From equation (3.19) in the discussion of the theory of the firm we may infer that it is the *ratio* of the marginal products of two inputs that plays a key role in production efficiency. Hence we also find it useful to define θ_i as the marginal rate of technical substitution of K for L – that is the ratio of the marginal product (9.9) to the marginal product (9.8).[3] Thus we have:

$$\theta_1 \equiv \frac{g_1(k_1)}{g_1'(k_1)} - k_1 \tag{9.13}$$

$$\theta_2 \equiv \frac{g_2(k_2)}{g_2'(k_2)} - k_2 \tag{9.14}$$

We may also show in Figure 9.1 the value of θ_1 that corresponds to a particular k_1. You are invited to experiment with different values of k_1 for a given $g_1(\,)$ function and to examine how θ_1 changes. This may also be examined using the isoquants in Figure 9.2.

---

1 See Exercise 2.11

2 Obviously $g_2(k_2)$ will look like this too, but may have a slightly different shape.

3 See Definition 2.2.

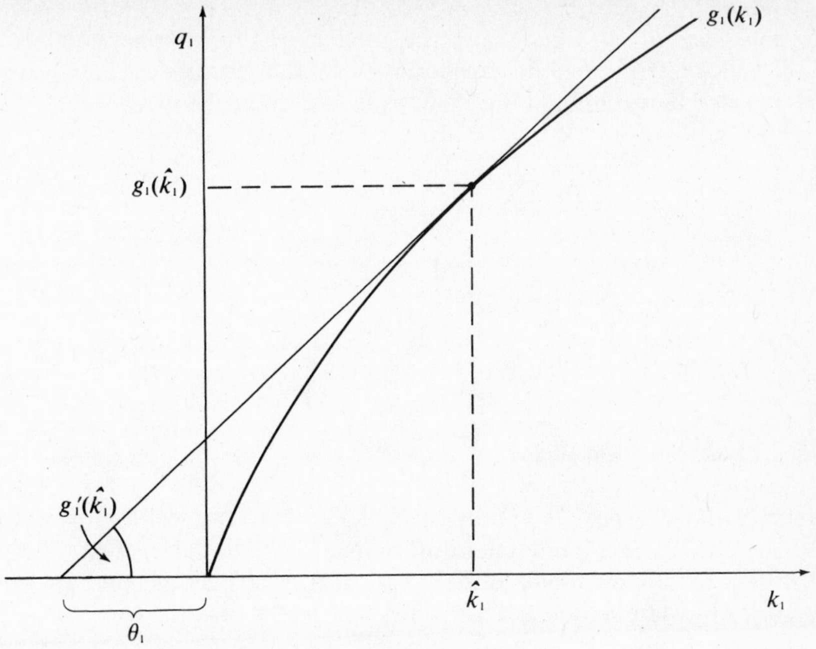

Figure 9.1

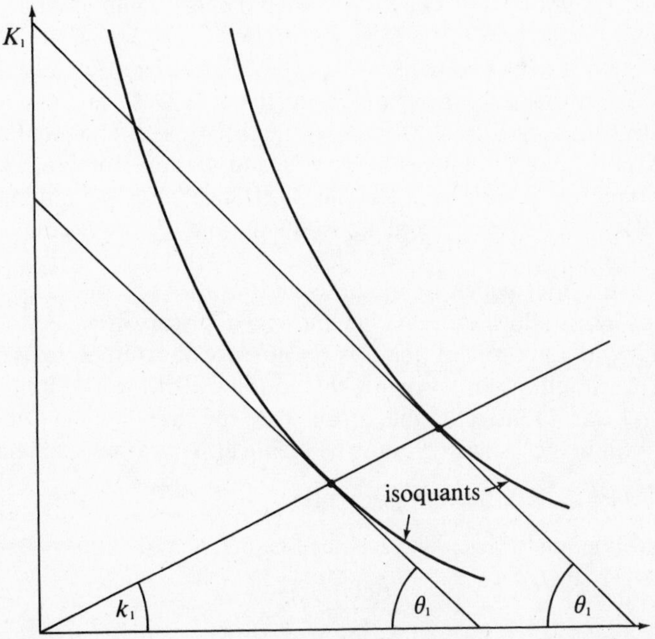

Figure 9.2 The relationship between k and θ in industry 1

Finally, consider θ_1 as a function of k_1. By definition (cf. Definition 2.5) the *elasticity of substitution* of the production function of good 1 is $\partial \log k_1/\partial \log \theta_1$. Hence on differentiating (9.13) and (9.14) we may write the elasticity of substitution in the production of each of the two goods as

$$\sigma_1 \equiv \frac{\theta_1}{k_1}\frac{dk_1}{d\theta_1} = \frac{-[g_1'(k_1)]^2\theta_1}{g_1(k_1)g_1''(k_1)k_1} \tag{9.15}$$

$$\sigma_2 \equiv \frac{\theta_2}{k_2}\frac{dk_2}{d\theta_2} = \frac{-[g_2'(k_2)]^2\theta_2}{g_2(k_2)g_2''(k_2)k_2} \tag{9.16}$$

Note that both are positive by S6.

9.2 The Production Box

The 'production box' is a convenient device for representing the set of technically efficient production allocations. Within the context of this diagram we may then look at the subset of these allocations that are candidates for consideration as Pareto efficient allocations.

Firstly, consider how much it is possible to produce goods 1 and 2 given the resource stocks $\bar{K}$, $\bar{L}$ in assumption S2. If (K_1, L_1) is being used in industry 1, yielding $Q_1 = G^1(K_1, L_1)$, then the maximum amount of good 2 that can be produced is $Q_2 = G^2(K_2, L_2)$ where $K_2 = \bar{K} - K_1$ and $L_2 = \bar{L} - L_1$. We plot these K and L values in Figure 9.3. The isoquants for industry 1 are drawn with references to the axes O_1K_1 and O_1L_1. The isoquants for industry 2 are drawn with reference to axes O_2K_2 and O_2L_2. The sides of the box are of dimension $\bar{K}$ and $\bar{L}$ and, by construction, any point in the box represents a particular technically efficient allocation of inputs, since it lies on both a 1-isoquant and a 2-isoquant, and of course conditions (9.3) and (9.4) hold.

Now consider which of the points within the box may correspond to Pareto efficient allocations. As we know, a necessary condition for Pareto efficiency with pure private goods in the absence of externalities is that equation (8.15) should hold. Applying this to the use of the two inputs K, L in industry 1 and industry 2, this means that the marginal rate of technical substitution in each industry must be identical. Hence we must have

$$\theta_1 = \theta_2 = \text{efficiency price ratio} \tag{9.17}$$

Denote this single efficiency price ratio by θ. Then obviously we have

$$\theta = \frac{g_1(k_1)}{g_1'(k_1)} - k_1 = \frac{g_2(k_2)}{g_2'(k_2)} - k_2 \tag{9.18}$$

as a condition for Pareto efficiency.

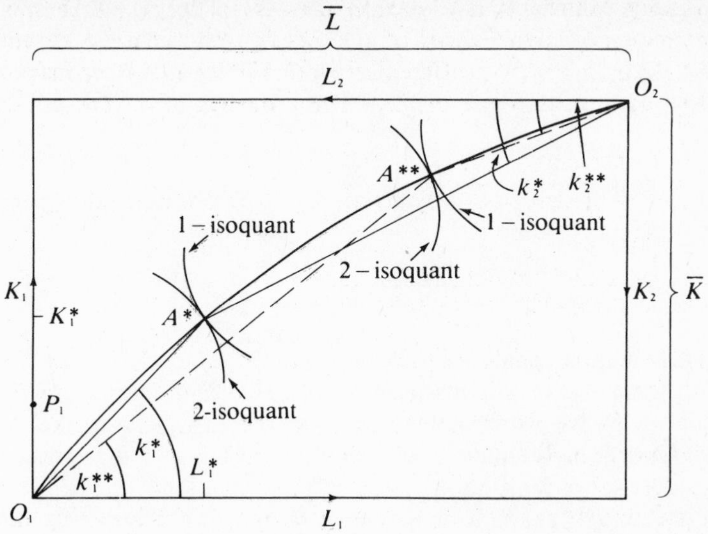

Note: $k_1 > \dfrac{K}{L} > k_2$; k_1 must *fall* as L_1, K_1 are increased.

Figure 9.3 The production box

Given any set of 1-isoquants and any set of 2-isoquants that each exhibit constant returns to scale we may now locate graphically the allocations that satisfy condition (9.18). Simply plot in the box those points at which a 1-isoquant and a 2-isoquant share a common tangent. This is represented by the curve $O_1A^*A^{**}O_2$ – which we shall call the *production efficiency locus.*[4] Let us consider the shape of this curve.

First notice that it must pass through each origin O_1 and O_2. To see this, suppose to the contrary that the curve did not pass through O_1 but instead through a point P_1 on the O_1K_1 axis above O_1, and consider the 1-isoquant that passes through P_1. *Either* this isoquant corresponds to a zero output for industry 1, in which case P_1 could not be technically efficient since a positive amount of the K-resource would then be producing a zero amount of output; *or* this isoquant corresponds to a positive output for industry 1, in which case assumption S5 is violated, since good 1 is then produced without using any L-resource. So the curve obviously cannot pass through any point on the boundary of the box other than the corners O_1, O_2.

---

[4] Note that this term must be treated with caution. Not *all* points on the locus will represent Pareto efficient allocations for every arbitrarily specified set of preferences. However it is true that all the Pareto efficient production allocations must lie on some part of this curve.

Next note that – unlike the contract curve of the exchange economy in Figure 7.1 – the curve cannot 'wiggle about' arbitrarily. To see this let us express the points on the production efficiency locus with reference to the origin O_1 as

$$K_1 = \Psi(L_1) \tag{9.19}$$

and consider the shape of the function Ψ. To do this note that we also have the obvious relationships

$$K_1 = k_1 L_1 \tag{9.20}$$
$$k_2 = [\bar{K} - k_1 L_1]/[\bar{L} - L_1] \tag{9.21}$$

which follow from equations (9.3), (9.4) and (9.7). Now (9.18), (9.20), (9.21) form a system of three simultaneous equations in four unknowns (K_1, L_1, k_1, k_2). In principle we may be able to eliminate k_1 and k_2 between the equations so as to leave a single equation in K_1 and L_1 which is of course nothing other than (9.19). So we can find the slope of Ψ by examining the differentials of (9.18), (9.20), (9.21) and solving. Let us do that.

Differentiating (9.18) and using (9.15) and (9.16) we obtain

$$\frac{\theta}{k_1\sigma_1}\mathrm{d}k_1 = \frac{\theta}{k_2\sigma_2}\mathrm{d}k_2 \tag{9.22}$$

Differentiating (9.21) and simplifying by using (9.3), (9.4) and (9.7) we have

$$\mathrm{d}k_2 = \frac{-L_1\mathrm{d}k_1 + [k_2 - k_1]\,\mathrm{d}L_1}{L_2} \tag{9.23}$$

Combining (9.22) and (9.23) to eliminate $\mathrm{d}k_2$ we find:

$$\frac{\partial k_1}{\partial L_1} = \frac{k_2 - k_1}{L_1 + L_2\dfrac{k_2\sigma_2}{k_1\sigma_1}} \tag{9.24}$$

Clearly the denominator of this expression must be positive. So (9.24) states that if (i) $k_2 > k_1$ (good 2 is relatively K-intensive) then as more labour and capital are shifted from 2-production to 1-production k_1 must always *rise*. Conversely if (ii) $k_1 > k_2$ (good 1 is relatively K-intensive) then as resources are switched away from the production of good 2 into the production of good 1, k_1 must always *fall*.

This latter case is illustrated in Figure 9.3. Clearly k_1 is always greater than k_2 (note that k_1^* is the tangent of the angle $A^*O_1L_1$). So if we move along the production efficiency locus away from O_1 towards O_2 (*increasing* the output of good 1) we find that k_1 falls. To see this compare k_1^* (at the point A^*) with k_1^{**} (at the point A^{**}). Note too that k_2 always goes in the same direction as k_1 along the efficiency locus – a result which is evident from (9.22) – which proves that Ψ *cannot* cross the diagonal between O_1 and O_2; for, if it did, then at some point k_1 would be rising and k_2 falling (or vice versa) – a contradiction. Moreover, in case (ii) since $\Psi(L_1)/L_1$ is decreasing for all $L_1 \geqslant 0$, $\Psi(0) = 0$, we see that Ψ must be concave. In case (i) a similar argument establishes that Ψ must be convex. Hence the efficiency locus must either have the shape illustrated in Figure 9.3 *or* the shape found by holding the page upside-down, as long as assumptions S1–S7 are satisfied.

Let us now look at what these relationships imply for the price system.

9.3 Product Prices and Factor Prices

If we now specifically examine a competitive system the 2-good, 2-resource model enables us to see the relationship between prices of the goods (commodities 1 and 2) and the prices of units of the resources, or factors (commodities 3 and 4). Write the prices of the two consumer goods 1 and 2 as p_1 and p_2 respectively. Since we have used K_i and L_i to denote the amounts of resource the K- and the L-resource that are being used in the production of the ith consumer good, and since we are making a clear distinction between commodities that are inputs and commodities that are outputs of the processes, we shall introduce special symbols for the prices of the resources. Accordingly

w_K (equivalent to p_3) is the price of the K-resource
w_L (equivalent to p_4) is the price of the L-resource

Let us suppose that each firm acts in a competitive, price-taking fashion, and is a profit maximiser. Then from equation (3.16) we know that if a positive output is produced and a positive amount of each input is demanded by the firm producing good i, then the first-order conditions for profit maximisation, using the production functions (9.1) and (9.2) are:

$$p_i \frac{\partial G^i(K_i, L_i)}{\partial K_i} = w_K \tag{9.25}$$

$$p_i \frac{\partial G^i(K_i, L_i)}{\partial L_i} = w_L \tag{9.26}$$

But, given assumption S4 (constant returns to scale) we can simplify (9.25) and (9.26) by using (9.8) and (9.9) to yield

$$p_1 g_1'(k_1) = w_K \tag{9.27}$$

$$p_1 [g_1(k_1) - k_1 g_1'(k_1)] = w_L \tag{9.28}$$

for firms producing good 1, and

$$p_2 g_2'(k_2) = w_K \tag{9.29}$$

$$p_2[g_2(k_2) - k_2 g_2'(k_2)] = w_L \tag{9.30}$$

for firms producing good 2. Of course, for firms in either industry the optimal choice of technique is determined simply by the unique ratio of the factor prices $\theta \equiv w_L/w_K$, where θ is given by the efficiency condition (9.18). We may thus simplify the problem by dividing (9.28) by (9.27) and dividing (9.30) by (9.29). In view of assumptions S4 to S7, g_i'' is strictly negative for $i = 1,2$ and we may invert (9.13), (9.14) – or, equivalently, solve the equations (9.27) to (9.30) – to yield explicit solutions for k_1 and k_2 thus:

$$k_1 = \varkappa_1(\theta) \tag{9.31}$$

$$k_2 = \varkappa_2(\theta) \tag{9.32}$$

For any θ, the resource price ratio that happens to be ruling in the market, we may read off from (9.31) and (9.32) the optimal techniques used in the two industries.

It is interesting to sketch the behaviour of the functions $\varkappa_1$ and $\varkappa_2$. First of all note that, from (9.13) and (9.14) we find that θ is a strictly increasing function of k_i (check this using either Figure 9.1 or 9.2). Hence the *inverse* functions (9.31) or (9.32) must also be strictly increasing. Next notice that $\varkappa_1$ may lie wholly above $\varkappa_2$ (or vice versa) or $\varkappa_1$ and $\varkappa_2$ may intersect an arbitrary number of times. Two possibilities are illustrated in Figure 9.4. In the left-hand panel, clearly k_1 will always be greater than k_2 for any factor-price ratio θ: we say that industry 1 is *unambiguously more K-intensive* than industry 2. In the right-hand panel a problem arises: for low values of θ, $k_1 > k_2$, but for high values of θ we have $k_2 > k_1$. This is known as a *factor intensity reversal.* Which case we get depends entirely on the production functions $g_1(k_1)$ and $g_2(k_2)$. The importance of this distinction will soon be evident.

We may also introduce a ratio of goods prices, $\rho \equiv p_1/p_2$. Now it is clear that we may also divide (9.27) by (9.29) and (9.28) by (9.30) to obtain, on rearrangement:

$$\rho = \frac{g_2'(k_2)}{g_1'(k_1)} \tag{9.33}$$

and

$$\rho = \frac{g_2(k_2) - k_2 g_2'(k_2)}{g_1(k_1) - k_1 g_1'(k_1)} \tag{9.34}$$

Substitute from (9.31) and (9.32) into (9.33) to obtain

$$\begin{aligned} \rho &= g_2'(\varkappa_2(\theta))/g_1'(\varkappa_1(\theta)) \\ &\equiv \rho(\theta) \end{aligned} \tag{9.35}$$

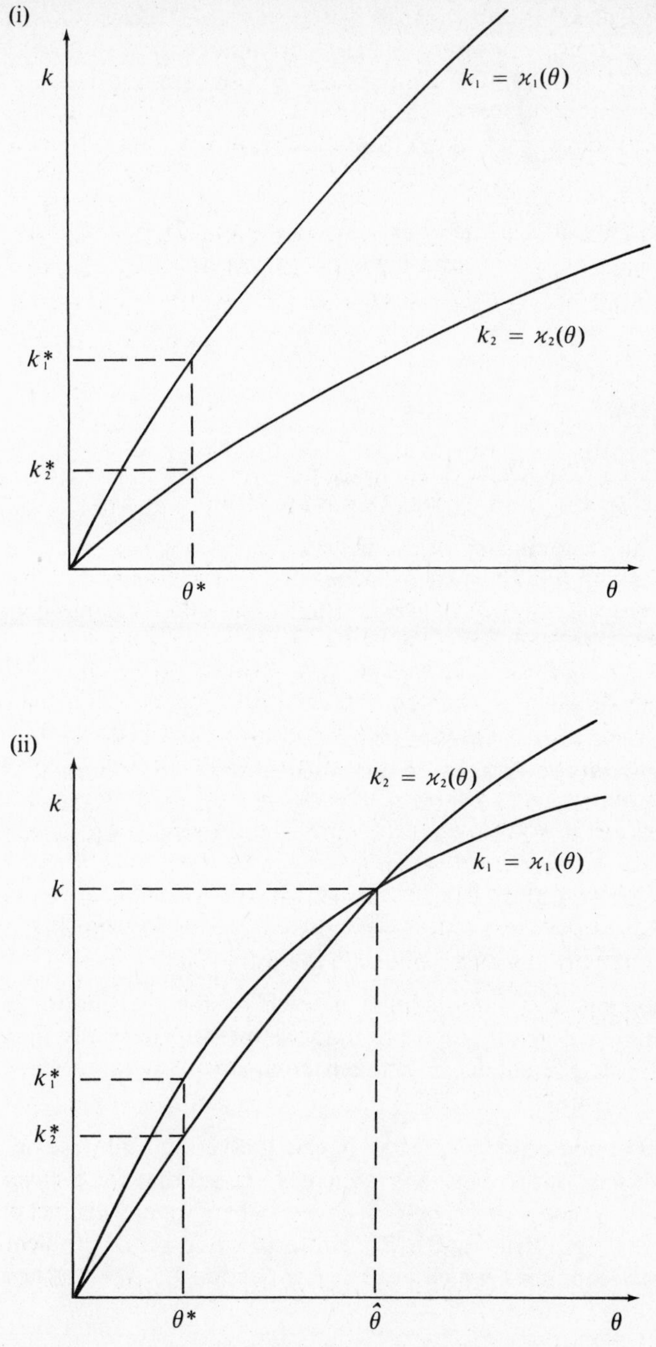

Figure 9.4

let us say. Equation (9.35) reveals that for any given factor price ratio θ there is a unique goods price ratio ρ. Let us examine this relationship.

Differentiate (9.35) logarithmically with respect to θ:

$$\frac{1}{\rho}\frac{\partial \rho}{\partial \theta} = \frac{g_2''}{g_2'}\varkappa_2'(\theta) - \frac{g_1''}{g_1'}\varkappa_1'(\theta) \tag{9.36}$$

Now, noting that $\varkappa_i$ is the inverse function of (9.13), (9.14) we find $\varkappa_i'(\theta) = -g_i'^2/g_i g_i''$, $i = 1,2$. Substituting in (9.36) we get

$$\frac{1}{\rho}\frac{\partial \rho}{\partial \theta} = \frac{g_1'}{g_1} - \frac{g_2'}{g_2} \tag{9.37}$$

which in view of (9.18) yields

$$\frac{1}{\rho}\frac{\partial \rho}{\partial \theta} = \frac{k_2 - k_1}{[k_1 + \theta][k_2 + \theta]} \tag{9.38}$$

Clearly the denominator of the fraction in (9.38) is non-negative. Hence ρ decreases with θ if $k_1 > k_2$; ρ increases with θ if $k_1 < k_2$.

Now apply this (i) to the case where industry 1 is unambiguously more K-intensive than industry 2, and (ii) to the case where there is a factor intensity reversal. In case (i) ρ is a monotonically decreasing function of θ – see the left-hand panel of Figure 9.5. Within the range of feasible price ratios[5] there is a one-to-one correspondence between ρ and θ. However if there is a factor-intensity reversal we need to distinguish two possibilities. Let $\hat{k}$ and $\hat{\theta}$ be the values of k and θ at the 'crossover' in Figure 9.4, so that $\hat{k} = \varkappa_1(\hat{\theta}) = \varkappa_2(\hat{\theta})$. Thus if $\theta < \hat{\theta}$, then $k_2 < k_1 < \hat{k}$ and ρ decreases with θ, the converse applies for $\theta > \hat{\theta}$. So in the factor-intensity reversal case, though there is a unique ρ for any given θ there will generally be *two* values of θ (one on each 'branch') for each value of ρ – see the right-hand panel of Figure 9.5. We can summarise these observations in the following theorem.

THEOREM 9.1: if (a) production in each of the two industries satisfies assumptions S1–S7, (b) there are no factor intensity reversals, then there is a one-to-one correspondence between competitive factor price ratios and goods price ratios.

In a *closed* economy, factor intensity reversals will pose no problem. We have seen this in Figure 9.3 where we noted that for a *given* $\overline{K}$ and $\overline{L}$ *either* $k_1 > k_2$ everywhere, *or* $k_2 > k_1$ everywhere for any distinct production functions g_1, g_2 satisfying S1–S7. However a number of problems do arise with open economies, which we discuss in Section 9.5. We may now state the

[5] Note that in a closed economy there is no possibility that $k_1 = k_2 = 0$, since $K_1 + K_2 = \overline{K} > 0$ so that either k_1 or k_2 or both must be positive.

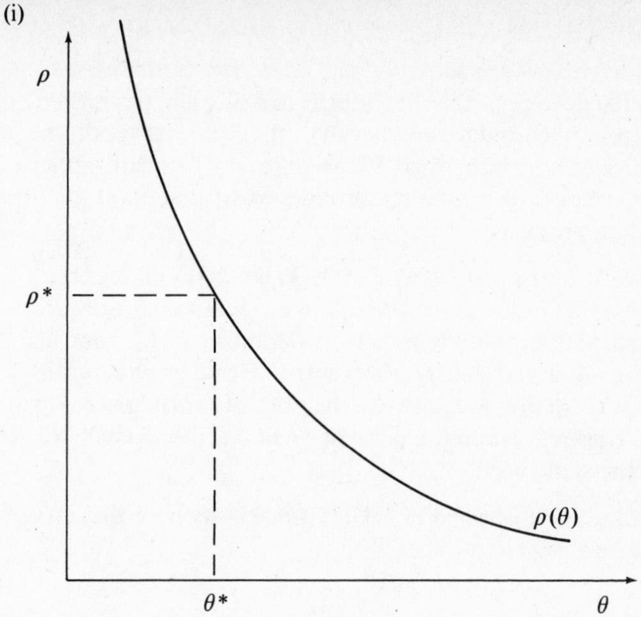

(i) No factor intensity reversals

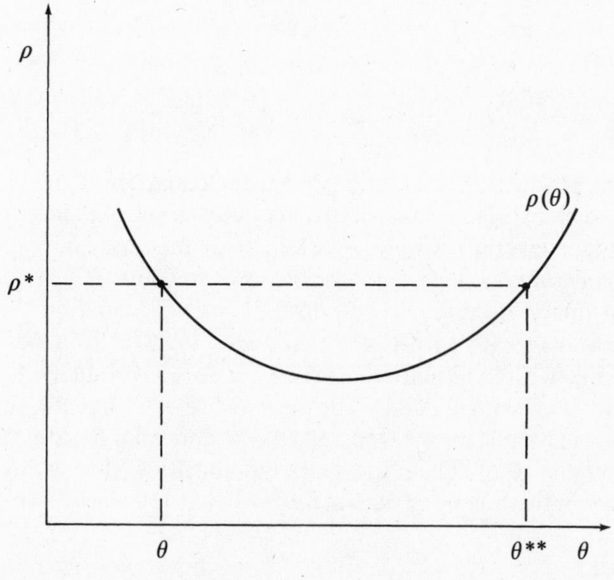

(ii) Factor intensity reversals

Figure 9.5

following:

THEOREM 9.2 (*Stolper–Samuelson*): in a competitive economy with two factors in fixed supply, constant returns to scale, and diminishing returns to either factor in the production of each of the two final goods, increasing the relative price of one of the final goods increases the relative price of the factor that is used intensively in the production of that good, if some of each good is being produced.

PROOF: we know that *either* $k_1 \lesseqgtr \bar{k} \lesseqgtr k_2$ holds for all feasible price ratios, *or* $k_2 \lesseqgtr \bar{k} \lesseqgtr k_1$ holds everywhere. So without loss of generality we may assume that in the economy under discussion $k_1 > k_2$: good 1 is relatively K-intensive, good 2 is relatively L-intensive. However equation (9.38) reveals that if the price of L rises relative to the price of K (θ increases) then the price of good 2 rises relative to the price of good 1 (ρ decreases). All other cases follow in the same way.

The result is illustrated in Figure 9.6. Firstly note that from (9.33) we have the efficiency condition

$$\rho = \frac{g_2'}{g_1'}$$

$$= -\frac{\partial G^2/\partial K_1}{\partial G^1/\partial K_1}$$

$$= -\frac{dQ_2}{dQ_1} \tag{9.39}$$

for efficient production of Q_1, Q_2 (we use the equations (9.1)–(9.8) for the intermediate steps). Hence, at an efficient allocation, ρ equals the slope in (Q_1,Q_2)–space of the aggregate production function – i.e. the slope of the *production possibility frontier* illustrated in Figure 9.6. Assuming $k_1 > k_2$ we find that ρ decreases monotonically with θ (equation (9.38)), θ increases monotonically with k_1 (equation (9.13)), and k_1 decreases monotonically with L_1 (equation 9.24)). Therefore as production of good 1 is increased by increasing L_1 and K_1 at the expense of L_2 and K_2, k_1 and θ fall and ρ rises. Hence one moves from A^* to A^{**} and from B^* to B^{**} in the two parts of Figure 9.6. This, incidentally, confirms that the production possibility frontier is convex outward.[6]

---

[6] We did not need to *prove* this, because the convexity of this curve follows as an immediate consequence of the convexity of the aggregate production set Y – see Chapters 2 and 6.

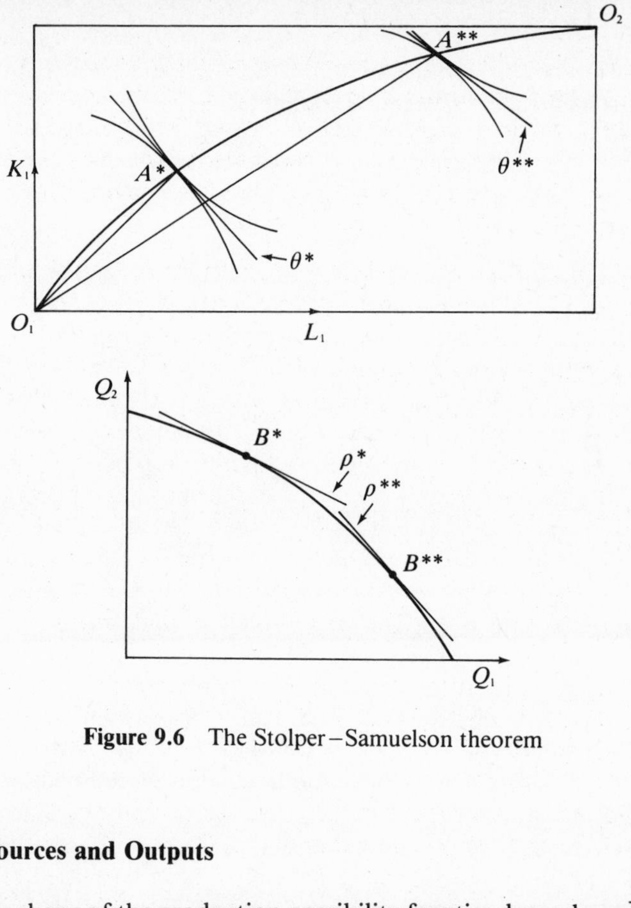

Figure 9.6 The Stolper–Samuelson theorem

9.4 Resources and Outputs

Clearly the shape of the production possibility frontier depends on $\overline{K}$, $\overline{L}$, the amounts available of the two commodities considered as fixed resources. What happens if the quantities of these resources are subject to exogenous change? We retain assumptions S1–S7 about the technology and about competition and examine a small exogenous variation in one resource.

THEOREM 9.3 (*Rybczynski*): if goods prices are held constant, an increase in the amount available of one resource will increase the output of the good that uses that resource intensively and will decrease the output of the other good.

PROOF: since ρ is held constant we know from (9.32) that θ remains constant and hence, from (9.28) and (9.29), k_1 and k_2 remain constant. Let $\overline{K}$ increase autonomously. Since we have equation (9.4) and also

$$k_1L_1 + k_2L_2 = \overline{K} \tag{9.40}$$

we see at once that

$$\frac{\partial L_1}{\partial \bar{K}} = \frac{1}{k_1 - k_2}$$

But we also have from (9.5) and (9.6) that

$$Q_1 = L_1 g_1(k_1)$$

$$Q_2 = L_2 g_2(k_2)$$

So we immediately get $\partial Q_1/\partial \bar{K}|_{\rho=\text{const}} = \dfrac{g_1(k_1)}{k_1 - k_2}$ which will be positive if $k_1 > k_2$. Likewise $\partial Q_2/\partial \bar{K}|_{\rho=\text{const}} = -\dfrac{g_2(k_2)}{k_1 - k_2}$ which will be negative if $k_1 > k_2$. The result for $\mathrm{d}\bar{L}$ follows by symmetry.

This result is illustrated in Figure 9.7. In the top part of the figure the original dimensions of the box are $(\bar{K},\bar{L})$ and the box has corners O_1 and O_2. Originally the particular factor price ratio θ determines an equilibrium allocation of resources at A (although the efficiency locus has not been drawn in, A must of course lie on that locus): the values $k_1 = \varkappa_1(\theta)$ and $k_2 = \varkappa_2(\theta)$ have been drawn in. The corresponding equilibrium allocation of goods is illustrated in the lower part of Figure 9.7 as point B on the original production possibility frontier. Now let $\bar{K}$ increase to $\bar{K} + \mathrm{d}\bar{K}$, keeping θ constant. Since θ is constant k_1, k_2 and ρ must be constant – see equations (9.31), (9.32) and (9.35). The new box of dimensions $(\bar{K} + \mathrm{d}\bar{K}, L)$ has corners O_1 and O_2'. The new equilibrium allocation of resources A' can be found by drawing rays of slope k_1, k_2 through O_1 and O_2'. Since $O_1A' > O_1A$ and $O_2'A' < O_2A$ it is clear that the production of good 1 must have increased and the production of good 2 must have decreased. The consequent shift in the production possibility frontier is illustrated in the lower part of the figure – compare points B and B'.

Note the interesting point about the result. Not only does the K-intensive good *increase*, but at constant prices the production of the L-intensive good must *decrease*: see Exercise 9.3.

9.5 Incomplete Markets

We know that in the case where all commodities (consumer goods, intermediate goods and primary resources alike) are traded in competitive markets in the absence of externality the competitive equilibrium, if it exists, will be Pareto efficient. Moreover if the economy is 'convex' we can be sure that any Pareto efficient allocation could be sustained by a competitive equilibrium. However what happens if there are some restrictions on trade? Will an equilibrium still be efficient? Will perfect competition in some markets work as well as perfect competition in all markets?

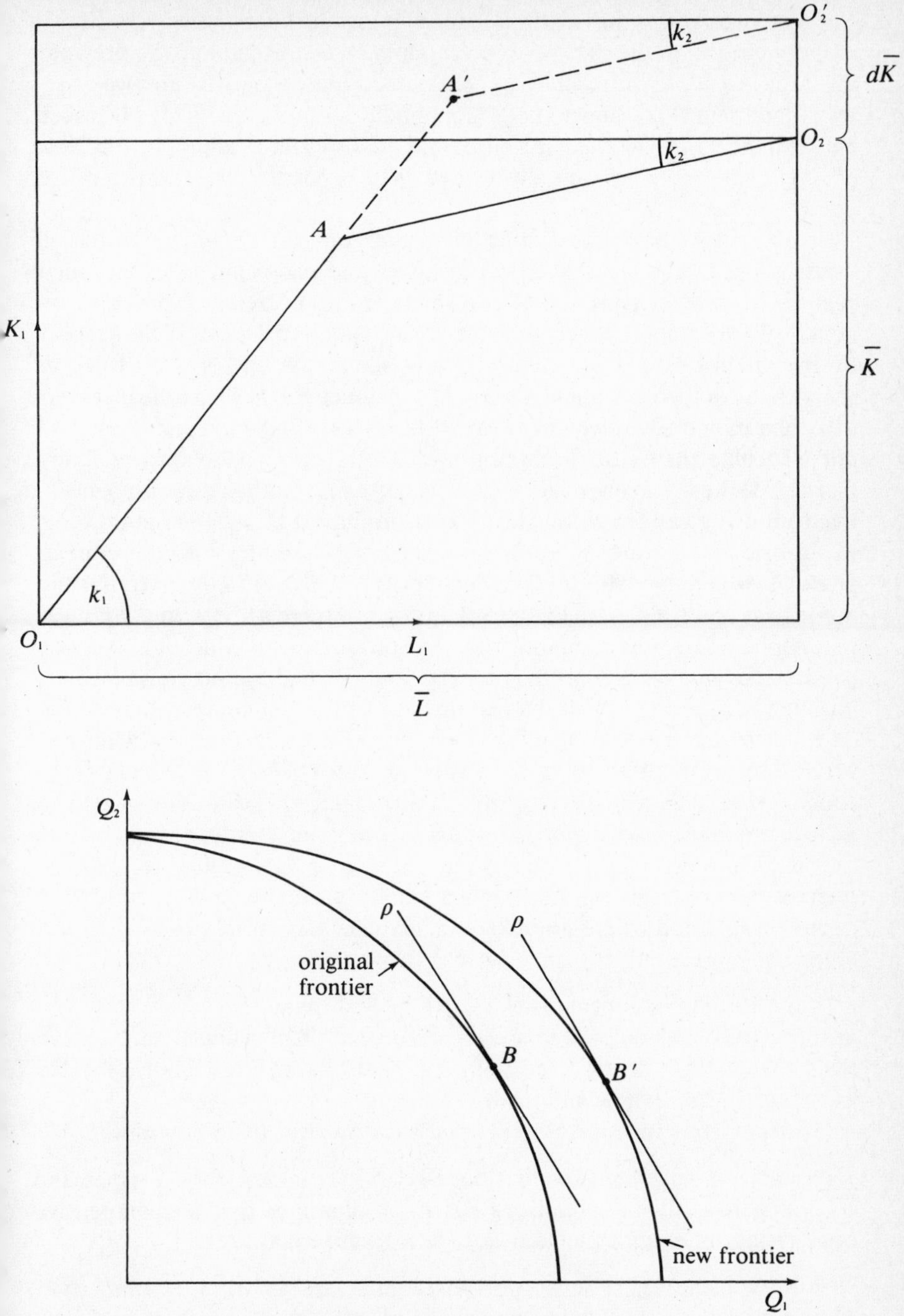

Figure 9.7 The Rybczynski theorem

The two-by-two model throws some interesting light on this, since this is an old question in the theory of international trade. Retain all the previous assumptions about the technology, but now suppose that there are *two* countries, and that the consumer goods (commodities 1 and 2) can be freely traded between them but that the K-resource and the L-resource cannot be traded at all. Will the countries actually trade? Which country will export which good?

Let country Alpha be a price taker. Suppose, for the moment, that all households in Alpha are identical in tastes and endowments so that their preferences may be represented by a single set of indifference curves. Competitive equilibrium is clearly at point B_α, with goods prices ρ_α, in the absence of any opportunity to trade elsewhere – see Figure 9.8. Now let there be access to a competitive world market in consumer goods where the members of Alpha may trade freely at given world prices. If resources are fixed and not tradeable then clearly nothing happens to the production possibility frontier. If the world price ratio p_1/p_2 should equal ρ_α, then there is no incentive to move away from consuming and producing at B_α. But suppose the world price ratio is $\rho^* \neq \rho_\alpha$. Then evidently the country may consume at point C_α (where, by definition, it is better off – it doesn't *have* to trade) and produce at point B'_α – see Figure 9.9. As drawn there $\rho^* < \rho_\alpha$ and it is clear that Alpha will export commodity 2 in the production of which it has a comparative advantage *vis-à-vis* the rest of the world, and import commodity 1, in the production of which the rest of the world has a comparative advantage. Clearly a motive for undertaking international trade arises whenever $\rho^* \neq \rho_\alpha$. So it is evident that in order to see how trade will emerge between two countries Alpha and Beta we must understand what causes international differences in the price ratios ρ_α, ρ_β that would prevail under autarky.

There are clearly a great many reasons by ρ_α and ρ_β might differ, so it is perhaps easier to state the additional assumptions that would be required to ensure that ρ_α and ρ_β are bound to be identical, assuming that S1–S7 still hold. These are:

ASSUMPTION T1: identical tastes for Alpha and Beta;
ASSUMPTION T2: homothetic preferences in both Alpha and Beta;
ASSUMPTION T3: identical technological possibilities (production sets) for Alpha and Beta;
ASSUMPTION T4: identical proportionate endowment of resources $\bar{K}/\bar{L}$.

THEOREM 9.4: given the assumptions S1 to S7 for both economy Alpha and economy Beta, then assumptions T1 to T4 guarantee that the competitive price ratios under autarky, namely ρ_α and ρ_β, are equal.

PROOF: consider first a proportionate increase in *both* $\bar{K}$ *and* $\bar{L}$ to $\bar{K}[1 + d\lambda]$, $\bar{L}[1 + d\lambda]$ respectively. Employing (9.4) and (9.40) we get

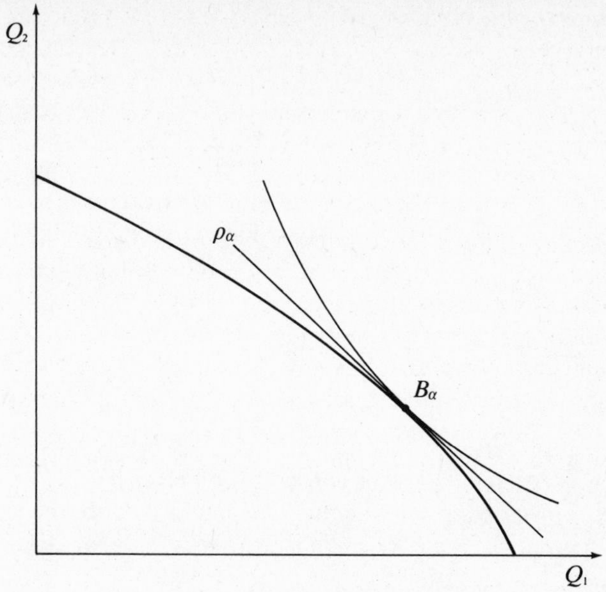

Figure 9.8

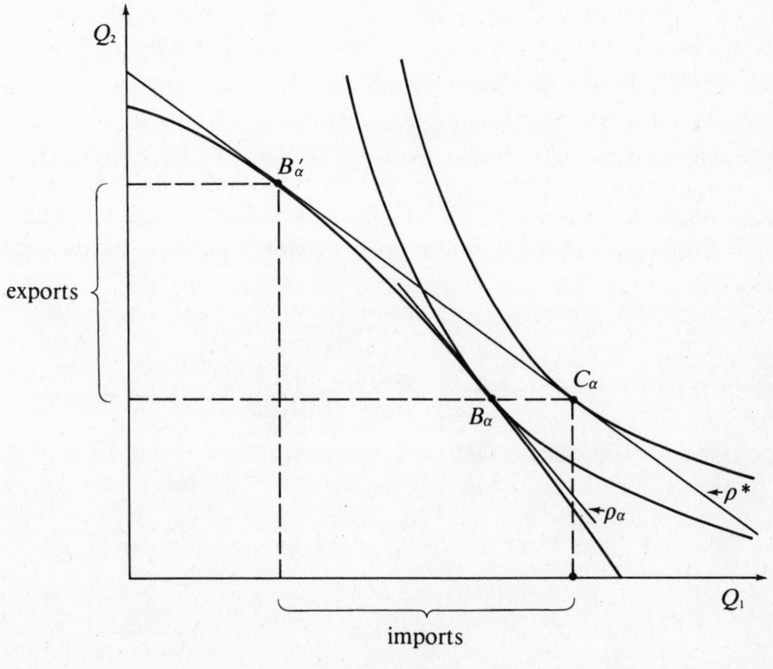

Figure 9.9

$$\left.\frac{\partial L_1}{\partial \lambda}\right|_{\rho=\text{const}} = \frac{\bar{K} - k_2\bar{L}}{k_1 - k_2} \tag{9.41}$$

$$\left.\frac{\partial L_2}{\partial \lambda}\right|_{\rho=\text{const}} = \frac{\bar{L}k_1 - \bar{K}}{k_1 - k_2} \tag{9.42}$$

Hence, in view of the fact that, because of constant returns to scale, a constant ρ implies k_1 and k_2 are constant, we have from (9.41) and (9.42)

$$\frac{\left.\dfrac{\partial Q_1}{\partial \lambda}\right|_{\rho=\text{const}}}{\left.\dfrac{\partial Q_2}{\partial \lambda}\right|_{\rho=\text{const}}} = \frac{g_1(k_1)}{g_2(k_2)}\,\frac{\overline{K/L} - k_2}{k_1 - \overline{K/L}}$$

Note that this expression must be constant for a given ρ and $\overline{K/L}$. Hence, as long as factor proportions remain the same, an increase in the 'scale' of the economy (λ) simply increases Q_1 and Q_2 proportionately for given ρ. The production possibility frontier is therefore homothetic. Given homothetic preferences, then the points of common tangency between this frontier and the indifference curve must all lie along a ray through the origin, and all common tangents must have the same slope. Clearly $\overline{K/L}$ and the production function determine the shape of the production possibility frontier, and so if these are identical for Alpha and for Beta, and if preferences are identical then the tangent, with slope ρ, must be identical.

If *any* one of T1 to T4 is not true, then the goods prices in Alpha and Beta will in general be different under autarky. The country with a high ρ will have a comparative cost advantage in producing good 2 and the country with a low ρ will have a comparative advantage in the production of good 1. If trade between countries then takes place we would expect a common price ratio ρ^* to emerge and we would expect each country to export that good in which it had the comparative cost advantage. Whilst dropping any one of the assumptions T1 to T4 – or indeed dropping assumptions S4 – can thus provide a basis for profitable international trade, attention is often focused on just one of these. This major inter-country difference is in the next theorem.

THEOREM 9.5 *(Heckscher–Ohlin)*: if all the assumptions of S1 to S7, and assumptions T1 to T3 hold, but the countries have different relative resource endowments then there is a basis for trade. The *K*-rich country will export the *K*-intensive good; the *L*-rich country will export the *L*-intensive good.

PROOF: from the Rybczynski Theorem it is clear that if $k_1 > k_2$, then, given a set of homothetic preferences in a closed economy, an increase in $\overline{K/L}$ will lead to a decrease in ρ – see Figure 9.7. Hence if Alpha is relatively well endowed with L (Beta is relatively poorly endowed with L) then $\rho_\alpha > \rho_\beta$

under autarky. The opening of trade in goods between Alpha and Beta will ensure a uniform price ρ^*. Now ρ^* must lie between ρ_α and ρ_β, for otherwise both countries would be exporting the same commodity and importing the same commodity, which is impossible. Hence Alpha exports good 2; Beta exports good 1 ($\rho_\alpha > \rho^* > \rho_\beta$).

Note that the statement of the above result ignores factor intensity reversals. A version of Theorem 9.5 will still hold if there are reversals, but the pattern of trade will obviously be more complicated to describe. However the following result holds *only* if there are no factor intensity reversals.

THEOREM 9.6: given the assumptions S1 to S7, a competitive equilibrium in the goods market, with competition within countries but not between countries in the market for resources, will be Pareto efficient.

PROOF: if there are no factor reversals we know that $\rho(\theta)$ is a monotonic relationship. Trade in the goods market will ensure everywhere that the $MRS_{12} = MRT_{12} = \rho$ for every household and every firm in each country. But if ρ is the same in each country and no factor intensity reversals are possible, θ must be the same in each country so the marginal rate of substitution in production of the *K*-resource for *L*-resource must be the same everywhere. Hence production is efficient.

However, if factor intensity reversals are possible, then the case is as illustrated in Figure 9.10. Autarky goods price ratios in each country are ρ_α, ρ_β; autarky factor price ratios are θ_α, θ_β. Equalisation of goods prices through trade at ρ^* does *not* imply equalisation of θ – we move instead to θ^*_α and θ^*_β.

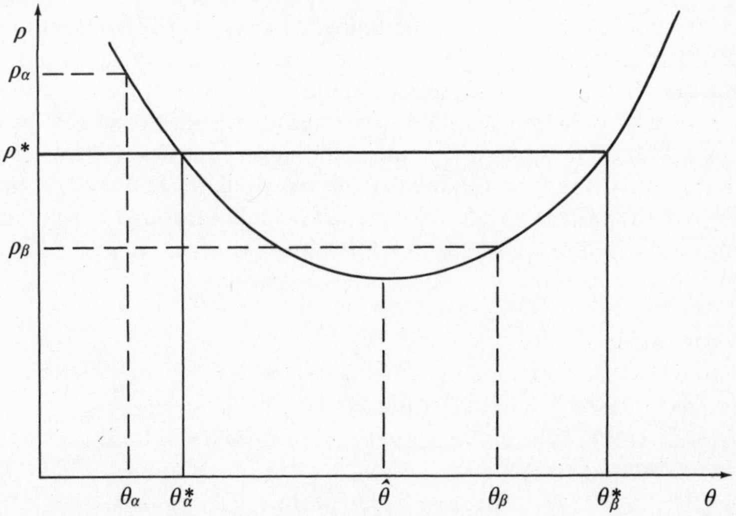

Figure 9.10

In such circumstances it is clear that the absence of trade in international factor markets results in a globally inefficient allocation of resources. This result is hardly amazing since Theorem 8.2 related only to a complete set of markets in *all* commodities – consumer goods and factors. The (slightly) surprising thing is that there should be relatively simple conditions under which this problem does *not* arise: it does not seem very demanding to require the absence of factor intensity reversals in the production function of each economy. However, in other cases where certain markets do not exist – for example in intertemporal economies that do not contain perfect forward markets for every good at every date – the problem of inefficiency of the equilibrium may be more common.

9.6 Summary

If we use a simple two-sector model (two non-produced inputs or 'factors', two outputs) using standard assumptions as to the technology, we can easily get useful results on the way a general equilibrium system operates. Final goods prices (ρ) are linked to the optimum input ratios (k_1 and k_2) which are in turn linked to factor prices (θ). This implies that in so simple a world:

- If endowments are given then there is an automatic link between changes in final goods prices (from changes in tastes or market distortions) and changes in factor incomes (Stolper–Samuelson).
- If final goods prices are given then there is an automatic link between endowments and the employment of factors in each of the sectors (Rybczynski).

The model can be applied in a number of ways, one of the most important of which is the analysis of international trade. However, it should be re-emphasised that all the manipulations in this chapter rest on a particularly simple form of comparative statics. No serious account has been given of how prices and quantities will immediately react in practice. Nor have we considered what happens if individual agents within the system have to take decisions in the light of well-known market data, but through a fog of uncertainty. The next chapter begins to address this issue.

Further Reading

The two sector model is conveniently set out in:

Baldry, J.C. (1980) *General Equilibrium Analysis: An Introduction to the Two-Sector Model*, Croom Helm.

Johnson, H.G. (1971) *The Two-Sector Model of General Equilibrium*, Allen & Unwin Parts I and II.

The applications to international trade theory are discussed more fully in:

Södersten, B. (1970) *International Economics*, Macmillan, Part I.

and

Dixit, A.K. and Norman, V. (1980) *Theory of International Trade*, Cambridge University Press, Chs 4, 5.

Other applications are to be found in:

Atkinson, A.B. and Stiglitz, J.E. (1980) *Lectures in Public Economics*, McGraw-Hill, Ch. 6.

Exercises

9.1 (a) In the context of the model of Section 9.1 suppose that the production function for each good i shifts over time thus:

$$\hat{G}^i(K_i, L_i; t) = A(t)G^i(K_i, L_i)$$

where $A(t)$ is an increasing function of t. Illustrate this using Figures 9.1 and 9.2.

(b) In the context of the same model suppose that the shift in the production function is given by

$$\tilde{G}^i(K_i, L_i; t) = G^i(K_i, A(t)L_i)$$

Again, illustrate this diagrammatically.

(c) Interpret each of the processes (a) and (b) as a model of technical progress.

*9.2 The government of Ruritania has to make reparation payments to another country. To do this it imposes a special tax. Assume that S1–S7 of Section 9.1 hold and that factors cannot move across Ruritania's frontier. Analyse the effects on prices, factor usage and outputs under each of the following assumptions about the way the tax is levied:

(a) Ruritania levies a tariff on imports;
(b) Ruritania imposes a tax on one good;
(c) Ruritania levies a tax on all interest income;
(d) A levy on capital is made which shifts some of Ruritania's capital stock abroad to its creditors.

9.3 Albion is a small state possessing limited quantities of labour and energy resources and having a technology that exhibits constant returns to scale. Oil is discovered in Albion. Use a simple General Equilibrium model to analyse the subsequent course of events assuming (a) that Albion is a price-taking trader in world markets of consumer goods; (b) that Albion is a closed economy with no international trade at all. State clearly any further assumptions you make.

9.4 Consider the 2-sector general equilibrium model. Labour becomes unionised in the labour intensive sector and negotiates a wage differential above that of the other sector. Analyse the new equilibrium in terms of relative goods prices, factor usage and factor rewards. Can the unionised labour lose out in terms of real income?

9.5 Examine the effect of each type of technical progress in Exercise 9.1 in a 2-good model of a small economy that trades in a perfectly competitive world market for consumer goods.

9.6 (a) Suppose that in the absence of trade, the situation in two countries is as follows:

	Price of good 1	Price of good 2
Country Alpha	\$5	\$4
Country Beta	£10	£2

Show that there is a basis for trade between the countries.

(b) Describe and explain the pattern of trading that will take place between the two countries.

(c) Suppose that on the international money market £1 may be bought for \$2.50: good 2 can be produced cheaper in country Alpha. Why is any of good 2 produced in country Beta?

9.7 In a certain economy two goods (labelled 1 and 2) can be produced from two resources (labelled K and L) according to the production functions

$$Q_1 = K_1^{1/2} L_1^{1/2}$$

$$Q_2 = [K_2^{-1} + L_2^{-1}]^{-1}$$

where Q_i, K_i, L_i are, respectively, the output of good i, the amount of factor K used in producing good i and the amount of factor L used in inputs in producing good i, $i = 1,2$. The economy is competitive with prices p_1, p_2 for the two goods and prices w_K, w_L for the two resources. Find the relationship between the resource price ratio w_L/w_K and the efficient input ratio K_i/L_i in each industry. Hence find the relationship between the goods price ratio p_1/p_2 and the resource price ratio w_L/w_K. The states of Banania and Republico each produce these two goods, subject to the production functions given above. Banania has a fixed K-endowment of two million units, and an L-endowment of one million units. Republico has endowments of one million units of K and two million units of L. Originally the economies are completely isolated; and the price ratio p_1/p_2 is $\frac{1}{4}$ in Banania and $\frac{1}{3}$ in Republico. Trade in the two consumer goods is then permitted, but *not* in resources. Describe the pattern of trade that emerges and the movement of resource prices in the two countries.

9.8 In the world descibed in Exercise 9.7 Banania and Republico consider forming a common market which will now permit free movement of resources as well as goods. Is there any point in doing so? What will be the equilibrium prices?

*9.9 Consider the 2-country example of the opening of international trade (p. 196, Section 9.5).

Suppose that each of the two countries, Alpha and Beta, consists of two homogeneous groups: those who own the K-resource (but no L) and those who own the L-resource (but no K). Compare the situation of each of the two groups in each of the two countries before trade, and after the international trade equilibrium has been established.

In the light of your answer are there any pitfalls in stating that a country will potentially gain from free international trade in goods?

10

Uncertainty

10.1 Introduction

Uncertainty means that you don't know what is going to happen. Having said that, there are quite different reasons *why* a person does not know what is going to happen, reasons which are important to distinguish in modelling the economics of people's choices. The primary distinction we shall make is between uncertainty that arises purely as a result of our not knowing exactly what the morrow will bring in terms of 'exogenous' events (whether it will be a fine day or not, whether your lottery ticket will come up, whether there is accidental nuclear war ...) and the uncertainty that arises because of the interaction between our own decision problem and those of other people (if I cut the prices in my store, will the fellow round the corner do the same?). In this chapter we shall concentrate on the former type of uncertainty in which the individual decision maker has to take action whilst not knowing the outcome of a roll of the dice over which he can have no influence. The issue of strategic interdependence – where the unknown events themselves may be influenced by the decision maker's choice – will be discussed in Chapter 11. However, the roll of the dice analogy need not be confined to natural phenomena. Some of the actions of government, for example, might be taken as exogenous yet uncertain by households or firms in making their consumption or production plans. Indeed, let us use this case to explain further the type of uncertainty that we shall analyse.

Imagine that you have to take a decision in the morning, the full consequences of which depend on the outcome of something that will happen later in the day. For example, suppose it is Budget Day in the UK. You have a small, unrefundable portion of your car's annual Road Fund Tax left unexpired, but you suspect that the Chancellor of the Exchequer may increase that tax. Should you renew your one-year licence (and risk simply losing the value of the unexpired portion if the tax does not go up) or leave the renewal until the licence expires in a month's time (and risk having to pay for the next eleven months at a much higher rate)? The various announcements that the Chancellor might make in the afternoon we shall call *states of the world* and the monetary gains or losses arising from your choice in the morning we shall

Table 10.1 Essential notation for Chapter 10: Uncertainty

ω	:	state of the world
Ω	:	set of states of the world
$\pi(\omega)$	:	(subjective) probability of state ω
$\upsilon(\mathbf{x}(\omega))$	:	cardinal utility of payoff $\mathbf{x}(\omega)$
ξ	:	certainty equivalent
$p_i(\omega)$	:	*ex-ante* price of good i contingent on state ω
P_ω	:	price of a \$1-security in state ω
p_i	:	*ex-post* price of good i in state ω

call the *outcomes*. In this case the outcome could be simply evaluated as a scalar, although more generally, it might be a vector of goods. We refer to the view of the situation as it appears in the morning as *ex-ante*, and the view in the evening, after the Chancellor has made his budget statement, as *ex-post*. The set of outcomes corresponding to a particular set of states of the world viewed *ex-ante* will be referred to as a *prospect*, and will be discussed further below.

Consider further the set of possible states of the world. In the example we have just given there are in fact infinitely many states which could be represented by an interval on the real line: the Chancellor could announce an increase in Road Fund Tax that is any number greater than or equal to zero.[1] But the choice under uncertainty might be made where there was a finite number of states of the world. To change the example, the afternoon might see the announcement of the result of an election: whichever party wins determines completely the outcome of any given choice made by an individual in the morning, and so the set of all states of the world consists simply of the parties which might take office.

We shall refer to the set of all possible states of the world as Ω, and refer to a particular state of the world by the letter ω. Note, incidentally, that the concept of a 'state of the world' is quite different from the concept of a 'social state', used in Chapter 8. An element of $\mathcal{S}$ (the set of all social states) is an exhaustive description of a particular 'snapshot' of the social and economic system (the consumption bundles received by each household, the outputs and inputs of each firm, who lives in which family . . .); the set Ω is a convenient way of describing all the possible outcomes of a roll of the dice, or a spin of the roulette wheel.

Obviously a mere description of the set of all possible states of the world – a listing of all the possibilities that the afternoon might bring – is going to

[1] I am assuing that there is no conceivable circumstance under which the Chancellor could or would *reduce* Road Fund Tax, and that you are not so important as to be able to influence the Chancellor's decision.

be inadequate for many types of choice under uncertainty. It is useful to know *ex-ante* what the *probability* of each state's occurrence might be: such information would reasonably be expected to influence the *ex-ante* choice of a rational decision maker and, indeed, for some applications would be an essential part of the description of a 'prospect'. Where states can be described by a continuous random variable ω (as in the tax example above) we may assume the existence of a probability density function. Whether one has a discrete or continuous state space, however, it is assumed that no individual can influence the *ex-ante* probability of any particular event.[2]

However one has to be rather cautious at this point. Whilst for a lot of elementary statistical examples – throwing dice, drawing balls from urns and so on – the probabilities associated with each state of the world are clearly defined, this is not always so in cases of economic choices under uncertainty. The uncertain event may well involve so much specialised information that it is impossible to provide any worthwhile objective description of the *ex-ante* probabilities. Consider, for example, the difficulty of trying to specify the frequency distribution of the profits of a firm about to market a revolutionary new product, or the probability of a particular individual being offered employment in a unique job that demands a complex of specialised skills. Must one therefore discard the idea of an *ex-ante* probability distribution under such circumstances? As we shall see in the next section, things may not be quite so hopeless. For, even in circumstances where an 'objective' probability distribution cannot usefully be defined, each individual may take decisions *as though* he knew of a probability distribution. Of course different rational agents might have quite different beliefs about such 'subjective' probabilities but, as we shall see, this need not destroy the main structure of the argument.

10.2 Preferences

Consider Figure 10.1 which gives a particularly simple version of the election example above. These are only two possible states: either red wins or blue wins, and the outcome in each case is a monetary payoff. Let us see how far the analysis of Section 4.3 of Chapter 4 can be applied: it seems reasonable to suppose that the elementary axioms on preferences should hold. For example, take a particular point A: obviously any point such as B to the 'north east' of A, which gives a greater payoff whether red or blue wins, would reasonably be assumed to be preferred to A (Axiom C4). And there seems little

---

[2] For a modification to the case where individuals *can* influence the probabilities see Ehrlich, I. and Becker, G.S. (1972) 'Market insurance, self-insurance and self-protection', *Journal of Political Economy*, Vol. 86, pp. 623–48. See also pp. 286–92 below.

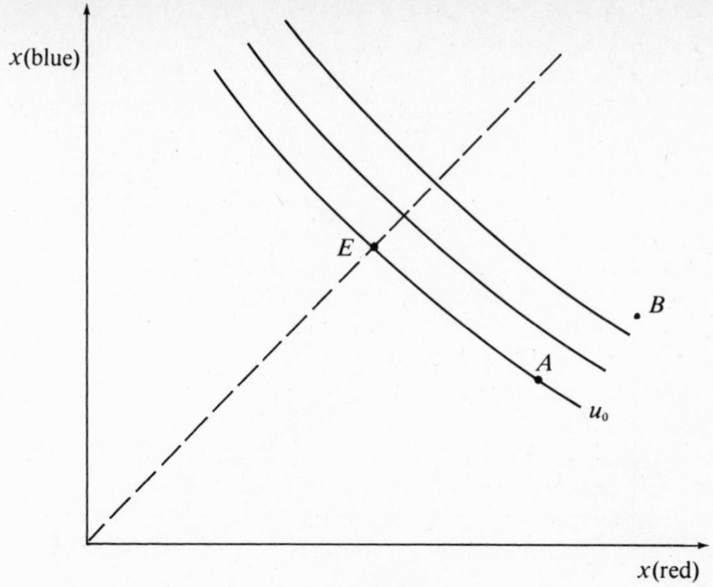

Figure 10.1

objection to imposing Axioms C1 to C3 in this model of choice as well,[3] which then implies the existence of a continuous ordinal utility function defined on the consumption set which is a subset of 'red–blue' space – see Theorem 4.1. We may, therefore, sketch in a family of indifference curves such as that depicted in Figure 10.1. However whilst, as we have argued, the existence of a utility function (C1 to C3) and the Axiom of greed (C4) seems reasonable, and whilst indeed the assumptions of smoothness (C6) seems fairly harmless, what about the assumption of a strictly concave-contoured utility function (C5) – is there a rationale for that?

To see the argument here, let us introduce a very simple idea. Draw a line through the origin at 45° and observe where it cuts a particular indifference curve u_0: call this point E. The point E is a prospect which offers the same outcome whatever the state of the world and is, by construction, indifferent to A. We shall call E the *certainty equivalent* of A for obvious reasons. Now examine Figure 10.2 where we find the preferences of an individual who happens to regard the proposed $A_0 = (6,12)$ as indifferent to $A_1 = (15,3)$: each prospect has the certainty equivalent $E = (8,8)$. With A_0 his payoff is bigger if the blue wins, with A_1 it is bigger if red wins. Now consider any

---

[3] In fact serious objection can be raised against the continuity axiom for certain kinds of uncertain events – see Arrow, K.J. (1970) *Essays in the Theory of Risk Bearing*, North-Holland, pp. 48, 49.

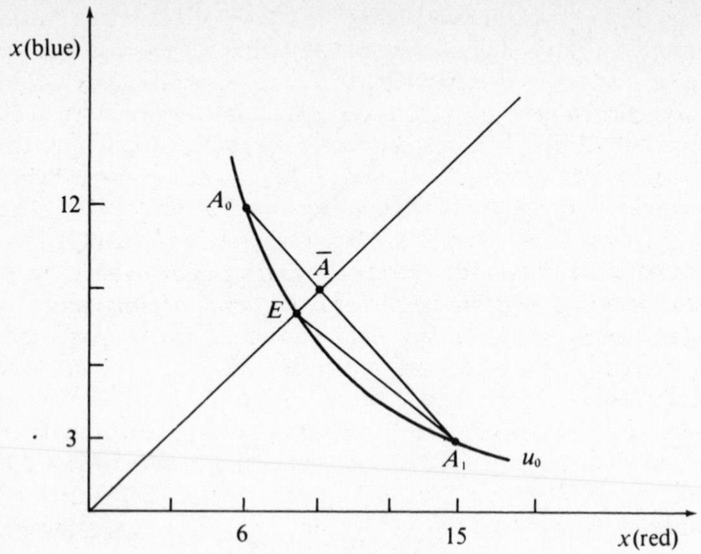

Figure 10.2

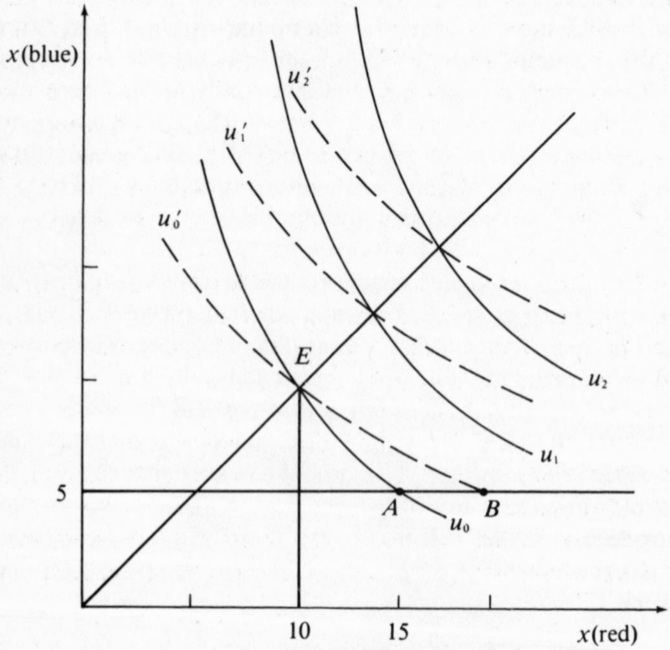

Figure 10.3

point lying on the straight line joining A_1 and E. If the utility function is strictly concave-contoured it is clear that any point in the interior of this line segment must be strictly preferred to either of the endpoints. So, we find that to 'mix' a particular prospect with its certainty equivalent is *always* preferred to the original prospect – a property known as *risk aversion*.[4] One can also see this point by considering A_0, A_1 and the 'mix' of the two $\bar{A}$ (which is $\frac{2}{3}$ of A_0 and $\frac{1}{3}$ of A_1). A risk-averse individual would *always* prefer $\bar{A}$ with its guaranteed return of (9,9) to either of the two bundles A_0 and A_1.

To restate the point: *risk aversion implies and is implied by strictly convex-to-the-origin indifference curves in the space of prospects.*

So far in this section we have managed to get by with only the most fleeting reference to the idea of probability. Let us now see how the individual's beliefs about which of the two events (red or blue winning) affect the choice problem. Suppose that we have a complete description of the person's indifference map at 10 o'clock in the morning represented by the system of curves labelled u_0, u_1, u_2, ... in Figure 10.3. Reflect on the significance of two points lying on the same curve: at 10 a.m., the way this person sees things, he would be prepared to swap an absolutely certain outcome of 10 whatever happens (point E) for an entitlement that says 'pay 15 if red wins, but only 5 if blue wins' (point A). Now suppose that at 10.05 a.m., after he has heard a news bulletin with a revised forecast of the electoral outcome, the person concludes that red is less likely to win than he first thought. It would be unusual indeed to suppose that he *still* regards A and E as indifferent: perhaps now he would only be prepared to swap the certain prospect E for the prospect B, for example. Indeed we may now find that the preferences he expresses are represented by the system of broken curves u_0', u_1', u_2', ... So we see that the 'degrees of belief' about, or the 'subjective probabilities' imputed to, the uncertain events affect the shape of the indifference map: they are an integral part of consumer preferences under uncertainty.

However this still leaves one with a rather unwieldy, general representation of a person's preferences. For example, where outcomes are each commodity vectors and Ω is a finite set $\{1,2,3, \ldots, \bar{\omega}\}$, preferences are represented by a continuous function

$$U(\mathbf{x}(1), \mathbf{x}(2), \ldots, \mathbf{x}(\bar{\omega})) \tag{10.1}$$

where the form of the function U itself depends on the personal evaluation of risks by the individual.

By introducing further axioms we can impose more structure on the expression (10.1) which may give us a more tractable criterion function with which to work.

---

[4] For obvious reasons if the person is indifferent to such mixtures we say that he is *risk neutral*, if he actually dislikes such mixtures, we say he is a *risk lover*.

AXIOM U1 (state irrelevance): whichever state ω is realised has no intrinsic value to the person.

AXIOM U2 (independence): let A_z and $\hat{A}_z$ be any two distinct prospects specified in such a way that the payoff in one particular state of the world ω is the *same* for both prospects: $\mathbf{x}(\omega) = \mathbf{x}(\omega) = \mathbf{z}$. Then, if prospect A_z is preferred to prospect $\hat{A}_z$ for *one* value of $\mathbf{z}$, A_z is preferred to $\hat{A}_z$ for *all* values of $\mathbf{z}$.

AXIOM U3 (revealed likelihood): Let $\mathbf{x}^0$ and $\mathbf{x}^1$ be two payoffs such that under certainty $\mathbf{x}^0$ would be (weakly) preferred to $\mathbf{x}^1$. Let Ω' and Ω'' be two given subsets of the set of all states of the world Ω and suppose the individual weakly prefers the prospect

$$A' = [\mathbf{x}^0 \text{ if } \omega \in \Omega', \quad \mathbf{x}^1 \text{ if } \omega \notin \Omega']$$

to the prospect

$$A'' = [\mathbf{x}^0 \text{ if } \omega \in \Omega'', \quad \mathbf{x}^1 \text{ if } \omega \notin \Omega'']$$

for *some* such $\mathbf{x}^0$, $\mathbf{x}^1$. Then he prefers A' to A'' for *every* such $\mathbf{x}^0$, $\mathbf{x}^1$.

We shall discuss the intuition underlying these three axioms in a moment: but let us note immediately that they impose a powerful, and useful, structure upon the utility function.

THEOREM 10.1[5]: Given Axioms C1 to C3 and U1 to U3 the utility function (10.1) may be written

$$\sum_{\omega \in \Omega} \pi(\omega) \upsilon(\mathbf{x}(\omega)) \tag{10.2}$$

where $\{\pi(\omega)\}$ is a set of scalars and $\upsilon(.)$ is a continuous, concave, real valued function.

Expression (10.2) is usually known as a *von Neumann–Morgenstern* utility function. It has a delightfully simple interpretation: $\upsilon(.)$ can be interpreted as the (cardinal) utility of any given outcome, $\pi(.)$ as the (subjective) probability of that outcome and hence the entire expression (10.2) as the *expected utility* $\mathscr{E}\upsilon$ of the prospect given by $[\mathbf{x}(\omega) : \omega \in \Omega]$. A number of writers have discussed the logical basis of the criterion function of choice under uncertainty in terms of this 'expected utility' function. But perhaps the particular axiomatic structure of which the above is a sketch brings out most clearly the issues involved. Whilst we shall retain this formulation for the simple discussions of the remainder of this chapter, two points should however be borne in mind: (a) the *special* form of utility function (10.2) is unnecessarily restrictive for many useful results in economic theory under uncertainty – in fact much can be achieved with theoretical constructs as general as that depicted in Figures 10.1 and 10.2: (b) the Axioms U1–U3

[5] For proof see Arrow, *Essays in the Theory of Risk Bearing*, Ch. 2.

receive far from universal support amongst economists and other social scientists. It is, perhaps, worthwhile reflecting further on the implications of these assumptions. Axiom U1 is perhaps not very troublesome. In many risk-taking problems the particular state that is realised is unimportant – it is only the associated monetary payoff that matters. But there *are* a few examples where this manifestly will not do, the most obvious example of which is perhaps where there is a risk of death. Here it would be quite reasonable to employ a *different* utility function for each of the two states ω = 'survive', ω = 'die' since in the one state monetary payoffs affect one's own consumption directly, in the other they benefit only one's nearest and dearest. Axiom U2 endows the utility function with an additively separable structure. Compelling arguments have been suggested for its reasonableness on the grounds that one and only one state will be realised and that therefore the hypothetical payoffs attached to other (*ex-ante*) possible states are irrelevant to the ordering of outcomes in the particular state that is realised *ex-post*.[6] The problem is that experiments suggest that people just do not seem to act that way. Axiom U3 suggests a degree of coherence about people's prognoses of forthcoming states of the world that not everyone would be prepared to accept.

However, let us accept for the moment the expected utility criterion, leaving aside for now the nature of the probability distribution that is implied in the use of the $\mathscr{E}$-symbol. In the simple two-state example of Figures 10.1 and 10.2 the slope of an indifference curve is $-\pi(\text{red})\upsilon'(x(\text{red}))/\pi(\text{blue})\upsilon'(x(\text{blue}))$ where a prime denotes the derivative. So along the 45° line, where the payoffs are equal, *the slope of the indifference curves equals the ratio of the subjective probabilities*. Furthermore if one computes the curvature of the indifference curve and evaluates it at a point on the 45° line we find that it is proportional to $-\upsilon''(x)/\upsilon'(x)$. Now we have already associated the convex-to-the-origin shape of the indifference curve with aversion to risk. Indeed a few experiments with Figure 10.2 suggest that the more 'sharply' curved is the indifference curve at any point, the more risk averse the person is. Hence the quantity $a \equiv -\upsilon''(x)/\upsilon'(x)$ is often referred to as the (absolute) *risk aversion* of the person.

Another way of seeing the usefulness of this concept is in terms of the *certainty equivalent* or the *risk premium*. Again let the payoff be in terms of a single consumption good x.

DEFINITION 10.1: for a given cardinal utility function υ and probability distribution of x,

(a) the *certainty equivalent* ξ is a non-stochastic variable such that

$$\upsilon(\xi) = \mathscr{E}\,\upsilon(x)$$

---

[6] See, for example, Deaton and Muellbauer, pp. 390–2.

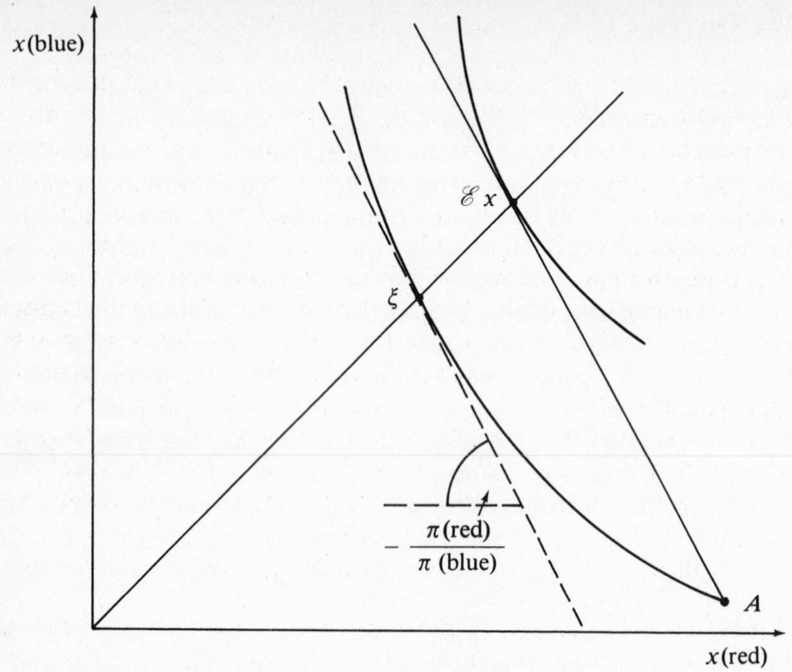

Figure 10.4

(b) the *risk premium* is $\mathscr{E}x - \xi$

For a risk-averse individual the certainty equivalent of x is less than the expected value of x; he demands a positive risk premium. This is illustrated in Figure 10.4. Note that in general the risk premium depends on both the utility function and the distribution of x, as we see in the next two theorems.

THEOREM 10.2:[7] for small risks

$$\mathscr{E}x - \xi = \tfrac{1}{2}\, a \operatorname{var}(x)$$

So, as an approximation, the risk premium equals half the absolute risk aversion times the variance.

THEOREM 10.3: let $\upsilon(x)$ and $\hat{\upsilon}(x)$ be two cardinal utility functions such that $\hat{\upsilon}$ is a concave transformation of υ. Then $\hat{a} \geqslant a$.

Hence the more concave – the more 'sharply curved' – is the cardinal utility function υ, the higher is the risk aversion and the higher is the risk premium on any given prospect.

---

[7] For proof of this and Theorem 10.3, see Exercise 10.4.

10.3 The Feasible Set

Let us now consider the kind of options that may be open to the decision maker under uncertainty – his market environment and budget constraint. In one sense we have already introduced one aspect of this in that we have considered whether an individual would swap a given random prospect x for a certain payoff ξ. Is there, however, an analogue to the type of budget set we considered in Chapters 4 and 5?

It is easiest to proceed carefully by means of example since there are a number of important practical pitfalls. Return once again to the two-state 'red/blue' examples above and examine Figure 10.5(i) which represents a simple portfolio composition problem. Imagine that an individual is endowed with an entitlement to a sum x_0 (denominated in dollars) whichever state of the world is realised. We may think of this as money. He may use one or more of these dollars to purchase bonds in dollar units. Each bond has a yield of r_1 if state blue is realised, and r_2 if state red is realised where we assume that

$$r_2 > 0 > r_1 > -1$$

So if the individual purchases B bonds and holds the balance $x_0 - B$ in the form of money then the payoff to him is

$$\begin{aligned} &\text{either} \quad x(\text{blue}) = [x_0 - B] + B[1 + r_1] \\ &\text{or} \qquad x(\text{red}) = [x_0 - B] + B[1 + r_2] \end{aligned}$$

Notice that, by construction of the example, for all positive B we have $x(\text{red}) > x_0 > x(\text{blue})$. In Figure 10.5(i) the points M and A represent, respectively the two cases where $B = 0$ and $B = x_0$. Clearly the slope of the line MA is r_1/r_2 a negative number.

Given that he has access to such a bond market, any point on the line MA must lie in the feasible set; and assuming that free disposal of his monetary payoff is available in either case, the feasible set must include all the points in the pentagon $OLMAK$. Are there any more such points? Perhaps.

First of all, consider points lying above the line LM. If one could 'buy' a *negative* amount of bonds, then obviously the line AM could be extended up beyond M until it met the vertical axis. What this would mean, of course, is that the individual is now *selling* bonds to the market. Whether this is a practical proposition or not depends on other people's evaluation of him as to his 'financial soundness' – will he pay up if red materialises? With certain small transactions – betting on horse races among one's friends, for example – this may be quite reasonable. Otherwise one may have to offer an extremely larger r_2 relative to r_1 to get anybody to buy one's bonds.

Secondly consider points to the right of AK. Why can't we just extend the line MA downwards until it meets the horizontal axis? In order to do this

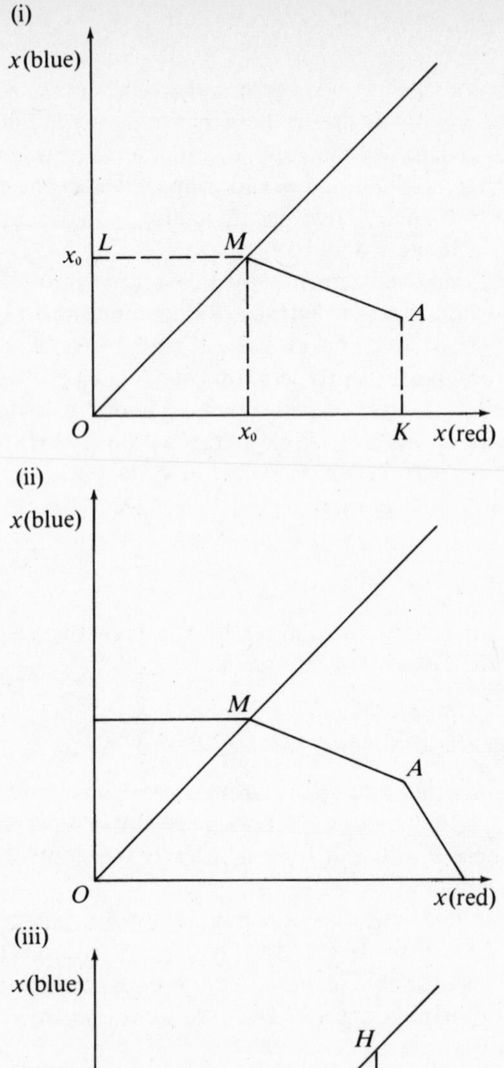
(i)
x(blue)
L
M
x0
A
O
x0
K
x(red)
(ii)
x(blue)
M
A
O
x(red)
(iii)
x(blue)
H
M'
L
M
x0
P
K1
A
K2
O
x0
x(red)

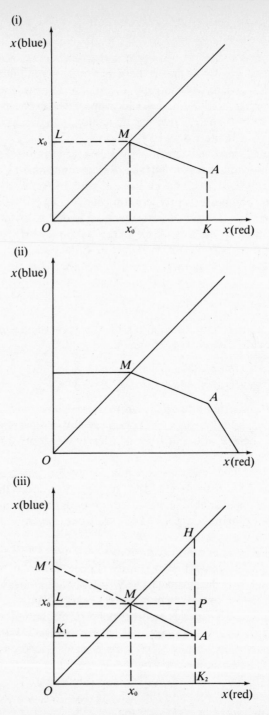

Figure 10.5

one would have to find someone ready to sell bonds 'on credit' since one would then be buying an amount $B > x_0$. Whoever extends this credit then has to bear the risk of the individual going bankrupt if blue is realised. So lenders might be found who would be prepared to advance him cash up to the point where he could purchase $-x_0/r_1$ worth of bonds. Again, we can probably imagine situations in which this is a plausible assumption, but it may seem reasonable to suppose that one may have to pay a very high premium for such a facility. Accordingly the feasible set might look something like Figure 10.5(ii), although for many purposes Figure 10.5(i) is the relevant shape. Of course if there were many possible states there might be a role for many such financial assets, a point to which we return in the next section.

Now consider a rather different problem in Figure 10.5(iii). Suppose that the individual's endowment is itself stochastic – it equals OK_1 if blue is realised and OK_2 if red is realised. To use the well-worn example here, state blue might be having one's house destroyed by fire and state red its not being destroyed: OK_1 and OK_2 represent the monetary values of one's assets in the two states. Let us suppose that fire insurance is available and interpret Figure 10.5(iii). Obviously the monetary loss from the fire, should it occur, is represented by the distance HA. If full coverage is available at a premium represented by the distance HP then the outcome for such full insurance will be at point M. If the individual may also purchase partial insurance at the same rates, then once again the whole of the line segment MA – and hence the whole pentagonal area $OLMAK_2$ – must lie in the feasible set.

In this case too we can see that it may be that there are no further points available to the individual. Again consider the implications of extending the line AM to the point M' on the vertical axis and taking all the points lying between it and the axes as part of the budget set. At any point between M and M' the individual would in fact be better off if his house burned down than if it did not. The person has over-insured himself, a practice which is usually frowned upon. The reason that it is frowned upon is to be found in the concept of *moral hazard*. Moral hazard refers to the influence that the actions of the insured may have on the probability of certain events' occurrence. Up until now we have taken the probabilities – 'objective' or 'subjective' – attached to different events as exogenously given. But in practice the probability of my house burning down depends in part on my carelessness or otherwise. And I may be more inclined to be careless if I know that I have the Surething Insurance Company to back me up if one day the house does burn down. And I may be inclined to be criminally negligent if I know I stand to *gain* by event blue being realised. So insurance companies usually prevent over-insurance and may indeed include an 'excess' clause ('co-insurance') so that not even all of the line AM is available to the person. Finally note that for reasons similar to those of the portfolio selection example it is unlikely that the points on the projections of MA beyond A can be included in the feasible set.

Finally a word about numbers. In the discussions above of the portfolio and the insurance problem it has been assumed that a market exists, for at least some risks. Whilst the subject in general is quite complex, it is interesting to consider under what circumstances such a market might exist. A little reflection on the insurance market reveals that the large numbers of consumers in the market permit the *pooling* of risks. A simple example might help. Suppose we have an economy consisting of clones. Each clone faces an identical independent risk on his wealth, and evaluates the risk with identical subjective probability: specifically each reckons on $2,000 with probability 0.4 and $4,000 with probability 0.6. Let us suppose the clones assemble themselves and agree to pool their wealth and share equally whatever the combined realised payoff turns out to be. Clearly the mathematical expectation is $3,200. Now consider Table 10.2. As we replicate the economy to 2, 4, 8, 16, ... persons, we can see that the distribution of payoffs to the individual soon becomes symmetric and concentrated about the expected value. In the limit, of course, the probability of any payoff different from the expected value becomes infinitesimal. If the insurance company (or companies) is owned by a large number of 'small' individuals – that is if the shares in the profits and losses from insurance are reasonably diffuse – then the risks are not only pooled but also *spread*. Under such circumstances it would appear that there is the basis for effective competition in both the demand side and the supply side of a market for insurance.

Table 10.2 Probability distribution of payoffs to an individual in economies of different sizes

	Number in Population				
	1	2	4	8	16
Payoff 2,000	0.400	0.160	0.026	0.001	0.000
($) 2,125	0	0	0	0	0.000
2,250	0	0	0	0.008	0.000
2,375	0	0	0	0	0.001
2,500	0	0	0.154	0.041	0.004
2,625	0	0	0	0	0.014
2,750	0	0	0	0.124	0.039
2,875	0	0	0	0	0.084
3,000	0	0.480	0.346	0.232	0.142
3,125	0	0	0	0	0.189
3,250	0	0	0	0.279	0.198
3,375	0	0	0	0	0.162
3,500	0	0	0.346	0.209	0.101
3,625	0	0	0	0	0.047
3,750	0	0	0	0.090	0.015
3,875	0	0	0	0	0.003
4,000	0.600	0.360	0.130	0.017	0.000

So it appears that with a very large number of agents each one ought to be able to 'buy insurance' against the risk on his income at an actuarially fair price corresponding to the probabilities given above. But the example also reveals some obvious pitfalls: (i) there is the 'moral hazard' problem as described above. We must assume that no person can have direct influence on the probability of any particular payoff being realised; (ii) each agent must be 'small' in the limit; (iii) the *risks must be independent* – the results will not work if all the agents' risks are closely correlated; (iv) finally, of course, the payoffs must be tradeable amongst the individuals. If not money, they must be in the form of some transferable commodity. Obviously there are some risks which people confront where the payoffs cannot be thus transferred, and where losses cannot be compensated for in money. For any of these reasons a market may simply not exist.[8]

10.4 The Individual's Optimisation Problem

We now draw together the rather simplified and fragmentary discussions of the last two sections to look at a fundamental issue: consumer optimisation under uncertainty. For reference, let us go back to the standard certainty model. Typically this can be represented as follows (see Section 4.4 of Chapter 4):

$$\max_{\{\mathbf{x}\}} U(\mathbf{x})$$

$$\text{subject to} \quad \sum_{i=1}^{n} p_i x_i \leqslant M \tag{10.3}$$

$$\text{and} \quad x_i \geqslant 0 \tag{10.4}$$

where $p_1, \ldots, p_n$ and M are determinate parameters. Obviously, there are several ways in which one might enrich this model to incorporate uncertainty:

(a) M, the budget, may be stochastic;
(b) one or more of the p_i may be stochastic;
(c) the *quality* of each purchased good i may be unknown *ex-ante*.

We shall particularly pursue course (a) because the results that are obtainable are readily interpreted and the techniques employed provide useful lessons for other types of optimisation under uncertainty.

As we noted in Section 10.3 there are a number of ways in which one might model the uncertainty of wealth M. For simplicity we shall take the case where the individual is endowed with a fixed amount K of some asset

8 A further problem, 'adverse selection', is discussed in Chapter 12, page 279.

with a non-random return of zero ('cash') and has the opportunity of purchasing quantities $B^j, j = 1, \ldots, N$, of N other assets with stochastic rates of return, $r^1, r^2, \ldots, r^N$, subject to prohibitions on *selling* bonds or borrowing cash to purchase bonds, as discussed in Section 10.3. Then we find that

$$M = \sum_{j=1}^{N} B^j [1 + r^j] + \left[K - \sum_{j=1}^{N} B^j\right]$$

$$= K + \sum_{j=1}^{N} B^j r^j \tag{10.5}$$

and $B^j \geqslant 0$, for all j, $\sum_{j=1}^{N} B^j \leqslant K$

Then the consumer's problem is to choose $x_1, \ldots, x_n$ and $B^1, \ldots, B^N$ to maximise $U(\mathbf{x})$ subject to (10.3)–(10.5).

It is not hard to see that this optimisation problem can be conveniently split up. Recalling that the $\{r^j\}$ and hence M are random variables, write the realisation of M in state ω, given a particular choice of $B^1, \ldots, B^N$ as $M(\omega)$. The stochastic budget constraint (10.3) must always hold and for any particular realisation $M(\omega)$ we can use the usual first-order conditions to get

$$x_i^*(\omega) = D^i(\mathbf{p}, M(\omega)) \tag{10.6}$$

Notice that the price vector $\mathbf{p}$ and the *form* of the demand function D^i are independent of the state ω. Hence, if U1 to U3 are satisfied, we can write the cardinal utility in state ω in the form of a simple indirect utility function

$$V(\mathbf{p}, M(\omega)) \tag{10.7}$$

where only M depends on the state of the world ω. One may then choose $B^1, \ldots, B^N$ to maximise $\mathscr{E}\, V(\mathbf{p}, M)$ subject to (10.5). To summarise, we have a two-stage problem:

(1) For any given realisation of M choose the consumption vector to maximise utility in the usual way, yielding an indirect utility function (10.7).
(2) By choice of financial assets maximise the 'expected utility of wealth' implicit in (10.7).

The vector of commodity prices $\mathbf{p}$ acts as a shift parameter in stage (2) of the problem. Since it is on this stage that we wish to concentrate, let us eliminate this surplus notation by taking $\mathbf{p}$ as invariant from now on and defining

$$\upsilon(M) \equiv V(\mathbf{p}, M) \tag{10.8}$$

For a finite set of states of the world $\Omega = \{1, 2, 3, \ldots, \overline{\omega}\}$ we may then write stage (2) of the problem as:

choose $B^1, \ldots, B^N$ to maximise

$$\sum_{\omega=1}^{\bar{\omega}} \pi(\omega)\upsilon(M(\omega)) \tag{10.9}$$

subject to

$$\begin{cases} M(1) = K + B^1r^1(1) + B^2r^2(1) + \ldots + B^Nr^N(1) \\ M(2) = K + B^1r^1(2) + B^2r^2(2) + \ldots + B^Nr^N(2) \\ \ldots \quad \ldots \quad \ldots \quad \ldots \quad \ldots \\ M(\bar{\omega}) = K + B^1r^1(\bar{\omega}) + B^2r^2(\bar{\omega}) + \ldots + B^Nr^N(\bar{\omega}) \end{cases} \tag{10.10}$$

Clearly the problem is structurally very similar to the 'household production' model of Chapter 5, Section 5.6. Note in particular the similarity between (10.10) and the production constraint (5.17). Here the monetary wealth values in each state $\omega = 1, \ldots, \bar{\omega}$ are the desired 'outputs' that are arguments of the utility function and the quantities of the bonds $B^1, \ldots, B^N$ represent the 'purchased inputs'. The problem of the selection of financial assets under uncertainty will therefore have a similar solution to that of the household production model.

In view of this we may make a few simple generalised deductions. We may obviously ignore as being of no interest any asset which is dominated by another – i.e. any asset where it is possible to find another asset that yields a higher return in every possible state of the world. But we should also ignore any asset which is dominated by some *convex combination* of other assets: if, for example, there is some α between zero and unity such that $\alpha r^1 + [1 - \alpha]r^2$ dominates r^3 then asset 3 is irrelevant. However, it is difficult to predict *a priori* how diversified a person's portfolio is likely to be, in terms of the number of different assets of which he holds positive amounts. As we saw in Chapter 5, even where some household techniques were not dominated, it was quite rational for a household not to purchase some 'inputs' at all at one set of prices and yet to purchase only those 'inputs' at another set of prices in order to achieve the desired combination of outputs. Figure 5.11 illustrates the case with only two outputs and a large number of purchasable inputs. So it is reasonable to expect that, even if we have excluded from our list of N assets any that would be dominated (and hence irrelevant) there may be a lot of zeros amongst the $B^1, \ldots, B^N$. This conclusion may still hold even if the set of all possible states of the world Ω is much larger than the set of desired goods in the household production example. Moreover, the demand for any particular asset is likely to have 'jumps' in it as we consider changes in income or in rates of return – again similar to the sudden switches in demand in the household production model.

For expository purposes, therefore, there is a lot to be gained by simplifying the analysis for any one *individual* by looking at his decision on how to allocate his endowment between just two assets: a safe, non-random asset, 'cash', and a risky asset which can be considered as a composite of the assets that he would have purchased, yielding a composite, stochastic return. The comparative static analysis of the problem – i.e. the analysis of the demand for financial assets in response to changes in K or in the distribution of one or more of the rates of return r^j – then avoids the complications of (a) having to consider the entire multivariate distribution of the rates of return and (b) having to consider the switches in the optimal mix of the risky assets.

So if we simplify the above problem in this fashion we may write the amount of the risky asset held as simply B, and the rate of return as r. The optimisation problem then becomes:

$$\max_{\{B\}} \mathscr{E}\upsilon(K + Br) \tag{10.11}$$

subject to $0 \leqslant B \leqslant K$. For an interior solution – i.e. one where the individual holds a mixed portfolio of cash and bonds – the obvious first-order condition for this is

$$\mathscr{E}(\upsilon'(K + Br)r) = 0 \tag{10.12}$$

This is illustrated in Figure 10.6(i) for the case where r can assume one of only two values, r_1, r_2 as in the example on page 213. Figures 10.6(ii) and (iii) show the two possible corner solutions where, respectively, the person holds all cash and the person holds all bonds. The proportion of resources devoted to the risky asset is chosen so that

$$-\frac{r_1}{r_2} = \frac{1-\pi}{\pi}\,\frac{\upsilon'(K + Br_2)}{\upsilon'(K + Br_1)} \tag{10.13}$$

where π is the subjective probability of state blue's occurrence. Obviously the right-hand side of (10.13) is nothing other than the individual's marginal rate of substitution and the equation is just a way of rewriting (10.12) for the two-state case.

In passing it is worth noting that with merely a few changes in notation the above model could be applied to the insurance problem as well. In this case we note that the slope of the line MA is $1 - 1/\rho$ where ρ is the ratio of the insurance premium to the insured loss. Now suppose π^* represents the *actuarial* probability of loss. Then, neglecting for a moment the moral hazard problem and supposing that an insurance company serves a large market, in which each customer's risk of loss is statistically independent, it is fairly easy to see that as long as $\rho \geqslant \pi^*$, the insurance company can stay in business. The reason for this is that the company's expected profits, per dollar of risk insured, are exactly $\rho - \pi^*$. Clearly if everyone perceived the probability of loss to be exactly π^* and if insurance were 'actuarially fair' so that insurance companies exactly broke even in terms of their expected profits we would have $\rho = \pi^* = \pi$. In view of our earlier observation that the slope of the indifference curves as they intersect the 45° line is the ratio of the

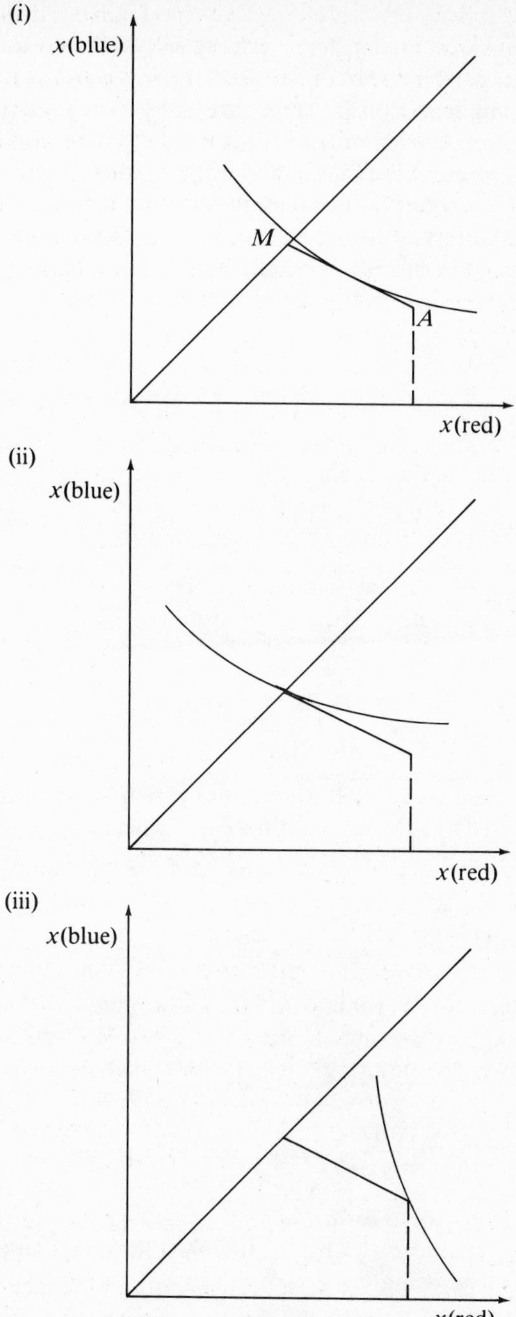

Figure 10.6

probabilities (in this case $1 - 1/\pi$) we may immediately deduce that every risk-averse person would want to be exactly fully insured: we would have a tangency solution at point M in Figure 10.6(i). However, in view of the problems we have noted in Section 10.3 there are likely to be good reasons in practice why such a pleasingly simple result is unlikely to obtain; Figure 10.6(ii) may be used to represent the case where the individual knows more than the insurance company about the probabilities of loss (and perhaps indeed can increase the probability of loss) and thus would wish to over-insure; Figure 10.6(iii) represents the case where excessively cautious insurance companies have set a rate $\rho > \pi$ so as to be sure of positive expected profits, and the individual does not find it worthwhile insuring.

Returning to the portfolio analysis version of the model let us examine the comparative statics of the solution. We shall consider three potentially interesting changes:

(a) an increase in the person's asset endowment K,
(b) a 'rightward shift' of the distribution of r,
(c) an 'increased spread' of the distribution of r.

In the first case we may examine the effect of wealth on risk taking simply by taking the first-order condition (10.12), differentiating with respect to K to find

$$\mathscr{E}\left(\upsilon''(M)\left[r + r^2\frac{\partial B^*}{\partial K}\right]\right) = 0 \tag{10.14}$$

and then solving for $\partial B^*/\partial K$. In the second case we may consider replacing the rates of return r by the rate of return $r + \tau$ where τ is a non-random shift parameter; one may then differentiate (10.12) with respect to τ:

$$\mathscr{E}\left(\upsilon''(M)\left[B^* + \frac{\partial B^*}{\partial \tau}[r + \tau]\right][r + \tau] + \upsilon'(M)\right) = 0 \tag{10.15}$$

It is usually convenient to evaluate $\partial B^*/\partial\tau$ at the point $\tau = 0$. Finally we may consider replacing r by the rate of return λr where λ is a positive non-random scale parameter. Differentiating (10.12) with respect to λ then yields

$$\mathscr{E}\left(\upsilon''(M)\lambda r^2\left[\frac{\partial B^*}{\partial\lambda}\lambda + B^*\right] + \upsilon'(M)r\right) = 0 \tag{10.16}$$

Once again one may solve for $\partial B^*/\partial\lambda$.

Simplifying equations (10.14) to (10.16), using (10.12) and setting $\tau = 0$ then gives us the following:

$$\frac{\partial B^*}{\partial K} = \mathscr{E}(\upsilon''(M)r)/\Delta \tag{10.17}$$

$$\frac{\partial B^*}{\partial \tau} = \mathscr{E}\upsilon'(M)/\Delta + B^* \frac{\partial B^*}{\partial K} \tag{10.18}$$

$$\frac{\lambda}{B^*} \frac{\partial B^*}{\partial \lambda} = -1 \tag{10.19}$$

where $\Delta \equiv -\mathscr{E}(\upsilon''(M)r^2)$. In view of υ being an increasing, concave function, Δ and $\mathscr{E}\upsilon'(M)$ must be positive. But what of the sign of the numerator in (10.17)?

In order to say something definite about this we have to enquire whether a further restriction on υ (over and above those cited in the last paragraph) might be reasonable. Consider the following:

AXIOM U4 (decreasing absolute risk aversion): for all values of the scalar payoff x, $a(x)$ decreases with x.

In view of the definition of a as $-\upsilon''(x)/\upsilon'(x)$ assumption U4 obviously imposes a condition on the *third* derivative of $\upsilon(x)$.[9] One might wonder what possible reason there might be for such an apparently arbitrary condition. The justification is in fact fairly intuitive. Note that, for a payoff with given variance, Definition 10.1 and U4 together imply that as one gets richer one demands less of a risk premium from any given distribution. This seems to accord with a fairly general presumption that rich people are better able to bear financial uncertainty than poor. Moreover it can be shown that U4 is equivalent to the following proposition about behaviour. Fix a particular level of wealth and consider the set of gambles that a person would be prepared to accept at that level; then increase the level of wealth: the new set of acceptable gambles should include the previous set. Once again this seems to accord with a generally accepted notion of how one's wealth is related to one's willingness to accept risks. Anyhow, if we accept U4 a very useful result follows. Note, first of all, that for any non-negative value of B and for all values of r, positive or negative, U4 implies

$$\begin{aligned} & ra(K + Br) \leqslant ra(K) \\ \Rightarrow\ & r\upsilon''(K + Br) \geqslant -ra(K)\upsilon'(K + Br) \\ \Rightarrow\ & \mathscr{E}(r\upsilon''(M)) \geqslant -a(K)\,\mathscr{E}(\upsilon'(K + Br)r) \end{aligned} \tag{10.20}$$

But the right-hand side of (10.20) is zero – see (10.12). Hence U4 implies that the numerator of (10.17) is positive. So we may now establish the following:

THEOREM 10.4: for any person holding a mixed portfolio of safe and risky assets:

---

[9] Namely $\upsilon'''(x) > (\upsilon'')^2/\upsilon' > 0$. For further discussion of such a restriction see Menezes, C., Geiss, C. and Tressler, J. (1980) 'Increasing downside risk', *American Economic Review*, Vol. 70, pp. 921–32.

(a) if U4 holds the demand for bonds increases with wealth;
(b) if U4 holds the demand for bonds increases with a rightward translation of the distribution of the rate of return;
(c) the demand for bonds falls with a scaling up of the distribution of r. The elasticity of demand for bonds with respect to λ, the scale of r, is unity.

Notice that part (c) of the result holds independently of U4. From this and part (b) one obtains a further simple corollary. Consider the following transformation of the rate of return: $\lambda\,[r - \mathscr{E}r] + \mathscr{E}r$ where $\lambda > 1$. Clearly the transformed rate of return has the same expected value as r, but a more 'spread out' distribution.[10] Also it is clear that the transformed rate of return can be written as $\lambda r - \tau$ where $\tau > 0$. Hence, in view of Theorem 10.4(b) and (c) this pure increase in spread would unambiguously reduce the demand for bonds.

10.5 Efficiency

In Chapter 8 we established that in a world of perfect certainty a competitive equilibrium, if it exists, is Pareto efficient. Will such a result be available for an economy in the presence of uncertainty?

As a preliminary step in answering this question we need to modify Definition 8.2 of Pareto efficiency to allow for the presence of uncertainty. To simplify matters let us suppose that, using the notation of Chapter 8 under perfect certainty, a social state $\mathscr{s}$ is completely described by the consumption allocation $[\mathbf{x}^h] \equiv [\mathbf{x}^1, \mathbf{x}^2, \ldots, \mathbf{x}^H]$. Now extend the concept of a consumption allocation to incorporate the idea that 'in the morning' one does not know which state of the world ω is going to be realised at lunchtime: let $[\mathbf{x}^h(\omega)]$ denote $[\,[\mathbf{x}^1(\omega), \mathbf{x}^2(\omega), \ldots, \mathbf{x}^H(\omega)] : \omega \in \Omega]$, the exhaustive list of the payoffs to each household in each possible realisation of the state of the world, where $\mathbf{x}^h(\omega)$ is the consumption vector that household h enjoys if state of the world ω is realised at lunchtime. We have now described an allocation of *prospects* over the households $1, \ldots, H$. Let u^h be the *ex-ante* utility level of household h when confronted with the prospect $[\mathbf{x}^h(\omega) : \omega \in \Omega]$; then looking at all the various feasible allocations $[\mathbf{x}^h(\omega)]$ as they appear to us 'in the morning' we may introduce the following definition.

DEFINITION 10.2: an allocation $[\hat{\mathbf{x}}^h(\omega)]$ is *ex-ante Pareto efficient* if it is feasible, and if there is no other feasible allocation $[\mathbf{x}^h(\omega)]$ such that

[10] This is an instance of the more general concept of 'increasing risk' discussed in the Rothschild and Stiglitz reference at the end of this chapter. More generally an increase in risk means changing the probability density function to one with the same mean, but 'more weight in the tails'.

$$u^h \geqslant \hat{u}^h \tag{10.21}$$

for all $h = 1, \ldots, H$ with strict inequality holding for at least one household h.

Definition 10.2 can be used even if Axioms U1 to U3 are not imposed on household preferences. If we *do* impose U1 to U3 then, of course, each household's utility can be written down in the form (10.2) and then expression (10.21) in the above definition can be rewritten

$$\sum_{\omega \in \Omega} \pi^h(\omega) v^h(\mathbf{x}(\omega)) \geqslant \sum_{\omega \in \Omega} \pi^h(\omega) v^h(\hat{\mathbf{x}}(\omega)) \tag{10.22}$$

for each household h. Observe that the functions π^h, v^h may differ for each household.

Using Definition 10.2 a simple result is available for an exchange economy in which there is a complete set of contingency markets.

Let $p_i(\omega)$ be the *ex-ante* price of good i contingent on state ω occurring. For example, suppose good 2 is bread and we have the two-state system described in Section 10.2. Then p_2(red) is the market price of a title deed that says 'bearer is entitled to one loaf if red wins the election'. Obviously p_2(red) and p_2(blue) could be regarded as the prices of two different 'goods' – respectively the price of an entitlement to a loaf if red wins and the price of an entitlement to a loaf if blue wins. So if there are n commodities (apples, bread, coconuts . . .) in the economy and $\bar{\omega}$ possible states we *could* regard the system as one consisting of $n\bar{\omega}$ 'goods' with an $n\bar{\omega}$-vector of prices $(p_1(1), p_2(1), \ldots, p_n(1), p_1(2), p_2(2), \ldots, p_n(2), \ldots, p_1(\bar{\omega}), p_2(\bar{\omega}), \ldots, p_n(\bar{\omega}))$. Hence if the conditions of Theorem 8.2 and 8.3 hold we may state for a simple exchange economy where markets in all such 'contingent goods' exist:

THEOREM 10.5: if a competitive equilibrium exists in the market for contingent goods then it is *ex-ante* Pareto efficient.

THEOREM 10.6: if consumers are greedy and have concave-contoured utility functions then any *ex-ante* Pareto efficient allocation with positive incomes, for all consumers can be supported by a competitive equilibrium.

Note that the conditions required for Theorem 10.6 are merely that each agent's indifference curves are convex to the origin – which of course implies that all agents are risk averse.

However, these two results are not all that encouraging because of the huge number of contingent goods and contingent prices involved – the product $n\bar{\omega}$ may be an enormous number – and, indeed, many of these markets may just not exist. Fortunately there is a helpful simplification. We introduce a market for securities payable in money. There are $\bar{\omega}$ different types of security, one for each possible state of the world, and the amount that household h holds of an ω-type security will be denoted m^h_ω and the market price of such a security is P_ω. A unit of such a security says 'bearer is entitled so \$1 if red wins', and the price P_{red} is, of course, the amount that you would pay at the bookmaker's or bank for such a title deed. One has the obvious constraint

$$\sum_{\omega} P_{\omega} m_{\omega}^{h} = M^{h} \tag{10.23}$$

Finally let p_i^{ω} be the *actual* (*ex-post*) price of good i given that state ω has actually occurred. A little thought reveals that in equilibrium

$$P_{\omega} \quad \times \quad p_i^{\omega} \quad = \quad p_i(\omega) \tag{10.24}$$

price of an ω-type security	×	price of good i in state ω	=	price of good i conditional on state ω occurring

Then, if the conditions of Theorem 10.1 hold, a very simple result is available.

THEOREM 10.7: if every individual has a utility function of the form (10.2) and each utility function satisfies the conditions required for Theorem 10.6, then any efficient allocation can be supported by a competitive equilibrium in the securities market and in the goods market in whichever state is realised.[11]

The reason for this result is as follows. Because of the additive structure of the utility function (10.2) – whereby, of course, the marginal rate of substitution of any pair of goods in state ω, $\upsilon_i(\mathbf{x}(\omega))/\upsilon_j(\mathbf{x}(\omega))$, must be independent of consumptions in any other state – any household may perform 'two stage budgeting' (see also Section 10.4, p. 218). So, it can proceed by (i) deciding how much of each ω-type security to purchase, subject to the constraint (10.21); (ii) given that state ω has occurred, purchasing quantities $x_i(\omega)$ so as to maximise the cardinal utility function $\upsilon(\mathbf{x}(\omega))$ subject to the budget constraint

$$\sum_{i=1}^{n} p_i^{\omega} x_i(\omega) \leqslant m_{\omega}^{h}$$

Because this two-stage procedure is possible, only the $n + \bar{\omega}$ markets (for the goods and for the securities) are required. Contrast this with $n\bar{\omega}$ markets presupposed in Theorems 10.5 and 10.6.

So the Axioms U1–U3 which yield the additive utility function in Theorem 10.1 also provide a considerable saving in informational requirements for efficient allocations since we can do without $[n-1]\bar{\omega} - n$ markets in the economy. Moreover it is interesting to note the apparently

[11] For proof see Arrow, op. cit., pp. 124–6.

remarkable point that the result holds even though no restriction has been placed on the subjective probabilities in (10.2). We could indeed have a *different* $\pi^h(1), \ldots, \pi^h(\omega)$ for each household and yet Theorem 10.7 would hold.

However there is a 'catch 22' in this result: the two-stage budgeting procedure requires that each household should know what all the *ex-post* prices p_i^ω *would* be were state ω to be realised, in order to decide how much of an ω-type security to buy in the first place. This is, to say the least, a somewhat demanding requirement.

Finally, note that *ex-ante* Pareto efficiency may not be the appropriate criterion on which to judge consumption allocations. As an alternative approach let us look at the concept of efficiency from the 'afternoon' standpoint, after the state of the world has been realised.

DEFINITION 10.3: an allocation $[\hat{\mathbf{x}}^h(\omega)]$ is *ex-post Pareto efficient* if it is feasible and if there is no other feasible allocation $[\mathbf{x}^h(\omega)]$ such that

$$\upsilon^h(\mathbf{x}^h(\omega)) \geqslant \upsilon^h(\hat{\mathbf{x}}^h(\omega)) \tag{10.25}$$

for all $h = 1, \ldots, H$ and all $\omega \in \Omega$, with at least one strict inequality in (10.25).

The relationship between the two views of Pareto efficiency can be clarified by the following theorem.

THEOREM 10.8: if there is no state of the world that is regarded by any household as impossible, then an *ex-ante* Pareto efficient allocation is also *ex-post* Pareto efficient.

PROOF: let $[\hat{\mathbf{x}}^h(\omega)]$ be any feasible allocation. If it is not *ex-post* efficient then there is some other feasible allocation $[\mathbf{x}^h(\omega)]$ such that (10.25) holds for all h and ω with at least one strict inequality. Hence, if $\pi^h(\omega) > 0$ for all h and ω we find that (10.22) is true. Thus, if an allocation is dominated *ex-post*, it is bound to be dominated *ex-ante*. Hence if there is no feasible allocation which dominates $[\hat{\mathbf{x}}^h(\omega)]$ *ex-ante* there cannot be any allocation which dominates it *ex-post*.

However the reverse is not true: an allocation that is *ex-post* Pareto efficient may be inefficient *ex-ante*. To see this, consider Figure 10.7. There is a single good (cake) which has a known total but which is to be allocated between two people (a and b) on a random basis. The indifference curves for each person's preferences concerning consumption in the two states and the resulting 'contract curve' have been sketched in. By analogy with Figure 7.1 of Chapter 7 we observe that points on this contract curve must be *ex-ante* Pareto efficient, but points *off* the curve (such as D) will be *ex-ante* inefficient (since we can increase the expected utility of person b without reducing the expected utility of person a by switching to point E, thus increasing person B's share of the cake), yet will be *ex-post* efficient (since, once the state

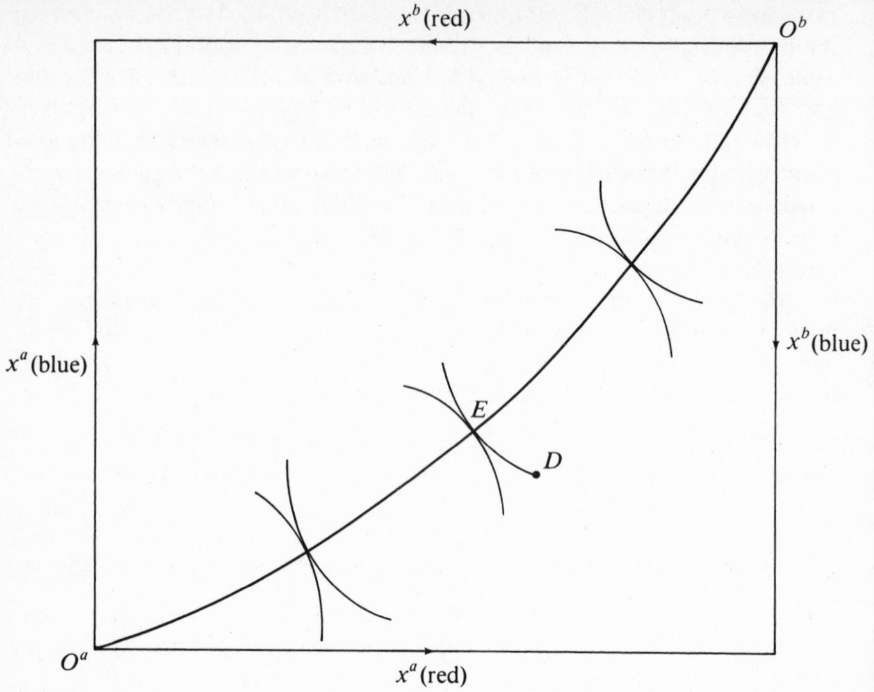

Figure 10.7

red or blue has been realised, one person's share can only be increased at the expense of the other).

As we have seen, competitive markets might be able to support *ex-ante* efficient allocations. But who is to say that one of the *ex-post* but not *ex-ante* efficient allocations is not in some sense desirable? A competitive market system as outlined above could not be relied to support such allocations, which provide a further reason – over and above the problems of externality and increasing returns – why one might find such an allocation mechanism inadequate as a method of social organisation. This is considered further in Chapter 13.

10.6 Summary

We have seen how the elements of Chapters 4 to 8 can be translated into a world where decisions must be made in the face of exogenous uncertainty. Much of the structure of individual preferences can be transferred – with some care – to preferences amongst prospects giving payoffs in different states of the world. If we impose a bit more structure on the preferences – Axioms U1 to U3 – subjective probabilities 'emerge' quite naturally.

However, there are some natural restrictions on the budget set which means that it may look rather different from that assumed in Chapter 4: these restrictions may also mean that complete markets in 'contingent goods' and insurance do not exist. If such markets *do* exist, then in some sense the efficiency results of Chapter 8 go through. But the stringent conditions required for this to happen do not give one much grounds for optimism. We shall find still less grounds for optimism when we consider the further problems raised in Chapter 11.

Further Reading

A useful general reference on decision making under uncertainty is:

Hey, J.D. (1979) *Uncertainty in Microeconomics*, Martin Robinson.

The following two references are useful guides to the expected utility models, and to what extent some of its restrictive assumptions may be relaxed:

Schoemaker, P.J.H. (1982) 'The expected utility model: its variants, purposes, evidence and generalizations', *Journal of Economic Literature*, Vol. 20, pp. 529–63.

Sugden, R. (1986) 'New developments in the theory of choice under uncertainty', *Bulletin of Economic Research*, Vol. 38, pp. 1–24.

A slightly more difficult paper is:

Machina, M.J. (1982) '"Expected utility" analysis without the independence axiom', *Econometrica*, Vol. 50, pp. 277–324.

The following pair of papers lay the formal foundation for much of the comparative static work involving changes in probability distributions:

Rothschild, M. and Stiglitz, J.E. (1970, 1971) 'Increasing risk', *Journal of Economic Theory*, Vol. 2, pp. 225–43; Vol. 3, pp. 66–84.

The notions of efficiency under uncertainty are discussed in

Hammond, P.J. (1981) '*Ex ante* and *ex post* welfare economics', *Economica*, Vol. 48, pp. 235–50.

Exercises

10.1 Consider the following definition of risk aversion. Let $A \equiv \{(x(\omega), \pi(\omega)) : \omega \in \Omega\}$ be a random prospect, where $x(\omega)$ is the payoff in state ω and $\pi(\omega)$ is the (subjective) probability of state ω, and let $\mathscr{E}x \equiv \Sigma_{\omega\in\Omega}\pi(\omega)x(\omega)$, the mean of the prospect, and let $A_\lambda \equiv \{(\lambda x(\omega) + [1-\lambda]\mathscr{E}x, \pi(\omega)) : \omega \in \Omega\}$ be a 'mixture' of the original prospect with the mean. Define an individual as risk averse if he always prefers A_λ to A for $0 < \lambda < 1$.

Illustrate this concept on a diagram similar to Figures 10.2 to 10.4 and contrast it with the definition of risk aversion given on page 209. Show that this definition of risk aversion need *not* imply convex-to-the-origin indifference curves.

*10.2 The following is an example of the so-called Allais paradox. Suppose you are offered a choice between exactly one of two lotteries. In one case the choice offered is between A^1 and A^2, and in the other case the choice offered is between A^3 and A^4, as specified below:

$$A^1: \quad \$1{,}000{,}000 \text{ with probability } 1$$

$$A^2: \begin{cases} \$5{,}000{,}000 & \text{with probability } 0.1 \\ \$1{,}000{,}000 & \text{with probability } 0.89 \\ \$0 & \text{with probability } 0.01 \end{cases}$$

$$A^3: \begin{cases} \$5{,}000{,}000 & \text{with probability } 0.1 \\ \$0 & \text{with probability } 0.9 \end{cases}$$

$$A^4: \begin{cases} \$1{,}000{,}000 & \text{with probability } 0.11 \\ \$0 & \text{with probability } 0.89 \end{cases}$$

Show that if A^1 is preferred to A^2 and also A^3 is preferred to A^4, then these preferences violate the independence axiom.

*10.3 (a) Consider a problem where the payoff in each state of the world is in terms of a scalar x and suppose the individual has a utility function of the form (10.2). Draw $\upsilon(x)$ as a function of x for (i) a risk-neutral person; (ii) a person who is a risk lover for small risks (relative to some original level x_0) but is risk averse for large risks.

(b) Take the model of part (a) and assume that the person is always strictly risk averse. Suppose the individual perceives that he confronts a prospect that has payoff of x_1 with probability π and x_0 with probability $1-\pi$. Show on the diagram the certainty equivalent and the risk premium of this prospect.

10.4 (a) Using Definition 10.1 and a Taylor expansion around $\bar{x}$ show that the risk premium ξ must satisfy

$$\upsilon'(\bar{x})[\xi - \bar{x}] = \tfrac{1}{2}\mathscr{E}(\upsilon''(\bar{x})[x - \bar{x}]^2) - \tfrac{1}{2}\upsilon''(\bar{x})[\xi - \bar{x}]^2 + \dots$$

where $\bar{x} \equiv \mathscr{E}x$. Hence prove Theorem 10.2 for small risks.

(b) Writing $\hat{\upsilon}(x) = \phi(\upsilon(x))$ where $\phi(.)$ is a concave function, prove Theorem 10.3.

*10.5 Analogous to the index of *absolute* risk aversion, the index of *relative* risk aversion, $-\ x\upsilon''(x)/\upsilon'(x)$ is sometimes employed. (a) Find a utility function that exhibits constant absolute risk aversion. (b) Find a utility function that exhibits constant relative risk aversion. (c) Prove the analogue of Theorem 10.3 for relative risk aversion.

10.6 An individual faces a prospect with a monetary payoff represented by a random variable x that is distributed over the bounded interval of the real line $[\underline{A}, \overline{A}]$. He has a utility function $\mathscr{E}\,\upsilon(x)$ where

$$\upsilon(x) = A_0 + A_1x - \tfrac{1}{2}A_2x^2$$

and A_0, A_1, A_2 are all positive numbers.

(a) Show that the individual's utility function can also be written as $\phi(\mathscr{E}x, \text{var}(x))$. Sketch the indifference curves in a diagram with $\mathscr{E}x$ and var(x) on the axes, and discuss the effect on the indifference map altering (i) the parameter A_1, (ii) the parameter A_2.

(b) For the model to make sense, what value must $\overline{A}$ have? [Hint: examine the first derivative of υ.]

10.7 An individual has an objective function $\mathscr{E}\,\upsilon(M)$ where υ is an increasing, concave, twice-differentiable function, and M is the *ex-post* monetary value of his wealth. He has *ex-ante* a stock of assets K which he may keep either in the form of bonds, where they earn a return at a stochastic rate r, or in the form of cash where they earn a return of zero. You may assume that $\mathscr{E}r > 0$ and that Prob$\{r < 0\} > 0$.

(a) If he invests an amount B in bonds ($0 < B < K$) and is taxed at a rate τ on his *income*, write down the expression for his *ex-post* wealth M, assuming *full loss offset* of the tax.

(b) Find the first-order condition which determines his optimal bond portfolio B^*.

(c) Examine the way in which a small increase in τ will affect B^*.

(d) What would be the effect of basing the tax on *ex-post wealth* rather than income?

10.8 Consider a competitive, price-taking firm that confronts one of the following two situations:

(a) 'uncertainty': price P is a random variable with expectation $\overline{P}$.

(b) 'certainty': price is fixed at $\overline{P}$.

It has a cost function $C(Q)$ where Q is output and it seeks to maximise the expected utility of profit.

(a) Suppose that the firm must choose the level of output *before* the particular realisation of P is announced. Set up the firm's optimisation problem and derive the first- and second-order conditions for a maximum. Show that, if the firm is risk averse, then increasing marginal cost is *not* a necessary condition for a maximum, and that it strictly prefers 'certainty' to 'uncertainty'. Show that if the firm is risk neutral then the firm is indifferent as between 'certainty' and 'uncertainty'.

(b) Now suppose that the firm can select Q *after* the realisation of P is announced, and that marginal cost is strictly increasing.

Using the firm's competitive supply function write down profit as a function of P and show that this profit function is convex. Hence show that a risk-neutral firm would strictly prefer 'uncertainty' to 'certainty'.

*10.9 Every year Alf sells apples from his orchard. Although the market price of apples remains constant (and equal to 1), the output of Alf's orchard is variable yielding an amount R_1, R_2 in good and poor years respectively; the probability of good and poor years is known to be $1 - \pi$ and π respectively. A buyer, Bill offers Alf a contract for his apple crop which stipulates a downpayment (irrespective of whether the year is good or poor) and a bonus if the year turns out to be good. Assuming Alf is risk averse, use a diagram similar to Figure 10.6 and 10.7 to sketch the set of such contracts which he would be prepared to accept.

Assuming that Bill is also risk averse, sketch his indifference curves in the same diagram. Assuming that Bill knows the shape of Alf's acceptance set, illustrate the optimum contract on the diagram. Write down the first-order conditions for this in terms of Alf's and Bill's utility functions.

*10.10 In question 10.9, what would be the effect on the contract if (i) Bill were risk neutral; (ii) Alf were risk neutral?

11

Strategic Behaviour

11.1 Introduction: Market Power

With two exceptions we have assumed throughout the previous chapters that people act as price takers, whether in their capacity of consumers or producers. It is time to deal with those exceptions, and in order to do this we need to examine, in outline at least, the concept of 'market power', which permits agents to engage profitably in strategic behaviour, rather than just accepting as inevitable the prices which they observe ruling in the market.

At its simplest level one might define market power as the ability to act as a 'price maker' rather than meekly accept the role of 'price taker'. This is rather an oversimplification, since there could be a variety of stratagems open to an agent with market power, whether he be a consumer, worker or a firm, which might involve a particular time profile of prices, collusion or co-operation with some potential rivals. If the agent is a producer, then a further option may be to vary the nature of the product itself by choice of quality.

This can be illustrated by reference back to the first of our two exceptions. The monopolist in Section 3.8 of Chapter 3 is, on reflection, in a remarkably privileged position: why *should* he assume that the entire market is his for the taking? There are a number of reasons why this might be so in practice: the firm may have been accorded a legal monopoly (as is the case with the Post Office); it may have a natural cost advantage over any potential rival (for example a patented process, or the property rights over access to some cost-reducing resource); or it may be able to prevent entry to the market by a potential rival through the use of some artificial blocking mechanism, such as brand loyalty advertising or even a protection racket. Whatever the reason in practice, the issue remains that simply writing down the optimisation problem for a profit-maximising monopolist in total seclusion is manifestly inadequate in a general model of the economy. At the very least one needs some account of why there are no other firms producing goods that are very close substitutes for the monopolist's product, why there are no other firms waiting in the wings ready to depose the monopolist and take over the role of sole producer themselves, and why the monopolist has to sell all the units of his output at an identical price to any customer. Market structure, market power, or the 'degree of monopoly' cannot be taken as immutably given.

The other exception occurred in Section 7.3 of Chapter 7. We noted there that if there were many traders, each of them appropriately small, a price-taking competitive equilibrium is the logical solution to the trading process. But if there are just a few traders it is soon apparent that one or more of them might, by his efforts alone, be able to exert a significant influence on the outcome of the process. Clearly this type of market power that results either from the small number of agents, or from the enormous size of one or more of their number, can arise either in the context of exchange amongst consumers, or in competition amongst firms. Indeed, for firms the forces that prevent entry (as mentioned in our first example) foster the exercising of power by those who are already in the market.

So, to understand the nature of market power in practice, and to analyse the pricing or output strategies that might sensibly be pursued in the light of that power, one needs to specify in much greater detail the 'rules of the game' that govern economic activity in situations where strategic behaviour is feasible. Such rules are trivial in the hypothesised models of perfect competition with which our discussion has been preoccupied thus far.

Section 11.2 introduces in an informal way some elementary concepts which assist one in analysing strategic behaviour. Sections 11.3 to 11.6 examine some applications of these concepts to firms and consumers.

11.2 Games

There is an enormous amount of literature on the theory of games and its application to economic analysis. However, examination of some specific examples can illuminate the issues of principle that arise in discussing strategic behaviour in economics.

By a 'game' we mean any activity involving two or more participants, each of whom recognises that the outcome for himself depends not only on his own actions, but also those of the other participants. This concept is broad enough to include, for example, cases of bilateral exchange of goods (as in Section 7.3 of Chapter 7), rivalry amongst firms in a market, and the relationship between union and employer. However our illustrative exposition will be greatly simplified in two important respects: (i) we shall consider games involving only two players. The oversimplification involved here is not simply a question of avoiding the complexity of sheer large numbers, but also that of neglecting the possibility that a player's moves may be influenced by the response of others who *might also join the game* if the rules specify that anybody may play; (ii) we assume that each of the players is identical so that their choice problems may be treated symmetrically.

Table 11.1 Essential notation for Chapter 11: Strategic Behaviour

$\overleftarrow{A},\overrightarrow{A}$	:	'left' and 'right' strategies of player A
$\phi^{lf}(Q^f)$	:	belief by firm f about firm l's response to f's output
$C^f(Q^f)$	:	cost function of firm f
$\overline{Q}_{-f}$	:	output of all firms *other than* f
$\chi^1(Q^2)$	:	Cournot–Nash reaction function of firm 1 to firm 2's output
$P(Q)$	:	inverse demand function (slope is P').

To fix ideas let us consider a family of games for two players, Alf and Bill, where each of the two players can play either one of exactly two 'moves' or strategies which we shall refer to as 'left' and 'right'. As a convenient shorthand, let us use the notation '$\overleftarrow{A}$' to denote 'Alf plays the left-hand move' and '$\overrightarrow{B}$' to denote 'Bill plays the right-hand move'. So in any particular play of the game there are four possible combinations of the participants' moves, namely $\overleftarrow{A}\overleftarrow{B}$, $\overleftarrow{A}\overrightarrow{B}$, $\overrightarrow{A}\overleftarrow{B}$ and $\overrightarrow{A}\overrightarrow{B}$. The result, or payoff, to each player depends, in general, on the moves played by each of them: the way in which the payoffs depend on the moves depends on the structure of the game.

Each agent explicitly recognises his interdependence with the other agent or agents (remember that in many practical applications the moves of *potential* players can be as important as those of the current participants in the game) when planning any particular move. Thus, *in a sense*, 'uncertainty' is essential to the model: but by contrast to Chapter 10 (where an exogenous state of the world was unknown), the unknown element here is *endogenous*, in that the prospective payoff to a particular course of action depends on other agents' conjectural response to one's own actions; it is the uncertainty of the chess board rather than that of the dice or the roulette wheel. Hence the concept of an 'optimal strategy' may itself not be well defined since in general such a strategy will be conditional upon an assumption about the course of action that other people will take. This, in turn will be influenced by the structure of the game. Under these circumstances it is not entirely surprising to find that equilibrium states may not be efficient (by contrast to well-behaved competitive models) since the individual agents' 'short-term' interests (based upon an assumption about *other* agents' short-term behaviour) may not be the same as their 'long-term' interests – the results of actions that agents would be prepared to agree to if all others changed their behaviour in an appropriate fashion.

Let us rank the possible outcomes for each player 1 (worst) to 4 (best): one can, if one wishes, consider these numbers to be monetary payoffs to the particular player concerned or as purely ordinal utility rankings. Write the payoffs to the two players as an ordered pair, so that, for example, '[4,2]' means 'Alf's payoff is 4, Bill's payoff is 2'. Recall our further simplifying assumption of symmetry so that, for example, if $\overrightarrow{A}\overleftarrow{B}$ produces the payoff [4,2], then $\overleftarrow{A}\overrightarrow{B}$ produces the payoff [2,4].

Consider Figures 11.1(i)–(vi). The box in each figure represents the payoff allocation under each of the four possible strategy combinations by A and B. Imagine, if you like, that each box represents a table: Alf sits at the west of the table, Bill sits at the south. So, for example, the 'top right-hand' corner of the box represents the allocation that emerges if Alf plays $\overleftarrow{A}$ and Bill plays $\overrightarrow{B}$. In each case the Pareto efficient allocation or allocations have been shaded in.

Case (i) is particularly simple. Whatever the rules of the game may be, it is difficult to think that anything other than $\overleftarrow{A}\overleftarrow{B}$ will be played, with the Pareto efficient outcome [4,4], since either party always gains from switching from playing 'right' to playing 'left'. This is an example of there being a *dominant strategy* for each player. The strategy of playing 'left' is always in the interests of either player, whatever the other player does.

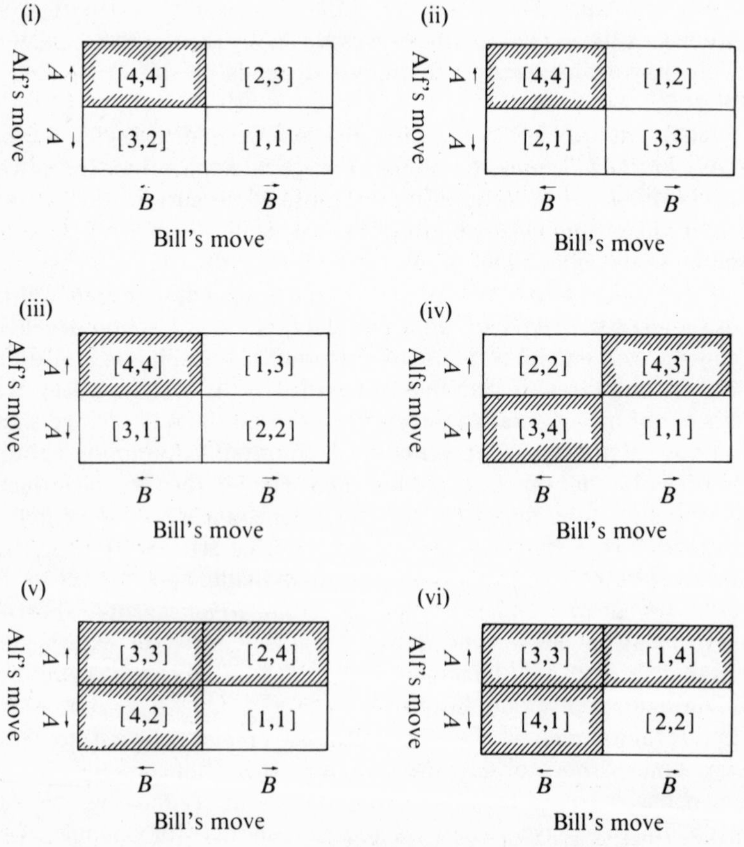

Figure 11.1

Cases (ii) and (iii) have an interesting twist. Here it is possible that the game gets stuck in a Pareto inefficient outcome: for if, for example, Bill through ignorance or stupidity plays $\overrightarrow{B}$, Alf may perceive it in his immediate interests to play $\overrightarrow{A}$, thus yielding an outcome allocation of [3,3] in case (ii) and [2,2] in case (iii). Of course, if Alf and Bill could communicate, change their minds and replay, it is quite reasonable for them to agree to switch back to $\overleftarrow{A}\overleftarrow{B}$ and ensure Pareto efficiency: once at $\overleftarrow{A}\overleftarrow{B}$ they could stay there. In case (iv) either $\overrightarrow{A}\overleftarrow{B}$ or $\overleftarrow{A}\overrightarrow{B}$ is a candidate for a solution; from the point of view of their own selfish, short-term interests neither party would be interested in the 'equitable' but Pareto inefficient outcome $\overleftarrow{A}\overleftarrow{B}$ yielding the allocation [2,2]. In case (v) again either $\overrightarrow{A}\overleftarrow{B}$ or $\overleftarrow{A}\overrightarrow{B}$ is a candidate for a solution as before: in contrast to case (iv), however, the outcome of $\overleftarrow{A}\overleftarrow{B}$ in case (v), which yields [3,3] is not only equitable but is also Pareto efficient; yet it is still not likely to be an equilibrium if each party is able to change his mind in the light of the other party's play.

Case (vi) is a real cracker. Although there are three Pareto efficient outcomes $\overleftarrow{A}\overleftarrow{B}$, $\overleftarrow{A}\overrightarrow{B}$ and $\overrightarrow{A}\overleftarrow{B}$, *none* of these is candidate for a solution if each party acts in his own short-run selfish interests: the so-called 'prisoner's dilemma'.[1] For, whatever Bill plays, *left to himself* Alf has an incentive to play $\overrightarrow{A}$; in view of the symmetry of the game we see that Bill also has an incentive to play $\overrightarrow{B}$. Thus each of the players perceives playing the right-hand move as a dominant strategy in a single round of the game. But each is aware that he (and, incidentally, the other fellow) would be unambiguously better off if there were to be a 'policeman' or 'umpire' to enforce the solution $\overleftarrow{A}\overleftarrow{B}$ on both of them: a problem to which we return in Chapter 12.

To summarise: (i) has one equilibrium which is Pareto efficient; (ii) and (iii) may each have two equilibria, only *one* of which is Pareto efficient; (iv) and (v) may each have multiple equilibria *all* of which are Pareto efficient; (vi) has one equilibrium to the short-term game which is inefficient.

It is evident that the type of solutions which are likely to emerge depends on the structure of the game and that the structure of the game itself depends on several things besides the mere pattern of payoffs that emerges from each possible combination of feasible strategies by the players; see Exercise 11.1.

For example, in some games the *status quo* at the outset of the game and the *order of play* may be crucial to the possible outcomes that are worth considering. As a practical example consider the question of entry-deterrence discussed in Section 11.1. The pricing strategy of a firm confronted by a potential rival may quite reasonably depend on whether the point from which one starts is one where the rival has actually entered, or one where he

---

[1] There is a huge literature on this type of problem. Under certain types of rules – and certain assumptions about individuals' rationality – for example if the game were to be repeated over and over again, each player *may* see it in his long-term interests to play the left-hand strategy indefinitely.

has not yet entered. Where the order of play matters – for example in case (iv) – neither the 'right' nor the 'left' strategy is going to be the optimal strategy under all possible circumstances in which the game may be played. Clearly it is in the interest of each party not to pre-announce to the other which of '←' or '→' he is going to choose. To deal with this one may introduce the concept of a *mixed strategy* which involves a randomisation by each player of his own policy. This may mean in effect that he follows a deliberate plan of tossing a coin to decide which of the moves to select each time he plays.[2]

Furthermore time can play an essential role, over and above the issue of 'who goes first'. If the players can change their minds and reverse their policies after they have seen the 'cards' that the others have played, or if everyone knows that the same game is to be played repeatedly, then common sense suggests that the players may well consider rather different strategies in pursuing their own interests from that which could be relevant to a 'once-only' game with no afterthoughts. For example the solution to games between rival firms where the moves involve output decisions may depend critically on whether changes in output require substantial commitment to irreversible investment in capital equipment.

Finally, we may mention the importance of *information* available to, and *beliefs* formed by the players, and of the *background institutions* available. For example, if the players are evenly matched then the realisation by the players that they *are* evenly matched may be crucial to the formation of beliefs by each of them about the likely course of action of the others. Again, if there is an attempt at a co-operative solution, then the possibility of enforcement by an outside agency possibly accompanied by transfers of the payoffs between the players administered by that agency[3] may greatly affect whether such an attempt may succeed.

It is clear from the above informal discussion that we have to be careful about what is meant by an 'equilibrium' or a 'solution' to the game. Very often this means an equilibrium must be defined relative to a particular set of beliefs by each player about what the others will do, or relative to a particular status quo point. Obviously there are exceptions to this, such as

---

[2] Of course a simple coin toss gives equal weight to the two strategies: any randomising device could be used to give the desired probability weights. The idea is analogous to the derivation of points on the straight-line isoquants in Figure 2.3: there one derives a non-basic technique by combining a proportion of α of the basic net output vector $\mathbf{y}^1$ with a proportion $[1 - \alpha]$ of the basic vector $\mathbf{y}^2$. In the case of strategy choice the player chooses the 'left' strategy (and its associated payoff prospects) with probability π and the 'right' strategy with probability $1 - \pi$. The choice of π and the use of mixed strategies is discussed succinctly in the McKinsey reference at the end of this chapter.

[3] The possibility of such transfers implies that the payoffs must have some sort of cardinal significance (like money) rather than being purely ordinal (like utility).

Figure 11.1 (i), where the same strategy would be played by each player regardless. But besides these convenient and very special cases, what solution concept may we use? In trading games we have already come across one such concept in Section 7.3 – the *core*. Two others are relevant to many applications of strategic behaviour and will be discussed in connection with the specific models introduced later in this chapter.

For any particular game let a *strategy* denote the move or collection of moves which a player may legitimately choose during one play of the game. Call any ordered collection of such strategies – one to each player – a *profile* of strategies.

DEFINITION 11.1: the *Nash* or *non-cooperative* equilibrium to a game consists of a profile of strategies such that no player could obtain a higher payoff for himself on the assumption that *all other players' strategies remain unchanged*.

Although the concept is extremely general, built into the Nash solution is a spirit of symmetry (of *status* rather than of substance) amongst the players. A contrasting approach assumes that everyone recognises a fundamental asymmetry: between one leader and one or more followers. A follower's behaviour is such that in any play of the game he maximises the payoff to himself, conditional on the currently observed moves by all other players in the game. The leader takes this behaviour by the followers into account.

DEFINITION 11.2: a *Stackelberg* equilibrium consists of a profile of strategies such that no follower could obtain a higher payoff for himself on the assumption that *all other players' strategies remain unchanged* and that the leader could not obtain a higher payoff for himself on the assumption that *all other players' strategies would be to respond to deviations from equilibrium as followers*.

In Sections 11.3 to 11.5 we examine the use of these concepts in a simplified approach to firms' strategic behaviour in the market for their output – the case of oligopoly.

11.3 Firms: Non-cooperative Behaviour

Take the simple case where there are exactly F firms in an industry such that firm f produces output Q^f and $Q \equiv \Sigma_{f=1}^{F} Q^f$. The products are regarded as identical and consumer demand can be represented by an *inverse demand function* yielding price as a function of aggregate output $P = P(Q)$. Let us consider the possible behaviour pattern of any one of the F firms. Obviously if F is a large number and if in some sense every individual producer regards himself as 'small' relative to the total market, then he may regard the impact of his own production decisions on Q and hence on P as of negligible importance: he then acts as a price taker.

Suppose that the opposite, more interesting, assumption is valid – that each producer recognises that his output decision has a significant effect on Q and hence on P. This immediately raises the question – what effect does firm f suppose that it has on the market?

There appear to be two types of assumption (1) (the *Cournot assumption*): although he recognises that his output decision has a direct effect on the aggregate output and price, the producer supposes that his output decision will not affect that of any other firm; or, (2), each producer recognises that, just as he takes account of all other firms' output decisions, so all other firms will take account of his output decision. He then incorporates into his own optimisation plan a belief about other firms' reactions.

More specifically, if one makes assumption (2) then producer f will assume that producer l will determine his output Q^l thus:

$$Q^l = \phi^{lf}(Q^f) \tag{11.1}$$

where ϕ^{lf} can be thought of as the belief by firm f about firm l's output response.

So if firm f has a cost function $C^f(Q^f)$ then its total profits are given by:

$$P\left(Q^f + \sum_{\substack{l=1 \\ l \neq f}}^{F} \phi^{lf}(Q^f)\right)Q^f - C^f(Q^f)$$

Clearly the firm's optimum strategy will depend crucially on the particular 'conjectures' that it forms about the responses by other firms to its own actions, ϕ^{lf}. It is not at all clear *a priori* how one ought to specify such functions. In practice a realistic approach would have to incorporate some account of the time sequence of adjustments in the market. This is a topic which is beyond the scope of the present discussion.

Of course the Cournot assumption (1) could be regarded as a special case of assumption (2), where each ϕ-function is assumed to be constant:

$$\phi^{lf}(Q^f) \equiv \bar{Q}^l \tag{11.2}$$

This statement is to be interpreted as 'firm f assumes that firm l will go on producing at output level $\bar{Q}^l$ regardless of the output decision Q^f made by firm f.' If so, then the specification of the optimisation problem becomes much easier, since any firm only needs to add up the outputs of all the other firms to work out its own impact on the market. Specifically let us write

$$\bar{Q}_{-f} \equiv Q - Q^f \tag{11.3}$$

for the output of all firms *other than* f. Then profits for firm f can be written:

$$\Pi^f(Q^f; \bar{Q}_{-f}) \equiv P(Q^f + \bar{Q}_{-f})\,Q^f - C^f(Q^f) \tag{11.4}$$

Maximising this with respect to Q^f yields

$$P'Q^f + P - C_Q^f \leqslant 0 \tag{11.5}$$

$$P'Q^f + P = C_Q^f \quad \text{if} \quad Q^f > 0 \tag{11.6}$$

$$PQ^f - C^f \geqslant 0 \tag{11.7}$$

where P' denotes the first derivative of $P(Q)$ and C_Q^f is the marginal cost of firm f. We assume that the second-order conditions for a maximum are satisfied. Now in each of these equations $\bar{Q}_{-f}$ appears as a parameter, since P and its derivative P' have total output as arguments. We may, therefore write optimal output for firm f as a function

$$Q^f = \chi^f(\bar{Q}_{-f}) \tag{11.8}$$

where Q^f is derived from the solution to (11.5)–(11.7); χ^f is known as the *reaction function*. This is illustrated in Figure 11.2.[4] The curve AB is derived from the first-order conditions (11.6); at $\bar{\bar{Q}}_{-f}$ maximum profits attainable by firm f are zero, so the firm stops producing and χ^f is discontinuous at that point.

Of course, every firm in the industry is in the same sort of position, so in actual fact we have a system of F equations of this type:

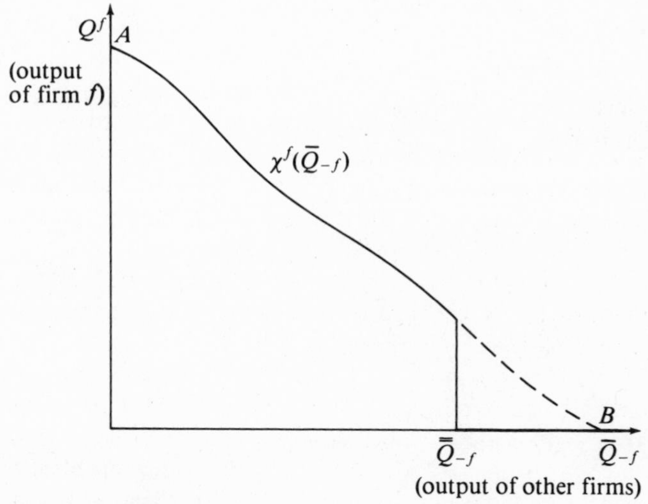

Figure 11.2 The Reaction Function

[4] Note that χ^f does not have to be a decreasing function. It is possible for it to be locally increasing if $-P''/P' > 1/Q^f$.

$$Q^1 = \chi^1(Q^2 + Q^3 + Q^4 + \ldots + Q^{F-1} + Q^F)$$
$$Q^2 = \chi^2(Q^1 + Q^3 + Q^4 + \ldots + Q^{F-1} + Q^F)$$
$$Q^3 = \chi^3(Q^1 + Q^2 + Q^4 + \ldots + Q^{F-1} + Q^F)$$
$$\ldots \quad \ldots$$
$$Q^F = \chi^F(Q^1 + Q^2 + Q^3 + \ldots + Q^{F-2} + Q^{F-1})$$

In principle we may solve this set of equations to yield a solution vector $(\hat{Q}^1, \hat{Q}^2, \ldots, \hat{Q}^F)$.[5] Referring back to Definition 11.1 we see that this represents a Nash equilibrium. Since the rules which lead to this equilibrium have been described as the Cournot assumption, it may be helpful to refer to this solution as the *Cournot–Nash* solution.

This is perhaps more easily seen with a two-firm example. Let

$$P(Q) = 2\alpha - \beta Q \tag{11.9}$$

$$\left.\begin{aligned} C^f(Q^f) &= C_0^f + c^f[Q^f]^2 \quad f = 1,2 \\ Q &= Q^1 + Q^2 \end{aligned}\right\} \tag{11.10}$$

Firm 1's profits, conditional on a *given* level of firm 2's output $\bar{Q}^2$ are:

$$\Pi^1(Q^1; \bar{Q}^2) = 2\alpha Q^1 - \beta[Q^1 + \bar{Q}^2]Q^1 - C_0^1 - c^1[Q^1]^2 \tag{11.11}$$

Likewise firm 2's profits, conditional on a *given* level of firm 1's output, are:

$$\Pi^2(Q^2; \bar{Q}^1) = 2\alpha Q^2 - \beta[Q^2 + \bar{Q}^1]Q^2 - C_0^2 - c^2[Q^2]^2 \tag{11.12}$$

Maximising (11.11) with respect to Q^1 we find, for any situation where firm 1 actually produces:

$$2\alpha - 2\beta Q^1 - \beta\bar{Q}^2 - 2c^1Q^1 = 0 \tag{11.13}$$

We may solve this for Q^1; doing so, and solving the equivalent problem for firm 2 we find

$$Q^1 = \chi^1(\bar{Q}^2) = \frac{\alpha - \frac{1}{2}\beta\bar{Q}^2}{\beta + c^1} \quad (\text{for } Q^1 > 0) \tag{11.14}$$

$$Q^2 = \chi^2(\bar{Q}^1) = \frac{\alpha - \frac{1}{2}\beta\bar{Q}^1}{\beta + c^2} \quad (\text{for } Q^2 > 0) \tag{11.15}$$

We may plot the reaction function χ^1 in Figure 11.3 – the line running from $(0, 2\alpha/\beta)$ to $\left(\frac{\alpha}{\beta + c^1}, 0\right)$; likewise we may plot χ^2 in Figure 11.3 – the line

[5] See Exercise 11.5.

running from $\left(0, \dfrac{\alpha}{\beta + c^2}\right)$ to $(2\alpha/\beta, 0)$. Of course we still need to check that each firm can make non-negative profits. Were either firm's output to become sufficiently small the presence of positive fixed costs C_0^f would make its profits negative if it attempted to produce: it would simply drop out of the market. So in fact for firm 2 we find that maximum attainable profits are zero if firm 1 is already producing at $\bar{\bar{Q}}^1$ and for $\bar{Q}^1 \geqslant \bar{\bar{Q}}^1$ the curve $\chi^2(\bar{Q}^1)$ lies along the horizontal axis.

Point C is the Cournot–Nash solution, consisting of the pair of outputs

$$(\hat{Q}^1, \hat{Q}^2) = (A[\tfrac{1}{2}\beta + c^2], A[\tfrac{1}{2}\beta + c^1])$$

where $A \equiv \alpha/[c^1c^2 + \beta[c^1 + c^2 + \tfrac{3}{4}\beta]]$

Notice that this solution has a powerful equilibrium property.

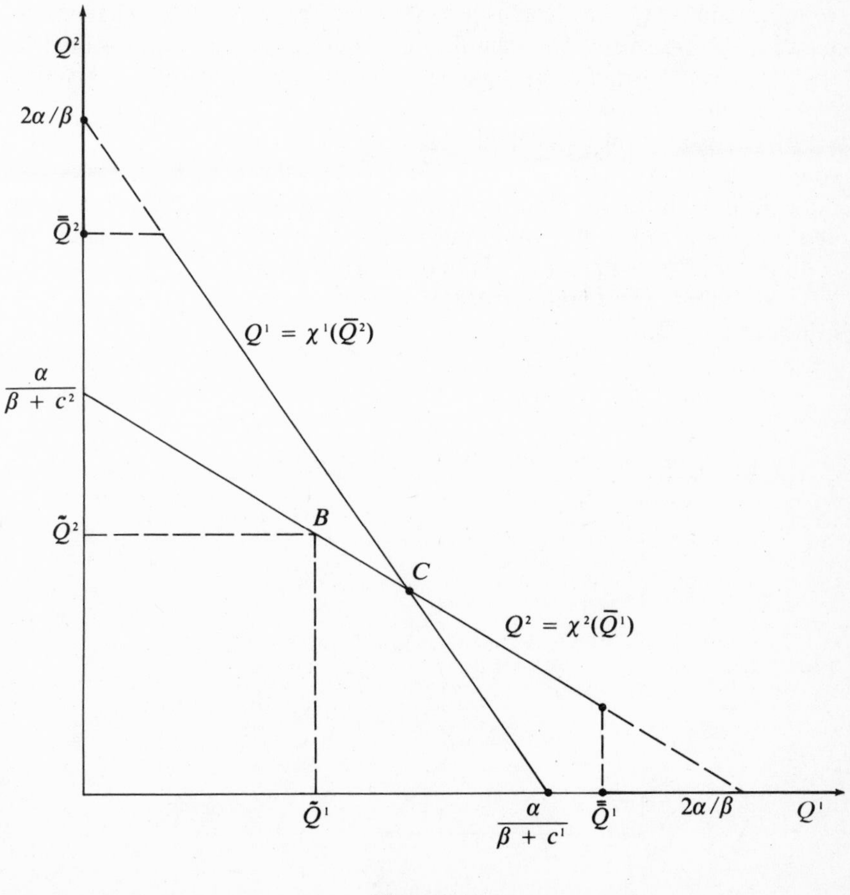

Figure 11.3

Everyone's beliefs about everyone else are simultaneously realised at that point. So if firm f were already producing at $\hat{Q}^f$ and it found every other firm were also producing at the Cournot–Nash solution, then it would not have the slightest incentive to revise its beliefs about the other firms.

However there are other respects in which the Cournot–Nash solution is less appealing. For example there may be no such solution at all. If C_0^1 and C_0^2 are sufficiently high, then we may have $\bar{\bar{Q}}^1 < \hat{Q}^1$, $\bar{\bar{Q}}^2 < \hat{Q}^2$; fixed costs are then so high that each firm can only make non-negative profits if the other firm produces a very small amount or nothing at all. Moreover we may note that whilst beliefs about each other are self-reinforcing at the point $\hat{Q}^1, \ldots, \hat{Q}^F$, they obviously are not so at any other point. For example, consider a point such as B which lies on χ^2, firm 2's reaction function, but *not* on χ^1: if firm 1 produces $\tilde{Q}^1$ then firm 2 produces $\tilde{Q}^2$, which is fine, so far. But if firm 2 produces $\tilde{Q}^2$ *firm 1 wouldn't plan to produce* $\tilde{Q}^1$, but a greater output, yielding a point on χ^1 to the right of B. But this would mean that firm 2's assumption that $\tilde{Q}^1$ was fixed is now seen to be erroneous. So, whatever the process of adjustment, why should one suppose for a moment that firms hold the curious belief of unchanged behaviour by the opposition except at the one point C?

There is a further very important respect in which the Cournot–Nash equilibrium is seriously deficient. Suppose every firm is at the Cournot–Nash equilibrium. Now imagine some government agent comes along and compels firm 1 to alter its output by a small amount. By definition of the equilibrium, firm 1's profits will not change (after all $(\hat{Q}^1, \ldots, \hat{Q}^F)$ has been defined so that at this point $\partial \Pi^1/\partial Q^1 = 0$). Now consider the profit of any other firm $f \geqslant 2$:

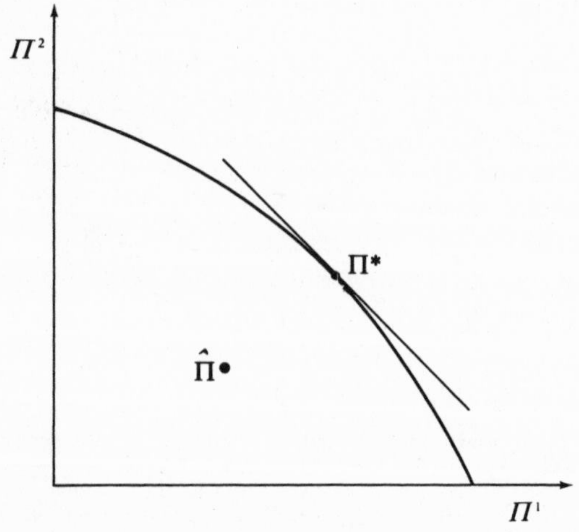

Figure 11.4

$$\frac{\partial \Pi^f}{\partial Q^1} = P'(Q)\,Q^f \tag{11.16}$$

which must be negative in view of the downward sloping demand curve. So if the government agent compelled firm 1 to decrease its output a little *every other firm's profits would increase and firm 1 would be no worse off than before*: the equilibrium is dominated by other feasible outcomes.

In Figure 11.4 is sketched the set of all possible profit configurations for the case where $F = 2$. The shape of the set will depend on the demand function for the industry and the cost function of each firm. The point $\hat{\Pi}$ represents the profit pair $(\hat{\Pi}^1, \hat{\Pi}^2)$ corresponding to the Cournot–Nash equilibrium, and is deliberately drawn in the interior of the set.

11.4 Firms: Co-operative Behaviour

An obvious alternative to the Cournot–Nash solution appears to be to maximise joint profits $\Pi^1 + \Pi^2$ and thus to reach point Π^* on the profit frontier. Explicit collusion of this sort is usually known as a cartel. The problem is then to choose the firms' outputs to maximise

$$P(Q)Q - \sum_{f=1}^{F} C^f(Q^f) \tag{11.17}$$

where $Q \equiv \sum_{f=1}^{F} Q^f$. Clearly this is achieved by setting

$$P + QP'(Q) - C^f_Q(Q^f) \leqslant 0, \quad f = 1, \ldots, F \tag{11.18}$$

where

$$P + QP'(Q) - C^f_Q(Q^f) = 0 \quad \text{if} \quad Q^f > 0 \tag{11.19}$$

It is immediate from (11.19) that every single firm that produces in positive amounts selects its output such that its marginal cost equals the same value, the marginal revenue. In effect the cartel solution works as though there were a single monopolist with F separate plants; the activity levels across the plants are optimised so as to equate marginal cost everywhere. Notice that it can never be optimal for any one firm (or plant) to make a loss even though others are making a profit. For, suppose firm 1 is making a loss but all other firms are making a profit; total profits are

$$\Pi^1 + \sum_{f=2}^{F} [P(Q)Q^f - C^f(Q^f)] \tag{11.20}$$

where $\Pi^1 < 0$. But if plant 1 were shut down Π^1 would then vanish (i.e. it would *increase* from a negative number to zero); but since Q will have fallen and $P(.)$ is downward sloping in Q, the profits of all the other firms will have risen. Hence

THEOREM 11.1: in a joint profit-maximising cartel each active firm sets its output so that its marginal cost exactly equals marginal revenue and loss-making firms are shut down.

There are obvious snags with this solution, however. Firstly, note that to implement it may involve making transfers or side-payments amongst the firms to secure the agreement of firms who would otherwise lose out. But if such compensatory arrangements are to be made, how is the overall size of the cartel, and hence the number of 'deserving cases', to be determined? Secondly, this co-operative solution may prove to be like the $\overleftarrow{A}\overleftarrow{B}$ outcome in Figure 11.1(vi): the participants would like to secure it, but the result will not stick.

To see this, consider the case where the industry is already at the joint profit-maximising solution depicted by Π^* in Figure 11.4 and examine the position of any one firm f. Could it improve on this by unilateral action? Obviously, by definition, it can only do so at the expense of some other firm in the cartel, because the initial point lies on the profit frontier. The temptation to 'chisel' – i.e. to increase one's own sales beyond the agreed level – is clearly there, however. For, suppose firm f perceived all other firms' outputs as being unresponsive to its own decisions; once again it perceives its profit function as being (11.4). Differentiating with respect to Q^f, and keeping output of all other firms constant, we have:

$$\begin{aligned}\partial\Pi^f/\partial Q^f &= P'Q^f + P - C^f_Q \\ &= [P'Q + P - C^f_Q] - P'\bar{Q}_{-f}\end{aligned} \tag{11.21}$$

But in view of (11.19) the first term on the right of (11.21) must vanish and so the net effect of an increase in Q^f on firm f's profits is $-P'\bar{Q}_{-f}$ which is positive in view of the downward sloping demand curve. Hence, *if any firm feels that the others will not react to its output decision it has an incentive to chisel* – see Exercise 11.6.

Of course this observation is not *in itself* fatal to the cartel solution, since the crude notion of chiselling outlined above presupposes an extreme, if not bizarre, assumption by each firm about its fellows, but it does raise an issue which is fundamental to the discussion of strategic behaviour. For it is immediately apparent that the problems that were seen to arise in Section 11.3 and this section could be greatly simplified if there were some pre-specified, and enforceable, 'rules of the game'. These rules might need to be quite detailed, since they would have to include a method of checking whether agreements were being respected, and a set of perceived penalties (which must be believable and believed) for violation of agreements, along with the institutions to carry them out. The difficulty is that, whilst such rules are commonly observed amongst established players in certain market games it is remarkably difficult to formulate a general 'rule of rules' to determine how these come about. With this warning in mind let us turn to a case that is of interest in a number of applications.

11.5 Firms: Follow-my-Leader

In Sections 11.3 and 11.4 we assumed that there was an essential symmetry amongst firms: each one formed more or less the same conjectures about the others' behaviour and thus acted in the same sort of way, for good or ill. But what if the players take distinct roles? This section and Section 11.6 examine two-agent situations which only illustrate two firms and trading between two consumers. The essential feature is that only one party acts in the fashion that we discussed in Section 11.3: he is then known as a 'follower'. The other party *knows* that the follower is going to act this way, come what may, and makes use of this information in deciding what his own policy shall be: in this way he acts as a leader.

So let us just suppose that firm 1 leads and firm 2 follows. The behaviour of firm 2 can now be written down immediately from equation (11.8), since it always takes firm 1's announcement of its output as all it needs to know. Firm 1 can then use the belief $\phi^{21}(Q^1) = \chi^2(Q^1)$ in its computation of its own profits thus:

$$P(Q^1 + \chi^2(Q^1))Q^1 - C^1(Q^1) \tag{11.22}$$

compare this with (11.4). The first-order condition for an interior maximum of (11.22) with respect to Q^1 is:

$$P + \left[1 + \frac{\mathrm{d}\chi^2}{\mathrm{d}Q^1}\right]Q^1P' - C^1_Q = 0 \tag{11.23}$$

Obviously this is a very simple modification of (11.6). Examine Figure 11.5:

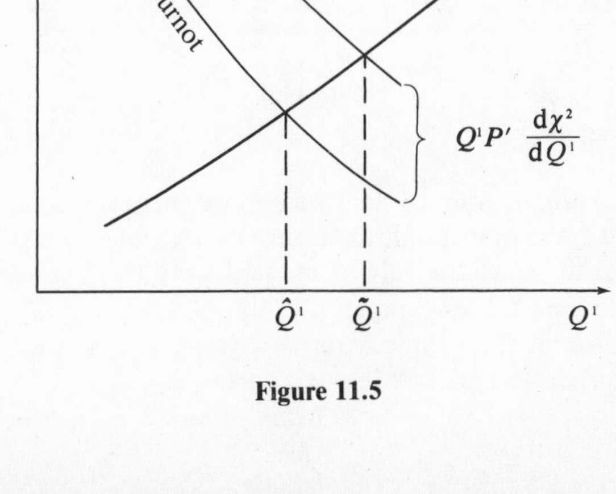

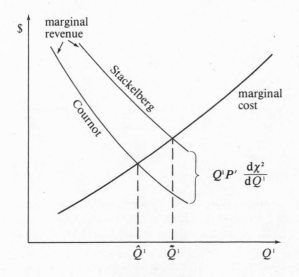

Figure 11.5

the left-hand marginal revenue curve is that which firm 1 perceives were it to conjecture that firm 2 will not react ($\phi^{21}(Q^1) = Q^2$), and the right-hand marginal revenue curve is that which firm 1 perceives on the assumption that it is the leader and firm 2 is the follower ($\phi^{21}(Q^1) = \chi^2(Q^1)$). Obviously, if χ^2 is downward sloping, firm 1 produces more under the follow-my-leader rules than it would do under the 'symmetric' Cournot rules; and so firm 2 must be producing *less* (along its χ^2 reaction function). This is illustrated in Figure 11.6 where the contours are those of $P(Q^1 + Q^2)Q^1 - C^1(Q^1)$, the iso-profits contours for firm 1, and point S represents the *Stackelberg equilibrium* where (11.23) is satisfied. This raises a couple of pertinent questions:

Why should anyone *want* to be a follower?
How is the casting of the two roles decided?

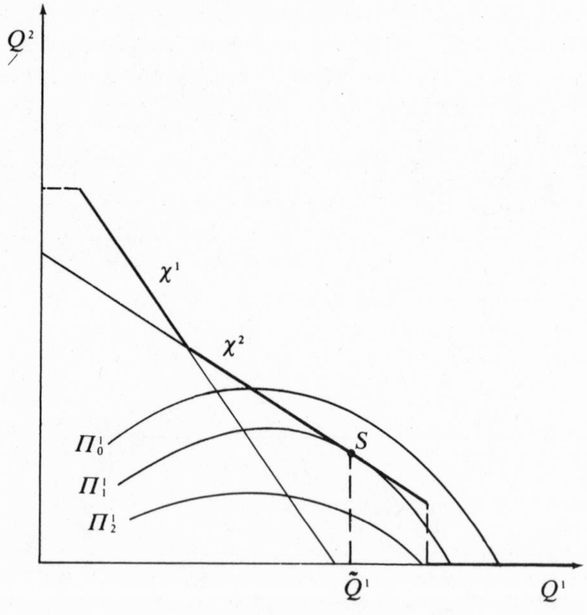

Figure 11.6

These issues are, of course, mainly a reiteration of the point raised at the end of Section 11.4: it is difficult to formulate a general rule of why certain rules emerge. In this case the rule seems odd since the follower gets lower profits than if he were at the 'symmetric' Cournot–Nash equilibrium. Clearly we have to account for some overwhelming reason why asymmetric behaviour should be accepted by the two parties.

In some cases the answer to this appears to be provided by the situation itself. For example, one party may have tremendous advantages because of sheer size or because of his possessing information about market conditions that would be costly to acquire (and which we have not attempted to model).[6] Again, if one changes the above example so that we consider instead a model of entry, in which firm 1 is the incumbent of a particular industry and firm 2 is a potential entrant, we see another possible reason for the acceptance by both parties of this behaviour. For it can be argued that the positions of incumbent and potential entrant in this type of set-up appear to be manifestly asymmetric[7] – it might be argued that the incumbent possesses advantages over the potential entrant in the form of market information, technological know-how and 'goodwill' amongst existing customers – and that a reasonable conjecture for the potential rival to make is that the incumbent would maintain his output level were the rival actually to enter. This then gives a rationale for the 'market power' of a monopolist (see the discussion in Section 11.1) and an account of the way in which such power may be fruitfully exercised. For, if the follow-my-leader rules apply then the leader (the incumbent monopolist) may find it in his interest to set his output level (or price) in such a way that the follower (the potential entrant) finds it just not worthwhile to produce at all.[8]

However, follow-my-leader behaviour is by no means confined to oligopoly. We shall consider further the application of this to models of public policy in Chapter 13, but we may turn to the way in which such behaviour may emerge in simple trading games in an exchange economy.

11.6 Consumers and Lies

In Section 7.3 of Chapter 7 we appealed to a 'large-numbers' argument to suggest that price-taking behaviour was a reasonable way of modelling what

---

[6] An illustration of this – price leadership – is given in Exercise 11.2.

[7] Actually one can think of exceptions. One such is where one has a monopoly that is 'perfectly contestable'. Suppose that the demand and cost functions are such as to permit only one firm to survive in the industry at any one moment, and that the component C_0^f in a firm's cost function (see equation 11.10) represents *fixed*, but not *sunk* costs. (The distinction is important: the idea is that although there may be a certain amount of 'overhead' capital equipment required before a single unit of output can be produced – the fixed cost component – this equipment could be sold off at virtually its purchase price should the firm decide to leave the industry.) Then one may have a situation where the identity of the single incumbent in the industry varies from year to year. And if this happens then in a long-run sense all the potential occupiers of the position are 'in the same boat'. But this is a very special case.

[8] See Exercise 11.3. Of course there are other means by which the monopolist may retain his position: for example, by making a threat to cut prices if anyone else enters (which may not be believed) or by exploiting the uncertainty that there might be about the true costs of producing in that industry.

was going on in an economy-wide equilibrium. Now, in such a competitive model, there is no point in misrepresenting one's preferences: if a person falsely states his marginal rate of substitution, all that happens is that he achieves a lower utility level than if he had selected a point on the boundary of his budget set at which his MRS equals the price ratio. But if he has market power – if he perceives that he is 'large enough' to influence the prices at which the market will clear, this may no longer be true.

A simple example of what happens when information is distorted by misrepresentation on the part of the agents yields important insights into what can go badly wrong when idealised competitive conditions do not hold.

Let Alf and Bill be two traders in an exchange economy with conventional utility functions as described in Section 7.3 of Chapter 7. Alf owns the entire stock of commodity 2, namely R_2, Bill owns all of R_1, so the initial property distribution is at point D in Figure 11.7. On Monday haggling takes place between the two traders, with each telling the truth, and revealing to the other his demand functions. A competitive equilibrium is agreed on (possibly by each side agreeing to abide by the rulings of an impartial arbitrating auctioneer), each trader acting as though he were a price taker – prices are p_1^*, p_2^* at point E in Figure 11.7. On Tuesday each trader arrives

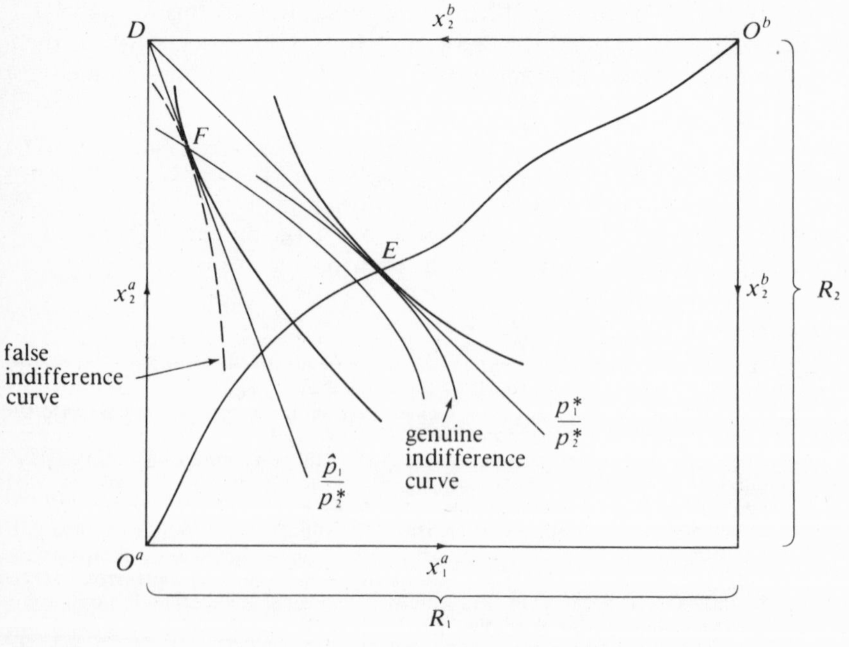

Figure 11.7

with stocks R_1, R_2 but Bill has now decided to lie – purely for material advantage of course. He realises that by trading at point F rather than point E he will be better off: he can induce honest, trusting Alf to accept point F by saying that his true preferences have changed, misrepresenting his indifference curves as shown, and once again securing agreement that a competitive equilibrium solution can be adopted.

Bill's strategy can be formalised thus. Take Alf's demand functions as given

$$x_1^a = D^{a1}(p_1, p_2, p_2R_2) \tag{11.24}$$

$$x_2^a = D^{a2}(p_1, p_2, p_2R_2) \tag{11.25}$$

Now choose p_1 so as to maximise

$$U^b(R_1 - x_1^a, R_2 - x_2^a) \tag{11.26}$$

subject to (11.24), (11.25).

Assuming p_2 remains at p_2^*, and that Alf *still* acts as a price taker, the solution to this is clearly given by $\hat{p}_1$ such that:

$$- U_1^b D_1^{a1} + U_2^b [D^{a1} + \hat{p}_1 D_1^{a1}]/p_2^* = 0 \tag{11.27}$$

where the subscripts on U^b and D^{a1} represent the appropriate partial derivatives. Equation (11.27) has the solution

$$\frac{U_1^b}{U_2^b} = \left[1 + \frac{1}{\varepsilon_{11}^a}\right] \frac{\hat{p}_1}{p_2^*} \tag{11.28}$$

where ε_{11}^a is the elasticity of Alf's demand for good 1 with respect to p_1. The *true* MRS_{21}^b at point F is given by the left-hand side of (11.28). The *revealed* MRS_{21}^b at point F is given by $\hat{p}_1/p_2^*$. Bill is better off than he would be at the competitive equilibrium allocation, but the solution is Pareto inefficient.

Obviously Bill has been getting away with behaviour that is similar to that of the Stackelberg leader discussed in Section 11.5. He may be able to do this if he is a single decision unit whilst the 'Alf' character is actually made up of thousands of tiny Alf people who cannot club together to act as a single unit. Otherwise, if Alf is a single individual, and if he hits on the same idea, then he may also reveal false indifference curves, and the outcome will be a point G in Figure 11.8: this is a point of common tangency of two false indifference curves, and is obviously Pareto inefficient. In fact the outcome with both parties lying is so bad (in this example) that point E is actually Pareto superior to point G – *both* parties would benefit from a restoration of the original competitive equilibrium.

Unfortunately it is not too hard to think of situations where the Alfs and Bills of this world can behave in this fashion, each attempting to exercise monopoly power: for example negotiations between unions and employers

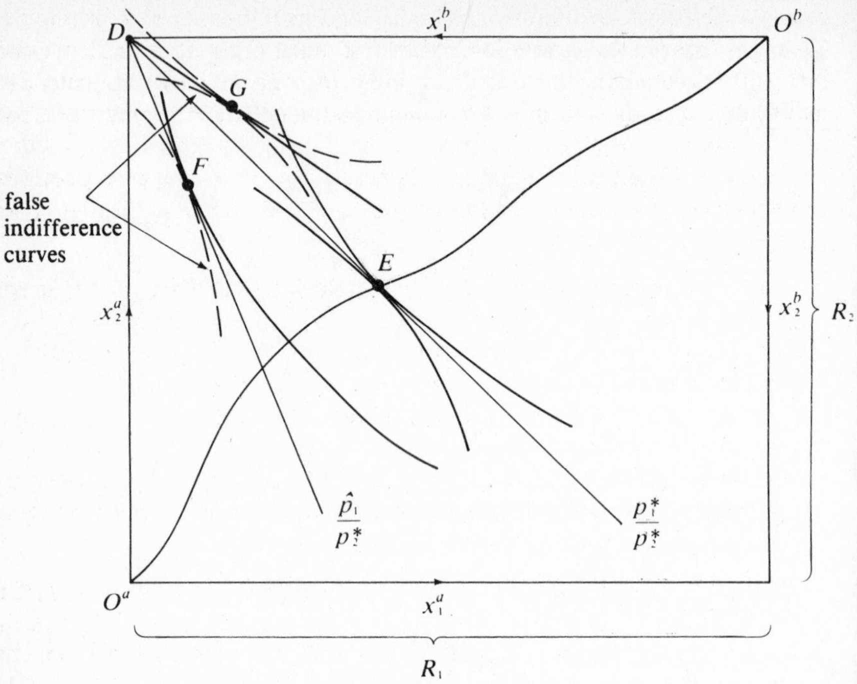

Figure 11.8

or trade agreements between countries.[9] It is perhaps a comfort, but only small comfort, to note that if the number of agents are large enough and the individual agents are small enough, then this type of inefficiency through misrepresentation cannot arise, see Section 12.3 of Chapter 12.[10]

11.7 Summary

Since strategic behaviour – by contrast to price-taking behaviour – is not neat and mechanical, it is hardly surprising that there are no neat and mechanical rules to be summarised at the end of this chapter. As we noted in Sections 11.4 and 11.5 the simplest rule is that there are no rules. Less flippantly, however, we do find the emergence of rules *for particular situations*:

---

[9] See Exercise 11.4.

[10] Also if Bill's market power is increased in a certain way the problem of inefficiency may be avoidable – see Exercise 11.9.

clearly such rules can simplify matters for the participants by reducing the costs of information-gathering, planning and negotiation that would inevitably accompany the search for rules in practice. How the rules are made and who makes them is a fascinating subject that is beyond the scope of this book.

Some, rather negative, points do stand out. In contrast to previous chapters where individuals respond passively – i.e. non-strategically – we find:

- individualistic behaviour can often lead to Pareto inefficient outcomes;
- hence there may be an incentive to invoke or introduce institutions other than the market to support certain solutions;
- the very concept of equilibrium depends on the set of rules and beliefs which are assumed to be in force;
- hence demand and supply responses by both firms and households depend on the appropriate assumed reactions by other agents, and *not* just on price.

Finally, a word of caution. To simplify the approach we again only paid scant attention to time and uncertainty. 'Uncertainty' in each of the models discussed here has only involved the conjectures that agents form about the actions of other agents: it is 'endogenous' in the sense explained on p. 235; some of the further issues that arise when exogenous random events are also present are discussed in Section 12.7 of Chapter 12. Moreover, it is arguable that the passage of time plays a much more important role in the analysis of strategic behaviour than in the models of Chapters 3 to 10 since, as we saw in Section 11.2, issues such as 'who plays first' and whether the game is repeatedly played significantly affect the character of the game itself; moreover time enters explicitly in the emergence of rules and the means by which rules are enforced. Introducing time into models of oligopoly and entry is a difficult task to accomplish neatly and plausibly: on this subject the interested reader should consult the references below.

Further Reading

On the principles of games theory and their applications, see:

McKinsey, J.C.C. (1952) *Introduction to the Theory of Games*, McGraw-Hill.

Shubik, M. (1981) 'Game theory models and methods in political economy', in K.J. Arrow, and M. Intriligator (eds) *Handbook of Mathematical Economics*, Vol. I, Ch. 7.

Shubik, M. (1982, 1984) *Game Theory in the Social Sciences*, MIT Press, Vols. I and II.

On the very important subject of strategic behaviour by firms see:

Friedman, J. (1981) 'Oligopoly theory', in K.J. Arrow and M. Intriligator (eds) *Handbook of Mathematical Economics*, Vol. II, Ch. 11.
Friedman, J. (1983) *Oligopoly Theory*, Cambridge University Press.
Waterson, M. (1984) *Economic Theory of the Industry*, Cambridge University Press.

A useful survey of recent adances in the oligopoly literature is given in the introductory chapter of Geroski, P.A., Phlips, L. and Ulph, A. (eds) (1985) *Oligopoly, Competition and Welfare*, Basil Blackwell.

On the question of strategic behaviour by agents in an exchange economy see:

Roberts, D.J. and Postlewaite, A. (1976) 'The incentives for price-taking behaviour in large exchange economies', *Econometrica*, Vol. 44, pp. 115–27.
Farrell, M.J. (1970) 'Edgeworth bounds for oligopoly prices', *Economica*, Vol. 37, pp. 341–61.

Exercises

11.1 (a) Discuss the difference in structure between games (ii) and (iii) in Figure 11.1.
(b) For which of the games illustrated in Figure 11.1(i)–(vi) does it matter whether there is a specific order of play?

*11.2 Consider a market in which there is one very large firm, which may act as a price maker, and several small firms each of which acts as a price taker. Let the quantity supplied by all the small firms together be given by a function $S(P)$ where P is the price of the product. Let the market demand for the good be given by $D(P)$. Analyse the profit-maximising behaviour of the large firm.

11.3 Consider a monopolist confronting a market where the demand curve is given by $D(P) = Q = A_0 - aP$ and for whom costs are given by $C(Q) = C_0 + cQ$. Write down Π, its profit, as a function of price charged. Plot Π as a function of P and find the firm's optimum.

Now suppose that there is a critical price $\bar{P}$ at which rival firms will enter the market. If they *do* enter let them behave as price takers and suppose that their (collective) supply can be represented by $S(P) = bP - B_0$ for $P \geqslant \bar{P} \equiv B_0/b$. In the light of your answer to question 11.2, write down the erstwhile monopolist's profits as a function of P on *the assumption that the rival firms have entered the market*. Hence examine the problem facing the profit-maximising monopolist facing the threat of entry. Will it be worthwhile its setting the price so as to keep the rivals out? Is there a well-defined optimum strategy?

11.4 Two countries, Alphaland and Betaland, engage in international trade: Betaland exports good 1 to Alphaland in exchange for good 2. Initially a perfectly competitive equilibrium prevails with the price ratio equal to marginal rate of substitution in each country.

Betaland is a much bigger country than Alphaland and gets the idea it can force its small neighbour into accepting terms of trade more favourable to Betaland. The Betan economic advisers suggest that this can be done by putting a tarriff on imports from Alphaland: they go so far as to suggest that knowledge of Alphaland's demand function will enable Betaland to determine an 'optimal' tariff. Are they right? Is such a tariff really 'optimal'?

11.5 A market contains F identical firms. The output of firm f is Q^f and the total cost of firm f is $C_0 + cQ^f$ where $C_0 \geqslant 0$ and $c > 0$ are constants and $f = 1, \ldots, F$. Market demand is given by the demand function

$$Q = \frac{a - P}{b}$$

where a, b are positive constants, P is the market price and Q the total quantity demanded, $\Sigma_f Q^f$.

(a) Write down the profit for firm f.

(b) Assuming that F is given and that each firm can make non-negative profits, show that if each firm acts as a Cournot oligopolist it will choose an output level

$$\hat{Q}^f = \frac{a - c}{bF + b}$$

(c) Show that if $C_0 = 0$, as $F \to \infty$ optimal output approaches that of perfect competition.

(d) Suppose $C_0 > 0$. Show that the maximum number of firms in the indsutry is no greater than

$$[a - c][bC_0]^{-\frac{1}{2}} - 1$$

*11.6 Suppose then firms in question 11.5 form a cartel and then jointly act as a profit-maximising monopolist, dividing output and profits equally amongst the members of the cartel.

(a) Find firm f's profits under the cartel and compare this with profits in question 11.5.

(b) Verify that firm f has an incentive to chisel.

11.7 Assume that F firms sell identical products. The cost curve for producer f is given by $C^f(Q^f)$ where Q^f is its output. The price of the product can be expressed $P = P(Q)$ where Q is aggregate output $\Sigma_f Q^f$.

If each firm maximises its own profits, assuming that the outputs of the other firms remain unchanged, show that in equilibrium:

(a) the market price exceeds the marginal cost of each firm. Under what circumstances will the difference between price and marginal cost be small?
(b) the outputs of the firms will be ranked in the exact opposite order to their marginal costs.

11.8 A firm sells its products in a market along with a number of other firms. The price at which the product can be sold is given by $P = 20 - Q/5$, where Q is aggregate output. Initially the prevailing price is 10 and the firm's output is 10. The firm assumes that if its output is reduced, then the other firms will not alter their output. However, any attempt to increase its share of the market will be met by a corresponding increase in the output of the other firms, thus maintaining the existing market shares.

Derive an expression for the marginal revenue curve faced by the firm. If the cost function is always of the form $C = \alpha [Q^f]^2$ and initially $\alpha = 0.25$, what changes in costs could occur without a change in the output of the firm?

*11.9 Imagine a 2-good exchange economy where there is a single b-trader with utility function $x_1^b x_2^b$ and a thousand a-traders each with utility function $\sqrt{x_1^a} + \sqrt{x_2^a}$, where x_i^h denotes consumption of good i by a trader of type h. The b-trader owns the entire stock R_1 of good 1. Each a-trader has a one thousandth share in the stock R_2 of good 2.

(a) Suppose that the b-trader is allowed to announce a single price ratio at which any of the as may come and buy from him. Show that the optimal purchases of the a-traders are given by

$$x_1^a = \frac{1}{\rho^2 + \rho} R_2$$

$$x_2^a = \frac{\rho}{1 + \rho} R_2$$

where ρ is the price of good 1 in terms of good 2. Show that if $R_1 = 20$ and $R_2 = 10$ then it is optimal for the a-trader to set $\rho = 1$.
(b) Now suppose that the b-trader can demand an 'entrance-fee' from each a-trader before allowing him to purchase anything. Describe the b-trader's optimal policy.
(c) Compare the solutions to (a) and (b) with the solutions to Exercises 7.5, 7.8 and 8.3. Are they Pareto efficient?

11.10 Use the example given on pages 242 and 243 to derive (a) the cartel solution, and (b) the Stackelberg solution where firm 1 is the leader.

12

Incentives

12.1 Introduction

Markets 'work' because each agent – buyer or seller – realises that he could not do better for himself than by accepting the ruling prices and maximising his objective function using those prices. Of course this is only true under certain carefully specified conditions: no one agent may have a significant effect on the trading opportunities of others for example. But under these circumstances we find that not only are markets 'efficient' but they also simplify greatly the amount of information required in the economic system – no one need know or care about the intentions, constraints or information pertaining to anybody else – and they ensure that the information is truthful – no one has any incentive to pretend that his preferences are other than they in fact are.

On the other hand markets do not 'work' in some important cases. As we have seen, problems arise if one agent's actions give rise to externalities or if there are 'large' non-convexities in the system (Chapter 8); more things can fall apart if individual agents realise that they *do* have substantial market power (Chapter 11).

In this chapter we shall extend the discussion of market failure in two ways.

We shall examine more closely the reasons for failure, other than those that arise purely from the technology (such as increasing returns and production externalities). The main point is that the situation in which individuals transact their business is such as to create an incentive for them to misrepresent important aspects of their own characteristics or their actions. This discussion draws on the material in both Chapters 10 and 11 since both 'exogenous' and 'endogenous' uncertainty will be found to be present in the problems that we shall examine.

However we should not, of course, suppose that the possibility of 'market failure' is the cue for throwing up hands in despair. If the reasons for such failure are understood, one may also begin to formulate a scheme that would circumvent that failure: indeed it would be rational for private or government agencies to take steps to protect their interests in instances where markets do not 'work'. Some of these issues overlap with the subject matter of Chapter 13 on 'Welfare': in the present chapter we shall examine the problems that arise in attempting to design such policies and in attempting to ensure that allocation schemes which require co-operation – such as the provision of public goods – do in fact work.

We begin with a case which, it has been argued, is soluble by an extension of the logic of the free market.

12.2 Externalities and the Private Sector

One of the most obvious reasons why the market fails to produce an efficient outcome arises from interdependence amongst agents that is not taken into account by transactions within the market: the 'externalities' discussed in Chapter 8. It may be worth examining whether economic mechanisms are readily available for circumventing this problem, since it is clear that all the firms involved (that is, all the firms' shareholders) could potentially benefit from such a move. To fix ideas let us return to the glue factory example of Section 8.4 in Chapter 8.

Firm 1 produces glue, and the other firms' production possibilities are affected as a result of its noxious by-products. For simplicity let us suppose that there is only one other firm in the economy, and let us further suppose that the production functions $\Phi^1(\mathbf{y}^1)$ and $\Phi^2(\mathbf{y}^2; y_1^1)$ are known.[1] If both firms are rational, self-interested profit maximisers, what will be the outcome?

Consider firm 2's self-interest. If it could identify the source of the pollution that is raising its costs it would obviously be worthwhile to take steps to reduce it. Having (a) correctly spotted firm 1 (the glue factory) as the source of the trouble, and (b) recognised that firm 1 might be open to financial inducements, firm 2 might consider offering firm 1 a cash payment *conditional* on firm 1's output.[2] The less firm 1 produces, the more firm 2 would be prepared to pay. In plain language firm 2 plans to bribe firm 1 to cut back output and hence the emission of pollution. How much should firm 2 offer? To answer this question, write the bribe B as a function of firm 1's output: $B(y_1^1)$ and write the inverse of the function $y_1^1(B)$. Now consider firm 2's optimisation problem. Clearly this is

$$\max_{\{\mathbf{y}^2, B\}} \left[\sum_{i=1}^{n} p_i y_i^2 - B\right] - \mu_2 \Phi^2(\mathbf{y}^2; y_1^1) \tag{12.1}$$

---

[1] In the example of Chapter 8, $y_1^1 > 0$ was the output of glue and $\mathbf{y}^f$ denoted the net output vector of firm f.

[2] We assume that market conditions are such that firm 2 is making positive profits so as to be able to afford the bribe.

Table 12.1 Essential notation for Chapter 12: Incentives

x_i^h	:	household h's consumption of good i
y_i^f	:	firm f's net output of good i
R_i^h	:	household h's endowment of good i
ρ^h	:	personalised price for household h (p_1^h/p_2^h)
F^h	:	fixed charge for household h
CV^h	:	compensating variation for household h
Φ^f	:	production function for firm f
s	:	social state
$\mathcal{S}$	:	set of social states
z	:	cost contribution or effort of servant
w	:	wage schedule
ω	:	state-of-the-world
Ω	:	set of states-of-the-world

where the expression inside the square brackets is the firm's profits and μ_2 is the Lagrange multiplier associated with the production constraint. The first-order conditions yield:

$$p_i - \mu_2 \Phi_i^2 = 0, \quad \text{if} \quad y_i^2 \neq 0, i = 1, \ldots, n \tag{12.2}$$

and

$$-1 + \mu_2 e_1^2 \frac{dy_1^1}{dB} = 0 \tag{12.3}$$

where, as before Φ_i^2 is $\partial \Phi^2/\partial y_i^2$ and e_1^2 is $-\ \partial \Phi^2/\partial y_1^1$, a negative number if firm 1 is producing a negative externality. These two conditions imply:

$$\frac{dB}{dy_1^1} = \mu_2 e_1^2 = p_i e_1^2/\Phi_i^2 \tag{12.4}$$

which is obviously negative in view of e_1^2 being negative. Clearly the marginal bribe offered is proportional to the marginal damage suffered.

Now look at the position of firm 1. Once firm 2 has made its offer of financial inducement, firm 1 must incorporate this in its profit function. So its problem is now

$$\max_{\{y^1\}} \sum_{i=1}^{n} p_i y_i^1 + B(y_1^1) - \mu_1 \Phi^1(\mathbf{y}^1) \tag{12.5}$$

The first-order conditions yield

$$p_1 + \frac{dB}{dy_1^1} - \mu_1 \Phi_1^1 = 0, \quad \text{if} \quad y_1^1 > 0 \tag{12.6}$$

and

$$p_i - \mu_1 \Phi_i^1 = 0, \quad \text{if} \quad y_i^1 \neq 0, i = 2, \ldots, n \tag{12.7}$$

Substituting in the expression for dB/dy_1^1 we find, on simplification:

$$\frac{\Phi_1^1}{\Phi_i^1} = \frac{p_1}{p_i} + \frac{e_1^2}{\Phi_i^2} \tag{12.8}$$

So firm 1 equates its MRT to the market price ratio *adjusted for* the relative valuation of the marginal damage caused by its output. *An efficient solution has emerged because firm 2 has made firm 1 respond to the full impact of its output decision by the suitable choice of bribe function.*

One way of visualising this result is to envisage the setting up of a market – really a pseudo-market – in 'pollution rights' which firm 2 sells to firm 1. In equilibrium the market price of such rights would be equal to the relative marginal damage caused by firm 1's output. The extended market system thus appears to support an efficient allocation, which would be a very attractive result indeed. However, whilst these are practical examples of arrangements that resemble such a pseudo-market, one is not immediately struck by their being everywhere present as a fact of commercial life. Why not?

One reason is that, even if negotiation were possible, the situation may nevertheless involve an allocation that *could* not be supported by a market arrangement because of an implicit non-convexity (compare Figure 8.5). Consider firm 2's output (of good 2) as a function of firm 1's output (of good 1). As firm 1 increases its output, along with its noxious fumes, firm 2's costs (average and marginal) rise and output falls; and if the output of glue is increased sufficiently, firm 2's average costs may increase so much that it is driven out of business altogether as firm 1 expands. Hence the production possibility frontier may look as depicted in Figure 12.1.

Now consider what happens if one introduces a price for the externality, that is a price for the right to pollute. Firm 2 may want to sell a very large number of such rights to firm 1 and in the process shut down production of good 2 altogether: the economy would operate at point *A* in Figure 12.1, rather than at any point where good 2 is actually produced. In this case it is clear that many Pareto efficient allocations (such as point *B*) *could* not be supported by an extended market system, although whether the problem arises in practice depends on the physical nature of the externality and thus whether this non-convexity is 'significantly large'.[3]

[3] In fact an artificial market in externalities may have no equilibrium under such conditions. This argument is considered further in Starrett, D.A. (1972) 'Fundamental nonconvexities in the theory of externalities', *Journal of Economic Theory*, Vol. 4, pp. 180–99.

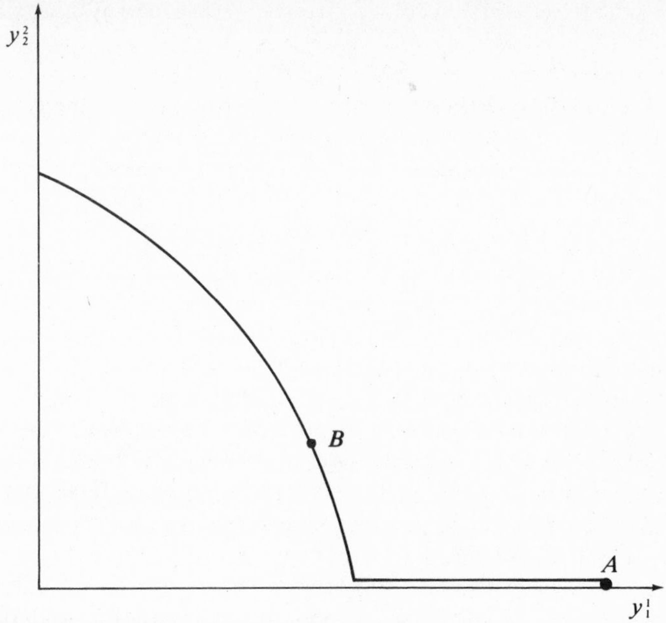

Figure 12.1

A second reason for being sceptical about the extended market solution to the efficiency problem with production externalities concerns numbers. If there is only a small number of firms involved then the 'market' will be thin – which is one reason why it is better to refer to it as a pseudo-market. But if there is a large number of firms the mere formulation of the solution – let alone its enforcement – may be very difficult to arrange.

The problem is closely analogous to the case of oligopolistic equilibrium which we discussed in Chapter 11. When there is a large number of firms, then policing a collusive agreement (the cartel) may be intractable because of the difficulty of identifying – and punishing – a 'chiseller'.

A third reason, linked to the second, is the problem of information. The computation of the inefficient marginal bribe, or the pseudo-market price for the externality, clearly relies on full knowledge – by *both* parties – of the firms' production functions. This might be quite plausible if few parties are involved in the externality – either as victims or as culprits – and if each of the parties is involved in a similar production activity. But if there are several potential polluters, or if the details of one party's production function are unlikely to be readily ascertained by others, then there is a motive for that party to attempt to convince the other that the marginal damage of the externality is greater than is really the case. If the other side suspects that this is going on then one would expect the fragile pseudo-market in externalities to break down immediately.

It is apparent that the misinformation argument applies with even greater force to consumption externalities. Indeed it is possible to think of several examples in this area where it is impossible even to check whether the externality is positive or negative – for instance the smoker's example on page 116 of Chapter 6. In fact we shall find that the problem of inefficiency arising from an incentive to misinform is fairly general: we examine these issues further in the next section.

12.3 Misrepresentation and Manipulation

The trading game of Section 11.6 illustrated an important point: if each agent perceives that he has market power then he may find that it appears to be in his interests to dissimulate. By not stating his true preferences over the goods being traded he hopes to use that power to exploit the passive – or gullible – nature of his trading partner's behaviour.

This is a pervasive problem in economic relations where one assumes, quite reasonably, that individuals pursue their own self-interest. In many cases it is plausible to argue that the presence in the market of large numbers of small agents will ensure an efficient, competitive allocation (as in Section 7.3 of Chapter 7); in some others one might legitimately argue that the allocational inefficiencies arising from externalities are small relative to the size of the economy. However as we noted in the Introduction, there is a large class of economic problems for which the problem cannot just be assumed away: for which the technology of production, consumption or the nature of the market means that there is a built-in motive for providing false information, and hence a built-in source of inefficiency. An instance of this which is of prime economic interest is the problem of how public goods are to be provided.

Notice that the issue here is not 'what is the "right" amount of public goods to be provided in the economy?' – we have already discussed this in Section 8.3 of Chapter 8, albeit in an elementary fashion. The question is rather: 'how are the people in the community to be persuaded to provide the resources to provide the right amount of goods in the economy?'.

Obviously we can invent a planner who, like an omniscient nanny, (a) knows what is good for everybody, and (b) has the power to enforce it upon everybody. Then an efficient allocation – satisfying equation (8.35) of Chapter 8 – could immediately be implemented. But suppose, for the moment, that we spurn such an invention: how is the provision of such goods to be determined? Let us begin by considering free will: could a public good be efficiently provided on the basis of voluntary contributions?

The essence of the problem can be conveyed in a simple 2-good example. Good 2 is a private good of which household h has a stock R_2^h. Household h actually consumes only x_2^h and contributes the balance, $R_2^h - x_2^h$, to the production of public good 1. The production of good 1 is a function ϕ of the total private contributions of all the households. Thus the amount x_1 of good 1 that is available for consumption by each household is given by

$$x_1 = \phi\left(\sum_{h=1}^{H} [R_2^h - x_2^h]\right) \tag{12.9}$$

Now consider the decision problem of household l. It wishes to maximise its utility function $U^l(x_1, x_2^l)$ by choice of x_2^l subject to the above production constraint. What it does not know, of course, is how *other* households will react in terms of *their* contributions if it varies its own contribution $R_2^l - x_2^l$. In a large economy it might be reasonable to suppose that household l takes $\sum_{h \neq l} [R_2^h - x_2^h]$ as a constant, c: it assumes that it is 'too small to matter' in influencing other households decisions. Then the optimisation problem for household l becomes:

$$\max_{\{x_2^l\}} \; U^l(\phi(c + R_2^l - x_2^l), x_2^l) \tag{12.10}$$

Obviously the first-order condition for an interior solution to this problem is

$$-U_1^l\phi' + U_2^l = 0 \tag{12.11}$$

which implies

$$\text{MRT}_{21} = \frac{1}{\phi'} = \frac{U_1^l}{U_2^l} = \text{MRS}_{21}^l \tag{12.12}$$

But, referring back to equation 8.25 of Chapter 8, efficiency requires

$$\text{MRT}_{21} = \frac{1}{\phi'} = \sum_{h=1}^{H} \frac{U_1^h}{U_2^h} = \sum_{h=1}^{H} \text{MRS}_{21}^h \tag{12.13}$$

So we find that individual voluntary contributions lead to consumption at point A in Figure 12.2 rather than at efficient point B – too little of the public good is produced.

It is useful to examine this problem using a 2-person example. In Figure 12.3 measure Alf's contribution to the public good along the horizontal axis, and Bill's contribution along the vertical axis. Now consider Alf's indifference curves in this diagram: If the MRS_{21} in equation (12.12) is large for $x_1 = 0$ and falls to zero as $x_1 \to \infty$, then in Figure 12.3 as Alf's contribution is increased ($R_2^a - x_2^a$ is increased) utility at first rises and then falls, producing

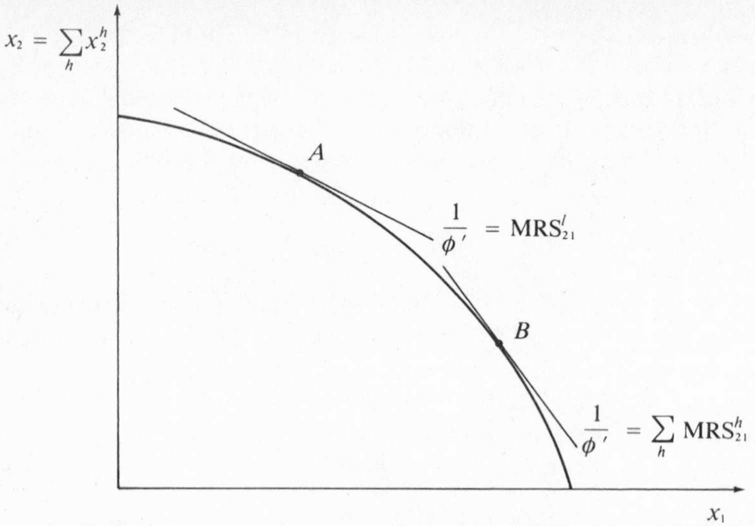

Figure 12.2

the U-shaped contour as shown.[4] What will Alf choose to do? If he takes Bill's contribution as exogenously given (i.e. if he makes the Cournot–Nash assumption of Section 11.2) then he fixes his own contribution at a point which is at the bottom of one such contour. For example, if he knows that Bill is stumping up an amount *OB*, and believes that this will continue to be the case whatever he chooses to do, then Alf will choose a contribution of size *OA*. Hence we may plot the locus of these lowest points as Alf's reaction curves. Of course the same thing may be argued for Bill: by turning the page at right-angles you can see his indifference curves in the space of the parties' contributions are similar in shape to those of Alf. In the same manner we may draw Bill's reaction curve.[5]

It is immediately obvious where the Cournot–Nash solution corresponding to (12.12) is located: point *C* at the intersection of the two reaction curves.

This is manifestly inefficient. Both Alf and Bill's utilities could be increased if it were possible to shift the allocation from *C* in a north easterly direction. Again it is easy to see where the locus of Pareto efficient points

---

[4] See Exercise 12.3.

[5] For further discussion of the use of this diagram see Cornes, R. and Sandler, T. (1985) 'The simple analytics of pure public good provision', *Economica*, Vol. 52, pp. 103–16.

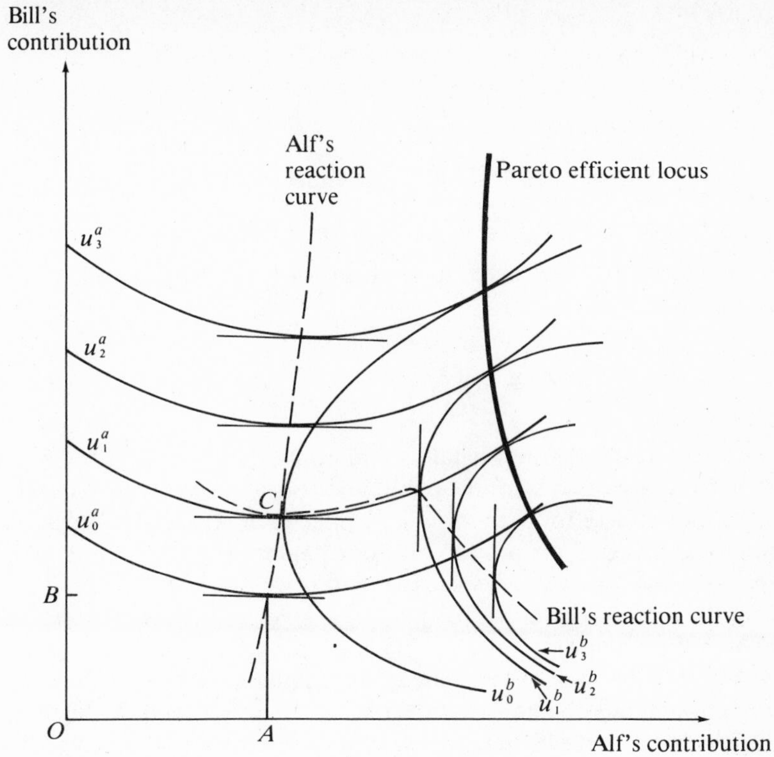

Figure 12.3

must be: the set of points of common tangency sketched in the top right-hand corner of the Figure 12.3.

So unguided free choice leads to inefficiency, a result which is unsurprising in view of Chapter 8's discussion of externalities and Chapter 11's discussion of the prisoner's dilemma game form. We would expect each agent to welcome, in principle, an external agency that would stipulate the amount that each person should pay. But will the introduction of such an external agency resolve the inefficiency problem noted above? Not necessarily.

Imagine that the agency that produces the public good is empowered to fix a discriminatory 'subscription price' that is specific to each household h, in the manner of the discriminating monopolist of Exercise 3.13 of Chapter 3. For convenience write this price as a ratio ρ^h that measures the cost per unit of good 1 in terms of good 2, following the same convention as in Chapter 9. The agency announces the set of personalised prices and then household h announces how much of the public good it would wish to purchase. The decision problem of household h is:

$$\max_{\{x_1, x_2^h\}} U^h(x_1, x_2^h) \tag{12.14}$$

subject to

$$\rho^h x_1 + x_2^h = R_2^h \tag{12.15}$$

Obviously the household will announce intended purchases (x_1, x_2^h) such that

$$U_1^h / U_2^h = \rho^h \tag{12.16}$$

Apparently all the agency needs to do to ensure efficiency is to select the ρ^h such that

$$\sum_{h=1}^{H} \frac{U_1^h}{U_2^h} = \sum_{h=1}^{H} \rho^h = \text{MRT}_{21} \tag{12.17}$$

This is often known as the Lindahl solution. Notice the interesting way in which individual demands for the public good are aggregated. By contrast to private goods (where for a given, unique price each household's demanded quantity is summed – see pp. 123–125 of Chapter 6) we find that for a unique *quantity* each household's subscription price is summed – see Figure 12.4 for the 2-person case.

There is, however, a rather obvious problem. Why should each household reveal its *true* MRS to the agency? After all, there may be no way of checking whether the household is telling lies or not, and the higher the MRS one admits to, the higher the subscription price one will be charged. So, once a household realises this, what will be the outcome? It then realises that it can effectively choose the price that confronts it by announcing an appropriate, false MRS. It seems reasonable to suppose that it will do this to maximise its own utility subject to the actions of all other households assumed to be given. Writing $\sum_{h \neq l} \rho^h x_1$ as c, which is taken as constant by household l, it then chooses ρ^l and x_2^l to maximise

$$U^l(x_1, x_2^l) \tag{12.18}$$

subject to

$$x_1 = \phi(c + \rho^l x_1) \tag{12.19}$$

and

$$\rho^l x_1 + x_2^l = R_2^l \tag{12.20}$$

But a brief inspection reveals that this is *exactly* the problem above where each household made its own voluntary contribution. *Because there is no incentive for any household to reveal its true preference and no way of checking the preferences independently, the inefficiency persists.*

Evidently we have re-encountered the problem of 'cheating' in the

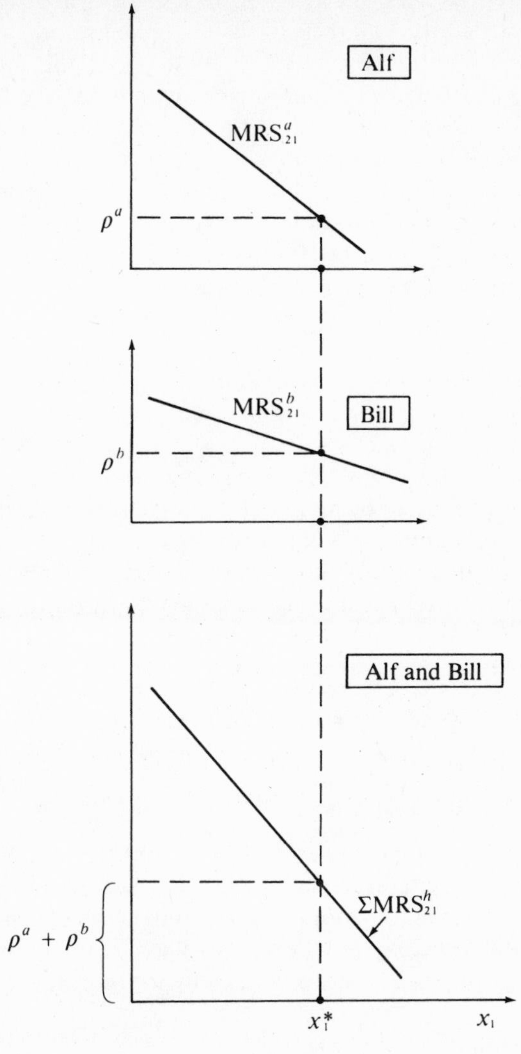

Figure 12.4

trading game of Section 11.6, of 'chiselling' in the oligopoly problem of Section 11.4, of misinformation in the simple externality problem of Section 12.2.

To consider this problem of dissimulation in a general way let us use the 'social state' notation of Section 8.1 in Chapter 8 – see Table 12.1. Imagine that all the information about the 'rules of the game' in society has been assembled – the resources, the available technology, the structure of property rights, the structure of markets, the system of allocation of public goods and the means of paying for them – in short all the minutiae of the mechanism which would determine a particular social state $\mathscr{s} \in \mathscr{S}$ once individual preferences are specified. Let household h have a utility function U^h (defined over $\mathscr{S}$) that represents its preferences over all possible social states. Call a particular set of such utility functions, one for each household, a *profile* of preferences, and assume that for a given profile a unique $\mathscr{s}$ is determined.[6] Write Γ for the function – or 'mechanism' – which transforms a profile of preferences into a social state thus:

$$\mathscr{s} = \Gamma(U^1, U^2, \ldots, U^H) \tag{12.21}$$

We say that the mechanism Γ is *manipulable* if there is some household h and some *other* function $\hat{U}^h(.)$ for that household such that the allocation

$$\hat{\mathscr{s}} = \Gamma(U^1, U^2, \ldots, \hat{U}^h, \ldots, U^H)$$

would be strictly preferred[7] by household h to $\mathscr{s}$. If this is *not* possible then Γ is known as *non-manipulable* or *cheat proof*.

As a final preliminary, if the $\mathscr{s}$ derived from Γ is always that which would have emerged from just using the utility function for one particular household h, $U^h(.)$, as a criterion function, then Γ is said to be *dictatorial*, with h as the dictator. We may now state:

THEOREM 12.1 (*Gibbard–Satterthwaite*):[8] if the number of individuals is finite, if $\mathscr{S}$ has at least three distinct elements, and if Γ is (i) defined over all logically possible preference profiles $(U^1, U^2, \ldots, U^H)$ and (ii) is cheat-proof, then it must be dictatorial.

There is thus a fundamental problem: unless the social mechanism is dictatorial then in the circumstances specified in Theorem 12.1 it appears to be in everyone's interest to dissimulate. As in the example shown in Figure 11.1(vi) on page 236 of Chapter 11, each agent perceives it to be in his interest to play a strategy that turns out to be socially irresponsible.

---

[6] Of course each utility function is defined up to a monotonic transformation – it is only the *ordering* over $\mathscr{S}$ that is important – so that the symbol U^h could everywhere be replaced by $\succ^h$: see Section 13.2 in the next chapter. If the social state $\mathscr{s}$ corresponding to a particular profile is not unique then the result below goes through in modified form.

[7] That is, 'preferred' according to its true utility function $U^h(.)$ and not the bogus utility function $\hat{U}^h$ used to manipulate Γ.

[8] For proof of this result see the Green and Laffont reference at the end of this chapter. (It is closely related to Theorem 13.1 in Chapter 13 below.) The original references are: Gibbard, A. (1973) 'Manipulation of voting schemes: a general result', *Econometrica*, Vol. 41, pp. 587–602; Satterthwaite, M.A. (1975) 'Strategy-proofness and Arrow's conditions: existence and correspondence theorems for voting procedures and social welfare functions', *Journal of Economic Theory*, Vol. 10, pp. 187–217.

The result appears to be pessimistic in the extreme. However it is of great value in showing the generality of the problem and in focusing our attention on the assumptions that may have to be changed in order to resolve a particular problem of economic incentives. For example, in a model of atomistic competition, with an effectively infinite number of small households and firms, manipulability will not be a problem (see Section 7.3 of Chapter 7). Again if one 'household' is in effect the government or some other public agency that is taken to represent the interests of the community, then having a dictatorial Γ may not matter (see Sections 12.5 and 12.7 below): however the very existence of such a representative body itself begs a number of questions (see Section 13.2 of Chapter 13). Or again some problems may admit of simplification down to one of binary choice (see Section 12.6 below). We now proceed to a closer examination of the various types of incentive problem.

12.4 The Ingredients of the Problem

The essence of the incentive problem which we shall examine is a kind of master-and-servant relationship, the type of relationship that may exist between a patient and his private physician, a firm and its employees, insurance firms and their clients or a central planning board and its satellite agencies. In fact there is a wide range of economic problems which can be fitted into this framework.

We shall assume that the roles of 'master and servant' (which in some cases are also known by the terms 'principal and agent'[9]) are clearly laid down. Associated with each of the roles is a certain type of optimisation problem, which specifies that role in economic terms. For the moment we shall suppose, as in Chapter 11, that we need only consider one particular actor taking on each of the two roles: in Section 12.5 we shall consider what happens when this rule is relaxed. Let us see how the two roles may be described, in general terms.

The 'master', as the very title implies, has a specific purpose that he wants to achieve, and the power to lay down rules for the servant in order to achieve that purpose. So, in order to set out the master's optimisation problem we need to specify the objective function which he is presumed to be maximising (profit or expected utility, for example), and the scope that he

[9] I have not used these terms here since the principal-and-agent problem is usually defined more narrowly than the general incentive problem here (it is often used to mean just the 'unseen actions' problem mentioned on page 271) and also because 'agent' is used elsewhere in a more general sense.

has for setting the rules. This latter point might seem rather odd, since it implies that there are some sets of rules which he may not lay down. But why can't the master, since he *is* the master, just do whatever he likes and make up the rules as he goes along?

There are two interlinked reasons: (i) he does not have all the information that would give him a completely free hand; (ii) the servant is not a *slave*, but a *servant*, whose co-operation must be obtained voluntarily. Let us deal with this point first.

The 'servant' has his own objective function too. In this respect he is, in economic terms, quite different from the Man Friday who appeared on the desert island in Section 5.3 of Chapter 5. Man Friday was purely an automaton whose sole existence was to facilitate Robinson Crusoe's objectives – he was part of the technology – whereas the actor whose behaviour we are now modelling has interests of his own which are presumably quite different from his master's. It is the recognition of this distinct set of interests, by both parties, that makes the incentive problem particularly interesting.

Apart from the explicit incorporation of his preferences into the model, the other way in which the servant differs from Man Friday is that we also allow him some freedom of action. Essentially he may choose whether or not to take up the deal on the terms offered by the master: if he does not like them he can get on his bike and go elsewhere. This 'participation constraint' limits the set of enforceable rules that the master may choose to lay down.

Now let us return to the problem of information. There are several interesting ways in which the issues raised by incomplete information, uncertainty and misrepresentation can be modelled. However many of the problems can be conveniently grouped into two main types:

(1) *private knowledge*: the servant knows something that could be kept hidden from the master. For example it might be some matter of personal taste (as in the case of the demand for public goods, discussed above), or it might be a personal characteristic (such as state of health). Even if the private knowledge is announced it may not be accepted at face value since the master may believe that it is in the servant's interest to dissimulate. The main point is that if the master were to know what the servant knows, he could use that information to his own advantage; indeed it may even be the case that *both* parties could be made better off in that resources may be used up by one or other party to overcome the problem that the private knowledge cannot be checked.[10]

[10] See Exercise 12.4.

(2) *unseen actions*: in this case we suppose that some action taken by the servant cannot be directly observed; what *can* be observed is some outcome which is determined in part by the unseen action and in part by random events. In this case exogenous uncertainty (and not just the misrepresentation that is endogenous to the problem) has an essential role to play, since otherwise *either* (i) the master could deduce the action from the observed outcome, or (ii) the problem is essentially the 'private knowledge' case again, in that the servant knows the connection between actions and outcome but the master does not.

The essential features of the two problems are summarised in Table 12.2; of course, elements of both of them might appear in mixed form but it is easier to bring out the main issues separately. In each case there is an authority system (as embodied in the two roles), and an enforcement system (incorporated into the set of rewards and penalties which the master may lay down) and in each case there is intrinsically more information available to the servant than to the master. As we shall see below, part of the master's problem is to choose the rules of the game so that some of this information becomes evident: ideally he would like to choose them so that 'telling the truth' becomes a dominant strategy for the servant. Of course he has to choose the rules in such a way that the servant still wants to play.

Table 12.2 Types of incentive problem

	'Master'	*'Servant'*
(a) Private knowledge		
Objective	Expected utility	Expected utility
Scope of power	Designs a system of rewards and punishments	*Either* (a) accepts the system and chooses action *or* (b) refuses to participate
Information	Observes the choice, but not *all* the information used in making it	Knows what the master knows plus some private information
(b) Unseen actions		
Objective	Expected utility	Expected utility
Scope of power	Designs a system of rewards and punishments	*Either* (a) accepts the system and chooses action *or* (b) refuses to participate
Information	Observes outcome, but *not* action, nor state-of-the-world which produced it	Knows system of rewards/ punishments, but *not* state-of-the-world

The rules of the game that are drawn up depend on the power that the master has to enforce his will. In turn the type of enforcement policies available and the extent to which they are employed will depend on the available information, the technology of consumption and production, and also on the market structure. In the next three sections we shall examine a number of important cases. Section 12.5 tackles the 'private knowledge' problem where the master can employ exclusion devices; Section 12.6 examines the 'private knowledge' problem in the presence of public goods – where individual exclusion is not possible. Section 12.7 analyses 'unseen actions'.

12.5 Private Knowledge and Excludability

In this section we shall examine the problem of using an economic device to get someone to reveal private information that might, if it were concealed, lead to market failure – an inefficient allocation. The devices considered here will involve cases where a firm (acting as 'master') can dictate the terms on which it is prepared to deal with its customers: for example charging an 'entrance fee' for the privilege of purchase, or rationing the amount of the commodity that the customer may buy. Since it is clear that this can only be done with goods that are 'excludable' (in the sense of Section 6.3 of Chapter 6), it might seem that the cases where the really interesting problems of private knowledge occur, such as those on pages 265–269 above, have been ruled out. In fact we discuss such 'pure public good' cases in Section 12.5; however, excludable good cases raise some interesting issues in their own right. First, where the production set is non-convex, market prices may not convey all the relevant information about preferences (as an example refer back to Figure 8.5 of Chapter 8): which social state is efficient depends on people's willingness to cover the substantial fixed cost as well as their marginal rates of substitution. Second, it may be that the nature or quality of the good itself differs as between different types of buyer or seller; an efficient allocation would require different prices for what are in effect different goods, but the available information may prevent this occurring if the quality of the good is unknown (or unknowable) at the time of the transaction.

We deal first with the problem of substantial fixed costs of production: here 'substantial' means that it is impossible to achieve a Pareto efficient allocation in competitive markets because firms could not break even just by charging a uniform price per unit of output. Suppose that production is undertaken by a single firm: as in the example of Figure 8.5 we may take it that there is one other good in the economy (good 2) which the firm uses as input to produce good 1. We know that if this firm acts as a 'simple monopolist' (i.e. one may only announce a uniform price for one's wares to all comers) then the outcome will be inefficient – see Section 3.8 of Chapter 3 and Exercise 8.11(b).

However, suppose the public monopolist is endowed with greater power. Imagine the good to be something that is effectively impossible to resell – like electricity, natural gas or telephone services – and that the monopolist knows the demand function of *each* customer. If the monopolist is allowed to deal with customers in a discriminatory fashion then it may be possible to ensure that an efficient allocation is supported. The situation is illustrated in Figure 12.5 for the case where two customers, Alf and Bill, have an endowment of good 2 given by R_2^a and R_2^b, respectively, and we suppose that each of the two customers can survive without consuming good 1 so that their indifference curves touch the vertical axis: 'reservation utility' is given by the indifference curve through the point $(0, R_2^h)$, $h = a, b$. The indifference curves have been drawn so that, at a given level of consumption of good 1, $\text{MRS}_{21}^a < \text{MRS}_{21}^b$ – Bill is willing to make higher marginal sacrifices of good 2 for good 1 than is Alf.

If the monopolist knows the identities of Alf and Bill, and if its objective is to maximise profits, then its optimal strategy is clear. Any household can be forced on to a particular consumption bundle by an appropriate income-adjustment and choice of prices (subject to the participation constraint being met). In the present case the monopoly can do it by fixing a so-called 'two-part tariff' (F^h, ρ^h) for household h, where F^h is a fixed charge[11] that is payable if h consumes *any* positive amount of good 1 and ρ^h is the price per unit of good h, denominated in units of good 2.

Profits for the monopoly are given by

$$\Sigma_h[\rho^h x_1^h + \delta^h F^h] - C(\Sigma_h x_1^h) \tag{12.22}$$

where δ^h is a dummy variable that equals 1 if household h is in the game ($x_1^h > 0$) and zero otherwise, and where C is the cost function. Differentiating (12.22) with respect to x_1^h it is clearly optimal to set $\rho^h = \rho^*$, where ρ^* equals marginal cost, for every household h. Obviously, it is also optimal for the monopoly to set F^h sufficiently large that household h is just in the game – i.e. such that h is forced back on to his reservation utility. This situation is illustrated by points A and B in Figure 12.5 where Alf and Bill consume x_1^{*a}, x_1^{*b}: clearly F^a and F^b are nothing other than the compensating variation to Alf and Bill for their being allowed the great favour of being able to buy its product at ρ^* rather than being banned from consuming it at all.

The solution in which Alf and Bill consume at points A and B is clearly Pareto efficient – in sharp contrast to the simple monopolist – each consumer's marginal rate of substitution equals the marginal rate of transformation of good 2 into good 1 (marginal cost). However of course it is also

---

11 F^h plays the role of an entrance fee for playing the game.

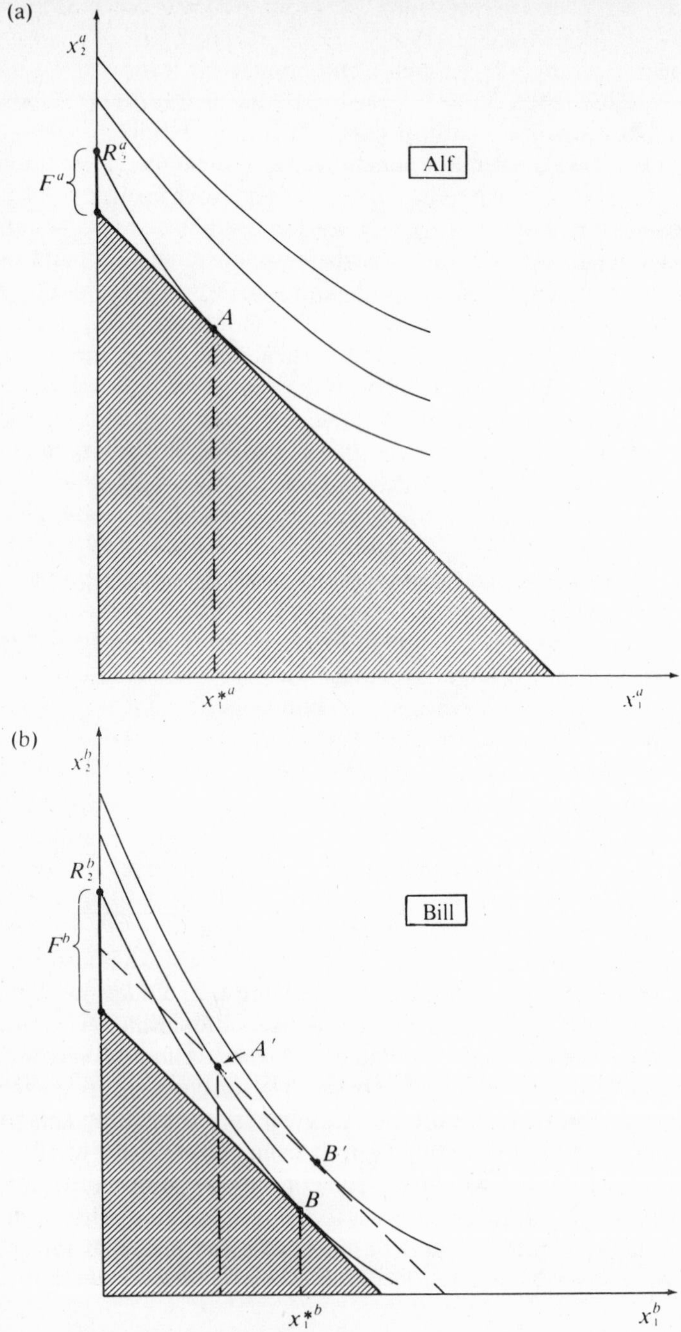

Figure 12.5

shamelessly exploitative since each consumer is forced down to his reservation utility level.[12] There is thus a nice paradox of market power – a monopolist that is given unlimited power over its customers (other than their right not to participate) will set a payment system that is extortionary, but not distortionary.

But what happens if the monopolist does *not* have enough information to know which consumer is which? To extend the example, let us suppose that there are still only the two *types* of consumers, but that now there are lots of each type (Alf, Arthur, . . . ; Bill, Ben, . . .). The monopolist knows how a-type and b-type consumers behave *as a type* (i.e. it knows the demand curves for each of the two groups in isolation) but it cannot identify any *particular* customer as being of one particular type.

The previous scheme, offering (F^a, p^*) to people like Alf and (F^b, p^*) to people like Bill, will not work. The reason is that, under the circumstances that we have specified, (i) b-type people would prefer to have the offer intended for a-type people, (ii) the monopolist has no way of telling that someone who claims to be an a-type person is not in fact Bill or Ben. It is worth considering point (i) a bit more closely. It is evident from Figure 12.5 that Bill would prefer the deal offered to Alf if he could get it, because then he could reach a higher point on his own indifference curve: observe the broken constraint superimposed on Bill's diagram. However, in the many-person case we are now considering, if a b-person succeeds in being offered an a-person's deal (F^a, p^*) then obviously he must not go ahead and maximise his utility subject to the budget constraint implied by (F^a, p^*) – i.e. consume at point B' – for then his behaviour would differ from the typical a-person and his masquerade would be discovered. So if Bill or Ben pretend to be an a-person they must not consume at B', but at A', where their consumption would be indistinguishable from Alf's or Arthur's consumption. There is thus apparently an inefficiency (marginal rates of substitution are no longer equal across households) arising from the possibility of misinformation.

However the monopolist can do something about the situation. He can do this by taking into account the decision problem faced by b-type people. As noted in Section 12.3, they have the fundamental option whether or not to participate in any scheme offered to them, so in this case, if the monopolist is to persuade them not to masquerade as a-people, he knows he has to offer them a deal that is as good as that which they can get by masquerading. In other words they must be enabled to purchase $\mathbf{x}^b = (x_1^b, x_2^b)$ such that

$$U^b(\mathbf{x}^b) \geqslant U^b(x_1^a, R_2^b - p^* x_1^a - F^a) \tag{12.23}$$

[12] See Exercise 11.9.

where x_1^a is the consumption of good 1 that a-type people are known to choose; (12.23) is known as a *self-selection* constraint.

Now if the monopolist continues to offer the Alfs of this world (F^a, p^*) so that they still consume at point A in Figure 12.5, then clearly the best that the monopolist can do is offer Bill and Ben, (F^{*b}, p^*), which would just induce such persons to consume at B^* in Figure 12.6: the expression (12.23) then becomes an equality. The indifference curve u_0^b is Bill's reservation indifference curve, *given that he can masquerade as Alf or Arthur, and that they are now consuming* x_1^a. The equilibrium with the a-types at A and b-types at B^* is Pareto efficient, since each consumer's MRS is equated to MRT.

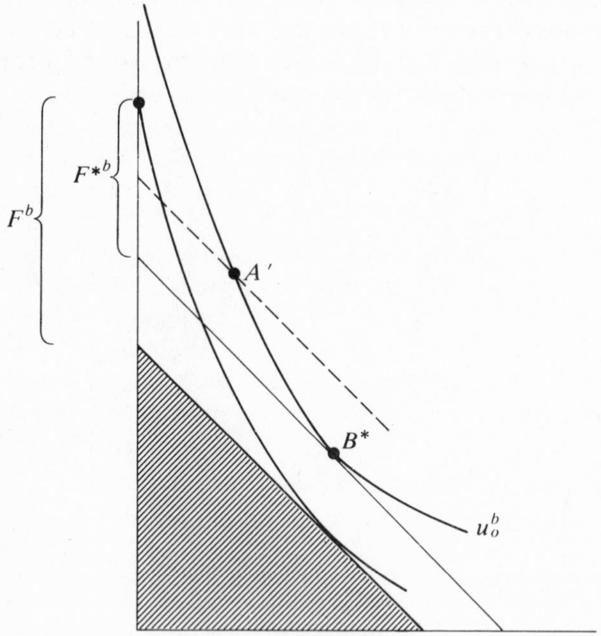

Figure 12.6

However, although it is efficient the above solution is not, in fact, profit-maximising for the discriminating monopolist, since Bill and Ben are still achieving a positive consumer's surplus at (F^{*b}, p^*). It could do better by reducing the consumption of the a-types a little (and compensating them to keep them on their reservation utility level): the reduction in their consumption would then permit an adjustment in the offer designed for the

b-type people with a view to grabbing a bit more of their surplus. Consider a small reduction in F^a, to $\bar{F}$, and an increase in ρ that keeps Alf on the same indifference curve as point A in Figure 12.5, but at a lower consumption level $\bar{x}_1^a < x_1^{*a}$. Consider how the right-hand side of (12.23) changes if x_1^a is reduced in this way. We find

$$\Delta U^b \simeq [U_1^b - U_2^b \rho^*][\bar{x}_1^a - x_1^{*a}] - U_2^b x_1^{*a} \Delta\rho \qquad (12.24)$$

The first term on the right-hand-side of (12.24) is positive (since, as seen in Figure 12.5(b) $\mathrm{MRS}_{21}^b > \rho^*$), and so since $\Delta\rho > 0$ and $\bar{x}_1^a - x_1^{*a} < 0$ (12.24) is negative. Since the b-type's reservation utility will have fallen, this enables the monopolist to raise their entrance fee from F^{*b} to $\bar{\bar{F}}$, such that (12.23) still holds. So the monopolist's optimal policy will involve specifying $\bar{\rho} > \rho^*$ and an entrance fee that is a step function, as illustrated in Figure 12.7. Customers select their own payment schedule: those who demand no more than $\bar{x}_1^a$ get charged the entry fee $\bar{F}$; those who demand more than this get charged $\bar{\bar{F}}$. *But in pursuing this policy so as to increase his profits the discriminating monopolist will have introduced a new distortion.*

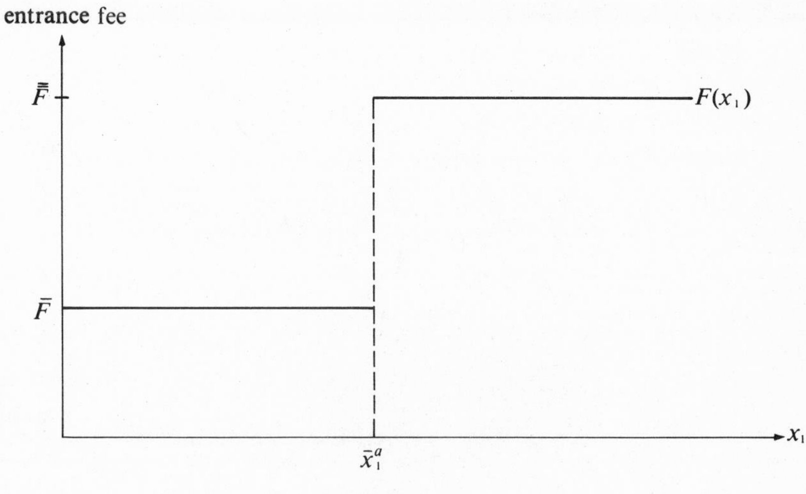

Figure 12.7

The analysis so far has assumed that there is a single actor – a monopolist – who takes on the role of 'master', and many 'servants' – the customers. The question naturally comes to mind: what happens if there are many masters? Suppose we are dealing with an unregulated industry, so that new firms could enter and produce as long as they can break even or make a profit. For example, imagine that Figures 12.5 and 12.6 and the accompanying discussion refer to a telephone service: the physical characteristics of the good make resale difficult, and the device of a discriminatory entrance fee may be used to distinguish between different categories of customers.

Although this case has sometimes been taken to be a 'natural monopoly', technological developments in the field of telecommunications may make it possible for a new company to offer a rival service alongside the incumbent. If a new firm enters it will see immediate advantages in making use of 'free' information provided by the incumbent firm. But if it sets up shop using this information then this is going to distort the equilibrium which so conveniently provided the information in the first place: it is not clear what the equilibrium solution would look like, if one exists.

A problem of this sort has been recognised for some time in the field of insurance, and is illustrated in Figure 12.8. In this case the underlying difficulty is not primarily one of non-convexity; but that insurance policies sold to different customers are in effect 'different goods'. Imagine that each consumer faces a situation in which there are exactly two states of the world 'red' (in which no accident occurs) and 'blue' (in which an accident of given severity occurs). There are, as in the previous monopoly example, two types of consumer a and b; if any uninsured customer does not have an accident he

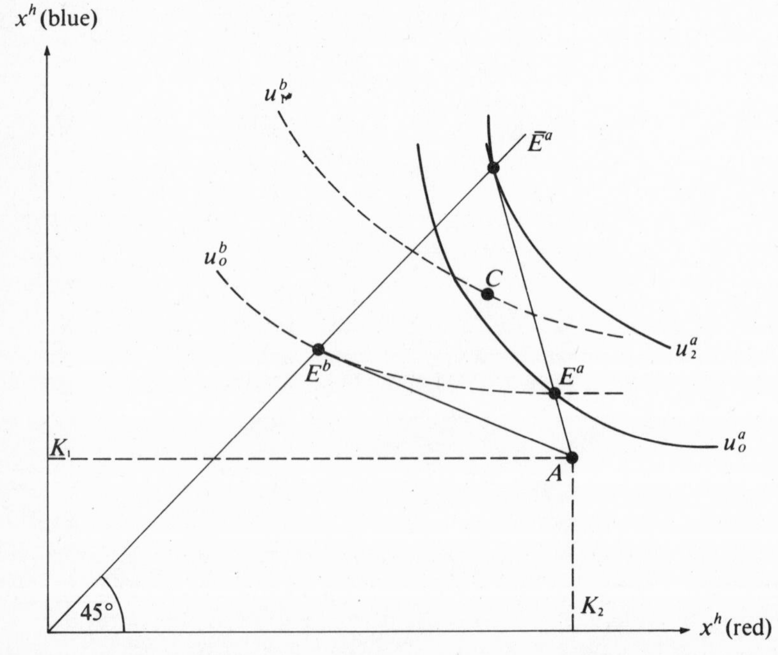

Figure 12.8

enjoys consumption OK_2, but if he has an accident, he only gets consumption OK_1: this situation is represented by point A. The diagram is based on Figure 10.5(iii) on page 214 of Chapter 10.

What makes the consumers different is their accident-proneness. People of type a are low-risk: this is interpreted to mean that the probability of state blue's occurrence, for them, is $\pi(\text{blue}) = \pi^a$, a small number. People of type b are high-risk: for them, we have $\pi(\text{blue}) = \pi^b > \pi^a$. The risk of accident to any one person is assumed to be independent of the risk to any other person. The difference in risk could arise from differences in personal characteristics discussed in Section 12.3. Thus in Figure 12.8 the indifference map for the a-type people is given by the broken curves, whereas that for the b-type people is given by the solid curves; of course, the slope of an indifference curve as it crosses the 45° ray is $1 - 1/\pi^h$, $h = a$ or b (see page 211 of Chapter 10).

Now consider the possibility of there being a 'separating' equilibrium, with the a-types and the b-types each buying insurance at different rates. Examine Figure 12.8. If insurance companies had perfect information about each risk class – i.e. they could identify whether each person was an a or b – then an equilibrium alloction would entail the a-types consuming at $\overline{E}^a$ and the b-types at E^b. Firms would break even in such a situation (see the argument on page 220 of Chapter 10 as to why this is so); moreover $\overline{E}^a$ and E^b are utility-maximising choices for the two types of households given budget constraints $A\overline{E}^a$ and AE^b, respectively. So the situation would appear to be consistent with a (Pareto efficient) competitive equilibrium.

But of course this will not do if firms cannot objectively distinguish between the two types of individuals. If it were possible for b-types to masquerade as a-types they would do so since clearly $\overline{E}^a$ lies on a higher b-indifference curve than E^b. So if the individual π^a and π^b cannot be readily identified this will not do as an equilibrium: were it to be tried, the influx of the high-risk b-types would cause firms to go bankrupt at $\overline{E}^a$, and if the terms to low-risk individuals are worsened (i.e. if $A\overline{E}^a$ were rotated anticlockwise) it is possible that low-risk people might drop out of the market altogether. One has the problem of 'adverse selection' whereby the insurance market breaks down because only the 'bad risks' want to buy insurance. In the light of our argument about the discriminating monopolist above, the answer may lie in restricting the types of trade that may take place. If insurance companies can prevent people buying unlimited amounts of insurance, or multiple contracts with different firms (which in practice they often do), then, rather than just offering *unlimited* choice to an a- or b-type person along a budget line through point A, insurance companies can offer a particular contract – i.e. one particular *point* on Figure 12.8 – on a take-it-or-leave-it basis. It is interesting to compare this power over the consumer with that exercised by the entrance-fee and price-fixing monpolist of Figure 12.5.

If insurance companies – the 'masters' – have this power then they can separate out the a's and the b's by offering an alternative contract such as E^a. The contract must not lie above u_o^b (otherwise the b-types will grab it); it must not lie to the right of $A\overline{E}^a$ (otherwise it would make a loss): so $\overline{E}^a$ is the best offer that companies can make to the a-types without the whole arrangement collapsing. However, the combination (E^a, E^b) may not itself be sustainable as an equilibrium. Consider a point such as C. If it were available as a contract it could be preferred by *everybody* to (E^a, E^b): so could firms provide a contract such as C? If there were a lot of high-risk b-types then C would make a loss; but if there were relatively few such consumers C could itself be profitable for competitive insurance companies. Furthermore C *cannot* be an equilibrium. For, suppose C would in fact break even, so that the slope of AC is $1 - 1/\overline{\pi}$ where $\overline{\pi}$ is the 'average' risk of an accident in the whole population ($\pi^a < \overline{\pi} < \pi^b$). Now another firm could offer a contract C' very close to C which the low-risk a-types would prefer and the high-risk types would reject: since C' is close to C the price at which the insurance is offered is close to $\overline{\pi}$, but since only a-people would now want the insurance, the risk of loss is now much lower, π^a. So C' would certainly be profitable, and therefore C cannot represent an equilibrium contract.

The reason for this possible lack of a competitive equilibrium is that there is a type of externality problem involved, which may be compared with the simple pollution example (Section 8.4 of Chapter 8 and Section 12.2 of this chapter) and the externality in consumption implicit in the public good problem cited earlier in this section. In this case it is an *informational* externality which is implicit in the way new firms form their observations in the insurance market: given a pre-existing set of contracts that break even the new entrant uses the information provided by those contracts to frame its own (profit-making) policy; this forces the original contracts to make a loss; since (as in the other situations of externality) the firm ignores the external consequences of its actions, it fails to take account of the fact that, once it has entered and rendered the previous policies unviable, its own policy will no longer be profitable. It is possible to construct models in which firms form more sophisticated conjectures wherein equilibrium may be possible; but this type of problem is endemic to the private-knowledge incentive problem where there are many actors to play the role of 'master'.

In each of the cases of the incentive problem examined in this section the 'master' has made extensive use of an economic exclusion device to force the servant to reveal information – entrance fees, quantity restrictions on purchases and so on. This approach can be employed in a number of other areas: 'screening' of workers with unknown aptitudes, the design of auction schemes, the targetting of tax and social security systems.[13] Let us turn to a case where these devices are inapplicable.

[13] See Exercises 12.9 and 12.10.

12.6 Private Knowledge and Public Goods

In the previous section we saw some elementary ways in which firms might force their customers to reveal information about themselves. The device that enables any firm to do this can be simply summarised as the power to dictate the terms on which it deals with any customer. We now consider a class of problem where this device will not work: the case of public goods. The essential point about public goods which makes them different for present purposes is their *non-excludability* (as noted in Section 6.3 of Chapter 6, public goods also have to be non-rival, but the issues raised by non-rivalness can be handled in a way similar to Section 12.5). So perhaps the first question one ought to address is: are there goods that are *really* non-excludable?

It is not hard to think of goods which, although usually classified as 'public', nevertheless are excludable in some sense. Although such goods do not carry a conventional price tag, some independent signal of willingness-to-pay – that is, some device of revealing preferences – might well be available. 'Local' public goods are a standard example: it has been argued that people may indicate their preferences concerning publicly provided services such as drains, libraries, and streetlighting, by selecting their place of residence in the light of the local level of provision of these services and the local level of taxes to pay for them. Again we may think of the demand for some public goods as being revealed by households' willingness to purchase complementary private goods: for example the demand for free access beauty spots in the countryside may to some extent be revealed in people's willingness to spend money on the cost of travelling there. However, even if we allow for these cases, and even if we allow for cases such as broadcast TV and radio where exclusion devices could be set up at some cost, there remains an element of the problem of non-excludability with many goods of this sort and there are arguably cases – such as national defence,[14] or law and order – where the non-excludability problem is overwhelming. Note that the issue of 'optionality' is irrelevant here: once the good has been provided it does not matter whether an individual *has* to consume it or not; the point is that his usage cannot be monitored.

Imagine that the public good provision problem is vastly simplified into an elementary, binary choice. Either a particular project is approved, in which case a unit amount of the public good is provided ($x_1 = 1$) and the consumption of private goods ($\Sigma_h x_2^h$) is appropriately reduced, *or* the project is rejected, none of the public good is provided ($x_1 = 0$) and private consumption remains unaltered. The public good itself does not have to be intrinsically

[14] Although one could argue that a person might be able to reveal preferences such as 'better dead than red' by migrating to another country.

indivisible; the binary choice setting of the problem can be seen as a convenient expository device rather than something that is imposed by the technology. If the project goes ahead ($x_1 = 1$) let $\bar{z}_2$ be its cost in terms of good 2: i.e. the minimum amount of private goods that have to be sacrificed in aggregate in order to produce this unit amount of public good. Using the notation of equation (12.9) above we may state this as:

$$1 = \phi(\bar{z}_2) \tag{12.25}$$

Let $\bar{z}_2^h$ represent the amount taken from household h to meet this cost, such that $\Sigma_{h=1}^{H}\bar{z}_2^h = \bar{z}_2$. Note that for present purposes, *how* the amounts $\{\bar{z}_2^h\}$ have been determined is unimportant[15] (as long as they do not depend on observed behaviour) – they could for example be determined on the basis of equal division, $\bar{z}_2^h = \bar{z}_2/H$, for all h; also note that, for some households, $\bar{z}_2^h$ will not represent the *total* amount of private good 2 that it will sacrifice, as we shall see. A complete description of the project then consists of (i) the unit amount of the public good and (ii) the list of cost burdens $\bar{z}_2^h$, $h = 1, \ldots, H$.

In the 2-person case, the situation is illustrated in Figure 12.9. Alf and Bill have, respectively, an endowment R_2^a and R_2^b of private good 2; the contribution to costs by each household, $\bar{z}_2^h$ is shown as a heavy black line. Points A_0, B_0 represent the situations of Alf and Bill *without* the public good (the status quo); points A_1, B_1 represent their situations *with* the public good and the above allocation of costs. The amounts CV^a and CV^b represent the compensating variations (i.e. the utility gains accruing to each household, measured in units of good 2) arising from a switch from (A_0, B_0) to (A_1, B_1). Observe that Alf would be a net gainer from the public project (after paying his whack of the costs his CV^a is still positive) but Bill is a net loser (CV^b is negative). The distances A_0A_2 and B_0B_2 represent the *total* 'willingness-to-pay' by each household – that is, approximately, the compensating variation for each of them if they were able to have a 'free ride' without actually paying any of the cost of the public good.

If all households were truthful, then the decision problem could be made quite simple. Suppose the issue of 'who pays what' is treated separately. The government as 'master' could simply ask each household to tell it the value of $CV^h + \bar{z}_2^h$, the household's total willingness-to-pay. If the government finds that the sum of these quantities over all the households is greater than or equal to $\bar{z}_2$, in other words if

$$\Sigma_h CV^h \gtreqless 0 \tag{12.26}$$

then in principle it would seem to be possible to achieve an allocation that is at least as good as, and possibly Pareto superior to, the status quo (i.e. a

[15] How the cost burden is to be allocated does of course matter very much in a wider context. This is an issue which is considered further in Section 13.3 of Chapter 13.

situation where Alf and Bill are on or above the indifference curves through A_0 and B_0). The inequality (12.26) could then be taken as a simple criterion for the project: 'go' if (12.26) is true, 'no go' if (12.26) is false.

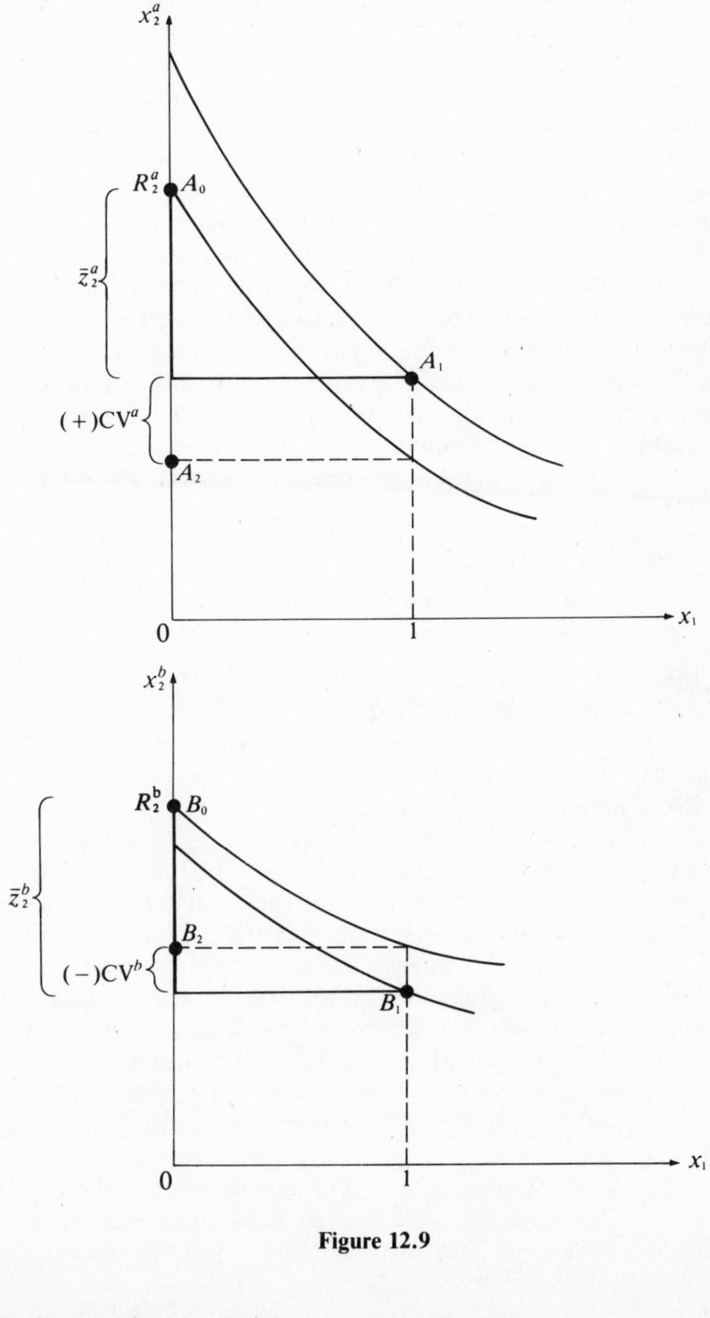

Figure 12.9

But of course this will not do. Irrespective of how the actual burden of cost will be resolved, the government knows that it cannot rely on the good nature of its citizens: it has to assume that each one will lie about his CV^h and will instead announce $\hat{CV}^h \lesseqgtr CV^h$ so as not to be saddled with so much of the share of the cost, as in Section 12.3. The recourse that the government has is to devise a set of rules – an incentive scheme – by which lying becomes pointless.

Let us consider a system of penalties, based on individual households' declarations. Note, first of all, that misrepresentation does not matter very much if it is not 'decisive'. In the binary choice case, suppose we were in the utopian situation where everyone told the truth and that (12.26) held with strict inequality. Then it would not matter very much if one or two people lied a little bit, because we might still find that the sum of the declared $\hat{CV}^h$ was positive, so that the project would still go ahead: all that would happen is that the liars would get a bit of surplus good 2 – a Pareto improvement over the status quo, whatever we might think of its morality. But there is always the danger that the sum of the declared $\hat{CV}^h$ turns out negative. The trick is to punish anyone who might tip the balance in this way.

To make this idea of 'tipping the balance' more precise, let us reinterpret (12.26) in a form that can be directly observed. Consider the two expressions:

$$\Sigma_{h=1}^{H} \hat{CV}^h \tag{12.27}$$

and

$$\Sigma_{h \neq l} \hat{CV}^h \tag{12.28}$$

where the '^' denotes that it is the *announced* CVs, not necessarily the *actual* CVs that are to be used. If (12.27) is non-negative then, analogous to (12.26) we can interpret this as meaning 'the announced willingness-to-pay for *all* the households is large enough to cover the costs of the public good'; if (12.28) is non-negative then we can interpret this as 'the announced willingness-to-pay for all households except l is large enough to cover their share of the cost of the public good' or, at the risk of slight oversimplification, 'everyone except l says "yes" to the project'. Take (12.27) as a criterion for going ahead with the project: 'no-go' if it is negative, 'go' otherwise. Suppose we find that (12.27) is indeed negative, but that (12.28) is positive or zero: then, in a sense, household l tips the balance, or is 'pivotal'; without the announcement of his CV^l it looked as if the decision ought to have gone the other way. In these circumstances the appropriate penalty for the government to impose on l would be the apparent gains foregone by all the other households now that the project is 'no go'; in other words a penalty equal to (12.28).

If we make the assumption of zero income effects[16] then the above

[16] The possibility of relaxing this assumption is discussed in Chapter 5 of the Green and Laffont reference at the end of this chapter.

Table 12.3 A Preference Revelation Mechanism

	Everyone else says 'yes'	*Everyone else says 'no'*
'go'	No penalty	Penalty = Σ costs imposed on everyone else
'no go'	Penalty = Σ forgone gains of everyone else	No penalty

system becomes 'reversible': in Figure 12.9 we could take A_1, B_1 as the status quo and apply the mirror-image criterion for 'go/no go' of a switch back to A_0, B_0, with a mirror-image penalty for any 'pivotal' household. The complete system is summarised in Table 12.3, and in the following theorem:

THEOREM 12.2: a scheme which (i) approves a project if and only if (12.27) is non-negative, and (ii) imposes a penalty of size $|\Sigma_{h \neq l} \hat{CV}^h|$ on household l if (12.28) and (12.27) have opposite signs, will guarantee that truthful revelation of the CV^h is a dominant strategy.

PROOF: the payoff to any household l from announcing either its true CV^l or some false $\hat{CV}^l$ consists of two parts (a) his own CV^l if the project is 'go' (zero otherwise) and (b) the penalty if l proves to be pivotal (zero otherwise). Define $K \equiv \Sigma_{h \neq l} CV^h$; assume that

$$K \geqslant 0, \tag{12.29}$$

and consider two sub-cases.

(1) The case $K + CV^l < 0$. If l tells the truth and declares CV^l, the project is 'no go' and l gets a payoff of $-K$; if l lies and announces $\hat{CV}^l$ then *either* the project is 'go' and l gets a payoff of CV^l (which is *less* than $-K$), *or* the project is 'go' and the payoff is again $-K$.

(2) The case $K + CV^l \geqslant 0$. If l tells the truth and declares CV^l, the project is 'go' and l gets the payoff CV^l ($\geqslant -K$). If l lies and announces $\hat{CV}^l$ then *either* the project is 'no go' and l gets a payoff of $-K$, *or* the project is 'go' and the payoff is again CV^l.

Thus in either sub-case there is an incentive for l to make a truthful announcement, for otherwise he might suffer loss. The case where the inequality in (12.29) is reversed follows by a similar argument.

Thus in this simple choice problem the pivotal penalty scheme is 'cheat-proof' in the sense of Section 12.3. However, whilst the incentive mechanism obviously provides an effective deterrent to misrepresentation of one's true preferences, it has a number of drawbacks. Even for moderate sized populations it may be administratively complex; it does not address the question of how the losers in the process[17] (such as Bill in Figure 12.9) are to be compelled to take part in the scheme; it is limited to situations of binary choice. Moreover there is a problem of what happens to the penalties that are paid by households who have the misfortune to find themselves as 'pivotal' as described above – they just seem to disappear into a black hole. If this incentive mechanism is to be used as a device for ensuring an efficient allocation of resources, then some satisfactory story must be provided about what happens to the resources diverted in this way.

Finally, note that an 'umpire' – a government or planning board – is essential to the operation of this mechanism. By contrast to Section 12.5 where the 'master' could be a self-interested participant in the game (a privately owned firm, for example), this role has now been assigned to an entity that is in a sense outside the community of individuals whose actions and preferences we are considering.

12.7 Unseen Actions

The final version of the incentive problem that we shall address specifically incorporates exogenous uncertainty. It is this particular version of the master-and-servant problem that is most commonly referred to as the 'principal-and-agent' problem. The master is interested in the output of some specific good; the level of output is affected both by the levels of input supplied by his servants and by random events; but the master finds it difficult to distinguish the impact of varying any specific input level from the effects of the random events. Since the servant or servants know there is this problem they see a golden opportunity to shirk and place the blame for poor output results on 'bad luck'. The master knows that there is this opportunity and wants to keep the servants working for him but dissuade them from cheating 'too much': he does this by devising an appropriate system of rewards. It is a problem that is common to (private) patient–doctor relationships, to litigants and their lawyers, to insurance companies and their clients where it is known as 'moral hazard' (see Section 10.3 of Chapter 10) and indeed to pollution-abatement problems such as that in Section 12.2. It combines elements of risk-sharing and design of incentives under asymmetric information.

However an elementary production example is one of the easiest ways of bringing out the issues involved. So let us take one of the simplest possible specifications of this type of model. Let Alf (a) be the servant and Bill (b) be the master (as a mnemonic, think of 'b' for 'boss'): Bill hires Alf to do some

[17] The reasonableness of using ΣCV^h as a criterion for selecting a social state is discussed further in Section 13.3 of the next chapter.

work for him: let us say Alf cultivates Bill's orchard.[18] There is a single output Q (apples), and Bill pays Alf a (total) wage w measured in apples. The problem is that the level of output depends on both (i) the amount of effort (z) Alf puts into his job, and (ii) the weather, represented by state of the world $\omega \in \Omega$ thus:

$$Q = G(z, \omega) \tag{12.30}$$

Note that Alf and Bill may agree to the wage w being tied to Q, z, or ω; how this is done depends on the information structure of the problem, as we shall see. Accordingly we shall refer to w as a wage *schedule*, and defer discussion of the specification of this schedule until other parts of the model have been explained.

Bill, the master, has a von Neumann–Morgenstern utility function which depends solely on his own consumption; once he has paid Alf, he has the rest of the output available for his own consumption, so that his utility is

$$\mathscr{E} \upsilon^b(Q - w) \tag{12.31}$$

where $\mathscr{E}$ denotes expectation taken over the probability distribution of the states-of-the-world ω. Alf, the servant, has a utility function which depends on his own consumption of apples *and* on 'leisure' which we may write as $1 - z$ (where $0 \leqslant z \leqslant 1$). So his utility is

$$\mathscr{E} \upsilon^a(w, 1 - z) \tag{12.32}$$

Now let us consider the optimisation problems of these two parties.

The servant (Alf) takes the wage schedule as given and selects his effort z so as to maximise (12.32) subject to the condition

$$\mathscr{E} \upsilon^a(w, 1 - z) \geqslant \bar{u}^a \tag{12.33}$$

where $\bar{u}^a$ is his reservation utility, i.e. the utility level he could achieve if he were to reject the master's terms and seek employment elsewhere. Note that the 'participation constraint' (12.33) plays a role similar to that of the non-negative profit constraint which we incorporated in the model of the firm on page 44 of Chapter 3. Note too that it is the wage *schedule* that Alf takes as given, so that in solving the maximisation problem he allows for the effect that his varying z will have upon the wages he actually receives.

The master (Bill) seeks to maximise (12.31) by choice of an appropriate wage schedule (which will induce Alf to put in an appropriate amount of effort) subject to the information at his disposal, and the servant's continued participation. Let us examine the information problem more closely. We shall take two distinct cases:

---

[18] This is another episode in the saga that has appeared in Exercises 10.9 and 10.10, and Section 11.6.

(1) The master *can* observe z, the effort put in by the servant.
(2) The master *cannot* observe z.

In each case the wage schedule, and the effort is fixed in advance of the realisation of the state of the world. Obviously case (2) is the really interesting one, but examination of case (1) provides a convenient introduction.

So, let us then suppose the master *can* directly observe the effort put in by the servant: this is equivalent to assuming that the master can always distinguish accurately between the role played by effort z and the role played by the state of the world ω in determining output Q (equation 12.30). In which case he can tailor-make a wage schedule for the servant that is contingent upon the state of the world. And since he can observe z and construct an appropriate incentive scheme for his servant, he can treat effort z as though it were a control variable, subject to the servant's still participating, of course (constraint 12.33). The master's optimisation problem is thus:

$$\max_{\{w(\omega)\},z} \mathscr{E} \upsilon^b(Q - w(\omega)) + \lambda [\mathscr{E} \upsilon^a(w(\omega), 1 - z) - \bar{u}^a] \qquad (12.34)$$

Since $w(\omega)$ may be specified separately for each $\omega \in \Omega$, the first-order conditions for an interior solution to (12.34) can be found by differentiating (12.34) with respect to each $w(\omega)$ and z, so as to give:

$$-\upsilon_1^b + \lambda \upsilon_1^a = 0 \qquad (12.35)$$

for all ω, and

$$\mathscr{E}(\upsilon_1^b G_z) - \lambda \mathscr{E} \upsilon_2^a = 0 \qquad (12.36)$$

where υ_1^a and υ_1^b represent the marginal utility of consumption (in state ω) for the two persons, υ_2^a represents the marginal utility of 'leisure' and G_z is $\partial G(z, \omega)/\partial z$, the marginal product of effort. These two conditions immediately yield:

$$\frac{\upsilon_1^b}{\upsilon_1^a} = \lambda = \frac{\mathscr{E}(\upsilon_1^b G_z)}{\mathscr{E} \upsilon_2^a} \qquad (12.37)$$

Since the marginal utilities in (12.37) are positive, we see that the Lagrange multiplier λ is positive, and thus constraint (12.33) is binding. So, if Bill, the master, has perfect information, he drives Alf, the servant, down in to his reservation utility $\bar{u}^a$ (this of course is exactly what should be expected from considering the elementary examples in Exercises 10.9, 10.10 and 11.9): Bill can do this by drawing up the contract in such a way that Alf would be greatly penalised if he supplied a less than ideal amount of (observable) effort. Moreover (12.37) also implies that there is ideal risk-sharing: the conditional payments are organised in such a way that the ratio of marginal utility of consumption for the two parties is equal across all states of the world.

Observe also that in the special case where the master is risk-neutral (so that υ_1^b is a constant, independent of ω) then (12.35) and (12.36) can be used to give the result

$$\mathscr{E}\left[\frac{\upsilon_2^a}{\upsilon_1^a}\right] = \mathscr{E}G_z \qquad (12.38)$$

Under these circumstances the master ensures that the servant's expected marginal rate of substitution of effort into output exactly equals the expected marginal rate of transformation of effort into output, which is clearly *ex-ante* Pareto efficient. What is happening here is that Bill has designed the conditional payment schedule $w(\omega)$ in such a way that Alf is perfectly insured against the vagaries of the weather. Alf is guaranteed to receive his expected marginal product in the orchard whatever happens: risk-neutral Bill has accepted all the risk. And risk-neutrality on the part of Bill may be perfectly reasonable if he represents a large consortium and Alf is a small trader.

Once again – as with the perfectly discriminating monopolist of Section 12.5 – we find that *complete market power combined with complete information leads to a perfectly efficient and perfectly exploitative solution.*

Now let us turn to the second, more interesting, case: Bill as the master *cannot* observe the effort, z.

It is useful to recast this problem in a slightly different form by reinterpreting the variables. Look at the problem from Bill's point of view. He has no way of effectively distinguishing the separate contributions of effort (z) and 'luck' (ω) in producing the output Q and so, from his point of view, Q itself might as well be the random variable. Of course the probability of any particular realisation of Q will depend on the effort z put in by Alf: so one might specify a probability density function for Q, namely $f(Q,z)$, where z is a shift parameter for the density function. We now examine this probability density function in more detail.

Let us assume that $\underline{Q}$ and $\overline{Q}$ are, respectively, the lower and upper bounds on Q, that $f(Q,z)$ is positive, continuous and differentiable throughout the interval $[\underline{Q},\overline{Q}]$ and that $f_z(\underline{Q},z) = f_z(\overline{Q},z) = 0$ (however hard the servant tries or fails to try, his efforts could not alter the best or worst possible outcomes), but that between $\underline{Q}$ and $\overline{Q}$ an increase in z increases the probability of high output and reduces the probability of low output,[19] as in Figure 12.10. For convenience write $\beta_z \equiv f_z(Q,z)/f(Q,z)$, the

[19] In other words, for every Q between $\underline{Q}$ and $\overline{Q}$ we find that $\int_Q^{\overline{Q}} f(\xi,z)d\xi$ is an increasing function of z. Of course, by definition of a probability density function $\int_{\underline{Q}}^{\overline{Q}} f(\xi,z)d\xi \equiv 1$ for all values of z which implies that $\mathscr{E}\beta_z = 0$.

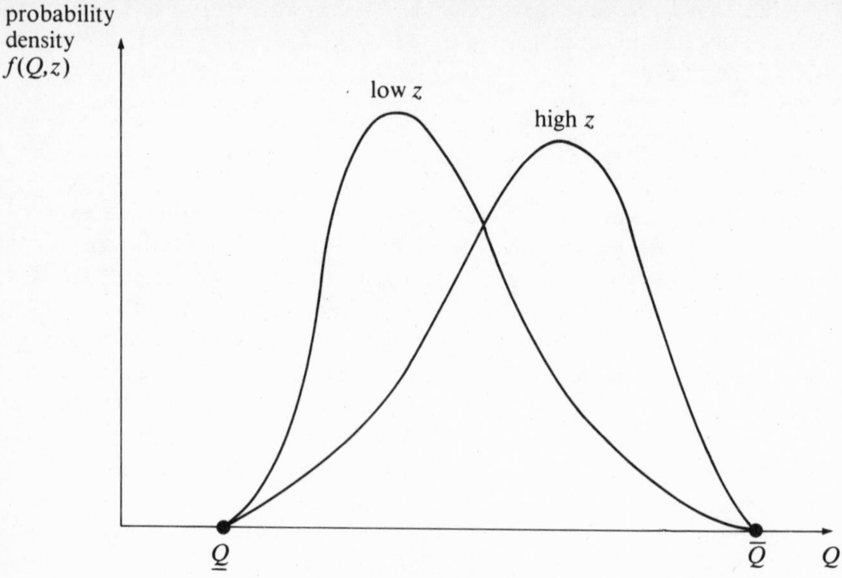

Figure 12.10

'proportionate shift' in the probability distribution from a small increase in z: observe that β_z is negative for low values of Q, and positive for high values of Q, and that $\mathscr{E}\,\beta_z = 0$.

The servant's maximand (12.32) thus becomes $\int_{\underline{Q}}^{\bar{Q}} \upsilon^a(w(Q),\ 1-z)\, f(Q,z)\mathrm{d}Q$. Maximising this with respect to z gives the first-order condition:

$$\mathscr{E}\,(\upsilon^a\beta_z) - \mathscr{E}\,\upsilon_2^a = 0 \qquad (12.39)$$

The first term in (12.39) gives the marginal change in expected utility if the probability density were to be shifted a bit in the direction of more favourable Qs (as illustrated in Figure 12.10); the second term is the expected marginal utility of leisure. Equation (12.39) implicitly determines a particular value of z for any given payment schedule $w(.)$: this behavioural condition acts as an effective constraint on the choice problem that the master has to solve in selecting $w(.)$.

We may now illustrate Bill, the master's, optimisation problem, using a simplified diagram. In Figure 12.11 the wage schedules $w(Q)$ have been arranged in such a way that for given z those on the right of the diagram yield higher expected utility for the master (whose indifference curves are given by $\bar{u}_0^a, \bar{u}_1^a, \ldots$). The curve $A_0A^*A_1$ is the combination of $w(Q)$ and z satisfying the servant's first-order conditions (12.39), given that the participation constraint is also satisfied. The master seeks the utility-maximising wage schedule that yields the solution A^*. Let us examine this algebraically.

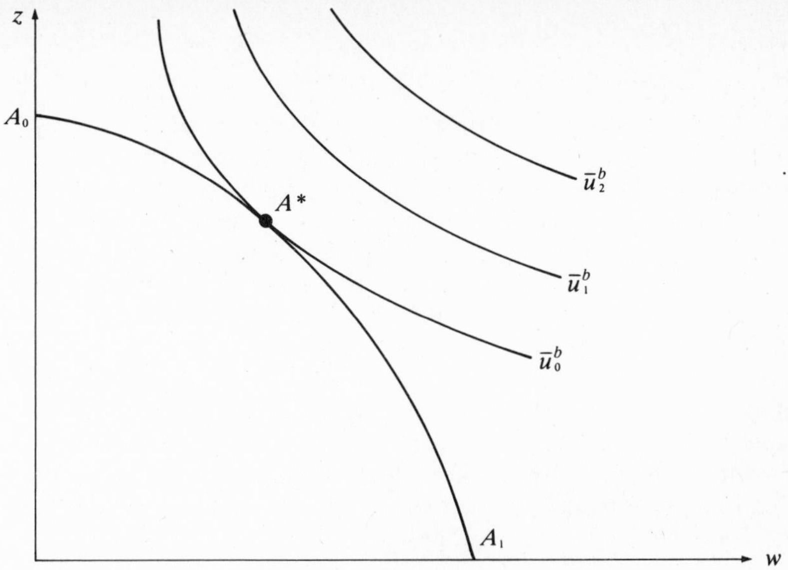

Figure 12.11

The master chooses $w(.)$ (i.e. a value $w(Q)$ for each realisation of Q) and z so as to maximise $\mathscr{E}\upsilon^b(Q - w(Q))$ subject to both the participation constraint (12.33) *and* the servant's first-order condition (12.39). Thus, instead of (12.34), he chooses $w(.)$ and z to maximise the Lagrangean

$$\mathscr{E}\upsilon^b(Q - w(Q)) + \lambda[\mathscr{E}\upsilon^a - \bar{u}^a] + \mu[\mathscr{E}(\upsilon^a\beta_z) - \mathscr{E}\upsilon_2^a] \quad (12.40)$$

where λ and μ are the Lagrange multipliers. In solving this we shall make a further simplifying assumption about the servant's preferences, namely that $\upsilon_{12}^a = 0$, so that the marginal utility of leisure is independent of income. Now let us write down the first-order conditions for the above problem. Differentiating (12.40) with respect to $w(Q)$ and z, and using the result (12.39), we now find:

$$-\upsilon_1^b + \lambda\upsilon_1^a + \mu\upsilon_1^a\beta_z = 0 \quad (12.41)$$

$$\mathscr{E}(\upsilon^b\beta_z) + \mu[\mathscr{E}(\upsilon^a\beta_{zz}) + \mathscr{E}(\upsilon_{22}^a)] = 0 \quad (12.42)$$

where $\beta_{zz} \equiv f_{zz}(Q,z)/f(Q,z)$. Contrast these two equations with (12.35) and (12.36), the case where z can be observed. The first term in (12.42) is positive because υ^b is increasing in Q; the term in [ ] must be negative in virtue of the second-order conditions in the servant's optimisation problem: so μ is positive. Hence the behavioural constraint (12.39) is binding at the optimum. Hence also, (12.41) implies:

$$\frac{\upsilon_1^b}{\upsilon_1^a} = \lambda + \mu\beta_z \tag{12.43}$$

(cf. equation 12.37). So now we find that for high values of Q (where $\beta_z > 0$) we find $\upsilon_1^b/\upsilon_1^a$ lies *above* λ: the payment to Alf (the servant) from Bill (the master) is relatively high, compared with the perfect information solution; conversely if Q turns out low (where $\beta_z < 0$) then the payment to Alf from Bill is relatively low compared with the perfect information solution. Once again the presence of imperfect information leads to an incentive scheme that has a built-in 'distortion'. The economic mechanism designed to offset the inducement to misrepresentation offered by the lack of information will itself introduce an apparent distortion.

One implication of this is that, in contrast to the result on page 289, even if Bill were risk-neutral (he represents a large apple-buying consortium) he no longer provides effectively perfect insurance to Alf against the effects of the weather. This can be seen from (12.43): putting υ_1^b equal to some constant we find that the optimal payment solution is still to pay Alf relatively well when Q is high and poorly when Q is low.

12.8 Summary

The concept of 'market failure' covers a number of different economic problems, each of which may preclude the use of a competitive equilibrium to support a particular allocation. In some cases the term refers to straightforward technological obstacles – such as non-convexities in the production set. And in some cases (such as externalities in production) the problem may only be one of *apparent* failure, in that the situation could conceivably be remedied by an 'extended market' system in which affected parties negotiate side-payments. However 'market failure' also covers important phenomena that are not so easily resolved and that are not attributable to quirks of the production set.

The difficulty lies in the concealment or misrepresentation of significant information by economic agents: this can upset some of the standard efficiency results of Chapter 8. The conditions under which agents might think it in their interests to dissimulate are not particularly unusual: the problem is, for example, endemic in an economy where there is a small number of agents and a large number of social states. These fundamental information problems may also beset cases of market failure that appear to be primarily technological in nature (such as externalities and public goods) and can be conveniently categorised into two main types: (a) private knowledge, and (b) unseen actions.

The question of economic incentives raised by each of these two types of problem can be analysed by the use of a 'master-and-servant' (or 'principal-and-agent') model: the master sets and enforces the rules, the servant decides whether or not to participate on those terms. In either case, if the master has perfect information, then he makes the servant an offer he cannot refuse: the servant ends down on his reservation utility level and the outcome is Pareto efficient. So a simplistic solution to the market failure problem in some cases may be to give some of the agents more information and more power (as with the perfectly discriminating monopolist). However if the information cannot be made available – because it would be expensive or immoral to do so – then the master constructs some form of incentive scheme – a test, conditional reward, or payment device – for the servant which makes it worth his while to behave, to a certain extent, in the manner that the master would have hoped. Nevertheless, whilst such a scheme may mitigate the effects of misrepresentation, it may still not achieve the Pareto efficient allocation that would have been possible under perfect information.

In some versions of the incentive problem the roles of 'master' and 'servant' are obvious: for example a firm and its employees. However, in some applications the role of master is assigned to a hypothetical independent umpire: this arises when considering schemes designed to ensure efficient provision of public goods. There is a logical snag with such an analytical device since the very existence of this law-making and law-enforcing umpire is itself a public good whose allocation is to be determined. In some respects this is reminiscent of the introduction of the 'auctioneer' who conveniently adjusts prices in the private good general equilibrium model (see page 149 of Chapter 7). Both the auctioneer and the umpire are convenient devices to make things work: but it is doubtful whether either of them is likely to be closely approximated by the type of economic institutions that exist in practice.

It is clear that the nature of a particular incentive problem may sharply limit what the 'authorities' – public or private, could hope to do. But what *should* the authorities do? We turn to this question in the final chapter.

Further Reading

Two straightforward and thought-provoking articles discussing the general problem of information incentives and uncertainty are:

Arrow, K.J. (1985) 'The economics of agency', in J.W. Pratt and R. Zeckhauser (eds), *Agency, The Structure of Business*, Harvard Business School Press.

Hirshleifer, J. and Riley, J.G. (1979) 'The analytics of uncertainty and information: an expository survey', *Journal of Economic Literature*, Vol. 17, pp. 1375–421.

Two classic references on pseudo-market solutions to the problem of externality involving side-payments are:

Buchanan, J.M. and Stubblebine, W.C. (1962) 'Externality', *Economica*, Vol. 29, pp. 371–84.

Coase, R.H. (1980), 'The problem of social cost', *Journal of Law and Economics*, Vol. 3, pp. 1–44.

For more on a general approach to the private knowledge problem the following two references are useful but more difficult:

Green, J. (1985) 'Differential information, the market and incentive compatibility', in K.J. Arrow and S. Honkapohja (eds) *Frontiers of Economics*, Basil Blackwell.

Laffont, J.-J. and Maskin, E. (1982) 'Theory of incentives: an overview', in W. Hildenbrand (ed.) *Advances in Economic Theory*, Cambridge University Press.

Three very interesting articles on the problem of market failure in the presence of private knowledge and on the use of economic devices to elicit that information are:

Akerlof, G. (1970) 'The market for lemons: qualitative uncertainty and the market mechanism', *Quarterly Journal of Economics*, Vol. 84, pp. 488–500.

Rothschild, M. and Stiglitz, J.E. (1976) 'Equilibrium in competitive insurance markets: an essay on the economics of imperfect information', *Quarterly Journal of Economics*, Vol. 90, pp. 629–49.

Spence, M. (1973) 'Job market signaling', *Quarterly Journal of Economics*, Vol. 87, pp. 355–79.

An exhaustive account of the incentive problems of public good provision is to be found in:

Green, J. and Laffont, J.-J. (1979) *Incentives in Public Decision-Making*, North-Holland.

Groves, T. and Ledyard, J. (1977) 'Optimal allocation of public goods: a solution to the 'free rider' problem', *Econometrica*, Vol. 45, pp. 783–809.

The details of the theory of the 'unseen actions' problem and its applications are surveyed in:

Rees, R. (1985) 'The theory of principal and agent', *Bulletin of Economic Research*, Vol. 37, pp. 3–25, 75–95.

Exercises

12.1 Suppose that in a certain community there is a law prohibiting the emission of pollution without compensation to victims of pollution. Show that, under the conditions specified on page 258, if firms can open costless negotiations, then the economy will achieve the same efficient allocation as that described in equation (12.8).

*12.2 Let an economy consist of two firms each producing a single output (y_1, y_2 respectively) from a single non-produced resource according to the production functions

$$y_1 = \sqrt{z}$$

$$y_2 = \max(\sqrt{(R - z)} - \alpha y_1, 0)$$

where R is the total amount of the resource, z is the amount of the resource used to produce good 1, and α is a parameter. Describe the phenomenon that this model represents. Sketch the production possibility set. Assuming that all consumers are identical, sketch (a) a set of preferences for which an efficient allocation may be sustained by a pseudo-market in externalities; (b) a set of preferences where this is not possible. What effect does the parameter α have on your answer?

12.3 In the 2-person voluntary contributions model of public good provision in Figure 12.3, show how the utility function (12.10) may be rewritten in terms of the two parties' contributions for the public good. Hence show that, under the conditions specified, the contours of Alf's and Bill's indifference curves must be U-shaped and that the Cournot–Nash solution is identical to the voluntary action model on page 263.

*12.4 Suppose a worker's productivity is given by an ability parameter α which is known to himself, but not to a potential employer ($\alpha \geqslant \alpha_0 > 0$). Firms pay workers on the basis of how much education (z) they have. The income received by a person with an amount z is $M(z)$; the cost to a person with ability α of acquiring an amount z of education is $ze^{-\alpha}$. Write down the first-order conditions which will determine the optimum amount of education for an α-person and show that this must satisfy $\alpha = -\log(M'(z^*))$. If individuals coming to the labour market with education z have the productivity that employers expect them to have ($M(z)$) show that the optimal wage schedule must satisfy $M = \log(z + k)$ where k is a constant. Compare net incomes (net of educational costs) in this system with incomes that would prevail if α could be directly observed.

12.5 In the model of two-part tariffs discussed on page 273, what will occur if resale of goods is not effectively precluded?

12.6 A simple monopolist serves a group of identical consumers; the characteristics of the product imply that it would be virtually impossible to prevent resale of the good. The government wants to induce the monopolist to produce efficiently. To do this it offers the monopolist a subsidy financed by lump sum taxation. Show that if this subsidy is set equal to a measure of the consumer's surplus enjoyed by the monopolist's customers the government can achieve its objective.

*12.7 Take the two-customer model of a perfectly informed, discriminatory monopolist, discussed on page 273. Analyse the effect of an increase in demand by one customer arising from a change in tastes.

12.8 Suppose there are only *two* possible social states: $\mathscr{S}_1$ in which there is a public good of fixed size provided and all the taxes required to finance the good are completely specified, and $\mathscr{S}_2$ in which there is no public good provided and each person just consumes his own resources. Show that under these circumstances taking a simple vote on $\{\mathscr{S}_1, \mathscr{S}_2\}$ will ensure truthful revelation of preferences.

12.9 I have a Ming vase to sell. Suppose I hold an auction for the vase with the following rules announced in advance: there is a reserve price $\bar{P}$ which is held secret; if the buyer makes a bid P, where $P \geqslant \bar{P}$, he gets the vase and pays just $\bar{P}$; if $P < \bar{P}$, he does not get the vase and pays nothing.

Show that this auction design will ensure a truthful revelation of a buyer's willingness to pay.

*12.10 An economy consists of two equal sized groups of people: the gifted (with an ability parameter $\alpha = 2$) and the deprived (with an ability parameter $\alpha = 1$). For all persons utility u, consumption x and earnings w are given by

$$\begin{aligned} u &= \log x + \log (1-z) \\ x &= w + T \\ w &= \alpha z \end{aligned}$$

where z denotes effort ($0 \leqslant z \leqslant 1$) and T is net transfer income. The government would like to set $T = \Delta$ for the deprived and $T = -\Delta$ for the gifted, where Δ is some positive number.

(a) If the government can observe each person's utility, and if each person chooses z so as to maximise utility, plot the graph of utility against earnings for a gifted person and for a deprived person, given some value of Δ. Find the optimum earnings for each person.

(b) If the government cannot observe ability and plans a transfer scheme which sets $T = -\Delta$ if $w > w^*$ and $T = +\Delta$ if $w \leqslant w^*$ (where w^* is the optimum earnings for a deprived person in part (a)), show that gifted people may find it in their interests to pretend to be deprived; on the same diagram as (a) plot the graph of utility against earnings for someone carrying on this pretence.

(c) Use the above diagram to show the case where a gifted person is just indifferent between being honest and pretending to be deprived.

(d) Hence show that the deprived people's utility could be increased by restricting the amount they are allowed to earn.

12.11 In the unseen actions model of Section 12.7, show that if the servant is risk neutral then the master can enforce a solution that is equivalent to the full-information solution given in (12.35) and (12.36).

12.12 Draw a diagram in the (incentive, effort) – space of Figure 12.11 in which the effort satisfying (12.39) for a given incentive scheme is not unique. Why might this situation arise?

Show that under these circumstances there will be some points satisfying the first-order condition (12.39) which will never represent (incentive, effort) – combinations that would be freely chosen by the servant. Hence show that the first-order conditions (12.41), (12.42) are no longer necessary conditions for an optimum.

13

Welfare

13.1 Introduction

A famous schoolboy's eye-view of English history once concluded that

> the French Revolution caused great loss of life, liberty, fraternity, etc., and was, of course, a Good Thing, since the French were rather degenerate at the time.[1]

The idea of a 'good thing' is central to the discussion of this chapter. Simply stated, welfare economics provides a system of analysis which is intended to throw light on what is meant by a 'good thing' in economics: which states of the economy ought to be regarded as particularly desirable, what changes from the status quo should be recommended. Thus in this chapter we move on to questions of how the economy *ought* to be run, as distinct from how we think it does run, in the light of Chapters 2 to 12.

We have already had some glimpses of this issue in the previous chapters: for example the reference to 'efficiency' in Chapters 2 and 8, and the discussions about individuals' preferences and rationality in Chapter 4. Yet the main text has necessarily glossed over some big issues.

As an example consider the remarkably simplified world of Chapter 9. When we examined changes in resources or trading opportunities that affected the households in the community we made some convenient, but perhaps quite unwarranted, assumptions about the representation of their preferences. For example in Figures 9.8 and 9.9 we drew indifference curves purportedly representing the tastes of the entire *communities* in country Alpha and country Beta, as though each community were a single individual. Plainly this would not do except in the simplest of models, since households will differ not only as to tastes but also as to their endowments of resources: so some people may be made *worse* off as the result of a move towards free trade. Thus it is evident that one needs a criterion for balancing the losses of one group against the gains of another within a community.

[1] Sellars, W.C. and Yateman, R.J. (1930) *1066 and All That*, Methuen.

Table 13.1 Essential notation for Chapter 13: Welfare

$s \in \mathcal{S}$	:	social states
$\succcurlyeq^h$	:	ordering of social states by household h
$\succcurlyeq$	:	collective ordering of social states
$\Sigma(\succcurlyeq^1, \ldots, \succcurlyeq^H)$	:	the constitution
$\hat{\mathcal{S}}(s)$	:	the subset of $\mathcal{S}$ which is accessible from s
$U^h(\mathbf{x}^h)$	:	household h's utility derived from bundle $\mathbf{x}^h$
$V^h(\mathbf{p}, M^h)$	:	household h's indirect utility
W	:	social welfare function
ξ	:	equally distributed equivalent income
ι	:	inequality aversion
$\pi^h(\omega)$	:	subjective probability held by household h
$\pi(\omega)$	:	social subjective probability

Depending on the type of questions one wishes to tackle and, to some extent, on one's philosophical standpoint, a 'good thing' in economics can variously be interpreted as having to do with something called 'social welfare' or to do with the welfare of individuals. Accordingly, the following questions appear to be particularly relevant: what do we mean by an individual's 'welfare'? What do we mean by 'social welfare'? How are the two related?

For the most part we shall continue to make a very simple assumption about the first issue – i.e. that an individual's (or household's) welfare is determined by the consumption of goods and services that he enjoys. However, larger issues may well be involved, as we have briefly noted in previous chapters. For example one person's utility may be affected by another person's consumption levels if he is afflicted with altruism or envy. So it is also useful to consider the wider aspects of individuals' preferences about social states, especially when we come to consider the second and third questions in the previous paragraph.

The issues raised are so many and varied that it is difficult to combine them all into a single unified theme. Accordingly, to bring out some of the main points, we shall adopt a piecemeal method of attack. We shall consider three approaches:

(1) We investigate whether 'social preferences', taken as an ordering over all possible social states, can logically be derived from individual citizens' orderings of all possible social states (Section 13.2).
(2) We examine whether certain 'reasonable' principles provide a satisfactory basis for evaluating social states (Section 13.3).
(3) We consider the implications of imposing a specific structure of social preferences that to some extent respect individual preferences (Section 13.4).

Of course these approaches are not necessarily incompatible, but they represent alternative, fruitful, lines of enquiry as to what can usefully be done in the name of welfare economics.

13.2 Social Choice and the Constitution

When one glances back at the first few sections of Chapter 4 it is apparent that the analysis is considerably simplified by the device of a utility function. Recall that this is simply a way of drawing a contour map of a decision maker's orderings over choices – in the context of Chapter 4, this means a map of preferences over different combinations of goods – and that relatively few assumptions (Axioms C1 to C3) are needed to derive these valuable tools. In this section we look at the analogous problem from the point of view of 'social preferences', and, as we shall see, the issue is a good deal more complex.

However, rather than attempting to define and specify in detail 'social indifference curves' as such, we shall investigate a more fundamental concept: that of the existence of a 'social ordering' – i.e. ranking by 'society' of all possible social states. Let us begin with some terminology and notation.

When we come to consider issues that affect the entire community it seems reasonable to allow social states to be described in very broad terms, as in the introduction to Chapter 8. A social state $\mathscr{s}$ may be taken to include, for example, the allocation $\boldsymbol{a}$ of all the named goods, the supply of public goods, and other non-economic entities; the set of all conceivable social states is $\mathscr{S}$.

Each household h has a well defined *ordering*[2] $\succcurlyeq^h$ over the social states in $\mathscr{S}$; this means that for everyone their rankings of social states satisfy the axioms C1 and C2 of completeness and transitivity, and is also reflexive (so that $\mathscr{s}$ is ranked at least as good as itself).

Denote by $\succcurlyeq$ (note the absence of h-superscript) the ordering over social states that is to be taken as the *social ordering*. It may be that there is some systematic way of deriving this $\succcurlyeq$ from all the individual $\succcurlyeq^h$, i.e. that we can write

$$\succcurlyeq = \Sigma(\succcurlyeq^1, \succcurlyeq^2, \ldots, \succcurlyeq^H) \tag{13.1}$$

The rule Σ will be termed a *constitution*.[3] Observe that it is rather a special

---

[2] Read the statement '$\mathscr{s} \succcurlyeq^h \mathscr{s}'$' as: '$h$ thinks social state $\mathscr{s}$ is no worse than social state $\mathscr{s}'$'.

[3] This concept is also referred to as a social welfare function in some of the literature. I use the symbols $\succ^h$ and $\succ$ to denote *strict* preference by household h and by society respectively. Note the difference between this and the function Γ defined in Section 12.3: Γ is also defined over the space of individual orderings as arguments, but it yields a particular social state, not an ordering, as its result.

animal since the arguments on the right-hand side of (13.1) are not scalars or vectors but *orderings*. It is a notional device for aggregating preferences. A central issue of welfare economics is whether such a constitution can be found that meets certain 'reasonable' preconditions. This is of primary interest in giving substance to the idea of 'social preferences' or a 'social ordering'. After all, one might argue, of what does society consist but its citizens? So, if the concept is to have any meaning, either social preferences are imposed from the outside, or they are somehow related to individual preferences about social states. The question that needs to be addressed immediately is this: what characteristics might the constitution Σ possess for it to be seen as a 'reasonable' way of relating $\succcurlyeq$ to the individual $\{\succcurlyeq^h\}$? Consider the following four requirements which we shall state as axioms.

AXIOM W1 (universality): the constitution shall be defined over all logically possible profiles of individual orderings.

AXIOM W2 (Pareto unanimity): for any $\mathscr{s}$, $\mathscr{s}' \in \mathscr{S}$ if $\mathscr{s} \succ^h \mathscr{s}'$ for all h then $\mathscr{s} \succ \mathscr{s}'$.

AXIOM W3 (independence of irrelevant alternatives): let two different profiles be identical over some subset $\hat{\mathscr{S}} \subset \mathscr{S}$. Then the social orderings corresponding to each of these profiles are identical over $\hat{\mathscr{S}}$.

AXIOM W4 (non-dictatorship): there is no individual h^* such that for all $\mathscr{s}$, $\mathscr{s}' \in \mathscr{S}: \mathscr{s} \succcurlyeq^{h^*} \mathscr{s}' \Rightarrow \mathscr{s} \succcurlyeq \mathscr{s}'$.

The first of these requirements is self-explanatory. Axiom W2 requires that the constitution is such that if there is unanimous agreement that one social state is strictly preferred to another, then 'society' strictly prefers the said social state. Axiom W3 is analogous to the requirement of 'independence' in the theory of choice under uncertainty: Axiom U2 in Chapter 10. Axiom W4 requires that there is no individual who is always decisive as to whether society shall rank one particular state above another.

We have run through this list of axioms quite rapidly, because the principal result that one has in this area is extremely simple and, unfortunately, rather negative in tone.

THEOREM 13.1 (*Arrow's Impossibility Theorem*):[4] there is no Σ satisfying W1 to W4.

Should this negative result be regarded as overwhelmingly disturbing? Not if one is careful about interpreting what it is actually saying. In fact, on reflection, it may not be all that surprising – given the potential conflicts of

---

[4] For a proof of this see Sen, A.K. (1970) *Collective Choice and Social Welfare*, Oliver and Boyd, Ch. 3*.

interest in a community one might be rather amazed if Theorem 13.1 did not hold.

There is obviously a close connection between this result and the Gibbard–Satterthwaite theorem, Theorem 12.1 of Chapter 12. Since we found there that if an individual was 'large enough to matter', manipulability of the social choice function could be a problem, we might expect that under such conditions a truly general social coherence of what constitutes a 'good thing' is impossible. Note that the result does *not* say that reasonable constitutions can *never* exist, which is a relief because societies obviously do seem to arrange for themselves constitutions that are not wholly bizarre. But it does suggest that it is too ambitious to expect a rule like Σ in (13.1) for deriving the 'social will' or 'social preferences' (i) to be a bona fide ordering; (ii) to be as general and as appealing as implied in Axioms W1 to W4; (iii) to be a function only of citizens' orderings over social states.

This remark suggests three possible ways forward from the apparent impasse posed by Theorem 13.1. One is to resign oneself to the unpalatable conclusion that if Axioms W1 to W4 are to be accepted, then 'social preferences' just will not work like ordinary household preferences in that they may not exhibit either the property of completeness (Axiom C1 in Chapter 4) or of transitivity (Axiom C2) which characterise an 'ordering' as conventionally understood. Collective choice, whether it is by a nation, a club, a corporation or a union, may therefore not be 'rational'. Some progress can be made by relaxing one or other of these two properties to some extent,[5] but even then some version of the above 'impossibility theorem' will still apply.

The second way forward is to examine whether one or more of W1 to W4 could, under certain circumstances, be done away with or modified to some extent. There are several ways in which this might be done, but let us take as given W2 and W4 (there does not seem to be much future in a specification of a social choice rule that perversely flies in the face of the Pareto unanimity criterion or that abdicates choice to a Führer). How may one usefully relax W1 and W3?

The problem with W1 is that one may be demanding far more of one's constitution Σ than one is ever likely to need, since W1 requires that Σ shall work for *every conceivable* pattern of individual preferences. In practice it may be reasonable to limit the range of 'relevant' preferences in some fashion, either by some empirical generalisation ('your average American wants less government interference'; 'no Frenchman puts ice cubes in red wine') or by restricting the jurisdiction over which individual preferences are to count. One aspect of this latter approach is pursued in Section 13.4.

---

[5] For example the requirement of transitivity may be relaxed to *quasi-transitivity* which could allow for the possibility that whilst (i) $\mathscr{s} > \mathscr{s}'$ and (ii) $\mathscr{s}'$ and $\mathscr{s}''$ are regarded as indifferent, yet (iii) $\mathscr{s}$ and $\mathscr{s}''$ are *also* regarded as indifferent.

Consider the possibility that only certain *types* of preferences may be empirically relevant. It might be true that, even though there is substantial disagreement in the relative desirability of social states, nevertheless all citizens' orderings have a similar structure. Consider, for example, a situation in which all the social states could be represented by a single variable – let us say the proportion of (homogeneous) national resources devoted to the production of a public good; every other possible variable is fixed. Now sketch the preferences of three individuals *a, b, c* in Figure 13.1: the horizontal axis measures the proportion of national resources devoted to the public

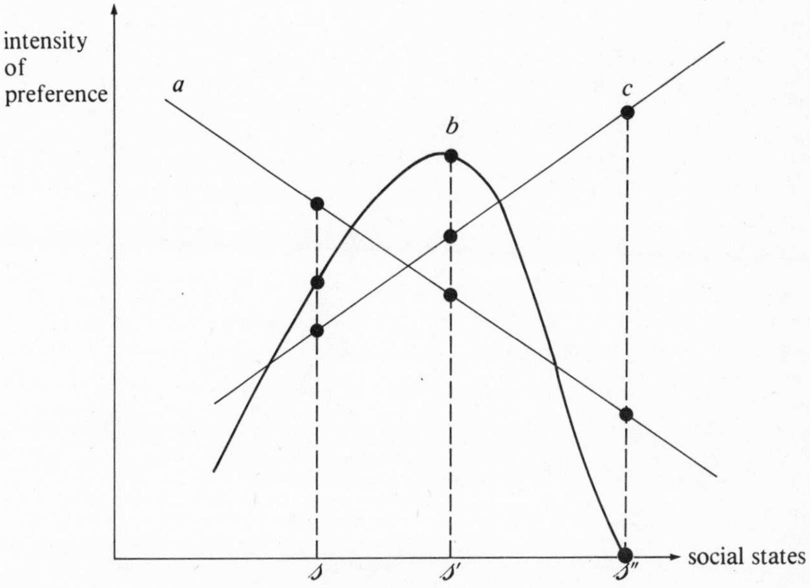

Figure 13.1

good and the vertical axis indicates intensity of preference of each person for each person over the range of $\mathscr{S}$. The scale of the vertical axis is arbitrary: if you like, you can imagine that this axis measures utility where utility scales need not be in any way comparable between people. Observe that person *a* prefers less resources to be devoted to the public good; person *c* has the opposite type of preference structure; person *b* dislikes extremes of either sort. All three are examples of *single-peaked* preferences – i.e. preferences where there is at most one peak along the line representing social states. Let us assume that *all* persons' preferences have this single-peaked structure, and consider a simple majority voting scheme as a possible candidate for Σ in

(13.1) (i.e. given a choice between s and s', then s is ranked over s' if and only if the number of people who prefer s to s' is greater than the number of people who prefer s' to s). Then simple experimentation will reveal that in Figure 13.1 this condition produces a well-behaved ordering of the states { s', s, s'' } – majority voting ranks the states in exactly that order in fact. By contrast, if preferences looked like those in Figure 13.2, then majority voting will *not* produce a well-defined ordering of the three states: in this case one will find apparent intransitivities in the social choice rule.[6] This property on preferences generalises.

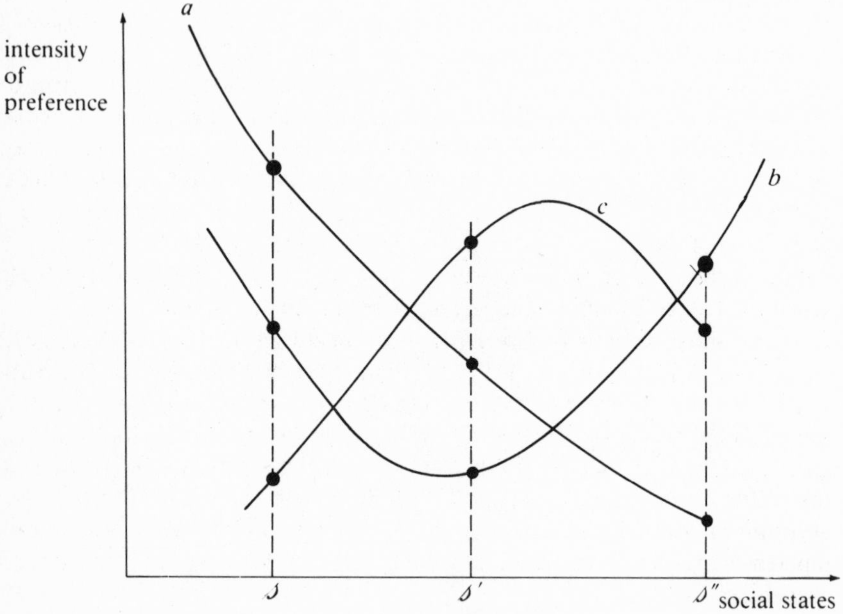

Figure 13.2

THEOREM 13.2 (*Black's Theorem*):[7] if the number of voters is odd and all individuals have single-peaked preferences, then the majority voting procedure produces a complete, transitive social ordering.

Unfortunately one should not get too excited about this result. In the first place single peakedness may be quite a strong assumption in some cases.

---

[6] See Exercise 13.1. See also p. 69 above for a discussion of transitivity.

[7] For a proof see Black, D.(1958) *The Theory of Committee and Elections*, Cambridge University Press. A slightly modified result is available for an even number of voters.

Secondly the 'single peakedness' idea is quite difficult to apply to cases where the set of social states $\mathcal{S}$ is multi-dimensional.[8] It appears that simply restricting the pattern of admissible preferences is not in itself of much help in dealing with the 'impossibility' result of Theorem 13.1.

If one relaxes W3, the independence of irrelevant alternatives, one can certainly obtain a well-defined social ordering; but again it is not clear whether this is necessarily a major step forward. A simple example of this is rank order point voting (or de Borda voting).[9] Let every household assign the number 1 to the worst alternative, the number 2 to the next worst, 3 to the next worst ... and so on. Let $v(s)$ be the total number of points voted for state s; then the constitution ranks s above s' if and only if $v(s) > v(s')$. Manifestly the use of $v(s)$ provides a complete, transitive ordering; but the ordering will depend crucially on the particular point system attached to the votes. For example if, instead of the points $\{1,2,3,4, \ldots\}$ one assigned the point system $\{1,2,4,8, \ldots\}$ then a different social ordering will emerge. However there is a more disturbing feature of this constitution, which illustrates directly why the independence of irrelevant alternatives assumption is so attractive. Consider the subset of social states that beat all others under this constitution; now reduce the size of the set of social states by discarding *only* some of the inferior states – one may find that even though the original subset of 'best states' is still available, they may not still be considered 'best' when the choice is made from the more restricted set of states.[10]

The third approach to coping with Theorem 13.1 is to change the domain of Σ. Recall that Σ is defined on a space of *orderings*; so if one imputed a utility function U^h to household h one might apply an arbitrary increasing transformation to U^h without affecting the social ordering generated by Σ. If one abandons this and imputes a cardinal significance to the utility functions U^h one is in effect allowing the constitution to take account of individuals' intensity of preference. This obviously demands much more information about households' preferences; we examine this further in Section 13.4.

13.3 Efficiency, Fairness and Welfare

We now switch to a consideration of the second approach: the sort of general principles one might bring to bear to determine whether a particular social state, or a particular proposed change in the social state, or a particular economic policy should be considered a 'good thing'. Once again we have

---

[8] See Exercise 13.2.
[9] See Exercise 13.3, for an example of how this violates Axiom W3.
[10] See Exercise 13.4.

had glimpses of this in earlier chapters, since the concept of 'efficiency' – first introduced in Chapter 2 – often has overtones of intrinsic desirability. Certainly technical efficiency seems eminently commendable (why throw away inputs or outputs?) and possibly the stronger concept of Pareto efficiency also has some intrinsic force as a principle for guiding economic policy. But how far will this kind of approach get us? What other general criteria of 'efficiency' and 'equity' might be fruitfully applied?

Let us begin by reconsidering the Pareto superiority criterion set out in Definition 8.1. Whilst it appears to have an attractive interpretation in social welfare terms – 'approve a switch from state s' to state s if no one is worse off in s than he would have been in s' and at least one person is strictly better off' – it is very limited as a general policy rule. A principal reason for this is that it is so wretchedly indecisive. To see this, consider Figure 13.3 which has the same axes as Figure 8.1, the utility enjoyed by each of the two individuals in various states of the world. For reference the boundary of the utility possibility set has been drawn in. Let A denote the

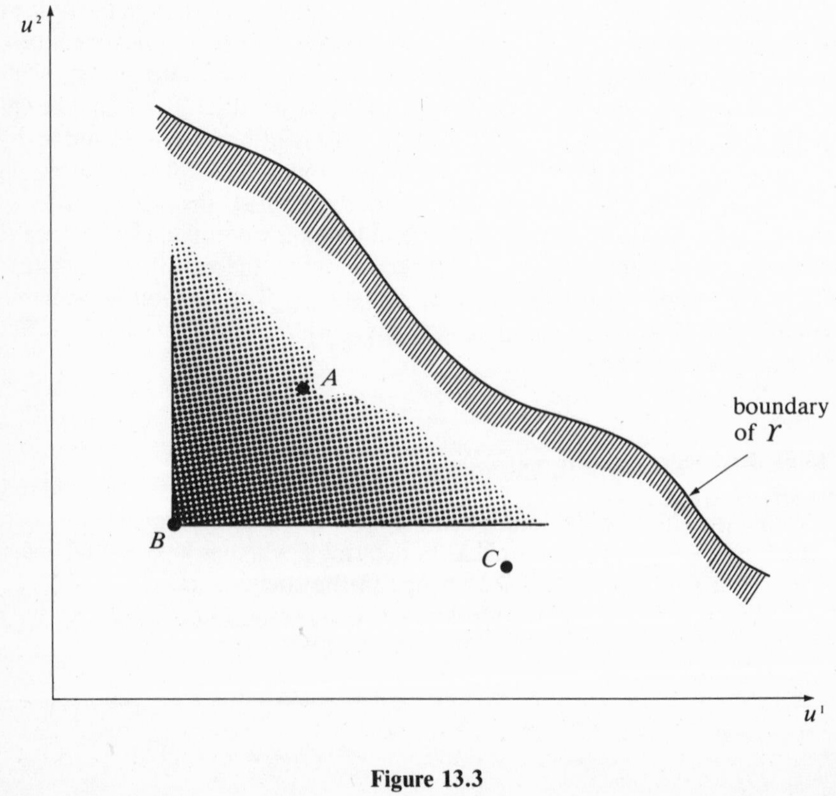

Figure 13.3

point $(u_{\mathscr{s}}^1, u_{\mathscr{s}}^2)$, the utility arising under state $\mathscr{s}$, and let B denote the corresponding point for state $\mathscr{s}'$. Now the Pareto superiority criterion is a strict north-east rule, A lies to the north and east of B so $\mathscr{s}$ is Pareto superior to $\mathscr{s}'$ (see the shaded area); but *nothing* could be said about whether C is to be preferred to B or vice versa (C does not lie in the shaded area); and, likewise, nothing could be said about the relative merits of A and C. So there are a lot of pairs of possible social states which just cannot be compared using this criterion; and, as it is quite difficult to think up lots of real-life examples where there have been demonstrable Pareto improvements, the Pareto superiority criterion does not strike one as overwhelmingly useful in practice.

Let us consider what might be done to make the Pareto superiority criterion more discriminating and, perhaps, more useful as a criterion for making welfare judgements. To do this, we convert the problem into a two-stage decision process.

To fix ideas, take the following example. Consider a government which has to decide whether or not to build an airport, and assume that the airport is a 'one-off' project – either one has an airport of given size and quality or one does not. There is in fact a huge range of possible social states associated with this decision even though there is only one type of airport which could be built: the reason for this is that there are all sorts of ways in which the gains and losses arising from the project may be distributed amongst the community. So it may make sense to consider (a) all the states of the world that could be obtained through a pure redistribution (e.g. by taxes and transfers) given that resources have been committed to the airport; and (b) all the states of the world that could be obtained (by similar methods) given that the airport is *not* built. In either case we describe these other states (obtainable through redistribution) as being 'accessible'[11] from the reference state. So the decision process is something like this: (1) look first at the resource commitment that is involved in building the airport; (2) then consider the states you can generate from the outcome of (1) by a further rearrangement of incomes.

On a more general note – with many possible projects of different types and sizes – the idea in step (1) is that the alternatives are mutually exclusive and irreversible, and that in step (2) all the states can be reached from one another by steps that are in principle reversible. Clearly the distinction between the two may be somewhat arbitrary and is reminiscent of the distinction between the 'short' and 'long run' which we made in Section 3.7 of Chapter 3. Nevertheless one can perhaps think of many practical decision where such a distinction could reasonably be drawn.

---

[11] Other, more sophisticated, definitions of accessibility are available, of course. For example, one might consider as accessible only those points that had the same (or less) aggregate consumption of each good as in the reference state.

To see how we may use this to extend the Pareto superiority criterion let $\mathscr{s}$ and $\mathscr{s}'$ be the two states under consideration ('airport' and 'no airport'), and let $\hat{\mathscr{S}}(\mathscr{s})$ be the subset of $\mathscr{S}$ that is accessible from $\mathscr{s}$. Then consider the following:

DEFINITION 13.1: the state $\mathscr{s}$ is *potentially superior* to $\mathscr{s}'$ if there exists $\mathscr{s}^* \in \hat{\mathscr{S}}(\mathscr{s})$ such that $\mathscr{s}^*$ is Pareto superior to $\mathscr{s}$.

The idea is this: $\mathscr{s}$ is potentially superior to $\mathscr{s}'$ if there is some other state, accessible from $\mathscr{s}$, which is actually Pareto superior to $\mathscr{s}'$. In the airport example, the rule says: 'building the airport (state $\mathscr{s}$) is potentially superior to not building the airport (state $\mathscr{s}'$), even if some people actually lose out thereby, if it can be shown that, once the airport is built, there is some *hypothetical* income redistribution which (were it to be actually implemented) would mean that everyone was at least as well off as before and no one was worse off (state $\mathscr{s}^*$).'

Again there are some obvious drawbacks to this criterion. One is on moral grounds. The state $\mathscr{s}$ is counted as being superior to $\mathscr{s}'$ on the above conditions *even though the switch by income redistribution to $\mathscr{s}^*$ never takes place.* To some people this will seem manifestly objectionable.

There is a second, powerful objection, this time on the grounds of logic. In Figure 13.4 again let A represent the utilities corresponding to $\mathscr{s}$ and let B correspond to $\mathscr{s}'$. The set of points (utility vectors) corresponding to states accessible from A, and the set of points corresponding to states accessible from B have been sketched in, as has the set of points that are Pareto

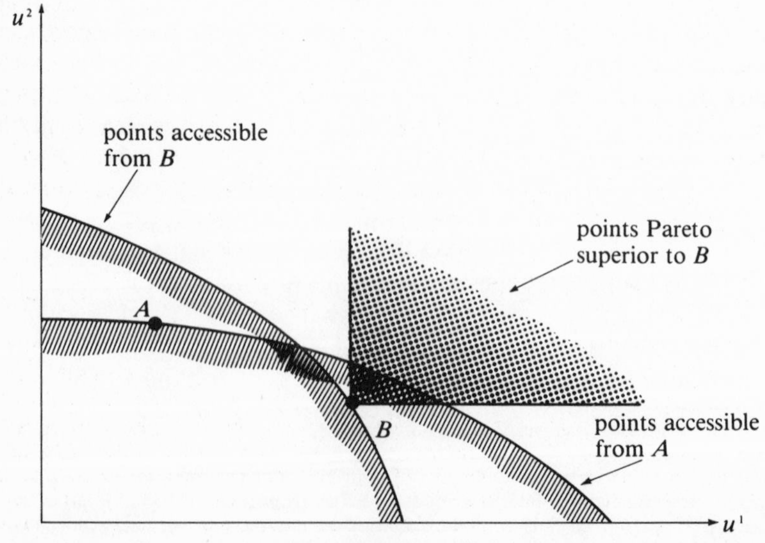

Figure 13.4

superior to B. Clearly, there are points in the set accessible from A that lie to the north east of B, and so $s' \in \hat{\mathscr{S}}(s)$ and thus, by Definition 13.1, s is potentially superior to s'. However we could just as easily turn the argument round, examine the points lying to the north and east of A and find that $s \in \hat{\mathscr{S}}(s')$. We have the extraordinary conclusion that s is potentially superior to s' *and* s' is potentially superior to s!

The solution to this problem that seems to suggest itself is to strengthen Definition 13.1 so that such apparent contradictions cannot occur. Consider the following:

DEFINITION 13.2: the state s is *unambiguously potentially superior* to s' if s is potentially superior to s' but s' is not potentially superior to s.

Unfortunately this apparently more attractive criterion may be vacuous since it may just restore the indecisiveness of the original Pareto superiority principle, and it may also lead to intransitive rankings of social states. However, despite the problem of 'reversals' associated with the simple 'potential superiority criterion' there is a useful connection between it and the decision criterion referred to in resolving the public good decision problem of Section 12.6 of Chapter 12. Recall that the essential concept there was the aggregate 'willingness to pay' expressed as $\Sigma_{h=1}^{H} \mathrm{CV}^h$, the sum of all households' compensating variations. Intuition suggests that this ought to be closely related to the criterion of Definition 13.1. Indeed it is; and, in the case where 'accessibility' is defined as above in terms of monetary transfers at given prices $\mathbf{p}$, the result is particularly simple.

THEOREM 13.3: a necessary and sufficient condition for s to be potentially superior to s' is that $\Sigma_h \mathrm{CV}^h(s' \to s) > 0$.

PROOF: let $\mathbf{p}$ be the prices in s. By definition of potential superiority there is some s^* such that (a) $\Sigma_h C^h(\mathbf{p}, u^h_{s^*}) \leqslant M^h$, and (b) $u^h_{s^*} \geqslant u^h_{s'}$ with strict inequality for at least one h. Part (b) implies $\Sigma_h C^h(\mathbf{p}, u^h_{s^*}) > \Sigma_h C^h(\mathbf{p}, u^h_{s'})$. Hence $\Sigma_h [M^h - C^h(\mathbf{p}, u^h_{s'})] > 0$, i.e. $\Sigma_h \mathrm{CV}^h > 0$. This proves necessity. If $\Sigma_h \mathrm{CV}^h > 0$ then let $M^{*1} = C^1(\mathbf{p}, u^1_{s'}) + \Sigma_h \mathrm{CV}^h$, $M^{*h} = C^h(\mathbf{p}, u^h_{s'})$, $h = 2, \ldots, H$. Clearly this produces a social state s^* that is superior to s' and accessible from s.

However this result relies on a rather strong definition of accessibility: for weaker versions it is usually the case that $\Sigma \mathrm{CV}^h > 0$ is necessary, but not sufficient for potential superiority.[12]

[12] The $\Sigma \mathrm{CV}^h$ criterion is equivalent to the potential superiority criterion if (1) the boundary of the set of aggregate consumption vectors $\mathbf{x}$ accessible from s is linear (as would be the case if 'accessibility' is defined in terms of income redistribution at constant prices), or (2) household preferences have the aggregation property referred to on pages 123, 124 of Chapter 6. See Boadway, R.W. (1974) 'The welfare foundations of cost-benefit analysis', *Economic Journal*, Vol. 84, pp 426–39; Gorman, W.M. (1953) 'Community preference fields', *Econometrica*, Vol. 21, pp. 63–80.

Finally let us examine another general principle which we might use to shape our notion of a 'good thing' in welfare economics. However, rather than an extension of Pareto efficiency – as in the case of potential efficiency – in this case it is a quite separate criterion that complements principles of efficiency: fairness.

To assist in the exposition of this principle it is convenient to suppose that each social state $\mathscr{s}$ is adequately described by the allocation $\mathscr{a}$ of goods embedded in it. In particular let a particular household's evaluation of a social state depend *only* on $\mathbf{x}^h$, the consumption vector that that household enjoys: households are selfish. Under this restricted interpretation it is convenient to use the conventional utility function $U^h(\mathbf{x}^h)$ as an index of household h's preferences – as in Chapters 7, 8 and 12.

DEFINITION 13.3: a consumption allocation $[\mathbf{x}^h]$ is *fair* if for every pair of households $h, l = 1,2, \ldots, H$ it is true that $U^h(\mathbf{x}^h) \geqslant U^h(\mathbf{x}^l)$. In other words an allocation is fair if it is such that no one in the community wishes he had somebody else's bundle instead of his own.

THEOREM 13.4: if all households have equal incomes then a competitive equilibrium is a fair allocation.

PROOF: let the competitive equilibrium be $(\mathscr{a}^*, \mathbf{p}^*)$, and denote the uniform income received by each household as M^*. By definition of such an equilibrium (see Definition 7.3) for every household h it is true that

$$U^h(\mathbf{x}^{*h}) \geqslant U^h(\mathbf{x}^h) \text{ for all } \mathbf{x}^h \text{ such that} \tag{13.2}$$

$$\Sigma_i p_i x_i^h \leqslant M^* \tag{13.3}$$

Now consider the utility h would enjoy were it to receive the consumption allocation of household l under this equilibrium, $\mathbf{x}^l$. Since all households face the same budget constraint $\mathbf{x}^{*l}$ satisfies (13.3); but then, by (13.2) we must have $U^h(\mathbf{x}^{*h}) \geqslant U^h(\mathbf{x}^{*l})$.

Of course not only would such an equal-income equilibrium be fair, it would also be Pareto efficient – see Theorem 8.2 which appears like a powerful endorsement. However one should *not* assume that such an equilibrium is ideal. Indeed one has only to imagine two households one of which consists of several physically handicapped people and the other composed of a single, fit person, to see that such an allocation of equal incomes, regardless of differences between households, is not very attractive. The 'fairness' concept of Definition 13.3 is, therefore, not of itself overwhelmingly powerful or compelling. We turn to a more explicit representation of social orderings.

13.4 The Social Welfare Function and National Income

One way of resolving the issue of what shall count as a 'good thing' for the community is to impose a specific structure on the method of aggregating individuals' preferences. We shall refer to such an imposed structure as a *social welfare function*. There are a number of ways in which the very general problem of social choice, discussed in Section 13.2, might reasonably be simplified down into a tractable form. The social welfare functions that we shall discuss employs the following four ingredients:

(1) a restriction on the range of issues on which each household's preferences is to count;
(2) an assumption that one either knows, or one may impute, the preferences of households;
(3) a basis for comparing the levels and scales of utility of one household with another;
(4) a function for aggregating the utilities enjoyed by (or imputed to) each household.

Take, for example, a social welfare function of the form

$$W(U^1(\mathbf{x}^1), U^2(\mathbf{x}^2), \ldots, U^H(\mathbf{x}^H)) \tag{13.4}$$

where W is increasing in each of its arguments. This social welfare function is said to be *individualistic* in that only individual utilities are used to evaluate social states.

Consider some change in the allocation of goods to households given by $\mathrm{d}x_i^h$, $i = 1, \ldots, n$; $h = 1, \ldots, H$. Differentiating (13.4) we find the change in social welfare given by:

$$\mathrm{d}W = \sum_i \sum_h W_h U_i^h \mathrm{d}x_i^h \tag{13.5}$$

Observe how each of the above points (1) to (4) is incorporated in equations (13.4) and (13.5). In (13.4) it is clear that each household h's views are counted only in so far as they relate to its own consumption $\mathbf{x}^h$. In (13.5) it is clear that the weight given to a marginal change $\mathrm{d}x_i^h$ in the amount of the ith good consumed by the hth household depends partly on U_i^h – the household's marginal utility for that good – and partly on W_h – the relative weight at the margin given to the utility of household h in the overall social welfare function.

Assume for the moment a government that has the degree of omniscience and social control necessary to maximise (13.4) by direct command. To complete the picture we might introduce production and a total resource constraint as in Definition 7.3 and equations (8.2, 8.3) of Chapters 7 and 8 respectively. Consider the conditions that would have to obtain at a maximum of (13.4), constrained by the resources and technology of the community. We see at once that, because of the individualistic structure of the social welfare function (W is just an increasing function of the Us), the maximisation problem is very similar to that carried out in Section 8.2 of Chapter

8.[13] So we may deduce straightaway that a constrained optimum of (13.4) will exhibit the first-order conditions for efficiency, namely: marginal rates of substitution for any pair of private goods equalled across all households, and equated to the marginal rate of transformation. Now consider a transfer of a small amount of good i from household l to household h: letting $\mathrm{d}x_i^l = -\mathrm{d}x_i^h$ in (13.5), and setting the result equal to zero to get the first-order condition, we find

$$W_h U_i^h = W_l U_i^l \tag{13.6}$$

where W_h is the differential of W with respect to U^h. The expression on either side of (13.6) – the weight of each household times the marginal utility of good i to that household – represents the 'marginal social value of good i if consumed by household h'. So the first-order condition for a maximum of 13.4 has the simple, appealing interpretation 'ensure that the marginal social value of any good is equated across households'.

Now let us examine the properties of the social welfare function (13.4) in the case of a market economy. Each household h maximises its utility $U^h(\mathbf{x}^h)$ subject to a budget constraint $\Sigma p_i x_i^h \leqslant M^h$ where M^h is the household's income: the argument can easily be extended to the case where M^h is endogenously determined, as in Chapters 7 and 8, if we wish. We may substitute from the demand functions for each household back into its utility function to obtain the indirect utility function for each household $V^h(\mathbf{p}, M^h)$.[14] This then yields the social welfare function in terms of prices and incomes:

$$W(V^1(\mathbf{p}, M^1), V^2(\mathbf{p}, M^2), \ldots, V^H(\mathbf{p}, M^H)) \tag{13.7}$$

Recall that for a consumer's optimum purchases in a free market we have $U_i^h = v^{*h} p_i$ if good i is purchased in positive amounts – see equation (4.11). The term v^{*h} is the marginal utility of money income and of course, equals $\partial V^h/\partial M^h$ – see equations (4.30), (4.31). So the social optimality condition (13.6) above can be rewritten, in the case of a market economy as

$$W^h V_M^h = W^l V_M^l \tag{13.8}$$

for any pair of households h and l. This is the effect on social welfare of giving one dollar to any household at the optimum; let us call it B_M. Hence it is immediate that if there is some economic change affecting individual

[13] Obviously, maximising $W(U^1(\mathbf{x}^1), \bar{u}^2, \bar{u}^3, \ldots, \bar{u}^H)$ where W is increasing in its first argument, and $\bar{u}^2, \bar{u}^3, \ldots, \bar{u}^H$ are fixed is exactly equivalent to the maximisation problem in Equation 8.4.

[14] See equation (4.15) for the demand function and Section 4.7 of Chapter 4 for the derivation of the indirect utility function.

incomes (for example a change in natural resource endowments or in the technology), the change in social welfare is

$$\sum_{h=1}^{H} W_h V_M^h \mathrm{d}M^h = B_M \sum_{h=1}^{H} \mathrm{d}M^h \tag{13.9}$$

The right-hand side of (13.9) is proportional to the change in *national income* $M^1 + M^2 + \ldots + M^H$.

Now consider a change in the prices **p** leaving incomes M^h unchanged.[15] Differentiating (13.7) we find that the effect on social welfare is

$$\Sigma_{h=1}^{H} W_h \Sigma_i V_i^h \mathrm{d}p_i \tag{13.10}$$

but, in view of equation (4.32) of Chapter 4 we have $V_i^h = -x_i V_M^h$. So, in the neighbourhood of an optimum, (13.10) becomes

$$-\Sigma_{h=1}^{H} W_h V_M^h \Sigma_i x_i^{*h} \mathrm{d}p_i = -B_M \Sigma_i x_i^* \mathrm{d}p_i \tag{13.11}$$

This is simply $-B_M$ times the change in the cost of aggregate expenditure (by all households on all goods) as a result of the change in the price vector. Since, in a market economy, aggregate expenditure equals national income, it is clear that whatever the reason for the change in the social state, the following result holds:

THEOREM 13.5: in the neighbourhood of a welfare optimum, welfare changes are measured by changes in national income.

What if the economy does not have an 'ideal' property distribution such that (13.8) is satisfied? Clearly there is in some sense a form of loss or 'social waste' that results not because prices are distorted (as in Section 8.6 of Chapter 8), but because households' money incomes have not been 'correctly' adjusted (according to the social welfare function W). To examine further the nature of this loss, let us make some further simplifying assumptions: all the V^h are identical[16] and W is a symmetric and concave function. Given that all the households are assumed identical, the assumption of symmetry is a natural one: it implies that there is no significance in the labelling of individual households $1, \ldots, H$.

---

[15] Of course a change in prices, for whatever reason will also change the incomes M^h; but we have already covered this situation above.

[16] The assumption of identical utilities is not necessarily as appalling as at first it might seem. Two issues are involved: identical taste patterns (indifference curves) and identical welfare levels for a given income M. The first point is not troublesome if we restrict attention to a *given* price vector **p**. The second point involves an assumption about compatibility of utility levels and scales of possibly unlike households. Given sufficient information about the characteristics of households of different types (single persons, families with children, the handicapped etc.) it may be possible to impute to each household a standardised income that takes account of its particular budgetary needs to attain a given living standard.

The assumption that W is concave[17] implies that a 'society' – as represented by the social welfare function – is weakly averse to an unequal distribution of income. Given total income $\Sigma_h M^h$ (equal to value of all the resources in the community plus all the profits made by companies, $\Sigma_i p_i R_i + \Sigma_f \Pi^f$, which will be fixed for a given price vector $\mathbf{p}$) then, for a given $\mathbf{p}$, W would be maximised when every household received mean income $\bar{M} \equiv \Sigma_h M^h / H$.

A natural way of measuring the apparent loss attributable to the less-than-ideal property distribution suggests itself in the light of the discussion in Chapter 8 of waste attributable to price distortion. Consider the income that, were it to be given identically to every household, would yield the same level of social welfare as the actual incomes $M^1, \ldots, M^H$. This income is clearly less than or equal to $\bar{M}$, and the difference between the two can be regarded as a money measure of the shortfall in social welfare attributable to the inequality of incomes.

DEFINITION 13.4: (a) the *equally-distributed equivalent income* ξ is a real number such that

$$W(V(\xi, \mathbf{p}), \ldots, V(\xi, \mathbf{p})) = W(V(M^1, \mathbf{p}), \ldots, V(M^H, \mathbf{p}))$$

(b) the *inequality index*[18] is $1 - \xi / \bar{M}$

This is illustrated, for a two-household example, in Figure 13.5. The ray OCB is at 45° to the axes: any point on this represents a situation of exact equality of income distribution. So, given an actual distribution of income (M^1, M^2) represented by the point A we find the mean by drawing a perpendicular from A to the 45° ray: this perpendicular meets the ray at B, the point $(\bar{M}, \bar{M})$. The contour of the social welfare function $W(V(\mathbf{p}, M^1), V(\mathbf{p}, M^2))$ that passes through A is symmetric about the ray, and cuts the ray at point C, the point (ξ, ξ). Clearly the more sharply curved is this contour, the greater the inequality $1 - \xi/\bar{M}$.

The similarity of these concepts to the concepts of certainty equivalence and risk premium discussed on pages 211, 212 of Chapter 10 may have already been spotted. This becomes even more evident if we impose a further restriction on the social welfare function W. If we assume that it is additively separable (analogous to the utility function in equation (10.2) of Chapter 10) then, suppressing the price vector $\mathbf{p}$ (assumed to be held invariant) we may rewrite (13.7) as[19]

---

[17] Concavity is a stronger assumption than is actually needed: Sen, A.K. (1973) *On Economic Inequality*, Oxford University Press, discusses the weaker concept of Schur-concavity.

[18] This inequality index is due to Atkinson, A.B. (1970) 'On the measurement of inequality', *Journal of Economic Theory*, Vol. 2, pp. 244–63.

[19] Note that this step has just been arbitrarily asserted rather than derived axiomatically as was the utility function (10.2) in Theorem 10.1.

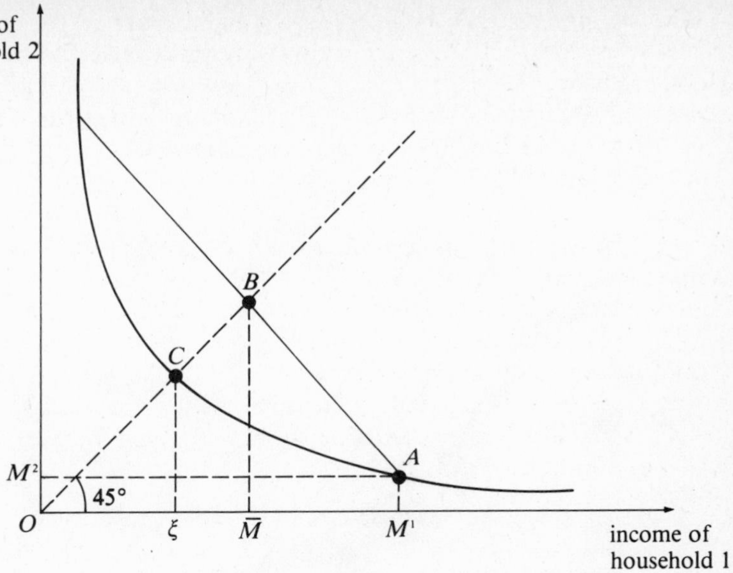

Figure 13.5 Contour of the Social Welfare Function

$$\sum_{h=1}^{H} \zeta(M^h) \tag{13.12}$$

where ζ is an increasing, concave function of one variable. Then the equation defining the equally-distributed equivalent income can be rewritten

$$\zeta(\xi) = \frac{1}{H} \sum_{h=1}^{H} \zeta(M^h) \tag{13.13}$$

Recall that in the case of choice under uncertainty the curvature of the function υ reflected the degree of risk aversion, and hence the risk premium to be imputed to any particular prospect. Likewise the curvature of ζ determines the degree of 'inequality aversion' that is implicit in the social welfare function: in fact, assuming differentiability of ζ, we conventionally define (relative) inequality aversion as $\iota = -M\zeta''(M)/\zeta'(M)$. Borrowing results from Theorem 10.3 (and Exercise 10.5) we may immediately state

THEOREM 13.6 let $\zeta(M)$ and $\hat{\zeta}(M)$ be increasing, concave functions of one variable, such that $\hat{\zeta}$ is a concave transformation of ζ. Then (a) $\hat{\iota} \geqslant \iota$; (b) $\hat{\xi} \leqslant \xi$.

The more sharply curved are the contours in Figure 13.5, the higher the inequality aversion and the lower the equally-distributed equivalent income.

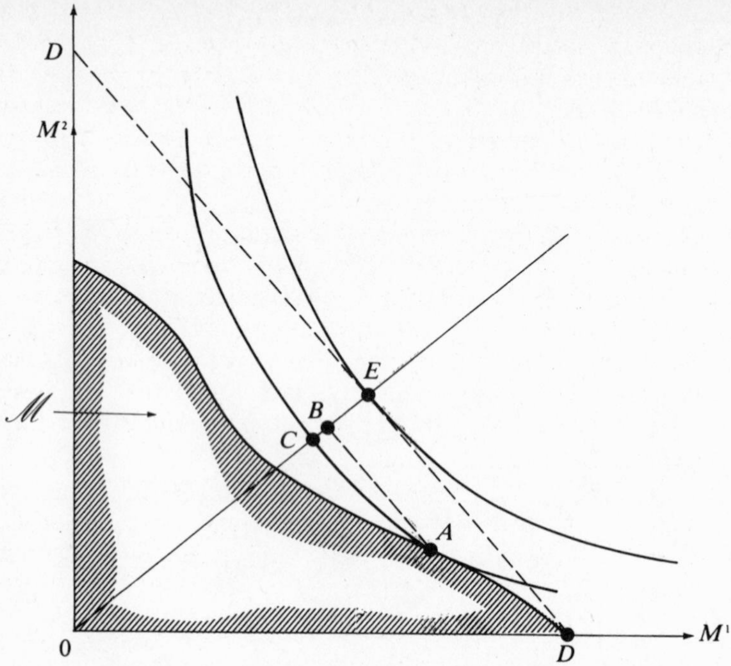

Figure 13.6

So the greater is the inequality aversion implicit in the social welfare function, the greater is the apparent loss attributable to any given unequal distribution of income.

It is important to emphasise that this is an *apparent* loss since there is no reason to suppose that in practice it is legitimate to take total income as *given* (as we did on page 314). If the property distribution is changed in a market economy then the total income in the community is also likely to change since the equilibrium price vector will also change. Consider Figure 13.6 which has the same axes as Figure 13.5 and suppose the economy is initially at point A. The incomes of the households are determined, (i) by $\mathscr{d}$, the property distribution of resources and shares in firms, and (ii) by the equilibrium prices at A. Now imagine all the possible income distributions corresponding to changes in the property distribution away from that which was in force at A: we may do this by using the equivalent variation concept discussed in Section 4.7 of Chapter 4 and taking as our starting point the household utility levels that were attained at point A. As is set out schematically in Figure 7.3, each $\mathscr{d}$ determines a particular equilibrium price vector, and thus each $\mathscr{d}$ fixes a market-determined income for household h, $M^h(\mathscr{d})$. We may thus construct the set of all feasible (market-determined) income distributions $\mathcal{M} \equiv \{M^1(\boldsymbol{d}), M^2(\boldsymbol{d}), \ldots, M^H(\boldsymbol{d}): \boldsymbol{d} \in \mathcal{D}\}$: this is illustrated by the shaded area in Figure 13.6. As we saw in Figure 13.5 the *apparent* welfare loss from being at point A is given by the ratio of the distances CB/OB. But, by construction, A is in fact a welfare optimum *on the assumption that* $\mathcal{M}$ *represents the set of feasible income distributions* (observe that the frontier of $\mathcal{M}$ is tangential to a contour of the social welfare function at that point). Whether A is an optimum in some wider sense depends on what one is prepared to assume about the scope for intervention in the economy (see Section 13.6). If, for example, lump-sum transfers of income were possible, then the set of all possible income distributions would be the set bounded by the 45° line DD', and the optimum would be at point E. If such transfers are just not practical policy, then the 'true' $\mathcal{M}$ may be somewhere intermediate between that determined by the market (as shown) and that which would have been relevant had lump-sum income transfers been attainable.

Without the structure of possible interventionist policies being specified it is, of course, impossible to specify $\mathcal{M}$, and so one cannot *in general* state that equality of incomes is a welfare-maximising condition. One simple result is available, however.

THEOREM 13.7: given identical individuals, an equal distribution of income is welfare maximising for *all* symmetric concave social welfare functions if $\mathcal{M}$ is symmetric and convex.

The proof is left to Exercise 13.7.

Clearly the above discussion of the nature of a welfare maximum is on an extremely limited basis: for the sake of simple, interpretable results we have swept aside difficulties that would be essential to practical policy making. Most notably we have assumed:

(a) that the choice of an appropriate social state effectively amounts to the choice of an allocation of pure private goods;
(b) that the social welfare function is individualistic and self-interested (W is a function of individual utility levels, and each U^h is a function only of household h's consumption). Each of these assumptions can be relaxed, at a cost.

Consider the problem of extending the analysis beyond a pure private-good economy. Obviously the problems of inefficiency arising from the presence of production or consumption externalities, discussed in Section 8.3 of Chapter 8 will mean that Theorem 13.5 is no longer applicable: prices will have to be 'corrected' if a social optimum is to be attained. The marginal benefit *to each household* of any change in the level of public good supply needs to be taken into account in determining the optimum: even if people are similar in tastes, differences in income between persons and the possible lack of a satisfactory preference revelation mechanism will make this information difficult to obtain.

A social welfare function that is not individualistic and self-interested may well be worth considering. For example if households had other households' incomes or utilities as arguments of their own utility functions (equation 8.31 and Exercise 8.9 of Chapter 8) then it is clear that a modified form of the above analysis will still go through. It may also provide a basis for assuming W to be strictly concave in incomes: if households 'feel bad' about income inequality (in a manner that is similar to the way they are adversely affected by other externalities) and if the social orderings respect individual tastes then the social welfare function will exhibit inequality aversion. However, this may not, in itself, be an entirely satisfactory reason for supposing the social welfare function to be inequality averse: a further reason will emerge in the next section.

13.5 Uncertainty

The discussion of Sections 13.3 and 13.4 was predicated on the assumption that there is a *known* set of alternative social states $\mathcal{S}$ from which one may select an appropriate state $\mathcal{s}$ under conditions of perfect certainty.

The situation is comparable to the problem of making a selection from a range of boxes of assorted chocolates on display: given that you know everybody's tastes, and you know the flavour inside each chocolate, and you have a rule for resolving conflicts of interest as to who is going to get which chocolates, you have enough information to solve the problem of which assortment to choose. Now introduce uncertainty in the manner of Chapter 10: none of the available boxes of chocolates has that useful bit of paper telling you what is inside each chocolate, and you have to select the appropriate box knowing that the state of the world will not be revealed until everyone bites into the chocolates.

The principal issue in welfare terms is that which was raised in Section 10.5 of Chapter 10 – whether welfare is to be assessed *ex-ante* or *ex-post*. To fix ideas let us suppose that individual households have utility functions of the form (10.2), although now we need to be careful to distinguish each household's preference map in the face of risk. So for a finite set of states of the world $\Omega = \{1, 2, \ldots, \bar{\omega}\}$ we may write

$$U^h(\mathbf{x}^h(1), \ldots, \mathbf{x}^h(\bar{\omega})) = \sum_{\omega \in \Omega} \pi^h(\omega) \upsilon^h(\mathbf{x}^h(\omega)) \tag{13.14}$$

Using this concept of (*ex-ante*) household utility under uncertainty in equation (13.4) gives one the following:

DEFINITION 13.5: an *ex-ante* social welfare function is a function W of household *ex-ante* utilities $W(u^1, u^2, \ldots, u^H)$ where, for each h, u^h is given by (13.14).

Alternatively we can imagine the social welfare criterion constructed as follows. Suppose state of the world ω were to be realised: in state ω the cardinal utility of household h is $v^h(\mathbf{x}^h(\omega))$. The collection of these cardinal utility numbers of individual households could be regarded as a 'payoff-vector' to society if state ω is realised. So we might consider the analogy in social welfare terms to the von Neumann–Morgenstern utility function (10.2), in which this payoff vector is the argument.

DEFINITION 13.6: an *ex-post* social welfare function is a linear combination of welfare that would be realised in each possible social state:

$$\sum_{\omega \in \Omega} \pi(\omega) W(v^1(\mathbf{x}^1(\omega)), \ldots, v^H(\mathbf{x}^H(\omega)))$$

Here the set of weights used in the linear combinations, $\{\pi(\omega) : \omega \in \Omega\}$ are playing the role of *socially* determined probabilities.

Definition 13.5 says 'take as your objective the welfare of individual expected utilities' and Definition 13.6 says 'take as your objective the expected welfare of individual utilities'. The former evaluates everyone's utility before they bite into the chocolates; the latter imagines all the possible combinations of pain and pleasure that could arise *after* the chocolates have been bitten as components of a risky prospect, and evaluates the welfare of that prospect in von Neumann–Morgenstern fashion. Given the differences in specification between the two definitions it is possible to imagine cases in which one might be able to adjust the $\mathbf{x}^h(\omega)$ for each h – that is adjust the payoffs to household h in each state of the world – such that h's expected utility (and therefore *ex-ante* social welfare) remains unchanged, but such that *ex-post* welfare is altered by the shifting of such payoffs. This obviously prompts the question: under what circumstances will *ex-ante* and *ex-post* welfare criteria be identical?

THEOREM 13.8: let each household have the utility function (13.14) and let *ex-post* social welfare function be as specified in Definition 13.6, and differentiable; then every *ex-post* welfare optimum will be *ex-ante* efficient if and only if the social welfare function can be written in the form

$$\sum_{h=1}^{H} \sum_{\omega \in \Omega} \pi(\omega) \lambda^h v^h(\mathbf{x}^h(\omega)) \tag{13.15}$$

where $\{\lambda^h\}$ is a set of positive constants and $\pi^h(\omega) = \pi(\omega)$ for all h.

PROOF: consider a set of variations in payoffs to each household in each state of the world such that $\mathrm{d}v^h(\mathbf{x}^h(\omega)) = 0$ for all $h \neq l$, and for all $\omega \in \Omega$. It follows that if *ex-ante* and *ex-post* criteria are to be identical then the following must be true:

$$\text{`}\sum_{\omega \in \Omega} \pi^l(\omega) \mathrm{d}v^l(\mathbf{x}^l(\omega)) = 0 \text{ implies}$$

$$\sum_{\omega \in \Omega} \pi(\omega) W_l(v^1(\mathbf{x}^1(\omega)), \ldots, v^H(\mathbf{x}^H(\omega))) \mathrm{d}v^l(\mathbf{x}^l(\omega)) = 0\text{'}.$$

But this can only be true for such an arbitrary variation if, for all $\omega \in \Omega$:

$$\pi(\omega)W_l(v^1(\mathbf{x}^1(\omega)), \ldots, v^H(\mathbf{x}^H(\omega))) = \lambda^l\pi^l(\omega) \tag{13.16}$$

for some constant λ^l. Since $\pi(\omega) > 0$ for some ω, we must have $\lambda^l > 0$. Again, if (13.16) is to apply for arbitrary values of $[\mathbf{x}^h(\omega)]$, we must have $W_l = \lambda^l$ for all $[\mathbf{x}^h(\omega)]$; hence $\pi^l(\omega) = \pi(\omega)$. Integration immediately gives the form (13.15). This establishes necessity; sufficiency is obvious.

We see that Theorem 13.8 imposes important restrictions on *both* (i) the social welfare function *and* (ii) the pattern of individual preferences. (i) The social welfare function has to be linear in the household utilities. This rules out any concern for *ex-post* inequality once the actual contents of the chocolates are known. (ii) Everyone's 'subjective probabilities' – i.e. their marginal rates of substitution between consumption in states of the world along the 45° line in Figure 10.1 – must all be the same.

Notice that this second point requires a remarkable degree of unanimity of view amongst the households: if all households do not possess the same subjective probabilities about the uncertain events then a maximum of *ex-post* social welfare will not generally be sustainable by means of competitive markets. If some individuals have the 'wrong' perceptions about the probability of finding certain flavours in the chocolates, then market intervention may be required to modify the relative prices confronting households. Of course this begs the question of what the $\{\pi(\omega)\}$ *should* be if the probabilities concerning the various risky outcomes cannot be objectively assessed.[20]

The *ex-post* welfare criterion may have much to recommend it if the problem of economic uncertainty cannot be safely incorporated into a model of efficiently operating markets for risk where all persons have correct perceptions of probabilities. If individuals' welfare is affected by the slings and arrows of outrageous fortune in ways that cannot be rationally anticipated, or if markets for trading in insurance and contingent goods do not exist, then risk aversion by individuals and by society provides an important argument for social preferences exhibiting inequality aversion – see Exercise 13.11.

13.6 Social Control

Once we have installed a social welfare function of the form (13.4) in our model of the economy, it is obviously interesting to see how agencies such as governments or planning boards might attempt to pursue the objectives represented by such a function, and on what economic principles they might

[20] See Exercise 13.10.

design suitable policies. Let us examine some of the preliminary issues which must be resolved if we are to apply the material of Sections 13.4 and 13.5 in this way.

For a start there is the 'They' problem. It is a convenient fiction to suppose that there is present in the community a kind Civic Fairy Godmother who can somehow bring about a desired social state by implementing the appropriate economic policies. There are two difficulties with this fiction: (1) as we have seen in Section 13.2, the notion of a 'social will' is somewhat illusory, to say the least; (2) the very existence, composition and powers of such an agency cannot just be taken for granted. Strictly speaking, the services of government themselves should be modelled as a 'public good problem' as discussed in Chapters 8 and 12.

However, if we set aside this issue and treat the 'government' as just one of a number of agents in the economy, how should its decision problem be modelled? Let us side-step the problems of Section 13.5 by assuming that the government knows with certainty the social welfare function for the community, defined over $\mathcal{S}$, the space of all social states. Next we assume that it has a well-defined and known opportunity set. There is, perhaps, more to this assumption than meets the eye. Clearly it rules out 'exogenous' uncertainty or risk of the type which we modelled in Chapter 10; but it also disposes of potential problems associated with the interaction between agents of the type discussed in Chapter 11.

As an example of the problems that can arise take the case where the government attempts to finance the production of a public good by imposing a commodity tax on a single private good, and the private good is being produced by a monopolist. Suppose that P is the price that the monopolist *receives*, that $P + \tau$ is the price that consumers *pay* for the private good, that the total quantity demanded of the private good is given by

$$Q = D(P + \tau) \tag{13.17}$$

(where for convenience we have suppressed the other arguments of D) and that the quantity of the public good is measured simply by the revenue raised from taxation of the private good, τQ. If the firm maximises profits then it chooses P to maximise

$$PQ - C(Q) \tag{13.18}$$

The first-order conditions for a maximum of (13.18) for any given τ gives the familiar 'marginal revenue equals marginal cost' result:[21]

$$\frac{P+\tau}{\eta} + P = C_Q \tag{13.19}$$

[21] See Section 3.8 of Chapter 3.

where η is the elasticity of demand (which may itself depend on the consumer price $P + \tau$) and C_Q is marginal cost. Equation (13.19) determines the firm's *reaction function* giving P as a function of τ.

What of the government? Suppose that it has an objective function $\Psi(\tau Q, Q)$ where the arguments are the quantities of the public good and the private good. It seeks to maximise this by choice of τ, allowing for the fact that Q is determined by (13.17). But how should we model its attitude toward the private sector monopolist? In the light of our discussion on strategic behaviour in Chapter 11, there are at least two possibilities leading to two different types of solution.

(1) *Nash*: the government acts in a manner similar to the private sector. It takes tne announced price P as *given* in the maximisation problem. This yields the first-order condition for a maximum:

$$\left[\frac{P+\tau}{\eta} + \tau\right]\Psi_1 + \Psi_2 = 0 \tag{13.20}$$

where Ψ_1 and Ψ_2 are the partial derivatives of Ψ. Equation (13.20) determines the government's reaction function giving τ as a function of P. Plotting these two reaction functions in Figure 13.7 would give us immediately the simultaneous Nash solution at point N.

(2) *Stackelberg*: alternatively we may assume that the government knows the price $P(\tau)$ that the firm fixes in response to any announced tax τ, so that its problem is, in effect, to choose τ so as to maximise

$$\Psi(\tau D(P(\tau) + \tau), D(P(\tau) + \tau))$$

Solving this in a fashion analogous to that in Chapter 11 yields point S in Figure 13.7 as the outcome.

As with our discussion of the interaction amongst firms in Chapter 11, which of the above two solution concepts (or of other possible solutions) is appropriate depends on the assumed information structure and market power of the agents involved. Whilst in some cases the Nash approach might be the appropriate way of modelling the relationships between the government and the private agents it would like to influence, if we make the assumption that the private sector is in some sense diffuse and passive whilst the government is well informed about the responses of the private sector to public policy instruments, then a Stackelberg type of solution would make much more sense. The argument applies with even greater force to the control of consumers rather than producers.

We shall take it that there is indeed a fundamental asymmetry between the government and the private sector. The government acts as 'leader' in that it chooses a structure of taxes or other controls which it

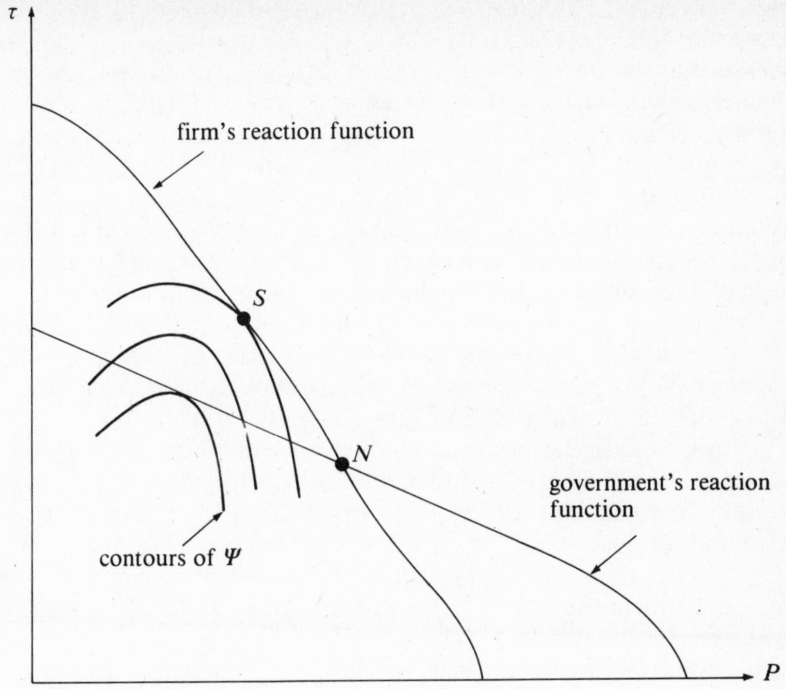

N is Nash solution
S is Stackelberg solution

Figure 13.7

assumes (rightly) will be taken by the private sector as exogenously given; in taking the structure of those taxes as exogenously given and responding thereto, the private sector is of course acting as a 'follower'.

Let us then use this analytical approach to proceed directly to a result that is almost obvious. Suppose the authorities are able, without loss of resources, to transfer income from one person to another: thus they can arrange for either a vector of exogenous income adjustments for all households (dM^1, dM^2, ..., dM^H) or an appropriate alteration in the (exogenous) property distribution $\mathscr{d}$.

THEOREM 13.9 given the assumptions of Theorem 8.3, a welfare optimum in a competitive market economy can always be achieved by the use of lump-sum transfers.

Apart from important technical difficulties (for example non-convexity of firms' technology sets or satiation of consumers) which may render Theorem 8.3 inapplicable, there are three major problems which stand in the way of Theorem 13.7 being a universal answer to the problem of policy making as it might at first appear. First, there may not be a full set of markets; we have already indicated important instances of such 'market failure' in Chapters 10–12. Second, there may be 'large' agents in the community that find it possible to achieve their objectives by using their size to distort free market prices: again it is evident from the analysis of previous chapters that the exercise of such power will mean that unfettered competition will not produce an efficient state of the economy, let alone a socially optimal one. Third, as we have seen in Section 13.6, if we attempt to extend the results to a world of uncertainty the *ex-post* welfare may not be supportable by competition because consumers differ as to their subjective probabilities. In some of these cases it may be possible for the government to use taxes on commodities to adjust relative prices so that, for example, the efficiency rules on MRS and MRT are satisfied (see Section 8.7).

However, even if we set these serious problems to one side – even if we assume a fairy tale 'convex' world of atomistic competition and pure private goods – there remains a further intractable difficulty. It concerns the *implementation* of a course of action such as is implied by Theorem 13.9: the lump-sum transfers required to remodel the property distribution may just not be practical policy. So it may just not be appropriate to assume that there is some mechanism by which society can arbitrarily manipulate $\mathscr{d}$ in order to get a desired $\mathscr{a}$, as we discussed in Chapters 7 and 8. Some types of redistribution may be prohibited by other rules of society: for example transferring the title deeds of labour power may involve some form of slavery. Or the application of transfers of specific commodities to particular people or groups of people may be perceived to involve injustices or inequality of treatment. However, it is arguable that the most serious problem is that of information: for, even if one can avoid the problem of transfer of title deeds of certain specific resource endowments (as cited above) by transferring money instead, one still has to identify which individuals deserve to have their incomes reduced in the social mechanism used to transfer income. Acquiring this information may again infringe social rules, such as those regarding personal privacy. And even where such formal restrictions do not exist, individuals may be able to dissimulate or provide false information, as we noted in Chapters 11 and 12. Finally, detailed transfer plans may involve substantial computational and transactions costs in their administration. For all these reasons governments may seek simple 'second-best' alternatives to property redistribution.

One such alternative is broadly based on taxation of commodities or factors of production. Of course this is by no means the only avenue which a government might follow, but common practice suggests that it might be one that is informationally not too demanding and does not obviously infringe personal rights in a completely unacceptable way.

A simple way of analysing this is to consider the following problem.

Suppose that a *given* sum T is to be raised by taxation – for the purpose of financing public goods, redistribution or whatever – and that the only way of doing this is to drive a wedge $\mathbf{\Delta p} = (\Delta p_1, \ldots, \Delta p_n)$ between consumer prices and producer prices: what choice of $\mathbf{\Delta p}$ will minimise the distortionary loss to the economy?[22] Noting the measure of loss in Section 8.6 then, if all households have identical demands, the problem is:

$$\min -\tfrac{1}{2}\Sigma_i\Sigma_j\hat{D}^i_j\Delta p_i\Delta p_j + \lambda\,[\Sigma_j\Delta p_j x_j - T] \qquad (13.21)$$

Differentiating (13.21) with respect to Δp_i we find[23]

$$-\sum_{j=1}^{n}\hat{D}^i_j\Delta p_j + \lambda x_i + \lambda\,\Sigma_j\Delta p_j D^j_i = 0 \qquad (13.22)$$

Using the Slutsky equation to substitute for D^j_i (see equation (4.23)) we find, on rearranging (13.22):

$$\frac{-\sum_{j=1}^{n}\hat{D}^i_j\Delta p_j}{x_i} = a, \quad i = 1, \ldots, n \qquad (13.23)$$

where $a = \dfrac{\lambda}{1-\lambda}\,[\Sigma_j D^j_M\Delta p_j - 1]$, some number which is the same for all i.

Equation (13.23) gives us a simple rule for the choice of price adjustments (taxes):

THEOREM 13.10 (*Ramsey*): the constrained optimal tax rule which minimises net loss to the community ensures that the proportionate reduction in demand (along with the *compensated* demand curve) is the same for all commodities.

Of course this simple rule is only a beginning; indeed it can be argued that such a tax rule is incomplete since it fails to incorporate the *uses* to which T is put – i.e. it fails to include the transfer incomes or the benefits from the public goods which would themselves affect households' demands. Moreover the assumption that households are effectively identical is clearly

---

[22] The list of goods 1, ..., n here is taken to be the list of all *taxable* goods. This is more limited than the set of all possible goods in the economy, see Exercise 13.12.

[23] Recall that substitution effects are symmetric: $\hat{D}^i_j = \hat{D}^j_i$: see page 49 of Chapter 3 and page 76 of Chapter 4. Observe also that we have omitted the 'production' terms from Λ as defined in equation (8.42) of Chapter 8. We may neglect these if production is effectively competitively organised and subject to constant returns to scale: see Diamond, P.A. and Mirrlees, J.A. (1971) 'Optimal taxation and public production', *American Economic Review*, Vol. 61, pp. 8–27, 261–78.

inappropriate if redistribution of incomes is to be considered one of the purposes of taxation. However (13.23) can be modified without too much trouble to take account of the heterogeneity of the population. Using the notation introduced above, let B^h_M denote the marginal social value of a dollar of income to person h; then, maximising (13.4) by choice of $\Delta p_1, \ldots, \Delta p_n$ subject to the above revenue constraint gives

$$\frac{-\Sigma_j \Sigma_h \hat{D}^{hi}_j \Delta p_j}{x_i} = a_i \quad i = 1, \ldots, n \tag{13.24}$$ [24]

where

$$a_i = 1 - \overline{\beta} - H\mathrm{cov}\,(x^h_i/x_i, \beta^h), \overline{\beta} \equiv \frac{1}{H}\Sigma_h \beta^h \text{ and } \beta^h \equiv B^h_M/\lambda + \sum_{j=1}^{n} D^{hj}_M \Delta p_j.$$

Observe that a_i will be small for those goods where purchases of the commodity are positively correlated with high β^h: i.e. the optimal proportionate reduction in demand is less if the commodity is likely to be heavily purchased by poor households (*high* B^h_M). It is possible to extend this type of optimal tax rule to include direct income taxation and to take account of the distributional impact of public goods; but these complications take us beyond the scope of the present chapter.

13.7 Summary

One of the principal problems of welfare economics is what constitutes a 'good thing': how social states – comprising consumption and production allocations, the level of provision of public goods and other features of the economic system – are to be ranked in terms of their desirability. This provides the basis for the specification of rules characterising an 'ideal' state and for designing policies to manoeuvre the economic system so as to obtain a welfare improvement.

In some respects it is possible to get considerable insight into such policy rules by treating the problem analogously to the optimisation problems of individuals discussed in Chapters 3 to 5. However, whilst it is convenient to model social objectives as though the entire community acted as a single, rational agent – as though it were a firm or a household – this procedure leaves open some important questions:

---

[24] See Exercise 13.16.

- is there a coherent, well-defined objective function?
- if so, where does it come from?
- how are the conflicts of interest resolved?

The answers provided to these questions depend, naturally, on factors such as the range of issues over which individuals' preferences are to be respected (only those concerning their own consumption bundle? the entire consumption allocation?) and the information structure one assumes (may one compare people's utility levels? their utility scales?). Indeed it may be impossible to specify in suitably general terms a 'constitution' that consistently bases social rankings on individual values. However if we abandon the problem of precise specification of a constitution in favour of more broadly-based criteria for making social welfare comparisons then we find that grand general principles, such as efficiency and equity, however defined, are usually insufficient to yield decisive social welfare rules.

If the problem of where the social welfare function comes from can be settled or side-stepped, then under ideal conditions there is a simple relationship between social welfare and national income. In less-than-ideal circumstances a measure of the performance of the economy (the level of social welfare) must take into account the inequality of the distribution of incomes amongst households as well as the size of national income itself.

However, even if an optimum member $\mathscr{s}^*$ of the set $\mathscr{S}$ can be specified, there remains a further problem: finding the economic and social machinery that will unerringly ensure that $\mathscr{s}^*$ is picked. This problem stems from the general incentive problem discussed in Chapter 12. Even if the government is assumed to be powerful and reasonably well-informed, and the private sector adopts the role of a passive 'follower', there are clearly practical limitations – personal privacy, administrative costs – on what the government can do. In many cases it is impractical to implement 'ideal' lump-sum transfers, intended to alter the property distribution or the distribution of income. So the government will usually have to adopt policies that are in themselves apparently distortionary in order to achieve a welfare improvement.

In trying to attain a 'good thing' one may have to settle for second-best.

Further Reading

A useful, and not overly technical, summary of the issues in social choice theory is to be found in:

Mueller, D.J. (1980) *Public Choice*, Cambridge University Press.
Sugden, R. (1981) *The Political Economy of Public Choice*, Martin Robertson.

A more difficult, but excellently thorough, treatment of these issues is given in:

Suzumura, K. (1983) *Rational Choice, Collective Decisions and Social Welfare*, Cambridge University Press.

For a discussion of the relationship between social welfare functions and the constitution problem see:

Boadway, R.W. and Bruce, N.M. (1984) *Welfare Economics*, Basil Blackwell.

The concept of fairness discussed in Section 13.3 is examined in more detail in:

Varian, H.R. (1974) 'Equity, envy and efficiency', *Journal of Economic Theory*, Vol. 9, pp. 63–9.

On social values and social welfare functions see:

Meade, J.E. (1976) *The Just Economy*, Allen & Unwin.

For an introduction to the literature on optimal taxation structures see:

Atkinson, A.B. and Stiglitz, J.E. (1980) *Lectures on Public Economics*, McGraw-Hill.

Auerbach, A.J. (1985) 'The theory of excess burden and optimal taxation', in A.J. Auerbach and M.S. Feldstein (eds) *Handbook of Public Economics*, North-Holland, Vol. I.

Sandmo, A. (1976) 'Optimal taxation: an introduction to the literature', *Journal of Public Economics*, Vol. 6, pp. 37–54.

Exercises

*13.1 Write out the preferences of individuals *a, b, c* over s, s', s'' in Figures 13.1 and 13.2 in terms of rankings. Show that for Figure 13.1 majority voting produces a well-defined order and that for Figure 13.2 majority voting does not produce such an order.

13.2 Consider a *two-dimensional* space of social states. Take three social states: s, s', s'' and three individuals: Alf, Bill, Charlie. Draw a set of indifference curves in two dimensions such that the following rankings are satisfied:

Alf	Bill	Charlie
s	s'	s''
s'	s	s'
s''	s''	s

Suppose dimension 1 of the social state is 'defence spending'; dimension 2 is 'expenditure on public welfare'; Alf always prefers more defence and less welfare; Bill prefers the opposite, Charlie prefers a middling amount of either to extremes of either. What restrictions on the set of alternatives $\{s, s', s''\}$ would be needed to ensure that the single-peakedness property obtains?

13.3 Consider a constitution Σ that is based on rank-order voting. Let there be three possible social states and two individuals, Alf and Bill. When each person announces his votes for the various social states, the best alternative gets given 3 points, the second choice gets

2 and the worst gets 1 point. Assume that the rule for determining social choice is 'rank states in order of their total voting points', Alf's ranking of social states changes during the week; Bill's stays the same:

Alf	Bill	Alf	Bill
s	s'	s	s'
s'	s	s''	s
s''	s''	s'	s''
(Monday)		(Tuesday)	

What is the social ordering on Monday? What is it on Tuesday? How does this constitution violate Axiom W3?

13.4 Consider an economy with four social states and three citizens: Alf, Bill and Charlie, where their preferences over the states are given by the following rankings:

Alf	Bill	Charlie
s	s'''	s'
s''	s	s'''
s'	s''	s''
s'''	s'	s

Assume that the above point-voting rule is used. Calculate v for each social state (a) on the assumption that all four social states are available and (b) that only the states $\{s, s'''\}$ are available. Show that under (a) s and s''' are ranked equal, and superior to other states, but that under (b) s''' is regarded as *superior* to s.

*13.5 Consider a simple economy consisting of three individuals, $\{a,b,c\}$ and four possible states of the world. Each state of the world is characterised by a monetary payoff M^h to each of the individuals thus:

	a	b	c
s	3	3	3
s'	1	4	4
s''	5	1	3
s'''	2	6	1

Suppose that person h has a utility function $U^h = \log(M^h)$. Show the following:

(a) If individuals know the payoffs that will accrue to them under each state of the world, then majority voting will produce a cyclic decision rule.

(b) The above conditions can rank unequal states over perfect equality.

(c) If people did not know which of the identities $\{a,b,c,\}$ they were to have *before they vote*, if they regard any one of these three identities as equally likely, and if they are concerned to maximise expected utility, then majority voting will rank the states strictly in the order of the distribution of the payoffs.

Comment on result (c).

*13.6 (a) Write down a social welfare function that exhibits constant relative inequality aversion.
(b) What is the inequality measure for such a function?
(c) Investigate the form of this function as $\iota \to -\infty$. [cf. Exercise 2.12].

13.7 Prove Theorem 13.7.

*13.8 Consider the model of Exerçise 7.5. Suppose that good 1 is a commodity that can be transferred between persons and that good 2 is a non-transferable commodity (such as labour): person a is endowed with three units of good 2 and person b with six units of good 2. There are 21 units of good 1 which are distributed between persons a and b. Using good 2 as *numéraire* plot the set of all possible income distributions. Assuming that the social welfare function is symmetric, will the optimum distribution of income be equal?

13.9 Use the analysis of Section 13.4 and Section 8.3 of Chapter 8 to write down the conditions for a welfare optimum when there are n private goods and m public goods.

*13.10 Consider an economy in which there is uncertainty as to which state of the world ($\omega \in \Omega$) will prevail, and in which there are H households. Household h has utility

$$\upsilon^h(\mathbf{x}^h, \omega) \equiv \psi^{h1}(x_1^h, \omega) + \sum_{i=2}^{n} \psi^{hi}(x_i^h)$$

in state ω, where the amount consumed by h of good $i (i > 1)$ is the same for all ω. The allocation $[\mathbf{x}^h]$ is fixed *before* the realisation of ω. Give an example of the kind of phenomenon that this might represent.

If the social welfare function is $\Sigma_{h=1}^{H} \lambda^h \Sigma_{\omega\in\Omega} \pi(\omega)\upsilon^h(\mathbf{x}^h, \omega)$ and if the aggregate amounts of goods 1, . . . , n satisfy the production possibility constraint $\Phi(\mathbf{x}) = 0$, write down the first-order conditions for a *social* optimum.

If household h has subjective probabilities $\{\pi^h(\omega) : \omega\in\Omega\}$, has income M^h and faces a price p_i^h for good i, find the first-order conditions for the *consumer's* optimum. Show that the two optima coincide when the 'personalised prices' p_i^h satisfy

$$\frac{p_i^h}{p_j^h} = \frac{\Phi_i}{\Phi_j}, \; i = 2, \ldots, n, \text{ and}$$

$$\frac{p_1^h}{p_j^h} = \frac{\Sigma_\omega \pi^h(\omega)\psi_1^{h1}(x_1^h, \omega)}{\Sigma_\omega \pi(\omega)\psi_1^{h1}(x_1^h, \omega)} \frac{\Phi_1}{\Phi_j}$$

*13.11 A group of identical schoolchildren are to be endowed at lunch time with an allocation of pie. When they look through the dining hall window in the morning they can see the unequal slices of pie lying on the plates: the only problem is that no child knows which plate he or she will receive. Taking the space of all possible pie distributions as a complete description of all the social states for these school children, and assuming that *ex-ante* there are perceived to be equal chances of any given child receiving any one of the plates, discuss how a von Neumann–Morgenstern utility function (equation 10.2) may be used as a simple social welfare function.

(a) What determines the degree of inequality aversion of this social welfare function?

(b) Consider the possible problems using this approach as a general method of specifying a social welfare function.

13.12 (a) Use equation (13.23) and Theorem 13.10 to discuss the conditions under which *ad valorem* tax at the same rate on all *taxable* commodities should be imposed.

(b) What would be the optimum taxation strategy if the government could tax *every* commodity in the economy (including leisure time)?

13.13 Consider an economy in which there are two goods and a large number of consumers who differ only in their incomes. Each person faces a price ratio $\rho \equiv p_1/p_2$, and has an income M (denominated in units of good 2); preferences are given by an indirect utility function:

$$u = V(\mathbf{p}, M) = \phi\left(\log M - \frac{1}{1-\beta}\rho^{1-\beta}\right)$$

where $\beta > 0$, and $\phi' > 0$.

(a) Show that a typical person's demand for good 1 is given by

$$x_1 = M\rho^{-\beta}$$

(b) Suppose that originally $\rho = 1$. Suppose also that the government wishes to raise a given tax revenue T, but it can only do this by taxing consumption of good 1 at a uniform rate τ, so that $\rho = 1+\tau$. What phenomenon might this represent? Show that if $\beta < 1$, T always increases with τ. What happens if $\beta \geqslant 1$? Interpret this.

(c) Show that if $\beta = \frac{1}{2}$ and ϕ' is constant, for given M, u is a decreasing, concave function of the required tax revenue T.

(d) Under what circumstances might u no longer be concave in T?

(e) Show that under the circumstances of part (d) for any given revenue requirement T the government can maximise expected utility of any person by randomising the tax rate amongst the large numbers of individuals.

13.14 Analyse the *ex-ante* and *ex-post* welfare properties of the answer to Exercise 13.13 (e).

13.15 Imagine a group of individuals whose income is only from labour: each person is endowed with a specific level of ability which is reflected in his or her market wage w, and chooses L, the amount of time he or she works $0 \leqslant L \leqslant 1$. The minimum value of w in the population is w_0, and the mean value is γw_0, $y > 1$. The government imposes a tax-transfer scheme such that a person with pre-tax cash income M has after-tax cash income of $x = [1-\tau]\ [M-M_0] + M_0$ interpret the parameters τ and M_0.

(a) Assume that every individual's preferences can be represented by the utility function $x^\alpha [1-L]^{1-\alpha}$. Find the optimal labour supply by a person with wage w. [Hint: compare Exercise 5.3].

(b) Suppose the government wants to ensure that everyone works. What constraint is imposed on the values of τ and M_0?

(c) Assuming that everyone does work, and that the tax raised is used solely for the purposes of redistribution, show that this implies that τ and M_0 must satisfy the constraint:

$$M_0 = \alpha \gamma w_0 \frac{1 - \tau}{1 - \alpha\tau}$$

(d) If the government seeks to maximise the after-tax cash income of the poorest person subject to the above constraints show that the optimal tax rate is

$$\tau^* = \frac{1}{\alpha}\left[1 - \sqrt{\left(\frac{\gamma - \alpha\gamma}{\gamma - 1}\right)}\right]$$

Interpret this result.

*13.16 (a) Write down the Lagrangean for the constrained welfare maximation problem of choosing $\Delta p_1, \ldots, \Delta p_n$ ('taxes') to maximise (13.7) given (i) that all consumers act as price takers, (ii) pre-tax prices $\tilde{\mathbf{p}}$ remain unchanged, and (iii) a given revenue T is to be raised by the government.

(b) Hence establish (13.24).

Appendix A: Selected Proofs

Some of the results cited in the main text require mathematical tools that are slightly harder than those advertised in Section 1.3 of Chapter 1 (the *really* difficult ones have been cited without proof, with a bibliographic reference for the dedicated reader).

A.1 Proof of Theorem 3.4(a)

We first show that, under the specified conditions, $\mathbf{z}^*$ is unique, given $\mathbf{w}$ and Q_0. Suppose $G(\mathbf{z})$ is strictly concave-contoured and let there be two *distinct* solutions $\mathbf{z}^*$, $\mathbf{z}^{**}$ to the problem: then, by definition, we would have $G(\frac{1}{2}[\mathbf{z}^* + \mathbf{z}^{**}]) > G(\mathbf{z}^*) = Q_0$. Hence there is some $\hat{\mathbf{z}}$ lying on the Q_0-isoquant ($G(\hat{\mathbf{z}}) = Q_0$) where $\hat{\mathbf{z}} \equiv \frac{1}{2}\alpha[\mathbf{z}^* + \mathbf{z}^{**}]$ where $\alpha < 1$. But the outlay on inputs at $\hat{\mathbf{z}}$ would be $\Sigma_i \frac{1}{2}\alpha [w_i z_i^* + w_i z_i^{**}] = \alpha C(\mathbf{w}, Q_0)$. If $\mathbf{w} > \mathbf{0}$ then $\alpha C(\mathbf{w}, Q_0) < C(\mathbf{w}, Q_0)$; but this implies that $\hat{\mathbf{z}}$ would have a lower input cost than $\mathbf{z}^*$ or $\mathbf{z}^{**}$: a contradiction.

Now let us write the unique z_i^* as a function $\hat{D}^i(\mathbf{w}, Q_0)$ for given $\mathbf{w}$ and Q; we investigate whether $\hat{D}^i$ is continuous under the above conditions. Let $\{\mathbf{w}^1, \mathbf{w}^2, \mathbf{w}^3, \ldots\}$ be a sequence of input price vectors which converge to $\mathbf{w}$: $\lim_{t\to\infty} \mathbf{w}^t = \mathbf{w} > \mathbf{0}$. Write $\lim_{t\to\infty} \hat{D}^i(\mathbf{w}^t, Q) = \bar{z}_i$; we need to prove that $\bar{\mathbf{z}} = \mathbf{z}^*$. The fact that $\mathbf{z}^*$ is cost minimising for $(\mathbf{w}, Q)$ implies

$$\Sigma_i w_i \bar{z}_i \geqslant \Sigma_i w_i z_i^* \qquad \text{(A.1)}$$

where one has equality if and only if $\bar{\mathbf{z}} = \mathbf{z}^*$. If $\bar{\mathbf{z}} \neq \mathbf{z}^*$ then there is some α, where $0 < \alpha < 1$, such that

$$\Sigma_i w_i \bar{z}_i = \frac{1}{\alpha} \Sigma_i w_i z_i^* \qquad \text{(A.2)}$$

Consider any member of the above sequence of input prices. By cost minimisation we have

$$\Sigma_i w_i^t \hat{D}^i(\mathbf{w}^t, Q) \leqslant \Sigma_i w_i^t z_i^* \qquad \text{(A.3)}$$

Subtracting (A.3) from (A.2) we have

$$\Sigma_i[\, w_i \bar{z}_i - w_i^t \hat{D}^i(\mathbf{w}^t, Q)] \gtreqless \Sigma_i \left[\frac{w_i}{\alpha} - w_i^t\right] z_i^* \tag{A.4}$$

However, as $t \to \infty$, the limit of the left-hand side is zero and, since $\alpha < 1$, the limit of the right-hand side is strictly positive, a contradiction. Hence $\bar{\mathbf{z}} = \mathbf{z}^*$.

Proof of Theorem 3.4(b) follows by a similar route; see the next section also.

A.2 Proof of a Modified Version of Theorem 3.4

It is instructive to look at the proof in a slightly different version of Theorem 3.4 which brings out more clearly the way in which the solution functions are derived from the first-order conditions (3.21).

THEOREM 3.4′: (a) If there is some transform of the production function which has the Hessian property, then the conditional input demand functions are always well defined and continuous.
(b) If the production function has the Hessian property, then input demand functions are always well-defined and continuous.

Note that the requirement in part (a) is weaker since the Hessian property is merely applied to some transform of ψ of G and not necessarily G itself. We present the proof of part (b) Theorem 3.4′ first since it is slightly more straightforward.

Combine steps (1) and (2) on page 38 of Chapter 3 to write the profit maximisation problem as

$$\max_{\mathbf{z}} PG(\mathbf{z}) - \sum_{i=1}^{m} w_i z_i$$

where we have substituted in $Q = G(\mathbf{z})$ from the conditions for technical efficiency (3.22). Assuming that attention is restricted to inputs that are actually purchased, the first-order conditions give us:

$$\left.\begin{aligned} G_1(\mathbf{z}) &= w_1/P \\ \cdots & \quad \cdots \\ G_m(\mathbf{z}) &= w_m/P \end{aligned}\right\} \tag{A.5}$$

a system of m equations in m unknowns $\mathbf{z}$. The implicit function theorem[1]

[1] See Theorem 7.6 in Apostol, T.M. (1957) *Mathematical Analysis*, Addison-Wesley.

assures us that we may solve for the unknowns in terms of the parameters $w_1/P, \ldots, w_m/P$ if the matrix

$$\mathbf{H} = \begin{bmatrix} \frac{\partial G_1}{\partial z_1}, \frac{\partial G_1}{\partial z_2}, \ldots, \frac{\partial G_1}{\partial z_m} \\ \frac{\partial G_2}{\partial z_1}, \frac{\partial G_2}{\partial z_2}, \ldots, \frac{\partial G_2}{\partial z_m} \\ \ldots \quad \ldots \quad \ldots \quad \ldots \\ \frac{\partial G_m}{\partial z_1}, \frac{\partial G_m}{\partial z_2}, \ldots, \frac{\partial G_m}{\partial z_m} \end{bmatrix} \tag{A.6}$$

is non-singular. But G_i of course is simply $\partial G(\mathbf{z})/\partial z_i$ and so the (i,j)-th element of the matrix **H** is just G_{ij}. **H** is the Hessian matrix of second partial derivatives (see page 9 of Chapter 1). But if we assume the Hessian condition to hold, **H** is negative definite and so is non-singular. Hence there exist continuous functions $\phi^1, \ldots, \phi^m$ such that we may write

$$z_i = \phi^i(w_1/P, \ldots, w_m/P) \tag{A.7}$$

as a solution to (A.5). A simple change in notation gives us (3.33).

The method of proof of Theorem 3.4′(a) is similar to the above. Minimising $\Sigma w_i z_i$ subject to $G(\mathbf{z}) \gtrless Q_0$ is clearly equivalent to minimising $\Sigma w_i z_i$ subject to $\hat{G}(\mathbf{z}) \gtrless \hat{Q}_0$ where $\hat{G}(\mathbf{z}) = \psi(G(\mathbf{z}))$, $\hat{Q}_0 = \psi(Q_0)$ and ψ is an increasing function. In view of the premise of the theorem we may select ψ such that $\hat{G}(\mathbf{z})$ has the Hessian property. The first-order conditions for this modified problem yield:

$$\begin{aligned} \lambda_0 \hat{G}_i(\mathbf{z}) &= w_i, \quad i = 1, \ldots, m \\ \hat{G}(\mathbf{z}) &= \hat{Q}_0 \end{aligned} \tag{A.8}$$

where λ_0 is the Lagrange multiplier, cf. equations (3.21), (3.22). This is a system of $m+1$ equations in $m+1$ unknowns $z_1, \ldots, z_m, \lambda_0$. Consider the matrix:

$$\hat{\mathbf{H}} = \begin{bmatrix} \lambda_0 \hat{G}_{11} & \ldots & \lambda_0 \hat{G}_{1m} & \hat{G}_1 \\ \ldots & & \ldots & \ldots \\ \lambda_0 \hat{G}_{m1} & \ldots & \lambda_0 \hat{G}_{mm} & \hat{G}_m \\ \hat{G}_1 & \ldots & \hat{G}_m & 0 \end{bmatrix} \tag{A.9}$$

$\hat{\mathbf{H}}$ is non-singular because $\hat{G}$ has the Hessian property so that the m-by-m submatrix $\|G_{ij}\|$ is non-singular, and $\hat{G}_i$ are not all zero. Hence by the implicit function theorem there exist continuous solutions of the form (3.32).

A.3 Proof of Theorem 7.3

The proof relies on the setting up of a continuous function Γ from the set of normalised prices J (which is convex and compact) into J itself. This function can be thought of as a notional 'price adjustment' for any given price vector selected from J, and is constructed so that no such 'adjustment' takes place if the vector selected happens to be an equilibrium price vector. Choose an arbitrary large positive number Δ, and define δ_i, $i = 1, \ldots, m$ thus

$$\delta_i = \begin{cases} \min\{E_i, \Delta\} & \text{if} \quad E_i \geqslant 0 \\ \max\{E_i, -p_i\} & \text{if} \quad E_i < 0 \end{cases} \tag{A.10}$$

Now consider the vector of 'adjusted' prices $\hat{\mathbf{p}}$ given by

$$\hat{p}_i = \Gamma_i(\mathbf{p}) = \frac{p_i + \delta_i}{1 + \sum_{j=1}^{n} \delta_j} \tag{A.11}$$

Observe that, by construction, Γ_i is a continuous function. Also $\hat{p}_i \geqslant 0$ and $\Sigma_j \hat{p}_j = 1$: so $\hat{\mathbf{p}} \in J$. Hence Γ is a continuous function from a convex set (J) into itself. Brouwer's theorem[2] assures us that there must exist $\mathbf{p}^* \in J$ such that

$$\mathbf{p}^* = \Gamma(\mathbf{p}^*) \tag{A.12}$$

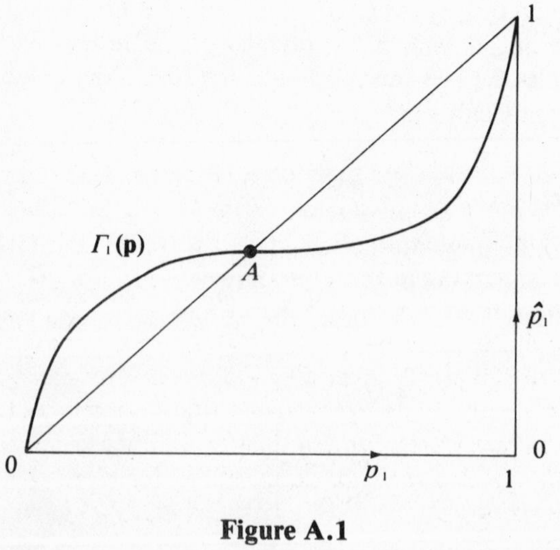

Figure A.1

[2] See Green, J. and Heller, W.P. (1981) 'Mathematical analysis and convexity with applications to economics', in K.J. Arrow and M.D. Intiligator (eds) *Handbook of Mathematical Economics*, Vol. I, Ch. 1.

Observe that $\mathbf{p}^*$ must correspond to Definition 7.8 of an equilibrium price vector, see page 140 of Chapter 7. For, suppose that for some i: $E_i(\mathbf{p}^*)>0$, then (from A.10) $\delta_i > 0$. If $p_i^* > 0$ then Walras' Law (7.26) implies that there is some l which $p_l E_l(\mathbf{p}) < 0$ so that (from A.6) $\delta_l < 0$; otherwise we must have $\delta_l = 0$ for some l. In either case we clearly would *not* have $\mathbf{p}^* = \Gamma(\mathbf{p}^*)$ thus violating the definition of $\mathbf{p}^*$ in (A.12). Again, suppose $E_i(\mathbf{p}^*) \leqslant 0$ for all i, but that for some i we have $E_i(\mathbf{p}^*) < 0$ and $p_i^* > 0$. Then (A.10) implies $\delta_i < 0$, and Walras' law implies that for some l we have $E_l(\mathbf{p}^*) > 0$, so that $\delta_l > 0$. So again, we would find $\mathbf{p}^* \neq \Gamma(\mathbf{p}^*)$, in violation of (A.12). Hence $\mathbf{p}^*$ is indeed the required equilibrium price vector. In the case of $n = 2$ the situation can be represented by Figure A.1. The 'original' price p_1 is measured horizontally, and the 'adjusted' price $\hat{p}_1$ vertically. The wavy line represents the function Γ_1, and A is the point at which we find $p_1^* = \Gamma_1(\mathbf{p}^*)$.

A.4 Proof of Theorem 8.3

The core of this proof is the demonstration of the existence of a so-called separating hyperplane. A hyperplane is a set in $\mathbb{R}^n$ thus:

$$\left\{\mathbf{x} \in \mathbb{R}^n \colon \sum_{i=1}^{n} p_i x_i = M\right\} \tag{A.13}$$

where $p_1, p_2, \ldots, p_n$ (not all zero) and M are constants. Two sets X^1, X^2 in $\mathbb{R}^n$ are said to be *separated* by a hyperplane if we can find constants $p_1, \ldots, p_n$ and M $(\mathbf{p} \neq \mathbf{0})$ such that

$$\Sigma_i p_i x_i \geqslant M \quad \text{for all} \quad \mathbf{x} \in X^1 \tag{A.14}$$

$$\Sigma_i p_i x_i \leqslant M \quad \text{for all} \quad \mathbf{x} \in X^2 \tag{A.15}$$

We now make use of an important result in convex sets.

Let X^1 and X^2 be two convex sets in $\mathbb{R}^n$, let X^1 have a non-empty interior, and let the intersection of X^2 with the *interior* of X^1 be empty: then X^1 and X^2 can be separated by a hyperplane.[3]

Let us apply this to Theorem 8.3. If $\hat{\alpha} \equiv ([\hat{\mathbf{x}}^h], [\hat{\mathbf{y}}^f])$ is the Pareto efficient allocation, then define the set $\overline{B}(\hat{\mathbf{x}})$ analogously to the definition in equation (7.41) of Chapter 7. Since all goods are private goods $\hat{\mathbf{x}} = \Sigma_h \hat{\mathbf{x}}^h$, and $\overline{B}(\hat{\mathbf{x}})$ represents the set of aggregate consumption vectors which correspond to allocations that are Pareto superior to, or are equivalent to $\hat{\alpha}$. By virtue of the assumption of concave-contoured utility functions this set is convex; by virtue of the assumption of greed any $\mathbf{x} \geqslant \hat{\mathbf{x}}$ must belong to $\overline{B}(\hat{\mathbf{x}})$, and any

---

[3] See Sydsaeter, K. (1981) *Topics in Mathematical Analysis for Economists*, Academic Press, p. 307.

$\mathbf{x} \geqslant \hat{\mathbf{x}}$ must be an interior point. Also define the set $Z \equiv \{\mathbf{x} : \mathbf{x} \leqslant \mathbf{y} + \mathbf{R}; \mathbf{y} \in Y\}$ where $\mathbf{R}$ is the vector of resource endowments for the economy: this is the set of feasible aggregate consumption vectors. Since it is assumed that each firm's technology set is convex and there are no externalities, Z is convex. By definition of a Pareto efficient allocation $\hat{\mathbf{x}} \in \bar{B}(\hat{\mathbf{x}})$ and $\hat{\mathbf{x}} \in Z$, but no vector in Z could also belong to the *interior* of $\bar{B}(\hat{\mathbf{x}})$ (for, if it did, then there would be some feasible allocation in which some greedy consumer could be made better off, without anyone else being made worse off). So there is a separating hyperplane (A.13) with (A.14) holding for $\bar{B}(\hat{\mathbf{x}})$ and (A.15) holding for Z. Obviously $\Sigma_i p_i \hat{x}_i = M$, since $\hat{\mathbf{x}}$ lies on the boundary of both sets, and in view of (A.14) we have

$$\Sigma_i p_i [x_i - \hat{x}_i] \geqslant 0 \quad \text{for all } \mathbf{x} \geqslant \hat{\mathbf{x}} \tag{A.16}$$

The inequality (A.16) reveals immediately that $\mathbf{p} \geqslant \mathbf{0}$.

It remains to be shown that the semi-positive vector $\mathbf{p}$ plays the role of a genuine competitive equilibrium price vector. Using (A.15) and the definition of Z we have

$$\Sigma_i p_i [y_i + R_i] \leqslant \Sigma_i p_i [\hat{y}_i + R_i] \quad \text{for all } \mathbf{y} \in Y \tag{A.17}$$

In view of the absence of externalities we have $\mathbf{y} = \Sigma_f \mathbf{y}^f$ and so (A.17) implies

$$\Sigma_i \Sigma_f p_i y_i^f \leqslant \Sigma_i \Sigma_f p_i \hat{y}_i^f \quad \text{for all } \mathbf{y}^f \in Y^f \tag{A.18}$$

But this implies $\Sigma_i p_i \hat{y}_i^f \geqslant \Sigma_i p_i y_i^f$ for any firm f: in other words, given prices $\mathbf{p}$, firm f would maximise profits at $\hat{\mathbf{y}}^f$.

Next observe that an analogous argument yields the result:

$$\text{`}U^h(\tilde{\mathbf{x}}^h) \geqslant U^h(\hat{\mathbf{x}}^h)\text{'} \quad \text{implies} \quad \text{`}\Sigma_i p_i \tilde{x}_i^h \geqslant M^h\text{'} \text{ for all } h \tag{A.19}$$

where $M^h \equiv \Sigma_i p_i \hat{x}_i^h > 0$.[4] In other words: any bundle that yields h at least as much utility as $\hat{\mathbf{x}}^h$ must cost at least as much as $\hat{\mathbf{x}}^h$ when valued at prices $\mathbf{p}$. So, consider any arbitrary $\mathbf{x}^h$ that h *could* afford at these prices, i.e. such that $\Sigma_h p_i x_i^h \leqslant M^h$. Take some positive scalar α. Obviously $\alpha \Sigma_h p_i x_i^h < M^h$ for all $\alpha < 1$. So, in view of (A.19) we have, for any $\alpha < 1$:

$$\text{`}\alpha \Sigma_i p_i x_i < M^h\text{'} \quad \text{implies} \quad \text{`}U^h(\alpha \mathbf{x}^h) < U^h(\hat{\mathbf{x}}^h)\text{'} \tag{A.20}$$

and in the limit, as $\alpha \to 1$ we see that we indeed have the result that, given prices $\mathbf{p}$, $\hat{\mathbf{x}}^h$ maximises $U^h(\mathbf{x}^h)$ over the budget set $\{\mathbf{x}^h : \mathbf{x}^h \geqslant \mathbf{0}, \Sigma_i p_i x_i^h \leqslant M^h\}$. Hence the allocation $\hat{a}$ and the associated price vector $\mathbf{p}$ is indeed a competitive equilibrium since each household is maximising utility, each firm is maximising profits and the allocation satisfies the materials balance condition (7.4) of Chapter 7.

---

[4] Observe that this follows from the assumption that $\hat{x}_i^h > 0$ for all h and i. This assumption could be weakened; but one must ensure that each household would have an income that would enable it to survive at $\hat{\mathbf{x}}^h$.

APPENDIX B: Answers to Exercises

Chapter 2

2.1 (a), (b)

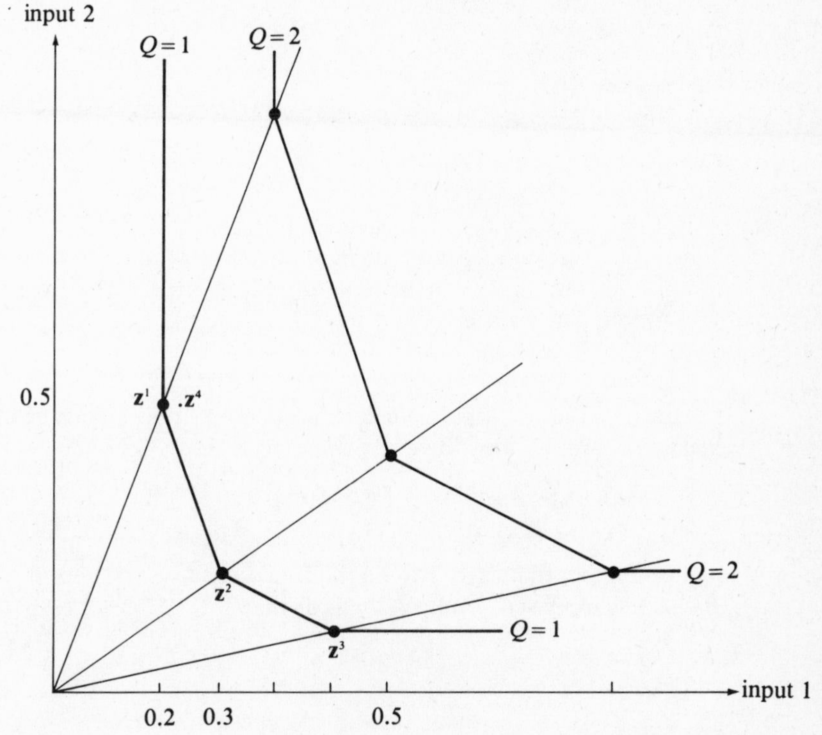

(c) Clearly $\mathbf{z}^4$ should *not* be included in the isoquant (since $\mathbf{z}^4$ requires strictly more inputs to produce one unit of output than does $\mathbf{z}^2$ so that it cannot be efficient).

2.2

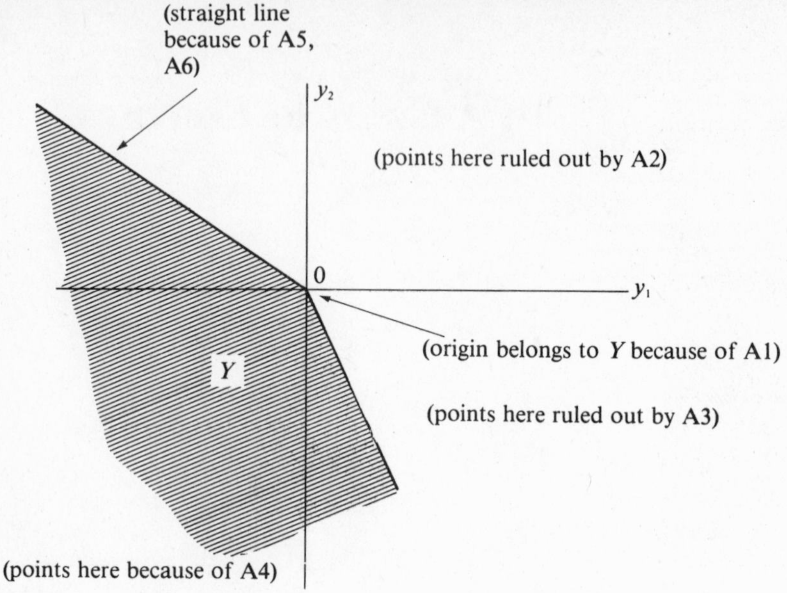

2.3 Note first that by Axiom A4, $Z \subset Y$ where $Z = \{\mathbf{z}:\mathbf{z} \in \mathbb{R}^n, \mathbf{z} \leqslant \mathbf{0}\}$, i.e. the entire non-positive orthant. Clearly, then, $(-Z) \subset (-Y)$. But $(-Z)$ is of course nothing other than $\mathbb{R}^n_+$, the entire non-negative orthant. We may, therefore, use Axiom A4 to write

$$(-Y) = \mathbb{R}^n_+ \cup X$$

where X is defined as the set of points belonging to $(-Y)$ that do not lie in the non-negative orthant (X may of course be empty). Now A3 implies

$$\{\mathbf{0}\} = Y \cap (-Y) = Y \cap [\mathbb{R}^n_+ \cup X]$$
$$\Rightarrow \{\mathbf{0}\} = [Y \cap \mathbb{R}^n_+] \cup [Y \cap X]$$

But this equation implies that each term on the RHS in square brackets must be *either* $\{\mathbf{0}\}$ *or* the empty set. Axiom A1 tells us that $Y \cap \mathbb{R}^n_+$ is not empty. So:

$$Y \cap \mathbb{R}^n_+ = \{\mathbf{0}\}$$

2.4 As illustrated in the figure, only processes 1, 2, 4 and 6 are technically efficient. Given the resource constraint, the economically efficient input combination is a mixture of processes 4 and 6.

Note that in the neighbourhood of this efficient point MRTS $= 1$. So, as illustrated in the enlarged diagram below, 20 extra units of input 2 clearly enable more output to be produced than 10 extra units of input 1.

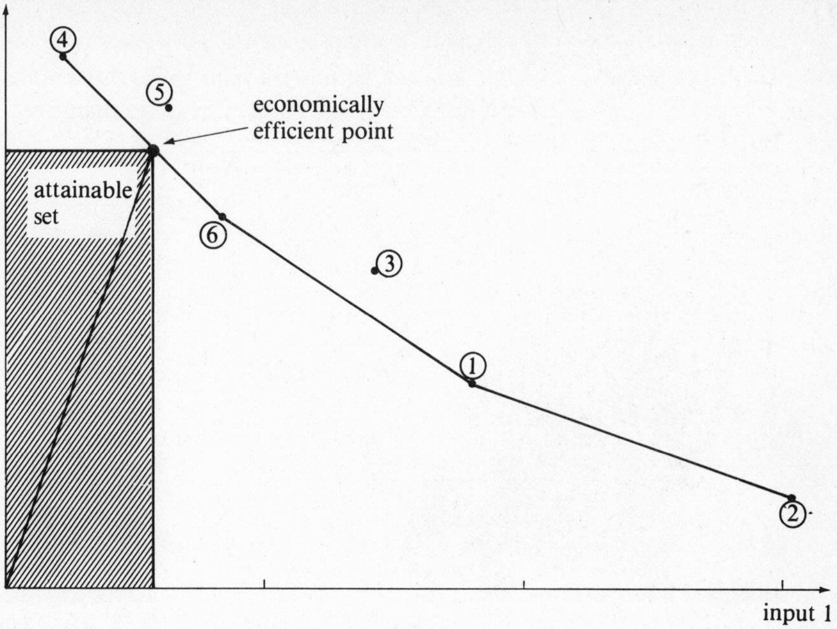
4
5
economically
efficient point
attainable
set
6
3
1
2
input 1

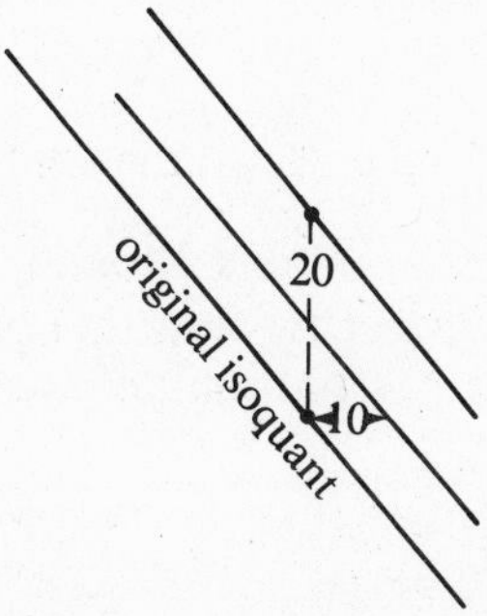
original isoquant
20
10

2.5

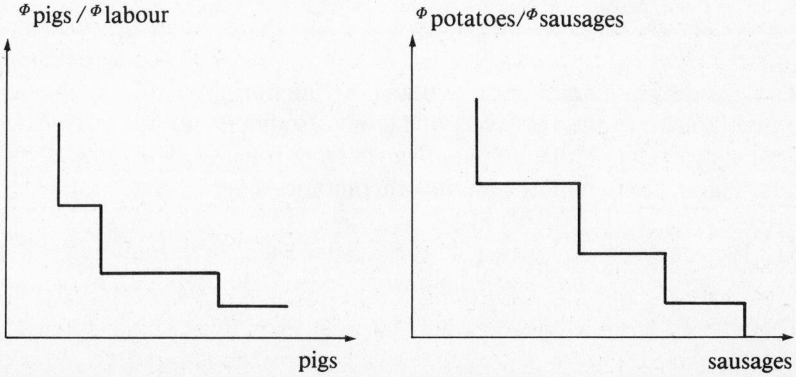
$^{\Phi}$pigs / $^{\Phi}$labour
pigs
$^{\Phi}$potatoes/$^{\Phi}$sausages
sausages

2.6 (a) Isoquants are straight lines. Production possibility frontier is a quarter circle. (b) All axioms satisfied if $\alpha = \beta = \gamma < 1$. Isoquants will then be similar to hyperbolas – cf. Exercise 2.8(a). (c) Similar to (b); all axioms satisfied. (d) Production possibility frontier is a straight line. Isoquants rectangular. All axioms satisfied if $\alpha > 0$.

2.7

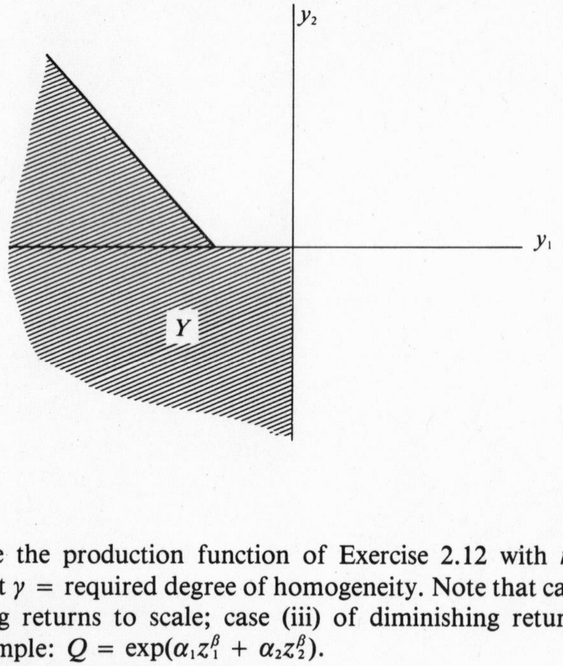

2.8 (a) Use the production function of Exercise 2.12 with $m = 2$, for example. Put γ = required degree of homogeneity. Note that case (ii) is that of increasing returns to scale; case (iii) of diminishing returns to scale. (iv) For example: $Q = \exp(\alpha_1 z_1^\beta + \alpha_2 z_2^\beta)$.
(b) Homogeneity of degree γ implies

$$G(\lambda \mathbf{z}) = \lambda^\gamma G(\mathbf{z}) \quad \text{for arbitrary } \lambda > 0$$

Differentiate with respect to z_i:

$$\lambda\, G_i(\lambda \mathbf{z}) = \lambda^\gamma G_i(\mathbf{z})$$
$$\Rightarrow \quad G_i(\lambda \mathbf{z}) = \lambda^{\gamma-1} G_i(\mathbf{z})$$

2.9 Consider as an example the production function $Q = [z_1^2 + z_2^2]^{\frac{1}{2}}$ where the two inputs are the two sorts of labour. Isoquants are quarter circles. Marginal product of either input is *always* higher when one is used on its own rather than in combination with the other input. A5 and A6 are violated.

2.10 We are going to investigate the behaviour in the neighbourhood of $\alpha = 1$ by letting $\alpha = 1 + \mathrm{d}\alpha$ and allowing $\mathrm{d}\alpha \rightarrow 0$. By definition of decreasing returns:

$$G([1 + d\alpha]\mathbf{z}) < [1 + d\alpha]G(\mathbf{z}), \quad \text{if } d\alpha > 0$$

Subtracting $G(\mathbf{z})$ from both sides and dividing by $d\alpha$ we get:

$$\frac{G([1 + d\alpha]\mathbf{z}) - G(\mathbf{z})}{d\alpha} < G(\mathbf{z})$$

The left-hand side is simply $\partial G(\alpha\mathbf{z})/\partial\alpha$. For increasing returns in this neighbourhood we would have $\partial G(\alpha\mathbf{z})/\partial\alpha > 1$.

2.11 (i) In view of the constant returns to scale assumption we may obviously write

$$\alpha\, G(z_1, z_2) = G(\alpha z_1, \alpha z_2)$$

for any arbitrary positive number α. Put $\alpha = 1/z_2$ and let $z_1/z_2 \equiv k$; then this yields:

$$G(z_1, z_2)/z_2 = G(k, 1)$$

Now, noting that $Q \leqslant G(z_1, z_2)$ and using the other definitions given, we have immediately: $q \leqslant g(k)$.
(ii) Consider the identity

$$g(k) = G(z_2 k, z_2)/z_2$$

Differentiate with respect to k

$$g'(k) = [z_2 G_1(z_2 k, z_2)]/z_2 = G_1(z_1, z_2)$$

(iii) Euler's theorem yields

$$z_1 G_1(z_1, z_2) + z_2 G_2(z_1, z_2) = G(z_1, z_2)$$

Divide by z_2 and substitute in from the definitions and result (b):

$$kg'(k) + G_2(z_1, z_2) = g(k)$$
$$\Rightarrow G_2(z_1, z_2) = g(k) - kg'(k)$$

The corresponding conditions on g and its first derivative are

$$g(0) = 0;\ \lim_{k\to\infty} (g(k)/k) = 0;\ g'(k) > 0,\ g(k) - kg'(k) > 0 \quad \text{for}$$

$$0 < k < \infty;\ \lim_{k\to 0} g'(k) = \infty;\ \lim_{k\to 0} (g(k) - kg'(k)) = 0$$

$$\lim_{k\to\infty} g'(k) = 0;\ \lim_{k\to\infty} (g(k) - kg'(k)) = \infty$$

Write down the MRTS, i.e. the slope of the contour (isoquant)

$$\frac{dz_2}{dz_1} = -\frac{G_2(z_1, z_2)}{G_1(z_1, z_2)} = \frac{-g(k)}{g'(k)} + k < 0$$

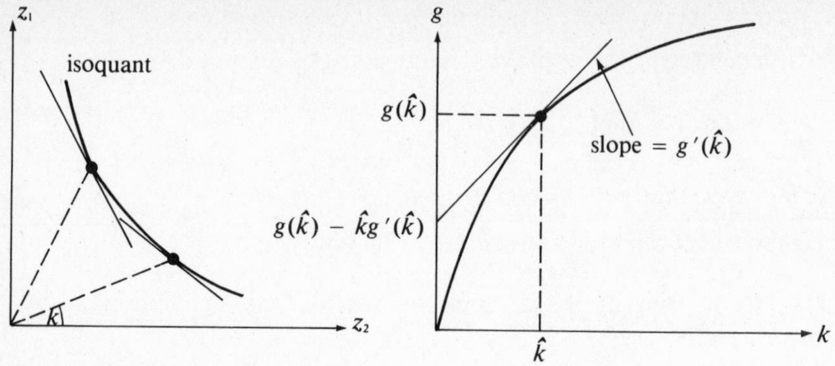

If G is strictly concave contoured then dz_2/dz_1 must strictly decrease with increases in k (i.e. the absolute slope must increase with increases in k – see diagram), i.e. increases in z_1/z_2. Differentiating the above formula with respect to k the condition is then:

$$-1 + \frac{g(k)g''(k)}{[g'(k)]^2} + 1 < 0$$

$$\Rightarrow g''(k) < 0$$

The function g is illustrated in the right-hand diagram.

2.12 Parameter γ determines returns to scale – see Exercise 2.8. Write the production function in logarithmic form:

$$\log G(\mathbf{z}) = \frac{\gamma}{\beta} \log (\Sigma_i \alpha_i z_i^\beta)$$

Differentiate with respect to z_i:

$$G_i(\mathbf{z})/G(\mathbf{z}) = \alpha_i \gamma z_i^{\beta-1}/\Sigma_l \alpha_l z_l^\beta$$

$$\Rightarrow \quad G_i(\mathbf{z})/G_j(\mathbf{z}) = \frac{\alpha_i}{\alpha_j} [z_i/z_j]^{\beta-1}$$

Take logs again and rearrange slightly:

$$\log (G_i/G_j) = \log (\alpha_i/\alpha_j) + [1-\beta] \log (z_j/z_i)$$

Differentiate:

$$\text{dlog} (G_i/G_j) = [1-\beta] \text{ dlog} (z_j/z_i)$$

Using Definition 2.5 immediately yields $\sigma = 1/[1-\beta]$. Note carefully the use, twice, in this proof of the device of taking logs and differentiating; this often saves a great deal of tedious manipulation.

To see the case where $\sigma = 1$ note that from the definition of the production function we may write:

$$\frac{[Q^{1/\gamma}]^{\beta}-1}{\beta} = \Sigma_i \alpha_i \frac{z_i^{\beta}-1}{\beta}$$

Let $\beta \to 0$ (so that $\sigma \to 1$). We get

$$\log Q^{1/\gamma} = \Sigma_i \alpha_i \log z_i$$

$$\Rightarrow Q = \left[\prod_{i=1}^{m} z_i^{\alpha_i}\right]^{\gamma}$$

If $\gamma = 1$, then from above we have $G_i = \alpha_i Q z_i^{\beta-1} \Sigma_l \alpha_l z_l^{\beta}$. Total factor payments would then be $\Sigma z_i G_i = \Sigma_i \alpha_i Q z_i^{\beta} / \Sigma_l \alpha_l z_l^{\beta} = Q$.

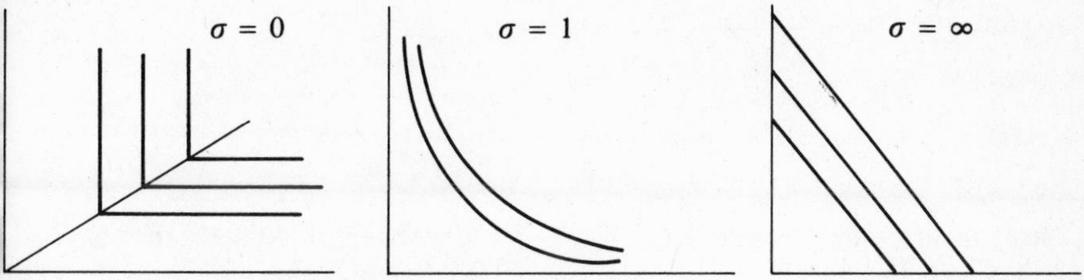

2.13 Consider $0 < \alpha < 1$ and a scalar $\lambda > 1$. In the case where $b > 0$ we find

$$[\lambda z_1]^{\alpha} + [\lambda z_2 - b]^{\alpha} > \lambda^{\alpha} z_1^{\alpha} + \lambda^{\alpha}[z_2 - b]^{\alpha}$$

$$\Rightarrow [[\lambda z_1]^{\alpha} + [\lambda z_2 - b]^{\alpha}]^{1/\alpha} > \lambda Q$$

It is easy to show that the above inequality also holds for $\alpha \lesseqgtr 0$. Hence for (a) we have increasing returns to scale. In like manner we can show that case (b) yields decreasing returns to scale.

Using the method of Exercise 2.12 and differentiating *along the isoquant* we may write the elasticity of substitution as

$$\sigma = \frac{1}{1-\alpha} \frac{1+A[1-b/z_2]}{1+A}$$

where $A \equiv \left[\frac{z_1}{z_2 - b}\right]^{\alpha}$

Clearly in case (a) $\sigma < \dfrac{1}{1-\alpha}$; in case (b) $\sigma > \dfrac{1}{1-\alpha}$ and as scale is expanded (z_1, z_2 get large) $A \to 1$, $b/z_2 \to 0$ and $\sigma \to \dfrac{1}{1-\alpha}$.

2.14 It is convenient to establish the second result first. From Exercise 2.11 we know we can write

$$\frac{G_2(\mathbf{z})}{G_1(\mathbf{z})} = \frac{g(k)}{g'(k)} - k$$

where $k \equiv z_1/z_2$.
So, using Definition 2.5 we have

$$\frac{1}{\sigma} = \frac{\partial \log (G_2/G_1)}{\partial \log (z_1/z_2)} = k\,\frac{\partial \log (g/g' - k)}{\partial k}$$

$$= -\frac{kgg''}{g'[g - kg']}$$

$$\Rightarrow \sigma = \frac{g'}{g''}\left[\frac{g'}{g} - \frac{1}{k}\right]$$

Now, noting that $G_1 = g'$, $G_2 = g - kg'$, we see immediately that $G_{12} = G_{21} = [g' - kg'' - g']\dfrac{1}{z_2} = -kg''/z_2$. Since, $z_2 g(k) = G(\mathbf{z})$ the first part of the result follows immediately.

Chapter 3

3.1 By Definition $C(\mathbf{w}^j, Q) = \sum_{i=1}^{m} w_i z_i^* = \sum_{i=1}^{m} w_i \hat{D}^i(\mathbf{w}, Q)$. But $\hat{D}^i$ is homogeneous of degree zero in $\mathbf{w}$, so it is immediate that C must be homogeneous of degree one in $\mathbf{w}$.

$C(\alpha \mathbf{w}^1 + [1-\alpha]\mathbf{w}^2, Q) = \alpha \sum_{i=1}^{m} w_i^1 z_i^* + [1-\alpha] \sum_{i=1}^{m} w_i^2 z_i^*$ where $\mathbf{z}^*$ is the cost-minimising input vector for Q at input prices $\alpha\mathbf{w}^1 + [1-\alpha]\mathbf{w}^2$. But, by definition, we also have $C(\mathbf{w}^j, Q) \leqslant \sum_i w_i^j z_i^*$, $j = 1,2$ with equality only if $\mathbf{z}^*$ is cost minimising for w^j. Therefore the RHS of the above equation must be $\geqslant \alpha C(\mathbf{w}^1, Q) + [1-\alpha] C(\mathbf{w}^2, Q)$.

Let $\mathbf{z}^*$ be the optimal input vector for producing given output Q at input prices $\mathbf{w}$. By virtue of homogeneity of degree γ we know that $Q = G(\mathbf{z}^*)$ implies $\alpha^\gamma Q = G(\alpha \mathbf{z}^*)$ for arbitrary $\alpha > 0$. Now consider $\mathbf{z}^{**}$, the optimal input combination required to produce an output $\alpha^\gamma Q$ given input prices $\mathbf{w}$.

Because G is homothetic we must have $\mathbf{z}^{**}$ proportional to $\mathbf{z}^*$; clearly $\mathbf{z}^{**}$ cannot be *less* than $\alpha\mathbf{z}^*$, for if so it would be infeasible to produce $\alpha^\gamma Q$; moreover $\mathbf{z}^{**}$ cannot be *greater* than $\alpha\mathbf{z}^*$, because if so it would not be a least cost input vector. Hence $\mathbf{z}^{**} = \alpha\mathbf{z}^*$. Thus we have

$$\begin{aligned} C(\mathbf{w},\alpha^\gamma Q) &= \Sigma\, w_i z_i^{**} \\ &= \alpha\, \Sigma w_i z_i^* = \alpha C(\mathbf{w},Q) \end{aligned}$$

Now, arbitrarily set $\alpha^\gamma = Q^{-1}$ in this equation. Then we get

$$c = Q^{-1/\gamma} C(\mathbf{w},Q)$$

where $c \equiv C(\mathbf{w},1)$. So:

$$C(\mathbf{w},Q) = cQ^{1/\gamma}$$

Hence, differentiating: $C_Q = \dfrac{c}{\gamma} Q^{\frac{1-\gamma}{\gamma}} > 0$ if $\gamma > 0$.

$$C_{QQ} = \frac{1-\gamma}{\gamma^2} c\, Q^{\frac{1-2\gamma}{\gamma}} \gtreqless 0 \quad \text{as} \quad \gamma \lesseqgtr 1.$$

For such functions: increasing returns $\Leftrightarrow$ falling MC; decreasing returns $\Leftrightarrow$ rising MC.

3.2 We establish first the relationship between output and AC given that diminishing returns hold everywhere. Consider two output levels $Q_1 < Q_2$ and their associated *cost-minimising* input vectors $\mathbf{z}^1$, $\mathbf{z}^2$, for some given vector of input prices. Now construct a vector $\mathbf{z}^3$ such that $\mathbf{z}^2 = \alpha\mathbf{z}^3$ where α is a scalar greater than 1 and $Q_1 = G(\mathbf{z}^3)$ where G is the production function. By diminishing returns $G(\mathbf{z}^2) < \alpha G(\mathbf{z}^3)$, so $Q_2 < \alpha Q_1$; and because $\mathbf{z}^1$ is cost minimising for Q_1 we must have $\Sigma w_i z_i^3 \geqslant C(\mathbf{w},Q_1)$. Hence

$$\frac{C(\mathbf{w},Q_1)}{Q_1} \leqslant \frac{\Sigma w_i z_i^2/\alpha}{Q_1} = \frac{C(\mathbf{w},Q_2)/\alpha}{Q_1}$$

But $\alpha Q_1 > Q_2$ and so

$$C(\mathbf{w},Q_1)/Q_1 < C(\mathbf{w},Q_2)/Q_2$$

Average cost is increasing in Q. Hence $\dfrac{\partial}{\partial Q}(C/Q) > 0$. But this implies $C_Q/Q - C/Q^2 > 0 \Rightarrow C_Q > C/Q$. Marginal cost is greater than average cost.

Similarly if returns to scale are increasing everywhere $C(\mathbf{w},Q)$ must be decreasing in Q and $C_Q < C/Q$.

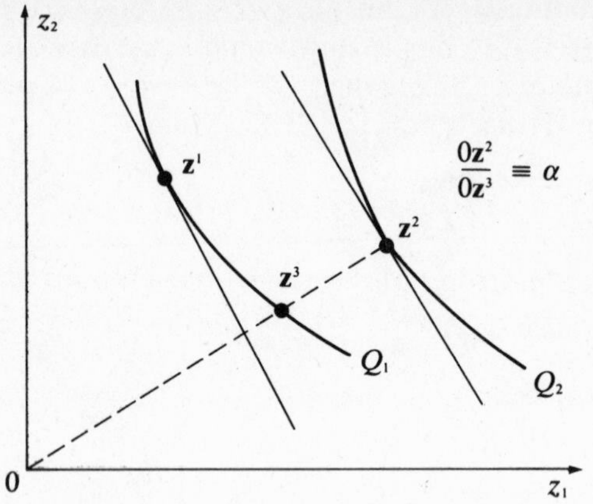

3.3 (a) We have to minimise the Lagrangean $z_1 w_1 + z_2 w_2 + \lambda[Q - z_1^\alpha z_2^\beta]$. Because of the shape of the isoquants an interior solution is bound to exist for all finite $\mathbf{w}$ (check this). The first-order conditions are:

$$w_1 - \alpha\lambda z_1^{\alpha-1} z_2^\beta = 0$$
$$w_2 - \beta\lambda z_1^\alpha z_2^{\beta-1} = 0$$

Substituting back for Q and rearranging these two expressions yields

$$Q = z_1^\alpha z_2^\beta = [\alpha\lambda Q/w_1]^\alpha [\beta\lambda Q/w_2]^\beta$$

$$\Rightarrow \lambda Q = A[w_1^\alpha w_2^\beta Q]^\gamma \quad \text{where } \gamma \equiv \frac{1}{\alpha+\beta} \text{ and } A \equiv \alpha^{-\alpha\gamma}\beta^{-\beta\gamma}$$

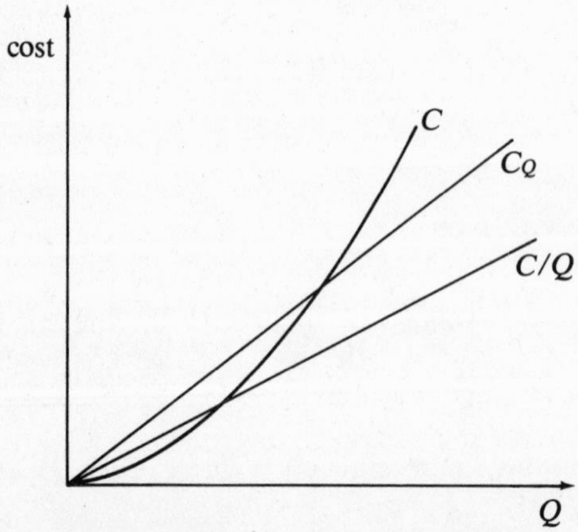

(the case where $\gamma = 2$)

Now $C(\mathbf{w},Q) = z_1 w_1 + z_2 w_2$ where $\mathbf{z}$ is the cost-minimising input. But using the two equations of the first-order conditions this implies

$$C(\mathbf{w},Q) = \alpha\lambda z_1^\alpha z_2^\beta + \beta\lambda z_1^\alpha z_2^\beta = [\alpha + \beta]\lambda Q$$

Therefore

$$C(\mathbf{w},Q) = A\,[w_1^\alpha w_2^\beta Q]^\gamma$$

the required cost function.
(b) Using the same approach as part (a) we find:

$$C(\mathbf{w},Q) = Q^{1/\gamma}\left[\sum_{i=1}^{m} [w_i/a_i]^\theta\right]^{1/\theta} \quad \text{for} \quad \beta \neq 0$$

where $a_i \equiv \alpha_i^{1/\beta}$ and $\theta \equiv \beta/[\beta-1]$. In the special case $\beta = 0$ we have a cost function similar to that in part (a). If $\beta \to 1$ then $\theta \to -\infty$ and $C(\mathbf{w},Q) = Q^{1/\gamma}\min\{w_i/a_i\}$. If $\beta \to -\infty$ then $\theta \to 1$ and $C(\mathbf{w},Q) = Q^{1/\gamma}\Sigma_i[w_i/a_i]$. Compare these with the special cases in the answer to Exercise 2.12.

3.4 If the firm produces at $Q^* > 0$, then the first-order conditions yield

$$P = C_Q(\mathbf{w},Q^*)$$

Differentiate this with respect to w_i keeping P and all other w_j constant and allowing Q^* to vary:

$$0 = C_{Qi} + C_{QQ}\frac{\partial Q^*}{\partial w_i}$$

Hence, by definition of inferiority, we must have

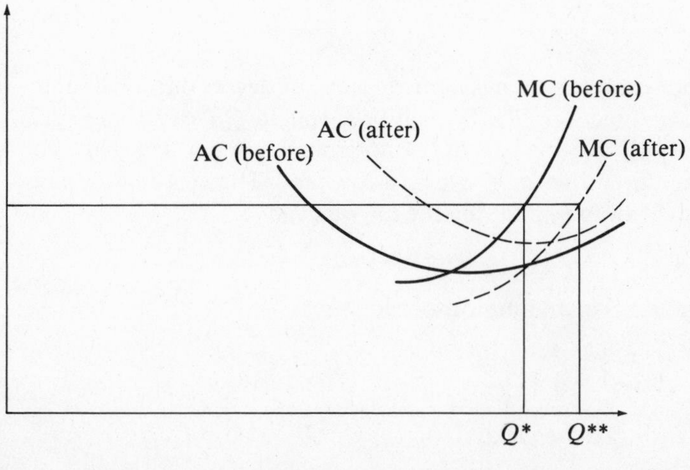

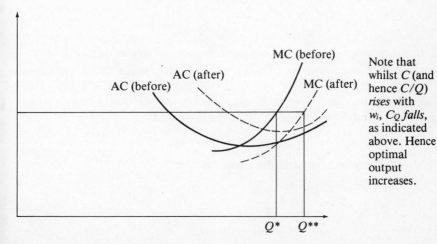

Note that whilst C (and hence C/Q) *rises* with w_i, C_Q *falls*, as indicated above. Hence optimal output increases.

$$- C_{Qi}/C_{QQ} > 0$$

Since $C_{QQ} \gtrless 0$ in the relevant region this implies $C_{Qi} < 0$ (compare equation 3.43).

3.5

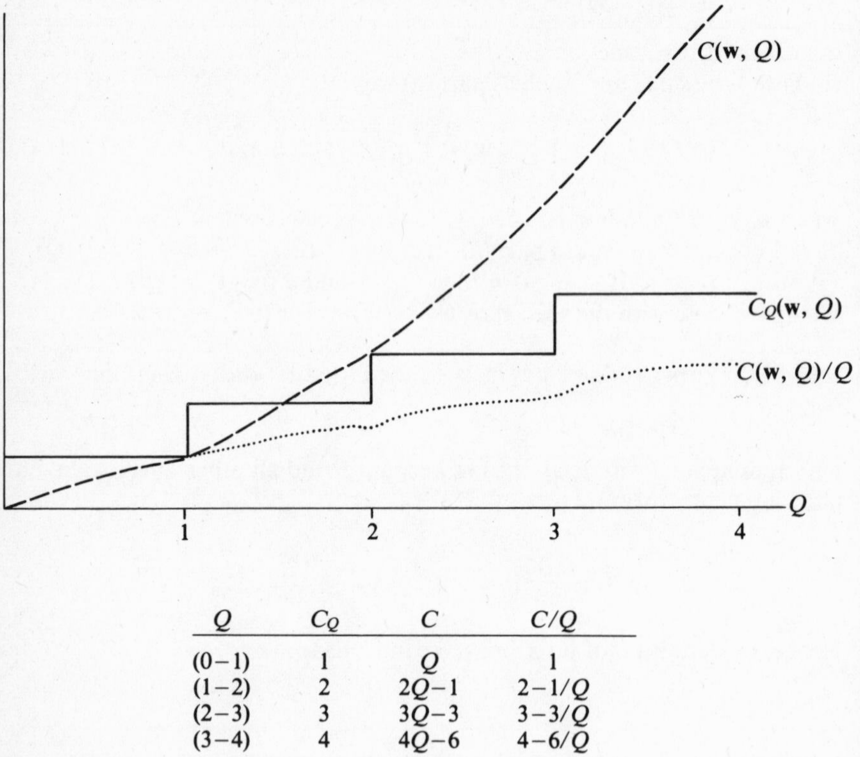

Q	C_Q	C	C/Q
(0–1)	1	Q	1
(1–2)	2	$2Q-1$	$2-1/Q$
(2–3)	3	$3Q-3$	$3-3/Q$
(3–4)	4	$4Q-6$	$4-6/Q$

3.6 Since production function is homogeneous of degree one in all inputs, the long-run cost function $C(\mathbf{w},Q)$ will be linear in Q (see Exercise 3.2). Hence long-run MC = long-run AC, a horizontal straight line. Now consider the short run and let $a \equiv \alpha_3 z_3^{-1}$, a constant. The cost-minimisation problem is equivalent to minimising the Lagrangean

$$w_1 z_1 + w_2 z_2 - \lambda [Q^{-1} - \alpha_1 z_1^{-1} - \alpha_2 z_2^{-1} - a]$$

First-order conditions at an interior solution are:

$$w_1 - \lambda \alpha_1 z_1^{-2} = 0$$
$$w_2 - \lambda \alpha_2 z_2^{-2} = 0$$

On substituting for Q these yield:

$$\lambda^{\frac{1}{2}} = \frac{[w_1\alpha_1]^{\frac{1}{2}} + [w_2\alpha_2]^{\frac{1}{2}}}{Q^{-1} - a}$$

Substituting back into the first-order conditions we find:

$$z_1 = \frac{\alpha_1 + [\alpha_1\alpha_2 w_2/w_1]^{\frac{1}{2}}}{Q^{-1} - a}$$

$$z_2 = \frac{\alpha_2 + [\alpha_1\alpha_2 w_1/w_2]^{\frac{1}{2}}}{Q^{-1} - a}$$

Therefore:

$$C(\mathbf{w},Q) = z_1 w_1 + z_2 w_2 = \frac{\phi Q}{1-aQ}$$

where $\phi \equiv w_1\alpha_1 + w_2\alpha_2 + 2[\alpha_1\alpha_2 w_1 w_2]^{1/2}$

Average cost: $C/Q = \dfrac{\phi}{1-aQ}$; marginal cost: $C_Q = \dfrac{\phi}{[1-aQ]^2}$

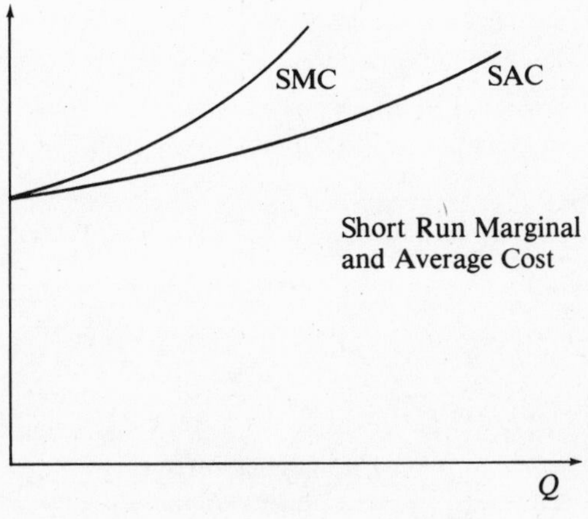

3.7 (a) Using $Q = S(P)$ and $\pi = PQ - C(\mathbf{w},Q)$ we find
(i) $\partial\pi/\partial P = [P - C_Q]S'(P) + Q = Q$
(ii) $\partial\pi/\partial w_j = - C_j = - z_j$
(b) Proof as for Exercise 3.1.

3.8 Differentiating $\dfrac{G_1}{G_2} = \dfrac{w_1}{w_2}$ we find

$$\frac{G_{11}}{G_2}\frac{\partial z_1}{\partial w_1} + \frac{G_{12}}{G_2}\frac{\partial z_2}{\partial w_1} - \frac{G_1 G_{21}}{G_2^2}\frac{\partial z_1}{\partial w_1} - \frac{G_1 G_{22}}{G_2^2}\frac{\partial z_2}{\partial w_1} = \frac{1}{w_2}$$

Now we also know $dz_2 = -\dfrac{G_1}{G_2}\, dz_1$, so this equation becomes on simplification

$$[G_{11}G_2 - G_{21}G_1 - G_{12}G_2 + G_{22}G_1^2/G_2]\,\frac{\partial z_1}{\partial w_1} = \frac{G_2 G_1}{w_1}$$

Now use the results $G_{11}z_1 + G_{12}z_2 = 0$; $G_{21}z_1 + G_{22}z_2 = 0$ (see Exercise 2.9) to eliminate G_{11} and G_{22} from the above equation.

Using also the result $G_1 z_1 + G_2 z_2 = G$ we find that this equation simplifies to

$$-\frac{G_{12}G^2}{z_1 z_2 G_2}\frac{\partial z_1}{\partial w_1} = \frac{G_2 G_1}{w_1}$$

Using the definitions of σ and v_1 $(= 1 - G_2 z_2/G)$, the result is immediate.

3.9 (a)

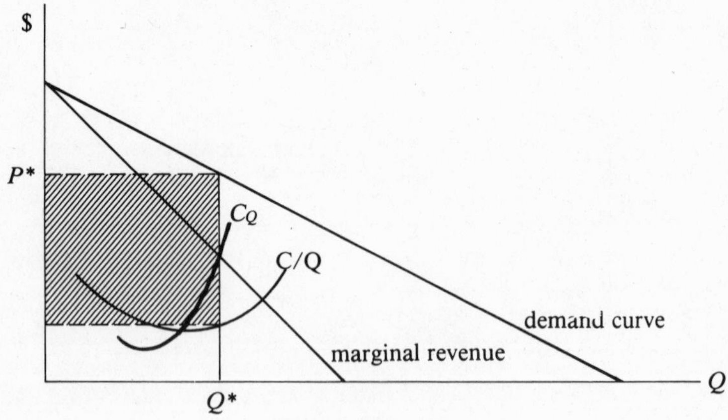

(b) From equation (3.61) we find $\partial\Pi/\partial Q = P_Q Q + P - C_Q = P[1+1/\eta] - C_Q$. Hence if $|\eta| < 1$ (i.e. if $\eta > -1$) we would find $\partial\Pi/\partial Q < 0$ for all $Q > 0$ but $\Pi = 0$ at $Q = 0$. No solution exists.

3.10 Yes. For otherwise the firm could, say, decrease one input *without increasing other inputs or reducing output*, and thus increase profits.

3.11 From the cost function and the monopolist's output decision (3.62) we have:

$$z_i = C_i(\mathbf{w},Q)$$
$$P_Q(Q^*)\,Q^* + P(Q^*) - C_Q(\mathbf{w},Q^*) = 0$$

Differentiate the second equation with respect to w_i

$$[Q^*P_{QQ} + 2P_Q - C_{QQ}]\frac{\partial Q^*}{\partial w_i} - C_{Qi} = 0$$

Now the term in [ ] must be non-positive (see condition 3.64). Hence $[\partial Q^*/\partial w_i > 0] \Leftrightarrow [C_{Qi} < 0]$. But from above we see that $[C_{Qi} < 0] \Leftrightarrow [\partial z_i/\partial Q < 0]$.

3.12 The monopolist's problem is

$$\max \Pi = PQ - w_1z_1 - w_2z_2$$

where $P = A - bQ$ and $Q = G(\mathbf{z}) \equiv [\alpha_1 z_1{}^{\beta} + \alpha_2 z_2{}^{\beta}]^{1/\beta}$. First-order conditions may be written:

$$\partial\Pi/\partial z_i = [A - 2bQ]G_i(z) - w_i = 0, \quad i = 1,2$$

Noting that $G_i = \alpha_i[Q/z_i]^{1-\beta}$, the first-order conditions thus yield

$$\alpha_i z_i^{\beta} = \alpha_i Q^{\beta}[w_i/[\alpha_i A - 2\alpha_i bQ]]^{\gamma}, \quad i = 1,2$$

where $\gamma \equiv -\beta/[1-\beta]$. Adding this last equation over $i = 1,2$ yields

$$Q^{\beta} = Q^{\beta}\sum_{i=1,2}\alpha_i[w_i/[\alpha_i A - 2\alpha_i bQ]]^{\gamma}$$

$$\Rightarrow Q^* = \frac{1}{2b}\left[A - \left[\sum_{i=1,2} w_i^{\gamma}\alpha_i^{1-\gamma}\right]^{1/\gamma}\right]$$

$$P^* = \tfrac{1}{2}\left[A + \left[\sum_{i=1,2} w_i^{\gamma}\alpha_i^{1-\gamma}\right]^{1/\gamma}\right]$$

(a) no reaction to profits tax

(b) Π would now be $[A - bQ][1-\tau]Q - w_1z_1 - w_2z_2$. So clearly new output and price are simply obtained by reducing A and b to $A[1-\tau]$ and $b[1-\tau]$ respectively; output falls.

(c) Clearly we would now have

$$Q^* = \frac{1}{2b}[A - [w_1^{\gamma}\alpha_1^{1-\gamma} + [1+\tau]^{\gamma}w_2^{\gamma}\alpha_2^{1-\gamma}]^{1/\gamma}]$$

Differentiating we find $\partial Q^*/\partial\tau < 0$.

3.13 Maximising the simple monopolist's profits

$$\Pi_0 \equiv [96 - 4Q]Q - [100 + 6Q + \tfrac{1}{2}Q^2]$$

with respect to Q yields optimum output of $Q_0 = 10$. Hence $P_0 = 56$ and $\Pi_0 = 350$.

Now let the monopolist sell Q_1 in market 1 for price P_1 and Q_2 in market 2 for price P_2. The new problem is to choose Q_1, Q_2 so as to maximise the function

$$\Pi_{12} = [96 - 4Q_1]Q_1 + [112 - \tfrac{4}{3}Q_2]Q_2 - [100 + 6Q_1 + 6Q_2 + \tfrac{1}{2}[Q_1 + Q_2]^2]$$

First-order conditions yield

$$9Q_1 + Q_2 = 90$$

$$Q_1 + \frac{11}{3}Q_2 = 106$$

Solving we find: $Q_1 = 7$, $Q_2 = 27$
hence: $P_1 = 68$, $P_2 = 76$
$\Pi_{12} = 1646$

If we abandon discrimination, a uniform price $\hat{P}$ must be charged. If $\hat{P} > 112$ nothing is sold to either market. If $112 > \hat{P} > 96$ only market 2 is served. If $\hat{P} < 96$ both markets are served and the demand curve is $\hat{Q} = 108 - \hat{P}$. Clearly this is the relevant region. Maximising simple monopoly profits we find

$$\hat{Q} = 34, \quad \hat{P} = 74, \quad \hat{\Pi} = 1634$$

Hence:

total output is identical to that under discrimination
$P_1 < \hat{P} < P_2$
$\hat{\Pi} < \Pi_{12}$

These results are quite general.

3.14 Differentiate equation (3.51) first with respect to w_i and then with respect to w_m (where $i < m$)

$$\hat{D}^i_i = \frac{\partial \tilde{D}^i}{\partial w_i} + \frac{\partial \tilde{D}^i}{\partial z^0_m}\,\frac{\partial z^0_m}{\partial w_i}$$

$$\hat{D}^i_m = \frac{\partial \tilde{D}^i}{\partial z^0_m}\,\frac{\partial z^0_m}{\partial w_m}$$

Note in the second case that w_m influences $\tilde{D}^i$ *only* through z^0_m – see the footnote on p.53. But of course in the long run $z^0_m = \hat{D}^m(\mathbf{w}, Q_0)$. Substituting in the terms $\hat{D}^m_i$ and $\hat{D}^m_m$ yields (3.56) and (3.57) immediately. Symmetry gives us $\hat{D}^i_m = \hat{D}^m_i$. So, eliminating $\partial\tilde{D}^i/\partial z^0_m$ between the two above equations immediately gives (3.58).

3.15

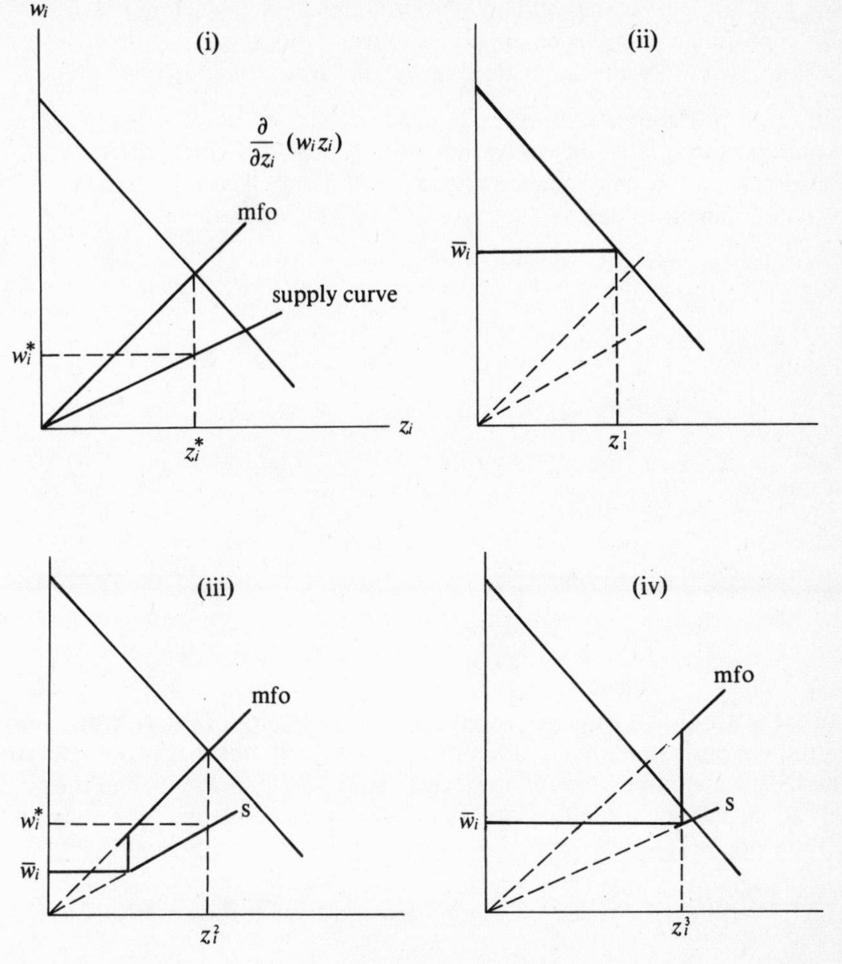

Diagram (i) illustrates the case where $G_i(\mathbf{z})$ is linear in z and supply curve of input i is given by $z_i = aw_i$. Case (ii) is the 'conventional' one. Imposition of a high $\overline{w}_i$ reduces input to z_i^1. This will be indistinguishable from the effect of the minimum price in the perfectly competitive case since the *effective* mfo = *effective* supply-curve = horizontal line at $\overline{w}_i$. Case (iii) is where $\overline{w}_i$ is so low that the equilibrium is unaffected: $z_i^2 = z_i^*$ and the wage paid is $w_i^* > \overline{w}_i$. Case (iv) is the interesting one. Input demand has *increased* to z_i^3, the wage paid being $\overline{w}_i$.

3.16 (a) The appropriate Lagrangean is $P(Q)Q - \lambda\,[\Pi_0 - P(Q)Q + \sum_i w_i z_i\,]$ ($\lambda \geqslant 0$). Clearly the firm will be a cost minimiser for any Q unless $\lambda = 0$. So if the profit constraint is binding the firm *will* be technically efficient since it will not want to waste inputs (see the answer to Exercise 3.10).

(b) If the profit constraint is binding ($\lambda > 0$) then, for any given Q and $\mathbf{w}$, input demands are obviously the same as for the competitive, profit-maximising firm. Once again we have $z_i = \hat{D}^i(\mathbf{w}, Q)$. If the profit constraint is not binding then demand functions D^i are not well defined.

(c) There are two main possibilities:

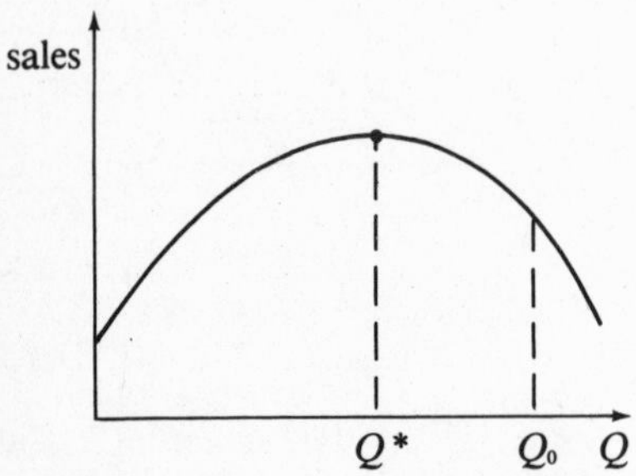

(i)

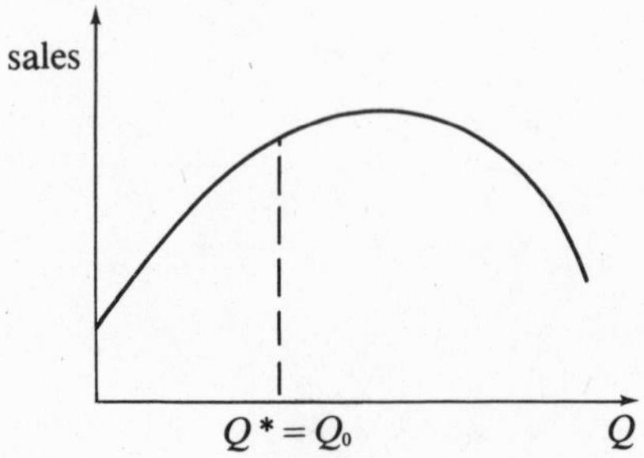

(ii)

In each case Q_0 is a value of output such that if $Q > Q_0$, $\Pi < \Pi_0$ (there may also be a positive *minimum* level of output as well, but that is not relevant here). In case (i) we have an interior maximum: $P_Q Q^* - P = 0$, and the profit constraint is not binding. In case (ii) the profit constraint is binding and $Q^* = Q_0$.

3.17 Writing profits as in (3.1) with demand given by $Q = \beta P^\eta$ and output as $Q = AK^\alpha L^{1-\alpha}$ first-order conditions for a maximum yield: $K = \dfrac{\alpha Q}{r}\lambda$, $L = \dfrac{[1-\alpha]Q}{w}\lambda$, $\left[1 + \dfrac{1}{\eta}\right]P = \lambda$ where λ is the Lagrange multiplier. Substituting back into the demand and production functions we find

$$\lambda = br^\alpha w^{1-\alpha} \text{ and } P = \frac{b}{1+1/\eta}\, r^\alpha w^{1-\alpha} \text{ where } b \equiv 1/A\alpha^\alpha\,[1-\alpha\,]^{1-\alpha}$$

Hence $K = \dfrac{\alpha Q}{b}\left[\dfrac{w}{r}\right]^{1-\alpha} = \dfrac{\alpha\beta}{b}P^\eta\left[\dfrac{w}{r}\right]^{1-\alpha}$. Investment is the rate of change of capital stock $\dot{K} \equiv dK/dt$. Differentiating we find

$$\dot{K}/K = \eta\dot{P}/P + [1-\alpha][\dot{w}/w - \dot{r}/r] + \dot{\beta}/\beta$$
$$= [1-\alpha][1+\eta][\dot{w}/w - \dot{r}/r] + \eta\dot{r}/r + \dot{\beta}/\beta$$

Chapter 4

4.1 Original choice was A – but he could have afforded B at the original budget. However new choice was B; yet he could still have had the original choice (A) under the new budget. This violates WARP.

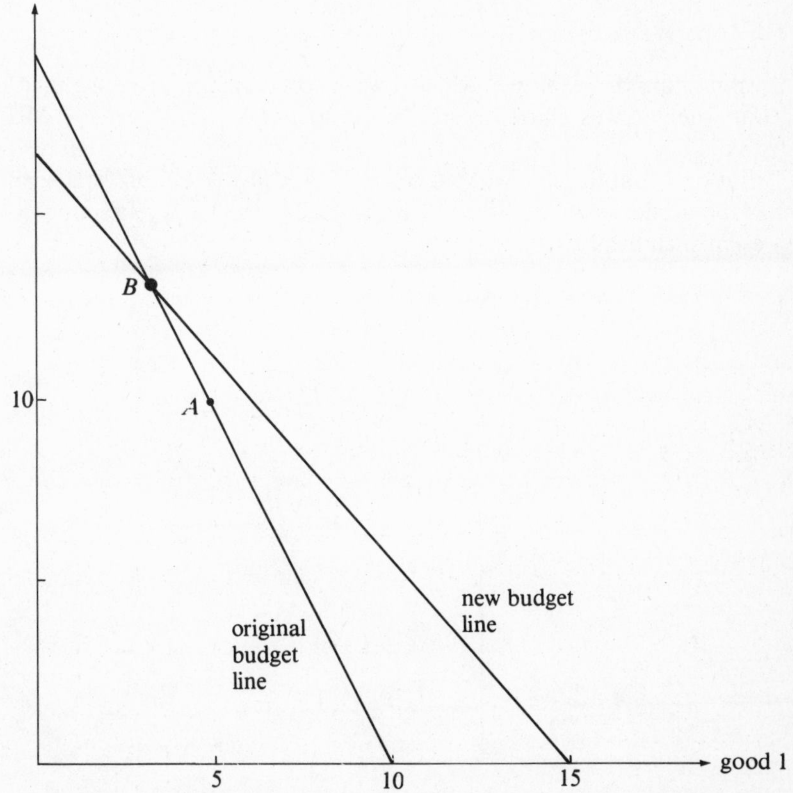

4.2 Let **x** be chosen at prices **p** and consider a price change $\Delta\mathbf{p}$ such that at the new prices the person could still afford the original bundle **x**, but in fact actually chooses a new bundle $\mathbf{x} + \Delta\mathbf{x}$. Then obviously

$$\Sigma_i [p_i + \Delta p_i][x_i + \Delta x_i] \gtreqless \Sigma_i [p_i + \Delta p_i]x_i$$

But, by WARP, this implies

$$\Sigma_i p_i \,[x_i + \Delta x_i\,] > \Sigma_i p_i x_i$$

Subtract the first equation from this second inequality:

$$- \;\Sigma_i \Delta p_i \,[x_i + \Delta x_i\,] > - \;\Sigma x_i \Delta p_i$$

$$\Rightarrow \Sigma \Delta p_i \Delta x_i < 0$$

From this we may deduce the required result.

4.3 Note the following totals:

$$\begin{array}{lll} \Sigma_i p_i^1 x_i^1 = 8; & \Sigma_i p_i^2 x_i^1 = 9; & \Sigma_i p_i^3 x_i^1 = 7 \\ \Sigma_i p_i^1 x_i^2 = 7; & \Sigma_i p_i^2 x_i^2 = 8; & \Sigma_i p_i^3 x_i^2 = 9 \\ \Sigma_i p_i^1 x_i^3 = 9; & \Sigma_i p_i^2 x_i^3 = 7; & \Sigma_i p_i^3 x_i^3 = 8 \end{array}$$

This shows that (for example) when $\mathbf{x}^1$ was chosen the person could have had $\mathbf{x}^2$; but when $\mathbf{x}^2$ was chosen he could not afford $\mathbf{x}^1$; etc. Hence WARP is satisfied.

But note that in *this* case $\mathbf{x}^1 \;\text{\textcircled{>}}\; \mathbf{x}^2 \;\text{\textcircled{>}}\; \mathbf{x}^3 \;\text{\textcircled{>}}\; \mathbf{x}^1$. Revealed preference turns out to be cyclic so that Axiom C2 is violated – no utility function could represent such behaviour.

4.4

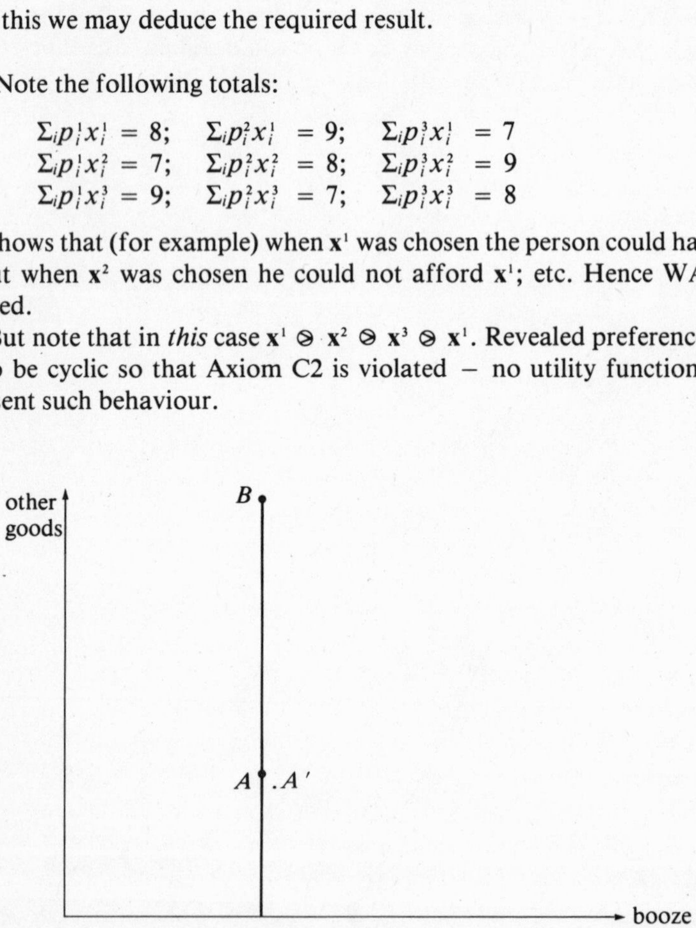

Consider an arbitrary point A. Old George might prefer B to A since B contains just as much booze but more of other goods. *But* he also prefers A' to B because A' contains just a *little* bit more booze. There is *no* point indifferent to A. More generally we have, in the case of n goods:

$$\mathbf{x}^1 \succcurlyeq \mathbf{x}^2 \;\text{ if }\; x_1^1 \geqslant x_1^2 \quad \mathbf{x}^1 \succ \mathbf{x}^2 \;\text{ if }\; x_1^1 > x_1^2;$$

$$\mathbf{x}^1 \succ \mathbf{x}^2 \;\text{ if }\; x_1^1 = x_1^2 \;\text{ and }\; x_2^1 > x_2^2;$$

$\mathbf{x}^1 > \mathbf{x}^2$ if $x_1^1 = x_1^2, x_2^1 = x_2^2$ and $x_3^1 > x_3^2$... and so on. C3 is violated.

4.5 (a) MRS and demand curves can be represented by downward-sloping curves. (b) MRS and demand curves will have 'horizontal' segments in them. (c) MRS will have a *rising* portion; demand will be discontinuous. (d) MRS and compensated demand curves have 'vertical' segments in them. Cf. Exercise 2.5 and Figures 3.3 to 3.5.

4.6 $\left.\begin{array}{l} U^2(\mathbf{x}) = \log(U^1(\mathbf{x})) \\ U^3(\mathbf{x}) = [U^1(\mathbf{x})]^2 \end{array}\right\}$ each of these is an increasing transformation.

Maximise $U^2(\mathbf{x})$ subject to $\sum_{i=1}^{n} p_i x_i \leqslant M$. Because of the shape of the indifference curves, we can be sure that there will be an interior solution. Forming the Lagrangean $\sum_{i=1}^{n} \alpha_i \log x_i + \lambda \left[M - \sum_{i=1}^{n} p_i x_i\right]$ we obtain the first-order conditions:

$$\frac{\alpha_i}{x_i^*} - \lambda p_i = 0, \quad i = 1, \ldots, n$$

From the first-order conditions we find

$$\sum_{i=1}^{n} \alpha_i = \sum_{i=1}^{n} \lambda p_i x_i^* = \lambda M$$

Substituting for λ back into the first-order conditions we find the demand function $x_i^* = D^i(\mathbf{p},M) = \alpha_i' \dfrac{M}{p_i}$ where $\alpha_i' = \alpha_i \Big/ \sum_{k=1}^{n} \alpha_k$. Denoting the maximised value of $U^2(\mathbf{x})$ by u we find:

$$u = \sum_{i=1}^{n} \alpha_i \log(\alpha_i' M/p_i)$$

$$\Rightarrow M = \exp\left(\frac{u}{\Sigma\alpha_i} - \sum_{i=1}^{n} \alpha_i' \log(\alpha_i'/p_i)\right) = C(\mathbf{p},u)$$

4.7 (a) We have the Slutsky equation

$$\varepsilon_{ij} = \hat{\varepsilon}_{ij} - v_j \varepsilon_{iM}$$
$$\varepsilon_{ji} = \hat{\varepsilon}_{ji} - v_i \varepsilon_{jM}$$

see equation (4.24). From the symmetry condition on $\hat{D}_j^i$ we have $v_i \hat{\varepsilon}_{ij} = v_j \hat{\varepsilon}_{ji}$. Simplifying these three equations we have:

$$\varepsilon_{ij} = \frac{v_j}{v_i}\varepsilon_{ji} + v_j[\varepsilon_{jM} - \varepsilon_{iM}]$$

(Cf. equation 4.26).

Clearly, even if $\varepsilon_{ji} > 0$, say, the sign of ε_{ij} will depend also on the relative magnitude of the two income elasticities ε_{iM}, ε_{jM}.
(b) Follows from (4.27) and the fact that $\hat{\varepsilon}_{ii} < 0$.

4.8 (a) Form the Lagrangean $U(\mathbf{x}) + \lambda[M - \sum_{i=1}^{n} p_i x_i]$. Once again we can be sure of an interior solution. The first-order conditions are

$$\frac{b_i}{x_i^* - a_i} - \lambda p_i = 0, \quad i = 1, \ldots, n$$

$\Rightarrow \sum_{i=1}^{n} b_i = \lambda \sum_{i=1}^{n} p_i x_i^* - \lambda \sum_{i=1}^{n} p_i a_i$. Letting $M_0 \equiv \sum_{i=1}^{n} p_i a_i$ and substituting back for λ in the first-order conditions we get

$$x_i^* = a_i + b_i \frac{M - M_0}{p_i}$$

Clearly a_i is a minimal consumption value for good i, M_0 is the minimum expenditure required to obtain the minimal bundle $\mathbf{a}$; b_i is the share of 'discretionary consumption' $x_i - a_i$ in 'discretionary expenditure' $M - M_0$.

(b) It is immediate that all goods are normal, since $\frac{\partial x_i^*}{\partial M} = b_i/p_i > 0$. Also for $i \neq j$ we have $\partial x_i^*/\partial p_j = -b_i a_j/p_i \leqslant 0$. Therefore all goods are (gross) complements.

(c) If income elasticity is >1 then $\frac{b_i M}{p_i x_i^*} > 1$

$$\Rightarrow \frac{p_i a_i}{M_0} < b_i$$

Note that the LHS of this expression is the share of the minimal expenditure on i as a proportion of M_0.

(d) $-\frac{p_i}{x_i^*}\frac{\partial x_i^*}{\partial p_i} = \frac{b_i p_i a_i + b_i[M - M_0]}{p_i a_i + b_i[M - M_0]} < 1$ if $a_i > 0$, since $b_i < 1$

4.9 $U_1 = 2[x_2/[x_1 + 2x_2]]^2 > 0$, $U_2 = [x_1/[x_1 + 2x_2]]^2 > 0$.

$$\text{MRS}_{21} = -\frac{dx_2}{dx_1} = \frac{U_1}{U_2} = 2\frac{x_2^2}{x_1^2}$$

Along an indifference curve we then have:

$$-\frac{\mathrm{d}}{\mathrm{d}x_1}\left(\frac{\mathrm{d}x_2}{\mathrm{d}x_1}\right) = \frac{4x_2}{x_1^2}\frac{\mathrm{d}x_2}{\mathrm{d}x_1} - \frac{4x_2^2}{x_1^3} = -\frac{8x_3^3}{x_1^4} - \frac{4x_2^3}{x_1^3} < 0$$

which establishes that U is concave contoured.

It is a little easier to work with $\log(U(\mathbf{x}))$. First-order conditions for a maximum are

$$\left.\begin{aligned} \frac{1}{x_1^*} - \frac{1}{x_1^* + 2x_2^*} &= \lambda p_1 \\ \frac{1}{x_2^*} - \frac{2}{x_1^* + 2x_2^*} &= \lambda p_2 \end{aligned}\right\} \text{where } \lambda \text{ is the Lagrange multiplier.}$$

$$\Rightarrow \lambda = 1/M$$

$$\Rightarrow x_1^* = \frac{M}{p_1 + \surd(\tfrac{1}{2}p_1p_2)}$$

$$x_2^* = \frac{M}{p_2 + \surd(2p_1p_2)}$$

Obviously the demand functions are indeed homogeneous of degree zero in $\mathbf{p}$ and M, and both goods are normal (since $\partial x_i^*/\partial M > 0$). Using the demand functions we find

$$V(\mathbf{p},M) = \frac{M}{2\surd(2p_1p_2) + p_2 + 2p_1}$$

The expression for $\partial V/\partial M$ is obvious. Hence we may differentiate with respect to p_i and immediately obtain

$$-\frac{\partial V}{\partial p_1}\bigg/\frac{\partial V}{\partial M} = M\frac{\surd(2p_2/p_1) + 2}{2\surd(2p_1p_2) + p_2 + 2p_1} = \frac{M}{p_1 + \surd(\tfrac{1}{2}p_1p_2)}$$

4.10

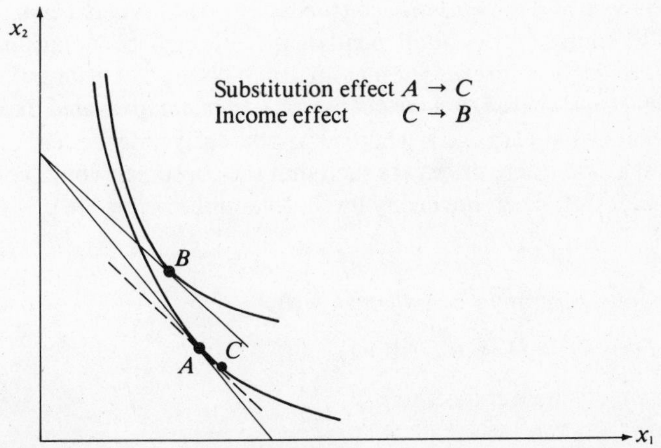

4.11

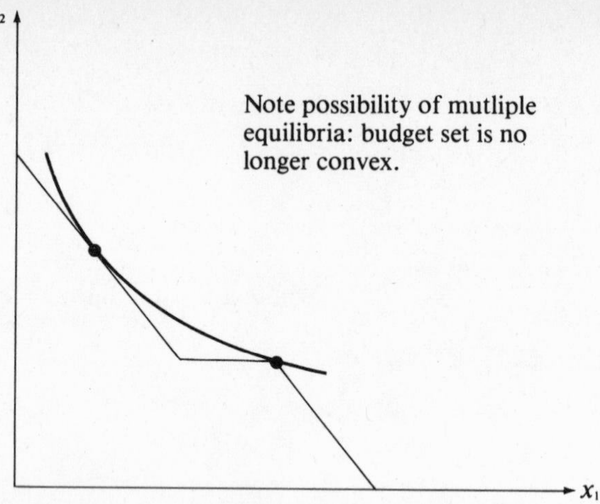
x_2
Note possibility of mutliple equilibria: budget set is no longer convex.
x_1

4.12 Consider the cost function $C(p_1,p_2,p_3,u)$. Clearly this may be written $C(p_1,\alpha\bar{p},\ [1-\alpha]\bar{p},u)=\bar{C}(p_1,\bar{p},u)$, say. (Recall that α is a constant.) Let us see if $\bar{C}$ is the cost function that would arise from maximising behaviour using the composite commodity $\bar{x}$. It is easy to see that $\bar{C}$ must be increasing in p_1, $\bar{p}$ and u, that it is concave in $(p_1,\bar{p})$ and is homogeneous of degree one in p_1 and $\bar{p}$. Also

$$\frac{\partial\bar{C}}{\partial\bar{p}} = C_2\alpha + C_3[1-\alpha] = x_2\alpha + x_3[1-\alpha] = \bar{x}$$

Hence $\bar{C}(p_1,\bar{p},u)$ is indeed the cost function that would result from the use of the composite commodity $\bar{x}$, so that maximising $U(\mathbf{x})$ is equivalent to maximising $\bar{U}(x_1,\bar{x})$ subject to $p_1x_1 + \bar{p}\bar{x} \leqslant M$.

4.13 Let $\tilde{C}(\mathbf{p},u,a)$ be the minimum cost of goods $2,\ldots,n$ when utility level is u, prices are $\mathbf{p}$ and the *quantity consumed of good 1 is constrained to be a*. Note that of course $\tilde{C}$ does not depend on p_1, although it is notationally convenient to write the entire vector $\mathbf{p}$ as an argument of $\tilde{C}$. Differentiating this with respect to p_i where $i > 1$ we get the *restricted* compensated demand for good i, $\tilde{D}^i(\mathbf{p},u,a) \equiv \tilde{C}_i(\mathbf{p},u,a)$, where $\tilde{D}^i$ is obviously independent of p_1 also. Consider the case where prices are such that the consumer would voluntarily purchase exactly a when the utility level is u and the prices are $\mathbf{p}$:

$$a = \hat{D}^1(\mathbf{p},u)$$

Then, obviously for any $i > 1$ we may write

$$\hat{D}^i(\mathbf{p},u) = \tilde{D}^i(\mathbf{p},u,\hat{D}^1(\mathbf{p},u))$$

Differentiate this with respect to p_1:

$$\hat{D}^i_1 = [\delta\tilde{D}^i/\delta a]\,\hat{D}^1_1$$

Differentiate the previous equation once more, this time with respect to p_i where $i > 1$.

$$\hat{D}^i_i = \tilde{D}^i_i + [\delta\tilde{D}^i/\delta a]\,\hat{D}^1_i$$

Substituting, to eliminate $\partial\tilde{D}^i/\partial a$, we find

$$\hat{D}^i_i = \tilde{D}^i_i + [\hat{D}^1_i]^2/\hat{D}^1_1$$

Therefore we find $\hat{D}^i_i < \tilde{D}^i_i < 0$. The constrained demands are less elastic.

4.14 (a) The Lagrangean is: $x_1 + x_2x_3 + \lambda\left[M - \sum_{i=1}^{3} p_i x_i\right]$

$$\text{First-order conditions:}\quad \left.\begin{array}{l} 1 - \lambda p_1 \leqslant 0 \\ x_3^* - \lambda p_2 \leqslant 0 \\ x_2^* - \lambda p_3 \leqslant 0 \end{array}\right\}$$

If $x_2^* > 0$ then $x_3^* = \lambda p_2 > 0$ (since $\lambda > 0$ given non-satiation). If $x_3^* > 0$ then, similarly $x_2^* > 0$. Hence there are three possible cases (a) $x_1^* > 0, x_2^* = x_3^* = 0$; (b) $x_1^* = 0, x_2^*, x_3^* > 0$; (c) $x_i^* > 0$, $i = 1,2,3$: Case (a) is not very interesting and case (b) is ruled out by the restriction in the question. Hence we have

$$\begin{aligned} x_2^* &= p_3/p_1 \\ x_3^* &= p_2/p_1 \\ \Rightarrow x_1^* &= M/p_1 - 2p_2p_3/p_1^2 \end{aligned}$$

Notice that goods 2 and 3 are independent of their own price and of income.

(b) $D^1_2 = -2p_3/p_1^2$; $D^1_M = 1/p_1$
$\Rightarrow \hat{D}^1_2 = D^1_2 + x_2^* D^1_M = -p_3/p_1^2$
Now also $D^2_1 = -p_3/p_1^2$; $D^2_M = 0 \Rightarrow \hat{D}^2_1 = D^2_1 = -p_3/p_1^2$

(c) $V(\mathbf{p},M) = [M/p_1 - 2p_2p_3/p_1^2] + [p_3/p_1][p_2/p_1]$
$= M/p_1 - p_2p_3/p_1^2$

Clearly V is homogeneous of degree 0 in $(\mathbf{p},M)$. Also $\partial V/\partial p_1 = 2p_2p_3/p_1^3 - \frac{1}{2}M < 0$; $\partial V/\partial p_2 = -p_3/p_1^2 < 0$; $\partial V/\partial p_3 = -p_2/p_1^2 < 0$ and $\partial V/\partial M = 1/p_1 > 0$ from which we may easily verify that

$$-\frac{\partial V}{\partial p_i}\bigg/\frac{\partial V}{\partial M} = x_i^*,\ i = 1, 2, 3$$

Now if p_3 were to fall from p_3^0 to p_3^1 we find that the total change in welfare would be given by

$$\int_{p_3^1}^{p_3^0} \partial V/\partial p_3 \, dp_3 = -\int_{p_3^1}^{p_3^0} [p_2/p_1^2]\, dp_3 = \frac{[p_3^1 - p_3^0]\, x_3^*}{p_1}$$

Likewise for good 2. We cannot write this in such simple terms for good 1, because the demand for good 1 is a function of its own price and income.

4.15 The lifetime budget constraint is

$$x_1 + x_2/[1+r] \leqslant A$$

Thus the Lagrangean is

$$\log x_1 + \alpha \log x_2 + \lambda [A - x_1 - x_2/[1+r]]$$

We can be sure that an interior maximum will exist (examine the indifference curve). First-order conditions are

$$1/x_1^* = \lambda$$

$$\alpha/x_1^* = \lambda/[1+r]$$

From this we find $A = \dfrac{1}{\lambda} + \dfrac{\alpha}{\lambda}$

$$\Rightarrow \lambda = \frac{1+\alpha}{A}$$

Therefore $x_1^* = A/[1+\alpha]$

$$x_2^* = \frac{\alpha}{1+\alpha} A[1+r]$$

Note that $\dfrac{x_2^*}{x_1^*} = \alpha[1+r]$. The larger is α (the lower is the level of impatience) the more consumption will the 'tilted' towards period 2. The larger is r, again, the more consumption is biased toward period 2. An increase in A has the following effect:

$$\partial x_1^*/\partial A = 1/[1+\alpha]; \quad \partial x_2^*/\partial A = \frac{\alpha}{1+\alpha}[1+r]$$

The ratio x_2^*/x_1^* is left unaltered. We also find $\partial x_1^*/\partial r = 0$ $\partial x_2^*/\partial r = \dfrac{\alpha}{1+\alpha} A$.

Now note that $\dfrac{1}{1+r}$ is the 'price' of future consumption. The substitution effect for x_1 of an increase in r may then be found to be

$$\left.\frac{\mathrm{d}x_1^*}{\mathrm{d}r}\right|_{u=\text{const}} = \frac{\partial x_1^*}{\partial r} - \frac{x_2^*}{[1+r]^2}\frac{\partial x_1^*}{\partial A} = -\frac{x_2^*}{[1+r]^2[1+\alpha]} < 0$$

4.16 (a)

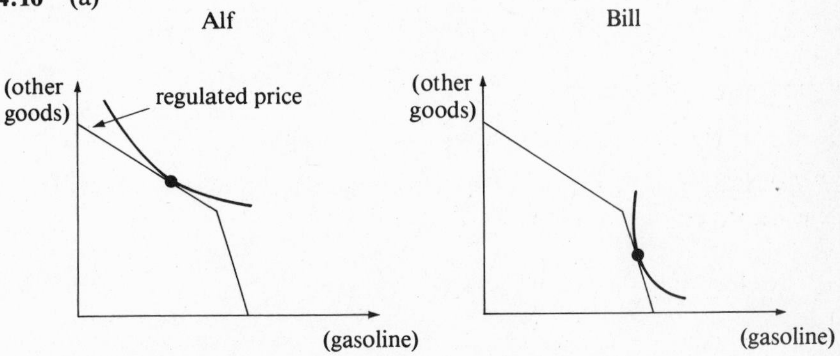

(b) Diagram is similar to above, but with budget constraint as in Figure 4.4. Equilibrium of Alf is unchanged; Bill is exactly on the kink.

(c) Anyone like Alf would want to sell coupons. The price that consumers like Bill would be prepared to pay equals the difference between the foreign (unregulated) price and the regulated price of gasoline: this then becomes the equilibrium price of coupons. The new budget constraint is found by projecting the 'lower branch' of the budget constraint in the above diagrams until it meets the 'other goods' axis. Alf gains.

4.17 Let p be the untaxed price, and τ the excise tax. Government revenue is $T = \tau x$, and the purchase price is $p+\tau$. Clearly an increase in τ would reduce consumption, and $\tau/[p+\tau] = 0.8$. The effect on tax revenue is given by $\partial T/\partial\tau = x + \tau\partial x/\partial\tau = x[1+0.8\varepsilon]$. If (a) $\varepsilon = -0.5$ then this is positive. If (b) $\varepsilon = -1.5$ then it is negative.

4.18 Let $\mathbf{x}^0$ be optimal for $\mathbf{p}^0$ at u_0 and $\mathbf{x}^1$ be optimal for $\mathbf{p}^1$ at u_0. Then because of homotheticity, $\alpha\mathbf{x}^0$ must be optimal for $\mathbf{p}^0$ at u_1 and $\alpha\mathbf{x}^1$ optimal for $\mathbf{p}^1$ at u_1. Hence $C(\mathbf{p}^0,u_0) = \Sigma p_i^0 x_i^0$, $C(\mathbf{p}^0,u_1) = \alpha\Sigma p_i^0 x_i^0$, $C(\mathbf{p}^1,u_0) = \Sigma p_i^1 x_i^1$, $C(\mathbf{p}^1,u_1) = \alpha\Sigma p_i^1 x_i^1$ and the result follows.

4.19 The problem is illustrated in the following diagram. Initial equilibrium is at A with the budget constraint EA tangential to the indifference curve labelled u_0. The new equilibrium is at point B with the budget constraint EB tangential to u_1. FD is parallel to EA and is tangential to u_1 at D; GC is parallel to EB and is tangential to u_0 at C. Because good 1 has a

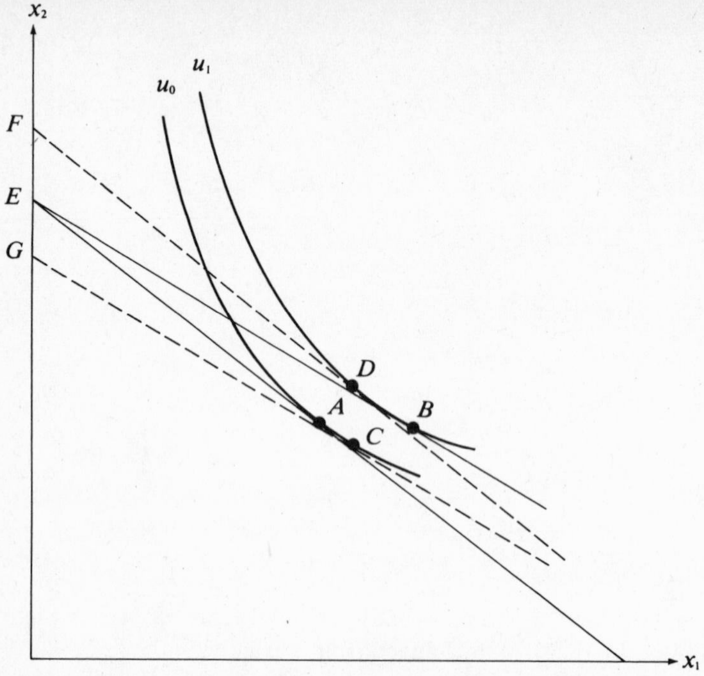

strictly positive income effect D lies to the right of A and B lies to the right of C. Let $|XY|$ denote the distance between any two points X and Y.

(a) The compensating variation for the price fall is $|EG|$; the equivalent variation is $|FE|$.

(b) Draw a vertical line through C and plot on it three points C', C'', C''' as follows: C' lies on EB; C'' lies on FD, C''' lies on EA (extended). Because of the parallel line construction note that $|CC'| = |EG|$ and $|C''C'''| = |FE|$. Because B is to the right of C, C'' must lie above C'; C''' must lie below C because of the negative own-price substitution effect. Therefore, in this case $|C''C'''| > |CC'|$: equivalent variation is greater than compensating variation.

Chapter 5

5.1 (a) It is convenient to solve the equivalent problem of maximising $\log U$. The Lagrangean is then

$$\log x_1 + 2 \log x_2 + \lambda [p_1R_1 + p_2R_2 - p_1x_1 - p_2x_2]$$

First-order conditions for an interior maximum are:

$$\begin{cases} 1/x_1 = \lambda p_1 \\ 2/x_2 = \lambda p_2 \\ p_1R_1 + p_2R_2 = p_1x_1 + p_2x_2 \end{cases}$$

which yield

$$\left.\begin{aligned} x_1 &= \frac{1}{3}R_1 + \frac{p_2R_2}{3p_1} \\ x_2 &= \frac{2}{3}R_2 + \frac{2p_1R_1}{3p_2} \end{aligned}\right\}$$

Clearly $x_1 > R_1$ if $p_2/p_1 > 2R_1/R_2$

(b) $\frac{\partial x_1}{\partial R_1} = \frac{1}{3}; \quad \frac{\partial x_1}{\partial R_2} = \frac{p_2}{3p_1}$ (normal)

$$\frac{\partial x_1}{\partial p_1} = -\frac{p_2R_2}{3p_1^2}; \quad \frac{\partial x_1}{\partial p_2} = \frac{R_2}{3p_1}$$

(c) $$\frac{\partial x_1}{\partial p_1} = -\frac{2M}{9p_1^2} - \left[\frac{p_2R_2}{9p_1^2} - \frac{2R_1}{9p_1}\right]$$

$$\frac{\partial x_1}{\partial p_2} = \underbrace{\frac{2M}{9p_1p_2}}_{\text{substitution effect}} - \underbrace{\left[\frac{2R_1}{9p_2} - \frac{R_2}{9p_1}\right]}_{\text{income effect}}$$

where $M \equiv p_1R_1 + p_2R_2$. Note the use of the *modified* Slutsky equation (5.13).

5.2 (a) We have $\phi_2 dy_1 + \phi_2 dy_2 + \phi_3 dz = 0$

$$\Rightarrow \frac{\partial y_i}{\partial z} = -\phi_3/\phi_i = 2z/2y_i = z/y_i; \quad i = 1,2$$

(b) $MRT_{12} = \phi_2/\phi_1 = y_2/y_1$

The Lagrangean is: $\underbrace{p_1y_1 + p_2y_2}_{(\mu)} + \lambda[\bar{z}^2 - y_1^2 - y_2^2]$

First-order conditions are

$$\begin{cases} p_1 - 2\lambda y_1 = 0 \\ p_2 - 2\lambda y_2 = 0 \\ \bar{z}^2 - y_1^2 - y_2^2 = 0 \end{cases}$$

$$\Rightarrow p_1^2 + p_2^2 = 4\lambda^2\bar{z}^2$$

$$\Rightarrow \lambda = \frac{\sqrt{(p_1^2+p_2^2)}}{2\bar{z}}; \; y_i = \frac{p_i\bar{z}}{\sqrt{(p_1^2+p_2^2)}} \quad i = 1,2$$

$$\partial y_1/\partial p_1 = p_2^2 \frac{\bar{z}}{[p_1^2+p_2^2]^{3/2}}, \quad \partial y_1/\partial p_2 = -p_1p_2\frac{\bar{z}}{[p_1^2+p_2^2]^{3/2}}$$

Hence $\mu = \sqrt{(p_1^2+p_2^2)}\bar{z}$

$$\Rightarrow \frac{\partial\mu}{\partial\bar{z}} = \sqrt{(p_1^2+p_2^2)}; \; \frac{\partial\phi}{\partial\bar{z}} = 2\bar{z}$$

The result gives a breakdown of the 'cost' of the production constraint.

5.3 Once again it is easier to work with log U. The Lagrangean is then

$$\frac{1}{6}\log x_1 + \frac{1}{6}\log x_2 + \frac{2}{3}\log(24-L) + \lambda[wL - p_1x_1 - p_2x_2].$$

First-order conditions are

$$\begin{cases} \dfrac{1}{6x_i} = \lambda p_i, \quad i = 1,2 \\ \dfrac{2}{3[24-L]} = \lambda w \\ -wL + p_1x_1 + p_2x_2 = 0 \end{cases}$$

Simplifying we find

$$-\frac{2L}{3\lambda[24-L]} + \frac{1}{6\lambda} + \frac{1}{6\lambda} = 0$$

$$\Rightarrow -\frac{2L}{24-L} + 1 = 0 \quad \Rightarrow L = 8$$

Hence $\lambda = \dfrac{1}{24w}$ and $x_i = \dfrac{4w}{p_i}$; $i = 1,2$

5.4 Original equilibrium is at A. Both parties are right!

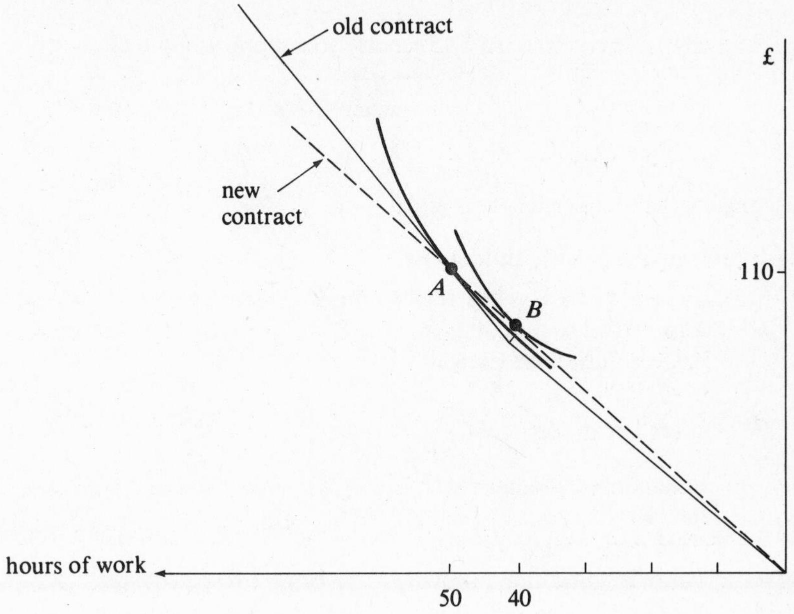

5.5 Using good 0 as numeraire, the budget constraint is

$$x_0 + w_1x_1 + w_2x_2 \leqslant \bar{M} + w_1T + w_2T$$

γ_i is the 'minimum consumption requirement' of good i, the sum $K \equiv \bar{M} - \gamma_0 + w_1[T-\gamma_1] + w_2[T-\gamma_2]$ may be regarded as 'discretionary' expenditure (i.e. income over and above that committed to the minimum requirements); α_i is the proportion of discretionary expenditure devoted to good i – compare this with Exercise 4.8. The maximisation problem has exactly the same form as that of Exercise 4.8. Hence we may immediately write down the demand for good i as:

$$x_i = \gamma_i + \alpha_i K/w_i, \quad i = 0, 1, 2$$

where $w_0 \equiv 1$. This immediately yields the required solution for the consumption good 0. Supply of labour by person 1 is

$$L_1 \equiv T - x_1 = T - \gamma_1 - \alpha_1[\bar{M} - \gamma_0 + w_1[T-\gamma_1] + w_2[T-\gamma_2]]/w_1$$

with a similar solution for person 2. We find

(a) $\partial L_1/\partial w_1 = \alpha_1[\bar{M} - \gamma_0 + w_2[T-\gamma_2]]/w_1^2$ which may be positive or negative depending on the size of $\bar{M}$ and w_2.

(b) $\partial L_1/\partial w_2 = -\alpha_1[T-\gamma_2]/w_1 < 0$
(c) $\partial L_1/\partial \overline{M} = -\alpha_1/w_1 < 0$

5.6 (a) The model of Exercise 4.15 yields (on suppressing the *s):

$$\left.\begin{array}{l} x_1 = M/[1+\alpha] \\ x_2 = \alpha M[1+r]/[1+\alpha] \end{array}\right\} \text{ where } M \equiv M_1 + M_2/[1+r]$$

So savings in the first period are $S \equiv M_1 - x_1 = \dfrac{\alpha M_1}{1+\alpha} - \dfrac{M_2}{[1+\alpha][1+r]}$.

Clearly this *increases* with an increase in r.

(b) If there is a ban on borrowing and M_1 is low then consumer may be constrained such that $x_1 = M_1$: cf Figure 4.4. A small increase in τ leaves solution unchanged.

5.7 (a) Budget constraint: $x_1 + \dfrac{x_2}{1+r} \leqslant M_1 - z + \dfrac{\phi(z)}{1+r}$

(b) The maximisation has two parts to the solution: (i) x_1, x_2 are determined as above with $M \equiv M_1 - z^* + \phi(z^*)/[1+r]$; and (ii) z^* is chosen such that $\phi'(z^*) = 1+r$.

(c) First-order condition (above) gives $\alpha\phi'(z^*) = 1+r$. For constant r

we find $\phi' + \alpha\phi'' \dfrac{dz^*}{d\alpha} = 0$. We immediately see $\dfrac{dz^*}{d\alpha} > 0$.

Raising α raises investment, second period income and hence consumption in *both* periods.

(d) Example contains elements of *human capital* model of education. Optimal 'purchase' of education z^* increaes with ability α, but is independent of income M_1.

5.8

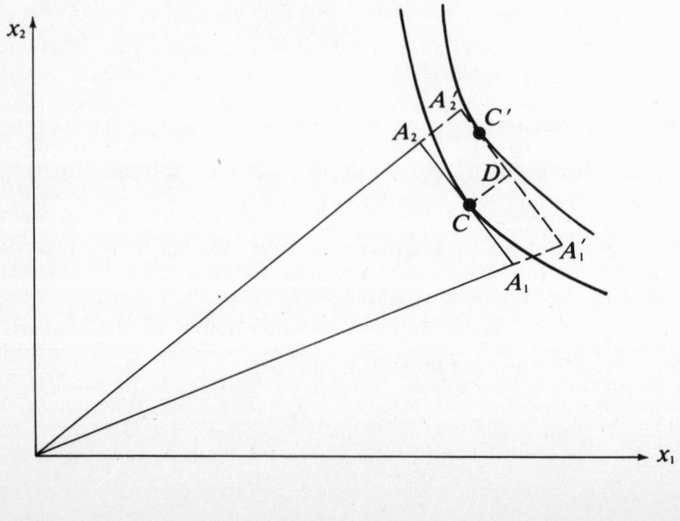

Original boundary of feasible set passes through A_1 and A_2. When income increases, boundary shifts to $A_1'A_2'$, chosen point moves from C to C': clearly neither x_1 nor x_2 is inferior. But at C' the absolute amount of market good z_1 has been reduced (compared to C). Had the amount of z_1 been kept constant the new consumption point would have been at D where D lies in $A_1'A_2'$ and CD is parallel to A_2A_2'.

Chapter 6

6.1 Consider an economy with F identical firms indexed $f = 1, \ldots, F$. Let input 1 have elasticity of supply ε, (aggregate) elasticity of demand η, and let all other inputs have constant price. Each firm in equilibrium produces an amount Q^f where

$$P = C_Q(\mathbf{w}, Q^f)$$

and where P is the output price, $\mathbf{w}$ the vector of input prices and C the cost function. Total output is given by $Q = \Sigma_{f=1}^F Q^f$. Clearly if we take firm f in isolation and assume $\mathbf{w}$ fixed for that firm we have:

$$\frac{\mathrm{d}Q^f}{\mathrm{d}P} = \frac{1}{C_{QQ}(\mathbf{w}, Q^f)}$$

Now allow P to increase for the industry as a whole; as Q increases the demand for each input will increase and so w_1 will rise, affecting the costs of all firms. For firm f we find:

$$\mathrm{d}P = C_{QQ}(\mathbf{w}, Q^f)\mathrm{d}Q^f + C_{Q1}(\mathbf{w}, Q^f)\mathrm{d}w_1$$

Now the demand by firm f for input 1 is given by $C_1(\mathbf{w}, Q^f)$. Therefore equilibrium in the market for input 1 is given by

$$z_1 = \sum_{f=1}^{F} C_1(\mathbf{w}, Q^f)$$

Differentiate and substitute in the elasticities:

$$\frac{z_1}{w_1}\varepsilon\,\mathrm{d}w_1 = \frac{z_1}{w_1}\eta\,\mathrm{d}w_1 + \sum_{f=1}^{F} C_{1Q}(\mathbf{w}, Q^f)\mathrm{d}Q^f$$

Since all firms are identical, we may take all the Q^fs as being identical. Hence we have

$$\mathrm{d}w_1 = \frac{w_1}{z_1}\,\frac{C_{1Q}(\mathbf{w}, Q^f)}{\varepsilon - \eta}\,\mathrm{d}Q$$

Using this result in the expression for $\mathrm{d}P$ we find

$$\frac{dQ}{dP} = \frac{1}{\dfrac{C_{QQ}}{F} + \dfrac{w_1}{z_1}\,\dfrac{C^2_{Q1}}{\varepsilon - \eta}}$$

Clearly dQ/dP increases with ε, the elasticity of supply of input 1.

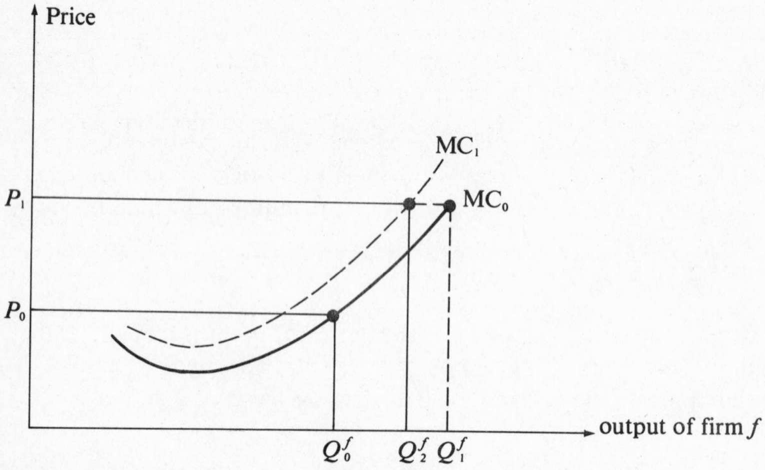

Original equilibrium of firm f is at Q^f on the marginal cost curve MC. If price rises from P_0 to P_1 *and we allow for the effect on all other firms in the market*, then as aggregate output rises, the marginal cost curve is shifted to MC_1 (because of the change in input price). Hence new equilibrium output is *not* at Q_2^f on the old supply curve, but at Q_1^f on the new supply curve. Hence the market supply curve must be *steeper* than $\Sigma_{f=1}^{F}$ MC.

6.2 If all firms are identical each firm will operate at the bottom of its average cost curve (where MC = AC) and, if input prices are fixed, an expansion of output can be met by a simple replication of the existing firms: the supply curve is horizontal.

6.3 Profits for firm i are

$$\Pi_i = AQ_i^{\alpha}/K - C_0 - mQ_i$$

where $K \equiv \Sigma_{j=1}^{n} Q_j^{\alpha}$. The first-order condition for maximising Π_i is

$$A\alpha Q_i^{\alpha-1}/K - A\alpha Q_i^{2\alpha-1}/K^2 - m = 0$$

If all firms are identical then, in equilibrium, $Q_i = Q_j$ for all i, and so $K = n[Q_i]^{\alpha}$. Substituting this in the first-order condition we get:

$$A\alpha/n - A\alpha/n^2 - mQ_i = 0$$

from which the first result follows immediately. Consider a variation in Q_i leaving Q_j constant, $j \neq i$: differentiating logarithmically the equation for p_i we find that the inverse of the elasticity is

$$-\frac{Q_i}{P_i}\frac{\partial P_i}{\partial Q_i} = -\alpha+1+\frac{1}{K}\alpha Q_i^{\alpha}$$

from which the result follows once one substitutes for K. The case $\alpha = 1$ represents a situation where the goods are perfect substitutes. In this case equilibrium profits of any one firm are $\Pi^* = AQ_i/K - C_0 - mQ_i = A/n - C_0 - mA[n-1]/n^2m$. The condition $\Pi^* \geqslant 0$ implies $A[1/n - [n-1]/n^2] - C_0 \geqslant 0$. This is equivalent to $n \leqslant \sqrt{(A/C_0)}$.

6.4 By definition $v_i(M,\mathbf{p}) = p_i x_i/M$, $i = 1, \ldots, 3$. Therefore $x_i = a_i(\mathbf{p})/p_i + Mb_i(\mathbf{p})/p_i$. For given $\mathbf{p}$, x_i plotted against M is thus a straight line.

Since, by definition $\sum_{i=1}^{3} v_i = 1$, we find

$$\sum_{i=1}^{3} a_i(\mathbf{p}) + M\sum_{i=1}^{3} b_i(\mathbf{p}) = M$$

for any value of M and $\mathbf{p}$. Put $M = 0$ in the above equation: we immediately see that $\sum_{i=1}^{3} a_i(\mathbf{p}) = 0$. Now put $M = 1$ in the above equation:

$$0 + 1\sum_{i=1}^{3} b_i(\mathbf{p}) = 1.$$

The expenditure by person h on good i is $a_i(\mathbf{p}) + M^h b_i(\mathbf{p})$. Hence total expenditure on good i is $3a_i(\mathbf{p}) + [M^1 + M^2 + M^3]b_i(\mathbf{p}) = 3a_i(\mathbf{p}) + 3M^3 b_i(\mathbf{p})$. Aggregate income, of course, is $M^1 + M^2 + M^3 = 3M^3$. Hence

$$\alpha_i = \frac{3a_i(\mathbf{p}) + 3M^3 b_i(\mathbf{p})}{3M^3} = \frac{a_i(\mathbf{p})}{M^3} + b_i(\mathbf{p})$$

6.5

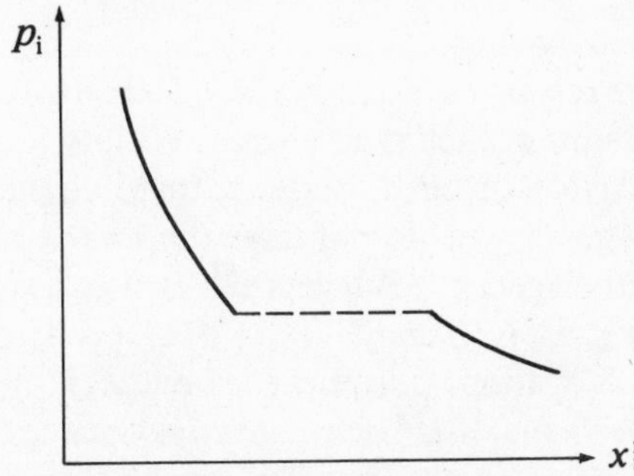

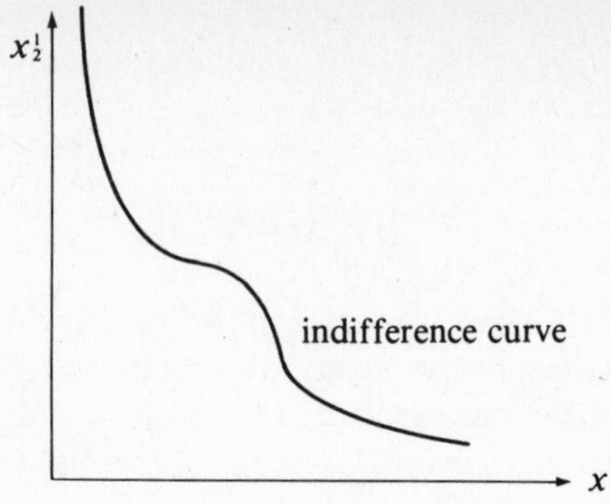

Clearly for $p_1 > a$ we must have $x_1^1 = x_1^2 = \frac{1}{2}[x_1^1 + x_1^2] = \dfrac{M}{4p_1}$. Likewise $p_1 < a$ we have $\frac{1}{2}[x_1^1 + x_1^2] = \dfrac{M}{2p_1}$. At $p_1 = a$ the following values of (x_1^1, x_1^2) are possible: $\left(\dfrac{M}{4a}, \dfrac{M}{4a}\right), \left(\dfrac{M}{4a}, \dfrac{M}{2a}\right), \left(\dfrac{M}{2a}, \dfrac{M}{4a}\right), \left(\dfrac{M}{2a}, \dfrac{M}{2a}\right)$. Evaluating $\frac{1}{2}[x_1^1 + x_1^2]$ for each of these yields $\left\{\dfrac{M}{4a}, \dfrac{3M}{8a}, \dfrac{3M}{8a}, \dfrac{M}{2a}\right\}$. In the case of n identical consumers, at $p_1 = a$, the following values of $\dfrac{1}{H}\sum_h x_1^h$ are possible:

$$\left\{\left[1 + \frac{h}{H}\right]\frac{M}{4a}: \quad h = 0,1,2, \ldots, H\right\}$$

Clearly, as $H \to \infty$ this set becomes dense in the interval $\left[\dfrac{M}{4a}, \dfrac{M}{2a}\right]$.

Chapter 7

7.1 (a) We prove the result for the case where there are two types of person (a and b) and two persons of each type where the utility functions U^a and U^b are each strictly concave-contoured. Suppose that in a particular allocation the two persons of a given type do *not* have the same consumption allocation: Alf gets $\mathbf{x}^{a1}$, Arthur gets $\mathbf{x}^{a2}$, Bill gets $\mathbf{x}^{b1}$, Ben gets $\mathbf{x}^{b2}$. Without loss of generality let $U^a(\mathbf{x}^{a1}) \leqslant U^a(\mathbf{x}^{a2})$ and $U^b(\mathbf{x}^{b1}) \leqslant U^b(\mathbf{x}^{b2})$. We shall show that this cannot be a core allocation. Consider the bundles $\hat{\mathbf{x}}^a = \frac{1}{2}[\mathbf{x}^{a1} + \mathbf{x}^{a2}]$ and $\hat{\mathbf{x}}^b = \frac{1}{2}[\mathbf{x}^{b} + \mathbf{x}^{b2}]$. By virtue of U^a being *strictly* concave contoured, $U^a(\hat{\mathbf{x}}^a) > U^a(\mathbf{x}^{a1})$ with a similar result applying for b. However since Alf and

Arthur each had endowment $\mathbf{R}^a$, and Bill and Ben each had endowment $\mathbf{R}^b$, it must be true that $\hat{\mathbf{x}}^a + \hat{\mathbf{x}}^b = \mathbf{R}^a + \mathbf{R}^b$. So a coalition of Alf and Bill would *block* the original allocation with unequal consumption.
(b) By construction the line *DK* must intersect the *a*-indifference curve passing through point *K*. Let *G* be any point on *DK* between that point of intersection and *K*: *G* must lie on a *higher a*-indifference curve than *K*. In view of the large-number assumption one may consider a coalition consisting of all of the *a*-people (who would be located at *G*) and a proportion *DG/DK* of the *b*-people (who would be located at *K*), leaving the remaining *GK/DK* of the *b*-people out of the coalition at *D*. This coalition could block the proposed allocation of *everyone* at point *K*.

7.2 (a) is not homogeneous of degree 0 in **p**; (b) violates Walras' Law; (c) is obviously homogeneous of degree 0 in **p** and, since $p_3 + p_3 - 2p_3 = 0$, Walras' Law is satisfied.

7.3 The result is easily established for $n = 2$ and will therefore apply for $n > 2$. Normalise so that $p_1 + p_2 = 1$. Then Walras' Law implies

$$[1 - p_1]E_2(\mathbf{p}) = -p_1E_1(\mathbf{p})$$

Now let $p_1 \to 1$, so that $p_2 = 1 - p_1 \to 0$. If (a) $E_2(\mathbf{p})$ remains finite in the limit, then the LHS of this expression must be zero at $p_1 = 1$; in which case $E_1(1,0) = 0$, so that E_1 must be discontinuous in the neighbourhood of $\mathbf{p} = (1,0)$. Obviously (b) if $\lim_{p_1 \to 1} E_1(p_1, 1 - p_1) = A$, then $[1 - p_1]E_2(p_1, 1 - p_1) \to -A$ and $E_2 \to -\infty$.

7.4 From Walras' Law $E_2(\mathbf{p}) = \rho^4 - 3\rho^3 + 2\rho^2$. Now $E_1 = 0 \Rightarrow -\rho[\rho - 1][\rho - 2] = 0$. Hence there are equilibria at $\rho = 0,1,2$, (see figure). If we

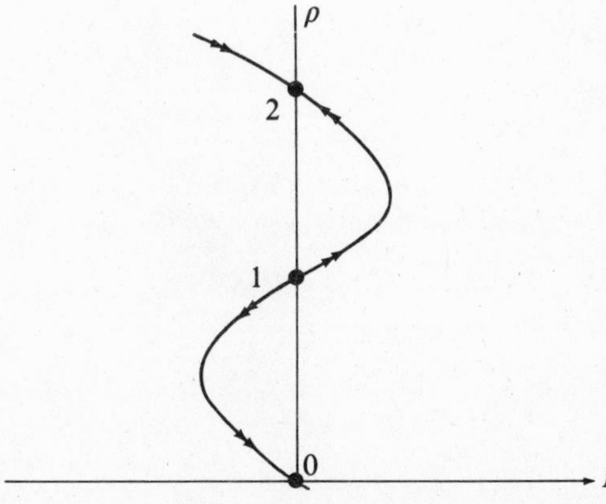

assume tâtonnement $\frac{d}{dt}(\rho)$ has the same sign as E_1 – see arrows in figure. Hence equilibria 0 and 2 are stable, equilibrium 1 is unstable.

7.5 The Lagrangean for person a is $\log x_1^a + 2\log x_2^a + v^a[9p_1 + 3p_2 - p_1x_1^a - p_2x_2^a]$ where v^a is the Lagrange multiplier. First-order conditions are

$$\left.\begin{aligned} 1/x_1^a - v^ap_1 &= 0 \\ 2/x_2^a - v^ap_2 &= 0 \\ 9p_1 + 3p_2 - p_1x_1^a - p_2x_2^a &= 0 \end{aligned}\right\} \Rightarrow \begin{cases} x_1^a = 3 + 1/\rho \\ x_2^a = 6\rho + 2 \text{ where } \rho \equiv p_1/p_2 \end{cases}$$

Similarly for person b we find $\begin{cases} x_1^b = 8 + 4/\rho \\ x_2^b = 4\rho + 2 \end{cases}$

Since $E_i = x_i^a + x_i^b - R_i^a - R_i^b$, $i = 1,2$, we find

$$E_1 = 5/\rho - 10; \quad E_2 = 10\rho - 5$$

so obviously $\rho E_1 + E_2 = 0$ and hence Walras' Law is verified. Clearly the equilibrium price is $\rho = \frac{1}{2}$. The contract curve is traced out by the twin conditions $\text{MRS}_{12}^a = \text{MRS}_{12}^b$ and $E_i = 0$. Writing $x_1^b = 21 - x_1^a$ and $x_2^b = 9 - x_2^b$ we have

$$\frac{2x_1^a}{x_2^a} = \frac{21 - x_1^a}{2[9 - x_2^a]}$$

$$\Rightarrow x_2^a = 12x_1^a/[x_1^a + 7]$$

7.6 For each group of traders the Lagrangean may be written

$$\tfrac{1}{2}\log x_1^h + \tfrac{1}{4}\log x_2^h + \tfrac{1}{4}\log x_3^h + v^h[M^h - p_1x_1^h - p_2x_2^h - p_3x_3^h]$$

where $h = 1,2,3$ and $M^1 = 10p_1$, $M^2 = 5p_2$, $M^3 = 20p_3$. From the first-order conditions we find for a trader of type h:

$$\begin{cases} x_1^h = M^h/2p_1 \\ x_2^h = M^h/4p_2 \\ x_3^h = M^h/4p_3 \end{cases}$$

Excess demands for goods 1 and 2 are then:

$$\begin{aligned} E_1 &= 100x_1^1 + 50x_1^2 + 50x_1^3 - 1000 \\ E_2 &= 100x_2^1 + 50x_2^2 + 50x_2^3 - 250 \end{aligned}$$

Substituting in for x_i^h and M^h and putting $E_1 = E_2 = 0$ (so that E_3 also equals 0) we find:

$$-500 + 125\,p_2/p_1 + 500\,p_3/p_1 = 0$$

$$250\, p_1/p_2 - \frac{750}{4} + 250\, p_3/p_2 = 0$$

$$\Rightarrow p_2/p_1 = 2, p_3/p_1 = \tfrac{1}{2}$$

Using good 1 as *numéraire* we immediately see that $M^1 = M^2 = M^3 = 10$. All are equally well off.

7.7 Indifference maps, utility functions and demand functions for the three individuals are as follows:

$$x_1^a = x_2^a = \frac{5\rho}{\rho+1} \quad \left\{ \begin{array}{ll} x_1^b = 2 + 4/\rho & x_1^c = 4/\rho \\ x_2^b = \rho + 2 & x_2^c = 0 \end{array} \right\}$$

where $\rho \equiv p_1/p_2$.

| $U^a = \min\{x_1^a, x_2^a\}$ | $U^b = 2\log x_1^b + \log x_2^b$ | $U^c = x_1^c$ |

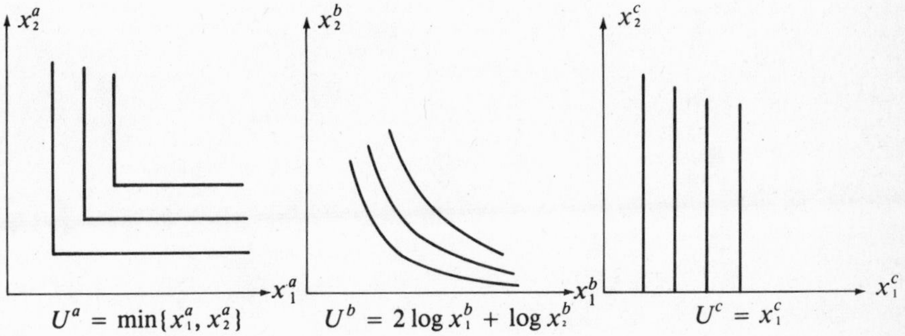

Excess demand for good 2 is: $E_2 = \dfrac{5\rho}{\rho+1} + \rho + 2 + 0 - 10$. Putting $E_2 = 0$

yields $\rho = -2$ or $\underline{4}$. Hence equilibrium price ratio is 4. Utility levels are $U^a = 4$, $U^b = \log(54)$, $U^c = 1$.

 (i) Excess demand is now $\dfrac{9\rho}{\rho+1} + \rho + 2 - 10 \Rightarrow \rho = 2$. Hence $U^a = 6$,
$U^b = \log(64)$, $U^c = 2$.

(ii) Excess demand function remains unchanged (Charlie just consumes the extra 4 units) so $\rho = 4$ still, and:

$$U^a = 4, \quad U^b = \log(54), \quad U^c = 4 + 1 = 5.$$

7.8 Lagrangeans for the two persons are

$$\mathscr{L}^a = -\tfrac{1}{2}[x_1^a]^{-2} - \tfrac{1}{2}[x_2^a]^{-2} + v^a\,[\rho R_1 - \rho x_1^a - x_2^a]$$
$$\mathscr{L}^b = x_1^b x_2^b + v^b\,[R_2 - \rho x_1^b - x_2^b]$$

where v^a, v^b are Lagrange multipliers, $\rho \equiv p_1/p_2$ and good 2 is *numéraire*.

Differentiating $\mathscr{L}^a, \mathscr{L}^b$ with respect to x_i^h, v^h ($i = 1,2$; $h = a,b$) and setting each derivative equal to zero, we find, on simplification:

$$x_1^a = R_1/[1 + \rho^{-2/3}]; \quad x_1^b = R_2/2\rho$$
$$x_2^a = \rho R_1/[1 + \rho^{2/3}]; \quad x_2^b = \tfrac{1}{2} R_2$$

Clearly the excess demand for good 2 is $\rho R_1/[1 + \rho^{2/3}] - \frac{1}{2} R_2$. Hence the equilibrium price ratio must satisfy:

$$\rho^2 = [2\rho R_1/R_2 - 1]^3$$

We can see that this cubic will have at most only one real root ρ^*:

If $R_1 = 5$ and $R_2 = 16, \rho^* = 8$.

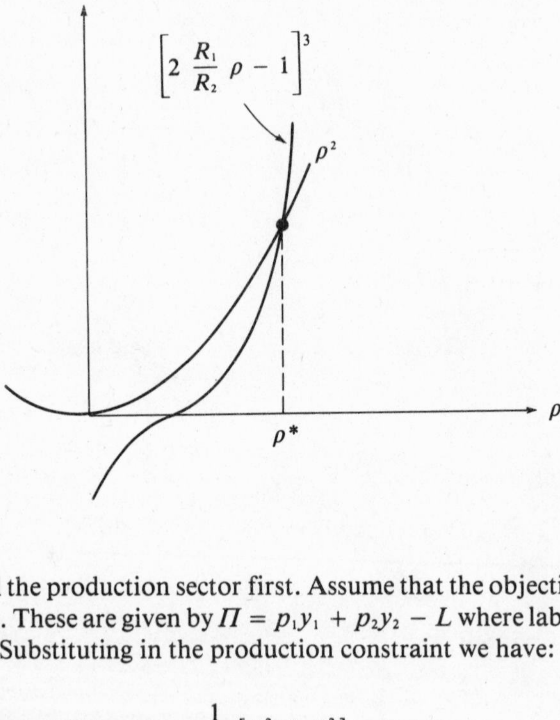

7.9 Model the production sector first. Assume that the objective is to maximise profits. These are given by $\Pi = p_1 y_1 + p_2 y_2 - L$ where labour is used as *numéraire*. Substituting in the production constraint we have:

$$\Pi = p_1 y_1 + p_2 y_2 - \frac{1}{A}[y_1^2 + y_2^2]$$

Maximising with respect to y_1, y_2 for given A, p_1, p_2 we find

$$y_1 = \tfrac{1}{2} A p_1, \quad y_2 = \tfrac{1}{2} A p_2, \quad \Pi = \frac{A}{4}[p_1^2 + p_2^2]$$

Now consider consumption of the capitalists. Maximising U^a subject to $p_1 x_1^a + p_2 x_2^a = \Pi$ yields

$$x_1^a = \Pi/2p_1, \quad x_2^a = \Pi/2p_2$$

Substituting for Π: $x_1^a = \dfrac{A}{8}[p_1 + p_2^2/p_1]$, $x_2^a = \dfrac{A}{8}[p_1^2/p_2 + p_2]$. Now consider the workers. Their budget constraint is $p_1 x_1^b = L$ (the wage is unity and they do not consume good 2). Maximising U^b subject to this constraint gives:

$$L = 1/2p_1, \quad x_1^b = \tfrac{1}{2}p_1^{-2}$$

For equilibrium excess demand for goods 1 and 2 must be zero:

$$\left\{\begin{array}{l} x_1^a + x_1^b - y_1 = 0 \\ \\ x_2^a - y_2 = 0 \end{array}\right\} \Rightarrow \left\{\begin{array}{l} \dfrac{A}{8}[p_1 + p_2^2/p_1] + \tfrac{1}{2}p_1^{-2} - \tfrac{1}{2}Ap_1 = 0 \\ \\ \dfrac{A}{8}[p_1^2/p_2 + p_2] - \dfrac{A}{2}p_2 = 0 \end{array}\right\}$$

The second equation immediately implies $p_1/p_2 = \sqrt{3}$.
Substituting this back into the first equation to eliminate p_2 we find $p_1 = \left[\dfrac{3}{2A}\right]^{1/3}$. This implies

$$\Pi = \left[\frac{A}{12}\right]^{1/3}, \quad L = \tfrac{1}{2}\left[\frac{3}{2A}\right]^{-1/3}$$

$$x_1^a = \tfrac{1}{2}[A^2/18]^{1/3}, \quad x_3^a = \frac{\sqrt{3}}{2}[A^2/18]^{1/3}, \quad x_1^b = \tfrac{1}{2}\left[\frac{3}{2A}\right]^{-2/3}$$

Since the wage is unity the total payments to labour are exactly L. So the share of profits is given by $\dfrac{\Pi}{\Pi + L} = [1 + L/\Pi]^{-1} = \left[1 + \tfrac{1}{2}\left[\dfrac{3}{2A}\,\dfrac{A}{12}\right]^{-1/3}\right]^{-1} = \tfrac{1}{2}$.
Hence, as A increases (technical progress) the share of profits remains constant.

7.10 Using Roy's identity we have, for each h and each i: $x_i^h = -V_i^h/V_M^h$. Now we have $V_i^h = -\beta_i^h[M^h - p_1\beta_1^h - p_2\beta_2^h]^{-1} - 1/2p_i$; $V_M^h = [M^h - p_1\beta_1^h - p_2\beta_2^h]^{-1}$. Also, of course, $M^h = p_1R_1^h + p_2R_2^h$ for each h. Combining these results we find:

$$x_i^h = \beta_i^h + \frac{1}{2p_i}[p_1[R_1^h - \beta_1^h] + p_2[R_2^h - \beta_2^h]]; \quad h = a,b; \quad i = 1,2.$$

Defining $\beta_1 = \beta_1^a + \beta_1^b$, $\beta_2 = \beta_2^a + \beta_2^b$, $R_1 = R_1^a + R_1^b$, $R_2 = R_2^a + R_2^b$ we obtain, for the excess demand for good 2:

$$E_2 = \beta_2 - R_2 + \frac{1}{2p_2}\,[p_1[R_1 - \beta_1] + p_2[R_2 - \beta_2]]$$

Hence, putting $E_2 = 0$, we get the equilibrium price ratio thus:

$$p_2/p_1 = \frac{R_2 - \beta_2}{R_1 - \beta_1}\quad .$$

7.11

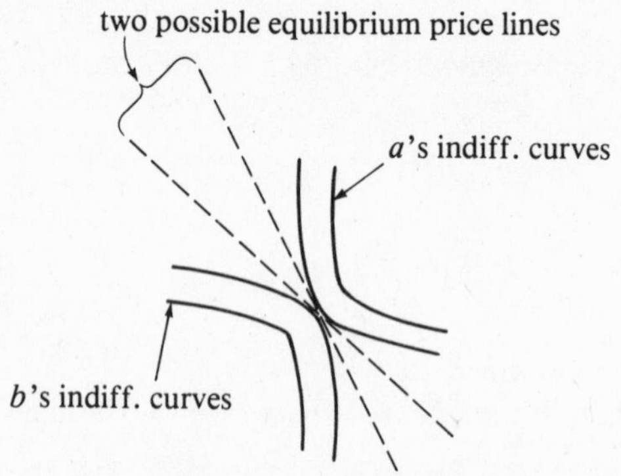

Note, both sets of indifference curves have a 'kink'.

7.12 Since no household is satiated we must have, for any h: $\Sigma_i p_i x_i^h = M^h$ where M^h is given by (7.10). Summing over the households and using (7.5) as an equality the result follows immediately. Expression (7.5) must hold with equality, for otherwise some (greedy) household's consumption of some good could have been increased.

Chapter 8

8.1

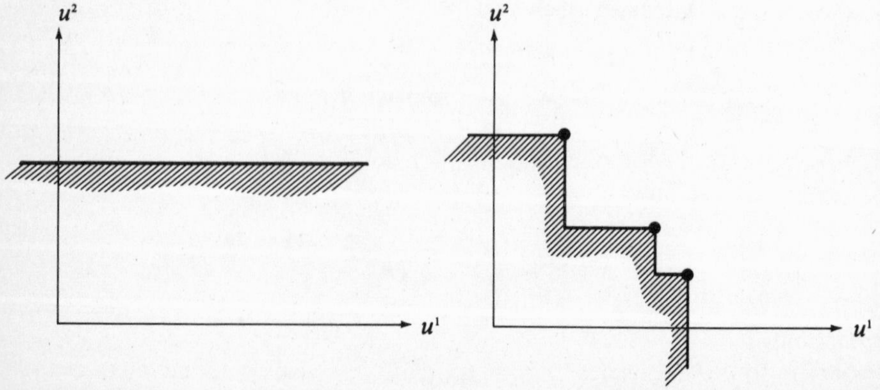

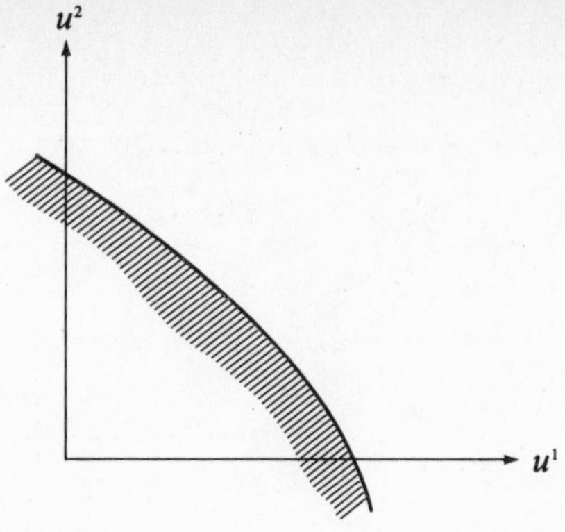

8.2

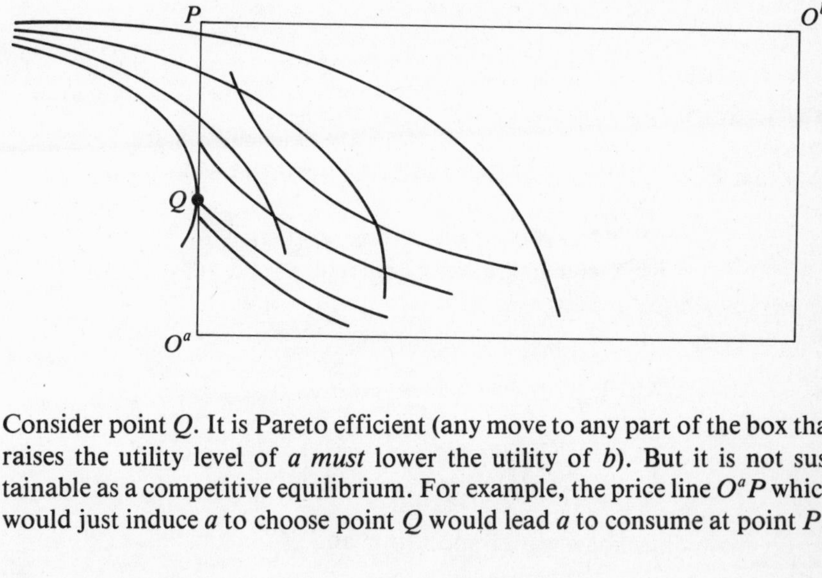

Consider point Q. It is Pareto efficient (any move to any part of the box that raises the utility level of a *must* lower the utility of b). But it is not sustainable as a competitive equilibrium. For example, the price line O^aP which would just induce a to choose point Q would lead a to consume at point P.

8.3 Given the data of Exercise 7.4 the initial allocation yields the utility levels $U^a = \log(91)$, $U^b = \log(864)$.
Since the equilibrium price ratio $\rho = \frac{1}{2}$ we have $\mathbf{x}^a = (5,5)$, $\mathbf{x}^b = (16,4)$. Hence utilities at the equilibrium are: $U^a = \log(125)$, $U^b = \log(1024)$.

8.4 Both production possibility set and indifference curve have a kink at A. Either of the two dotted lines represent possible equilibrium prices.

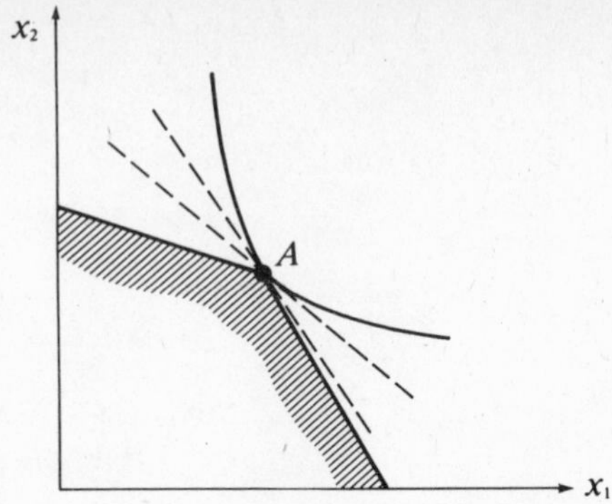

8.5 Let i and j be two commodities for which x_i^h, x_j^h, y_i^f, y_j^f are all non-negative – i.e. they are two (final) consumer goods. Furthermore, let j be such that $x_j^h > 0$ and $y_j^f > 0$. Then for household h and for firm f we must have:

$$\text{MRS}_{ji}^h \leqslant \frac{v_i}{v_j} \leqslant \text{MRT}_{ji}^f$$

where v_i/v_j is the shadow price ratio. If the first inequality is strict, then we know that $x_i^h = 0$; if the second inequality is strict then we know that $y_i^f = 0$.

8.6 To evaluate the efficiency conditions, maximise the utility of household 1 whilst keeping all other households on reference utility levels, subject to technological and resource constraints. The Lagrangean is

$$U^1(x_1^1, x_2^1, x_2) + \sum_{h=2}^{H} \lambda_h [U^h(x_1^h, x_2^h, x_2) - \bar{u}^h] - \mu\Phi(y_1, y_2)$$
$$+ v_1\left[y_1 - \sum_{h=1}^{H} x_1^h\right] + v_2\left[y_2 - \sum_{h=1}^{H} x_2^h\right]$$

Differentiating the above with respect to x_1^h and x_2^h for some h we get:

$$\lambda_h U_1^h - v_1 = 0$$

$$\lambda_h U_2^h + \sum_{j=1}^{H} \lambda_j U_3^j - v_2 = 0$$

where we have ignored corner solutions and where $U_i^h = \dfrac{\partial U^h(x_1^h, x_2^h, x_2)}{\partial x_i^h}$, $i = 1,2$, $U_3^h = \partial U^h(x_1^h, x_2^h, x_2)/\partial x_2$ and λ_1 is a dummy variable set at unity for notational convenience. These two conditions yield

$$\frac{U_2^h}{U_1^h} + e = \frac{v_2}{v_1}$$

where $e \equiv \sum_{j=1}^{H} \frac{\lambda_j U_3^j}{\lambda_h U_1^h}$, is the combined value of the externality, measured in units of good 1. The λs act as social weights in the utilities U^h. Differentiating the Lagrangean with respect to y_1, y_2 and simplifying we get

$$\Phi_2/\Phi_1 = v_2/v_1$$

Combining the results we have $\text{MRT}_{12} = \text{MRS}_{12}^h + e$. Let p_2 be the price consumers pay for good 2 (in terms of units of good 1) and $\hat{p}_2$ the amount received by the firm for each unit it produces. Then an efficient, price-taking solution could be ensured if

$$p_2 = \hat{p}_2 - e$$

Clearly if $U_3^h > 0$, $e > 0$ and e may be interpreted as a government subsidy designed to augment the output of good 2 from the (inefficient) pure competitive amount to the efficient quantity. If $U_3^h < 0$, $e < 0$ and $-e$ is a tax designed to choke off production and consumption of good 2, the collective consumption of which produces harmful side effects.

8.7 The two *technically* efficient points are $\mathbf{x}^0 \equiv (0,1)$ and $\mathbf{x}^1 \equiv (1,\frac{1}{2})$. The issue is: which is Pareto efficient? The situation can be summarised in the table and diagram below

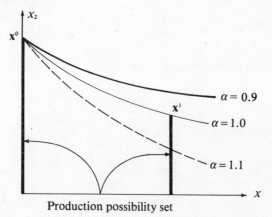

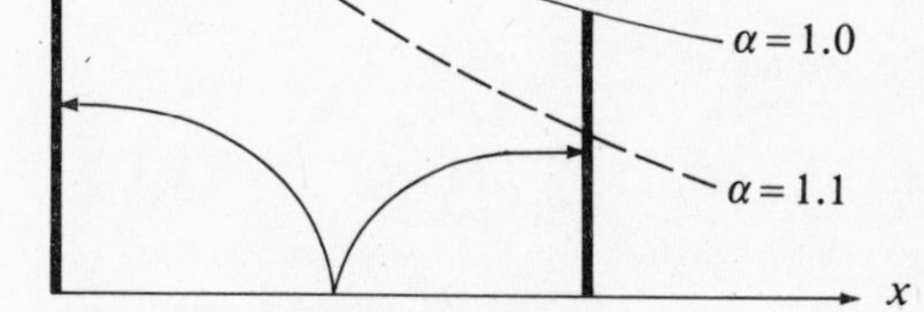

Production possibility set

α	U^0	U^1	MRS$_{21}$ $\mathbf{x}^0$	$\mathbf{x}^1$
0.9	1	.933	.9 log 2	1.8 log 2
1.0	1	1	log 2	2 log 2
1.1	1	1.072	1.1 log 2	2.2 log 2

Clearly the precise value of α is crucial to the decision whether to build ($\mathbf{x}^1$) or not to build ($\mathbf{x}^0$) the broadcasting system.

8.8 (a) The proof follows directly from Definitions 7.5, 7.6 and 8.1. Suppose an allocation $\hat{a}$ were in the core but *not* Pareto efficient. Then there must be a feasible allocation a^* such that

$$U^h(\mathbf{x}^{*h}) \geqslant U^h(\hat{\mathbf{x}}^h) \text{ for every } h$$

and $$U^l(\mathbf{x}^{*l}) > U^l(\hat{\mathbf{x}}^l) \text{ for some household } l.$$

But this implies that a coalition of all households would *block* $\hat{a}$. Therefore $\hat{a}$ cannot lie in the core – a contradiction.

(b) The proof is similar to that of Theorem 7.1. We proceed by demonstrating that no state that is Pareto superior to a competitive equilibrium allocation can be feasible. Let $\mathbf{p}^*$ be the equilibrium price vector, and a^* the associated equilibrium allocation. Let $\tilde{a}$ be any allocation Pareto superior to the equilibrium. Then for all households $h = 1, \ldots, H$: $U^h(\tilde{\mathbf{x}}^h) \geqslant U^h(\mathbf{x}^{*h})$ with strict inequality for some h. However, if households are rational and non-satiated, this implies:

$$\sum_{i=1}^{n} p_i^* \tilde{x}_i^h \geqslant \sum_{i=1}^{n} p_i^* x_i^{*h}, \quad h = 1, \ldots, H$$

with strict inequality for some h. Summing over the households we have, then:

$$\sum_{i=1}^{n} p_i^* \tilde{x}_i > \sum_{i=1}^{n} p_i^* x_i^*$$

Now, by definition $[\mathbf{y}^{*f}]$ is a profit-maximising allocation for the price vector $\mathbf{p}^*$. So, adding up over the firms:

$$\sum_{i=1}^{n} p_i^* \tilde{y}_i \leqslant \sum_{i=1}^{n} p_i^* y_i^*$$

subtracting this from the above and deducting $\sum_{i=1}^{n} p_i^* R_i$ from each side of the resulting inequality we have:

$$\sum_{i=1}^{n} p_i^* [\tilde{x}_i - \tilde{y}_i - R_i] > \sum_{i=1}^{n} p_i^* [x_i^* - y_i^* - R_i]$$

But the right-hand side of this is just $\sum_{i=1}^{n} p_i^* E_i(p^*)$, which by Walras' law must be zero. So the left-hand side must be strictly positive. This is only possible if

$$\tilde{x}_i - \tilde{y}_i - R_i > 0$$

for at least one good i. But this implies that $\tilde{a}$ is infeasible. So no feasible point exists that is Pareto superior to a^*.

8.9 Consider the problem max $U^1(\mathbf{x}^1; \bar{u}^2, \bar{u}^3, \ldots, \bar{u}^H)$ subject to equations (8.1)–(8.3). Since $\bar{u}^h$ is constant for $h = 2,3, \ldots, H$, the first-order conditions will be

$$x_i^1 \left[U_i^1 \left[1 + \sum_{l=2}^{H} \partial U^l / \partial u^1 \right] - v_i \right] = 0$$

for household 1 and otherwise much the same as equations (8.5)–(8.9).

8.10 The Lagrangean for a type-1 household is

$$\log x_1^1 + 2 \log x_2^1 + v^1[10p_1 - p_1x_1^1 - p_2x_2^1]$$

The consumption levels which maximise this are given by $x_1^1 = 10/3$, $x_2^1 = 20\rho/3$ where $\rho = p_1/p_2$ – compare Exercise 7.5. Likewise the utility-maximising consumption levels for a type-2 person (who takes x_1^1 as *given*) are $x_1^2 = 10/3\rho$, $x_2^2 = 20/3$. Market clearing for good 1 yields

$$10/3 + 10\rho/3 = 10$$

which implies $\rho = \frac{1}{2}$. Hence in the competitive allocation we have $\mathbf{x}^1 = (10/3, 10/3)$; $\mathbf{x}^2 = (20/3, 20/3)$. Consider a redistribution such that $dx_1^2 = -dx_1^1 > 0$ and $dx_2^1 = -dx_2^2 = \frac{1}{2}dx_1^1$. We find that in the neighbourhood of the equilibrium $dU^1 = 0.3[dx_1^1 + 2dx_2^1] = 0$, $dU^2 = 0.3[dx_1^2 + 2dx_2^2 - dx_1^1] > 0$. Hence a type-2 person's utility could be increased without reducing the utility level of the type-1 persons. The reason for this is that there is an obvious consumption externality: x_1^1 *reduces* U^2.

8.11 (a) Equilibrium is at A. Slope of broken line is $-p_1/p_2$, the ratio of producer prices; slope of solid line is $-\hat{p}_1/p_2$, the ratio of consumer prices; where $\hat{p}_1 = [1+\tau]p_1$ and τ is the *ad valorem* tax rate.

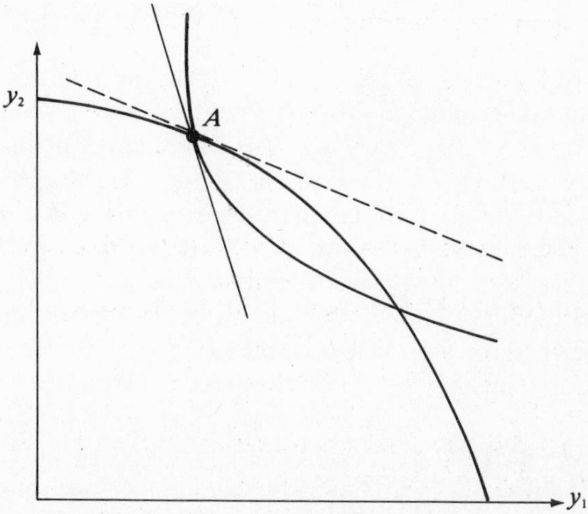

(b) In the monopolistic case take the model of part (a) and let p_1 denote the marginal cost of producing good 1 and let $\hat{p}_1$ the price charged to consumers.

8.12 Model is essentially that of Exercise 8.6.

Chapter 9

9.1 (a) Observe that the production function may be written in intensive form as $A(t)g_i(k_i)$, using an obvious notation. Hence the ratio of the marginal products, θ_i, is given by $[A(t)g_i(k_i)]/[A(t)g_i'(k_i)] - k_i = g_i(k_i)/g_i'(k_i) - k_i$: thus for a given k_i, θ_i will be unchanged by $A(t)$. Hence, in Figure 9.1, as t increases, the curve shifts upwards (but still passes through the origin) in such a way that at any k_i the tangent to the curve still has the same intercept on the *horizontal* axis. In Figure 9.2 the isoquant map remains unchanged: as time passes each isoquant corresponds to a larger value of output.
(b) Clearly the production function in intensive form is $q_i = A(t)g_i(k_i/A(t))$ which has slope $g_i'(k_i/A(t))$. This slope is constant over time if $k_i/A(t)$ is constant; but $k_i/A(t)$ is constant if and only if $q_i/A(t)$ is constant, that is if and only if q_i/k_i is constant. So, as the production function shifts upwards through time in Figure 9.1 the pattern of curves traced out must be of the 'homothetic' form: i.e. any given ray through the origin intercepts each production function at a point where it has the same slope for all values of t.
(c) Case (a) is so-called 'Hicks-neutral' technical progress. As time rolls by output increases for a given combination of inputs in such a way that, at a given factor price ratio θ, the technique remains unchanged. Case (b) is so-called 'Harrod-neutral' technical progress: as time rolls by the production function shifts in such a way that the L-factor appears to be augmented.

9.2 (a) and (b) can be analysed together, from the point of view of the Ruritanian domestic economy. The tariff or tax drives up the price of one good [cf. the answer to Exercise 9.4]. This will raise the price of the factor used intensively in the production of that good (the Stolper–Samuelson theorem). (c) Since the tax is on *all* interest income there is no distortion in relative factor prices between the two sectors. If Ruritania engages in international trade at given world prices the tax leaves the relative prices of the consumer goods unaltered too. The assumption of constant returns to scale will ensure that the same proportions of the two goods are still produced. (d) The result is simply the reverse of that illustrated in Figure 9.7.

9.3 Assume S1–S7. (a) Relative goods prices are fixed in world markets, so the Rybczynski theorem is immediately applicable. Energy-intensive

industry expands, labour-intensive industry contracts. Factor prices remain unchanged.
(b) Factor prices will change. Since labour is now relatively more scarce, relative price of labour intensive goods rises and price of labour rises relative to that of energy.

9.4 Interpret K to mean capital, L to mean labour; good 2 is labour intensive. Initially equilibrium is at A on the efficiency locus O_1AO_2. The curve through A and B is a 2-isoquant. Unionisation in sector 2 forces up the relative wage there so that $\theta_2 = [1+\alpha]\theta_1$, say, where $\alpha > 0$ is the union differential: this produces a new locus O_1BCO_2. (Check this by drawing some 1-isoquants that are tangential to 2-isoquants along O_1AO_2 – observe the difference in their slopes, α, along O_1BCO_2.) Price of good 2 rises relative to good 1, so less good 2 is produced (compare Figure 9.6). Therefore new equilibrium lies in the segment BO_2 of the locus $OBCO_2$. Clearly k_1 *must* fall; k_2 falls if the new equilibrium lies in the segment CO_2, but rises if the new equilibrium is in BC. Therefore w_1/p_1 and w_2/p_2 must fall; real wages in industry 2 may rise or fall, depending on movement of k_2.

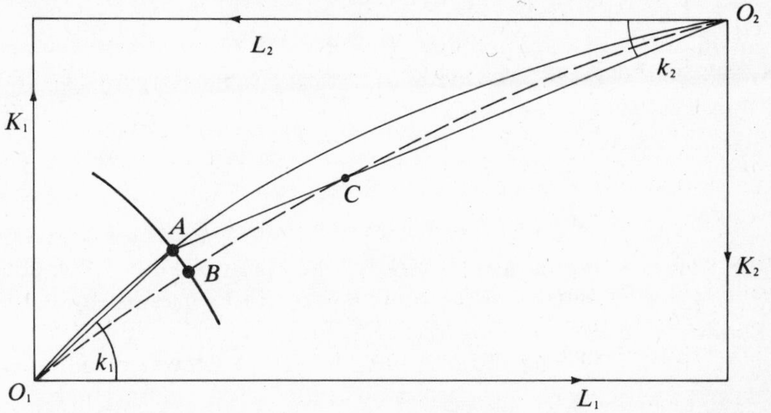

9.5 The 'Hicks-neutral' shift in part (a) of Exercise 9.1 leaves unchanged the relationships (9.31, 9.32) in each industry. Hence if world prices p remain unchanged θ, k_1 or k_2 remain unchanged as technical progress proceeds. The 'Harrod-neutral' shift in part (b) has an effect that is equivalent to augmenting the L-resource used in each sector. Define $\bar{\bar{L}}(t) = \bar{L}A(t)$. Then it is clear that the effect of technical progress in this model is equivalent to an exogenously growing stock of the L-resource. Hence we may use the Rybczynski theorem to show that as time passes production of the L-intensive good steadily expands, and production of the K-intensive good contracts. Observe that this cannot be taken as a complete model of economic development of an economy unless K is taken to be a strictly non-produced resource such as land.

9.6 (a) Before trade p_1/p_2 is 1.25 in Alpha and 5 in Beta: hence there is a basis for mutually beneficial trade. Alpha has a comparative advantage in the production of good 1, beta has the comparative advantage in producing good 2.
(b) Equilibrium price ratio lies between 1.25 and 5. Alpha exports good 1 and imports good 2.
(c) It makes sense for Alpha to import good 2 from Beta since the cost (in terms of forgone good 1) is less than it would have been had good 1 all been produced domestically.

9.7 Using equations 9.5 to 9.14 we may construct the following table for the production functions of the two goods.

	good 1	good 2
$g_i(k_i)$	$k_1^{\frac{1}{2}}$	$k_2/[1+k_2]$
w_K/p_i	$\frac{1}{2}k_1^{-\frac{1}{2}}$	$[1+k_2]^{-2}$
w_L/p_i	$\frac{1}{2}k_1^{\frac{1}{2}}$	$k_2^2/[1+k_2]^2$
θ_i	k_1	k_2^2

From this we see that in equilibrium $k_1 = \theta$ and $k_2 = \sqrt{\theta}$; so $k_1 < k_2$ for $\theta < \hat{\theta} = 1$ and $k_1 > k_2$ for $\theta > \hat{\theta}$. Dividing the second element in row 2 by the first we find $\rho \equiv p_1/p_2 = [w_K/p_2]/[w_K/p_1] = 2k_1^{\frac{1}{2}}/[1+k_2]^2$. Substituting for k_1 and k_2 we have

$$\rho = 2\sqrt{\theta}/[1+\sqrt{\theta}]^2$$

Hence $\partial\rho/\partial\theta = [1 - 1/\sqrt{\theta}][1 + \sqrt{\theta}]^{-3} \lesseqgtr 0$ as $\theta \gtreqless \hat{\theta} = 1$; ρ is an inverse U-shaped function of θ. Banania's $\bar{K}/\bar{L}$ is 2, and pre-trade $\theta > \hat{\theta}$; Republico's $\bar{K}/\bar{L}$ is $\frac{1}{2}$ and it thus has a pre-trade $\theta < \hat{\theta}$: in Figures 9.5(b) and 9.10, Republico is on the left of the diagram, Banania on the right. When trade opens ρ rises in Banania and falls in Republico to some value intermediate between $\frac{1}{4}$ and $\frac{1}{3}$; Banania exports good 1; Republico exports good 2; θ falls in both countries.

9.8 Since θ differs in the two countries in the free trade equilibrium above there *is* a point in introducing free trade in factors to eliminate the inefficiency in factor allocation. The combined economy has $\bar{K}/\bar{L} = 1$. Hence in the common market $\theta = 1$ so that $\rho = \frac{1}{2}$.

9.9 Label the countries and goods as on p. 196: Alpha is relatively well-endowed with L, and on opening of trade, exports good 2 (the L-intensive good). Then, using equations (9.27)–(9.38) we can set out the following table to indicate what happens when trade is opened:

	Alpha	Beta	
p_1/p_2 (ρ)	↓	↑	
w_L/w_K (θ)	↑	↓	
w_K/p_i	↓	↑	(9.27)
w_L/p_i	↑	↓	(9.28)

It is clear from the third and fourth lines of the table that in country Alpha the budget constraint for the K-owners shifts unambiguously inwards (and hence their utility falls) and the budget constraint for the L-owners shifts unambiguously outwards (hence their utility rises). The situation is the opposite in country Beta.

So, if the two factors are owned by distinct groups ('capitalists' and 'workers') trade is a mixed blessing in terms of each group's actual welfare levels. Note that we are here explicitly rejecting the assumption, used in Section 9.5, that the interests of *all* the members of one country can be represented by a single set of indifference curves.

Chapter 10

10.1

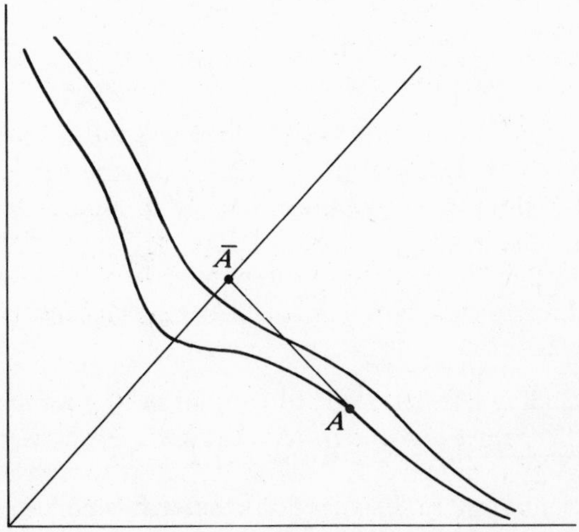

Let A be the prospect and $\bar{A}$ its mean; A_λ can be any point in the line joining them. The definition implies that moving along this line towards $\bar{A}$ puts the person on successively higher indifference curves. In the diagram it is clear that this condition is consistent with there being indifference curves that violate the conve-to-the-origin property locally.

10.2 Let there be only three possible states of the world: red, blue and green, with probabilities 0.01, 0.10, 0.89 respectively. Then the payoffs in the four prospects can be written

	red	blue	green
A^1	1	1	1
A^2	0	5	1
A^3	0	5	0
A^4	1	1	0

where all the entries in the table are in millions of dollars. Note that A^1 and A^2 have the same payoff (1) in state green; A^4 and A^3 (in that order) form a similar pair, except that the payoff in state green is 0. Axiom U2 states that if A^1 is preferred to A^2 then any other similar pair of prospects $(1,1,z)$ and $(0,5,z)$ ought also to be ranked in the same order, for arbitrary z: but this would imply that A^4 is preferred to A^3, the opposite of the preferences as stated.

10.3

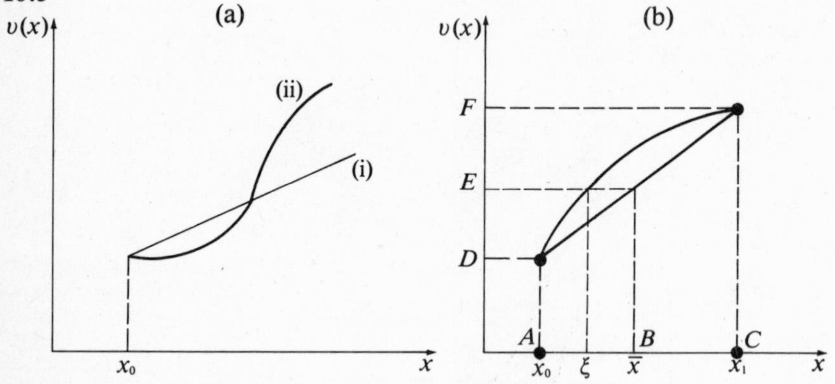

note: $AB/AC = DE/DF = \pi$

10.4 (a) Expanding left-hand side of Definition 10.1 we have

$$\upsilon(\bar{x}) + \upsilon'(\bar{x})[\xi - \bar{x}] + \tfrac{1}{2}\upsilon''(\bar{x})[\xi - \bar{x}]^2 + \ldots$$

Similarly the right-hand side, expanded around $\bar{x}$, becomes:

$$\upsilon(\bar{x}) + \upsilon'(\bar{x})\mathscr{E}[x - \bar{x}] + \tfrac{1}{2}\upsilon''(\bar{x})\mathscr{E}[x - \bar{x}]^2 + \ldots$$

Equating these gives the result. For small risks we may neglect terms in $[\xi-\bar{x}]^r$ for $r \geqslant 2$. So, dividing the equation in the question by $\upsilon'(\bar{x})$ we get the Theorem 10.3.

(b) Suppressing the x-argument for notational ease we find:

$$\hat{\upsilon}_1 = \phi(\upsilon) \Rightarrow \hat{\upsilon}' = \phi'\upsilon' \Rightarrow \hat{\upsilon}'' = \phi'\upsilon'' + \phi''[\upsilon']^2$$

Dividing the last equation by $-\hat{\upsilon}_1'$ we find

$$\hat{a} = a + \upsilon'\phi''/\phi'$$

But this last term is non-positive if $\phi'' \leqslant 0$. Hence the result.

10.5 (a) If $-\upsilon''/\upsilon' = a$, a constant, then integrating we find $\log \upsilon' = \log A - ax$ where A is a constant. Integrating again we find the utility function is $\upsilon(x) = -e^{-ax}$, up to a linear transformation.

(b) Likewise if $-x\upsilon''/\upsilon' = b$, a constant, we find $\upsilon = \dfrac{1}{1-b} x^{1-b}$.

(c) Multiply last equation in answer 10.4(b) by x. Answer is then immediate.

10.6 Clearly $\mathscr{E}\upsilon(x) = A_0 + A_1\mathscr{E}x - \frac{1}{2}A_2\mathscr{E}x^2 = A_0 + A_1\bar{x} - \frac{1}{2}A_2[\bar{x}^2 + \sigma^2]$, using the definitions $\bar{x} \equiv \mathscr{E}x$, $\sigma^2 \equiv \mathscr{E}x^2 - x^2$

Marginal utility is $A_1 - A_2x$. For this to be non-negative (i.e. for x to be a 'good') we must have $\bar{A} \leqslant A_1/A_2$; hence $\bar{x}$ is always a 'good' and σ^2 a 'bad'.

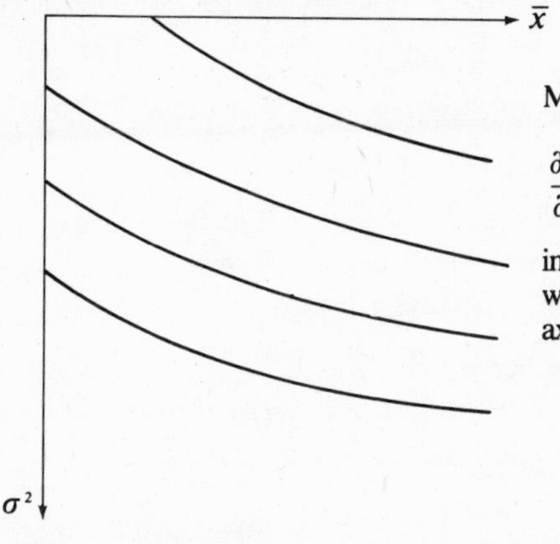

Marginal rate of substitution

$$\frac{\partial\phi}{\partial\bar{x}} \bigg/ \frac{\partial\phi}{\partial\sigma^2} = -2[A_1/A_2 - \bar{x}]$$

increases with A_2, decreases with A_1. Intercept on σ^2 axis is independent of A_1.

10.7 (a) Income (positive or negative) is Br, which therefore gives disposable income $Br[1-\tau]$. Hence, *ex-post* wealth is $M = A + Br[1-\tau]$ (which is $\gtrless A$).

(b) Maximising $\mathscr{E}v(M)$ with respect to B we find, for an interior solution:

$$\mathscr{E}(\upsilon'(A + B^*r[1-\tau])r)[1-\tau] = 0, \quad \text{or } \mathscr{E}(\upsilon'r) = 0$$

(c) Differentiating (b) we find $\mathscr{E}(\upsilon''r^2)[1-\tau]\dfrac{\partial B^*}{\partial\tau} - \mathscr{E}(\upsilon''r^2)B^* = 0$.

Hence $\dfrac{\partial B^*}{\partial\tau} = \dfrac{B^*}{1-\tau}$: an increase in the tax rate *in*creases the demand for bonds.

(d) We now have $M = A[1-\tau] + Br[1-\tau]$. Following through as in (a) to (c) we find $\mathscr{E}(\upsilon'' r^2)[1-\tau]\dfrac{\partial B^*}{\partial \tau} - \mathscr{E}(\upsilon'' r^2)B^* - \mathscr{E}(\upsilon'' r)A = 0 \Rightarrow \dfrac{\partial B^*}{\partial \tau} = \dfrac{B^*}{1-\tau} + \dfrac{\mathscr{E}(\upsilon'' r)A}{\mathscr{E}(\upsilon'' r^2)}$. First term on the right-hand side is positive; denominator of second term is negative, numerator positive if absolute risk aversion is decreasing. Hence $\partial B^*/\partial\tau$ is ambiguous.

10.8 (a) Maximising expected utility of profit $\mathscr{E}\upsilon(PQ - C(Q))$ by choice of Q requires $\mathscr{E}(\upsilon' P) = \mathscr{E}(\upsilon')C_Q$ for the first-order condition. This will represent a maximum if $\dfrac{d^2\mathscr{E}\upsilon}{dQ^2} < 0$. We find that this implies

$$\mathscr{E}(\upsilon''[P - C_Q]^2) - \mathscr{E}(\upsilon'')C_{QQ} < 0$$

Note that since the first term is negative for a risk-averse firm then the condition can be satisfied not only if $C_{QQ} > 0$ but also if $C_{QQ} < 0$ and $|C_{QQ}|$ is not 'too large'.

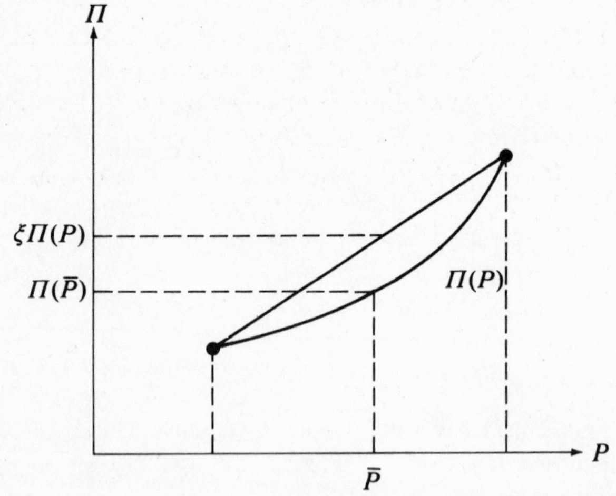

Now consider transforming P to $\hat{P}$ thus: $\hat{P} = [1 - \lambda]P + \lambda\bar{P}$; if $0 < \lambda \leqslant 1$, then $\hat{P}$ has the same mean as P, but is less dispersed. Maximised utility for the random variable $\hat{P}$ is

$$\mathscr{E}\upsilon([[1-\lambda]P + \lambda\bar{P}]Q^* - C(Q^*))$$

where Q^* is the output satisfying the first-order conditions for a maximum. Differentiate this expected utility with respect to λ:

$$\frac{\partial \mathscr{E}\upsilon^*}{\partial\lambda} = [\mathscr{E}(\upsilon'[\bar{P} - P])]Q^* + \mathscr{E}(\upsilon'[\hat{P} - C_Q])\frac{\partial Q^*}{\partial\lambda}$$

The last term vanishes of the first-order conditions. So $\partial \mathscr{E} \upsilon^*/\partial\lambda$ has the sign of $\mathscr{E}(\upsilon'[\overline{P} - P])$. But this must be positive if υ' is decreasing with Π and will be zero if υ' is constant. Hence the firm strictly prefers 'certainty' if it is risk averse and is indifferent between certainty and uncertainty if it is risk neutral.

(b) For any *known* realisation of P we may write $Q = S(P)$ where S is the competitive firm's supply curve (see Chapter 3). Profits as a function of P may thus be written:

$$\Pi(P) = PS(P) - C(S(P))$$
$$\Rightarrow \Pi'(P) = [P - C_Q]S'(P) + S(P) = S(P)$$
$$\Rightarrow \Pi''(P) = S'(P) > 0$$

Hence $\Pi(P)$ is increasing and convex (cf. Exercise 3.7). So it is immediate that $\mathscr{E}\Pi(P) > \Pi(\overline{P})$.

Alf accepts any contract that puts him in the shaded set; $u_0^a, u_1^a, \ldots$ denote Alf's indifference curves; they intersect the 45° ray through O^a at slope $[1-\pi]/\pi$. Bill has an endowment of K, irrespective of the state of nature; draw his indifference curves $u_0^b, u_1^b, \ldots$ with reference to O^b: they intersect the 45° ray through O^b at slope $[1-\pi]/\pi$. Point D represents the initial endowment point i.e. the consumption that Alf and Bill would each enjoy if they did not do a deal. Point E represents the optimum contract (from Bill's point of view) since it is a point of common tangency of two indifference curves. The contract specifies a payment of FE, whatever happens, and a bonus of $[O^aF - FE]$ if it is a good year. At E we have $\upsilon^{a\prime}(x_1^a)/\upsilon^{a\prime}(x_2^a) = \upsilon^{b\prime}(x_1^b)/\upsilon^{b\prime}(x_2^b)$ where x_i^h denotes consumption by h in state i; $h = a,b$; $i = 1,2$.

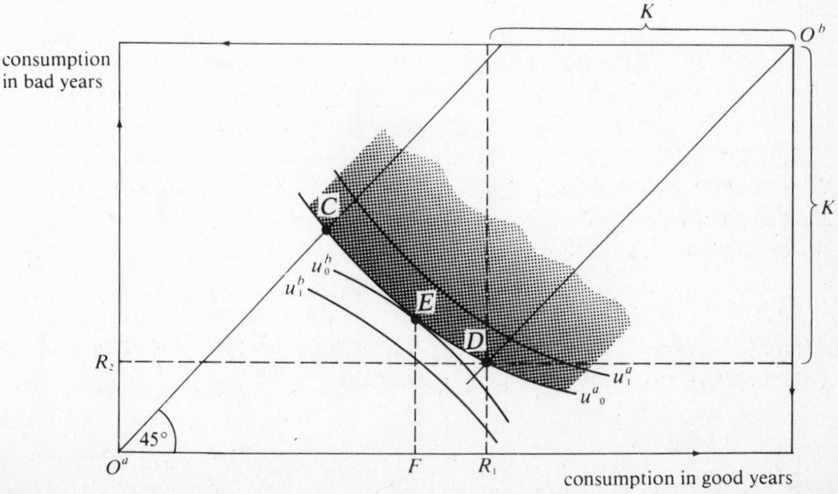

10.10 (a) Bill's indifference curves become lines with slope $[1-\pi]/\pi$: optimum is at *C*.
(b) Alf's indifference curves become lines with slope $[1-\pi]/\pi$: optimum is at *D*.

Chapter 11

11.1 (a) Game (iii) has the property that each party would like the other to play ← under all circumstances: so if each were allowed to choose the *other's* move they would automatically end up at the Pareto efficient ← ← solution; game (ii) does not have this property.
(b) Games (iv) and (v).

11.2 If the output of the other firms is $S(P)$ and the quantity sold in the market is $D(P)$, then the sales of the large firm must be $D(P) - S(P)$. Hence profits of the large firm are given by $[D(P) - S(P)]P - C(D(P) - S(P))$. The solution is almost exactly that of the monopolist in Section 3.7 of Chapter 3, with the demand function $D(P)$ replaced by $D(P) - S(P)$.

11.3 $\Pi = [A_0 - aP][P - c] - C_0$. Differentiating we find that Π has a maximum at $P^* = [A_0 + ac]/2a$. Substituting in the expression for Π we find $\Pi^* = [A_0 - ac]^2/4a - C_0$ as maximum profits. *If* the other firms enter then, from Exercise 11.2, we know that the profit-maximising solution for the incumbent firm is to treat $D(P) - S(P)$ as its new demand curve. Hence we merely have to replace A_0 by $A_0 + B_0$ and a by $a + b$ in the above to get the optimal price *conditional on entry* as $P^{**} = [A_0 + B_0]/2[a + b] + \frac{1}{2}c$ and $\Pi^{**} = [A_0 + B_0 - [a + b]c]^2/4[a + b] - C_0$. Two possibilities:

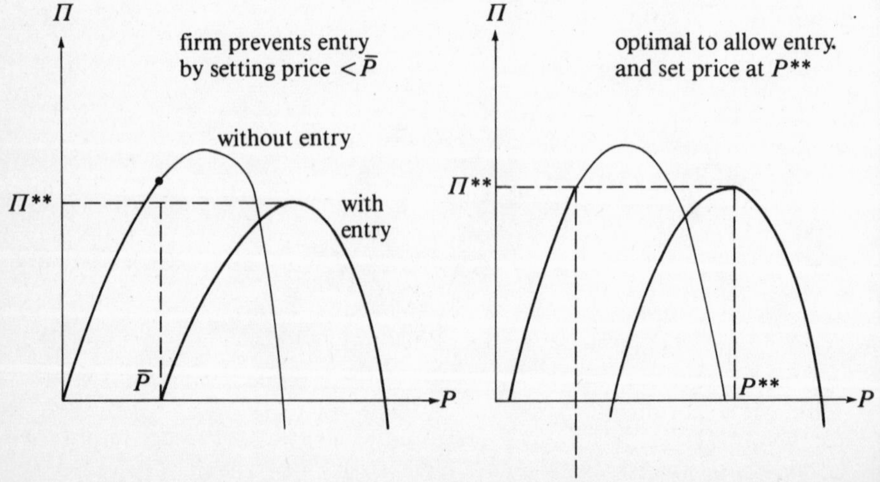

11.4 The left-hand side of (11.28) can be taken as price country b (Betaland) pays for good 1 (the good it exports) measured in units of good 2; call this $\tilde{p}_1$. Setting $p_2^* = 1$ we see $\tilde{p}_1 = [1 + 1/\varepsilon_{11}^a]\hat{p}_1$; or, rearranging, the price that country a (Alphaland) has to pay for good 1 (the good it imports) can be written as $\hat{p}_1 = [1 + \tau]\tilde{p}_1$ where $\tau(\equiv -1/1 + \varepsilon_{11}^b)$ is the tariff and is well defined for $\varepsilon_{11}^a < -1$. Obviously the solution is Pareto inefficient, irrespective of whether Alphaland retaliates.

11.5 (a) $\Pi^f = [a - b\overline{Q}_{-f} - bQ^f]Q^f - C_0 - cQ^f$.
(b) Differentiating (a) with respect to Q^f, assuming $\overline{Q}_{-f}$ is constant, yields an interior solution where $0 = a - b\overline{Q}_{-f} - c - 2bQ^f$. If all firms are identical then $\hat{Q}^1 = \hat{Q}^2 = \ldots = \hat{Q}^F$ hence $\overline{Q}_{-f} = [F - 1]Q^f$ and we immediately find $\hat{Q}^f = [a - c]/[bF + b]$.

(c) At the Cournot equilibrium $P = a - bF\hat{Q}^f = \dfrac{ab/F + bc}{b + b/F}$. As $F \to \infty$, $P \to c$, marginal cost.

(d) Profits in equilibrium are $\dfrac{ab + bcF}{[bF + b]^2}[a - c] - C_0 - c\dfrac{a - c}{bF + b}$ which, on simplification, are found to equal $\dfrac{1}{b}\left[\dfrac{a - c}{F + 1}\right]^2 - C_0$. Writing down the condition that profits be non-negative we find immediately the condition that $F \leqslant [a - c][bC_0]^{-\frac{1}{2}} - 1$.

11.6 (a) Joint profits are $[a - bQ]Q - FC_0 - cQ$. Optimum output, derived from first-order condition, is therefore at $Q^* = \dfrac{a - c}{2b}$. Maximised joint profits are thus $\dfrac{[a - c]^2}{4b} - FC_0$; so profits for each firm are $\dfrac{[a - c]^2}{4bF} - C_0$, which are clearly greater than in 11.5(d).
(b) If firm f assumes all other firms' outputs are constant, then differentiating the Π^f given in 11.5(a) at the point $Q^f = \dfrac{a - c}{2bF}$ gives $\partial\Pi^f/\partial Q^f = a - c - 2bQ + b\overline{Q}_{-f} = b\overline{Q}_{-f} > 0$. Hence firm f has incentive to increase output beyond $\dfrac{1}{F}Q^*$.

11.7 (a) First-order conditions give $P + Q^fP' = C_Q^f \Rightarrow P > C_Q^f$. Gap between P and C_Q^f small if Q^f small or P' small.
(b) Clearly $Q^f = [C_Q^f - P]/P'$. Since P' is negative, the larger the marginal cost, the smaller the output.

11.8 If the prevailing price is initially 10, then the total quantity supplied must be $5[20 - P] = 50$; given that this particular firm produces at $Q^f = 10$, everyone else is producing 40. For $Q^f < 10$ the firm believes that everyone else *stays* at 40: so the *total* revenue for firm f in this region is given by $[20 - [40 + Q^f]/5]Q^f = [12 - Q^f/5]Q^f$. For $Q^f > 10$ the firm believes that others will alter output so that market share is just maintained, i.e. such that $Q^f/Q = 10/50 = 1/5$. Hence total revenue in this region is given by $[20 - 5Q^f/5]Q^f = [20 - Q^f]Q^f$. Hence marginal revenue is

$$\begin{array}{ll} 12 - 0.4\,Q^f, & Q^f < 10 \\ 20 - 2\,Q^f, & Q^f > 10 \end{array}$$

Marginal cost is everywhere given by $0.5\,Q^f$, so that at $Q^f = 10$ we have MR (left hand) $= 8 >$ MC $> 0 =$ MR (right hand). Clearly MC continues to lie between 0 and 8 (and this equilibrium remains undisturbed) as long as $0 \leqslant \alpha \leqslant 0.4$.

11.9 (a) Maximising the Lagrangean for a price-taking a-trader we find the first-order condition $\frac{1}{2}/\sqrt{x_i^a} = \lambda p_i$, where λ is the Lagrange multiplier and $i = 1,2$. Hence $x_i^a = [2\lambda p_i]^{-2}$, $i = 1,2$. Using the budget constraint we find that $M = [2\lambda]^{-2}\,[p_1^{-1} + p_2^{-1}]$ where M is the income of a a-trader. Substituting we find $x_i^a = Mp_i^{-2}\,[p_1^{-1} + p_2^{-1}]^{-1}$. Aggregating and substituting for M we find the result.

The b-trader maximises $x_1^b x_2^b$, which involves choosing ρ to maximise $\left[R_1 - \dfrac{1}{\rho+\rho^2}R_2\right]\left[R_2 - \dfrac{\rho}{1+\rho}R_2\right]$. Maximising this when $R_1 = 20$, $R_2 = 10$ gives on simplification:

$$[\rho - 1][2\rho^2 + 4\rho + 1] = 0$$

which yields $\rho = 1$ as the only admissible solution.

(b) The b-trader can now drive the a-traders down to their reservation utility at $\sqrt{x_1^a} + \sqrt{x_2^a} = \sqrt{10}$.

(c) Solution (a) is not efficient; (b) is.

11.10 (a) Joint-profit maximising solution at

$$Q^{*1} = \frac{\alpha}{\beta[1 + c^1/c^2] + c^1}\,;\; Q^{*2} = \frac{\alpha}{\beta[1 + c^2/c^1] + c^2}$$

(b) Stackelberg solution at

$$\tilde{Q}^1 = \frac{\alpha}{\beta[1 + c^1/[\beta + 2c^2]] + c^1}\,;\; \tilde{Q}^2 = \frac{\alpha - \frac{1}{2}\beta\tilde{Q}^1}{\beta + c^2}$$

Chapter 12

12.1 Let the compensation to be paid from firm 1 to firm 2 be $\gamma(y_1^1)$. Firm 2's Lagrangean then becomes $\Sigma_i p_i y_i^2 + \gamma(y_1^1) - \mu_2 \Phi^2(\mathbf{y}^2; y_1^2)$; firm 1's Lagrangean is $\Sigma_i p_i y_i^1 - \gamma(y_1^1) - \mu_1 \Phi^1(\mathbf{y}^1)$ – compare (12.1) and (12.5). Clearly all the results go through with $\gamma = -B$.

12.2 There is an externality here since $\delta y_2/\delta y_1 = -\alpha$; y_2 is positive if $z < \bar{z}$ where $\bar{z} = \dfrac{R}{1+\alpha^2}$. In this region the boundary is given by $y_2 = \sqrt{(R - [y_1]^2)} - \alpha y_1$. If preferences are given by the dotted indifference curve, then A can be supported as a profit-maximising equilibrium. If preferences are given by the solid curve, then point B could not be supported. The larger is α, the closer is point C to the origin.

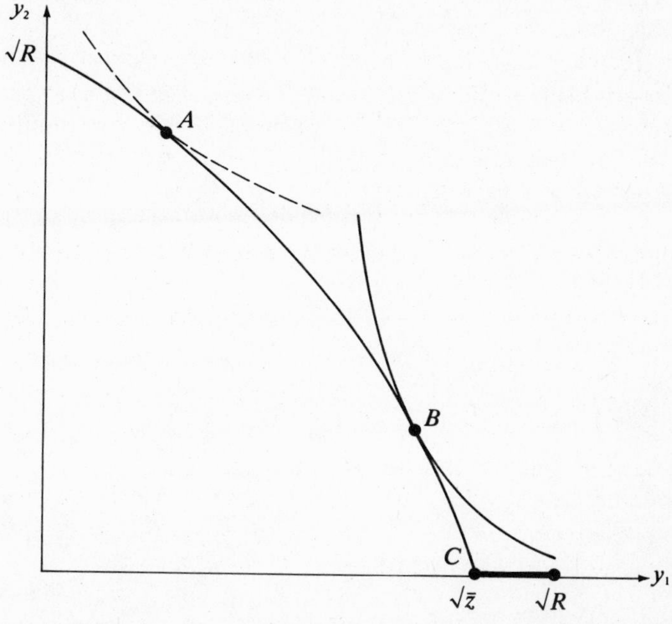

12.3 Let z^a, z^b be the amounts of good 2 that Alf and Bill contribute for the production of good 1. Then in a two-person case (12.10) becomes $U^a(\phi(z^a + z^b), R_2^a - z^a)$. Consider the slope of this in (z^a, z^b)-space: $[\partial U^a/\partial z^a]/[\partial U^a/\partial z^b] = 1 - U_2^a/U_1^a\phi'$. Clearly this slope is $\gtreqless 0$ as $\text{MRS}_{21}^a \gtreqless 1/\phi'$. Alf maximises U^a with respect to z^a assuming z^b constant: he chooses a point where $\partial U^a/\partial z^a = 0$: i.e. where $\text{MRS}_{21}^a = 1/\phi'$.

12.4 Individual income, net of educational costs is $M(z) - ze^{-\alpha}$. Maximising this with respect to z gives the first-order condition $M'(z) - e^{-\alpha} = 0$, from which the first part of the question follows immediately. If employer's expectations are fulfilled then the realised marginal product (α) equals the wage ($M(z)$) so we find:

$$-\log(M'(z)) = M(z),$$

which is a first-order differential equation. Solving this gives the second result, with k as a constant of integration. In this model the costs of education ($ze^{-\alpha}$) are a net loss to the workers who would have been paid α anyway if it could have been observed.

12.5 Customers could form themselves into retailing firms and undercut the incumbent firms.

12.6 Let the subsidy to the producer be denoted ($B(Q)$ (it is contingent on output). Profits for the monopolist are then $P(Q)\,Q - C(Q) + B(Q)$. Maximising this with respect to Q gives the first-order condition: $P + QP'(Q) - C'(Q) + B'(Q) = 0$. Efficiency requires $P = C'(Q)$; clearly this can be achieved if the function B is chosen such that $B'(Q) = -QP'(Q)$; integrating this we find $B(Q) = \int^{Q} P(x)dx - PQ$ which is a measure of consumer's surplus.

12.7 The change in the unit price depends on what happens to marginal cost: if marginal cost is rising in the neighbourhood of the equilibrium (it need not be) then this price rises.

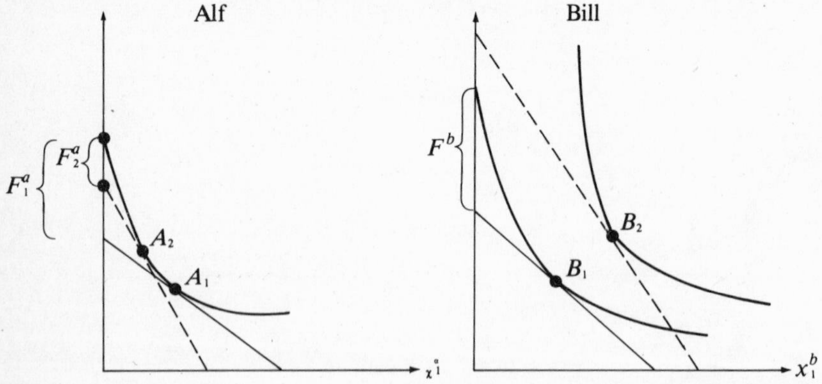

Bill's demand increases because of an increase in income, say. The slope of the solid line represents original marginal cost (equal to the unit price). The slope of the dotted line represents the unit price at the new, higher marginal cost. Entry fee for Alf *falls* from F_1^a to F_2^a; Bill's entry fee may rise or fall.

12.8 Let compensating variation of person h for the switch $\mathcal{S}_2 \rightarrow \mathcal{S}_1$ be CV^h, and take two cases: (a) $CV^h \geqslant 0$, (b) $CV^h < 0$. Let v be the number of votes *other than in his* favour of 1 rather than 2, and let $v^* \equiv \frac{1}{2}H - 1$. The project goes ahead if the *total* number of votes is $\geqslant v^* + 1$. Now consider the following table giving the payoff to person h's vote:

	$v < v^*$	$v = v^*$	$v > v^*$
h votes for $\mathscr{s}_1$	0	CV^h	CV^h
h votes for $\mathscr{s}_2$	0	0	CV^h

Clearly the payoffs from voting $\mathscr{s}_1$ dominate the payoffs from voting $\mathscr{s}_2$; case (b) follows from a similar table.

12.9 Let P^* be a buyer's *true* willingness to pay and P his announced bid. Consider the following payoff table for the bidder:

	fails to meet reserve ($P<\bar{P}$)	gets the vase ($P \geqslant \bar{P}$)
(a) underbids ($P<P^*$)	0	$P^* - \bar{P}(>0)$
(b) bids truthfully ($P=P^*$)	0	$P^* - \bar{P}(\geqslant 0)$
(c) overbids ($P>P^* \geqslant \bar{P}$)	0	$P^* - \bar{P}(\geqslant 0)$
(d) overbids ($P>\bar{P}>P^*$)	0	$P^* - \bar{P}(<0)$

It is not worth underbidding because the buyer might lose the sum $[P^* - \bar{P}]$. If the buyer overbids, then either there is no advantage vis-à-vis telling the truth (case (c)) or he may *lose* (case (d)).

12.10 (a)–(b)

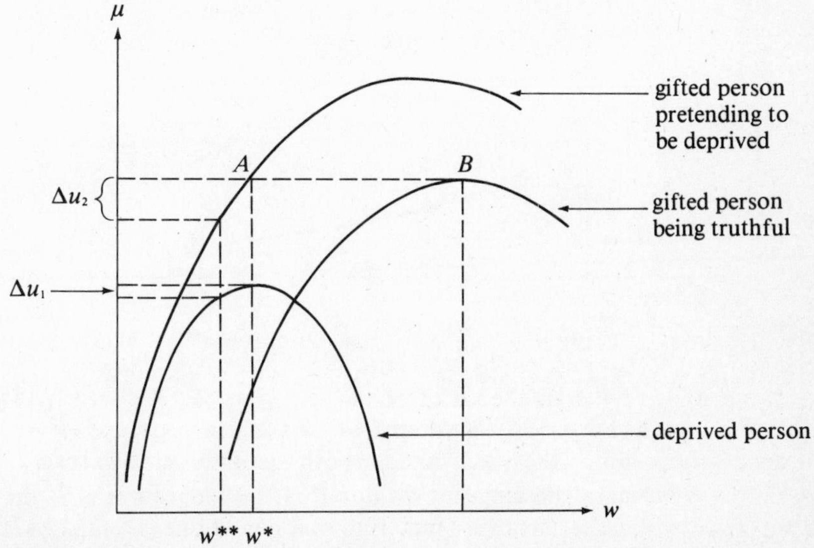

Using w as the control variable and noting that $z = w/\alpha$ the problem is to maximise $\log(w+T) + \log(1-w/\alpha)$. This has the solution $w = \max(0,\frac{1}{2}[\alpha-T])$.
(c) If w^* is as shown, then a gifted person is just indifferent between being truthful (point B) and pretending to be deprived (point A).
(d) If w^* is reduced a little to w^{**} the utility change of the deprived is small (Δu_1), but in the neighbourhood of A the utility loss of the gifted would be large (Δu_2): they switch to point B and pay the transfer.

12.11 If the servant is risk neutral, then u_1^a is non-stochastic, independent of Q. Recall that $\mathscr{E}\beta_z = 0$ and take expectations in (12.41): we find $\mathscr{E}\,\upsilon_1^b = \lambda \upsilon_1^a$, independent of Q and z. If b is risk averse, this can only be true if $w(Q)$ has been designed so that $\upsilon^b(Q-w(Q))$ is independent of Q; in which case the first term in (12.42) becomes $\upsilon^b \mathscr{E}\beta_z$ which is zero. Hence $\mu = 0$ and, from (12.41), $\upsilon_1^b/\upsilon_1^a = \lambda$.

12.12

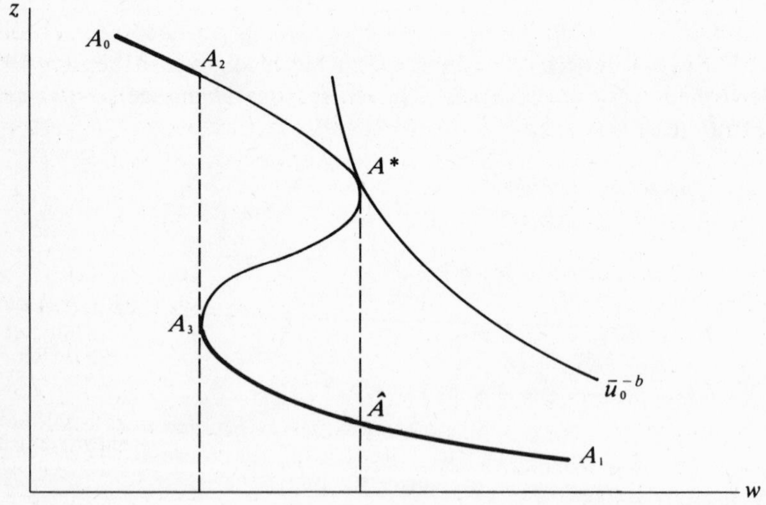

The curve $A_0A_2A^*A_3A_1$ is the set of points satisfying (12.39): clearly the point A_3 is regarded as *strictly better* than A_2 (since it involves less effort), and so only the points on the heavily shaded position of the curve will ever be chosen by the servant. The tangency 'solution' A^* no longer works – the servant would choose $\hat{A}$; hence we may find that conditions (12.41, 12.42) are no longer necessary for a maximum.

Chapter 13

13.1 The rankings in the two cases are

a	*b*	*c*
s	s'	s''
s'	s	s'
s''	s''	s

(13.1)

a	*b*	*c*
s	s''	s'
s'	s	s''
s''	s'	s

(13.2)

Let the symbol '$x > y$' denote 'x beats y in a simple vote'. In (13.1) we find $s' > s > s''$ and also $s' > s''$, a transitive ordering; in (13.2) we have $s > s' > s''$ but also $s'' > s$, which is intransitive.

13.2 Given the independent 'single peaked' rankings of each of the two characteristics we only get single peaked rankings over the social states if the set of alternatives can be represented along a straight line in the space of the two characteristics. This clearly imposes a serious restriction on the applicability of the 'single-peak' criterion.

13.3 Use '$>$' to denote strict preference and '$\sim$' to denote indifference.
The voting points scored for the three states s, s', s'' are as follows; Monday: [5,5,2], Tuesday: [5,4,3]. So the social ordering changes from $s \sim s' > s''$ to $s > s' > s''$. Notice that the rankings by Alf and Bill of s and s' remain unchanged; yet their reranking of s'' with reference to other alternatives *changes* the social ordering of s and s' from indifference to strict preference.

13.4 (a) The votes cast for [s, s', s'', s'''] are [8,7,7,8].
(b) The votes cast for [s, s'''] (when other states have been *excluded*) are [4,5]: inspection of the voting points yields the result.

13.5 (a) As in Exercise 13.1 we find that voting produces $s' > s > s'''$ but also $s''' > s'$; i.e. we have a cycle. (b) s' would be strictly preferred to the state of perfect equality s. (c) Since the probability of being assigned any one of the three identities is $\frac{1}{3}$, we find the utility payoffs of [s, s', s'', s'''] are [(log 27)/3, (log 16)/3, (log 15)/3, (log 12)/3]. But this is also the exact order of the states by income inequality: each state in the list can be reached from the one preceding it by a 'poor-to-rich' transfer and a permutation: the largest income (regardless of the person to whom it accrues) is made larger still at the expense of an income or incomes below it. Clearly concavity of the utility function implies (in a state of primordial ignorance about identity) a preference for equality. See Harsanyi, J.C. (1955) 'Cardinal welfare, individualist ethics and interpersonal comparisons of utility', *Journal of Political Economy*, Vol. 73, pp. 309–321.

13.6 (a) Put $\zeta(M^h) = \frac{1}{1-\iota}[M^h]^{1-\iota}$ in (13.13), cf. Exercise 10.5 in Chapter 10.

(b) $1 - \left[\frac{1}{H}\sum_{h=1}^{H}[M^h/\bar{M}]^{1-\iota}\right]^{1/1-\iota}$

(c) The limiting case is $W = \min_h \{M^h\}$, the *Rawls* social welfare function.

13.7 Suppose to the contrary that **M*** maximises a concave social welfare where **M*** is *not* perfectly equal. Let **M**** be some vector, distinct from **M***, that is formed from a permutation of **M***; by symmetry of $\mathscr{M}$ we have $\mathbf{M}^{**} \in \mathscr{M}$; by symmetry of the social welfare function welfare at these two vectors is identical. Now consider $\tilde{\mathbf{M}} = \alpha\mathbf{M}^* + [1-\alpha]\mathbf{M}^{**}$; by convexity we have $\tilde{\mathbf{M}} \in \mathscr{M}$; by concavity of the social welfare function, welfare at $\tilde{\mathbf{M}}$ is at least as great as at **M***. Hence, for any distribution of income that is unequal we can always find an equalising redistribution that yields an income distribution vector for which social welfare is at least as high.

13.8 Let the endowments be $\mathbf{R}^a = [\mathrm{K},3]$, $\mathbf{R}^b = [21-\mathrm{K},6]$, $0 \leqslant \mathrm{K} \leqslant 21$. Using the answer to Exercise 7.5 we find that the equilibrium price ratio is given by $\rho = 15/[21+\mathrm{K}]$. Writing $M^h = \rho R_1^h + R_2^h$, $h = a,b$ we find

$$\frac{63-21M^a}{M^a-18} = \mathrm{K} = \frac{441-21M^b}{M^b+9}$$

Simplifying this we find $2M^a + M^b = 27$. This is the equation for the boundary of the income-possibility set $\mathscr{M}$. Clearly it is linear, but asymmetric. A symmetric social welfare function will always imply that b gets more income than a.

13.9 The social welfare function is $W(U^1(\mathbf{x}^1, \mathbf{z}), \ldots, U^H(\mathbf{x}^H, \mathbf{z}))$ where $\mathbf{x}^h$ is an n-vector of consumption goods enjoyed by household h ($h = 1, \ldots, H$), and **z** is an m-vector of public goods enjoyed by all. The Lagrangean is

$$W - \lambda\Phi(\mathbf{x},\mathbf{z})$$

where $\mathbf{x} = \Sigma_h \mathbf{x}^h$, Φ is the aggregate production function (with $\Phi(\mathbf{x},\mathbf{z}) \leqslant 0$ for feasibility). First-order conditions for an interior solution are given by

$$W_h U_i^h - \lambda\Phi_i = 0 \quad i = 1, \ldots, n \quad \text{(private goods)}$$
$$\Sigma_h W_h U_j^h - \lambda\Phi_j = 0 \quad j = 1, \ldots, m \quad \text{(public goods)}$$

Hence $\Sigma_h U_j^h/U_i^h = \Phi_j/\Phi_i$ (i private, j public). See also Samuelson, P.A. (1954), 'The pure theory of public expenditure', *The Review of Economics and Statistics*, Vol. 36, pp. 387–389.

13.10 If good 1 represents health care provision that must be bought *before* you know whether you are going to be sick, the utility of good 1 depends on which state of the world is realised. The Lagrangean for the social optimum problem is $\Sigma_h \Sigma_\omega \pi(\omega) \upsilon^h (\mathbf{x}^h, \omega) - \lambda\phi(\mathbf{x})$. The first-order conditions for a maximum give for each household $h = 1, \ldots, H$:

$$\Sigma_\omega \pi(\omega) \psi_1^{h1}(x_1^h, \omega) = \lambda \Phi_1(\mathbf{x}) \qquad \text{(good 1)}$$
$$\psi_1^{hi}(x_i^h) = \lambda \Phi_i(x), \quad i = 2, \ldots, n$$

Consumer h's Lagrangean is $\Sigma_\omega \pi^h(\omega) \upsilon^h (\mathbf{x}^h, \omega) + \mu[M^h - \Sigma_i p_i^h x_i^h]$. The first-order conditions are

$$\Sigma_\omega \pi^h(\omega) \psi_1^{h1}(x_1^h, \omega) = \mu p_1^h \quad \text{(good 1)}$$
$$\psi_1^{hi}(x_i^h) = \mu p_i^h, \quad i = 2, \ldots n$$

Rearrangement of the above expressions gives the result. To see the interpretation, consider two states of the world ω = 'sick' where the marginal utility $\psi_1^{h1}(x_1^1, \omega)$ is large and positive and ω = 'healthy' where the marginal utility is virtually zero. The 'personalised pricing' rule says that good 1 should be subsidised (p_1^h/p_j^h biased downwards) for consumer h if he is likely to underestimate the probability of falling sick. See Sandmo, A. (1983), 'Ex post welfare economics and the theory of merit goods', *Economica*, Vol. 50, pp. 19–34.

13.11 Let there be H schoolchildren, and let the pie received by child h be M^h, $h = 1, \ldots, H$. The space of all possible pie distributions is $\mathcal{M} = \{(M^1, \ldots, M^H) : M^h \geqslant 0, \Sigma_h M^h \leqslant 1\}$. If each child perceives an equal chance of being allocated any particular plate, the expected utility of the perceived pie distribution $M^1, \ldots, M^H$ is $\Sigma_{h=1}^H \upsilon(M^h)/H$ where υ is an increasing, concave function. Used as a social welfare function this will consistently rank more equal distributions as being preferable to less equal distributions. (a) Inequality aversion is identical to risk aversion. (b) In practice the probability of receiving a particular pie-allocation will not be the same for all individuals; personal risk aversion for small risks may be inappropriate basis for inequality aversion with reference to life chances. See also answer to Exercise 13.5.

13.12 (a) Conditions include identical income elasticities for all commodities. See Atkinson, A.B. and Stiglitz, J.E. (1972) 'The structure of indirect taxation and economic efficiency', *Journal of Public Economics*, Vol. 1, pp. 97–119.

(b) From the budget constraint $\Sigma p_i x_i \leqslant M$ it is clear that if we could tax *all* the commodities this is equivalent to being able to tax M itself. Hence one would be able to impose lump sum taxes.

13.13 (a) Using Roy's identity (4.32) we have

$$x_1 = -V_1/V_M = \phi' \rho^{-\beta}/[\phi'[1/M]] = M\rho^{-\beta}.$$

(b) If good 2 is labour time (unobservable) and good 1 is observable consumption, this is a simple income tax. We have $T = \tau M[1+\tau]^{-\beta}$; so $\partial T/\partial \tau = M[1+\tau]^{-\beta-1}[1+\tau-\beta\tau]$ which is clearly positive if $\beta < 1$. If $\beta \geqslant 1$ taxes will *fall* with τ whenever $\tau > 1/[\beta-1]$; the substitution elasticity is so large that increases in τ become self-defeating.

(c) If $\beta = \frac{1}{2}$ then, from above, $\partial\tau/\partial T = [1+\tau]^{3/2}/M[1+\frac{1}{2}\tau]$. Hence $\partial u/\partial T = -\phi' \rho^{-\frac{1}{2}}\partial\tau/\partial T = -a[1+\tau]/[1+\frac{1}{2}\tau] < 0$ where $a \equiv \phi'/M$, a constant; so $\partial^2 u/\partial T^2 = -\frac{1}{2}a/[1+\frac{1}{2}\tau]^2 \partial\tau/\partial T < 0$.

(d) If $\phi'' > 0$ for large T and $\beta < 1$ the curve may be non-concave – see Stiglitz, J.E. (1982) 'Utilitarianism and horizontal equity: the case for random taxation', *Journal of Public Economics*, Vol. 18, pp. 1–33.

(e)

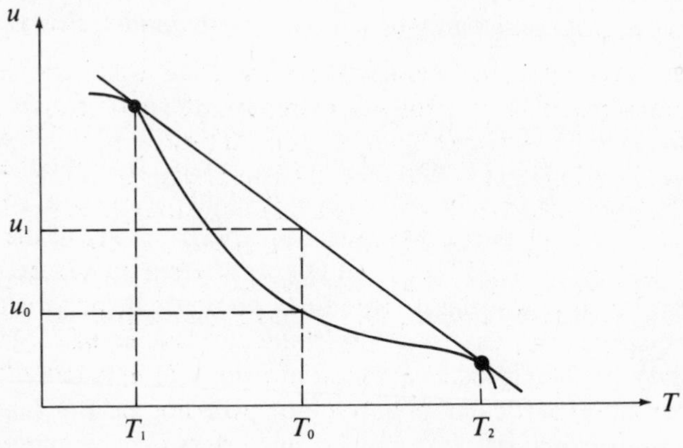

Suppose the government wants to raise an amount T_0. If all households are identical, let $\tau(T_0)$ be the tax rate required to raise T_0 overall. Each household then enjoys utility u_0. Suppose instead half the population face a tax rate $\tau(T_1)$ and the other half $\tau(T_2)$: then T_0 is still raised overall but, if everyone is allocated randomly (with equal probability) to the two classes, *expected utility* is higher at u_1.

13.14 Let $\mathscr{S}_0$ be the social state with uniform taxation and $\mathscr{S}_1$ the state with random taxation. The switch $\mathscr{S}_0 \rightarrow \mathscr{S}_1$ is a Pareto improvement *ex-ante*, but is *not* a Pareto improvement *ex-post* since half the population have a realised utility level less than u_0.

13.15 The system operates as a simple income tax: τ is the marginal tax rate, and for $M \geqslant M_0$, M_0 is an exemption level; for $M \leqslant M_0$ the system operates as a negative income tax scheme with minimum guaranteed income τM_0.

(a) The individual seeks to maximise $[M_0 + [1-\tau][wL - M_0]]^\alpha [1-L]^{1-\alpha}$ subject to $0 \leqslant L \leqslant 1$. Writing down the first-order conditions and solving in the usual way gives

$$L = \max\left\{0, \alpha - [1-\alpha]\frac{\tau M_0}{[1-\tau]w}\right\}.$$

(b) Since everyone has a wage $w \geqslant w_0$ the government can ensure $L > 0$ by setting τ and M_0 such that $\frac{\tau}{1-\tau} < \frac{\alpha}{1-\alpha}[w_0/M_0]$.

(c) The government's budget constraint (written as an equality) is $\mathscr{E}[Lw - M_0]\tau = 0$, where the expectation is taken over the distribution of w. If everyone works then, from part (b), $Lw - M_0 = \alpha w - \frac{1-\alpha\tau}{1-\tau}M_0$; taking expectations gives the result.

(d) The specified social welfare function requires that the income of the poorest person be maximised: in this case the poorest person's income is $\alpha w_0[1-\tau] + \alpha\tau M_0$ which, on substitution for M_0, becomes $\alpha w_0[1-\tau][1+\alpha\gamma\tau/[1-\alpha\tau]]$. Differentiating with respect to τ and setting the result to zero yields a quadratic in $\alpha\tau$ that has as its solution $\alpha\tau = 1 \pm \sqrt{(1-[\gamma\alpha-1]/[\gamma-1])}$; neglecting the irrelevant root the result follows. Note that as γ increases τ^* rises: as the mean wage rises relative to the minimum, so, too, does the optimal tax rate.

13.16 The Lagrangean is

$$W(V^1(\mathbf{p},M^1), \ldots, V^H(\mathbf{p},M^H)) + \lambda[\Sigma_i\Sigma_h x_i^h \Delta p_i - T]$$

Maximising this with respect to Δp_i gives the first-order condition

$$-\Sigma_h B_M^h x_i^h + \lambda[\Sigma_j \Delta p_j \Sigma_h D_i^{hj} + x_i] = 0$$

where B_M^h is the social marginal utility of income to person h, and the first term utilises Roy's identity. Rearrangement of this, using the Slutsky equation, gives the result.

Index